The relationship between changes in (inflectional) morphology and the consequences of these changes in syntax has been a perennial issue in historical linguistics. The contributors to this volume address the issue of how to model the phenomena of syntactic and morphological change within recent frameworks, including the Minimalist Programme. Topics addressed include the way categories like aspect and mood interact over time with the valency of verbs; the nature of changes in verb placement; the changing division of labour between different types of argument marking – case, word order, clitics, agreement.

The volume contains chapters by many of the leading scholars in the field. There is a substantial introduction which reviews the development of ideas in generative historical syntax over the last fifteen years, and assesses the distinctive properties of the generative position. The volume will appeal to those working in theoretical syntax, and also to specialists in the history of German, French and the Romance and Germanic languages more broadly.

Parameters of morphosyntactic change

Parameters of morphosyntactic change

Edited by

Ans van Kemenade

Vakgroep Taalkunde/HIL
Vrije Universiteit Amsterdam

and

Nigel Vincent

Department of Linguistics
The University of Manchester

PUBLISHED BY THE PRESS SYNDICATE OF THE UNIVERSITY OF CAMBRIDGE
The Pitt Building, Trumpington Street, Cambridge CB2 1RP, United Kingdom

CAMBRIDGE UNIVERSITY PRESS
The Edinburgh Building, Cambridge CB2 2RU, United Kingdom
40 West 20th Street, New York, NY 10011-4211, USA
10 Stamford Road, Oakleigh, Melbourne 3166, Australia

© Cambridge University Press 1997

This book is in copyright. Subject to statutory exception
and to the provisions of relevant collective licensing agreements,
no reproduction of any part may take place without
the written permission of Cambridge University Press.

First published 1997

Printed in the United Kingdom at the University Press, Cambridge

A catalogue record for this book is available from the British Library

Library of Congress cataloguing in publication data

Parameters of morphosyntactic change / edited by Ans van Kemenade and
Nigel Vincent.
   p. cm.
Includes bibliographical references and index.
ISBN 0 521 58402 7 (hardback : alk. paper). – ISBN 0 521 58643 7
(paperback : alk. paper)
1. Linguistic change. 2. Grammar, Comparative and general –
Morphology. 3. Grammar, Comparative and general – Syntax.
4. Generative grammar. I. Kemenade, Ans van, 1954– .
II. Vincent, Nigel.
P142.P37   1997
415–dc21   96–46074   CIP

ISBN 0 521 58402 7 hardback
ISBN 0 521 58643 7 paperback

Contents

List of contributors   ix

Preface   xi

Parameters and morphosyntactic change   1
Ans van Kemende and Nigel Vincent

Part 1
Aspect, argument structure and case selection   27

1. The interdependence of case, aspect and referentiality in the history of German: the case of the verbal genitive   29
Werner Abraham

2. The rise of the article in the Germanic languages   62
Julia Philippi

3. The diachronic development of a modal verb of necessity   94
Paola Benincà and Cecilia Poletto

4. Auxiliary verbs in Old and Middle French: a diachronic study of substitutive *faire* and a comparison with the Modern English auxiliaries   119
Philip H. Miller

5. Commentary on part 1: aspect, argument structure and case selection   134
Alessandra Tomaselli

Part 2
Clitics   147

6. The emergence of the D-system in Romance   149
Nigel Vincent

7. On two locations for complement clitic pronouns: Serbo-Croatian, Bulgarian and Old Spanish   170
María Luisa Rivero

8. On the integration of second position phenomena   207
Josep M. Fontana

Part 3
Verb second and comp — 251

9. Shifting triggers and diachronic reanalyses — 253
   David Lightfoot

10. Viewing change in progress: the loss of V2 in Hiberno-English imperatives — 273
    Alison Henry

11. Verb movement in Old and Middle English: dialect variation and language contact — 297
    Anthony Kroch and Ann Taylor

12. V2 and embedded topicalization in Old and Middle English — 326
    Ans van Kemenade

13. Qu'est-ce que *ce que*? The diachronic evolution of a French complementizer — 353
    Laurie Zaring and Paul Hirschbühler

14. The structure of parametric change, and V-movement in the history of English — 380
    Anthony Warner

Part 4
Scrambling and morphological case — 395

15. Directionality and word order change in the history of English — 397
    Ian Roberts

16. On the relation between morphological and syntactic case — 427
    Fred Weerman

17. The rise of positional licensing — 460
    Paul Kiparsky

18. The chapters by Kiparsky, Roberts and Weerman: an epilogue — 495
    Höskuldur Thráinsson

References — 509

Index — 539

Contributors

Werner Abraham
University of Groningen
Dept of German
O. Kijk in 't Jatstraat 26
9712 EK Groningen
Netherlands
abraham@let.rug.nl

Josep M. Fontana
Inst. Univ. de Lingüística Aplicada
Universitat Pompeu Fabra
La Rambla, 30–2
08002 Barcelona
Spain
jfontana@upf.es

Paul Hirschbühler
Univ. d'Ottawa
Dept de Linguistique
Ottawa, Ontario KIN 6N5
Canada
phhaf@acadvm1@uottawa.ca

Paul Kiparsky
Stanford University
Linguistics Dept, Building 10
Stanford, CA 94305
USA
kiparsky@csli.stanford.edu

David Lightfoot
Dept of Linguistics
Univ. of Maryland
College Park
Maryland, 20742 USA
dwl@umdd.umd.edu

Paola Benincà
Centro di Studio per la
Dialettologia Italiana
Fracoltá di Lettere e Filosofia
Universitá degli Studi di Padova
Via Beato Pellegrino 1
35137 Padova, Italy
beninca@ipdunidx.unipd.it

Alison Henry
Dept of Communication
U. of Ulster at Jordanstown
Newtonabbey
Co. Antrim BT37 OQB
Northern Ireland
fehn23@ujvax.ulster.ac.uk

Ans van Kemenade
Vrije Universiteit
Vakgroep Taalkunde/Engels
De Boelelaan 1105
1081 HV Amsterdam
Netherlands
kemenade@let.vu.nl

Anthony Kroch
University of Pennsylvania
Dept of Linguistics
Williams Hall 618
Philadelphia, PA 19104-6305
USA
kroch@babel.ling.upenn.edu

Philip H. Miller
113, Rue de la Victoire
B-1060 Bruxelles
Belgium
pmiller@ulb.ac.be

Julia Philippi
Avenariusstrasse 16
22587 Hamburg
Germany

María Luisa Rivero
Univ. d'Ottawa
Dept de Linguistique
Ottawa, Ontario KIN 6N5
Canada
mrivero@acadvm1.uottawa.ca

Ann Taylor
University of Pennsylvania
Dept of Computer Science
200 South 33rd St
Philadelphia, PA 19104-6389
USA
ataylor@linc.cis.upenn.edu

Alessandra Tomaselli
Strada Campeggi 63
27100 Pavia
Italy
tomas@chiostro.univr.it

Anthony Warner
University of York
Dept of Language and Linguistics
Heslington, York YO1 5DD
Great Britain
aw2@vaxa.york.ac.uk

Laurie Zaring
368 Rutherford Ave.
Delaware
Ohio, 43015-1176
USA
lzaring@carleton.edu

Cecilia Poletto
Centro di Studio per la
Dialettologia Italiana
Facoltá di Lettere e Filosofia
Universitá degli Studi di Padova
Via Beato Pellegrino 1
35137 Padova, Italy
diplin@ipdunivx.unipd.it

Ian Roberts
UCNW Bangor
School of English and Linguistics
Bangor, Gwynedd LL57 2D6
Great Britain
i.g.roberts@bangor.ac.uk

Höskuldur Thráinsson
University of Iceland
Institute of Linguistics
101 Reykjavik
Iceland
hoski@rhi.hi.is

Nigel Vincent
University of Manchester
Dept of Linguistics
Manchester M13 9PL
Great Britain
nigel.vincent@man.ac.uk

Fred Weerman
University of Utrecht, OTS
Trans 10
3512 JK Utrecht
Netherlands
weerman@let.ruu.nl

Preface

This collection of articles is a spin-off of the Third Diachronic Generative Syntax conference, held at the Vrije Universiteit Amsterdam, Holland Institute of Generative Linguistics, 30 March – 2 April 1994. The support of the following institutions for the conference is hereby gratefully acknowledged: The Royal Dutch Academy of Arts and Sciences; The Foundation for Language, Speech and Logic of the Netherlands Organization for Scientific Research (NWO); the Holland Institute of Generative Linguistics (HIL) as part of the Netherlands Graduate School of Linguistics (LOT); the Faculties of Arts of the Vrije Universiteit Amsterdam and the University of Amsterdam. Many thanks to Aafke Hulk, Bettelou Los, Marga Petter, Erik Reuland and Fred Weerman for their help in pulling the conference together, and to Frank Beths for valuable practical assistance with this volume. Thanks are also due to Judith Ayling, our editor at Cambridge University Press, and to René Mulder of Holland Academic Graphics, who produced this beautiful typescript. Finally, we wish to thank the following colleagues for their assistance with the refereeing: Marcel den Dikken, Jack Hoeksema, Anders Holmberg, Ans de Kok, Anthony Kroch, Susan Pintzuk, Lorenzo Renzi, Maggie Tallerman, Höskuldur Thráinsson, Alessandra Tomaselli, Anthony Warner.

Ans van Kemenade and Nigel Vincent
Amsterdam and Manchester, July 1996

Parameters and morphosyntactic change

Ans van Kemenade and Nigel Vincent

1 Background

The relation between changes in (inflectional) morphology and consequences thereof in the syntax has been a perennial issue in historical linguistics. Recent theoretical developments have yielded on the one hand a surge of work on grammaticalization as the source of inflectional markers and on the other an articulated theory of the relation between inflectional morphology and syntax and a consequent boost of historical work in that area. Most of the articles in this volume belong to the latter category. The framework they adopt is broadly speaking the Principles and Parameters approach to grammar developed in Chomsky (1981) and subsequent work, and whose application to language change was instigated by Lightfoot (1979). They continue the debate on topics on which a good deal of fruitful work has been done since 1979: historical change in the position of the finite verb (e.g. Adams 1987; van Kemenade 1987; Roberts 1993a); the interaction of that change with the loss of the so-called null subject phenomenon (the papers in Hulk & van Kemenade 1993a; Battye & Roberts 1995); the relation between changes in case-marking and changes in constructions such as passives and impersonals (Allen 1995); the history of English modals in particular (Lightfoot 1979; Warner 1993), and auxiliarization in general (for a formal approach see Warner 1993, and from the grammaticalization perspective, Heine 1993).

The aim of this introductory chapter is to review, as a backdrop for the chapters in this volume, the development of ideas in historical syntax from a generative point of view since the early 1980s.[1] We shall discuss some of the distinctive properties of the generative position as compared to other approaches, trying in the process to correct a few of what we see as prevalent misapprehensions. Sections 2 and 3 will lay out the generative approach to language change. Sections 4 and 5 provide some theoretical and technical background about the relation between structure and morphology as viewed from a generative perspective. Section 6 will compare and contrast the generative approach to morphosyntactic change with the grammaticalization approach. We will conclude with an overview of the volume in section 7.

2 Reanalysis

Ever since Lightfoot's pioneering monograph (1979), the generative approach to syntactic change has considered that the key mechanism of change is reanalysis. A problem with this term is that it has been used in many senses by scholars working on language change from a variety of perspectives, so a degree of terminological clarification seems in order. A fundamental distinction is between those changes that involve the redistribution of existing patterns, and changes in which genuinely new patterns are created. The latter are commonly called 'reanalyses', whereas the term 'analogy' is traditionally applied to the former. For example, the use of plural -*s* in PDE represents a generalization of the OE masculine and neuter *a*-noun plural, but there is nothing intrinsically new about the use of -*s* to mark plurality. On the other hand, -*hood* as an abstract noun marker is an innovative formation deriving from the earlier independent word *hād* meaning 'state, condition'. In other words, the latter change involves the creation of a new association of form and content rather than the extension of an existing one.

For older scholars, such as Meillet (1912), the category of reanalysis seems to have been equivalent to grammaticalization. More recently, however, scholars such as Lightfoot (1979, 1991) have seen their work as starkly opposed to latter-day theorists of grammaticalization, such as Hopper & Traugott (1993). How does this divergence come about? The answer lies in the relative importance attached to the historical discontinuity that a reanalysis necessarily implies. Consider the notorious case of the English modals. For Lightfoot, the essential change lies in the abrupt categorial shift from Old and Middle English premodals, a class of main verb, to a modern separate category of modal, for him crucially distinct from the category V. Grammaticalization theorists by contrast, while not denying the categorial shift, are more concerned to see such a change as part of a larger development whereby full lexical verbs come to be the markers of modality and other aspects of grammatical meaning (Plank 1984). The English change would then in turn be seen as but one instance of the recurrent crosslinguistic tendency for markers of mood and modality to derive from independent lexical items (Bybee *et al.* 1994).

Lightfoot in a sense continues the Saussurean tradition of seeing diachrony as no more than the sum of a sequence of synchronies. The only continuity is at the genetic level of UG, whose effects are necessarily punctuated by the discontinuities implicit in the acquisition of language by each new generation of speakers. For Traugott, on the other hand, an individual change only makes sense if it is embedded in a larger sequence for which the diachronic perspective is essential. In this sense, modern grammaticalization theory reverses Saussure's claim for the logical priority of synchronic over diachronic linguistics. The conflict between these two approaches inevitably raises larger metaphysical issues, as is evidenced by the exchange between Lightfoot (1995) and Traugott & Smith (1993). We will discuss these as we provide a more detailed characterization of the separate approaches.

3 Parametric change

Generative theory conceives of UG as a system of principles and parameters. Subsystems of UG include Case Theory, Binding Theory, Government Theory. Parameters form part of these subsystems and define dimensions along which languages may differ. It is by now commonly accepted that parametric differences between languages are restricted to properties of that part of sentential structure where morphological information such as tense, agreement, main/subordinate are expressed. Consider the following simplified illustration, with what we shall for the moment dub 'the V2 parameter'.[2] V2 refers to the word order constraint by which, in languages like Dutch and Modern German, the finite verb is fronted to second constituent position in main clauses. This is illustrated by the following sentences from German:

(1) a. Er hat ihn gestern   gesehen
       he has him yesterday seen
    b. Gestern   hat er ihn gesehen
       yesterday has he him seen
    c. ... daß er ihn gestern   gesehen habe
       ... that he him yesterday seen   has
    d. *... daß gestern   hat er ihn gesehen
       ... that yesterday has he him seen
    e. *... daß hat er ihn gestern   gesehen
       ... that has he him yesterday seen
       '... he saw him yesterday'

In (1a, b), the first constituent and the finite verb are purportedly fronted with respect to the rest of the sentence, to some pre-sentential position, the same position as that of the subordinating conjunction *daß* in (1c, d, e). The V2 parameter would then be the abstract property of this pre-sentential position that is responsible for attracting the finite verb to it.

In a parameter-setting model of language acquisition and change, the task of the language learner is to decide, on the basis of the evidence in her language environment, how to fill in the values for the various parametric options allowed by UG. Choosing the values for the parameters for any particular language is the main task of language acquisition.

In the course of the 1980s increasing emphasis has come to be attached to the question of how the language learner comes to set parameters in a different way. With this development, it has become important to appreciate the nature of the triggering evidence for the language learner. Lightfoot (1991) lays particular emphasis on the need to find acquisition triggers for the resetting of parameters, i.e., we should try to formulate clearly what the changes in the language environment are that induce the language learner to set a parameter in a novel way. Such evidence must be robust, Lightfoot argues. An important constraint that he formulates on the robustness of that evidence is that it should come from simple, unembedded clauses, including the initial functional domains of the embedded clause, so-called degree-0 learnability. The rationale is that the language environment of the learner consists largely of main clauses. These should therefore contain the evidence for the resetting of a parameter. Hence, if a language change formulated as a parametric change has to appeal primarily to embedded clauses for evidence, this does not qualify as an appropriate explanation for that change, according to Lightfoot.

It may be useful to consider how the type of change called reanalysis in Lightfoot (1979) and in grammaticalization theory is related to the type of change we here dub parameter resetting. Hopper & Traugott (1993: 40) fully identify Lightfoot's radical reanalysis with parametric change. It is easy to see how such a misunderstanding could arise, since they are both cases of abrupt change. A definition of reanalysis fully compatible with recent generative interpretations of the notion comes from Langacker (1977: 58): 'change in the structure of an expression or class of expressions that does not involve any immediate or intrinsic modification of its surface manifestation'. In other words, a different structure is assigned to an utterance or set of utterances that remains the same on the surface. The recategorization of the English modals mentioned above is an appropriate example of this. However, this is not an instance of parametric change. Roberts (1993a: 311) makes a clear distinction between the two: the parametric change relevant to the history of the English modals is the loss of V2. Such a parametric change entails a resetting of a grammatical option that affects the whole grammar, not just a set of utterances. It will be visible as a clear shift in surface patterns, in this case a marked decrease in the number of V2 patterns. This is in contrast to reanalysis, which is a hidden change in the sense that it constitutes a grammatical reorganization of existing surface patterns.

In the preceding paragraphs, we have seen that in generative work on change, the emphasis is on abrupt change. This is primarily a consequence of the theoretical framework. Since parameter settings are typically an all-or-nothing phenomenon, a new parameter setting will represent an abrupt change in the I-language of the speaker with respect to those of the speakers in her language environment. As we all know, however, language change as it emerges from our historical descriptions is typically gradual and it is not immediately obvious how the analysis of change as putatively abrupt can be reconciled with its surface graduality. Moreover, this raises an interesting issue with respect to the causality of change. There are many cases of change that occur across several generations of speakers. What is it that pushes such change forward? This is a point where grammaticalization theorists' appeal to notions of diachrony is vehemently opposed by Lightfoot (1979, 1991, 1995) who insists that the language acquisition perspective excludes any idea that change could have independent causation. But it is not clear how longterm change can be accounted for from the parametric perspective.

Anthony Kroch, in important work, has made a principled attempt to deal with the friction between the notions of abrupt change on the one hand and surface graduality on the other, establishing a coherent way of looking at synchronic variation (Kroch 1991). Syntactic change, indeed change in general, follows an S-shaped curve, taking off slowly, booming after it has passed a certain threshold level, and petering out slowly when nearing completion. During this period of change, speakers are in a sense bilingual speakers of their native language: they may acquire two grammars that compete with each other with opposed values for the relevant parameter, thus representing the old form beside the innovative form. A case in point is Old English phrase structure, which is argued by Pintzuk (1991) to be variable between a grammar in which IP is head-medial and one in which IP is head-final. Eventually only the innovative grammar remains as an option. It should be noted, however, that this type of approach, while providing a coherent rationale for modelling the time course of change, has very little to say on the causality of change, or on the question of what gives any particular innovation its momentum. This applies in a similar fashion to the approach to synchronic variation advocated in Falk (1993). Falk, writing on the loss of nonreferential empty subjects in early Modern Swedish, notes the problem of synchronic variation for restrictive theorizing, and attempts to pinpoint the source for it in ambiguities within the system of subject agreement marking rather than in competing grammars. Although the restrictiveness of the theory presumably requires that such ambiguities be eliminated, it is hard to ensure that the innovation 'wins out'. Lightfoot (this volume) insists strongly that the theory of grammar, in conjunction with the language acquisition perspective, leaves no scope for what he calls an unduly deterministic approach. Here he criticizes Roberts (1993b) whose distinction between parametric change and D(iachronic) R(eanalysis) we have already noted. According to Lightfoot, the DR as formulated by Roberts is a device that relates the grammars of speakers of subsequent generations rather than the grammar of the new generation to the output of the older generation. Hence, the DR cannot be triggered by robust evidence from the language environment.

Other attempts to deal in some fashion with the causation of change try to do this in terms of preferences inherent in the system. Thus Clark & Roberts (1993) try to relate natural selection, language acquisition and language change in the light of current computational models of language learning. In this model, the language learner computes the language input by so-called genetic algorithms. Beside fixing the values for each parameter separately, this involves combining parameter values to arrive at the combination generating the model output. In addition, a genetic algorithm contains a fitness metric, which evaluates the combination of parameter values with respect to how it covers the data in the language environment (together with such weighting factors as the elegance of derivations). The fittest combination will survive. Clark & Roberts propose that parametric change typically occurs when the target of acquisition contains parameter values that cannot be uniquely determined on the basis of the language environment. This can happen when the evidence presented to the learner is formally compatible with a number of different and conflicting parameter settings. The input data do not put pressure on the learner to set certain parameters to a definite value and several alternative grammars can adequately account for the input stream. Clark & Roberts suggest that in such a situation the learner 'will turn in on itself, abandoning external pressure, and rely on its own internal structure to select from the alternatives at hand' (302). In such a model, the language learner can potentially make choices that are not forced by the input of acquisition. This is also true of the approach in Henry (this volume), who suggests that the language learner may ignore positive evidence in selecting from the alternatives offered by UG. And Kiparsky (this volume) claims: 'A third approach, to my mind the most promising, is to build the appropriate preferences (whether formal or substantive) into the theory, and to view acquisition and change in terms of a push-pull mechanism where preferences, if sufficiently strong, may override available evidence, if sufficiently weak' (473). These approaches are of course not necessarily incompatible with that of Lightfoot. As long as the UG preferences are formulated in terms of well-established principles of grammar and language acquisition, and the amount of evidence ignored by the language learner falls below Lightfoot's threshold of robustness, there need be no conflict. But this remains to be seen.

4 Functional categories

Since Chomsky (1986a) replaced the sentential structure in terms of S/S' by one in terms of CP/IP both conforming to the standard phrase structure format, these two projections have come to be split ever further. The rationale is that each such projection hosts relevant morphology, e.g. tense and agreement, and a verb requiring association with such morphology then moves to that projection to 'pick up' tense and agreement endings.

Functional categories (FCs) firmly put inflectional morphology in the syntax. Each syntactically (semantically) relevant morphological category heads its own phrasal projection, conforming to the general phrase structure rules:

(2) a. XP → {spec X'}
    b. X' → {X'   YP}
           {X   ZP}

There is now an emerging consensus that (3) represents the sequence of functional heads, each of them projected as in (2). C stands for Comp, Agr_S for subject agreement, Neg for negation, T for tense.[3]

(3) C Agr$_S$ Neg T Agr$_O$ V

The underlying claim is that parametric differences between languages (and historical stages of one language) are differences in functional properties only.[4] Parametric change is therefore change that should be located in shifts in functional properties like case, agreement, tense, etc., hence in the relationships within and between functional projections and the lexical projections for which they are relevant. The first major application of these ideas to syntactic change is Roberts (1993a), who relates historical changes in the French and English systems of verb agreement to changes in the English auxiliary system, and word order changes in French.

Throughout the early 1990s, FCs have boomed. For historical applications, see the contributions in van Kemenade & Hulk (1993) and Battye & Roberts (1995). Foremost among the FCs that play a role in the articles in this volume are the MoodP, to express modality; Agr$_O$P to express object case; D(eterminer)P to extend the lexical projection of the noun; Clitic Phrases (ClPs) of various sorts; and K(case)P provides an obvious rationale for thinking about morphological case.[5] We will come back to the role of KP in section 5.

Chomsky (1991) constrains the theory of FCs in an important way: movement of any element (head or XP) to any functional position only takes place when it is required for the licensing of the relevant functional feature. This has come to be known as the Economy condition; elements can only move when they must to have their morphological features licensed.

So far we have considered the motivation for head movement: the movement of lexical heads to functional heads to pick up morphology. We now turn to the elements that occupy the specifier position. Only phrasal categories can move to the specifier position. It follows from Economy that phrases do so for the purpose of licensing functional properties. Assuming that the morphological properties of an FC are on the head, movement of a phrase to the specifier related to that head establishes a locality relation between head (and associated morphology) and the phrase in the specifier. This relation of specifier–head agreement is central to the theory of functional categories. We conclude our discussion of functional categories by a brief discussion of the Minimalist Programme.

Although the Minimalist Programme (Chomsky 1993a) follows up naturally a number of notions we already knew from Chomsky (1991), it nevertheless represents in some ways a radical departure from previous theorizing. The most radical ingredient of minimalism is that the derivational levels D-structure and S-structure are abolished; the derivation is now built up by means of the structure-building operation Generalized Transformation (GT). The order of FCs is universal. Lexical elements are inserted in the structure fully inflected. Inflectional morphology is checked against the relevant functional features. Functional features are now defined in a different way. There are specifier features and head features. Each of these can be weak or strong, independent of each other. Weakness vs strength of features does not correlate in any way with morphological weakness or strength; they merely determine at what point 'movement' takes place: if T (the head of the Tense Phrase) has a strong head feature, the verb will move to T to check its tense morphology 'overtly' in the syntax (i.e. in the process of GT). If the head feature of T is weak, this checking takes place at the semantic interface level LF, and will not be overtly visible as movement.

One problem that arises in the new framework is exactly how to interpret the notion of 'strength' of features, since there is apparently no necessary correlation between overt morphology and strength. The matter is raised in different ways in the chapters by Roberts and by Philippi, but no completely satisfactory conclusions are reached.

4.1 V2, head movement and related issues

Let us now consider some more specific issues relating to the chapters on V2 in part 3 of this volume. The term V2 refers to an absolute word order constraint which requires that the *finite* verb be preceded by exactly one constituent. Let us take some examples from Modern German(Gm) as a starting point:

(4) a. Der Johann hat ihm gestern   das Buch gegeben
        the John   has him yesterday the book given
    b. Gestern   hat der Johann ihm das Buch gegeben
        yesterday has the John   him the book given
    c. Das Buch hat der Johann ihm gestern   gegeben
        the book has the John   him yesterday given
       'Yesterday John gave him the book'

The finite verb (Vf) in these sentences immediately follows the first constituent, whether that is the subject (a), an adverb (b) or an object (c). This phenomenon is distinct from the rest of the clausal structure. For German we may assume that the basic word order is SOV, as the position of the nonfinite verb in (4) testifies. Other languages, like the Scandinavian languages, have SVO order. Nevertheless, the Mainland Scandinavian languages have the same XP–Vf–... order that German has.

The V-movement illustrated in (4) is restricted to root clauses, a more precise term than main clauses for reasons that will become clear below. The following sentences from Gm show that it is blocked in most embedded clauses:

(5) a. ... daß er ihn gestern   gesehen habe
       ... that he him yesterday seen   has
    b. *... daß gestern   hat er ihn gesehen
       ... that yesterday has he him seen
    c. *... daß hat er ihn gestern   gesehen
       ... that has he him yesterday seen
      '... he saw him yesterday'

This is the main reason why V2 is widely analysed as movement of Vf to Comp, which is blocked in nonroot clauses by a base-generated complementizer, as shown in the German examples in (5b–c), while (5a) shows that in the presence of a base-generated complementizer *daß*, Vf remains in its VP-final position. Examples (5b–c) show that fronting of Vf is ungrammatical in the presence of a complementizer. Hence, it is assumed that lexical material in the C-position blocks fronting of Vf to that position.[6]

The finite verb moves to I and subsequently V/I moves to C, iff C is nonlexical. This explains why V/I to C is blocked when C is lexically filled as in embedded clauses introduced by *daß* or another lexical element.

(6)

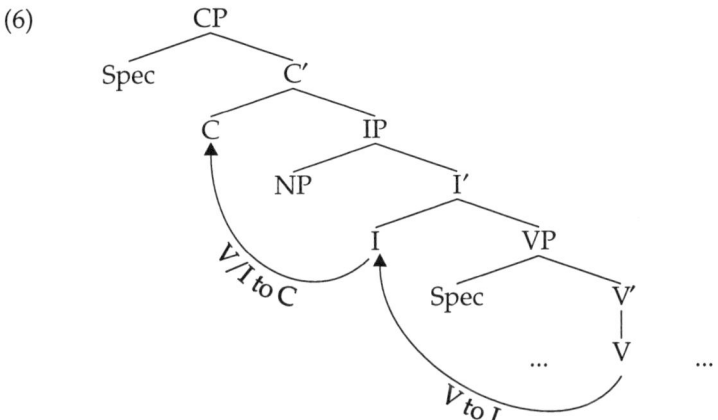

4.1.1 Symmetric and asymmetric V2

Even in languages like Gm, the V2 phenomenon is not entirely restricted to main clauses. V2 in embedded clauses is essentially of two types. The first type is represented by languages like Dutch, German, Frisian, Continental Scandinavian, Old French. These allow embedded V2 only in the complements of 'bridge' verbs, which are verbs that allow complementizer deletion (see, e.g., Vikner 1990). This is illustrated with (7) from Danish:

(7)   a.   Vi ved   (at) denne bog har Bo ikke læst
          we know that this   book has Bo not read
    b.   Vi ved   (at) Bo har ikke denne bog læst
          we know that Bo has not this   book read
    c.   Vi beklag *(at) Bo har ikke læst denne bog
          we regret   that Bo has not read this   book

This type of embedded V2 is usually analysed as CP-recursion, e.g. Vikner (1991). In terms of the structure (6), we get V/I-to-C movement as in root clauses.[7] Indeed, complements of bridge verbs can essentially behave as root clauses. The requirement that C be lexical is found in various guises in recent proposals for the analysis of V2. We shall be referring to V2 languages of the sort discussed so far as *asymmetric V2* (also variously called CV2,

CP-V2) languages. Crucial for this notion is a root/nonroot asymmetry for V2. In this language type, Spec,IP is the canonical position for the nominative subject.

The second type of embedded V2 is represented by languages like Yiddish and Icelandic, as analysed in Santorini (1989), Diesing (1990), Rögnvaldson & Thráinsson (1990). In these languages, embedded V2 occurs more or less freely and is compatible with a base-generated complementizer. This is illustrated in (8) with some examples for Icelandic from Rögnvaldsson & Thráinsson (1990):

(8) a. Jón efast um að á morgun fari María snemma á fætur
John doubts that tomorrow get Mary early up
'John doubts that Mary will get up early tomorrow'
b. Jón harmarað þessa bók skuli ég hafa lesið
John regrets that this book shall I have read
'John regrets that I have read this book'

Given the compatibility of lexical complementizers and V2 in such languages, there is no root/non-root asymmetry with respect to V-fronting. We will call this type of language *symmetric V2*: XP–Vf–subject sequences occur more or less freely in both root and non-root contexts. However, these are to be analysed as instances of V to I. The asymmetry between root and non-root contexts can only emerge in a CV2 language. An important consequence of this is that Spec,IP in these languages is a topic position, an A' position; it is not the canonical position for the nominative subject. The distinction between symmetric and asymmetric V2 is an important one with respect to the history of English: the chapters in part 3 by Kroch & Taylor on the one hand and van Kemenade on the other, explore evidence for the precise nature of early English V2. In the same way, it is central in Fontana's chapter in part 2 of the book. And Henry's chapter in part 3 analyses three stages in the development of Belfast English imperatives: from a stage with V/I to C through one with restricted movement to a lower position, to one with no V2 at all.

4.1.2 The V2 parameter

Given current generative thinking, V-movement should be derivable from independent principles of grammar. One of the foci of work on V2 since the mid 1980s has been to give an accurate characterization of the parameter(s) responsible for V-movement. Descriptively speaking, the above observations could be captured by three parameters along the following lines:

(9) a. V moves to I (yes/no)
b. V/I moves to C (yes/no)
c. Spec,IP is an A position (yes/no)

But, preferably, one would like to couch these in more general terms; (9a) and (9b) could be viewed as instantiations of a more general property, which could be formulated as follows: if a functional head I or C in the functional extension of VP has a certain property X, then V must move to that head position.

Many attempts have been made to define this property X. Among the recent ones, there is a marked tendency, in the spirit of economy/ minimalism, to formulate X in terms of morphological strength. Examples are Pollock (1989) and Zwart (1993). The virtue of this notion is that it can be generalized to derive other instances of movement. On the other hand, attempts to correlate 'morphological' strength with overt morphology in any empirically contentful way have not yielded much result so far. Relevant discussion of this is found in the chapter by Lightfoot in part 3 and in the chapter by Roberts in part 4. We will leave this issue for now.

4.1.3 The directionality of change

Recent proposals often relate the presence of overt V-movement to the relative morphological strength of the landing site. This raises interesting and nontrivial questions with respect to the directionality of change. Recent studies about the diachrony of V2 are mainly concerned with accounting for its loss in the histories of English, French, Portuguese, as a number of the papers in Battye & Roberts (1995) testify. This ties in naturally with the notion that the loss of V2 can be related to the loss of morphological strength. But this would imply that the earlier stages of the languages in question, with presumably richer morphology, had V-movement, and there is evidence against this. V2 arose out of patterns in which the verb was not fronted. Adams (1994a, b) shows that in Classical Latin the copula was attached to particular kinds of (second position) hosts and thus establishes the rise of a V-movement dependency. Vennemann (1974) reconstructs an earlier Germanic stage where the verb was always in nonfronted position. Weerman (1989), assuming that V2 is V-movement to C, speculates that the rise of V2 structures was motivated by the *loss* of morphological specification on C, arguing for a scenario in which C was first licensed by inherent morphological specifications. When these were lost, C had to be licensed by being lexicalized. Longobardi (1991) offers some evidence from Gothic for a similar scenario. And Abraham (1993c) argues that older stages of German did not have V-to-C movement; this arose out of an older stage with paratactic IP organization, and was a spin-off of the rise of hypotaxis. The latter is in line with the insights in Kiparsky (1995). These case studies suggest that there are morphological and syntactic ways of licensing functional material and that these should exist as functionally equivalent alternatives. Similar issues with respect to case will be addressed in section 5. How such developments can be reconciled with declining morphological strength of the landing site of V is an intriguing question which we will leave for the moment.

5 Case and change in morphology and syntax

An important issue which arises in different ways in a number of the contributions in this volume is the relation between morphological and syntactic ways of marking grammatical function (cf. Abraham, Kiparsky, Philippi, Roberts, Vincent, Weerman). It is of course a classic line of argument within traditional grammar to see a causal connection between the erosion of morphological case marking, usually attributed to the disruptive effects of 'blind', Neo-grammarian-style sound change, and the emergence of patterns of more or less fixed word order, and the increased use of prepositions as markers of syntactic dependency.

Another way of referring to these postulated correspondences is to label the patterns evinced in Latin as 'synthetic' and those found in Romance as 'analytic', and then to argue that the change from Latin to Romance can be summed up in a single general shift dubbed 'synthesis to analysis' (cf. Vincent 1996 for more details and a critical discussion). And indeed in spirit this style of explanation is not very far removed from that to be found more recently under the banner of 'parameter resetting' (Lightfoot 1991; Roberts 1993a). Phenomena whose surface expression is very diverse are brought under a single dimension of grammatical variability (synthesis vs analysis), and the change is located in the switch from one grammatical mode to the other. Thus, compare Harris (1978a), who equates synthetic with morphological and analytic with syntactic and then argues that the Romance languages prefer a 'more syntactic' type of grammatical marking, with Roberts (1985a), who sees the key to the emergence of the category of modal in Modern English as lying in the replacement of morphological with syntactic government. On the other hand, while Harris (1978b) explicitly dissociates himself from the traditional view in that he argues that syntactic shifts must precede and not follow on morphological erosion, Roberts (1985a) represents a direct continuation of the nineteenth-century position that syntactic change follows and responds — in a therapeutic rather than prophylactic way (cf. Lightfoot 1979) — to the effects of phonological change.

In sum then the debates go on around the same topics — the relation between phonological and (morpho-)syntactic change; the nature of the link between functionally equivalent but structurally different sub-systems; etc. This however is not to say that progress is not being made. Kiparsky's chapter here provides one striking instance among several. Whereas traditional grammarians had assumed a loose correlation between presence/absence of inflectional morphology and fixedness of word order, Kiparsky refines the insight into a unilateral implication: 'lack of inflectional morphology implies fixed order of direct nominal arguments' (Kiparsky, p. 470). By contrast, as he further notes, 'The converse is not true, and hardly even a tendency.' To take another instance, Weerman explores a Modern version of the idea that there is an equivalence between case-marked NP and the combination of a preposition and NP. More generally, our detailed understanding of the nature and mechanisms of grammar is incommensurably greater than twenty, let alone a hundred, years ago, so that even when Modern researchers such as those whose work is represented in the present volume broach similar questions to those posed by their predecessors, they do so with greater refinement and sharper analytical and conceptual tools.

One respect in which Modern work both sharpens and complicates the traditional question concerns the nature of case. Earlier grammarians operate with a notion of morphological case as the surface exponent of grammatical relations (see Blake 1994), and this notion underlies a number of current theoretical models, notably the various mapping theories which we will discuss further below and of which the article by Kiparsky in this volume is a prime example. Other current syntactic theories include a notion of abstract, syntactic case.[8] What is then the relation between syntactic and morphological case? This would seem an obvious question, but it is one to which surprisingly little attention has been given. In most GB work on case, it is tacitly assumed that s-case is the same as m-case except for the matter of overt realization. This is essentially Vergnaud's original idea which led to the Case Filter (Chomsky 1981). On this view English and Latin differ only in that the latter requires case always to be overtly spelt out in the form of the word whereas the former does not. There is then a parameter controlling realization of case, just as there is a parameter determining whether subjects of finite main clauses are phonetically null or not. For an expression of this view, see Haegeman (1994b: 158) who writes: 'We assume that abstract case is part of universal grammar. The degree of morphological realization of abstract case varies parametrically from one language to another'.[9] What is crucial, however, is that the Case Filter requires s-case in order for any NP to be realizable at PF, regardless of whether that NP bears m-case. The issue is complicated, moreover, by the introduction into Case Theory of the Visibility condition, according to which s-case is required to make an argument visible for θ-marking.[10] This shifts attention away from the Case Filter seen as a condition on PF and seems to bring the notion of s-case closer to the traditional grammatical functions subject and object. Indeed, Johnson (1991: 578, note 1) observes à propos of quirky case phenomena: 'These facts indicate that there is no direct relationship between "structural case" ... and morphological case. ... we may understand "structural case" to have a closer affinity to the OBJECT relation defended in Zaenen, Maling & Thráinsson.'[11] On such a Mapping view too — found also in the system proposed by Kiparsky (this volume) — there has to be a further theory to determine the mapping between s-case and m-case (cf. Holmberg 1986 and Sigurðsson 1992 for proposals), an issue to which we return below.

On either view, there will be a further question as to the best way to assign s-case — whether by *LGB*-style assignment under government or by the minimalist notion of checking. A third possibility canvassed by Weerman in part 4 of this volume is that s-case is an unnecessary and even confusing luxury within grammatical theory and one which can readily be dispensed with.

Case Theory is one module of grammar where the burgeoning of functional categories discussed above has had important consequences. As originally conceived, s-case is a feature assigned under government to DPs. Such s-cases could be either 'structural', that is assigned by a governing head in a given configuration at S-structure, or 'inherent' and assigned by a governing lexical category at D-structure. Inherent s-case involves a fixed association with a given θ-role also assigned by the governor whereas elements bearing structural s-case may have a variety of θ-roles.

More recently within the Minimalist Programme (MP — see Chomsky 1993, Marantz 1995), the notion of s-case-assignment has been replaced by that of s-case-checking, which can only take place in a Spec–head configuration. This in turn requires additional functional categories to host the moved elements. Whereas, within the *LGB* model of Chomsky (1981), the Agr property of a finite Infl was what determined the assignment of [+nominative] to the subject argument, so there now has to be an Agr_S projection, and the subject argument raises to Spec,Agr_S where its s-case is checked. Similarly, an object DP must raise to Spec,Agr_O for s-case-checking purposes. An important aspect of this new approach is that the core mechanism of Case Theory is not assignment under government but checking under agreement. What, it may be asked, is the significance of this shift for theories of syntactic change? We will consider these questions in a discussion of each of the three positions that are represented in the chapters of the present volume:

i. the current minimalist view sketched above where s-case is assigned under agreement with an appropriate functional head (Roberts);
ii. the subsumption of Case Theory into a non-derivational theory of Mapping between semantic and syntactic argument structure (Kiparsky);
iii. the view that Case Theory (whether in a government or a checking variant) should be abandoned (Weerman).

Let us consider each in turn.

5.1 Minimalism, case and word order

Roberts' chapter explores the consequences for a theory of change of the model elaborated by Kayne (1994), according to which the universal underlying order is:

(10) S(pecifier)   H(ead) C(omplement)

This order follows as a theorem from Kayne's theory of phrase structure and forces the abandonment of the classic directionality parameter. For students of change this in turn means that shifts such as the postulated passage of head-final OE to head-initial ME can no longer be treated as due to parameter resetting. Roberts articulates an alternative view — compatible with Kayne's conclusions — according to which the order OV in OE is derived by leftward movement of the object, licensed by the morphological strength of the functional head hosting the moved material. Simplifying somewhat, it follows therefore that erosion of the m-case system leads to a failure to license movement, which in turn requires the object to remain *in situ*. On this view, then, deviations from the universally determined underlying head-first order require overt morphological licensing, and hence loss of such licensing material will cause the underlying order to (re-)appear.

Roberts' argument is an elegant illustration of how an approach in terms of FCs captures the relation between word order and m-case familiar already to nineteenth-century students of change. Note first that the parametric shift, to the extent that there is one, concerns not the cross-linguistically identifiable property of head–complement order, but the language-particular one of the 'strength' of the morphological marking. This is in line with the general view (Chomsky 1993a) that parameters are associated with functional material. If the relevant functional material is strong, then case is checked by overt movement (i.e. before Spell-Out); otherwise procrastination ensures that checking is delayed until LF (after Spell-Out). In either circumstance, what is checked is s-case (i.e. abstract case); the 'strength' or not of the functional feature determines which of the interface levels is the locus of the checking.

There is an asymmetry in the Kayne/Roberts approach in that order is primary (though in turn reducible to c-command), and 'strength' simply the licenser of deviations therefrom. However, on this view one would still look for — as Roberts notes (p. 43) — a bilateral relation between m-case and position. If a language does not have m-case, we would not expect leftward movement; in particular scrambling ought not to be possible. Yet Dutch, which does not have m-case, is OV and allows scrambling. The obvious move, and the one Roberts makes, is to assume that in Dutch the relevant functional projection, Agr_O, is strong even though morphologically unrealized. This removes the possibility of a simple correlation between overt morphology and overt movement and raises the problem of the empirical content of the property 'strong'. Icelandic by contrast, is problematic in the opposite sense: although the case morphology is overt, and therefore presumably 'strong', the order is VO and scrambling is not possible. It is not at all clear how to accommodate this situation within the theory.

A further problem with the Kayne/Roberts position is noted by Weerman, namely that it is not readily compatible with optional or free word orders. One would expect strict patterning in one of the two directions but not the widely attested alternative that the morphology (whether of a head- or dependent-marking kind) does all the necessary syntactic work and makes questions of linear order irrelevant (cf. for example Warlpiri (Simpson 1993) or Mohawk (Baker 1991)).

We will turn now to the alternative mapping approach, elaborated here by Kiparsky, in which both the Icelandic and Dutch constellations of properties and the more general problem of the relation between position and other types of argument coding are claimed to find natural explanations.

5.2 Mapping Theory

In the paper which launched the Minimalist Programme, Chomsky (1993) reviews the deficiencies in grammatical theory that follow from a concentration on (head) government as the key structural notion. He advocates instead a system in which the core relation is that between a specifier and a head, in other words agreement. Viewed, however, from a wider cross-linguistic perspective, case-marking as determined by a governing item (a V or a P) and agreement are simply two of the ways in which languages may signal their structural relations (corresponding roughly to the typological distinction established by Nichols 1986 between dependent-marking and head-marking patterns). On this view it makes no sense to privilege either type of relation, especially when there is a third category of language in which relations are signalled neither by overt case nor by overt agreement, but by linear position.[12] Rather, what advocates of this view seek is a model which defines the grammatical relations in their own terms and only then specifies how these abstractly represented relations are expressed or realized in the languages of the world. Such an approach, which has much in common with the logic leading to the development of relationally based models such as Relational Grammar and Lexical-Functional Grammar, lies behind the account that Kiparsky offers. Syntactic argument structure is seen as a direct projection of semantic roles, and the task is to find an economical and perspicuous way to map theta-roles into syntax: hence the label Mapping Theory.

Mapping theories have their origin in models of grammar that assume monotonicity and monostratality: in other words, there are no movements, no empty categories and in general no grammatical operations which 'destroy' structure that has already been compiled. They are also non-configurational models in the sense that syntactic constituency is only postulated when the overt morphosyntactic properties of the language require it. The architecture of such systems and the general constraints within which they operate do not require configurationally based notions such as c-command, government, Spec–head agreement, etc. Order and constituency can therefore be treated as being exactly on a par with m-case or agreement: part of the component that provides the realization or expression of abstract grammatical relations, and not part of the underlying system that defines those relations. For the most part (Gerdts' model is an exception), they involve the use of grammatical features to capture generalizations (much in the same spirit as the features [± N, ±V] define categories in X-bar theory).

The distinctive properties of Kiparsky's system *vis-à-vis* other mapping theories can be summarized under the following heads:

(i) The number of levels. In the model proposed by Bresnan & Kanerva (1989) and Bresnan & Moshi (1990) there is a mapping from theta-structure to a level of grammatical relations. There is of necessity also a connection to be established between the GRs and the ways in which they are formally realized, though the references cited above have very little to say on that score. There are, then, three stages in the mapping: theta-roles, GRs, realization.[13]

Kiparsky's model by contrast has four levels and we compare it here with the very similar system of Gerdts (1993). Kiparsky notes that his concept of abstract case bears some resemblance to the similarly labelled notion within the Principles and Parameters model, and is also equivalent to what other people call grammatical relations. Morphosyntactic case by contrast is rather harder to define in terms that translate into other systems. It is something like the final, surface GR but shorn of any form of realization.

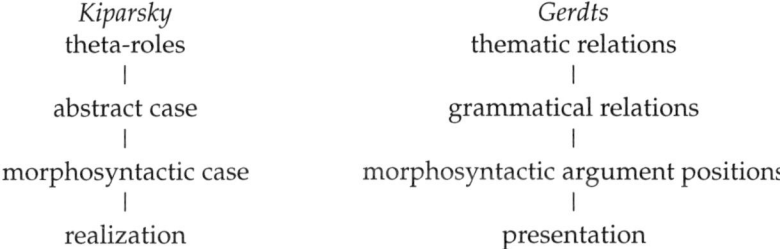

In naming the third level, Gerdts privileges the concept of position and Kiparsky that of case; in truth neither term is strictly appropriate at this level since both case and position are aspects of realization (presentation). What we have rather is a level of morphosyntactically realizable argument structure. It is the composition of this level and its mapping onto the level of realization which may be the locus of syntactic change in Kiparsky's conception (see point (iv) below).

(ii) The system of features. Bresnan *et al.*'s LMT cross-classifies GRs in terms of two features, [± (semantically) r(estricted)] and [± o(bjective)], and then provides a separate set of correspondences between the features and the items on a hierarchy of theta-roles. Alsina (1993) does something similar though with a different pair of features, [± subj(ect)] and [± obl(ique)]. Kiparsky's features, [± H(ighest)R(ole)] and [± L(owest)R(ole)], instead directly exploit the ranks within the hierarchy and apply to all levels of the representation. In this respect, his system works rather like the features in phonology which are present at all levels of representation.

(iii) The extension of features to include position. A special case of the preceding point is that the features characterize syntactic positions as well as relations or morphological case. In this way all aspects of the level of realization/presentation can be encompassed within the same notation so that equivalences and changes can be more transparently stated. Since change takes place precisely between these two levels, this is an important advance.

(iv) The application to change. As noted, Kiparsky's is the first Mapping Theory to be directly responsive to the facts of change and the needs imposed by extending enquiry to include data from this source.

Here is not the place to enter into the comparative merits of mapping and minimalism as synchronic systems; readers will have to form their own view on that score.[14] However, we may legitimately ask where the advantage of mapping lies for the student of language change. The main answer is in the independence and formal as well as functional equivalence of m-case and position. Roberts' result is still derivable: if a language loses m-case for whatever reason, an alternative has to be found at the level of realization. This may well be a recourse to position, which, as Kiparsky notes, is always available, and may even be the default strategy, not for reasons of underlying structure but because of the inevitable linearity of language. Equally, however, the answer may lie in agreement. Indeed, Vincent in his chapter argues that within Romance both options are available but for different relations: subjects are typically marked by agreement and objects by position, though in Latin both were marked by m-case.

5.3 Case and the role of prepositions

Weerman's contribution focusses on the consequences of the loss of morphological case in the history of Dutch. Recall that Roberts had identified Dutch as a problem for his account insofar as the language lacks morphological case but yet still has scrambling and OV order. Roberts' solution is to postulate that the head of Agr_O must contain 'strong' N-features despite the lack of overt morphology. There is an obvious danger of circularity here: if Dutch N-features are not presumed to be strong, then the language counterexemplifies the proposal, but the only reason to believe that the features are strong is to avoid the counterexample! Weerman confronts this issue and argues for the abandonment of Case Theory altogether. The theoretical burden borne by Case Theory is instead claimed to be attributable to an independently motivated principle, to wit the ECP.

In making this move, Weerman brings back into focus another aspect of traditional discussions, namely the functional equivalence between case inflections and prepositions. Traditional grammars assume the replacement of Latin dative and genitive endings by prepositions parallel to the replacement of nominative and accusative by positional identification of the roles they express. What would this mean in modern terms? Weerman points to the following paradigm of equivalences:

a) [case DP]   Middle Dutch
                (or any case-inflecting language)

b) [Ø DP] Modern Dutch
            (or any 'analytic' language)
c) [P   DP] Modern Dutch
            (or any language with the category P)

He then argues, in much the same spirit as Roberts though with different theoretical assumptions and consequences, that case-marked DPs have a richer range of distributional possibilities. The data he focusses on are complementary to those discussed by Roberts, namely instances in which a DP has been moved rightwards (extraposed) beyond V. This pattern was possible in Middle Dutch where such DPs were case-marked and is possible in Modern Dutch only if the extraposed DP is preceded by a preposition. Hence the conclusion that Ps may license 'misplaced' DPs just as case could, but a non-case-marked DP is blocked. This distribution would follow quite naturally if the difference lay in whether the case-marker was overt or not. If it is, then the element is free; if not — i.e. if the structure in question contains an empty category — then the distributional possibilities will be constrained by an old and well-tried principle, namely the ECP.

When set beside the contributions of Roberts and Kiparsky, Weerman's chapter highlights an interesting issue about the mutual dependence of theoretical constructs. Recall that Kiparsky retains the equivalent of a GB-style system of abstract case, but dispenses with the configurational structure that is normally taken to determine it (either under government as in *LGB* or by Spec–head agreement as in the MP). Weerman by contrast dispenses with case but must keep government in the form of the ECP to keep track of his empty categories. Mapping theories such as Kiparsky's in turn do not have empty categories — indeed part of the original rationale for the development of such systems was the desire to avoid empty categories (cf. Bresnan 1982). The MP system has all three (though see Chomsky 1995 for some new thoughts on these matters). That historical data may be germane to the resolution of these important questions is of course fully in the spirit of Lightfoot's early plea for the significance of diachronic syntax (extending from Kiparsky's seminal doctoral dissertation where the same mode of argumentation is applied in the realm of phonology).

5.4 The role of case and the DP and KP

One natural question that the reader may have asked is: what is the category label of the constituents in (a–c) above? For (c) the answer would seem to be straightforward, viz PP. It would then follow that the case in (a) is also the head of a constituent — call it KP. For the circumstance where the *ec* is postulated it is not clear whether PP or KP or simply DP is appropriate. What is clear is that subject arguments must escape the distributional limitations imposed by the ECP, and thus that subjects are categorially different in kind from all other arguments. This conclusion is also reached within a different and much more elaborate theory of the relation between m-case and argument structure developed recently by Bittner & Hale (1996).

Another issue which has not received a great deal of attention in the literature concerns the locus of the case marking. In a case-inflecting language like Latin the morphological answer is that case is attached to nouns (or better perhaps to members of the archi-category [+N] since adjectives may also be case-inflected). Yet s-case and related notions such as Kiparsky's morphosyntactic case are clearly properties of arguments, in turn realized as NPs in the traditional view. As long as Ns are heads of NPs there need be no contradiction here — the m/s-case properties hold of the NP and are realized by percolation on its head (following the criterion for headship identified by Zwicky 1985 as the 'morphosyntactic locus'). Recently, of course, it has become the standard view that arguments are of the category DP, thus requiring syntactic movement of N to D (Longobardi 1994) and/or K to explain the surface position of m-case.

More evidence for the intrinsic connection between m-case and the category D is offered in the chapters by Abraham, Philippi and Vincent, in which the loss of m-case within Romance and Germanic is shown to correlate — though in different ways within the different families — with the rise of articles, that is to say with overt exponents of the category D. For Germanic, Abraham shows how there was an original system in which, as in Modern Russian and Polish, a choice of different m-case for the object of a verb could lead to different semantic interpretations. As the case marking is lost, so an alternative means has to be found to signal definiteness and thus the article is born. Confirmation of this line of thinking is found in the differential evolution of the definite and indefinite articles. Only the former are required to fill the structural gap left by the loss of m-case. The indefinite article is a later, and in origin independent, development. Where Abraham starts with the interaction of case and aspect, Philippi focuses on the role of the article and its relation to other members of the emerging German system of determiners and quantifiers. Taken together the two chapters are complementary and mutually supportive, and offer a valuable new perspective on the historical development of functional categories.

The situation in Romance is rather different, as Vincent shows. Once again the daughter languages all have articles although their historical ancestor, Latin, demonstrably did not. In this instance, however, there is no evidence of m-case subserving an aspectual or quantificational function. Rather, its function was principally one of marking arguments. Vincent notes that whereas Latin subjects were encoded twice, once via the case — nominative — of the (pro)noun in question and once via the rich system of person/number agreement on the verb, objects could only be identified by their case form and, to a lesser extent, by their position. Since order was relatively free in Latin and subject largely to discourse conditions, displaced objects would need to be identified as such. The erosion of morphological case leads to this function being carried out by unstressed pronouns from which the clitics subsequently emerge, these in turn becoming a system of pronominal agreement in several of the modern languages. Discourse status is also identified by the former deictic elements *ipse* and *ille* attached to the nouns, and it is from these that the articles develop in different daughter languages. The nominal substitutes (clitics) and the nominal escorts (articles) thus converge in systems which provide overt morphological evidence in favour of the DP hypothesis.

The comparison of these grammatical sub-systems in Romance and Germanic offers a salutary lesson for the historical syntactician. In both instances the older languages have a similar property, namely morphological case, and their historical descendants share another feature, namely definite (and indefinite) articles, yet the historical paths and the driving forces behind the changes are very different. There is nonetheless one quality in common between the two, namely that the new grammatical elements have derived from items that in origin had more clearly definable independent semantic functions. It is precisely the insistence on this aspect of change — the recruitment of new members of grammatical systems via the semantic 'bleaching' of formerly autonomous items (cf. Meillet 1912) — that characterizes the mechanism of grammaticalization (Hopper & Traugott 1993). We see here then a valuable point of possible convergence between two largely independent traditions of historical enquiry (cf. Roberts 1993b and Postma 1995, for more work in this vein). The further ramifications of the relations between the categories K, D and P are ripe for historical exploration, and functional categories as deployed in the articles discussed here provide an interesting perspective for developing the insights of grammaticalization theory in formal terms.

6 Grammaticalization

All the authors whose chapters have been touched on in the previous section address historical scenarios in which the central empirical issue is what Weerman calls deflection, in other words the loss of (inflectional) morphological marking (in traditional terms the move from synthesis to analysis). Inflectional morphology is seen as licensing various structural possibilities; if the morphology is lost, then the structures it licenses are also lost (Roberts) or an alternative and partially non-overlapping mode of licensing is found (Kiparsky, Weerman). A logically complementary problem, and one by no means so central to debates in generative diachronic syntax in general or to the chapters of this volume in particular, is the emergence of inflectional morphology, whether of the case (dependent-marking) or agreement (head-marking) type.

It is perhaps not a coincidence that this aspect of change has been less frequently addressed within generative grammar. Whereas the kind of change known traditionally as synthesis to analysis logically requires an abrupt discontinuity (see Vincent 1996), analysis to synthesis seems to argue for a view of change as a continuous and gradual process whereby formerly autonomous elements evolve into markers of grammatical function, losing their status as independent elements in the process. It is scarcely surprising therefore that the study of such changes has been the staple fare of proponents of grammaticalization theory (GT) as an alternative approach to grammatical change (cf. Hopper & Traugott 1993; Traugott & Heine 1991; Heine et al. 1991).

Areas of research within the grammaticalization tradition that are pertinent to studies in this volume are the emergence of articles from markers of distal deixis (Greenberg 1991), the development of adpositions into case markers (Blake 1994: ch. 6) and of pronouns into agreement morphemes (Hopper & Traugott 1993: 16-17). What all such studies demonstrate beyond dispute is that there are recurrent semantic pathways along which grammatical categories appear to pass in the course of their historical development. These semantic dimensions can be detected even when the detailed morphosyntactic changes are rather different. Thus, there is a common semantic evolution to both definite and indefinite articles in Romance and Germanic even though, as we have noted, the chapters in this volume show that the evolving relations between morphological case and the determiner system are by no means parallel in the two case histories. Moreover, the same semantic patterns seem to be involved in languages of very different genetic types, as shown by the similarities in the evolution of Romance clitics and Bantu pronominal agreement. Lightfoot may well be right in his analysis of the discontinuity of change in grammars — what he calls the logical problem of (morpho-)syntactic change — but the fact remains that such apparent semantic continuities are there as an empirical datum. Some attempts to incorporate the directionality of change into formal models of change were briefly discussed in section 3. Functional categories provide the formal vehicle for analysing such change, as noted and to some extent worked out in Roberts (1993b), Vincent (1993), van Kemenade (1993), Postma (1995).

Another area in which grammaticalization theorists have made considerable progress in documenting change types across language families and reducing them once again to a set of morphosemantic dimensions concerns the marking of tense, mood and aspect (Bybee et al. 1994). A first step towards incorporating such data into a generative model is Roberts (1993b). In the present volume two more case studies which move in this direction are offered by Benincà & Poletto and by Miller. The former address the changes that are involved when an independent lexical item becomes a marker of modality, and they demonstrate within a minimalist framework how this is reflected in the evolving functional structure. Miller adopts a rather different formal approach — that of HPSG — and shows how the verbs *avoir* and *être* in Old French start out with properties similar to those of their Modern English counterparts and evolve away from that in the transition to Middle French.

To the extent that the Modern English auxiliaries seem more grammaticalized than their French counterparts (which share more properties with main verbs — see Pollock 1989), such a development would appear to reverse the process of grammaticalization and thus offer a potential counterexample to Hopper & Traugott's unidirectionality hypothesis (1993: ch. 5). More such carefully documented and appropriately formalized studies are a prime *desideratum* if there is to be a real dialogue between two approaches to language change which are as often as not complementary.

7 Overview of the volume

As in any volume that derives from a conference, there is an inevitable heterogeneity (or perhaps better multi-dimensionality) about the collected papers when they emerge in published form. However, some of the disparities have been eliminated in the refereeing process and the sectioning of the present volume is designed to highlight similarities and parallelisms. We will explain briefly our thinking behind this grouping into parts, noting that different groupings would have been possible.

All the papers published here except one were presented at the 3rd Diachronic Generative Syntax Conference held in Amsterdam, 31 March – 2 April 1994. The exception is Miller's paper, which was presented at the almost immediately preceding 24th Linguistic Symposium on Romance Languages held at UCLA/USC in early March 1994, and which is included here by invitation of the editors. Some of the papers that were presented at the conference were subsequently withdrawn or did not survive the rigours of refereeing. All that remain were substantially revised in the light of at least two and sometimes three or four rounds of referees' comments.

Part 1: this is one of the most varied parts and reflects the complexity of the core issue: the way a predicate selects and marks its arguments. Classically, of course, there are argument-changing constructions such as passives and causatives, and these have been well studied. Less attention has by contrast been devoted to the ways a verb's argument-array varies with a particular mood or aspect (Abraham), and the way nominal properties such as m-case and definiteness interact with the verb to determine particular semantico-syntactic effects (Abraham, Philippi). Loss of argument structure — in particular loss of theta-assigning properties — is a natural way to model grammaticalization (Benincà & Poletto), while the shift of argument structure may provide a route away from grammaticalization (Miller).

Part 2: this section on clitics contains one chapter (Vincent) which is in part at least a link with the preceding one, since it studies the emergence of clitics and articles in Romance as part of wholesale restructuring of the system of argument marking in that family. Fontana and Rivero, by contrast, are principally concerned to advance our understanding of the syntactic structures that clitics inhabit, and how those change in the course of the history of Spanish.

Part 3: the chapters grouped here focus on the landing sites of V-movement and the properties of Comp, though they share an interest with Fontana and Rivero in the nature of clause structure and how to model changes which can be observed in this domain. The longstanding debate on the history of English V2 and clause structure continues (Kroch & Taylor and van Kemenade), while Zaring & Hirschbühler add a new case study from French. Henry gives a case study of change in progress: the loss of V-movement in Hiberno-English imperatives. Lightfoot teases out the implications of current empirical work and raises the issue of indeterminacy, discussed above (sections 3 and 6).

Part 4: the connections between the chapters here have already been laid out in some detail in section 5 above. Essentially, they are united by a common interest in how the different forms of argument marking — agreement, case and position — interact, and how in turn the historical study of these phenomena illuminates and is illuminated by theoretical developments. There is therefore a natural, cyclical continuity back to Part 1, and we now leave it to our readers to make their own selection from the riches of the chapters that follow.

Notes

1. For other recent surveys of a more or less introductory kind, see Lightfoot (1988), Kroch (1992), Vincent (1994).
2. We use this example because it provides a clear illustration, although it does not really do justice to the vast amount of literature on V2, in which it becomes clear that 'V2' is not a unitary phenomenon. This is illustrated, for instance, by the chapters on V2 in this volume.
3. This is in the spirit, though not to the letter of Pollock (1989). Pollock (1989) proposes a different order of the FCs. However, as noted, there is now an emerging consensus that (3) is the appropriate order.
   For more detailed discussion of these issues, see the introduction to Battye & Roberts (1995).
4. Of course this does not preclude other types of change, such as change in lexical properties of, e.g., verbs. But these would not be examples of parametric change.
5. MoodP was first introduced, as far as we know, by Rivero (1986); DP by Abney (1987); Agr_OP by Chomsky (1991); ClP by Sportiche (1992); KP by Lamontagne & Travis (1987) and Laughren (1989).
6. We will leave the possibility that IP consists of a multitude of different FCs on the side for the moment, since it is not relevant to the current discussion. IP subsumes Agr_SP and TP at the very least.
7. Note, however, the argument in Vikner (1990) that Continental Scandinavian has no V-to-I movement.
8. The usual convention is to spell abstract case with a capital C to distinguish it from the traditional morphological sense of the term. Rather than rely on this uncertain typo-

graphical practice, which anyway not all authors adopt, we will henceforth refer to s-case and m-case to distinguish the two senses.
9. See van Kemenade (1987: ch. 3) for an application of this.
10. For discussion of the introduction of the Visibility condition, see Webelhuth (1995: 41ff.).
11. The OBJECT relation of ZMT is that of LFG — cf. Bresnan (1982).
12. Blake (1994: 16–18) adds adverbs, relator nouns and possessives to the list of ways that languages may realize relations without having recourse to m-case.
13. A variety of possible terms suggest themselves here — e.g. expression, exponence, presentation (the term used by Gerdts) or even Spell-Out. We choose realization in acknowledgement of the lucid and prescient discussion of the whole problem in Matthews (1981: ch. 13).
14. For example, mapping theories do not require extensive functional structure *pace* the claim of Kayne (1994: 132): 'I do not think that other theories can do without such entities.'

Part 1

Aspect, argument structure and case selection

1 The interdependence of case, aspect and referentiality in the history of German: the case of the verbal genitive

Werner Abraham

*To the memory of Herbert Penzl, Berkeley —
eminent linguist and philologist, and friend 1910–95*

1 Introduction*

In the history of the grammar of German, there is a recalcitrant problem related to the case paradigm: how is the decay of the verbally governed genitive from late Middle High German (around 1450) onwards to be motivated and how is it to be related to developments in other components of syntax, morphosyntax and their semantics (see, most recently, Schrodt 1992)? One attractive solution was proposed by Leiss (1991) who sketches an intricate interplay between the decay of the morphologically marked aspectual morphology, the emergence of the definite (and, not without a remarkable temporal delay, the indefinite) article, and the opposition between the accusative and the genitive cases and their specific roles as objects. While it is enticing to follow Leiss' speculations, which still await empirical, quantitative support from the side of philology, it is likewise attractive to place this speculation in a wider framework of a theory of aspect and its relation to verbal argument structure. In the process, Leiss' account, which has nothing to say about the specific structural distinction of the accusative and the genitive cases as governed by verbs, will be expanded and deepened.

The emergence of Det-categories and the decay of the case morphology such as the German genitive has invited an abundance of speculations about the very function of the article category as such (see, e.g., Behaghel 1923, Paul 1959, Holmberg 1993). The main tenet is that the article morphemes developed because both nominals and adjectivals[1] gave up a good deal of their inflection for case. Although the (partial) decay of nominal inflection as such is not at all untenable for German (primarily for the genitive), the causal link still appears ill motivated, as Leiss (1991: 1408) has argued. Both the assumption that the article is superfluous, given that a language has articulate case distinctions, and the claim that adjectival, prenominal agreement inflection suffices for the syntactic marking of valency meet with typological counterevidence. For example, Modern Greek has had, throughout its history, both (definite) articles and nominal and adjectival agreement inflection. Thus, it appears that the rise of the article categories cannot be linked directly to inflectional morphology in the attributive adjective.

The present chapter takes up the above issues. Its main line of argument is that, as long as the Old High German (OHG) aspect system was intact, case distinctions helped to identify the referential status of verbal arguments. When, in the course of late OHG, aspectual morphology weakened, thereby increasingly disallowing referential identification by means of case distinctions alone, the need for explicit article morphemes to take over this function arose. Section 2 discusses the genitive in Modern German(ModG) and its structural vs its lexical status. Section 3 shows that the verbal genitive in Middle High German (MHG) has a much wider distribution. Furthermore, its status is illustrated in context in OHG. Particular emphasis is placed on the structural status of the partitive (nominal) genitive as opposed to the verbally governed genitive. In section 4, we discuss the relation between verbal aspect, case and nominal reference primarily in Russian, with the purpose of showing that the proposal made for the diachrony of German can be generalized. Section 5 illustrates how the definite and the indefinite article emerged compensating the loss of verbal aspectual morphology. In Section 6 the aspectual systems of Slavic, OHG, MHG, and ModG are compared. This enables us to correlate the two verbal cases, genitive vs accusative, with the emerging articles.

Since the relation between the genitive and the accusative arguments prompts our reflection, let us first look at the status of these cases in ModG.

2 Case distribution in ModG — the diachronic plot

2.1 Genitive vs accusative: lexical vs structural

There are only a few verbs in Modern Standard German governing the genitive — and none in any of its dialects or oral regiolects! Otherwise, where the genitive occurs, it is selected by the nominal category as partitive case. In those cases where the (old) genitive government is retained, the genitive-bearing argument is always the most direct argument to the verb (= verb-closest, and thus structurally the deepest, argument), or 'VCA' ('verb-closest argument', where 'close' is to be taken both with respect to linear order and structurally deepest embedding). See (1a–c), where capitals denote focal accent within the clause, which is always on the structurally deepest, V-closest position (I take German to be an SOV-language). See Abraham (1992b) and Cinque (1993a) for the structural identification of main clausal accent in terms of UG. Note that the genitive cannot be separated from the V–closest position.

(1) a. ich <heute> den Mann   <heute> des VERRATS
       I   today the man-ACC today the treason-GEN
       <*heute> bezichtige
          today accuse

b. ??daß ich des Verrats   den MANN   bezichtige
   that I the treason-GEN the man-ACC accuse
c. *daß ich des VERRATS den Mann bezichtige
          GEN   ACC

This type of object genitive, i.e. the genitive object in a three-place valency configuration, is restricted to a small number of verbs, which can be unified only *ex negativo*: it is not a partitive in semantic terms. See the examples in (2a–c) below. On the other hand, the genitive in two-place valency verbal classes has shrunk considerably more, and where some tokens are still retained they are strongly reminiscent of the partitive function. According to the *Akademiegrammatik* (Heidolph et al. 1981: 348ff.), the thematic Goal combines with some privative sense or an abstract experience. Thus, one is likely to find it with privative two-place predicates or two-place verbs of learning such as:

(2) a. *bedürfen, entbehren, ermangeln; bedürftig sein* 'be in need of, miss'
    b. *(un)kundig/gewiß/mächtig* '(in)competent, certain, capable'
    c. special predicates: *(un)fähig/verdächtig/geständig/schuldig sein* 'be (in)competent, suspicious, confessed, guilty'

The common denominator is sought by Heidolph et al. (1981: 351) in the domain of negation, of modal conditions of various kinds, and extra thematic roles like 'effected object' or 'communicated object'. Whereas such characteristics mark the predicates in (2a) and (2b) as selectors of 'weak' (non-referential, or abstract, or non-count nominal) objects in some intuitive, non-formal way, there is hardly any similarity with the set of predicates in (2c). On the other hand, the common feature of (2a–c) may be sought in the fact that the partitive case is selected by features within the DP or the noun-head, whereas the 'three-place genitive' (exemplified by (1a–c)) is clearly selected by the verb.[2] See (3) for an illustration of the clausal relations covered by the old partitive relation.

(3) a. weil   ich [$_{VP}$ [$_{DP}$ das/ein [$_{NP}$ Glas] [$_{PP}$ (des)   Wasser(s)]
       because I   the/a   glass   the-GEN water(-GEN)
       trinke]]
       drink
    b. weil   ich [$_{VP}$ [$_{DP}$ das/ein [$_{NP}$ Glas] [$_{PP}$ (vom)   Wasser]
       because I   the/a   glass   of(-the) water(-DAT)
       trinke]]
       drink

The general idea behind the present description of the partitive genitive is, counter to Belletti (1988), that partitives are genitives subjacent to, and dependent on, some instantiation of Q in QP above the NP in question. The partitive genitive is selected once the nominal head *Glas* selects a [−count] noun like *water*. This means that the partitive genitive is not a verbal case in that it is not in the structural domain of V. Note in passing that partitive genitive objects, despite the fact that they may use a definite article, are invariably non-count and therefore indefinite. In other words, if you say *Ich trinke des Wassers* 'I drink (of) the water', there is nothing definite-referential about the object nominal. We take partitive genitives to be governed by their non-count head nominals, with the case form percolating upwards to $Spec_1$ following the Spec–head-agreement relation. See (36)–(38) in section 5 below on verbal government.

I have argued elsewhere at some length that the case system in German is subject to a strict categorial distribution, in which the structural genitive is selected only by nominals and no longer by verbs (Abraham 1995a, ch. 1 and 3). If this is correct, the decay of the structural genitive appears to be subject to a systematic paradigmatic reshuffling. According to a suggestion made by Donhauser (1992), this development does not capture lexical genitives, e.g. the partitive genitive. See again (3a, b). This would explain why the genitive type subcategorized by three-place verbs is still retained. See the overall distribution of cases in three-place verbs in ModG in (4) below. The assignment of any case other than the accusative, including the genitive, is always in collocation with the accusative, which makes the genitive in three-place configurations a candidate for inherent verbal government. Note that the subcategorial verbal class represented in (4a) is very marginal in ModG.

(4) a. (ACC + GEN + V_1)   three-place predicates
      b. ACC + PO + V_2
      c. DAT + ACC + V_3
      d. *DAT + GEN + V_4
      e. *DAT + DAT + V_5
      f. *GEN + GEN + V_6
      g. (GEN + V_7)   two-place predicate

The verbal class represented by (4a) (often called the *genetivus criminis* class: viz. *anklagen, beschuldigen, bezichtigen*, all meaning more or less 'accuse') belongs to the written register.

Turning back to (1a), the deepest constituent head is the genitival *Verrats*, which receives focal accent by default. (1b, c) show that the order in (1a) is the basic order, with the genitive as (structurally and linearly) verb-closest argument (VCA), despite the fact that there is also a structural accusative object, *den Mann*. While (1b) deviates from the basic order, but retains the focus assignment under default conditions, (1c) alters two basic principles: that of the linear order as well as that of the syntactic distribution of focal accent. Consequently, clear ungrammaticality ensues. The very same holds for prepositional objects (likewise in Dutch and Frisian, where the genitive case is replaced throughout by prepositional objects, as in the dialects of German). See (5a–c) from ModG:

(5) a. dass ich <heute> Maria <heute> um ihre GELDBÖRSE
that I today Maria today for her wallet
<*heute> bitte
today ask
b. ??daß ich um ihre GELDBÖRSE MARIA bitte
c. *daß ich um ihre GELDBÖRSE Maria bitte

Note again that the notion of VCA, which is identified uniquely by its clausal default accent, does not necessarily cover the accusative object in German. The verbal genitive in ModG, if present, is the uniquely identified VCA. Its semantics suggest that it is to be accounted for as verb-incorporated (i.e. the genitive DP to be within the V^0) $[_{V^\circ} [_{DP}$ NP-GEN] $V^0]$. It is not *a priori* clear that this must have been the case in MHG or OHG, too.

3 Diachronic stages: case distribution in modern and older German stages

In this section we will argue for the following generalization for earlier German: the accusative object governed by either a perfective or an imperfective verb (reading) refers to the specific object noun in the former case and to a non-specific reading in the latter case. The genitive, on the other hand, selected by perfective verbs, or by perfective readings of aspectually open verbs, always yields a non-specific reading on the object.

3.1 The verbal vs the partitive genitive in MHG and ModG

The following MHG verbs took an object in the genitive (selection from Paul, Wiehl & Grosse 1989: 341; Behaghel 1923: 564–606):

(6) a. two-place: *(be)gern, muoten, (ge)ruochen* 'demand', *geniezen* 'enjoy', *ergetzen* 'make forget', *entgelten* 'have the disadvantage of', *vergezzen* 'forget', *bîten* 'wait for', *warten* 'wait for', *hüeten* 'heed', *walten* 'have power over', *pflegen* 'be busy with', *gehugen* 'think of', *(ge)dingen* 'hope for', *volgen* 'follow', *darben* 'miss', *(be-)durfen, enbern* 'be in need of', *jehen* 'confess', *swern* 'swear', *zîhen* 'accuse'
b. three-place (reflexive): *sich — bewegen* 'insist on; renounce', *gelouben* 'do away with', *genieten* 'be busy with', *vlîzen* 'busy oneself with', *verstân* 'be competent in', *underwinden* 'meddle with'
c. two-place impersonal: *mich — be-/verdriuzet, bevilt, beträget* 'resent', *gelüstet* 'like, feel lust for' *mir — gebristet, gebricht* 'miss'

Except perhaps for some verbs under (6c), there is no partitive meaning available for the objects. Note the high number of prefixed verbs in this list of genitive governors.

Examples (7) and (8) below illustrate changes in case government between pre-ModG (including MHG) and ModG. The old genitive was replaced by accusative or by a preposition or PP.

(7) *Shift from genitive object to accusative object:*

object places	pre-Modern German: genitive object	Modern German: accusative object
1	*eines Heimes* (be)gehren want a home	*ein Heim* begehren
1	*eines Verhältnisses* pflegen take care of a relation	*ein Verhältnis* pflegen

(8) *Shift from genitive object to prepositional object:*

object places	pre-Modern German: genitive object	Modern German: prepositional object
1	*der Gefallenen* gedenken to think of those who have fallen	*an die Gefallenen* denken
2(1)	sich *des Sommers* erinnern to think of the summer	sich *an den Sommer* erinnern
2(1)	sich *Peters* entsinnen remember Peter	sich *an Peter* entsinnen
1	*einer Aufgabe* vergessen forget a task	*auf eine Aufgabe* vergessen
2(1)	sich *einer Sache* wundern be surprised about something	sich *über eine Sache* wundern

According to Schrodt (1992: 364), there is a preliminary verbal classification that handles the case government distinction in OHG. The purported distinctive property is in the referential weight of the object-NP or PP.

(9) a. *Independent* objects (existing referentially independent of the verbal event) affected by the verbal event, but not brought into being.
   b. *Resultative* objects, whose existence is dependent upon the verbal event in that it comes into being because of the verbal event.

This distinction may not be general enough since Schrodt's list (Schrodt 1992) covers only a small fraction of Otfrid's OHG texts as well as some of the Heliand for Old Saxon. In this respect, Donhauser's (1992) book-length investigation may well be more general and therefore more reliable. In fact, there is reason to believe that Schrodt's distinction is a biased generalization in the light of prevalent typological generalizations to be discussed in section 4 below. There are interconnections between referentiality and case in Russian and Polish. Note, on the other hand, that Finnish appears to corroborate Schrodt's conclusions. However, it will be argued below, in line with Donhauser (1992) and Leiss (1992), that there exists an intricate interplay between the referential status of the object NP and Aktionsart, or aspect, of the verb or verbal group. This link co-determines the choice of verbal object case. It cannot be *a priori* excluded that both the aspectual characteristic and the referentiality status are inherent properties of the predicate involved. Likewise, they may have morphological carriers of such information, such as verbal aspectual affixes and nominal cases or prepositions. But it seems improbable that there are indeed verbs whose semantics motivate strong object interpretations, as opposed to other verbs. Since Schrodt's distinction between referentially 'dependent' and 'independent' NPs is too strong and does not directly relate to crosslinguistic restrictions on the object case distinctions, I will not make use of the distinction in (10) and hence will stick to the generalization about a tripartite distinction as made in (36a–c) below.

Beyond the latter reservation with respect to Schrodt's generalization in (10), there is one piece of solid evidence which is shared without exception by the three investigations (Schrodt, Donhauser and Leiss). Whatever the genitive case signals in terms of the referentiality of the object noun in the older stages of German, this genitive co-occurs, with more than arbitrary frequency, with inherently perfective[3] predicates or else with predicates with perfectivizing verbal prefixes. See (10a, b) (see Abraham 1994 for details).

(10) a. verbal prefixes: *ge-, er-, ent-, ver-*, etc. as well as perfectivizing prepositions, adjectives and adverbials (both as X^0 and XP) such as:
b. prepositions: *aus-, vor-, auf-, an-* 'out, in front of, on, at', etc.
adjectivals: *weg-, tot-, krank-* 'away, dead, ill', etc.
adverbs: *vorüber-, hinein-* 'past, into', etc.

From the dichotomy between simple verbs as duratives and prefix verbs as perfectives, it appears logical and pre-theoretically plausible to assume that it is the verbal prefix as well as the preposition that trigger definiteness on the governed object-NP.

We therefore provisionally conclude that in ModG perfective verbs as such and perfectivizing verbal prefixes, affixoids and adverbials strongly correlate with referentially strong (definite) objects (and, in the case of perfective intransitives, with strong subjects). Unlike in ModG, such aspectually marked verbs in OHG and partly also in late MHG co-occur freely with referentially strong (definite or specific) and weak (indefinite or non-specific) objects. Non-perfective verbs, on the other hand, govern weak object nominals only. We shall come back to this issue in section 5.

3.2 Genitive vs accusative in OHG

So far we have looked at verbs of perception as in (8). Further verb classes that lend themselves to genitive objects for purely referential reasons are, e.g., verbs of eating and drinking, which — Schrodt (1992: 381ff.) makes a particular point of this — presuppose an external, *a priori* existing object and consequently take genitive objects. Note, however, that verbs of feeding prototypically select mass nouns as objects. As expected in this case, the partitive genitive is the default case with these verbs. Therefore, the partitive genitive is realized if the object (of eating and drinking, respectively) is indeterminate, i.e. remains unspecific. The accusative is the non-default for these verbs and needs particular motivation, e.g. by way of a verbal prefix denoting exhaustion of the act or event meaning of the prefix-verb. See, for example, *an(t)bîtan* (cf. Dutch *ontbijten*) 'eat', originally something like 'set teeth (= bite) toward', with the genitive usually 'enjoy, taste' according to (11). Examples (11)–(14) are taken from Schrodt (1992: 382).

(11) [...] Sô   thô the treulogo   *that môs*   antfeng endi mid
     when then the unfaithful that meal(ACC) began   and with
     is   muđu *anbêt*, sô   afgaf ina thô thiu godes craft
     his mouth bit   there left him then *det* god's power

(OS, Heliand 4620)

The meaning of (11) above is that he (=Simon, the unfaithful), receiving the Lord's Supper, sets his teeth at the bread, the eating of which is the all-pervasive topic of the story in the first place. As soon as he takes the first bite (with his mouth) he loses God's power. In other words, the meaning of the verb is not the complex 'eat (up)', but, rather, the componential '(set the) bite toward', with a perfective prefix. Likewise, with *drinkan*, the typical governing case is the genitive, as in (12a), not because the genitive is the structural case under government by referential default (as Schrodt assumes), nor for any other structural reason (in terms of Belletti 1988), but because of its typical [–count] reference for what is drunk. See the formal account for the partitive in (12a).

(12) a. [$_{DP}$ Spec [$_{D'}$ e [NP [$_{KP}$ [$_K$ t_i][$_N$ uuater- [–es]$_i$]]]]] drinkan
                                            water-GEN   drink
     b. drincan suôties   brunnan
         drink   sweet-GEN fountain-GEN (partitive)

Clearly, the partitive genitive is not a verbally governed case (counter to Belletti 1988). Both object NPs designate a determinate object. However, no determiner category expresses this. By contrast, the accusative is used when the object referent is determined on contextual grounds as in (13)–(14).

(13) ne mornont an iuuuomu môde, *huuat*   gi   eft   an
     not worry   in your   spirit what-ACC you then in (the)
     morgan sculin etan eftho drinkan
     morning shall eat or   drink

(OS, Heliand 1663)

Here the reference of the relative clause object is indefinite. This is in line with the extended use of the accusative. On the other hand, where the object of drinking is pre-conceived by the Saviour and thus definite in some specific sense, the accusative (*huuat* instead of *huues*) is also used. Consider (14).

(14) [...] ik nimu thene kelik   an   hand, drinku *ina*
     I take the   chalice by (my/the) hand drink it-ACC
     thi   te   diurđu
     (to) you for glorification

(OS, Heliand 4764)

Here it is not wine that is drunk, but the chalice, i.e., a specific object and an exhausted, countable quantity. To distinguish the partitive genitive ((**eines*) *Wassers trinken* 'drink of some water') from the indefinite accusative (*einen Helden sehen* 'see a hero') we might make the following qualification.

(15) a. ein- + NP_i-ACC iff i = individuated
       ... *einen Helden sehen*   'see a hero'
    b. 0 + NP_i-GEN iff i = non-individuated
       ...(**eines*) *Wassers trinken* 'drink water'

Take another verb of eating. As Schrodt (1992: 386) has observed, the government of Old Saxon *niotan* 'use' and that of the corresponding OHG etymon, *niozzan* 'enjoy', is determined in accordance with the semantic and deictic property of the object NP. Since the verb is durative, the genitive on the direct object *thera heimwisti* in (16b) below is indefinite, despite the deictic demonstrative *thera*, i.e. 'some home place'. On the other hand, concrete-definiteness goes with accusative (*drutscaf* 'companion') as in (16a) below.

(16) a. Ewiniga   drûtscaf *niazen* se   iamer, sôsô ih quad,
        (the) eternal-ACC friendship enjoy they always as   I said
        in himile zi wâre mid   Ludowige thare!
        in heaven as with   Ludowige there

(OHG, LudwigsLied: 85)

    b. So thu *thera*   heimwisti *niuzist* mit gilusti, so   bistu
       if you this-GEN home   enjoy with pleasure then are-you
       gote   liober,   ni intratist scadon niamer
       (to) god (a) dear (one) not dread   harm   never

(1.18,45 — OHG)

More clearly so than with the Old Saxon Heliand, in early OHG (Otfrid) the genitive object with *etan* need not be triggered (in Schrodt's sense) when the object referent has been mentioned before. Where *etan* is used in the sense of the perfective *firslintan* 'devour', the accusative is used invariably, i.e., whether or not the governed object is specific. Gothic makes the very same distinction: *itan* 'eat' takes the (partitive) genitive for non-count object referents, whereas the prefixed perfective *fraitan* takes the accusative whether or not the object referent is specific in the respective event. Thus, this accusative, if governed by a perfective verb, is ambiguous with respect to the reference of the object noun, whereas the genitive object allows the conclusion that the reference is non-specific.

Let us take a look at another subclass of verbs. Among the verbs of perception MHG *denken* 'think, believe' has almost totally lost its accusative government. This may mean that a semantic change has taken place such that the 'believe'-semantics, which is amenable to some preconceived object referent, is no longer available. Schrodt's survey appears to support the idea that this morphologically simple durative verb acquires perfectivity by way of prefixation, although both accusative and genitive government are available (Schrodt 1992: 388). See (17), where perfective *gedenken* occurs also with the genitive.

(17) case distribution with MHG *denken*

	referential/strong object referent [+ accusative]	non-referential/weak object referent [+genitive]
bedenken	consider	conclude
erdenken	find (out) something	ask for something
gedenken	find (out)	think of something past
verdenken	capture meaning of	remember something
voldenken	think something to the end	—
überdenken	forget	—

This allows the generalization that verbs selecting direct objects both in the accusative and the genitive are ambiguous between a definite and indefinite reading only when perfective with accusative (left column in (17)). Otherwise, i.e. when imperfective, only the genitive occurs, yielding an indefinite reading.

The question of unifying the three cases discussed, the two genitives and the accusative, can be looked at also against a different background. As Baker (1988) has observed, verbal Cases can be classified in the following tripartite way[4] — to which we add a fourth option (18d).

(18) a. structural Case: under government; any θ-role; ModG: ACC; (ACC+) DAT; (ACC+) GEN
    b. inherent Case: under government; fixed D-structure θ-role; ModG: DAT for two-place verbs
    c. semantic Case: not governed; fixed D-structure θ-role; ModG: PART-GEN; privative GEN in any-place verb
    d. lexically incorporated verbal genitive: ungoverned; any θ-role; ModG: *jemandes harren* 'someone-GEN wait'

Under this characterization, the accusative in ModG is the structural Case; the verbally governed genitive is an 'inherent Case' (according to Baker's terminology; see Baker 1988); and the partitive genitive is the 'semantic Case'. The distinction in (18) is similar to Baker's distinction except that Baker's distinctive characteristic 'not governed' is not addressed at all, since the partitive features are mapped from the category N and, consequently, are not licensed by V-government.

3.3 The 'pre-article' periods in OHG and MHG: the transition from the demonstrative to the definite article

Clearly, there were restrictions on the occurrence of the definite article and, to an even larger degree, the indefinite article. The illustrations from MHG below show nouns without articles, both subjects and objects, where the modern language cannot do without a determiner; the definite form with a demonstrative meaning; and the indefinite form with the reference of the cardinal numeral. Generally, neither article form has yet developed the ModG meaning.

(19) *Definite ['(_)' for empty DET-position]:* MHG
    a. ist   zwîvel (_)   herzen nâchgebur
       is (?the) doubt (of the) heart neighbour
    b. über (_)   mêr, über (_) sê, von (_)   himile
       across (the) sea across lake from (the) heaven
    c. si (_)   saelec wîp
       she (the) blessed woman
    d. (_) sumeres, (_) morgens
       '(of/in-the-) summer; morning'
    e. hin ze (_) herbergen
       'there to (the) hostel'   (Veldeke, *Eneit* 6471)
    f. ob   in (_)   ertrîche niht mêr fröuden wære
       whether on (the) earth   not more pleasures were
                                                     (Veldeke, *Eneit* 13268)
    g. daz her dâ mit   mohte heilen
       that here therewith could heal
    h. alliu unfrôhiu herzen
       all   sad   hearts
    i. von (_)   rouweclichem smerzen
       from (the) deep   pains   (Veldeke, *Eneit* 13273)

(20) *Indefinite vs cardinal numeral:*
    a. wir sin *ein*   fleisch und *ein*   blût
       we are one (single) flesh and one (single) blood   (Veldeke 6600)
    b. ichn vernam von (_)   hochzîte in allen wîlen mâre
       I-not heard about (a) feast   in all   times wonderful   (13222)
    c. nu   uns got hât *ein*   lîb geben
       now (to) us god has one/a life given   (6607)
    d. ich vernam von (_) swertleiten
       I   heard about (a) knighting   (13238)
    e. als ez (_)vrouwen wol gezam
       as it (a) woman well befitted   (13453)

f. az   der kunech Éneas daz rîche   eine   gewan
    when the king   Aeneas the kingdom together won
g. daz im   nie weder (_) maget noch (_) wîb â   vor nie sô
    that him not again (a) maiden nor (a) woman for not so
    lieb ne wart
    dear not became   (10988f.)

The OHG examples in (21)–(23) below provide evidence against the assumption that the form of the indefinite article (derived from the cardinal for 'one') has the reference of the modern indefinite. This can be shown in various ways.

(21) *Indefinite pronoun and indefinite numeral instead of indefinite article:*
    a. dhea *einun* godnissa   OHG
       the one deity
    b. wir *einon*
       we alone

(22) *Plural of the 'indefinite article':*
    a. *eino* zîti
       certain times
    b. in *einen* buachon
       in some books

(23) *No article in clearly definite contexts:*
    a. giuuîhit   bistu   in (_)   uuîbon ioh untar
       consecrated are-you among (_) women and among
       uuoroltmagadon
       maidens   (Otfrid.8(I,6).7)
       'You are consecrated among (the) women and among (the) maidens'
    b. Uuio uuard ih io   sô uuirdig fora (_)   druhtine,
       how was   I   ever so worthy before (_) woman
       thaz (_) selba (_) muater sîn giangi innan (_) hûs   mîn?
       that (_) self (_) mother be gone into (_) house mine
                                                  (Otfrid.8(I,6).9)
    c. Allo uuîhi   in (_) uuorolti, thir gotes boto
       all consecrations in (_) world (to) you god's messengers
       sageti, ... Nu singemes alle mannolîh bî (_) barne: uuola (_)
       tell   now sing   all humans at (_) child will (to) (_)
       kind diuri, forasago (_) mâri!
       child dear tell   tales   (Otfrid.8(I,6).13)

The generalization made below, i.e. in (36a–c), about the link between case assignment and aspect-triggered referentiality distinctions predicts that duratives such as *thenken* would govern the accusative. Note first example (24), with perfective *gedenken*.

(24) in   wirdetvile   ture, den schalken, *des*   si   hânt
      (to) them it will be very tough to the bastards what-GEN they had
      *ge*dâht, daz si   mit schiffen bî der naht hine entrinnen wolden, ...
      planned that they with boats wanted to flee

(Middle Dutch/MHG, Veldeke *Eneit*: 6489)

The perfective verbal prefix, *ge-*, selects a genitive object relative pronoun, *des*. Naturally, in this particular case of the relative pronoun no (in)definiteness evaluation is possible. Now consider (25) with a simple, non-prefixed verb. The OHG author Otfrid rendered the original Latin perfective sense of the present tense in *videtur* 'appears' with the simple, seemingly durative verb *thenken*. In fact, however, it was meant to be perfective, which Otfrid made plausible to the reader by the accusative relative pronoun, *waz*. Note that (25) (indirect question) shows that this relative could as easily occur in the genitive: *waz inan thesses thunke* in (25). Examples (25)–(27) are from Schrodt (1992: 373–4):

(25)   Waz   er selbo   hiar nu   quît, thaz eigut ir   gihôrit;
      (everything) that he himself here now says that have you heard
      mannilîh nu   thenke *waz* inan   thes*es* thunke!
      everyone now (may) consider what him (of-) this   deems-SUBJ

(OHG, Otfrid.4.19.67)

'What he himself says here you have heard. Now everyone should consider himself what to think of it!'
(cf. Matthew 26,66: '...quid vobis videtur' = what (to) you appears 'has been seen')

The original Latin version shows that *thenken* is used perfectively here. Consider also (26) with a complement clause and accusative object selected by *thenken*.

(26) Thie buah duent   thaz mâri, theiz sambazdag thô   wari,
      the books tell (do) that story that-it Saturday   there were
      thô Krist   *thes* wolta *thenken*, this[GEN]/*thiz*[?ACC]
      then Christ (of-) this would think (of-) this
      selba wuntar   wirken
      self   wonder (to) work

(OHG, Otfrid.4.19.67)

As in (25) above, *thenken* here can be taken as inchoative, i.e. meaning something like 'make occur to oneself' or 'make come to one's mind'. As a perfective, as was observed before, the V-governed genitive is licensed.

Now consider (27) with *thâhta* seemingly in the sense of 'considered', i.e. non-perfective. This demonstrates the use of the accusative despite the fact that the object has independent, definite reference. This would license, according to the generalization reached so far, the genitive rather than the accusative.

(27) Er *thâhta*   imo   ouh in gâhi *thia* managfaltûn wîhi,
    he considered (by) himself also quickly the manifold   holyness
    joh *thia* hôhun wirdi   ni wolta   thaz   wurdi
    and the high   dignity; not would (-he) that (to) become

(OHG, Otfrid.1.8.13)

However, as in cases discussed above, the accusative is appropriate since the predication may be interpreted as perfective. Consider the following interpretation. Joseph (= *er (thâhta)*!) took as a fact Mary's pregnancy considering all of a sudden (*in gâhi*) also the salvation that would result from it. Here we can take the phrase *thâhta imo in gâhi* to be perfective, which is consistent with selection of accusative with a definite reading.

The appropriate generalization seems to be that the accusative governed by either the perfective or the imperfective verb (reading) refers to the definite object noun in the former case and to indefiniteness in the latter case. On the other hand, the genitive, selected by perfective verbs, or by perfective readings of otherwise aspectually open verbs, only and always renders an indefinite reading on the object noun. This is supported even by examples which, by their mere form (simple durative verbs, without the perfective prefix *ge-*), appear as counterexamples to the generalization.

4 Aspect and object case interlocked in Slavic, Finnish and in early German

What exactly does it mean to say that there is a link between aspect (or Aktionsart), referentiality on the object nominal, and nominal case under verbal government? What is the evidence for the claim that articles compensate for the loss of the aspectual system in general, and for the loss of paradigmatic perfectivity in particular? Let us begin with a few general typological observations. The idea that aspect (or Aktionsart),[5] case, and object referentiality (in the determiner phrase) can be inter-dependent as soon as certain accompanying conditions are met draws on the following typological assumptions and insights.

(28) There appears to be a complementary distribution between languages with strong (morphologically and paradigmatically identified) aspectual systems and the surface representation of determiner forms in the following sense: if some language makes a systematic formal distinction between perfectivity and non-perfectivity, it *can* (but need not) do without surface articles. Examples are Russian, Polish and Czech (and in fact to some extent all Slavic languages except Bulgarian, which has a definite article). Also the Indic languages (Hindi, Bengali; see Chatterjee 1988), Chinese and Finnish (albeit in a particular sense), and both Gothic and OHG.[6]

(29) Case oppositions are adequate substitutes for referentiality distinctions such as [±definite][7] on NP under verbal government as long as certain aspect and/or Aktionsart conditions are met. Representatives of this generalization are again the Slavic languages as well as Gothic and OHG. There is overwhelming agreement that the classical Indo-European languages reflect, in the form that has come down to us, the non-tensing, aspectual system of Proto-Indo-European (for a survey of the relevant literature, see Chatterjee 1988: 6ff.).

(30) Romance languages provide evidence that the emergence of the definite article does not necessarily result from changes in the aspectual system. However, if a language loses its strong aspectual paradigm and develops article forms as a result, it will develop the definite article category first; this may even be restricted to the definite article. Cases in point are Icelandic and Old Irish as well as Sanskrit and Modern and Ancient Greek, all of which have a definite article only. If, on the other hand, a language develops both the definite and the indefinite articles, no condition prevents the emergence of the indefinite article both in the singular and the plural (certain dialects in Spanish and southern German dialects, including Carinthian in southern Austria).[8]

Examples (31a, b) illustrate for Russian the generalization in (28)–(29) that there are direct relations between aspectual verbal morphology, definiteness of the object noun, and case morphology (following Birkenmaier 1977, Brunnhuber 1983; Leiss 1991: 1406, Birkenmaier 1979: 108, 115). ('α PERF', here and later on, stands for 'α perfectivity'; PRET = preterite, PERF = perfective, DEF = definite (reference).)

(31) a. [−PERF] On kolo-l   drov-a
                he split-PRET wood-ACC-[−DEF]
                                        kolot' = *im*perfective verb
     b. [+PERF] On *ras*-kolo-l   drova
                he PERF.PREF-split-PRET (the) wood-ACC-[+DEF]
                                        raskolot' = perfective verb

Note that Russian, like many other Slavic languages, does not lexically realize the determiner category. Nevertheless, it does mark NPs distinctly with respect to referentiality, in part by those mechanisms depicted in (31a, b). In other words, the (in)definiteness of the object-NP can be distinguished by aspectual morphology on the verb. Non-perfective verbs, such as *kolot'* in (31a), mark indefiniteness on the accusative direct object NP. The very same accusative, however, marks definiteness on the object nominal when governed by a perfective verb. Notice that the verbal genitive is incompatible with the imperfective (since, semantically, it describes an event in progress).[9]

Now consider an inherently perfective verb such as *prinosit'* 'bring'.

(32) a. [+PERF]   On prinës   papir-os
                  he brought-PERF cigarettes-GEN-[−DEF]
     b. [+PERF]   On prinës   papir-os-y
                  he brought-PERF (the) cigarettes-ACC-[+DEF]

No derivational prefix is needed to signal perfectivity on verbs like *prinosit'*, as opposed to the inherently imperfective *kolot'*. The marking of accusative on the object signals definiteness. On the other hand, genitive marking on the object with the same perfective verb signals indefiniteness. Note, however, that an imperfective verb governing an object in the genitive case in direct object function does not generally signal specificity, or definiteness, since this is also signalled by accusative with imperfective verbs. The tree graph in (33) schematizes the interplay between case, perfectivity and definiteness in Russian:

(33)

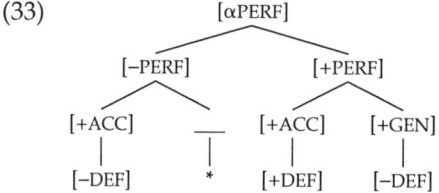

This mechanism expressing referentiality on the object-NP on the basis of case assignment and aspect is not unique to Russian. It is shared by equally articleless languages such as Czech and Serbo-Croatian, albeit without the same strict aspectual complementarity as in Russian, and also by Polish.[10]

Gothic seems to be another language that shows an interplay between perfectivity and case selection. According to Streitberg (1891) and Krause (1987), Gothic had a great number of systematic verbal pairs, simple and prefixed, which were distinguished exclusively by their aspectual meaning.

(34) *taujan — gataujan*   'do — complete'
     hausjan — gahausjan   'hear — hear that something is said'
     fraujinon — gafraujinon 'rule — dominate'
     auknan — biauknan   'grow'
     kukjan — bikukjan   'kiss' (from Leiss 1994: 315)

Such verbal pairs were frequent — which is remarkable for a text corpus as small as the Gothic one.

Let us now assume that 'accusative' and 'genitive', which play such a major role in Russian, Finnish, and, as we have seen in section 3 above, also in the early stages of the development of German, are somehow distinguished not only by morphological form, but also by structural position. Several questions arise, in this context, against the assumptions sketched in (28)–(30) above.

(35) a. How is the link between an aspectual verb or VP and the determiner category in terms of case to be expressed? In particular, what is the structural position of ACC vs GEN? What is the positional distribution of ACC vs GEN?

b. If case is to determine a feature within the Det-category, how are the definite/referential/specific vs the indefinite/non-referential/non-specific Det-categories distinguished structurally?

c. What makes the assumption in (30) plausible in structural terms? More specifically, which structural characterization in the DP allows the indefinite feature to remain unrealized, while the definite one is captured more readily by a lexical representation?

The following options come to mind with respect to (35a): the accusative is a structural(ly defined) case, but the genitive is lexical; or both were lexical originally, but one (i.e. the accusative) developed into a structural case.[11] See also (4) above. Before we address (35b, c), however, let us wrap up the generalizations made so far. The observations on Russian lend support to the assumption that in OHG the case options for object nouns, the aspectual distinction, and nominal referentiality were interlocked in a similar way. The following section discusses these links in OHG and in Russian in detail.

5 Introducing the article morpheme

5.1 Interlocking verbal aspectual classes, case assignment, and (in)-definiteness on the verbal argument in the diachrony of German

The question to be asked is this: what were the triggering forces for the decay of the verbal genitive government in favour of accusative and prepositional government? Following Schrodt (1992: 368f.) we may consider the following possibilities: (a) replacement of the verbal genitive by the neutral, or structural, case, the accusative; this development presupposes no semantic change, but just a formal shift under semantic constancy; or (b) the accusative indeed marks a different semantic category, as do prepositions, and the shift is motivated accordingly. We may add a third alternative, (c): the genitive gives way to accusative or some prepositional valency when any accompanying genitive-supporting restriction disappears. Leiss (1989) and others before her (such as Brunnhuber 1983) have argued that such a restriction is the aspectual system in OHG, which, in the course of MHG, is replaced by a tense system. The first two options, (a) and (b) above, do not have anything to say on the parallel emergence of the article category, and there is also no connection to the decay of the aspectual paradigm. We therefore opt for (c). See (36a–c) for the essential links between the aspectual markers, case and referentiality on the object NP. Notice that (36c) pinpoints a difference between OHG and Russian (in that Russian had [+DEF] in this place).

(36) a. The GENITIVE governed by a perfective verb (whether explicitly perfective by prefixation such as {ge, etc.}-V, or inherently perfective) had a [−DEFINITE] reading.

b. The ACCUSATIVE if governed by a perfective verb (marked as {ge, etc.}-V, or inherently perfective) had a [+DEFINITE] reading.
c. The ACCUSATIVE governed by a perfective verb was ambiguous, [±DEF], with respect to the determiner status.
d. OHG stage: see the marked DET-feature and compare with Russian in (36e) below.

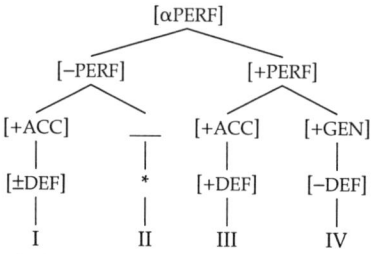

e. Modern Russian (from (31)–(32)): the marked Det-feature in (36d) for OHG.

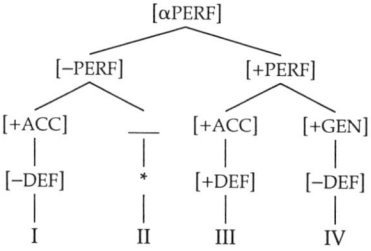

The genitive government in OHG thus has only one reading: indefinite. The accusative on the other hand had both options, i.e. either [+DEF] or [–DEF], depending on the aspectual classification of the predicate. Admittedly, the basis for this generalization for OHG is as yet limited and is in need of more solid statistical support gained from texts in OHG and MHG as well as the critical period of early ModG. However, the observations in the literature provide a solid lead in this direction.

We suggest the diachronic scenario in (37a, b) to complete the OHG picture in (36):

(37) Loss of aspectual opposition DURATIVE VS PERFECTIVE (see Leiss 1991: 1408, based on the classical literature on OHG):
    a. The durative verbs lost their paradigmatic status as morphologically marked imperfectives to the extent that their selectional properties no longer distinguished them from paradigm II (in 36d). As a consequence, they became defective with respect to the definite pole of the categorial opposition 'definite' vs 'indefinite'. In other words, whereas there was a case-marked indication for [αDEF]-objects for perfective verbs, there was no longer one for non-perfective verbs.

b. Unlike the imperfective/durative verbs, and even after losing the aspectual (i.e. the durative) partner, perfective verbs still have means of expressing indefiniteness, i.e. by alternating case. See (38) below.

The expressions for the DET-category in Gothic and, less regularly, in OHG and MHG (except for demonstrative *der/die/das* and the numeral *ein-*), stabilized in Late MHG simultaneously with the loss of the genitive. There was, however, a striking imbalance between the definite article and the indefinite one, the definite expression (deriving from the demonstrative pronoun) developing earlier (by a noticeable temporal distance) than the indefinite one (emerging from the cardinal numeral for *one*). Example (38) below charts this out. The variation expressed by different clusters of '+' and '−' plus additional parentheses is to indicate that, except for Gothic, no language stage, neither OHG nor MHG, is clearly without indefinite articles. Nor does either have the definite article in a statistically significant way. This is due to difficulties in interpreting morphological 'forms' of the relevant categories and their meaning.

(38) *Temporal co-incidences*

	1 definite article	2 indefinite article	3 genitival VCA	4 aspectual paradigm
Gothic	−	−	+	+
OHG	±	(+)−	+	+
MHG	+	+(−)	+++	±
(early) ModG	+	+	−	−

As (38) shows, OHG still has unsystematic definite article realizations (viz. '±' in (38), second column), whereas the indefinite article is almost absent ('(+)−', second column). MHG, on the other hand, shows progress on the overt realization of the definite article ('+', first column) as well as the indefinite one ('+(−)', second column). Finally, the 'explosion' of verbal genitives ('+++', third column) is accompanied by a diffused picture of aspectual morphology ('±', fourth column). ModG has both article forms, virtually no verbal genitive government, nor does it have a grammatical aspect. The chart in (38) above shows this relative distribution of the definite vs the indefinite article; the latter did not clearly emerge in the indefinite — i.e. the non-numerical and non-referential — meaning until early New High German (see second column). Note that the definite article emerged from the morpheme for the demonstrative pronoun, whereas the indefinite one developed from the indefinite cardinal numeral, 'one', as in most other languages where the indefinite article emerged. Thus, the clusters relate to the relative weight that the categories have in the different historical stages of German.

Recall that strong (accusative) object nominals are candidates for the definite article at some point in the historical development, whereas the genitive is not. See the arguments in connection with the charts in (48) and (50) below. We have seen in (36a–c) that this was not the case for OHG and early MHG, where the accusative was open to both the definite option (governed by a perfective verb) and the indefinite option (governed by an imperfective verb). It appears furthermore that where the prepositional alternative exists already in pre-ModG or where it comes to replace the genitive object (see (19)–(20) above as well as (50) and (51) below), the preposition correlates with the perfectivizing verbal prefix. It is the verbal perfective prefix, or an adequate preposition governing the accusative, that licenses the referentiality feature [–DEF] on the DET-category in those places where originally the verbal genitive was licensed. Since, as we have seen in (36a, b), the accusative object case can be selected both by the perfective and the imperfective verb, we may conclude that the accusative somehow carries the functional load of the perfective verbal and/or the stative local preposition to yield the same result, i.e. determining [–definiteness] in the category DET. Compare again the examples under (27) above. Consider also note 6.

5.2 Perfectives as small clauses

Let us now assume that perfective Aktionsart verbs in ModG must be represented (as has been claimed by various linguists) syntactically as small clauses (secondary predications), while non-perfectives never are (Abraham 1991a, 1993b, 1994a; see also, for Dutch, van Dijk 1994). Then the following syntactic distinctions for ModG are available. In (39), the italicized NP is the object in question. By way of convention, X(P) stands for a variety of predicative categories, such as adjectives, adverbials and prepositional phrases (with the directional accusative).

(39) *Case syntax chart for ModG*

Case	object structure under a perfective verb	object structure under a non-perfective verb
accusative	[$_{SC}$ *NP* AgrP X(P)]	[$_{V'}$ *NP*, V]
preposition+ACC	[$_{SC}$ *NP[+ACC]* AgrP X(P)]	[$_{V'}$ *PP*, V]
genitive	—	[$_V$ *NP*, V]

See the following examples. The small clause predicates, whether phrasal or lexical, are in italics.

(40) a. Sie$_i$ tanzte [e_i [$_{PP}$ *an den Rand*]]   XP=ACC-governing directive P
       she danced   to the side [= ... until she was at the side]

b. Sie tanzte   [sich [$_{Adj}$ *müde*]]   XP=resultative adjective
   she danced   herself   worn-out
c. Sie *zer*tanzte   ihre Schuhe   X=verbal prefix *zer-*
   she*pref*-danced her shoes
   'She danced until her shoes were all worn down'

X(P) in the small clause (SC) encompasses a number of divergent categorial phrases, in both zero and in maximal projections: directional adverbials and adjectives as well as affixes. The pattern is also illustrated in (41) below.

Recall that, in contrast to the accusative, the genitive in ModG never collocates with directional PPs (DIR-PPs, which invariably govern the 'directional' accusative). Rather, the genitive and the directional PP (P+accusative) are in complementary distribution. Since perfectives are always SCs containing a structural accusative (or a VP–internal, 'ergative' or 'unaccusative' structural nominative) as SC-subject (see Abraham 1993b), and since accusatives but not genitives carry the semantics of directionals, it is concluded that the ModG genitive is not a SC-subject.

However, the relevant conclusion that these patterns allow with respect to earlier stages of German is different. Since the genitive in OHG was governed also by perfective verbs and since perfective verbal structures are always secondary predicates (small clauses, as in (39)), the genitive must have had structural status in OHG, unlike the genitive in ModG.[12] See (41). This conclusion appears to be empirically correct. What we can say, in descriptive terms, is summarized in the last line in chart (41) on OHG.

(41) *Partial case syntax chart for OHG (see (39) for comparison)*

Case	object structure under a perfective verb	object structure under a non-perfective verb
accusative	[$_{SC}$ NP[+ACC] AgrP XP]	[$_{V'}$ NP, V]
genitive	[$_{V}{}^{0}$ [$_{QP}$ Q] [NP]]	[$_{V'}$ [$_{QP}$ Q][NP]]

It will be for future work to see whether this conclusion is supported by data from the history of German. It is important to note, however, that the roles of the genitive in OHG and ModG were probably different. From this it follows that the accusative has received a special role in terms of direction and theta-marking in Modern German. This entails also a different role of secondary predication in OHG with both genitival and accusatival small clause subjects.

5.3 The emergence of the article morphemes

This section makes an attempt to align the different referential functions of the two article categories, definite and indefinite, with the assignment and categorial status of the two relevant object cases, the accusative and the genitive. Let us assume that case within DP is expressed by a functional category, in the spirit of Uriagereka (1992) and Philippi & Weerman (1993).

In (42) below, the partitive genitive, Case$_1$ [+GEN], is assigned according to a selectional feature by the head-noun, NP$_1$. The verbal genitive, on the other hand, Case$_2$, is selected by verbal subcategorization and needs to be higher up in the structural tree to be in the domain of verbal government, either as Case$_2$ as in (18) or even higher up as suggested by Bittner (1991). See (42) and (43) below, where (42) shows the distinct positions of the V-governed Case (such as the accusative) and the N-selected (partitive) genitive; and see (43) for the verbal government of the accusative and genitive (showing just the structural essentials).

(42) Partitive genitive: non-V-determined Case$_1$; the genitive is selected by the [−count] noun under the quantifier phrase QP dominated by DP; Q=cardinal numeral ε {0, 1, 2, ...}; Case$_1$=genitive; and with a Q-filter such that DP ⇒ D + *(Q) + Case$_1$ + N[−count]

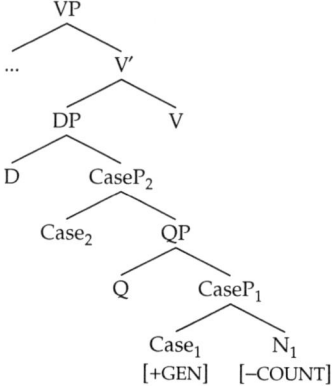

This expresses the idea that the [−count]-feature of N$_1$ always percolates to yield the genitive case under Case$_1$ dominated by QP (the ultimate source of the indefinite article).

(43) Verbal genitive: the genitive is V-determined: in Gothic and OHG by the aspectual verb classification (with or without perfective prefix; see also (45b) vs (45a) below); DP ⇒ D + Case$_2$ (+QP) + N[+count]

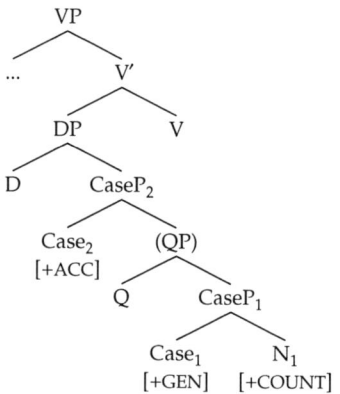

The assumption for the diachronic emergence of the two article forms is that, where different cases distinguish the two types of reference, such functional Case categories will appear in exactly the domains that have been reserved for the two distinct determiner types in (42)–(43). The specific reference, then, should be represented in CaseP$_2$ as in (42) or (43), whereas the non-specific reference would be lower down in Case$_1$, subjacent to Q^0, which is the lexical source of the emerging indefinite article morpheme, *ein-*. As mentioned before, the genitive is lexically licensed, at least in ModG. See, further, the discussion regarding (45a, b), where this issue is taken up again.

Let us now briefly consider the pre-modern periods of German, anticipating the direction of the argument. Bear in mind our suggestion that if there is a structural distinction between the [+definite] and the [−definite] determiners for any historical stage of German, and since accusative and genitive correlate with [+DEF] and [−DEF] respectively in ModG, then in the historical pre-articles stage of German, the genitive and the accusative should also appear in different structural positions. The intuition behind this assumption is that the syntactic positions in which the historical cases with definiteness distinctions were generated were taken over seamlessly by the later article morphemes. My claim to this end is that the accusative is in the structurally higher Case position, Case$_2$, in the c-command domain of the verb, whereas the genitive is in the lower Case position, Case$_1$, dominated by Q^0 in the c-command domain of the nominal head. See again (42)–(43)[13] as well as (44) below where the distribution between [+count] and [−count] nouns and its relation to the corresponding values of perfectivity forms the basis for the unification of Case selection and referential distinction.

(44) a. [−term] = [−count] as a verbal property
    b. [+term] = [+count] as a verbal property
    c. partitive genitive = [−count] as a nominal property
    d. verbal genitive   = [+count] as a nominal property
    e. [[+count]-V + [+count]-N] selects Case$_2$ (= accusative), which emerges as the [+DEF]-position
    f. [[+count]-V + [−count]-N] selects Case$_1$ (= partitive), which emerges as [−DEF]-position
    g. [[−count]-V + [+count]-N] selects Case$_1$ (= genitive), which emerges as [−DEF]-position

The unification of the verbal accusative and the verbal genitive departs from the [−count] features for imperfective verbs and may be thought of as follows: [−count]-verbs (imperfective or durative verbs) either select lexically [−count]-nominals as objects, or they copy the count-feature on the verb-closest argument, which we assumed is incorporated. See (45a) below. This mechanism triggers the verbal genitive on the nominal object by way of reaching no higher than the deepest Case node, Case$_2$, embedded below QP. This is the derivational mechanism realizing (44d) above. Duratives and statives are [−count] to the extent that their inherent event characteristic does not distinguish countable subentities of the event (see Abraham 1990). Perfectives (telics, or resultatives), on the other hand, figure as delimiting, and thus counting, event entities with distinct event properties (see also Verkuyl 1993). For duratives it is assumed that the following mechanism is operative. Any durative, [−count], verb of the early German period copies its [−count]-feature onto the lower object nominal, irrespective of its inherent count-characteristic (cf. (45a)). The first domain will then be defined as the structurally lower Case node, which is reserved for genitive. In the case of the nominal [−count]-characteristic, the lower Case node will be targeted, thereby realizing the genitive. Only in the case of no [−count]-feature on either verb or object nominal will the structurally higher Case node be targeted yielding the accusative object. See (45a, b) below for the two language states in question.

The mechanism just sketched holds for the older periods of German. Its earliest stage is sketched in the charts (7)–(8), left columns. Since, in the diachronic development, German loses its aspectual verbal paradigms, the feature-copying mechanism from the verb onto the lower Case node will be lost, too, yielding realizations of the structurally higher Case node only. In other words, all that remains is the partitive genitive — that genitive which is due to the inherent [−count]-feature on the object nominal in the first place (cf. (45a, b) disregarding technical details), where this transition is sketched from aspectual verbal marking in older German to morphologically unsignalled aspect in ModG and, consequently, to the loss of the verbally governed genitive.

(45)

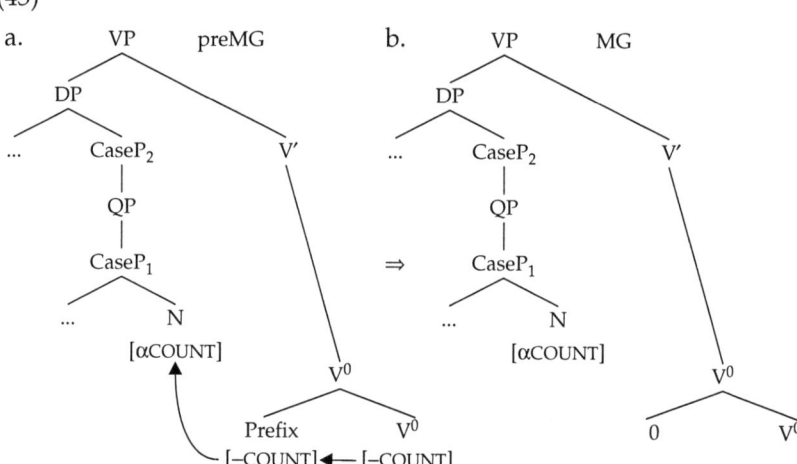

Notice that no transfer of features is licensed in the case of the verb that has lost its aspectual prefix in ModG (cf. (45b) above).

Case, aspect and referentiality 53

We are now in a position to give a unified description of the verbal genitive, the partitive genitive, and the accusative (cf. (44a–d)).

Unifying the two genitives and the accusative:
(46) a. strong Case, Case$_2$: selected by D (anticipating the definite article *d-*)
  b. (nominal) partitive, Case$_1$: selected by Q
  c. weak Case, Case$_1$: subjacent to Q (anticipating the indefinite article *ein-/Ø*)

Compare with (42)–(43) above. If the indefinite article and the homonymic cardinal numeral for 'one' in ModG are in different structural positions — with *ein* 'a(n)' in D and *der/die/das* 'the-M/F/N' in Spec,DP — then this would also provide some explanation for the fact that the indefinite article emerged later than the definite one. Any process of disambiguating a lexeme such as the cardinal 'one' in syntactic terms would seem to take its time. The definite article, on the other hand, arising from the demonstrative use of the homonymic determiner never needed to change its structural position (Spec,DP) in the first place.

6 Comparison of aspectual systems in terms of case and the nominal epistemics

6.1 The diachrony of case, perfectivity and definiteness

What remains to be sketched is a diachronic line connecting OHG, MHG and ModG in minimal stepwise changes. To this end, let us turn back to the Russian examples in (31)–(32) as well as the OHG case–aspect distribution, (36a–c), above. As we saw, the two systems are very similar. They share the distribution exemplified for Russian examples by (31b)–(32a, b) and summarized for OHG in (36a, b) (for inherent and analytical (prefixed) perfectives: [+PERF] + ACC yields [+DEF], whereas [+PERF] + GEN yields [−DEF]). Where they differ, however, is in the less restricted consequence of the feature pair '[−PERF] + ACC' in OHG, which, unlike Russian ([−PERF] selects just [−DEF]!), yields both [−DEF] and [+DEF] characteristics. In other words, if a [−PERF]-verb wants to express [+DEF] on an object-NP, it must perfectivize. This is an option Russian does not have.

The correlations as argued for in the previous sections are summarized in the following charts, (47) for Russian, (48) for OHG:

(47) *Case/aspect/definiteness distinctions in Modern Russian*

illustration	case (+ ⇒ ACC, − ⇒ GEN)	perfectivity of verb	definiteness	Det lexically filled
(31b)	+	+	+	Ø
(31a)	+	−	−	Ø
(32a)	−	+	−	Ø
—	−	−	*	*

(48) *Case/aspect/definiteness distinctions in Old High German*

illustration	case on noun	perfectivity of verb	definiteness	Det lexically filled
(36b)	+	+	+	+
(36c)	+	−	±	+/Ø
(36a)	−	+	−	Ø
-	−	−	*	*

In the light of the foregoing discussion and (36), it is not surprising that the two case–article correlating systems, that of Modern Russian and that of OHG, are congruent except for one position, i.e. where OHG provides '±' for the characteristic 'definiteness'. Compare (36d, e). By contrast, Russian displays the negative feature on this complex characteristic. Note, furthermore, that the [−DEF]-selections are more numerous by type characteristics than the [+DEF]-selections which are restricted in type. We may speculate that it was this mismatch that evoked the early emergence of the explicit [+DEF]-determiner category.

Let us take stock and see what we have achieved so far. Clearly, what the material in sections 2 and 3 showed requires answers to the following general questions:

(49) a. What triggers, and explains, the loss of the verbal genitive under the loss of aspectual reinforcement in the course of MHG up to ModG (see (36a–c))?
   b. What is the cause for the explosion of the genitive in early NHG, i.e. before the onset of ModG (cf. (38))?
   c. How is the asymmetry between the emergence of [+DEF] and [−DEF] articles to be explained?
   d. What is the dependence of case on perfectivity ([±PERF]) in formal terms?

The following further parameters appear to be of relevance for answers to these questions. Aspect was not only lost, but it was gradually replaced by a tense system, in particular as a full-fledged paradigm to serve the explicit expression of the sequence of tenses. This development was accompanied by the emergence and continuous extension of grammatical features of subordination (notably, the emergence of the subjunction *daß* 'that' from the complement object demonstrative *das*), as well as the emergence of the grammatical status of markers for backgrounding and foregrounding (such as modal particles).

Let us turn back to the Russian set-up in (47), based on (31), and the one for OHG in (48) supported by (36a–c). As already observed, what turns out to be different in OHG as compared to Russian is the second line with '±' for the strength composition '+Case/−V'. On this characteristic, OHG turns out to be ambiguous with respect to the DET-decision, whereas Russian only has the [−DEF]-realization. The OHG situation, to be sure, presents a very obscure and difficult-to-learn system because of its apparent arbitrariness at this point.[14]

Let us now chart the further development of the case-aspect-reference scenarios through MHG up to ModG. See (50) and (51) below.

(50) *Case/aspect/definiteness distinctions in Middle High German*

case	perfectivity of verb	definiteness	Det lexically filled
+	−	Ø	+
+	−	−	+/Ø
−	−	−	Ø
−	−	−	Ø

'Ø' stands for the lack of 'inherent', i.e. genitive-derived, signal for [−DEF] due to the co-temporal rise of the lexical representation of [−DEF] in the fourth column. Note that there is no longer any aspectual marking on the verb (column 2). In this respect, MHG differs from OHG (cf. (48) above). What we have retained, merely for the purpose of comparison with (47)/(48) and (51), are the four lines, although they no longer have separate parameterizations in terms of strength of case and aspect. The former four classes of verbs, which are no longer distinguished on the basis of aspectual morphology, will only have partial reflexes in terms of referentiality on their object nominals. 'Ø' in the third column indicates that the indefinite article is to be identified only by contrast to the definite article form, which is realized morphologically (viz. '+' in the fourth column). Crucially, the first two verbal classes distinguished by aspectual morphology (first two lines) have collapsed and are distinct from the third and fourth line classes in terms of allowing only for indefinite nominal reference ('Ø' by contrast to the definite article morpheme). Note, further, that the second to fourth lines, third column (all yielding indefinite readings on the object nominal), reflect the explosive rise of genitive government. The reason for this sudden rise is that the last genitive-governing verbs conflated to one single expression class due to the fact that the governing verb no longer marks its aspectual classification, while there was still a need to distinguish aspectual verb classes. See (38), fourth column, again for the generalization of this fact. Note that the former accusative governed by a non-perfective verb (second line) yields indefinite article forms, albeit inconsistently ('+/Ø'). Note, further, that in MHG there are still genitive objects beside accusative objects (first column)!

To what extent is ModG (see (51) below) different from MHG?

(51) *Case/aspect/definiteness distinctions in Modern German*

case	perfectivity of verb	definiteness	Det lexically filled
+	−	Ø	+
+	−	Ø	+
+/P	−	Ø	−
+/P	−	Ø	−

Note, first of all, that the verbal genitive objects have been replaced by either accusatives or prepositional cases (third and fourth lines, first column). Second, there are no more inherently identified article references (third column); they have all become lexically represented (fourth column). In MHG there was an explosion in the number of genitive-governing verbs due to the loss of aspectual marking and the continuing need to distinguish imperfective verbs by way of genitive-government (see (50), second to fourth lines). But verbal genitive government was eventually lost in ModG because supportive aspectual distinctions were no longer available, and there was no longer any reason for case distinctions to be linked with aspect marking. See (51), third column, and compare with (50) above. This is my answer to the questions (49a, b) above.

6.2 Two diachronic stages of case in OHG

In section 6.1 an account was given of the development of the relation between case, aspect and definiteness from OHG to ModG. I will now attempt a formalization of this, and suggest a way of conceptualizing the changes. Recall our account for OHG above, represented as in (36d), which is here repeated as (52):

(52)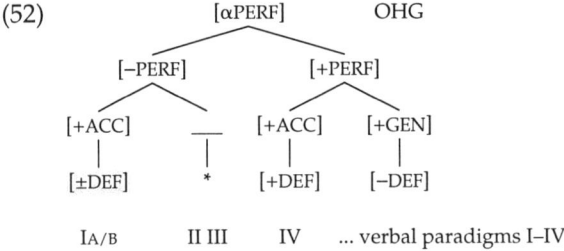

This is presumably the earliest stage, pre-OHG as well as OHG (and, presumably also Gothic). We now postulate a (younger generation) variety of OHG, OHG$_2$, which had to cope without the morphological paradigm for perfectives.[15] This is accounted for by the chart in (53) below, postulating a change that involved the reranking of the main triggering features, i.e., from the perfectivity feature to the case feature. This change anticipates the total decay of the paradigmatic aspectual triggers and leads, in Late MHG, to the direct correlation of ACC with [+definiteness], on the one hand, and GEN with [−definiteness], on the other. Recall also the 'genitive explosion' in early ModG (cf. (38), fourth column and fourth line, as well as (50) above), which is indicative of this type of genitive selection and which was anticipated already in OHG$_2$. This accounts for (36b) and (36c). But what about (36a), under which perfective verbs can select GEN to determine [−DEF]-referentiality on their arguments? Perfectives should be in a SC-configuration. However, GEN does not qualify for a subject in a SC. Thus, this does not appear as a viable solution unless the [±DEF] reference triggered by [−PERF] + [+ACC] is taken to stand for a system that is split as a result of systematic variety across different generations of OHG speakers. This is the scenario I would definitely prefer, subject to further philological research.[16]

Note that (52) accounts for the empirical observation that [−PERF] selects no genitive complement.

On both decision lines, the main path distributor was the perfectivity feature, [αPERF], whereas the decision made on the basis of case distinctions was secondary. In (53), OHG$_2$, all that changes is the priority of these conditioning features, with perfectivity losing in prominence.

(53)

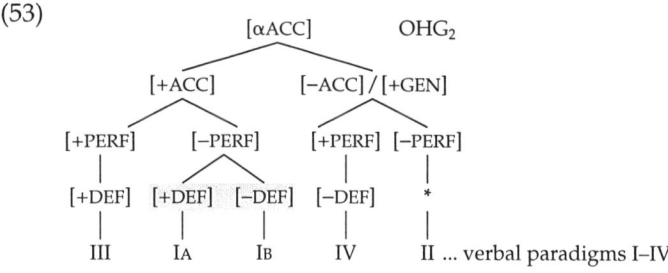

Example (53) already specifies that OHG$_2$ no longer needs the perfective feature to decide on the definiteness of its complement NP, since [+DEF] is selected under both [−PERF] and [+PERF]. Recall that the definite article had emerged already, while the indefinite one still surfaced unsystematically (cf. the two left-most branches in (53)). This rearrangement of (52), in terms of (53), I propose, is the crucial step toward the total disappearance of the perfectivity feature as a trigger for the definiteness contrast. At the same time, it is easy to see why the genitive verbs reclassified as those interlinked with indefiniteness: there was a heavy majority of accusative–definiteness links (cf. the classes III and I in (53) above), pushing the minority of indefinites to merge with that class in IV which was unthreatened by competing case triggers. This resulted in what has been called the 'genitive explosion' in late MHG and early ModG. Compare again (38) above, third column. The next step to be reached no longer contains any reference to perfectivity. See (54) from late MHG.

(54)

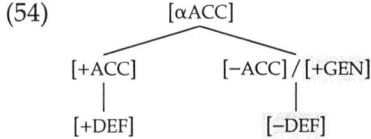

It is crucial to see that the two stages of development, i.e. the loss of the aspectual condition in OHG_1 as well as the 'genitive explosion', in a way are anticipated by what can be identified as a chain shift. See again (52), (53) and (54). The ultimate trigger is the definiteness ambiguity under the combined condition of [+ACC] and [−PERF]. This is an unstable situation, which will eventually be resolved at the cost of the weaker feature. Since the feature combination of [−ACC] and [−PERF] (see the verbal paradigm II in (53)) does not yield any result, the case feature of the accusative will remain as the identifying condition for [+DEF], whereas [−DEF] will have to look for another identifying locus — in terms of the case opposition, this will be the [−ACC]/[+GEN] feature; see IV in (53) and the transfer of IB to IV. Simultaneously, this locates a number of governing non-perfective verbs under the definiteness-identifying feature of [−DEF], but not until the aspectual opposition has lost its distinguishing force. Compare the change between (53) and (54) and the shadowed nodes. Recall that Russian does not have this instability (branch I in (52)). This may be a partial explanation for the fact that, unlike in OHG, no such profound change took place in Russian. On the other hand, it can be assumed that the definiteness ambiguity in OHG is the visible result of an ongoing weakness of the aspectual trigger in the first place. None of all this explains yet another striking loss, namely the total loss of verbs governing only the genitive originally (see Schrodt 1994). We assume that, together with the independently emerging lexical indefinite article morpheme, not only the verbal genitive government as a case relation disappeared, but also all only-genitive governing verbs, due to a radical change from lexical selection toward categorial selection. This process redistributed case selection on the basis of categorial status, with genitive remaining fully deployed for nominal selection (see Abraham 1995a: ch. 3).

6.3 The asymmetrical emergence of the definite over the indefinite article

Let us now briefly consider how we can account for the asymmetrical emergence of the definite over the indefinite article, against the background of the diachronic scenario sketched in sections 6.1 and 6.2. It needs to be emphasized that in the light of the interconnections displayed here and the sudden and unprecedented, but only temporary, increase of the verbal genitive for non-perfective verbs in early ModG, the emergence of the indefinite article cannot be regarded as a separate development independent of the processes triggering the emergence of the definite article. On the contrary, the overall picture is that the genitive, erstwhile dependent on the specific co-condition of [α count]-properties of both verb and complement-DP, came to serve as a classifier for durative verbs once the perfective/non-perfective morphology had disappeared as a case and definiteness identifier. Clearly, the rise of the indefinite article may have been a totally different, and independent, story in other languages without such intricate and powerful interconnections as in the history of German, Russian and other Slavic languages, and Finnish, to mention just a few. From early ModG on, this durative case-classifier rapidly disappeared. It was argued that this is due to the disappearance of the [α count]-mark on the verb as a consequence of the loss of morphological aspectual distinctions (cf. (45a, b)). What disappeared with this loss of count-features was the triggering force of the [−count]-feature on the verb onto the count-feature of the complement NP. Since the copying mechanism 'saw' only the structurally lowest NP and its functional category, Case$_1$, this feature loss yielded the following result: (a) only *a priori* nominally [−count] object-NPs trigger the genitive, which is a (nominally inherent) partitive; and (b) where such an inherent [−count] characteristic on the object is absent, the genitive can no longer be licensed by the verb. Under the new tense system, taking over from the aspect paradigm, the property of text deixis is invoked — which is a completely novel scenario devoid of verbally inherent triggers for case and nominal reference.

7 Conclusion

The most general conclusion to our discussion so far is that the loss of specific perfectivity as marked morphologically and identified paradigmatically led to the shrinking of the verbally governed (not partitive!) genitive and, simultaneously, to the dominance of the accusative, since that had less restricted status. We have argued for a system of aspect-triggered case selection and definiteness in OHG, which developed via a postulated intermediate stage of case-triggered aspect and definiteness in MHG. During the time when definiteness was expressed by the interaction of case and aspect, there was no significant need to employ articles to express definiteness. When the interaction of case and aspect was gradually obliterated, articles came to assume the role of expressing definiteness. The definite article emerged noticeably earlier than the indefinite article. We have accounted for this by postulating distinct structural representations for the definite and indefinite articles (45). The definite article arose from the demonstrative use of the homonymic determiner and occupied a relatively high structural position, i.e. Spec,DP. The indefinite article developed out of the cardinal numeral, which originally occupied a lower position.

Notes

* The present version of this chapter has profited greatly from the intelligent and helpful remarks extended by the two volume editors, Ans van Kemenade and Nigel Vincent. Likewise, it would not have been possible without the stimulating observations made by Elisabeth Leiss (1991 as well as in personal communications), Karin Donhauser and Richard Schrodt. As always, my Groningen colleagues John Nerbonne and Tette Hofstra read earlier versions and suggested valuable corrections. H. R. Mehlig (Kiel) and W. Klimonov (Berlin) have rightfully drawn my attention to the empirical and conceptual intricacies of aspect and its morphological representation in Russian. Further special thanks are due to Harry Bracken, Peter Gallman, Herbert Penzl, Willy Mayrthaler, and Julia Philippi. Several audiences in Amsterdam, Graz, Berkeley, Florence, Los Angeles, Münster, Stuttgart and Tübingen have helped me to clarify the issues as well as to avoid and correct misconceptions — hopefully not in vain.

1. Adjectives in German carry 'strong' or 'weak' inflection dependent on the preceding category filled in the subtree.
2. Note that in assuming this particular [±]-partitive, or V- vs N-government distinction we are still discarding the structural explanation of the partitive genitive in languages that distinguish between accusative vs genitive objects, such as Finnish and Polish. See Abraham (1989 and 1995a, ch. 9) vs Belletti (1988).
3. I will not speak about TERMINATIVITY, or TERMINATIVE verbs, although it makes absolute sense, and is strictly maintained in the Slavic tradition of grammar, to distinguish carefully between perfective features of lexical (verbal) elements and the type of perfective paradigmatic morphology represented in the Slavic languages. Yet, to keep in line with English grammatical terminology and sidestep a terminology which, in Vendler's sense, applies to events, I stick to the ambiguous PERFECTIVE throughout.
4. Nigel Vincent has pointed this out to me. See, in more detail for German, Czepluch (1988).
5. Conceptually, the latter is a lexical variety of the clausal or phrasal notion of 'aspect'. Note, also, that aspect, as it is used here, has more to do with (locative) telicity vs nontelicity, rather than temporal aspect (as in Ancient Greek). It is this (typological) background that served the purpose of distinguishing between 'aspect' and 'Aktionsart' in the first place. No terminological distinction has been made in the present paper.
6. As John Nerbonne points out to me, the objection may be raised that, given Latin with no aspectual distinctions or articles, this generalization can at best be a tendency, or an option. This may be so. On the other hand, the situation in the history of German was different to the extent that the case system was involved, too, unlike in Latin. Given this unique, threefold connection, one could hypothesize that it was case (with its relation to (in)definiteness all along) that formed the catalyst between aspect and the epistemics of case-bearing nominals.
7. I differentiate between definite and indefinite as concepts under the general denominator of referentiality. In the modern literature (de Hoop 1992; Ritter & Rosen 1994) the terms 'strong' (for 'definite') vs 'weak' (for 'indefinite') have been used on the basis of a distinction involving 'perfective' vs 'imperfective'.
8. Note that Bulgarian, which has both a definite article and aspect and case distinctions (unlike Russian and the other Slavic languages), is not to be regarded as a counterexample since it acquired the article rather late under areal influence from neighbouring Greek. Moreover, it would not be a counterexample anyway since Bulgarian has retained a full-fledged aspectual system. A serious counterexample would be an articleless language that has lost aspectual distinctions and that has not gained articles at all. Languages with both categories, i.e. both aspectual distinctions and article morphemes, are simply 'double-marked'.
9. Note that the perfective verb is incompatible with the periphrastic future (with *budu*, something like German *werden* 'become'), since perfectives inherently plot two event components: one of 'approach', and a subsequent one resulting from the first one and bringing it to an end state. Compare the small clause structures in (40) below, where the

small clause refers to state dependent on a previous event predication leading to this state.
10. Modern Finnish has a similar distribution (cf. Karlsson 1982; Chesterman 1991; Larsson 1983; Korchmáros 1983; Wexler 1976), and grammarians traditionally speak about RESULTATIVITY vs IRRESULTATIVITY, despite the lack of a verbal aspectual paradigm as displayed by the Slavic languages. See (34)–(35) below (from Karlsson 1982: 101; cf. also Denison 1957). This is also discussed in Philippi (this volume).
11. In the generative framework, lexical case is assigned *in situ*, whereas structural case is checked for strong nominal features in a local Spec–head configuration. In other words, structural case should be identifiable by movement to an agreement node where it can pick up the case feature, whereas lexical case should be identified by staying close to the verb (in the case of German, immediately to the left of the—lexically—governing verb).
12. Unless the distinction between definite and indefinite objects, and, parallel to this distinction, between accusative and genitive objects has to be seen as one between VP-external (thematic, in the sense of Heim 1982; see Abraham 1993a) and VP-internal (rhematic). I cannot exclude this option, although I will not pursue it here.
13. The following option is possible. We may think, in the presence of the genitive case marker, of the verbal terminative prefix, or else of the accusative-governing preposition, as licensing the indefinite Det-category in the presence of the genitive case marker. Since, as we have witnessed, the accusative case (marker) does not presuppose any aspectual restriction on the governing verb, we may conclude that the accusative somehow carries the functional load of the terminative verbal marker and/or the directional, telic preposition, to yield the same result, i.e. determining [+specificity]. This clearly characterizes a purely lexical mechanism, below the level of syntax proper. I will not pursue this option any further because of its intricate representational problems.
14. One may consider, as a way out of this impasse, that the OHG system as sketched in (36a–c) and charted in (48) is in fact a scenario of sociolectically competing grammars: a Russian-like system embodying the aspectual condition leading to some OHG_1 (including, presumably, also Gothic); as that of the parent generation; and another, of the younger generation, with the following feature implications: GEN ⇒ [–DEF], ACC ⇒ [+DEF], irrespective of aspectual considerations. Let the latter be called OHG_2. Quite obviously, this speculation can only be confirmed by scrutinizing sociolectal and sociostratal parameters across the texts.
15. Recall that this system is very similar to that of Modern Russian as in (36e) above.
16. Otfrid would definitely represent the earlier OHG stage as opposed to the rest of the scarce OHG literature. I have nothing to say about whether Otfrid can be said to stand for the distinct OHG_1 claimed above.

Primary texts taken from:

Behaghel, O. and W. Mitzka (eds) 1958. *Heliand und Genesis*. Tübingen: M. Niemeyer. [Altdeutsche Textbibliothek 4]. 7th edition.
Braune, W. and E. A. Ebbinghaus (eds) 1962. *Althochdeutsches Lesebuch*. Tübingen: M. Niemeyer. 14th edition.
Sievers, E. (ed.) 1960. *Tatian. Lateinisch und altdeutsch mit ausführlichem Glossar*. Paderborn: F. Schöningh. 21st edition.

2 The rise of the article in the Germanic languages

Julia Philippi

1 Introduction*

1.1 The problem

Using an article is not universally necessary; there are languages like Arabic and Icelandic which do not have an indefinite article, and languages like Finnish and Russian which have no article at all. In the Germanic (Gmc) languages, the emergence of articles is a relatively recent development; languages like Gothic (Got), Old High German (OHG), Old Saxon (OS) and Old English (OE) do not have a definite or an indefinite article.

(1)   a.   iþ sa inngaggands þairh *daur hairdeis* ist *lambe*   Got (J.X.2)
         but who goes through *the door* is *a shepherd* for *the sheep*
      b.   uuantra giboran ist *man* in *mittilgart*   OHG (Tatian.174.5)
         because (it) was born *a man* in *the world*
     c.   stonc ða æfter *stane stearcheort* onfand *feondes fotlast*   OE (Beo.2288)
         jumped then behind *the stone the stouthearted*, found *enemy's footstep*
     d.   ef eo *man* mid sulicun dadun *dodes* gesculdien   OS (Heliand.5244)
         if sometimes *a man* with such actions deserves (*the*) *death*

Occasionally, we find in all these languages demonstratives used in a way similar to the article of the modern Gmc languages (2). In much the same way, there are indefinite pronouns and numerals used in an article-like manner (3). However, it will be shown that the use of these pronouns is so restricted that we cannot label them as articles, the latter acting as obligatory definiteness markers in the modern Gmc languages.

(2)   a.   jah andhafjands *sa hundafaþs* qaþ   Got (M.VIII.8)
         and answering *the captain* said
      b.   so er bifora wardh chichundit dhuruh *dhen forasagun*
         so he before was foreseen by *the prophets*   OHG (Isidor.28.5.6)
     c.   that *all thia eliledun man* iro vothil suohtin   OS (Heliand.345)
         that *all the strange men* their home looked-for
     d.   Men ne cunnon secgan to soðe ... hwa þæm hlæste onfeng
         people cannot say for sure who *the cargo* received   OE (Beo.50)

(3) a. ni magt *ain tagl* hveit aiþþau swart gataujan Got (M.V.36)
   not can-you *a/one hair* white or black dye
b. inti findet ira *eina eselin gebuntana* OHG (Tatian.116.1)
   and you will find a donkey tied up
c. legda im *ena boc* in an barm OS (Heliand.232)
   layed him a book in (the) bottom
d. ða bær *sum wudewe* hire suna lic to bebyrgenne OE (ÆHom.i.66.15)
   then bore a/some widow her son to be buried

In the Middle High German (MHG) and Middle English (ME) periods the use of lexical reference markers increased steadily and finally became obligatory in late MHG/ME, and indefiniteness markers became obligatory in early ModG and early Modern English (eModE). This is discussed in some detail in traditional works on the development of the Gmc languages such as Grimm (1837), Behaghel (1923), Mustanoja (1960) and others.

What are the grammatical factors that trigger such a development? In principle, it could be a purely language-specific choice, hence a coincidence from the point of view of the grammar whether an article is used or not in order to distinguish definite from indefinite NPs. Given the striking parallels in the development of the article in the Gmc (and even Romance) languages, this is not very likely. In traditional linguistics, various theories have been put forward to account for the rise of the article.

Heinrichs (1954) claims that, in Proto-Gmc, definiteness was expressed by weak adjectival inflection. Weak adjectives were formed by adding a demonstrative suffix *en/on* to mark definiteness and substantiation. In the course of time, however, the demonstrative force of the suffix eroded and was no longer sufficient to indicate the demonstrative character of the adjective. Therefore, the need for a new reference marker arose. The East and West Gmc languages used the demonstrative pronoun *sa/thata/so* which was realized in pre-adjectival position. Later, the use of the definite article was extended from the substantivized adjective to all NPs.

Other scholars (Behaghel 1923; Paul 1959; Giusti 1993; Holmberg 1993) assume that it was the loss of nominal morphology which led to the rise of the article. Holmberg (1993) observes that there is a partial complementary distribution between case morphology and articles in the European languages. Languages without articles (most Slavic, and Finno-Ugric, languages, but also Latin and the Old Gmc dialects) have a rich system of case morphology. Languages which have a poor system of case morphology (the Celtic, most of the Romance and modern Gmc languages) have lexical determiners. Giusti observes that all languages with articles develop them at a stage when they were losing or weakening case morphology. It is therefore considered probable that the article had to develop to identify the case information that was no longer visible on the noun.

Note that both theories have some appeal. Arguing in favour of Heinrichs' approach, we can show that the earliest forms of demonstrative pronouns are in fact found with weak (or nominalized) adjectives. On the other hand, in languages like German, it is in fact on the article that case is realized (see Giusti 1993).

(4) das Buch *(der)   Studentin
     the book   the(GEN-FEM) student(FEM)

However, it can also be shown that both approaches meet with striking counterevidence. Looking first at Heinrichs' approach, we find three arguments against the essence of his theory. First, although the article is commonly associated with the weak adjective, the weak adjective does not necessarily take an article (5). Second, it is also possible to combine demonstratives with strongly inflected adjectives (6).

(5) a. *libains aiveno* '(the) life(NOM) eternal(NOM-WEAK)'; *auhumistans gudjans* '(the) oldest(NOM-WEAK) priests(NOM)' Got
    b. *engil gotes guato* (the) angel(NOM) god(GEN) good(NOM-WEAK) 'the good angel of god'; *bi himilischin gote* by (the) celestial(DAT-WEAK) god(DAT) 'by the celestial god' OHG
    c. *helagon Criste* 'the holy(ACC-WEAK) Christ'; *winterscaldon snewe* '(the) winter-cold(ACC-WEAK) snow' OS

(6) a. *thiu ewingiu sunna* 'the(NOM) eternal(NOM-STRONG) sun'; *thes wares* the(GEN) true(GEN) 'the truth' OHG
    b. *thes odages mannes* 'the(GEN) rich(GEN) man(GEN)'; *thes mahtiges Kristes* 'the (GEN) mighty(GEN-STRONG) Christ' OS

The third argument against Heinrichs is that, although in the older stages of the Slavic languages we find a distinction between strong and weak adjective inflection like in the older Gmc languages, the loss of weak and strong adjectival inflection in languages like Russian did not prompt the emergence of the article (Abraham, this vol.; Leiss 1989, 1994).

Turning to the second theory, there are four counterarguments. First, it is not necessarily the case that the article is superfluous in a language that also has case morphology. In Ancient Greek, we find (definite) articles as well as a rich case morphology. Second, it is not correct that languages without case morphology necessarily have articles. Languages such as Chinese do not have articles in spite of the fact that they do not have inflectional morphology. Third, the introduction of an article does not help to identify grammatical features when the same process of deflection which takes place in the noun also takes place in the determiner. This is what happened in the development of most Gmc and Romance languages. Fourth, the loss of case morphology may be compensated in principle without using an article. In languages like Dutch and English, for instance, there is a variety of prepositions that take over the function of the case markers in the older stages.

1.2 General outline

In this paper, I will provide an alternative explanation for the emergence of determiners. In my theory the article acts as a reference marker for the NP from the very beginning. I will argue that languages universally must be able to make the definite/indefinite or specific/non-specific distinction visible; however, its referentiality marking is different between languages. In the modern Gmc languages, the article is used as a default reference marker. In the Old Gmc languages, definite or indefinite NPs are distinguished by different structural case markings as is known from languages like Finnish (see Belletti 1988; de Hoop 1992; Meinunger 1993; Runner 1993, among others). Here, an indefinite (or weak) NP is marked genitive, while a definite (or strong) NP is marked accusative (Abraham 1994; Donhauser 1991; Leiss 1989, 1994), as in (7) and (8).

(7) a. hvas haldiþ aweþi jah miluks þis aweþjis ni matjai   Got (K.IX.7)
    who tends a flock and does not milk(GEN) of the flock drink
   b. skancta sinan fianton bitteres lides   OHG (Ludwigsl.II.53–4)
    (he) poured out to his enemies a bitter drink(GEN)
   c. an is handun dragan hluteres waters   OS (Heliand.4536)
    on his hands carry clear water(GEN)

(8) a. jah insandida ina haiþjos seinaizos haldan sweina   Got (L.XV.15)
    and (he) sent him out to his field to look after (the) pigs(ACC)
   b. Inti dir gibu sluzzila himilo riches   OHG (Tatian.90.3)
    and to you I give (the) key(ACC) of the kingdom of heaven
   c. gisahun then mahtigan, godes angil chuman   OS (Heliand.394–5)
    (they) saw (the) mighty(ACC) god's angel(ACC) come

In the late MHG period the verbal genitive is lost and is replaced by an accusative NP or PP; in ME, genitive and accusative are replaced by one neutral objective case. It is therefore no longer possible to mark definiteness on NPs by different cases. A new system of definiteness marking emerges. The demonstrative pronoun, formerly a purely emphatic element severely restricted by context, is finally reanalysed as the new definiteness marker within the NP.

The outline of this chapter is as follows. In section 2, I will show that so-called weak and strong NPs are syntactically different, and we will give an account for these differences. In section 3, I will discuss the relationship between case marking and NP interpretation in the older Gmc languages. In section 4, I will sketch the development of the Gmc languages from a stage where no articles were employed to one where they are obligatory and I will relate this development to the loss of genitive as an object case.

2 The structure of NP in the modern Gmc languages

In this section I want to argue that the semantic interpretation of NP is reflected at least partially in its syntactic structure. I will show that there are fundamental differences between so-called strong NPs, i.e. NPs introduced by a determiner like *most* or *all*, and weak NPs, i.e. NPs introduced by a determiner like *some* or *many*. These differences are primarily semantic in nature, but they also interact with the syntactic structure of NP. Finally, I will show how weak and strong NPs differ in their syntactic behaviour, and how these differences may be represented structurally.

Let us take the DP-hypothesis (Abney 1987) as a point of departure. This theory claims that NPs are maximal projections of a functional head D, where D^0 is the position where the referential interpretation of the NP is determined. The NP acts semantically as a predicate. Generally, predicates have at least one argument position in their argument structures, namely the referential argument, which appears in addition to a lexically fixed number of thematic arguments (cf. Williams 1981; Higginbotham 1985 and 1987; Hudson 1989; Zwarts 1992) The referential argument corresponds to the individual (or to the group of individuals) denoted by the NP. While thematic roles are discharged inside the maximal projection of N, the referential argument position must be bound from outside the NP. I believe that this is done by some determiner: either by an element in D^0 (as, for instance, the definite article), or by an operator in Spec,DP, which is coindexed by Spec–head agreement with an abstract feature within D^0. Let us assume as a preliminary that this feature is something like [±strong], foreshadowing the weak/strong distinction on quantifiers which I will introduce below. The structure of the nominal projection is therefore parallel to that of the sentential projection, where the referential argument of the verb — i.e. the Davidsonian argument (see Zwarts 1992) — is saturated by some complementizer: either by an element in C^0 — for instance the complementizer *that* — or by a *wh*-operator in [Spec,CP] which is coindexed via Spec–head agreement with an abstract element [+*wh*] within C^0. Thus, a NP like *most dogs* is analysed as in (9)

(9)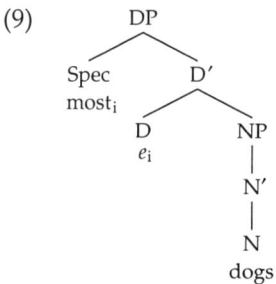

Note that we have to distinguish between weak quantifiers/determiners, such as *a*, *some* and *many*, and strong ones (*the*, *all*, *most*). A weak NP, i.e. an NP introduced by a weak quantifier/determiner, is allowed in existential sentences, while a strong NP, i.e. an NP introduced by a strong quantifier, is not (Milsark 1977). Consider (10).

(10) a. There is/there are a/some/many/few/three dog/dogs in the garden.
b. *There is/there are the/all/most/both/every dog/dogs in the garden.

In Barwise & Cooper (1981) weak quantifiers are characterized as 'symmetric' or 'intersective'. This is not the case with strong quantifiers. Symmetry is defined as in (11).

(11) Symmetry
   DetAB ↔ DetBA

(11) says that a determiner is symmetric if it may saturate the referential argument position of either the subject or the predicate NP in a simple predicative sentence. The examples in (12) show that quantifiers like *some* and *many* are symmetric, while the quantifiers *most* and *all* are not.

(12) a. Some/many linguists are lazybones =
       Some/many lazybones are linguists
   b. Most/all linguists are lazybones ≠
       Most/all lazybones are linguists

The sentences in (12a) are truth-conditionally equivalent. Quantifiers like *some* and *many* are symmetric, since the functions they denote may be applied either to the set of linguists or to the set of lazybones, with no difference to the truth conditions. The examples in (12b) show that this analogy is not possible for NPs introduced by strong quantifiers. A quantifier is symmetric if and only if it is intersective; in other words, intersectivity is equivalent to symmetry. The formal definition of intersectivity is given in (13).

(13) Intersectivity
   DetAB ↔ Det(A∩B)(A∩B)

Intersective determiners are only concerned with the intersection of the two sets A and B. (12a) says that the intersection of the set of the linguists and the set of the lazybones contains some or many members. Thus, it is irrelevant which of the sets is denoted by the NP and which by the predicate. However, strong quantifiers place a condition on the cardinality of the intersection of A and B relative to the cardinality of A (Ruys 1992). Example (12b) says that the set of lazy linguists makes up a certain proportion (most/all) of the set of linguists.

Following Higginbotham (1987) let us assume that weak quantifiers cannot bind the referential argument position in the noun, but rather behave like adjectives, also showing a referential argument position which is identified with the referential argument position of the noun (see also Diesing 1992; de Hoop 1992; Hudson 1989). Thus, a NP like *a linguist* receives an interpretation like in (14a).

(14) a. a(x) linguist(x)

The claim that a weak quantifier does not act as a binder for the referential argument position of the noun is supported by the fact that weak NPs may act as predicates with the sentential subject saturating the referential argument position (14b).[1]

(14) b. John is a linguist

The referential argument position is bound only in a strong NP. Only this may be interpreted as a quantificational expression in a logical interpretation. A weak NP on the other hand has an unbound referential argument position. This acts as unsaturated predicate, introducing variables in the logical representation of the sentence. For a weak NP to be realized in an argument position, it must have its referential argument position bound from outside. In the default case, this is done by a process called *Existential Closure* where an Existential Quantifier is inserted into the logical representation which is in the scope of all quantifiers in the sentence. This Existential Quantifier binds the unsaturated referential argument positions of all weak NPs in the sentence, thereby yielding an existential interpretation on the NP (cf. Heim 1982, Zwarts 1992).

I believe that the semantic behaviour of weak NPs is syntactically reflected in that weak determiners are not realized in D^0, but rather occupy an adjective-like position (cf. Hudson 1989, Zwarts 1992 *inter alia*) in that they obey distributional tests for adjectivehood. First, it is in principle possible to combine weak quantifiers with strong ones. Weak quantifiers may generally occur with the definite article (15a). In German, numerals may also be combined with other strong quantifiers such as *alle* 'all' (15b).[2]

(15) a. the few/many/three linguists
    b. alle drei Linguisten
       all three linguists

Second, there are weak quantifiers which clearly show adjective-like behaviour in that they may form comparatives and superlatives, allow for modification by degree expressions such as *very*, and may show up in contexts like *as* Adj *as*:

(16) a. fewer linguists than logicians
    b. very few linguists
    c. as many linguists as logicians

Consequently, the D-position in a weak NP is always empty while it is obligatorily filled in a strong NP. According to the Principle of Minimal Projection suggested by Grimshaw (1993) a functional projection is realized only if it makes a functional contribution to the extended projection it is part of, i.e. if it can be functionally interpreted. If Grimshaw is right, this means that only strong NPs are DPs, because their functional head D has the function of binding the referential argument position of N, thereby yielding a quantificational interpretation of NP. Weak NPs, on the other hand, are NPs since they get their existential interpretation from outside. Hence, the empty D-head would not get any functional interpretation.

This hypothesis is supported by the differential behaviour of weak and strong NPs with respect to *wh*-extraction. Bowers (1988) observes that *wh*-extraction from a weakly quantified NP is possible while it leads to ungrammaticality in a strong NP.

(17) a. Who did you see a picture of?
  b. Who did you see many pictures of?
  c. Who did you see some pictures of?

(18) a. *Who did you see the picture of?
  b. *Who did you see every picture of?
  c. *Who did you see most pictures of?

The contrast between (17) and (18) receives a simple account if we assume weak NPs to be NPs and strong NPs to be DPs. In (17), where a *wh*-phrase is extracted out of a weak NP, NP is L-marked by the verb and is therefore not a blocking category. In (18), on the other hand, the *wh*–phrase is extracted out of a strong NP, i.e. a DP. NP is not L-marked by the functional head D and is therefore a blocking category and a barrier. The DP-node inherits barrierhood from the NP. This results in the extraction crossing two barriers, yielding a Subjacency violation (Chomsky 1986a).

Note that the existential interpretation is not the only possible interpretation for weak NPs. Rather, they are neutral between an existential and a quantificational reading. I therefore conclude that not only lexical properties of the quantifier are responsible for the interpretation of the NP. Let us assume that discourse grammatical facts are relevant too. What is special about existentially interpreted NP is that it introduces a new individual into the universe of discourse. Strong NP on the other hand is discourse-linked, i.e. it is mapped onto a discourse referent which is a proper subset of another discourse referent already introduced into the universe of discourse (see Enç 1991). Consider (19).

(19) [There are several dogs living in my neighbourhood]
  Some dogs are sitting in my garden this afternoon

The most salient reading of (19) says that the dogs sitting in my garden belong to the dogs living in my neighbourhood. Thus, the NP *some dogs* refers to a subset of a set of contextually given dogs, and has, therefore, a quantificational rather than an existential reading. I believe that a weak NP with a specific reading is base-generated as a DP headed by an abstract feature [+strong] binding the referential argument position of N. The weak quantifier is base-generated in Spec,NP. In the course of the derivation, it must raise to Spec,DP where it is coindexed with D^0 (see Zwarts 1992). This is parallel to *wh*-operator moved to Spec,CP in order to be coindexed with an abstract feature [+*wh*] in C^0.

(20) $[_{DP}[_D[+ \text{strong}]][_{NP} \text{some dogs}]] \rightarrow [_{DP} \text{some}_i [_D[+ \text{strong}]_i][t_i \text{ dogs}]]$

One argument in favour of analysing weak NP on its specific interpretation as DP is the impossibility of extracting from indefinites as objects directly affected by the event denoted by the verb (21):[3]

(21) *Who did you destroy a picture of?

Summarizing, we have seen that a weak NP differs from a strong NP in that the former does not have a quantificational force of its own; there is an unsaturated referential argument position which must be bound by Existential Closure. In order for the special binding requirements on weak NPs to be met, their syntactic distribution must be fairly restricted. This is in fact the case. It is, for instance, a well-known fact that in German the ordering of adverbials and arguments is free. The object NP may precede or follow the sentential adverb. Generally it is assumed that the structure in (22b) is derived from (22a) by a process which is called 'scrambling' in the literature. However, existential NP seems to be barred from scrambling. Example (22b) is grammatical only if the NP *zwei Linguisten* 'two linguists' has a specific interpretation. (22c), where the NP has an unambiguously existential interpretation, is ungrammatical.[4]

(22) a. daß die Polizei gestern   zwei *Linguisten* festgenommen hat
          that the police yesterday two   linguists   arrested   has
      b. daß die Polizei *zwei* Linguisten gestern   festgenommen hat
          that the police   two linguists   yesterday arrested   has
      c. *daß die Polizei Linguisten gestern   festgenommen hat
          that the police   linguists   yesterday arrested   has

How can the contrast in (22) be accounted for? In what follows, I will show that the restrictions on weak NPs receive a straightforward explanation in terms of what has recently been called 'Mapping Hypothesis'.

The Mapping Hypothesis (Diesing 1992) is based on the Discourse Representation Theory (DRT) proposed by Heim (1982) and Kamp (1981). According to Heim the logical representation of a sentence is a tripartite structure, consisting of a quantifying expression, a Restrictive Clause specifying the set of individuals the quantifier operates over, and a Nuclear Scope specifying the truth conditions of the sentence. Existential Closure is a process which typically applies to the Nuclear Scope of a sentence. Recall that weak NPs have an unsaturated referential argument position which has to be bound via Existential Closure.[5] We therefore expect weak NPs — as far as interpreted existentially — to be realized within the Nuclear Scope. NPs realized within the Restrictive Clause must have quantificational force of their own, i.e. only strong NPs are admitted in the Restrictive Clause. Accordingly, (23a) is interpreted as in (23b).

(23) a. Every dog eats a bone.
      b. Every x   [x is a dog]   ($\exists$y) [bone (y) & x eats y]
         Quantifier   Restrictive Clause   Nuclear Scope

Diesing claims that there is a correspondence between the syntactic and the semantic representation of a sentence. She suggests a mapping procedure splitting the syntactic tree into two parts which are mapped into two parts of the logical representation. According to Diesing, material from inside VP is mapped into the Nuclear Scope while material from outside VP ends up in the Restrictive Clause.

Meinunger (1993) and Runner (1993) attempt to reconcile the Mapping Hypothesis and Chomsky's 'Checking Theory' (Chomsky 1993a). These theories at first sight seem to be incompatible. Chomsky reduces case assigment to a 'checking' mechanism which uniformly takes place in a Spec–head configuration. Chomsky claims that an NP is base-generated as a fully inflected form within VP. In the course of the derivation it must leave its base-generated position and move to the Spec of an Agr-projection in order to get case features 'checked'. Checking principles force movement of all NPs from their base-generated position within VP.

Meinunger and Runner argue that combining Chomsky's Checking Theory with Diesing's Mapping Hypothesis leads to the expectation that all NPs must receive a specific interpretation, since all NPs leave VP in the course of the derivation for checking purposes. This is clearly an incorrect prediction. Therefore, they revise Chomsky's theory slightly and claim that only strong NPs move to the Spec of an Agr-projection for case checking. Weak NPs cannot leave VP. This is because the unsaturated referential argument position must be bound by Existential Closure within the Nuclear Scope. Therefore, weak NPs remains in their base-generated position where they are assigned a default case.[6] Meinunger and Runner end up with the tree-splitting algorithm in (24).

(24) $[_C...[_{Agr}...\quad\quad|\quad[_{VP}...]]]$
     Restrictive Clause | Nuclear Scope

We are now in a position to give an explanation for the data in (22) above. Let us assume that scrambling is a case-driven process where NP moves to Spec,Agr$_O$P for case checking (see Mahajan 1990). The NP *zwei Linguisten* 'two linguists' is realized in a scrambled position, which can be seen from its position on the left of the adverb *gestern* 'yesterday'. From here it is mapped into the Restrictive Clause of the logical representation of the sentence. Therefore, the only possible interpretation of the NP is a specific one presupposing that there is a set of linguists established in the universe of discourse, two of them being arrested by the police. This can be seen from the focal stress which is realized on the numeral, indicating that it is not the fact that linguists are arrested which is new, but rather the number of linguists in question.

One caveat is in order here. Note that while a weak NP is only allowed in VP-internal position, a strong NP does not necessarily move to the Spec of an Agr-projection. It can be seen from (25) that, for instance, scrambling is by no means obligatory for strong object NPs in German.

(25) daß die Polizei gestern   alle Linguisten festgenommen hat
     that the police yesterday all linguists   arrested   has

We therefore have to refine the theory developed so far. Let us assume that movement of a NP to Spec,Agr is not only determined by semantic properties of NP, but also by discourse-functional concepts such as theme and rheme. A thematic NP (which is necessarily strong) has to move out of VP overtly, i.e. before Spell-Out. A rhematic strong NP moves to Spec,Agr$_S$P or Spec,Agr$_O$P as long as it has a specific interpretation, but this movement takes place covertly, i.e. after Spell-Out (see also Meinunger 1993).

There is evidence that one and the same syntactic process may occur before or after Spell-Out. In multiple *wh*-constructions, for instance, only one *wh*-phrase is moved to Spec,CP before Spell-Out; other *wh*-phrases may move to an operator-position at LF.

(26) a. John forgot why he should tell Mary what
 b. *John forgot why what he should tell Mary
 c. John forgot [what]$_j$ [why]$_i$ $t_i$he should tell Mary t_j

At the moment, we can only speculate why it should be that only thematic NPs move to Spec,Agr$_O$P or Spec,Agr$_S$P. Note that it is a basic assumption in the minimalist framework that movement before Spell-Out must be triggered by some PF-specific condition; movement that is not triggered by PF-conditions takes place after Spell-Out for Economy Principles like PROCRASTINATE. However, the informational structure, i.e. the partitioning of a sentence into a thematic and a rhematic part, is clearly performance-oriented and must be visible at PF. We may therefore assume that overt movement of NP to Spec,Agr may be triggered by a feature [Theme] which is realized on a thematic NP. This feature is 'strong' in as much as it has to be checked before Spell-Out. A rhematic strong NP does not have a feature triggering movement, hence raising is delayed until LF.

Runner (1993) shows that the Mapping Hypothesis sketched above can give an explanation for the so-called Definiteness Effect, i.e. the inability of strong NP to show up in existential sentences. Consider again (10):

(27) a. There is/there are a/some/many/few/three dog/dogs in the garden.
 b. *There is/there are the/all/most/both/every dog/dogs in the garden.

Runner establishes two peculiarities of existential sentences. First, as pointed out, they do not allow for a specific NP, i.e. an NP in an existential sentence must remain *in situ* and therefore be realized within the Nuclear Scope. Second, there are only a few verbs which allow productively for a *there*-subject; interestingly enough the class is restricted to a small subset of unaccusative verbs. Existential sentences with unergative verbs are always ungrammatical.

(28) a. There appeared a/some/many/few/three dog/dogs in the garden.
 b. *There appeared the/all/most/both/every dog/dogs in the garden.
 c. *There ran a/some/many/few/three dog/dogs in the garden.
 d. *There ran the/all/most/both/every dog/dogs in the garden.

One of the claims traditionally made about unaccusative verbs is that they do not assign accusative case (Burzio 1986). In Chomsky's system, not being able to assign accusative case presumably means not having an active Agr_O-projection.

Since only unaccusative verbs are allowed in English existential sentences, and since unaccusative verbs lack an Agr_O-projection, we may conclude that there is no Agr_O-projection available in existential sentences. Since strong object NPs have to move to Spec,Agr_OP at least at the level of LF, and since this position is not available in sentences containing unaccusative verbs, only weak NPs are allowed to show up in existential sentences.

To summarize, in this section I have shown some structural differences between weak and strong NPs, and how these account for differences in syntactic behaviour. Weak NPs were analysed as NPs, and these NPs function semantically as predicates whose referential argument position is unsaturated. Strong NPs, on the other hand, are DPs; the referential argument position of the noun is saturated by some determiner: either by an element in D^0 (for instance, the definite article), or, indirectly, by an operator in Spec,DP which is coindexed with an abstract feature [+strong] which is realized in D^0. In order to be licensed in an argument positon, weak NPs must be bound from outside by Existential Closure. In order for this binding to be possible, I assumed weak NPs to be fairly restricted in distribution. In fact, weak NPs are barred from scrambling, analysed here as movement to Spec,Agr_OP. This fact, I argued, can be explained by the Mapping Hypothesis claiming that material from inside VP is mapped into the Nuclear Scope of the logical representation of a sentence, while material from outside VP is mapped into the Restrictive Clause (Diesing 1992; Meinunger 1993; Runner 1993). On the assumption that only strong NPs may be realized within the Restrictive Clause, while weak NPs must be bound within the Nuclear Scope, movement to Spec,Agr necessarily correlates with a specific interpretation on NPs.

The proposal above was to analyse the articles in the modern Gmc languages as default reference markers.[7] Note, however, that not all languages use articles to mark weakness vs strength on NPs. If I maintain our initial claim that all languages must mark definiteness, I conclude that there must be different reference marking systems. I want to turn to these questions in the following section.

3 The weak–strong distinction in the older Germanic languages

In the previous section I have claimed that all languages have formal ways of marking definiteness on NPs. I have claimed that in the modern Gmc languages articles and determiners function as means to mark NPs as weak or strong. However, there are many languages — including the older Gmc languages — which do not have articles. In the introduction, I said that there must be different language-specific mechanisms to visualize the referential interpretation of NPs. In what follows, I want to show that in the older Gmc languages referentiality was marked by different cases.

3.1 Case and referentiality

It is known from recent studies that there is a close interaction between case marking and the referential interpretation of NPs (see Abraham, this vol.; Belletti 1988; de Hoop 1992, *inter alia*). In some languages with rich case morphology, there are two structural cases which can be assigned to the object of a transitive verb, a so-called strong one, which occurs if NP has a strong interpretation, and a so-called weak one, which is found if NP has a weak interpretation (Belletti 1988; de Hoop 1992). In Finnish, for instance, weak NP is marked partitive, while strong NP is marked accusative. Likewise, in Russian a genitive NP has an existential reading; if it is marked accusative, it receives a strong interpretation (Abraham, this vol.; Leiss 1989, 1994); see (28), where PART stands for *partitive*.[8]

(29) a. Anne tapaa vieraita (Finnish, de Hoop 1992)
       Anne meets guests(PART)
       'Anne meets (some) guests'
   b. Anne tapaat vieraat
       Anne meets guests(ACC)
       'Anne meets the guests'
   c. On prinës papiros (Russian, Abraham, this vol.)
       he brought cigarettes(GEN)
       'He brings (some) cigarettes'
   d. On prinës papirosy
       he brought cigarettes(ACC)
       'He brought the cigarettes'

The same correlation between case and referentiality is found in the older Gmc languages. Here, the NP bears genitive case if it has an existential interpretation. It bears accusative if it has a specific reading.[9] Reconsider data like (7) and (8) repeated for Gothic here.

(7) hvas haldiþ aweþi jah miluks þis aweþjis ni matjai Got (K.IX.7)
    who tends a flock and does not milk(GEN) of flock(DEF) drink

(8) jah insandida ina haiþjos seinaizos haldan sweina Got (L.XV.15)
    and (he) sent him out to his field to look after (DEF) pigs(ACC)

The above data receive a straightforward acccount in terms of the Mapping Hypothesis introduced in the previous section. The basic idea was that only strong NPs move to Spec,Agr for case checking. A weak NP cannot leave its base-generated position; it remains *in situ* and is assigned a default case. Finnish and the older Gmc languages are special in that the default case assigned to weak NPs within VP and the structural case checked in Spec,Agr$_O$P have different morphological forms; the former is genitive/partitive, the latter is accusative. This means that Finnish and the older Gmc languages behave exactly like the modern Gmc languages. Why is it that weak NPs cannot move to Spec,Agr in Finnish and the older Gmc languages?

I proposed that a weak NP cannot leave its base-generated position since there is an unsaturated referential argument position which must be bound by Existential Closure within the Nuclear Scope. A strong NP has quantificational force of its own; the referential argument position is bound by a determiner. However, there is no determiner present in the examples in (8), and still the NPs have a definite interpretation. Nevertheless, let us assume that it is a functional head governing the maximal projection of N that discharges the referential argument position of the NP. What is it that saturates the referential argument positon of a strong NP in the older Gmc languages? I think that the functional head in question is occupied by an abstract case element which is related to accusative case realization. A weak NP on the other hand is analysed uniformly as an NP in which the referential argument position is unsaturated. In the previous section, I took the fact that a weak NP may function as a predicate noun as evidence for the claim that it has an unsaturated referential argument position. If genitive is the case of weak object NPs in the older Gmc languages, we expect genitive NPs to be potentially predicative as well. This is in fact the case.

(30) a. ibai jah þu þize siponje is þis mans   Got (Ulfilas)
whether also you (of) those disciples(GEN) are of this man
b. thu bist rehto in wara thesses mannes fuara   OHG (Otfrid.IV.18.14)
you are surely in truth of this man an adherent(GEN)
c. si uuaren is hiuuiscas   OS (Heliand.365)
they were of his family(GEN)

Do we have evidence favouring the idea that case acts as a functional head saturating the referential argument position of NP? The most convincing data come from languages like Turkish, where the direct object bears an accusative morpheme -(y)ı if the NP has a specific reading. If the NP does not carry case morphology, it is interpreted existentially (see Enç 1991).[10]

(31) a. Ali bir   kitab-ı   aldı   (Enç 1991)
Ali a certain book(ACC) bought
b. Ali bir   kitap aldı
Ali some book bought

It is very probable in (30a) that it is the the case morpheme -(y)ı that acts as a functional head saturating the referential argument position of the noun in Turkish, thus yielding a specific interpretation on the NP. In (30b), there is no F⁰–element present to saturate the referential argument position of N. The NP does not have quantificational force of its own, but must be bound by Existential Closure. Therefore, the NP has a weak interpretation. In order for this binding to be licit, we expect the syntactic distribution of existential NPs in Turkish to be restricted in a way similar to that of object NPs in German. The following examples show that this is in fact borne out (see de Hoop 1992; Lamontagne & Travis 1987).

(32) a. Hasan dün pasta yedi (Lamontagne & Travis 1987)
 Hasan yesterday some cake ate
 b. *Hasan pasta dün yedi
 Hasan some cake yesterday ate
 c. Hasan pasta-yi dün yedi
 Hasan one cake(ACC) yesterday ate

In (31a), the indefinite object occurs inside VP, which can be seen from its position to the right of the sentential adverb *dün* 'yesterday'. According to the Mapping Hypothesis, the NP is mapped into the Nuclear Scope and thus may be bound by Existential Closure in a logical representation. In (31b), on the other hand, the object is moved out of VP, which can be seen from its position to the left of the sentential adverb. In a logical representation it is mapped into the Restrictive Clause of the sentence. Note that there is no morphological case marker present in the object NP, so that the referential argument is unsaturated and needs to be bound within the Nuclear Scope. The sentence is ungrammatical since the NP occurs in a position where such binding is impossible. Example (31c) shows that object scrambling is possible as soon as a morphological case marker is present. Here, the referential argument position of the object is saturated by F^0.

What about the distribution of genitive and accusative object NPs in the older Gmc languages? If the assumption that genitive objects are NPs is correct, we expect them to be severely restricted in distribution. This is because they must get their referential argument position bound by Existential Closure within the Nuclear Scope. Scrambling, for instance, should not be allowed for genitive NPs. In fact, it was suggested recently that genitive NP only occurs in its base-generated position as the most direct argument of the verb (or verb-closest argument (VCA) in the sense of Abraham (this vol.) as in (32)). An accusative NP is also found in VCA-position; it is, however, realized in scrambled position as well, as in (34).

(33) a. (inti sliumo liof ein fon in intfagana spunga)
 and quickly ran one of them taking a sponge (and)
 fulta$_i$ sia ezziches t$_i$ OHG (Tatian.208.3)
 filled it with vinegar(GEN)
 b. that he thene siakon man sundeono tomean weldi
 that he the sick man (the/his) sins(GEN) remit wanted
  OS (Heliand.2319.20)

(34) a. vato mis ana fotuns meinans not gaft Got (L.VII.44)
 water(ACC) I(DAT) for feet my not gave(2.PL)
 b. ni uuelda an is kindiski is craft mikil mannun marean
 not wanted in his childhood his strength big (the) people show
  OS (Heliand.840–1)

The data in (33) and (34) above suggest that it is in fact impossible for a genitive object NP to leave its base-generated position. This is corroborated by the fact that in ModG, where there are still some relics of the verbal genitive, scrambling of genitival objects leads to ungrammaticality. Consider (34). In (34a), the deepest constituent is the genitive NP *der Lüge* 'the lie', which is preceded by the accusative NP *den Freund* 'the friend'. In (34b), the order of the verbal complements is the other way around; the sentence is ungrammatical or at least very marked.

(35) a.   daß Johann den Freund der Lüge   bezichtigte
          that Johann the friend the lie(GEN) accused
     b.*/??daß Johann der Lüge   den Freund bezichtigte
          that Johann the lie(GEN) the friend accused

In the previous section, I explained the definiteness effect in Modern English proposing that the only verbs possible in existential sentences are unaccusative verbs which are special in that they cannot assign accusative case. Verbs which cannot assign accusative case, I claimed, do not have an active Agr_O-projection; therefore, a possible object NP can only be realized in its base-generated position; it must therefore be assigned a default case. Consider now existential sentences in the older Gmc languages.[11]

(36) i   was   im   rumis   Got (L.II.7)
     not was(3SG) him   fame(GEN.SG)
     'He did not have fame'

In (36) the object NP bears genitive. Above, genitive was analysed as a default case assigned within VP to NP that cannot move to Spec,Agr. It seems as if we can explain the data in (36) in much the same way as those in (10) above. Since there is no Agr_O-projection available in existential sentences, accusative case cannot be checked in sentences like (36). The NP is realized in its base-generated position, where it is assigned a default case.

To summarize, I have associated accusative case with a specific reading and genitive case with an existential reading on the object NP. I assumed a weak NP to be special in that it cannot move to Spec,Agr for case checking. Rather, it remains *in situ* and is assigned a default case, which in the older Gmc languages is genitive. This is because they have an unsaturated referential argument position which has to be bound by Existential Closure within the Nuclear Scope. A strong NP has quantificational force of its own; thus, it may leave its base-generated position and move to Spec,Agr_OP or Spec,Agr_SP for case-checking.

3.2 Excursus: case and aspect

In section 3.1 I have shown that two different object cases are assigned in the older Gmc languages to object NPs, depending on their referential interpretation. If the NP has a strong interpretation, it has accusative; if it has an existential interpretation, it has genitive case. Note, however, that the alternation between genitive and accusative is not only dependent on the referential interpretation of the object NP, but also on aspectual features of the governing V^0 (see Abraham, this vol.; Donhauser 1991; Erdmann 1973;

Leiss 1989, 1994).[12] The same is true for Russian and Finnish, the languages we compared with the older Gmc languages, although the interrelation between case, aspect and definiteness is slightly different in these languages.

According to Abraham (this vol.) and Leiss (1989, 1994), the older Gmc languages behave like Russian. In Russian, it is only possible for inherently perfective verbs to select alternatively for accusative or genitive objects, where the former correlates with a strong and the latter with a weak reading on the object. Imperfective verbs cannot govern an object in the genitive case in direct object function. Therefore, definite and indefinite NPs have accusative case. Nevertheless, the referential status of the object NP can be expressed, namely by aspectual morphology. Imperfective verbs such as *kolot'* 'split' in (37a) take an indefinite object NP. An inherently imperfective verb can perfectivize by adding a certain prefix to the stem. In that case, the object NP has a strong interpretation (Abraham, this vol.; Leiss 1989, 1994).

(37) a. On kolo-l   drov-a
     he split(PRET) wood(ACC [–DEF])
  b. On ras-kolo-l   drov-a
     he (PERF)-split(PRET) wood(ACC [+DEF])

These authors argue that the same is true for the older Gmc languages. Like Russian, these languages have a productive aspectual system. Perfectivity is expressed either as an inherent lexical feature of the verb, or it is morphologically derived by adding a perfective morpheme *ge-*, *gi-* or *ga-* to the stem (see also van Dijk 1994).[13] This can be seen from the Gothic verb pairs in (38).

(38) a. *taujan* 'do(IMPERF)'   – *ga-taujan* 'do(PERF)', 'fulfill'   (Leiss 1994)
  b. *hausjan* 'hear(IMPERF)' – *ga-hausjan* 'hear(PERF)', 'perceive'

As in Russian, only perfective verbs may alternatively assign genitive or accusative; imperfective verbs select only for accusative NP. Accordingly, many verbs allowing for case alternation on the object in the older Gmc languages were prefixed verbs. The following is a partial list of MHG verbs allowing for genitive complements (39), quoted from Abraham (this volume).

(39) *(be)-gern, muoten, (ge)-ruochen* 'demand', *ge-niezen* 'enjoy', *er-getzen* 'make forget', *ent-gelten* 'have the disadvantage of', *bîten* 'wait for', *hüeten* 'heed', *warten* 'wait for', *walten* 'have power over', *pflegen* 'be busy with', *ge-hugen* 'think of', *darben* 'miss', *(be)-durfen, en-bern* 'be in need of', *swern* 'swear', *zîhen* 'accuse'

The restriction of case alternation to perfective verbs is corrobated by the fact that the few verbs in Modern German allowing for genitive objects are without exception prefixed verbs which have a strong tendency toward perfective aspectuality (Abraham, this vol.).

(40) *der Gefallenen ge-denken* 'think of the fallen persons(GEN)', *sich des Sommers er-innern* 'remember the summer(GEN)', *sich des Freundes ent-sinnen* 'remember the friend(GEN)', *der Hilfe be-dürfen* 'require for help(GEN)'

However, the theory developed so far cannot account for verbs only allowing for genitive complements. According to Erdmann, these verbs are often inherently imperfective.

With these verbs, the accusative is an exceptional case which needs further motivation, e.g. by a verbal prefix denoting exhaustion of the act or event denoted by the verb (cf. Abraham). Consider (41):

(41) a.   *itan* 'eat' vs *fraitan* 'devour'   Got
     b.   joh sinero worto er horta filu harto   OHG (Otfrid.II.9.57)
          still to his(GEN) words(GEN) he listened(IMPERF.) very carefully
     c.   thaz imbot sie gihortun joh iro ferti iltun   OHG (Otfrid.I.17.53)
          the instruction(ACC) they heard(PERF.) and on their way they hurried away

Some verbs even acquire an imperfective interpretation by being combined with a genitive complement and a perfective interpretation by being combined with an accusative complement. This can be seen from (42) where *eiscon* must be translated as an imperfective verb 'ask for' if it is combined with a genitive object, and as a perfective verb 'find out' if it is combined with an accusative object (Donhauser 1991).

(42) a.   Sie eiscoton thes kindes   OHG (Otfrid.I.17.11)
          they asked for-the child(GEN)
     b.   Thia zit eiscota er fon in   OHG (Otfrid.III.2.29)
          the time(ACC) he found out from them

Note that the conditions for the genitive/accusative alternation on the object form a hierarchy with the perfective/imperfective distinction on the VP ranking over the weak/strong distinction on the verb. This can be seen from (42a) where the genitive NP only stands for imperfectivity on the dominating VP. The NP itself refers to the Christ-child and is therefore necessarily definite. With these data in mind, Donhauser suggests that the genitive/accusative alternation correlates with the weak/strong distinction on object NPs only if the governing verb is either inherently perfective or if perfective aspect is derived by prefixing a perfective morpheme to the stem. If the verb is neutral with respect to aspect, or inherently imperfective, the genitive case stands for imperfectivity and accusative for perfectivity.

(43) perfective   imperfective
     genitive

     strong interpretation   weak interpretation
     accusative   genitive

The same is true for Finnish, which has no aspectual system. However, grammarians distinguish between resultative verbs denoting a temporally limited event and irresultative verbs denoting an action which is not regarded as complete. Partitive case may also mark the object of an irresultative verb, i.e. one whose action is not regarded as complete. An irresultative verb (e.g. a verb expressing an emotion) allows only for partitive complements (44a). Other verbs are used in both resultative and irresultative senses and then the aspectual distinction is marked by case alternation. If the verb is irresultative, the object bears partitive case (44b); if it is used in a resultative sense, the object bears accusative (44c). Note again that the aspectual interpretation of the VP overrides the referential interpretation of the object NP. The object in (44a) is obviously definite, in (44b, c) the object NP is neutral with respect to definiteness, i.e. the referential interpretation of NP must be determined by the context.

(44) a. Minä rakastan sinua (Chesterman 1991)
I love you(PART)
b. Henry rakensi taloa
Henry was building a/the house(PART)
c. Henry rakensi talon
Henry built a/the house(ACC)

The question arises whether we may explain the interaction of case and aspectual interpretation of the verb in terms of the theory developed here. In what follows, I want to suggest a theory which is purely semantic in nature. This theory will lead me to refine my concept of the semantics of genitive object NPs in the older Gmc languages.

Note first of all that phenomena similar to the facts in (42) are attested also for English. Here, the VP describes a telic event if the object NP denotes a countable entity; it describes an atelic event if the object NP denotes a non-countable entity (Verkuyl 1988). Consider (45):[14]

(45) a. John ate all the cookies (in an hour/*for hours)
b. John ate cookies (*in an hour/for hours)

In (45a), the object NP refers to a set of cookies which is possibly contextually given. The VP *eat all the cookies* describes an event which in the literature is classified as an *accomplishment*. Accomplishments are complex events consisting of a process of successive stages and a natural end point (which occurs when all cookies in the set are eaten). In (38b), nothing is known about the cardinality of the cookies eaten by John; the event of 'cookie-eating' could in principle continue indefinitely. The VP describes an event which is called *activity*. An activity is an atelic event, i.e. it does not have a goal or natural end point; its termination is merely the cessation of the event (see Smith 1991).

Recent works on aspectual semantics consider the aspectual interpretation of VP as compositional (see Smith 1991; Tenny 1989; Verkuyl 1988). The verb is the aspectual center of the sentence which is associated with a certain situation type (state, activity, accomplishment, achievement) in the lexicon, each situation type being characterized by a bundle of semantic features (see (46)).

(46)

situations	static	durative	telic
state	[+]	[+]	[−]
activity	[−]	[+]	[−]
accomplishment	[−]	[+]	[+]
achievement	[−]	[−]	[+]

The aspectual information provided by the verb may be overridden in certain contexts. As shown above, quantificational features of the object NP, such as *countability* ([±count]), are relevant for the situation type referred to by the VP. NP referring to a countable set of objects may delimit an event; NP referring to an uncountable set may not. When the object NP is not countable, VP as a whole is atelic, even if the a verb itself denotes a telic event. If the verb is atelic, on the other hand, the VP as a whole is atelic, independent of the quantificational features of NP. Taking these observations as a point of departure, Verkuyl suggests a feature algorithm as a tool to compute the aspectual interpretation of the VP (Verkuyl 1988).[15]

(47) a. (John) ate   all the cookies
         $_V$[+telic] + $_{FP}$[+count]   = $_{VP}$[[+telic]]
     b. (John) ate   cookies
         $_V$[+telic] + $_{NP}$[−count]   = $_{VP}$[[−telic]]
     c. (John) likes   all the cookies
         $_V$[−telic] + $_{FP}$[+count]   = $_{VP}$[[−telic]]
     d. (John) likes   cookies
         $_V$[−telic] + $_{NP}$[−count]   = $_{VP}$[[−telic]]

In order to account for the data in (36) and (42) above, we may conclude that in the older Gmc languages the countability of the NP is expressed by case. Genitive objects, which refer to non-countable entities, cannot measure out the event denoted by VP; the VP then receives an atelic interpretation. If the NP bears accusative case, it refers to a countable entity. If the VP contains an accusative object, the VP as a whole is delimited and therefore receives a telic reading. This shows again that case alternation has a similar function in Old Gmc to that in Modern English and German. One caveat is in order here. The notion of 'countablity' of NP does not exactly correspond with the notion of weakness and strength given above. NPs such as *six cookies*, which are introduced by numerals are analysed as weak NPs in our approach. However, they are countable expressions and a VP *eat six cookies* is clearly delimited by the object NP. Generics, analysed as strong NPs in the literature, cannot be interpreted as countable NPs, and VPs containing a generic object NP generally denote habitual statives rather than telic events. This leads to the expectation that partitive NPs cannot refer to countable sets in the older Gmc languages. This prediction is in fact borne out. Genitive NPs with an agreeing numeral are not found in the older Gmc languages. If an object NP referring to a countable set is constructed, the quantifying element bearing accusative occurs in the head position, which selects a genitive NP as a complement (48).[16]

(48) a. insandida twans siponje seinaize   Got (Ulfilas)
(he) sent out two(ACC) (of the) disciples(GEN) his(GEN)
b. ein solta finfhunt pheningo, ander solta finfzug   OHG (Tatian.138.9)
one gave five hundred (of the) farthings(GEN) the other gave fifty
c. that fuaren ok fan Hierusalem thero iungrono twene
there went also from Jerusalem the disciples(GEN) two

                                                                  OS (Heliand.5956)
d. & þara consula twegen ofslog, & þone þriddan gefeng
the consuls(GEN) two he killed, the third (one) captured

                                                                 OE (Oros.101.13)

4 The development of the article in the Gmc languages

In this section I want to sketch the transition of the Gmc languages from a stage where no articles were employed to a stage where articles were obligatory, and relate this development to the loss of genitive as an object case. In section 4.1 I will show that the lexical definiteness markers occasionally found in the older Gmc languages are not articles, but rather demonstrative and indefinite pronouns. In section 4.2 I will describe the increase of definiteness markers in the MHG and ME periods and relate this to the loss of the verbally governed partitive genitive.

4.1 Demonstrative pronouns in the older Gmc languages

Lexical definiteness markers already existed in the Old Gmc languages. However, they cannot be treated as articles. They are rather demonstrative pronouns which are allowed in emphatic contexts only. Let me start with a few remarks on differences between demonstrative pronouns and definite articles. Later on, I will examine the syntactic distribution of definite determiners in the older Gmc languages. I will show that they are severely restricted in distribution. The restrictions on definite determiners receive a straightforward account if we consider them as demonstratives rather than articles.

I will draw on Neale's theory of definite NPs (Neale 1990), in which he takes a Russellian view of definiteness as a point of departure. According to this definite NPs are interpreted as follows.

(49) A sentence [*the* α] β expresses a proposition which is true, iff there is exactly one individual α of which β holds and false otherwise.

In the recent literature it is unanimously assumed that definite NPs — like strongly quantified NPs, proper names and pronouns — belong to the class of strong NPs. Above, I defined a strong NP in terms of Enç's theory (Enç 1991), where it is claimed that a strong NP refers to proper subsets of previously introduced discourse referents. According to Enç, a definite NP is special in that the set of individuals denoted by it equals an existing discourse referent, i.e., although it is a subset of another discourse referent, it is not a proper one. However, there is no consensus as to whether they have to be analysed as referring expressions - and therefore treated on a par with proper names — or as quantifying expressions, hence treated like strongly quantified NPs. Here, I want to analyse a definite NP as a referential expression.

Let me provide two important arguments given in literature in favour of this analysis. A definite NP is special in that the individual (or the set of individuals) denoted by it is presupposed to exist. If this condition is met, the NP denotes this individual and the sentence is either true or false depending on what the world looks like at the moment the sentence is uttered. Consider (50a). Intuitively, (50a) says that it is not the case that the king of France exists, which is a true proposition. However, under the assumption that a definite NP is a referential expression, (50a) can never be true. Suppose that there exists a king of France, in which case (50a) is still false. Now suppose that there exists no person who is king of France, or more than one person who is king of France. In those cases the presupposition that there is exactly one king of France fails, and (50a) does not express a proposition to which a truth value can be assigned. If we interpret the definite *the king of France* as a quantified expression, (43a) is ambiguous between two propositions, namely (50b) and (50c), where (50c) is exactly the desired interpretation.

(50) a. The king of France does not exist.
      b. There is exactly one king of France who does not exist
      c. It is not the case that there is one king of France who exists

Now consider (51). If we interpret the definite NP as a quantified expression, (51a) is ambiguous between a reading in which the definite NP may either be interpreted as having wide scope relative to the temporal operator, cf. (51b), or a reading in which it has wide scope with respect to the temporal operator, as in (51c). Referential expressions, however, are always interpreted as if they have wide scope relative to all operators within the sentence. Thus, if we analyse the definite NP *the president of the United States* as a referential expression it is impossible to get an interpretation (51b) for (51a), which is intuitively the more appropriate one.

(51) a. The president of the United States will always be white
      b. It will always be the case that the president of the United States is white
      c. For the (present) president of the United States it will always be the case that he is white

In other words, we have to analyse a definite NP as a quantified expression rather than as a referring expression. The definite article was assumed to be a default reference marker, yielding a strong interpretation on the NP. If it is correct to analyse a strong NP as a quantifying expression, we may conclude that the definite article belongs to the class of strong determiners.

Now, let us turn to demonstrative pronouns. According to Neale (1990), an NP introduced by a demonstrative pronoun must be analysed as a referring expression. This is similar to analysing them as proper nouns and pronouns. The fact that in a proposition containing a demonstrative expression the existence of the individual denoted by the demonstrative expression is presupposed clearly suggests this. Therefore, a sentence like (52), uttered in our world, cannot be true or false because at the present time a king of France does not exist.

(52) This king of France is bold

In much the same way, (53) can only receive a wide scope reading.

(53) This president of the United States will always be white

Syntactically, demonstrative pronouns differ from the definite article in the position they occupy in the syntactic tree. While the definite article is realized in F^0, demonstrative pronouns occur in Spec,FP. Consider demonstrative NPs in languages like Ancient Greek and Norwegian. Here, we find NPs which contain both demonstrative pronouns and articles. The article occupies the D^0 position which is also the landing site for the N-movement in Greek (54). The demonstrative is realized in FP-internal position preceding D^0, i.e. in Spec,FP.

(54) houtos ho aner   Ancient Greek
      this   the man

More evidence for this comes from German, where we find contractions of the definite article with a preposition.

(55) *am Strand* 'on-the beach'; *im Wald* 'in-the forest'; *ins Wasser* 'into-the water'; *zum Haus* 'to-the house'; *vom Ufer* 'from-the shore'; *beim Vater* 'with-the father'; *ans Herz* 'at-the heart'; *zur Schule* 'to-the school'

Contractions of demonstratives with a preposition, on the other hand, are not found in early German. This is expected if we assume contractions to be the result of head movement, as suggested in Grimshaw (1991). Demonstratives cannot move to P governing NP since they occupy Spec,FP. Movement from Spec,FP to P violates the Head Movement Constraint, according to which a head may move only to the head governing its maximal projection.

In what follows, I will show that definite determiners in the older Gmc languages are demonstratives rather than articles. We can see this by looking at their distribution. First and foremost, definite determiners are found in directly anaphoric contexts where a definite NP refers back to a previous mention (56).

(56) a. (was *manna* in Jairusalem) jah *sa manna* was garaihts   Got (Ulfilas)
         ((there) was (a) man in Jerusalem) and the man was righteous

b. (in anabeginne was *uuort*) inti *thaz uuort* uuas mit gote
   (In the beginning there was the word) and the word was with god
   OHG (Tatian.1.1)
c. (tho thar te theme lerende quam *en jung man*)...tho sprak eft *the*
   but there to the teacher came a young man... there said again the
   jungo man OS (Heliand.3256–7)
   young man
d. (þa Eadmund clypode *ænne bisceop* þe him þa gehendost wæs) ...
   (then Eadmund summoned a bishop who him the nearest was)
   þa forhtode *se bisceop* OE (ÆLS.XXXII.56)
   then was afraid the bishop

In OHG, OS and OE, but not in Gothic, definite determiners are also found in indirectly anaphoric contexts where the definite NP refers to an individual not previously mentioned, but implicitly familiar by the context (57a). Very often, an indirect anaphoric determiner may be translated either as an article or as a possessive pronoun (57b, c). However, even in the above languages, this is not a rule, and there are also cases of indirect anaphora, where the determiner is missing (58b, c).

(57) a. (Samaso man, þer elilento farenti forliez *sin hus*...)
        (like a man, who leaving for a foreign country left his house)
        inti *themo duiruuarte* gibot þaz her uuahhteti OHG (Tatian.147.6)
        and ordered the door-keeper that he would take care
    b. (tho sahun si thar [...] enan *liflosen* lichamon) [...] *thiu moder*
        (but saw they there a lifeless(GEN) body) Mother(DEF/POS)
        after geng an iro hugi hriuuig OS (Heliand.2180–3)
        went behind, in her head sad
    c. (Grap þa togeanes, *guðrinc* gefeng atolan clommum) ... *hring* utan
        ymbbearh þæt heo *þone fyrdhom* ðurhfon ne mihte OE (Beo.1501)
        ((the dragon) snatched then at (him), hero(DEF) seized (with her))
        terrible(DAT) claws(DAT)) Armour(DEF/POSS) was around (him)
        (from) outside that she the arming wreck not could

(58) a. (jah galeiþun in *Kafarnaum*) jah suns sabbato galeiþans
        (and they went into Capernaum) immediately on Sabbath going
        in *swanagogen* laisida ins Got (M.I.27)
        into synagogue(DEF) he taught them (the inhabitants of C.)
    b. inti mittiu *her* thaz qad, arougta in *henti, fuozi*
        and as he said this, he showed the/his hands, the/his feet
        inti *sita* OHG (Tatian.230.6)
        and (the/his) side
    c. that them *blindun*...wurdun *ogun* giopanod OS (Heliand.3580)
        that the blind man got the eyes opened
    d. Gecyste þa cyning æþelum god, þeoden Scyldinga, ðegn betstan
        ond be healse genam OE (Beo.1870)
        kissed then (the) king, (the) Lord of Scyldings, warrior best, and by
        (the) neck took

Furthermore, determiners are seldom found with NPs referring to an abstract entity.

(59) a. swaei nu *dauþus* in uns waurkeiþ, iþ *libains* in izwis Got (Ulfilas)
thus now death(DEF) in us works, but life(DEF) in you
b. thie thar in *finstarnissen* inti in *scuuen todes* sizzent OHG (Tatian.4.18)
who there in (the) darkness and in (the) shadow of death sit
c. er dan ik selbo her fon *dode* astande, arise fon *restu*
before I self then rise from (the) death, and raise from the grave
 OS (Heliand.3166–8)
d. ..., gif mec *deað* nimeð. Byreð blodig wæl OE (Beo.446)
if me (the) death takes, (it) takes away a bloody corpse

Finally, determiners do not show up if NP has a generic interpretation.

(60) a. *sabbato* in *mans* warþ gaskapans, ni *manno* in *sabbato* Got (Mk.II.27)
(The) Sabbath was made for (the) man, not (the) man (the) Sabbath
b. ist arloubit *manne* zi uorlassanna sina quenun OHG (Tatian.100.2)
is (it) allowed to (the) man to leave his wife
c. quað that salige uuarin man an thesero middilgardun
(he) said that blessed were (the) people in this world
 OS (Heliand.1300)
d. sægde se þe cuþe frumsceaft fira feorran reccan OE (Beo.90)
talked the one who could (the) source of people from the early time tell

The distribution of definite determiners in the older Gmc languages seems to be very similar to the distribution of demonstrative pronouns in the modern Gmc languages. First of all, demonstratives are found in directly anaphoric contexts. In (55a), for instance, the definite determiner *sa* may also be translated as a demonstrative without altering the meaning of the second sentence.

(61) There was a man in Jerusalem and this man was righteous

Demonstratives may not show up in indirectly anaphoric contexts. The NP *that man* in (62) cannot be related anaphorically to the NP *a couple*.

(62) A couple came into the bar. That man was a friend of mine.

Moreover, definite determiners do not show up with NPs referring to abstract entities or generic NPs (63). (63a) does not mean that people are afraid of the truth in general. Rather, they are afraid of a specific fact that is true (for instance the fact that they are mortal). (63b) is only acceptable if we have one specific tiger in mind who is a dangerous hunter; a generic interpretation is impossible.

(63) a. Humans are afraid of that truth
b. That tiger is a dangerous hunter

Therefore, it seems to make sense to analyse definite determiners in the older Gmc languages as demonstratives rather than as articles. Above, I argued that referential expressions are special in that they presuppose the existence of exactly one individual realizing the property denoted by the NP. In order to understand an utterance containing a referential expression, the hearer must be able to identify the individual referred to. In the case of demonstratives, the referent must be identified by a pointing gesture of the speaker or it must be directly given in the previous discourse. The above data suggest that in the older Gmc languages, definite determiners are allowed only if the individual denoted by NP can be at least inferred from the context. NPs referring to abstract entities or generic NPs not referring to any specific individual at all cannot realize a determiner.

The idea to analyse definite determiners as demonstrative pronouns in the older Gmc languages is supported by the fact that in the Bible translations of Gothic and Old High German, the definite determiner often translates a demonstrative pronoun (Jäger 1917).

(64) a. *sa broþar* < houtos adelphos 'this brother'; *þei sunjoi þis aiwis* < hoi hyoi aionos toutos 'the suns of this world', etc. Got
 b. Lat. ille: *in then tagon* < in diebus illis 'in these days'; *in thaz hus* < in domum illam 'in that house'; *in thero ziti* < in illa hora 'in this time'; *thuruh then uueg* < per viam illam 'through this way'
 Lat. hic: *umbi then samon* < de hoc semine 'from that family'; *after then tagon* < post hos dies 'after those days'; *thaz uuort* < hoc verbum 'that word'; *fon themo kinde* < de puero hoc 'from that child'
 Lat. is: *thiu scaf* < eos oves 'these sheep'; *thero uuorto* < eorum verborum 'of these words'; *thia stat* < eum locum 'this city' OHG

Furthermore, definite determiners may also act as pronouns (65).

(65) a. jah *sa* was miþ Iesua Nazoraiou Got (Mt.XXVI.71)
 also he was with Jesus from Nazareth
 b. inti *ther* was Samaritanus OHG (Tatian)
 and he was Samaritan
 c. *the* scal Heliand te namon egan mid eldin OS (Heliand.266)
 he shall Heliand as name own with people(DEF)
 d. *se* wæs moncynnes mægenes strengest OE (Beo.196)
 he was mankind(GEN) power(GEN) strongest

In Modern English, the definite determiner *the* cannot be used as a pronoun. The definite determiner in German may act as pronoun only when used demonstratively. The phrase in (66b) can be uttered in an anaphoric context, for instance in a dialogue situation, when one of the participants asks for a friend he has not seen for hours. Or it may be uttered deictically, if a speaker points to a person sitting on a bank without moving for a certain time.[17]

(66) a. *the sleeps
 b. (DER) schläft

If we analyse definite determiners as demonstratives rather than as articles in the older Gmc languages, we expect contractions of determiner and preposition to be unattested. This is because demonstratives are realized within Spec,FP. Movement from Spec,FP to P violates the Head Movement Constraint according to which a head may move only to the head governing its maximal projection. In fact, contractions of determiners and prepositions are not found in German until the fourteenth century (Behaghel 1923).

To summarize, we have seen that there is good reason to analyse definite 'determiners' as demonstratives in the older Gmc languages. First, they have the same distributional properties that demonstratives in the modern Gmc languages have. Second, they are used to translate demonstrative pronouns from the source text. Third, 'determiners' may be used pronominally in the older Gmc languages, which is at most possible for demonstrative pronouns in the modern Gmc languages. Finally, definite 'determiners' cannot move to a governing P-head in Gothic and Old High German, which can be explained if we assume determiners to be realized in Spec,FP in the older Gmc languages.

4.2 The expansion of articles in MHG and ME

We will now consider how the definite determiners in the Old Gmc languages, analysed as demonstrative pronouns, developed into articles, and how this is related to the loss of the aspect-triggered case alternation. In the course of history, genitive is lost as an object case. This development takes place at different times in English and German. While the verbal genitive is nearly lost in ME (Mustanoja 1960), in German the genitive/accusative alternation on verbal objects is still productive in the early MHG period, although the set of verbs allowing for genitive objects has shrunk considerably since OHG times (van der Elst 1984) (67). In German, the verbal genitive is lost in the fourteenth century — apart from a small set of verbs allowing for genitive complements even in Modern German.

(67) a. man gap uns spise, diu was guot   MHG (Iwein.367)
       one gave us food(GEN) that was good
    b. nu trincen wir di minne   MHG
       now drink   we love(DEF)

The reason for the loss of the object genitive may be the gradual erosion of inflectional morphology at the end of the OHG and OE periods. As a result, the genitive was collapsed with other cases (see van der Elst 1984). In Modern German, for instance, the genitive is homophonous with the accusative case:

— with weakly declined masculine singular and plural NPs (*dën hanen – dës hanen; die hanen – dër hanen*)

— with weakly declined feminine singular and plural NPs (*die zungen – der zungen ; die zungen – dër zungen*)

- with weakly declined neutral plural NPs (*die herzen – der herzen*)
- with masculine plural NP of the strong a-class (*die tage – dër tage*)
- with masculine plural NP of the strong ja-class (*die hirte – dër hirte*)
- with feminine singular NP of the strong ô-class (*die gëbe – dër gëbe*)
- with masculine plural NP of the strong i-class (*die geste – dër geste*)
- with feminine plural NP of the strong i-class (*die krefte – dër krefte*)

Simultaneous with the loss of the verbal genitive, the use of demonstrative pronouns as definiteness markers is extended. In indirectly anaphoric contexts, where determiners were impossible in Gothic and optional in OHG and OE, lexical definiteness markers become obligatory in the MHG and in the ME periods.

(68) a. (si komen da man *messe* sanc dem turegen künec
(they came when one mess(DEF) sang (for the) sad(DAT) king(DAT)
von Zazadam) [...] als *der bendiz* wart getan,
of Zazadam) when blessing(DEF) was done
do kam vrouw Herzeloyde an MHG (Parzival.93.28)
there came lady Herzeloyde on
b. (at nyght was come into that *hostelrye* well nyne and twenty
(at night was come to that hostel around nine and twenty
in a compagnye) *the cambres and stables* were wide
in a group) the chambers and stables were wide
  ME (CT.Prol.23–8)

The use of definite determiners with abstract NPs becomes an option in the MHG and ME period and is obligatory in Modern German.[18]

(69) a. wir sin in dem ellende MHG (Parzival)
we are in the misery
b. nu ist in *triuwe* unmaere MHG (Iwein.3174)
now is you fidelity not important
c. til that *the deeth* departe shal us tweyne ME (CT.Kn.1134)
until that the death(GEN) divide us two
d. to þolenn *dæþ* o rodetre ME
e. ich will *die Gerechtigkeit* zum Gewicht machen ModG (Luther)

Generic NPs allow for definite determiners in MHG as well as in ME (69); however, they are by no means obligatory (70).

(70) a. der vogel in den lüften, der visch in dem wage,
the bird in the air the fish in the waggon
die wurme in der erden...daz dienet allez gote MHG (Berthold)
the worm in the ground, that serves all god
b. the hinde in pes with the leoun, the wolf in
the hind in peace with the lion, the wolf in
pes with the moltoun, the hare in pes with the hound
peace with the sheep, the hare in peace with the hound
  ME (Gower.CA.Prol.1059–61)

(71) a. ditze buch redonot unde zellet von tieren und fogilin
this book talks and tells about (the) animals and (the) birds
aller ersit von dem lewen   MHG (Wilhelm)
first and foremost about the lion
b. that man shall yelde to his wyf hire dette   ME (CT.WB.130)
that (the) man shall pay for his wife her possessions

In the early ModG and eModE periods the use of definite determiners in generic contexts corresponds to the Modern German and Modern English uses.

(72) a. alle die meister die die geister künnen twingen   eModG
all the masters who the ghosts can force

Summarizing, in the ME and MHG periods, the restrictions on the use of definite determiners are gradually lost. Determiners are no longer used as demonstrative elements, and their function becomes one of marking NPs for definiteness. The distribution corresponds to that of articles in the modern Gmc languages.

Putting the above observations into the generative framework we are adopting here, let us assume that the definite article originates as a demonstrative. Demonstratives optionally occupy the Spec,FP (Uriagereka 1992a). F^0 is occupied by case such that the determiner in Spec,FP may only act as a redundant reference marker which is only allowed in emphatic contexts (73a). In the course of history, case morphology is weakened and it is no longer possible to mark definiteness of NP morphologically. Therefore a new reference marker becomes necessary. At that point the emphatic determiner is reanalysed as the functional head of NP. In this position it takes over the function of specifying the referential interpretation of the NP (73b).

(73) a.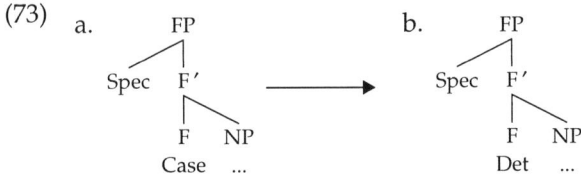

One consequence of this development is that it becomes possible for the determiner head to move to a governing preposition via head movement in German. Contractions of determiners with prepositions are found for the first time in the fourteenth century (Behaghel 1923).

(74) *zum Rade* to-the wheel; *zum Roden Juden* to-the red jew; *am Ryne* at-the R.; *zum Luchtenberge* to-the L.; *zum Schilde* to-the shield; *vom Hertzhorne* from-the H.

5 Conclusion

In this paper I focussed on the development of the article and related facts in some West Gmc languages. The central question was how the article developed from the early Gmc dialects and how this process is related to other historical developments like the loss of morphological case.

The starting point of my analysis was a revised version of the Mapping Hypothesis (Diesing 1992; Meinunger 1993; Runner 1993), in which it is assumed that the syntactic tree is split into two parts, one being mapped onto the Nuclear Scope, the other one to the Restrictive Clause of the logical interpretation of the sentence.

(24) [$_C$...[$_{Agr}$...   [$_{VP}$...]]]
      Restrictive Clause   Nuclear Scope

While a strong NP moves to Spec,Agr in the course of the derivation for case checking, a weak NP remains in its base-generated position and is assigned a default case there. This is because a weak NP has an unsaturated referential argument position which has to be bound by Existential Closure within the Nuclear Scope.

A strong NP is universally dominated by a functional projection FP with the functional head F^0 saturating the referential argument position of N. A strong NP therefore has quantificational force of its own, and is therefore free to move out of VP. I have shown that this functional head may have a different morphological spell-out in different languages.

I have shown that the weak/strong distinction is realized differently in different languages. While the modern Gmc languages have different determiners to mark NP weak or strong, in the Old Gmc language this is determined by an interaction of case and aspect. An object NP realizes accusative case if it has a strong interpretation. It is assigned genitive case if it has a weak interpretation. This can be represented by assuming two different manifestations for F^0 in different languages, determiners on the one hand, on the other hand an abstract case-element which is related to accusative case realization.

In a diachronic perspective the rise of lexical determiners is related to the process of nominal deflection under the above scenario. In the older Gmc languages, the determiner might in fact be a demonstrative pronoun that takes the specifier position of FP, which is headed by case. As a reference marker the demonstrative pronoun is redundant. Consequently, it is found only in emphatic contexts. In the course of history case morphology is weakened such that it can no longer function as a syntactic head of FP; the emphatic determiner is reanalysed as the functional head of the NP.

Notes

*   I am grateful to Werner Abraham, Peter Ackema, Gisella Ferraresi, Katja Göllner, Klaus von Heusinger, Ans van Kemenade, Ellen-Petra Kester, Andre Meinunger, Eddy Ruys, Maaike Schoorlemmer, Heike Tappe, Nigel Vincent, Fred Weerman, Petra de Wit and Joost Zwarts for discussion and for helpful comments on earlier versions of this chapter.
1.   I am not claiming that a sentence *John is the linguist* is ungrammatical. The noun phrase *the linguist* is not used predicatively; rather, the sentence has to be interpreted as an identity statement.

2. Note that other strong quantifiers such as *both* and *most* cannot combine with weak quantifiers since they are semantically incompatible with each other.
   (i) *both some/many linguists
   *most few/three/many linguists
3. Verbs of destruction such as *destroy* presuppose the existence of the individual denoted by the object NP and are therefore incompatible with an existential interpretation on the object.
4. In this chapter, I will only investigate the syntactic behaviour of object NPs, leaving subject NPs for future research.
5. Henceforth, I will call NPs weak only when they have an existential interpretation. NPs introduced by a strong quantifier as well as weakly quantified noun phrases with a quantificational interpretation I will designate as strong noun phrases.
6. Note that the term 'default case' is used here in the classical sense, referring to a type of case which is found in a position where one would not expect to find case at all. One typical example for default case assignment in the classical sense is given in the German example below, where nominative case is assigned to a noun phrase realized in a position where no case governor is present (cf. de Hoop 1992).
   (i) Dieser Mann,   den   kenn'   ich nicht.
       this(NOM) man(NOM) that-one(ACC) know I   not
7. The relationship between definite NP and strong NP is discussed in detail below.
8. In what follows, I will concentratre merely on objects.
9. There is some controversy in the literature on whether languages like Gothic, OHG, OS and OE behave like Finnish (Finnish Hypothesis) or like Russian (Russian Hypothesis) which differ subtly with respect to the interconnection between case, referentiality and aspect. Abraham (1994) and Leiss (1989, 1994), who adhere to the Russian Hypothesis, assume that only perfective verbs select alternatively for an indefinite genitive or a definite accusative complement. Non-perfectives, on the other hand, select for weak and strong accusative objects. Donhauser (1991, 1992), on the other hand, subscribes to the Finnish Hypothesis. She claims that the restriction of the genitive/accusative alternation to perfective verbs is too strong, and shows that there are not only imperfective verbs allowing for genitive complements but also verbs which acquire an imperfective interpretation by being combined with a genitive complement. I will come back to the interconnection between aspectuality and case in section 3.2 below.
10. Note that the case marker in strong NPs is obligatory. Thus, if an accusative marker is lacking, for instance, in universally quantified NPs, ungrammaticality results (Enç 1991).
    (i) Ali her kitab-i   okudu
        Ali every book(ACC) read
    (ii)*Ali her kitap okudu
11. Note that in the older Germanic languages, postverbal subjects are not only found with unaccusatives and not only in existential sentences, but also in purely rhematic statements. Furthermore, a postverbal subject is not necessarily weak, and does not necessarily bear genitive case.
    (i) duatiddja imma hundafaþa   Got
        came   to-him a-captain
    (ii) jah qaþ Iesus þamma   hundafaþa   Got
         and said Jesus the(DAT) captain(DAT)
    However, I think that different operations may be at work to generate postverbal subjects. The above examples, for instance, are generated by subject–verb inversion. I do not want to go into the discussion of postverbal subjects any further.
12. Other criteria relevant for alternative case assignment are: the affectedness of the object by the event denoted by the verb; whether the NP appears in an affirmative or negative sentence. I believe that these facts can be reduced to the aspectual structure of the sentence, treating negation and affectedness as features typical of irresultativity (see de Hoop 1992; Tenny 1989; Verkuyl 1988).

The rise of the article in the Germanic languages 93

13. Note that there were other prefixes such as *be-*, *ver-* and *ont-* which also acted as perfectivizing morphemes.
14. The adverbial expressions are sensitive to the aspectual structure of the VP and are used in the literature as diagnostics for delimitedness, i.e. *in an hour* is only compatible with a delimited event while *for hours* is only compatible with a non-delimited event.
15. The situation type associated with the verb may be overridden also by semantic features of the prepositional complement such as [locative], [directional]. A directional preposition may delimit the event denoted by the VP; a process such as *walk to school* stops after the arrival at school.
    (i) (John)   walks   in the park
          $_V$[–telic] + $_{PP}$[+locative]   = $_{VP}$[[– telic]]
        (John)   walks   to school
          $_V$[–telic] + $_{PP}$[+directional] = $_{VP}$[[+ telic]]
16. Although weak quantifiers do not agree with a genitive object NP, this is quite possible with accusative object NPs. However, these NPs do not have an existential but rather a specific interpretation.
    (i) Ioannes uuarlihho thiu her gihorta Cristes uuerk, giholate sine iungoron zwene   (Tatian.64.1)
        J. now with that he heard in prison Christ(GEN) work, called his disciples two
    This is exactly what Meinunger observes for object NP in Russian. Weak quantifiers are followed by a genitive NP when they are the direct object of the verb. However, when the weak quantifier is interpreted specifically, it switches to a normal adjective inflectional pattern exactly as strong quantifiers, and the whole NP is assigned accusative.
    (ii) vodele gotovogo plat'ja Nataša pomerilla mnogo jubok   (Meinunger 1993)
         in clothing departement Natasha tried on many skirts
    (iii) segodnja v magazine leshit 30 jubok. Nataša pomerila mnogije
          today in shop lay 30 skirts. Natasha tried on many
17. The use of demonstrative determiners as bare pronouns in English is not as productive as in German; however, it is not completely excluded. An example is: *This is an idiot*.
18. The use of articles with abstract nouns is still only optional in Modern English.

3 The diachronic development of a modal verb of necessity

Paola Benincà and Cecilia Poletto

1 Introduction*

In Benincà & Poletto (1994) we have presented evidence, drawn from modal auxiliaries of necessity in some Italian varieties, that the loss of forms in a verbal paradigm is connected to the loss of certain semantic properties of the verb. The idea we have put forth is that a verb's syntax and morphology are determined in some respects by its thematic grid. In this chapter, we will show that the loss of a verb's thematic grid is accompanied by a change in its syntax and morphology. Thus, the diachronic change described in this chapter as a process of grammaticalization provides further confirmation for an analysis originally based on synchronic data.

The morphosyntactic limitations that we will observe for modal auxiliaries shed light on the syntactic relations between tense and modality, which have been studied by many authors from a semantic point of view. The correlations we observe support a syntactic implementation of the interaction between tense and mood within a very restrictive theory.

This paper is organized as follows. In section 2 we abstract from Benincà & Poletto (1994) a description of the properties of Modern Italian *bisogna* ('must/is necessary'), which has the 'most reduced meaning' among Italian verbs of necessity. We then list its possible and impossible forms and the constraints which govern its syntactic behaviour. In section 3 we give an overview of other modal auxiliaries: Venetan *toca* 'touch', standard Italian *va* 'go' and Polesano *vuole* 'want'; they all share with *bisogna* the observed constraints only if a particular reading is selected. These verbs can be used as regular main verbs, but they can also be used as modal auxiliaries indicating a pure state of necessity where no theta-role is assigned (we will define this as the 'deontic reading'). When they assume the meaning of 'pure necessity' of Italian *bisogna*, or, better, when they lose a theta grid as *bisogna* does, they also undergo the same impoverishment of their paradigm and acquire the same syntactic constraints. In section 4 we present our analysis of the synchronic data and discuss the hypothesis that modal auxiliaries lacking a thematic grid are directly inserted under Mod^0.

In section 5 we examine the diachronic development of *bisogna*, showing how it has developed from a regular transitive verb into a pure modal head. Old Italian *bisogna* does not show any of the morphosyntactic restrictions that we observe in Modern Italian: it can be inflected for the whole paradigm, it can host clitics and it has two arguments (an experiencer and a theme). It seems then that Old Italian *bisogna* is still a full verb that projects a VP with its arguments, while Modern Italian *bisogna* is a purely functional element that is inserted directly into a modal head Mod^0. Therefore, the diachronic data strongly support our claim that grammaticalization goes hand in hand with the impoverishment of the thematic grid.

2 Surface properties of *bisogna*

2.1 *Bisogna* has a defective paradigm

The verb *bisogna* only means a pure state of necessity; its meaning does not involve any cause of the necessity itself nor a particular person or object individually concerned with it. This semantic characteristic will be clear when contrasted with one of the readings of the modal auxiliary *toca*. *Bisogna*, as the examples in (1) show, can be followed either by a CP with a subjunctive complement clause, or by an infinitive clause: they express 'what is necessary'.

(1) a. Bisogna partire subito
    it-is-necessary to-leave immediately
  b. Bisogna che Mario parta subito
    it-is-necessary that Mario leave(SUBJ) immediately

Its morphological paradigm is defective: it is always inflected in the third person singular, and it only occurs in the forms listed below in (2), no matter what type of sentence follows it:

(2) a. Bisogna farlo/che lo faccia
    it-is-necessary to-do-it/that it he-do
  b. Bisognava farlo/che lo facesse
    it-was-necessary (IMPERF) ...
  c. Bisognerà farlo/che lo faccia
    it-will-be-necessary ...
  d. Bisognerebbe farlo/che lo facesse
    it-would-be-necessary (CONDITIONAL) ...
  e. ?Credo che bisogni farlo/che lo faccia[1]
    I-think that it-be-necessary (PRES SUBJUNCT) ...
  f. Penso che bisognasse farlo
    I-think that it-was-necessary (IMPERF SUBJUNCT) ...

The possible forms of *bisogna* are then the present, imperfect and future indicative, the present and imperfect subjunctive and the present conditional. All other forms are impossible, as the following list illustrates:

(3)[2] a. *Potrebbe bisognare farlo /che lo faccia
   it-could   be-necessary (INFIN) ...
b. *Bisognando farlo, lo fece
   being-it-necessary (GERUND) ...
c. *E' (era, etc.)/ ha ... bisognato farlo
   it is (was, etc.)/has been-necessary (PAST PART and compound tenses)
d. *Bisognò farlo[2]
   it-was-necessary to do it

The sets of possible and impossible forms are less mysterious if we recall well-known observations regarding the possible forms, which are often referred to as forms having 'modal quality'. More formally, we hypothesize that:

i. They are not marked for a specific aspectual feature and are compatible with an unspecified time localization. The Italian present indicative is also an 'atemporal' or 'generic' tense (see Giorgi & Pianesi 1991 for a syntactic characterization of this observation).

ii. On the contrary they can have a modal specification. The imperfect, future and conditional have epistemic [+irrealis] possible interpretations; both subjunctives can be [+irrealis] forms. These properties can be thought of as sharing a precise structural correlate, namely that they have to be checked in a position higher than the functional head of RootMod, a hypothesis that we will discuss in section 4.

2.2 *Bisogna* lacks a subject

The morphological gaps are accompanied by severe syntactic limitations: *bisogna* apparently has no subject. The following test — set out to discover non-argumental subjects — shows a clear difference in grammaticality among the sentences in (4), in which the PRO subject of the infinitive takes a controller in the subject position of the governing sentence. An argumental or a quasi-argumental subject in the matrix clause is able to control the PRO subject of the untensed clause in (4a, b), while the expletive subject of the impersonal verb in (4c) is able to do so with some difficulty. On the other hand, the subject of *bisogna* in (4d, e) is completely unable to give PRO any content; (4f) illustrates the fact that, with a different locution of necessity, formed with the verb *essere* 'be', the structure becomes (marginally) possible:

(4) a. Andrò   a Roma senza   vedere il   papa
       (I) will go to Rome without seeing the pope
   b. Nevica senza   necessariamente fare   molto freddo
       it-snows without necessarily   it-being very cold

c. ?Sembra che si tratti di un delitto senza esser chiaro
   it-seems that it is   a murder without it-being clear
   chi sia il colpevole
   who the culprit is
d. *Bisogna   che lo leggiamo senza   esser   necessario
   it-is-necessary that we read-it   without it-being necessary
   che lo facciamo subito
   that we do so immediately
e. *Bisogna   leggerlo   senza   esser   necessario farlo
   it-is-necessary to-read-it without it-being necessary to-do-so
   subito
   immediately
f. ?C'è bisogno che lo leggiamo senza   esser   necessario
   there is need that we read it   without it-being necessary
   che lo facciamo subito
   that we do so immediately

The contrast between (4c) and (4d, e) shows that there is a difference between the non-argumental subject of a verb like *sembrare* 'seem' and the subject of *bisogna*, as the subject of *sembrare* can marginally control a PRO while the subject of *bisogna* cannot. We suggest that this stems from the fact that *bisogna* completely lacks a subject position, while this is not the case with the impersonal verb *sembrare*.

Further evidence in this sense comes from the behaviour of northern Italian dialects. In these varieties subject clitics are heads that appear when the syntactic projection of Agr$_S$ weakens, losing its *pro*-drop properties. Subject clitics appear in order to restore the *pro*-drop capacity of Agr$_S$. Within the domain of northern Italian dialects there is considerable variation regarding which type of subject clitic (argumental, quasi-argumental or expletive) is required. Expletive subject clitics imply the presence of argumental subject clitics in a given dialect (see Poletto 1993). Even in those varieties that show an obligatory subject clitic with expletives, there is a single verb that can occur without a subject clitic, and this verb has precisely the semantic properties of *bisogna* (see Benincà & Poletto 1994: 5). We will interpret this observation as indicating the impossibility of any type of subject in the Spec,Agr$_S$ position of the deontic modal auxiliary.

Furthermore, in Italian as in the dialects, a verb with the semantic properties of *bisogna* cannot host a raised subject coming from the following clause. The sentences in (5) may be compared with the behaviour of the impersonal *sembra* 'it seems' given in (6):

(5) a. *Mario bisogna   leggere
       Mario is-necessary to-read
    b. *Bisogna   partire Mario
       is-necessary to-leave Mario

(6) a. Mario sembra leggere
       Mario seems to-read
    b. Sembra conoscerlo Mario
       it-seems to-know-him Mario

The contrast between (5) and (6) shows that *bisogna* does not have a subject position available to the raised subject. We will come back to this in section 4.

2.3 *Bisogna* cannot host clitics

The third property to be outlined is the impossibility for *bisogna* to have clitics attached to it, whether thematically related to it (see (7a)) or to the embedded predicate via restructuring (7b). This is true even for benefactive clitics that in Italian are possible with any verb. This behaviour is again to be compared with that of *sembra* on the one hand and that of other modal locutions on the other, given in (8):

(7) a. *Gli bisogna   mangiare
       him is-necessary to-eat
       'He needs to eat'
    b. *Lo bisogna   incontrare
       him is-necessary to-meet
       'It is necessary to meet him'

(8) a. Lo sembra   fare volentieri
       it he-seems do willingly
       'He seems to do it willingly'
    b. Gli   sembravate parlare   amichevolmente
       to-him you-seemed to-speak friendly-ADV
       'You seemed to speak to him in a friendly way'
    c. Gli   è necessario partire
       to-him is necessary to-leave
       'He needs to leave'

Let us thus summarize the special properties that we have observed for *bisogna*:

(9) a. *bisogna* can be inflected only for those forms which can express modality;
    b. neither an overt nor a null subject is available;
    c. *bisogna* is not a raising verb;
    d. no clitics can co-occur with *bisogna*.

In the following section we will present arguments that are developed in more detail in Benincà & Poletto (1994).[3]

3 Other deontic modals

3.1 Venetan *toca*

The idea that the morphological and syntactic restrictions of *bisogna* are related to its defective thematic structure is supported by the comparison with a verb that acquires the same meaning as *bisogna* in the Venetan dialects of Padua and Venice. This verb is *tocar(e)*, a transitive main verb which can be also used as a deontic. When it is used as a main verb, *tocar(e)* is a regular transitive verb meaning 'to touch', as the corresponding Italian *toccare*: it has all tenses and normally hosts a subject DP, corresponding to a thematic agent, in the Spec,Agr_S position; it has a DP object, which can be an object clitic, and it can have a benefactive dative clitic too.

Tocar(e) can also have an impersonal use with a number of modal readings, one of which is very similar to *bisogna*. The others all involve, with some differences, a dative experiencer (or possibly a benefactive clitic). Let us call *toca1* the various uses, and *toca2* the reading that corresponds to *bisogna*. The argument of *toca1* is expressed by a dative element, and, with this reading, *toca* can only be followed by an infinitival clause:

(10) a. Me   toca   partire
       to-me touches to-leave
       'I have to leave'
    b. Ghe   toca   Mario partire
       to-him touches Mario to-go
       'It is Mario's turn/duty to leave'

When the complement is an infinitive, the subject of the embedded clause is always the person affected by the necessity expressed by the governing verb *toca1*.

The meaning of *toca1* goes from 'someone decided that it is someone else's duty to do something', to 'someone is obliged to do something that he would have preferred not to do', or 'someone is concerned with doing something', or else 'it is someone's turn to do something'. With these readings, *toca* has all tenses. It is interesting to observe that the form of the dative element is related to the choice of the reading of *toca1*. In particular, if the dative is realized by a clitic element the reading can only be 'someone is obliged to do something that he would have preferred not to do', while a dative DP only admits one of the two remaining readings (note that in (10b) the DP is doubled by a clitic, but this is a general fact in Venetan). This observation will become relevant later on in order to correctly interpret the data from Galileo and understand the diachronic change of *bisogna*.

The purely deontic reading of *toca*, very similar to Italian *bisogna*, is expressed by *toca* when it governs an inflected complement clause. We will use this distinctive feature to isolate the syntactic and morphological properties of this variant. In (11) *toca* has only the purely deontic reading:

(11) Toca che lo fasa mi
'I have to do it'
'*It's up to me/it is my turn to do it'

Toca2, corresponding to the purely deontic reading, shows the same morphological restrictions that we have examined in section 2 for the verb *bisogna*: it cannot be inflected in the infinitive, participial and gerund forms. We cannot test if the simple past is possible as in this dialect the simple past does not exist for any verb.

(12) a. *Ga tocà che lo fazese mi
      has touched that it did   I
      'I have had to do it'
   b. *Podaria tocare che lo fazese mi
      I might have to do it
   c. *Tocando che lo fasa mi,...
      having to do it myself

The tenses that are admitted with *bisogna*, the imperfect, future, conditional and subjunctive, are grammatical also with the purely deontic *toca2*:

(13) a. Tocava che 'ndase mi
      I had to go
   b. Tocarà che vaga mi
      I will have to go
   c. Tocarìa che 'ndase mi
      it-would-be-necessary for me to go
   d. Credevo che tocase che te 'ndasi ti
      I-thought that you had to go

If the hypothesis presented in section 2 is correct, we should expect *toca2* to also present the syntactic properties already discussed for *bisogna*, namely the impossibility of having a subject DP and the impossibility of realizing a clitic on the modal auxiliary. This is indeed the case:

(14) a. *Nisuni toca che vaga
      nobody has to go
   b. *Me toca che parla doman
      I have to speak tomorrow

Example (14a) shows that *toca* cannot have a subject DP, (14b) illustrates that no clitic can be hosted by it.

The parallelism of *bisogna* and *toca2* shows that the cluster of properties shown by *bisogna* is not an idiosyncratic fact connected to this verb, but is strictly related to the purely deontic meaning: we will analyse these properties in section 4 as an effect of the impoverished thematic structure. When *toca/tocare*, which is a regular transitive verb, assumes the meaning of *bisogna* thus disactivating its VP as a site of thematic role assignment, there are effects both in syntax and morphology, and they are exactly the same ones that characterize *bisogna*. In this perspective, the difference from an impersonal verb such as *sembrare* 'seem' is basically the fact that this verb always has an intended argument, i.e. the experiencer, no matter whether it is lexically filled or left unexpressed.

3.2 Two more deontic modals

In this section we will examine two more cases of deontic modals which are partially similar to *bisogna* and *toca*.

The first verb is standard Italian *andare* 'to go', which is a regular main verb of the unaccusative class and as such can be used in all inflected forms. As an auxiliary, it gives rise to two distinct readings: one is purely passive, the other is passive plus deontic. The purely passive reading is only possible with a subclass of verbs which entails the 'loss' of the object (it includes verbs such as *perdere* 'lose', *bruciare* 'burn', *distruggere* 'destroy', etc.). A sentence such as the following is ambiguous, admitting both readings of the auxiliary *andare*:

(15) La sterpaglia andava bruciata tutti gli anni
      the brushwood went(IMPERF) burnt every year
      'The brushwood was burnt every year'
      'The brushwood had to be burnt'

The passive–deontic reading shows some morphological restrictions which parallel those found with *bisogna* and *toca*;[4] the simple past, participial, infinitive and gerund forms cannot be used with the passive–deontic reading: they are possible only with the pure passive one. Moreover, as for *bisogna* and *toca2*, the passive plus deontic reading is possible with the future, conditional and subjunctive forms.

As the morphological restrictions parallel those found with *bisogna* and *toca2*, we should also expect that the same syntactic restrictions be present: the modal auxiliary *andare*, like *bisogna*, should not tolerate a subject DP in its Spec,Agr$_S$ position. However, (15) can have the deontic reading and the subject position is occupied by the DP *la sterpaglia*.

The syntactic restriction regarding the subject is also present with *andare*, but it is limited to first and second persons: only the third person singular and plural can be realized in the subject position of the deontic *andare*.[5] This seems to be the effect of restrictions that require a very detailed analysis of the Agr$_S$ projection and of its sub-components.

(16) a.??Io vado bocciato
        I   go   failed
        'I have to be failed'
     b.??Tu vai   bocciato
        you have-to-be failed
     c. Questo studente va   bocciato
        this   student has-to-be failed

d. ??Noi andiamo   bocciati
   we have-to-be failed
e. ??Voi andate   bocciati
   you have-to-be failed
f. Questi studenti vanno   bocciati
    these students have-to-be failed

The fact that the restriction on the subject is more limited with *andare* than with *bisogna* and *toca2* is parallel to another difference between these verbs: *bisogna* and *toca* are followed by a complete CP as their complement, while *andare* is followed by a passive past participle:

(17) a. Bisogna   [che vada io]
        it-is-necessary that go   I
        'I have to go'
     b. Toca   [che vaga mi]
        it-touches that go   I
        'I have to go'
     c. La sterpaglia   va [bruciata]
        the brushwood goes burnt
        'The brushwood is/has to be burnt'

It may be hypothesized that these two facts are connected, and that the possibility of realizing a third-person subject is related to the presence of the passive past participle (see also note 14).

This preliminary hypothesis is confirmed by data coming from other Italian varieties, where the verb *volere* 'want' is used in a deontic sense and is followed again by a past participle. The surface subject is the object of the past participle, which becomes the subject of the passive:[6]

(18) El vole   magnà
      it wants eaten
      'It wants eating, it is necessary to eat it'

The deontic reading of *volere* cannot be obtained when the verbal form is the infinitive, gerund or past participle (the simple past is not possible in this variety).[7] The possible forms are the present, the imperfect, the future indicative, the present conditional and the simple subjunctive. The parallel regarding the morphological restrictions (cf. Benincà & Poletto 1994: 32) with the other deontic modals is striking.

With respect to the syntactic restrictions regarding the subject, *vuole* behaves as *andare*: the deontic reading of *vuole* can only be used with a third person subject:

(19) a. *Mi voio petenà
        I   want combed
        'I need to be combed'
     b. *Ti   te voi petenà
        you want combed

c. El vole petenà
   he wants combed
d. *A volemo petenà
   we want combed
e. *A vulì petenà
   you want combed
f. I vole petenà
   they want combed

At this point we have two types of deontic modals: *bisogna* and *toca2*, which do not admit any subject, and *andare* and *vuole*, which only admit third-person subjects. *Bisogna* 'it is necessary' and *toca2* 'touch' are followed by a full CP while *andare* 'go' and *vuole* 'want' are followed by a passive past participle. Moreover, all deontic modals examined so far show the same morphological gaps in the verbal paradigm.

Thus, the evidence presented above leads us to conclude that:

— some morphological and syntactic restrictions are connected with the deontic reading of a modal auxiliary;
— the syntactic restriction on the subject depends on the type of embedded structure: if it is a complete CP no subject is permitted, if it is a past participle only third-person subjects are possible.

4 Deontic modals as functional heads

4.1 The problem

Let us sum up what we have seen so far: some modal auxiliaries have a particular reading that we have defined as 'deontic reading' of pure necessity, where no thematic role is assigned. They show some particular morphosyntactic properties: some verbal forms are impossible (simple past, infinitive, gerund and past participle) and there are also restrictions on the occurrence of a subject; furthermore, deontic modal auxiliaries cannot host object clitics. We have formulated the hypothesis that there exists a relation between the deontic reading and the morphosyntactic properties observed. In this section we will discuss our analysis of the relation we have hypothesized on a synchronic basis. The observations based on the diachronic development of the verb *bisogna* that we will present in section 5 will further support the relation we have hypothesized between the morphosyntactic restrictions and the thematic structure of the verb.

We have five different properties to explain:

i. The connection between the thematic grid and the morphological gaps in the verbal paradigm. This property is shared by all modal auxiliaries that can have the particular deontic reading of pure necessity.
ii. The fact that only some verbal forms (past participle, gerund and infinitive) are excluded and not others. In particular we would like to

find out what the possible or impossible forms have in common that renders them grammatical and ungrammatical.

iii. The impossibility for *bisogna/toca2* to host clitics.
iv. The relation between the possibility of having a subject and the structure embedded under the modal auxiliary. If the modal auxiliary embeds a CP, no subject is possible (see *bisogna* and *toca2*); if it embeds a passive past participle, only a third-person subject is possible (cf. *andare* and *vuole*).
v. The difference between verbs like *bisogna/toca2* and *sembra* 'seem' with respect to subject raising. Both types of verbs take a [+finite] or [−finite] CP as their complement. Why is it the case that with *bisogna/toca2* the subject of the embedded verb cannot raise while this is permitted with *sembra*?

We will frame our account in terms of an articulated functional structure of the sentence such as has been proposed in Cinque (1995) on the basis of the surface relative order of adverbs and functional heads. Of the sentence structure discussed by Cinque (1995) we will give here only as much as is relevant to our topic. In (20) we have indicated the adverbs corresponding to each relevant functional head:[8]

(20)

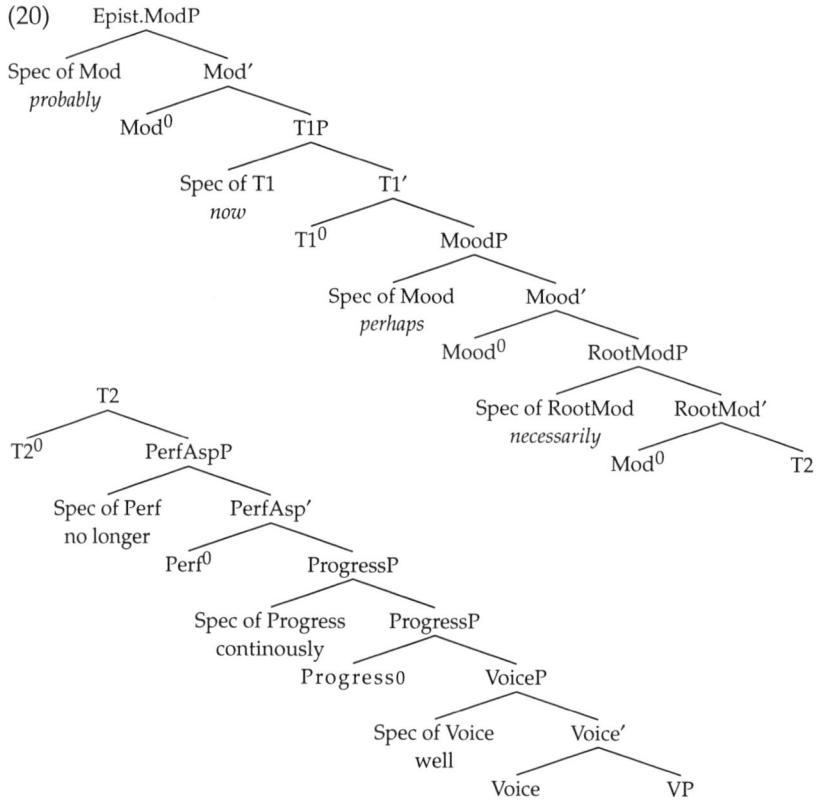

Cinque (1995) presents evidence that there are three distinct modal phrases in the structure of the sentence. One of them is located above T1P and two are located below T1P. The highest one hosts epistemic modality and its specifier position hosts adverbial elements like *probably*; this phrase does not concern us here directly. The second one is a MoodP that hosts a [±irrealis] feature (connected in Romance to grammatical mood such as subjunctive and conditional). Its specifier hosts adverbs like *perhaps*. The third modal phrase is a 'root modality' projection, whose specifier hosts subject-oriented adverbs like *necessarily*. Following Cinque's proposal, we will assume that a F^0 head has marked or default values. For instance, the marked value of the perfect/imperfect aspect head is 'perfect', the marked value of the progressive/generic aspect head is 'progressive'.

Following Giorgi & Pianesi (1991), we take T1 to mark the relation between Reference Time and Speech Time (where 'coincidence' between the two is the default value and 'non-coincidence' the marked one); T2 instead marks the relation between the Event time and Reference time (coincidence/non-coincidence are again respectively default and marked value).

A verbal form raises to check its features in the appropriate head, and can only move upward. When a verbal form (auxiliary, modal,...) is inserted directly in a higher functional head rather than in VP, it can only check features corresponding to functional heads above it.

4.2 The analysis

The central idea we want to exploit is that a modal auxiliary with the deontic reading of 'pure necessity' lacks a theta-grid. We can therefore conceive of it as a functional element directly inserted into the head of a functional projection corresponding to its semantics, namely the head of RootModP (cf. (20)). In other words, we propose that the deontic reading is provided by a purely functional element.[9] Cinque's proposal gives us the more articulated structure that we need in order to connect the morpho-syntactic properties of deontic auxiliaries to their semantics.

If deontic modals are inserted under RootMod^0, what is the status of functional projections that occur lower than it in the structure of the sentence? We can envisage two possibilities:

i. the lower FPs could be present but unmarked;
ii. the lower FPs could be totally absent.

In any case, if the deontic auxiliary is directly inserted in RootMod^0, all the projections below it are unavailable.

There is some evidence for the presence of functional structure (but not necessarily the VP) below the root modality projection but higher than the embedded CP. It is provided by the fact that it is possible, also with *bisogna* and *toca2*, to have adverbs such as *mica, più, già* that are hosted, following

Cinque 1995, in the specifier positions of functional projections lower than the root modality projection but clearly higher than VP:

(21) a. Bisogna   già   accendere il termosifone
        it-is-necessary already to-turn-on the heater
   b. Non bisogna   più   parlarne
        not it-is-necessary anymore to-speak-of-it
   c. Toca   zà   impissare el termo
        it-is-necessary already to-turn-on the heater

This could mean that the lower structure is present, but the corresponding head positions cannot be checked by the deontic modal auxiliary which is 'base-generated' in a higher head. However, we assume instead that the VP of the modal auxiliary is not projected, as a consequence of the fact that deontic modal auxiliaries do not have a theta-grid.

Independent support for this assumption comes from the status of the CP embedded under modal auxiliaries such as *bisogna* or *toca2*. The embedded CP does not behave as a true thematic argument of the modal auxiliary. Some cases that are revealing for our discussion are analysed in this sense by Stowell (1981). He concludes that the different syntactic properties of the sentential complements of verbs such as *murmur* or *shout*, and near-synonyms such as *claim*, come from the fact that the latter but not the former thematically mark their sentential complement. It is possible to perform a simple test based on the observation that a noun morphologically related to the verb can have the same clause as its complement only if the clause is a thematic complement of the verb (see Stowell 1981, §6.3). We can apply this test to our verb *bisogna* and see that the related noun *bisogno* — like the nouns *shout* or *murmur* related to the verbs *to shout* and *to murmur* in English — cannot have a sentential complement:[10]

(22) a. *[Bill's shout that I should get out of the way] surprised me
                                                         (Stowell 1981: 51)
   b. Bill's claim that I should get out of the way surprised me
   c. *Il   bisogno che tu   parta è grande
        the need   that you leave is strong
   d. La necessità che tu parta è grande

The fact that the embedded CP does not behave as a thematic argument of the modal auxiliary confirms the hypothesis that a verb like *bisogna* or *toca2* does not have a VP as a site of theta-role assignment.[11]

4.2.1 Morphological gaps in the paradigm

Summarizing, we have proposed that a deontic modal auxiliary like *bisogna* is directly inserted under RootModP; that the structure below this projection is present, since adverbs related to the lower portion of the clause can be very naturally used with *bisogna*, but all FPs must have their default values. This means that morphological forms which are associated with marked values of a lower head and thus require checking cannot be formed.

Verbal forms such as the active or passive past participle, which have a marked value for [voice], T2 or [perfect], and the simple past, which has a marked aspectual feature, cannot thus be checked, because these FPs are lower than the point in the structure where the deontic modal auxiliary is inserted. Although we do not have clear evidence on the precise position of the F heads hosting gerunds and infinitives, we conjecture that they belong to a portion of the structure situated below the RootMod head (for the gerund, for example, this is rendered plausible by the fact that *-ndo* suffix is associated with the marked value of the [progressive/generic] FP).

Concerning the forms which are possible, we observe that they can all have a marked [+irrealis] value of Mood, which is higher than RootModP. The subjunctive and conditional can have both an irrealis value, and the same is true for the future and the imperfect. Even the present tense form can be interpreted as irrealis, and can work as a substitute of the present subjunctive precisely with *bisogna*.[12] These forms can then check this [+irrealis] feature on a projection higher than RootMod where a *bisogna* type deontic modal auxiliary is inserted.

4.2.2 Restrictions on the presence of a subject and object clitics

Let us now turn to the other two questions: why is it that the possibility of having a subject depends on the type of embedded structure? We will begin with the analysis of *bisogna* and *toca2*, neither of which can have a subject. As deontic modal auxiliaries do not have a theta-grid, they cannot have a thematic subject. However, one might hypothesize that they could have a raised subject. This question is connected to the other one, which concerns the difference between *bisogna* and a raising verb.

From a purely descriptive point of view, it seems that the difference between *bisogna* and a raising verb lies in the presence of a thematic structure. A verb like *sembrare* always has an (explicit or implicit) experiencer theta-role. If this is really the discriminating factor that distinguishes between a raising verb and a non-raising one, we can treat raising as a non-primitive property. One could hypothesize that the raising property depends on the presence of a VP. We will not go into detail but will restate our observation in the form of a descriptive generalization:

(23) A raising verb must have a thematic grid.

As modal auxiliaries do not assign any thematic role, they do not have a VP. Hence, they cannot be raising verbs. The difference between *bisogna* and raising verbs can thus be derived from our assumption that deontic modals lack a VP.

The only possibility that remains open to *bisogna* is to have an expletive subject. Recall however the data illustrated in section 2: there is no subject of *bisogna* that can control a PRO, and *bisogna* lacks expletive subject clitics in the northern Italian varieties. It thus seems that the Agr$_S$ projection of *bisogna* and *toca2* is not available at all. In order to explain these facts, we will assume that the lack of a VP implies the lack of all AgrPs related to the arguments of the verb. This also explains why *bisogna* and *toca2* cannot host object clitics: as object clitics are also related to Agreement projections, they cannot occur.[13]

5 The diachronic perspective

5.1 Introduction

In this section we will analyse the syntax of *bisogna* as it developed through the history of Italian. The diachronic facts considered here will constitute a further argument in favour of the idea that the morphological and semantic properties of deontic auxiliaries go hand in hand. In fourteenth century Italian and, in the literary style, up until the nineteenth century, the distribution of *bisogna* differs in an interesting way from that of modern *bisogna*: all the restrictions which hold in Modern Italian are absent.

5.2 *Bisogna* through the history of Italian: the data[14]

5.2.1 Boccaccio's *Decameron*

It is readily apparent that in Boccaccio's *Decameron* (second half of the fourteenth century) the thematic structure of *bisogna* is different from the modern one: an experiencer theta role is realized with a dative and a theme with a nominative argument. Moreover, the verb agrees with the theme-subject (recall that this is never the case in Modern Italian).

(24) a. E   quivi da   una vecchia   procacciato quello
        and here from an   old-woman taken   what
        che le   bisognava, ...   (II, 9, 42)
        that to-her was-necessary
        'And having taken from an old woman what she needed ...'

  b. Saper   far ciò che a   ciò   bisognava, ...   (II, 10, 17)
     can(INF) do (INF) what that to-this was-necessary
     'To be able to do what was necessary for this ...'

  c. Oltre a questo non vi   bisognerebbe
     above this   not to-you would-be-necessary
     d'aver pensiero...   (III, 1, 16)
     to worry
     'Beyond this you would not need to worry ...'

  d. Per ciò   che egli   ci   bisogna ...   (III, 1, 16)
     for what that he(NOM) to-us is-necessary
     'For that for which we need him ...'

  e. E quando la gelosia   gli   bisognava del tutto ...
     and when the jealousy to-him was really necessary
     'And when he really needed to be jealous ...'

f. Mi   bisognano   fiorini dugento   d'oro
    to-me are-necessary florins two hundred of gold
    'I need two hundred gold florins'
g. E per ciò che tu ci bisognavi   per dir
    and for what that you to-us were-necessary to say
    certe orazioni   (VII, 3, 31)
    some prayers
    'And since we needed you to say prayers ...'

As predicted by our hypothesis, non-finite forms are possible (we could not find an infinitive form, but the occurrences of *bisogna* are very limited in this text):

(25) a. ... in più lunghi digiuni che loro   non sarien
         in longer   fasts   than to-them not would-be
         bisognati   (past participle) (II, 6, 41)
         been-necessary
         '... in longer fasts than they would have needed'
     b. ... bisognandogli   una grande quantità
         being-necessary-to-him a large   amount
         di denari ...   (gerund) (I, 3, 6)
         of money
         '... (with) him needing a large amount of money ...'

(24) and (25) are consistent with the analysis developed for modern *bisogna* in section 4, and show that the connection between the forms and the thematic structure postulated in section 2 is correct. Old Italian *bisogna* has two arguments in its theta grid and can be inflected for all tenses: our analysis predicts that these two phenomena are expected to appear together.

Also present in the corpus are some examples of impersonal *bisogna* (parallel to the modern usage) which do not show any overt argument:

(26) a. E   perciò   non bisogna   che io vi   dimostri, ... (III, 5, 11)
         and therefore is not necessary that I to-you show
         'and therefore it is not necessary for me to show you ...'
     b. Che egli, se bisognasse,   gli   spezzerebbe delle legne
         that he   if were-necessary to-him would-break some wood
                                                            (III, 1, 13)
         'that he, if it were necessary, would break some wood for him ...'

In the *Decameron* there are very few examples of this type. All of them are consistent with the modern use of *bisogna*. The most frequent verb of necessity is *dovere*. Also *tocca* (cf. section 3) is not much used and it only has the construction *tocca*+NP or *tocca*+*di* infinitive, meaning 'it is someone's turn to do something'. No case of *tocca*+bare infinitive has been found. This means too that the verb *tocca* was different both from the Modern Italian and from the Venetan counterparts.

5.2.2 Machiavelli

Il Principe by Machiavelli (1513) shows the same type of *bisogna* found in the *Decameron*, as it has two theta roles, an experiencer and a theme.

(27) a. E   quando pure li   bisognassi   procedere contro al
        and when also to-him were-necessary to-go   against the
        sangue di alcuno   (p. 82)
        blood of anyone
        'and if he must take someone's life'
   b. Et   a   tenere indietro li   Veneziani, bisognava
        and in-order to-keep-back   the Venetians was-necessary
        la   unione di tutti gli altri   (p. 55)
        the union of all the others
        'and to restrain the Venetians the alliance of all the rest was necessary'

There are also some examples of impersonal *bisogna* with no overt arguments. However, the impersonal has all the forms that are not possible in Modern Italian:

(28) a. ... se fussino venuti tempi che fussi   bisognato
         if were   come times that had-been necessary
         procedere con   respetti ...   (p. 124)
         to-go-on with caution
         '... if times which necessitated caution had come ...'
   b. Cioè   se uno principe ha tanto   stato che possa,
        that is if a   prince has so much state that he can
        bisognando,   per sè   uno destino reggersi, ...   (p. 51)
        being-necessary for himself a   destiny rule
        'that is, whether the prince has so much power that he can, if necessary, stand on his own ...'

The examples in (28) seem to contradict our hypothesis that whenever *bisogna* lacks a theta grid it loses non-finite inflection, as it can be found in the present perfect (a verbal form which is excluded in Modern Italian).

However, one could hypothesize that impersonal *bisogna* is only apparently similar to its modern counterpart, but still has a thematic grid in Old Italian. We will present here a test based on coreference showing that the subject position of *bisogna* is still present in Old Italian. Note the contrast between Old Italian in (29) and Modern Italian in (30):

(29) a. Chi vuole operar bene bisogna   allontanarsi
        who wants to-act well is-necessary to-distance-self
        da   tutte le cure   (Vasari, III, 507)
        from all   the cares
        'He who wants to act well must distance himself from all care'

      b. Chi voleva entrare in essa, bisognava per forza
         who wanted to-enter in it   was-necessary
         inchinarsi con il capo   (Giulio Cesare Croce, 95)
         to bow his head
         'Anyone who wanted to enter was obliged to bow his head'
(30) a. *Chi voleva entrare in essa bisognava
         who wanted to-enter in it   was-necessary
         inchinarsi con il capo   (Modern Italian)
         to bow his head
      b. Chi voleva entrare in essa, bisognava
         who wanted to-enter in it   was-necessary
         che si inchinasse con il capo
         that he bowed his head
      c. Chi voleva entrare in essa, doveva inchinarsi con il capo
         who wanted to-enter in it   had to bend his head

In (29) the anaphoric pronoun *si*, cliticized to the infinitival verb, is bound by a PRO in subject position of the infinitival sentence, which is controlled by the free relative clause. This means that the free relative clause must be interpreted as an argument of *bisogna* in order to bind the reference of the embedded PRO. This argument is thematically an experiencer, presumably realized as a nominative subject. Hence, even the impersonal *bisogna* in Old Italian has at least one argument in its thematic grid, represented by a free relative clause in our examples.

This structure is not possible in Modern Italian. The ungrammaticality of (30a) can be derived assuming that Modern Italian *bisogna* has no subject position which can bind the reference of PRO (which in turn binds the anaphor). An infinitival sentence embedded under *bisogna* can only have an arbitrary PRO and the anaphoric pronoun *si* cannot be coreferent with the free relative clause. Therefore, the contrast between (29) and (30a) concerning the binding of a PRO and of an anaphor shows that in Old Italian there is a subject position which can be occupied by the free relative clause; this position is not available in Modern Italian. (30b) is possible, with the free relative clause left-dislocated from the subject position of the embedded tensed clause. (30c) is possible with another deontic modal auxiliary, *dovere*, which has a subject position.

Hence, even the impersonal forms are different from the modern version of *bisogna*, as in Old Italian there is always at least one argument while this is not the case in Modern Italian. Therefore, these cases do not constitute counterexamples to our hypothesis. On the contrary, they confirm our idea that thematic roles and functional projections are tightly linked.

5.2.3 Case alternations

Another possible structure which is found in Old Italian but has disappeared in Modern Italian is the following, where the experiencer is not realized with a dative but with a nominative and the theme is in the genitive case:

(31) ... coloro che   ne bisognano
     those that(*wh*-subject) of-it need   (Fra' Bartolomeo Amm. ant. volg. 207)
     '... those who need it'

This possibility is present, though less frequent, throughout the history of Italian up to the nineteenth century:

(32) Quasi tutte le giovani   si   fanno più belle
     almost all the young.FEM themselves make more beautiful
     in viso e   non bisognano d'altri ornamenti   (Foscolo IV 342)
     in face and not need.3PL of other ornaments
     'Almost all the young women make their faces more beautiful and do not need any other ornaments.'

We thus have two possible case realizations of the two arguments of *bisogna*:

(33) a. experiencer → dative
         theme   → nominative
     b. experiencer → nominative
         theme   → genitive

The existence of these two possible case realizations gives us a hint about the functional and argumental structure of *bisogna* in Old Italian, as we will see in section 5.3.

5.2.4 Galileo Galilei

We have examined the *Dialogo sui massimi sistemi* (1632) by Galilei, whose language seems to be less artificial than that of literary works.

Most examples of *bisogna* show the same pattern that we find in the modern language: the verb has no subject or object DP, it can take an inflected or infinitive sentence, and it is never inflected for participle, gerund and infinitive:

(34) a. Bisogna   dunque   che voi diciate che ...   (p. 114)
         is-necessary therefore that you say   that
         'and therefore it is necessary for you to say that ...'
     b. Bisognerebbe   detrarne   quello che
         would-be-necessary to subtract-from-it what   that
         avesse fatto l'artiglieria   (p. 156)
         had   done the-artillery
         'it would be necessary to subtract from it the distance that the artillery had travelled'

Only 8 examples out of 260 show the older structure with two arguments, an experiencer and a dative:

(35) Che non vi   bisogna   chiamar   principio interno
     that not to-you is-necessary to-invoke neither principle internal
     né esterno per ...   (p. 317)
     nor external to
     '(so) that you have no need to invoke either an internal or an external principle ...'

In each case the dative experiencer is realized as a clitic pronoun. Note that this version of *bisogna* shows up in the present perfect, which does not occur when it is used without arguments:

(36) Mi   è   bisognato   tardar   lì   (p. 335)
      to-me has been-necessary to-linger there
      'I had to wait there'

No gerund has been found. There are two examples with an infinitive, both of them embedded under the verb *concludere*:

(37) a. vengono calcolando ... e   concludendo bisognare
        they-are calculating and concluding be-necessary
        in dottrina del Copernico ammettere che ...   (pp. 427–8)
        in doctrine of Copernicus to-admit that
        'they are calculating ... and conclude that, according to Copernicus' doctrine, it would be necessary to admit that ...'
     b. vo   meco medesimo concludendo necessariamente bisognare
        I-am myself   concluding   necessarily   be-necessary
        che quelli che restano ...   (p. 425)
        that those that remain
        'I myself conclude that it would necessarily have to be the case that those who remain ...'

The verb *concludere* takes an inflected clause as its complement in Modern Italian.[15] It is interesting to observe that when *bisogna* is used without arguments it never shows these forms in a sample of 252 sentences. It thus seems that the correlation between the presence of arguments and the activation of some functional projections that we have hypothesized for Modern Italian holds in this case too.

Another interesting observation concerns the number of occurrences of *bisogna*, which is very limited in the texts by Boccaccio and Machiavelli, while it increases dramatically in Galilei's *Dialogo*. We will come back to this in section 5.3.

A brief remark on *tocca*: in this stage it maintains the meaning 'it is someone's turn' but it can also mean 'it falls to/on someone, it happens to someone':

(38) a. secondo   il   numero che gli è toccato   (p. 91)
        according to the number that fell to him
     b. adunque non vi   è   toccato   ma a veder la Terra (p. 110)
        then   not to-you has happened ever to see the earth
        'then you have never happened to see the earth'

It is construed with a DP or with an infinitive preceded by *a*. No bare infinitive has been found.

5.2.5 Collodi

As a third stage we have examined Collodi's *Pinocchio* (1883), a tale written for children using the everyday language; the author intended to use a standard colloquial language based on spoken Florentine. This work presents the same distribution that we find in Modern Italian, as *bisogna* is only used without arguments and only in the forms possible in Modern Italian:

(39) a. Bisogna   sapere   che ...   (p. 236)
          is-necessary to-know that
     b. Bisognava   pensarci   prima   (p. 295)
          was-necessary to-think-about-it before

This shows that in the second half of the nineteenth century *bisogna* has already developed into its modern form. On the other hand, the use of the verb *tocca* is similar to that present in Galilei's language:

(40) Non   sai   la fortuna che mi   è   toccata?   (p. 287)
     not (you) know the luck   that to-me is fallen
     'Do you not know the luck that befell me?'

However, *tocca* has already acquired the modern deontic reading, even though it is construed with a prepositional infinitive:

(41) ... o per forza   mi   toccherà a   studiare   (p. 220)
     or necessarily to-me will-touch (PREP) study.INF
     '... or I will necessarily have to study'

No bare infinitive has been found.

5.3 Diachrony and synchrony come together

The three diachronic stages that we have exemplified show that *bisogna* has changed in the course of time. In Old Italian *bisogna* is a verb with two arguments: an experiencer and a theme. These two arguments can be realized with two possible case configurations:

i. the experiencer is realized with a dative and the theme with a nominative; or, alternatively,
ii. the experiencer takes the nominative and the theme the genitive.[16]

In the first stage impersonal *bisogna* is present, but in a limited number of occurrences. In Boccaccio's *Decameron* we have very few examples of impersonal *bisogna*, which is only attested in the forms which are also possible in Modern Italian. In Machiavelli, on the other hand, impersonal *bisogna* also occurs in the forms that contemporary Italian does not allow (past participle, infinitive and gerund). However, there are reasons to believe that even in this period impersonal *bisogna* is not identical to the modern one, having a subject position which can control a PRO in the embedded infinitive (as we have seen above in commenting on cases such as (29)). This suggests that the status of the embedded sentence under impersonal *bisogna* (cf. examples such as (26a)) is the same as that of the sentence selected by lexical *bisogna*, i.e. it has a complete thematic grid (cf.

(24c)). We conclude that, at this stage, *bisogna* always has a thematic grid and therefore projects a VP.

The second stage, represented by Galileo Galilei's *Dialogo*, shows a majority of examples where *bisogna* has no argument. As it behaves as in the modern language (it lacks the same verbal forms, it lacks a subject and cannot host clitics), we assume that at this point the change from a lexical into a purely functional element has already taken place. As noted above, the frequency of use of *bisogna* is much higher in the text by Galilei than the other two texts examined (the whole *Decameron* contains only 44 examples and Machiavelli's *Principe* 15, while Galilei has 260 occurrences): it is tempting to interpret this fact as connected to the development of *bisogna* as a modal auxiliary. In fact, functional elements tend to occur in a given corpus with much higher frequency than lexical elements.

Only 8 examples in Galilei's text show properties which partly overlap with the older usage. In these cases, *bisogna* takes a dative experiencer, which is always realized as a clitic and in one case it appears in the past participle. Note that 'modern' *bisogna* occurs in 252 examples in Galilei's text and no past participle, infinitive or gerund has been found in this set, while a past participle occurs precisely when a dative experiencer is present: this constitutes evidence in favour of our proposal regarding the connection between the theta grid and the morphosyntactic restrictions. The fact that the experiencer is always realized as a clitic pronoun strongly recalls the behaviour of Modern Venetan *toca* noted in section 3.1: only when the experiencer is realized as a clitic, does the following infinitival sentence have the meaning 'someone has to do something which he does not like' (see example (10)). This suggests that there are two different structures involved in the realization of the experiencer theta role. As the reading just mentioned is available only with a clitic, it could be hypothesized that the experiencer is realized as a sort of benefactive only when the verb is a deontic modal auxiliary. If this is true, we could think that even the 8 examples found in Galilei do not have the same structure as those found in Boccaccio's *Decameron*. It could be hypothesized that the structure with the dative clitic represents an intermediate stage of evolution from the deontic modal verb with a rich thematic grid to the purely functional modal auxiliary which has lost all its arguments. Dative clitics also realize a benefactive, which cannot be expressed by a tonic pronoun or by a DP. In these structures the clitic can be analysed in two ways: it can realize the experiencer — and as such be connected with a position inside a VP — or it can be a sort of benefactive, which is not necessarily an argument of the verb. If the clitic is interpreted as a true experiencer, *bisogna* will necessarily have a VP layer; if the clitic is interpreted as a benefactive, the VP is not necessarily projected.[17] This ambiguity might have favoured the passage from the lexical to the functional element.

In the third stage, Collodi's *Pinocchio*, there is no trace of the older construction with two arguments and the verb behaves like the modern *bisogna* with respect to the possible forms: both the thematic grid and some verbal forms have disappeared.

Thus, the development of *bisogna* constitutes an argument in favour of our hypothesis that functional and argumental structure go together: when there are arguments, all forms are possible; when no argument appears to be selected by *bisogna*, only modal forms are found.

6 Conclusion

Let us now sum up the analysis we have presented here. We have examined synchronic and diachronic instances of the process that changes a lexical item into a functional element. We have found that the loss of a thematic grid appears to be a necessary requirement for this evolution. We have supposed that the morphological lacunae observed for deontic auxiliaries with the semantic properties of *bisogna* are not historical accidents, but reflect the syntactic consequences of the semantic poverty of the verb.

Modern *bisogna* has no thematic grid and, as such, has no VP. It is directly inserted into the head of RootMod, a functional projection consistent with its semantics, and the lower portion of the syntactic structure is present but the modal auxiliary cannot move through it. Therefore, morphological forms which have to be checked in FPs lower than the RootModP are not possible. The agreement projections are also blocked: for this reason clitics and a nominative subject cannot appear. The observation of older records of Italian provides support for the idea that the semantic and syntactic properties of the verb are strictly connected to its morphology. When the modal verb *bisogna* expresses not simply a deontic modality but a necessity which affects a theme and is represented by a lexical element, these arguments appear as surface arguments of the modal; with this structure, the verb can be inflected for the forms that are impossible in the modern language. Apparent cases of impersonal *bisogna* in Old Italian have been shown to be different from the purely functional deontic modal present in Modern Italian, as they still preserve a thematic grid, and, as such, do not show the other morphosyntactic restrictions typical of the modern functional modal auxiliary.

An interesting question concerns the reason why most Italian varieties have developed a class of functional modal heads. We do not have a clear idea of which properties may be related to this change in the history of Italian, but it is certain that this cannot be connected to the loss of verbal agreement morphology as seems to be the case for English modals.

Notes

* Although the research for this chapter was carried out jointly, Paola Benincà is responsible for sections 1, 2, 3.1 and 5.1 to 5.2.4, and Cecilia Poletto is responsible for sections 3.2, 3.3, 4 and 5.2.5 to 6.

The diachronic development of a modal verb of necessity

We would like to thank Ans van Kemenade, Gennaro Chierchia, Guglielmo Cinque, Diana Cresti, Charlotte Galves, Richard Kayne, Maria Pia Lo Duca, Kathleen Parker, Gertjan Postma, Paolo Salvi, Laura Vanelli, Nigel Vincent and Raffaella Zanuttini for comments and discussion.

1. For reasons that are not clear, the present subjunctive (ex. (2e)) is not as natural, for many speakers, as the imperfect subjunctive is, though it is not impossible as the infinitive, gerund and past participle are. We will idealize the data and treat the present subjunctive as a possible form of *bisogna*.
2. In northern Italian the simple past tense is not used, but speakers of most of those Central and southern varieties that admit it do not find (3d) grammatical.
3. Note that the lack of non-finite forms strongly recalls the development of English modals (cf. Lightfoot 1979 and Roberts 1985b). The behaviour of the Italian verbs of necessity under consideration presents striking similarities with English modal verbs on the one hand, and with the French deontic *falloir* on the other.
4. Also the pure passive reading shows some restrictions: for instance, no agent can be realized in these structures (see Salvi 1988 for evidence in this sense).
5. If the modal is inflected in the conditional form, these sentences are only marginal:
   (i) ?Tu andresti   bocciato
       you should-go(COND) failed
6. The variety used for the examples is Basso Polesano, a southern Venetan dialect.
7. A southern variety spoken in Puglia presents the same phenomenon and has the simple past which is excluded in this construction.
8. Cinque does not discuss AgrPs in his analysis, as they have different properties.
9. We are familiar with functional elements that are independent words in one language while they are morphemes in others. In this regard, we can recall that in Classical Latin there is a morphological suffix *-ndum* which, added to the verb root, gives it deontic meaning:
   (i) a. lege-re   b. lege-ndum
          read (INFINITIVE)   to be read
       c. legendum est
          it is necessary to read

   For reasons of this kind, we chose to treat these verbs as pure functional elements. A possible alternative which deserves to be more extensively analysed, and is for the moment equivalent, is to consider *bisogna* as generated under V^0 but only capable of moving directly to RootMod^0, bypassing the intermediate head positions or, more precisely, passing through them vacuously.
10. The test is not applicable to *toca1, 2*, for which there is not in the language a related noun which has the deontic meaning (but only the transitive meaning).
11. The new syntactic theory presented in Chomsky (1995) gives us a new possibility to capture the connection between the morphological gaps and the absence of a thematic grid. Chomsky's (1994) proposal about syntactic structure only admits that a set (a set of sets) of features is projected and then merged with others. Thus, it is not possible to have a totally empty V^0 category, there must be at least one phonologically empty verbal head in order to project its features to the maximal node.

    Our analysis needs to be further refined to account for intermediate cases where the absence of some FPs seems connected with the absence of some thematic role. An auxiliary like *andare* 'go' in its purely passive reading, for instance, cannot have an agent expressed and at the same time cannot be inflected in the simple present form.
12. Notice the contrast regarding the acceptability of the present indicative with two different deontic modal auxiliaries, the defective *bisogna* and the non-defective *dovere* (see, for other, independent evidence, Bertinetto 1993):
    (i) Temo che si *deve/debba   andare
        (I) fear that we have(INDIC)/have(SUBJUNC) to-go
    (ii) Temo che bisogna/?bisogni   andare
        (I) fear that it is necessary/it be necessary to-go

13. The other two modal verbs that we have examined, namely *vuole* 'want' and *andare* 'go', tolerate a subject. However, their embedded clause is not a complete CP, as is the case of *bisogna* and *toca2*, but a passive past participle (probably a VoiceP, following Cinque's theory). We can hypothesize that verbs like *vuole* 'want' and *andare* 'go' are inserted under the root modality head but embed a marked VoiceP (following Cinque 1995 the passive is the marked value for the Voice head) and not a complete CP as *bisogna* and *toca2*. As the structure with verbs like *vuole* and *andare* is monoclausal, the AgrPs can be activated if they are parasitic on the VP of the embedded verb. Thus, the object of the embedded past participle can occur as the subject of the modal auxiliary.

    A more difficult question concerns the features of the subject: why are only third-person subjects permitted, while first- or second-person subjects are not possible? In order to answer this question, we need a more articulated theory of Agreement projection(s), which we do not have at present. A possible line of investigation could exploit Kayne's modular analysis of auxiliary verbs (see Kayne 1993). He assumes the presence of an Agr_S projection associated with the past participle. This Agr_S is clearly sensitive to person features, as it triggers syntactic differences related to person specifications. We could advance the hypothesis that this Agr_SP must be located higher than VoiceP but lower than the root modality head. In the spirit of the hypothesis we are developing, it could also be hypothesized that the lower Agr_SP cannot be activated as it is contained in the inactive portion of the sentence. This suggestion is clearly not a satisfactory answer to the facts that we have observed, but we hope that it may lead to future research exploring the connections that exist between the structure of VP and functional projections.

14. There is no established division of the history of the Italian language: we will use Old Italian for the language represented by texts up to the fourteenth century, Modern Italian for the language from the nineteenth century onwards, and we will refer to the language of the intermediate periods by the names of the single authors.

15. It seems plausible to think that in Old Italian the infinitive could show some of the properties connected with finite forms in Modern Italian, especially because it could license an overt subject (cf. the Aux to C construction, which is still possible at a high stylistic level).

16. Recall that a similar pattern was found in the case of auxiliary alternation between BE and HAVE (see Kayne 1993). If the explanation adopted by Kayne for auxiliaries can be exploited in order to account for the development of *bisogna*, then the pattern FP [DP] is not confined to aspectual auxiliaries.

17. However, it might be the case that the modal auxiliary is not yet inserted in the RootMod head but perhaps in a lower functional projection.

4 Auxiliary verbs in Old and Middle French: a diachronic study of substitutive *faire* and a comparison with the Modern English auxiliaries

Philip H. Miller

In this chapter, I will argue that there were two distinct syntactic constructions for substitutive uses of *faire* in Old and Middle French (OFr and MFr), one in which *faire* is simply an instance of the main verb *faire* (similar to substitution by main verb *do* in Modern English (ModE), e.g. in constructions using *do so* or *do that*), and a second in which *faire* is an auxiliary verb (similar to substitution by auxiliary *do* in ModE, e.g. in VP-Ellipsis).* The two central properties distinguishing substitution by main verbs *faire* and *do* from substitution by auxiliary *faire* and *do* are the same in French and English. First, main verbs *faire* and *do* are subject to a semantic restriction on substitution, namely they can only substitute for verbs of which they are a hyperonym (i.e., verbs which have a more specific but compatible meaning), whereas there is no such restriction on the auxiliary uses. Second, auxiliary *faire* and *do* can generally inherit the complementation properties of any verb they substitute for, whereas substitutive uses of main verbs *faire* and *do* are much more restricted in the types of complementation they allow (essentially, they are restricted to complement structures available for nonsubstitutive uses of the main verb). I will show (sections 4 and 5) that the auxiliary uses of *faire* disappear in the sixteenth and seventeenth centuries leading to the Modern French (ModFr) situation where substitution is only possible by main verb *faire*.

More generally, I will argue that OFr and MFr had a distinct syntactic class of auxiliary verbs, namely *avoir*, *estre* and *faire*, which were involved in a number of specific syntactic constructions distinguishing them from ordinary verbs. These constructions are strikingly parallel to those of the ModE auxiliaries, e.g. substitutive constructions such as VP-Ellipsis (VPE) and Pseudogapping (PG) (section 2). Related constructions in OFr and MFr depending on this property are the *si/non faire/estre/avoir* construction and the *ce faire/estre/avoir mon* construction (section 3). I will show that these constructions all disappear together during the sixteenth and seventeenth centuries, leading to the ModFr situation where VPE and PG do not exist (section 4). This supports the view that these constructions all depend on a single common property, distinguishing *avoir*, *estre* and *faire* from other verbs, the loss of which led to their disappearance.

The relevant data can be found in the literature on OFr and MFr, but to my knowledge the relations between these data, and their theoretical consequences, namely the existence of a syntactically distinct class of auxiliaries including *faire*, have not been noticed.[1] On the contrary, previous studies (e.g. Moignet 1973) have assumed that the status of *faire* is essentially the same in OFr and ModFr, and have failed to recognize that there were two very different types of substitution in OFr and MFr, respectively based on the main verb and on the auxiliary, as is the case in ModE. I will sketch an analysis of the substitutive constructions involving the auxiliaries *avoir*, *estre* and *faire* in the framework of Head-Driven Phrase Structure Grammar (cf. Pollard & Sag 1987, 1994), parallel to that proposed for VPE and PG in English in Miller (1990, 1992).

1 VP-Ellipsis and Pseudogapping in Modern English

To begin with, I will briefly sketch the unified analysis of VPE and PG proposed for ModE in Miller (1990, 1992). This will allow me to exhibit the crucial similarities between these constructions and those in OFr and MFr. Sentences (1) are classic examples of VPE, a construction which has received extensive attention in the literature (cf., e.g., Sag 1976; Williams 1977; Schachter 1978; Webber 1979; Dalrymple, Shieber & Pereira 1991; Hardt 1993; Warner 1993). Sentences (2), on the other hand, illustrate PG, a much less studied construction (cf. though Levin 1986 [1979], Visser 1963; § 573 and § 580ff.; Warner 1993). (In all examples, I will note the substitutive auxiliary in **bold** and its antecedent in *italic*.)

(1) a. Mary *saw John* and Anne **did** too.
 b. Mary may *see John* when Anne **will**.

(2) a. Does that *annoy* you? It **would** me.   (Levin 1986 [1979]: 17 (25))
 b. The small flower-bed that as yet *showed* more sticks and string and labels than it **did** flowers.   (Priestly, in Visser §581)

(3) a. Mary *saw* John and Anne Ø Peter.
 b. —Mary *saw* John. —*Anne Ø Peter.

VPE is characterized by the ellipsis of a VP leaving behind one (or more) auxiliaries. If the understood VP has no auxiliary, then supportive *do* appears (see (1a)). PG is a construction similar to Gapping (illustrated in (3)) in that the main verb is ellipsed and that there are overt remnants on both sides of the ellipsis site, specifically a subcategorized complement on the right, but it is different from Gapping in that there is an overt auxiliary. The latter property makes PG similar to VP-ellipsis. Furthermore, PG is not restricted to coordinate structures as is Gapping (see (3b)). PG has often been considered a marginal and/or somewhat deviant construction, although the references cited clearly indicate that this is not the case. Levin

(1986 [1979]) collected a large corpus of spontaneous occurrences of PG in conversation and Visser (1963) exhibits a considerable collection of literary examples. Furthermore, these studies show that it is not the case, as has sometimes been claimed (cf., e.g., Kuno 1981), that PG is restricted to comparatives. Though the construction is particularly frequent in comparatives, it also occurs regularly in other types of subordinate clauses ('or *felt* the pain which I **did** for him once — Visser: §581), in independent clauses (2a), and in coordinate structures with *but* or with a change of auxiliary or polarity in the second conjunct ('I won't *ride up* streets the wrong way, but I **will** alleys' Levin 1986: 17). It thus seems that PG appears regularly in all contexts where gapping is excluded.

VPE and PG were both initially analysed in terms of deletion under identity. However, following especially Webber (1979), numerous arguments have been put forth against this approach (cf., e.g., Hardt 1993 for recent discussion). These are based, *inter alia*, on antecedent-contained deletion, split antecedents, and more generally, the lack of an appropriate syntactic antecedent in the discourse context. The following examples illustrate these problems for cases for which we will find similar data in OFr and MFr. Well-known solutions exist for the cases of type (4) (cf., e.g., Fodor & Sag 1982). However, active/passive alternations of the type illustrated in (5) and (6) are much more problematic.

(4) — I *saw you* — You **did** not   [did = see me, VPE]

(5) Business needs to be *developed* differently than we **have** in the past
 (5/24/91 NPR 'Morning Edition' interview) (VPE, Hardt 1993: 37)

(6) The arms were *hidden* by the rebels as a woman **would** her most precious jewels   (PG, Miller 1992: 94)

Miller (1990, 1992) proposes a unified analysis of VPE and PG based on the idea that auxiliaries can function as pro-predicates (cf. Schachter 1978). Syntactically, auxiliaries are verbs which can take any subcategorization frame available for main verbs. Semantically, their translation involves a predicate variable which can be instantiated to any predicate of the appropriate semantic type present in discourse. The type of the variable depends on the subcategorization frame chosen for the auxiliary. It is a function from the types of the subcategorized arguments to the VP type. For instance, in (1a), *did* has as its subcat frame [—] and simply translates as a variable of type VP; in (2a), *would* has as its subcat frame [–NP] and translates as **would**$'(v_{\langle NP, VP\rangle})$ where $v_{\langle NP, VP\rangle}$ is a variable of type $\langle NP, VP\rangle$, and **would**$'$ is a constant representing the semantic contribution specific to the auxiliary.

This analysis leads to considering VPE and PG as essentially instances of the same construction (as also suggested in Warner 1993). This is supported by the fact that the conditions on the appearance of the auxiliary(ies) are identical, and by the fact that the discourse distribution of the constructions is identical: neither is restricted to coordinate structures, and both are instances of surface anaphora in the sense of Hankamer & Sag (1976), namely they require a linguistic antecedent in the preceding (or, more rarely, following) discourse (see however Hardt 1993: 17ff. for a defence of the opposite view). Furthermore, the parallel situation in OFr and MFr, and the subsequent simultaneous disappearance of both constructions in ModFr, support the view that VPE and PG are based on a single property of the auxiliaries. More generally, on the basis of this unified analysis, Miller (1992) argues against the validity of a distinction in structural attachment (VP-internal vs VP-external) between subcategorized and nonsubcategorized complements of the verb. Indeed, the most central criterion for this distinction (see McCawley 1988: 48–9 for a recent pedagogically oriented statement of this classical criterion), namely the impossibility for a subcategorized complement to appear after a VPE site, turns out to be invalid, since clearly subcategorized complements (direct objects, specifically) appear in that position in the PG examples (see (2a, b)).

It is noteworthy that the analysis proposed here involves no empty categories in the ellipsed clauses. It is clear that an extremely similar analysis could be proposed where the auxiliary is followed by an empty V having the same syntactic and semantic properties as those attributed here to the auxiliaries themselves, namely an arbitrary subcat frame and a translation as a predicate variable. I avoid postulating such an empty verb here essentially for reasons of conceptual economy. Furthermore, recent psycholinguistic evidence against empty categories in *wh*-constructions (cf. Pickering & Barry 1991) may extend to cases of the type examined here, and in any case reduces the general plausibility of postulating empty categories where they are not necessary.

2 VP-Ellipsis and Pseudogapping in Old and Middle French

In this section, I present a representative set of examples of VPE and PG in Old and Middle French. As the examples show, they function in a way that is clearly parallel to the corresponding English constructions discussed in the preceding section. It should be noted that I have conducted no systematic corpus search for these examples, but that they are relatively easy to find in classical sources, e.g. OFr dictionaries such as Tobler & Lommatzsch (1915–89, henceforth T&L), under *faire*, *estre* and *avoir*, and classical OFr and MFr grammars (e.g. Foulet 1972 [1919]; Marchello-Nizia 1979). Furthermore, Marchello-Nizia (1985, henceforth MN) provides a wealth of relevant examples.

— *VP-Ellipsis*
(7) Si *souffrira*. —C'est bien dit, voirement **fera**.
    (Th. frç. au m.â., in T&L, under *faire*)
    So he suffer-FUT. — Well said, he does-FUT indeed.
    'He will suffer indeed'

(8) Amors ne m'en faudrat mie,
car je *l'ai trop bien servie*
et **ferai** tote ma vie
senz nule fause pansee
(Colin Muset ±1230, quoted in Foulet 1972 [1919], § 341: 236)
'I won't lack for love, for I have served it very well and do-FUT [= will serve it] for all my life [...]'

(9) Si ne moi pot nuz *engenier*
Com **sui** or par un mollier
(Vie de Sainte Juliane, beg. 13th, quoted in Tobler 1905)
'So nobody could mislead me as I am now [misled] by a woman'

(10) 'Je vous jur que *vostre secré*,
Dame, ce n'est de vostre gré,
Nul ne *sara*.
— N'aussi par moi ja ne **fera**.' (MN, p. 131)
'"My Lady, I swear that no one will know your secret, if it is not by your will.
— Nor by me will any one [know it]"'

Example (7) is a typical case, showing that when the understood VP (*souffrira*, in this case) has no auxiliary verb, supportive *faire* appears just as supportive *do* does in English. This is also true for (8) and (10) (where the ellipsed VPs are respectively *la servirai trop bien* and *sara mon secré*). On the other hand, when the ellipsed VP has an auxiliary *avoir* or *estre*, that auxiliary appears. This is shown in example (9) where the ellipsed VP is the passive *sui engenié*. Furthermore, (9) is a remarkable example because it shows that active/passive alternations between antecedent and ellipsed VP were possible in OFr just as they are in ModE (cf. (5) above). Indeed, *engenier* appears as an active verb with the direct object *moi* in the antecedent. Thus, the same kind of arguments against deletion approaches which have been made for English appear to be available for OFr. Extensive corpus studies would be required to establish the frequency of such active/passive alternations, and the existence of other types of examples where there is no appropriate syntactic antecedent for controlling deletion. Furthermore, example (10) shows that we get the same type of discrepancies with pronouns between antecedent and ellipsed VP as those in English, illustrated in (4) above. The ellipsed VP in (10) is understood as *sara **mon** secré*, but the antecedent is *sara **vostre** secré*.

— *Pseudogapping*
(11) L'*ont* miex *ben'ie et sacree*
Que il n'**ont** une autre contree (Barb. & M., quoted in Tobler 1905: 135)
'They have blessed and sanctified it better than they have another land'

(12) Li fil ne *conoistra* le peire
Ne **fera** le fille la meire (Antéchrist, 13th century, quoted in T&L, under *faire*)
'The son will not recognize the father, nor will the daughter the mother'

(13) Nous li *avons valu* souvent; Aussi **avons** nous mainte gent
(Adenet le Roi, quoted in Tobler 1905: 135)
'We have defended her often; We have many other people too'

Examples (11)–(13) illustrate PG in OFr. Once again, we see the appearance of supportive *faire* as in (12), if the ellipsed V (*conoistra* in (12)) involves no auxiliary, and the appearance of the expected auxiliary otherwise, as in (11) and (13), where *ont* and *avons* appear for *ont ben'ie et sacree* and *avons valu* respectively.

Moignet (1974 [1960]) provides a discussion of the substitutive uses of *faire* of the types just given, arguing that *faire* should not be analysed as a grammatical morpheme, namely a pro-verb. Moignet thus fails to point out the clear syntactic parallels with *avoir* and *estre*, and the existence of a separate syntactic class of auxiliaries. In fact, he suggests that substitutive *faire* usage both in OFr and in ModFr is based on the semantic properties of *faire*, namely the fact that it expresses activity in the most general way (Moignet 1974 [1960]: 17, 31). This is a problem, however, since the semantic constraints on substitution by *faire* in ModFr, which can be understood on the basis of this idea (cf. section 5 below), clearly do not apply in OFr. For instance, non-agentive verbs like *souffrir*, *savoir* and *connaître*, for which *faire* substitutes in examples (7), (10) and (12) above, do not allow substitution by *faire* in ModFr. These facts force Moignet (1974 [1960]: 8) to claim that *faire* was more 'subductive' (i.e. had a more general meaning) in OFr than in ModFr, an idea for which there is no evidence independent of the fact that it could replace any verb but the auxiliaries *avoir* and *estre*.

Furthermore, Moignet clearly mischaracterizes the syntactic conditions on substitutive *faire*, claiming that it is restricted to comparative contexts except in the *si/non faire* construction (discussed below in section 3), and when *faire* is accompanied by the object pronoun *le* (cf. Martin & Wilmet 1980: § 322, for a similar statement for MFr). Moignet does mention the *aussi/autresi faire* construction, claiming that it has the same meaning as ModFr *en faire autant*. But it is not clear whether he classifies these constructions as some sort of comparative or, if not, why he distinguishes them from a case of *faire* alone in a noncomparative context. Actually, it is clear that *aussi faire* is not an instance of main verb *faire*, since it does not exhibit the semantic restrictions on possible antecedents typically associated with the latter. For instance, example (14) has *aussi faire* with *savoir* as its antecedent.

(14) L'empereres *seut bien*, ossi **fist** ses consaus,
Que de Melens a Romme n'estoit pas kemins saus (T&L, under *aussi*)
The emperor knew well, also did his consuls,
that from M to R was not a safe route

Furthermore, the auxiliaries *avoir* and *estre* also enter into the same construction with *aussi/autresi*, as shown in (13) above (see T&L under *aussi* and *autresi* for further examples). Moreover, as examples (7), (8), (10) and (12) above show, it is simply not true that substitutive *faire* without *le* is limited to comparatives and to the above-mentioned constructions. Such examples do not appear to be especially rare: there are four occurrences in T&L under *faire* as 'verbum vicarium' (including (7) and (12)) and two in Foulet (1972 [1919]: 236) (including (8)). It is not clear why comparative contexts favour PG in both ModE and OFr and MFr, but it is patently not the case that PG is restricted to such contexts.

The VPE and PG constructions discussed here, limited to the three verbs *avoir*, *estre* and *faire*, provide strong evidence for the existence of a syntactically distinct class of auxiliaries in OFr and MFr, with properties very similar to those of ModE auxiliaries (note however that there are no modal auxiliaries in OFr and MFr). Given this similarity, it is clear that the type of analysis sketched in section 1 for VPE and PG in ModE, based on the idea that auxiliaries can function as pro-predicates, can be immediately extended to these OFr and MFr data.

3 *Si/non* + AUX and *ce* + AUX + *mon*

In this section, I discuss two other constructions which are restricted to the verbs *avoir*, *estre* and *faire*, further supporting the notion that they form a specific syntactic subclass of auxiliary verbs. These are the *si/non* + *faire/estre/avoir* and *ce* + *faire/estre/avoir* + *mon* constructions. Henceforth I will refer to these as the *si/non* + AUX and *ce* + AUX + *mon* constructions, on the basis of the generalization established in the preceding section. The *si* + AUX construction, and the related *non* + AUX construction are discussed extensively in Marchello-Nizia (1985, cf. especially pp. 65–70, 116–33 and 211–16). In the first of these, *si* connects two clauses C1 and C2. The second clause C2 may not be negative. C1 may either be positive (this is what Marchello-Nizia calls the '*si faire* de reprise') as in (15), (16) and (18) or C1 may be negative and/or interrogative (this is what Marchello-Nizia calls the '*si faire* marqueur d'inversion') as in (17). (16) and (17) respectively illustrate the *si+estre* and *si+avoir* constructions. In all cases, *si* must immediately precede the auxiliary. In (15), (16) and (17), *fist*, *ert* and *as* respectively substitute for the whole italicized VP. Once again the syntax of this construction is remarkably similar to VPE in ModE, as the glosses show. In (18), we have a PG type variant of the *si* + AUX construction, where *fai* substitutes for *hais*, and is followed by the direct object *leur lignage tout*.

(15) *Del dol s'asist* la medre *jus a terre*,
 Si **fist** la 'spose dan Alexis   (Vie de saint Alexis, 1050–1100, T&L, *faire*)
 'The mother sat on the ground because of her pain,
 So did the wife of Sire Alexis'

(16) S'ele ot peor, ne l'en blasmez,
 qu'ele cuida qu'il *fust pasmez*
 Si **ert** il,... (Chrétien de Troyes, ±1180, quoted in MN, p. 119)
 'If she was scared, don't blame her for it,
 for she thought that he was unconcious.
 Indeed he was, ...'

(17) Certes ge ne pans ne ne croi
 que ge *onques mes vos veïsse*
 ne rien nule vos meisfeïsse.
 —Si **as**, fet ele,... (Chrétien de Troyes, ±1185, quoted in MN, p. 123)
 'Certainly, I don't think or believe
 that I ever saw you
 nor did anything bad to you.
 — You have so, she said, ...'

(18) 'Je *hais* mout ses louveaus et dout,
 Si **fai** je leur lignage tout, ...'
 (Philippe de Novare, ±1230, quoted in MN, p. 117)
 '"I hate his wolf-pups very much and, so do I their whole lineage"'

The *si* + AUX 'de reprise' construction appears to have a very similar discourse function to the *so* + AUX + subject construction in ModE, and the *si* + AUX 'marqueur d'inversion' appears similar to the subject + AUX + *so* construction in ModE, as the glosses of the above examples show. The PG type examples, illustrated in (18), appear to be rarer than the VPE type, (18) being the only instance found in T&L under *si*, and in MN. Note that the parallel construction in English is also rarer, though attested (e.g. '"I adore you." — "So do I you", said Jenny' — Visser § 583).

As discussed by Marchello-Nizia (1985: 131), the *si* + AUX construction is incompatible with negative *ne*. Examples like (19) are impossible. Instead, the *non* + AUX construction, illustrated in (20)–(22) appears (see T&L under *non* and Moignet 1973: 274–6 for numerous examples). As the glosses reveal, this construction is similar in meaning and discourse function to the subject + AUX + *not* construction in English.

(19) 'Je vous jur que vostre secré...
 Nul ne sara.'
 — *'Ne si par moi ja ne fera.' (MN, p. 131, cf. (10) above)

(20) 'Tu as *vëu* [...] *les anges* [...]'
 —'Non **ai**, voir, mere [...]' (T&L under *non*)
 ' "You have seen the angels." —"I have not, truly, mother." '

(21) 'Dame, c'est mesire Gavains!' —'Non **est**!' (T&L under *non*)
 ' "Lady, it is sire G!" — "It is not!" '

(22) 'Car *retornons en France* ..!' —'Non **ferons**' [...] (T&L under *non*)
 ' "Let us return to France!" — "We shall not" [...] '

Let us now turn to the *ce* + AUX + *mon* construction. The use of this construction is revealingly described in the following passage, from an early fifteenth-century French manual for English speakers, partially quoted by Marchello-Nizia (1979: 254) (cf. T&L under *mon* for numerous examples):

Oultre scachez que quant vous vouldrez o[trier ou] nier ce que un aultre a dit, donc il vous fault escouter que est son verbe, se il soit cest verbe *je suis* ou cest verbe *je ay* ou un aultre quelque il soit; car s'il soit cest verbe *je suis*, ou *je ay* tu respondra[s] par le mesmes verbe. Mais s'il soit un aultre verbe, donques tu respondras par cest verbe *je feis, tu feis*. Et tousjours tu mettras devant le verbe cest mot *ce* et apres le verbe cest mot *mon*, sicome es cestz exemples *le meistre est en la escolle*, tu respondras ottroiant *ce est mon* ou nient *ce n'est mon*, aussi *les disciples sont ove le meistre* tu respondras *ce sont mon* ou *ce ne sont mon*, aussi *le meistre a belcoup d'argent* tu respondra[s] *ce a mon* ou *ce ne a mon*, aussi *nous avons bonnes regles* tu respondras *ce avez mon* ou *ce ne avez mon*, aussi *le meistre nous ensaigne bien* tu respondras *ce fait mon* ou *ce ne fait mon*, aussi *mes compaignons apreinnent bien* tu respondras *ce font mon* ou *ce ne font mon* et aussi par toutz les autres verbes. ('Donait francois', in Stengel 1879: 32, partially cited in Marchello-Nizia 1979: 254).[2]

Once again, the similar distribution of the verbs *avoir*, *estre* and *faire* supports their status as a separate syntactic subclass. This specific construction is also clearly based on the status of the auxiliaries as pro-predicates, and the analysis sketched above in section 1 can be extended to account for it. It should be noted that I have found no cases of the *ce* + AUX + *mon* construction of the PG type (i.e. where the auxiliary has a subcategorized complement) in T&L or other sources for OFr and MFr. However, this is probably a random consequence of the selections presented by T&L since such examples can be found in sixteenth century French: cf. below, example (27).

4 Diachronic development of the auxiliaries

Further evidence that the OFr and MFr constructions discussed in the preceding sections are all based on a single property distinguishing the auxiliary verbs *avoir*, *estre* and *faire* from other verbs can be found in the diachronic development of these constructions. It appears indeed that all of these constructions disappeared together during the sixteenth and seventeenth centuries, leading to the ModFr situation where *faire* is no longer an auxiliary, and where *avoir* and *être* function in ways that are completely different from those described above (see, e.g., Abeillé & Godard 1994a, b, for discussion of the situation in ModFr). Specifically, they no longer license VPE.[3] Although serious corpus-based research would be required to establish the details of these developments, a preliminary sketch can be made on the basis of secondary sources such as Huguet (1925–73; henceforth Huguet), Marchello-Nizia (1979, 1985), Moignet (1974 [1960]), as well as a preliminary investigation of the usage of *faire* in Montaigne's *Essais*, based on the concordance of Leake (1981).

In Montaigne's *Essais*, substitutive *faire* continues to appear in comparatives with an apparently unconstrained range of subcategorization frames, and no semantic restrictions on substitution. Outside of comparative contexts, substitutive *faire* can appear accompanied by *le, si, aussi, de même*... The construction *le faire* will be discussed in section 5. As for the others, the following points should be made. According to Marchello-Nizia (1985: 212), the *si* + AUX construction disappears during the sixteenth and early seventeenth centuries, and is replaced by *aussi* + AUX. It appears from Montaigne's *Essais*, and from the examples given in Huguet under *faire*, that the *faire* of *aussi faire* and *si faire* is still an auxiliary, and that it still functions in parallel with *estre* and *avoir*. Almost all cases of *aussi faire* have subcategorized complements that would be impossible for *(le) faire* in ModFr, and are apparently also impossible for *le faire* in Montaigne's *Essais*. Furthermore, there are no semantic restrictions on substitution in the *aussi/si faire* construction. The following examples illustrate these points. (23) also shows that *si faire* and *aussi faire* are in a paraphrastic relation.

(23) S'il [l'homme] me [un oison] *mange*, aussi **faict** il bien l'homme son compaignon, et si **fay**-je moy les vers qui le tuent et qui le mangent
(PG, Montaigne, Essais)
'If he [man] eats me [a little bird], he also does man his companion, and I do the worms that kill and eat him'

(24) Nous *en* avions bien aultrefoys *refusé de bon argent* de ceulx de Londres et Cahors, si **avions** nous de ceulx de Bourdeaulx en Brye
(PG, Rabelais, quoted in Huguet vol. 6, p. 789, under si)
'We had formerly refused some in good silver from those from L&C, and so had we from those of B en B'

(25) Comme les ames vicieuses sont *incitées souvent* à bien faire *par quelque impulsion estrangère*, aussi **sont** les vertueuses à faire mal
(PG, Montaigne, Essais)
'Just as vicious souls are often pushed to do good by some external impulsion, so are virtuous [souls] [pushed] to do wrong'

(26) —*Partez d'icy, et me rendez mes patenostres*... —Non **feray**, par mon sergent   (Rabelais, quoted in Huguet vol. 4, p. 17, under *faire*)
'Go away from here, and give me back my rosaries ...
—I will not, by my servant'

The *ce* + AUX + *mon* construction also persists through the sixteenth century; see Huguet under *mon* for numerous examples. The example given in (27) is one of those of the PG type, where the auxiliary has a direct object (*ceulx qui veulent entreprendre sur mon authorité*).

(27) Vrayement, syre Agesilaus, tu sçais tres bien comment il fault ravaller tes amis. — Ce **fais** mon, respondit Agesilaus, ceulx qui veulent entreprendre sur mon authorité (Amyot, quoted in Huguet, vol. 5, p. 310)
'"Truly, sire Agesilaus, you know quite well how to put down your friends. I do indeed, replied Agesilaus, those who want to question my authority"'

This system seems to disintegrate during the seventeenth century. Examples of all the above constructions can still be found as shown in (28)–(32), but it is clear that they are rarer. It is probably not due to chance that the only example with *non, si* or *aussi* and auxiliary *être* quoted in grammars of seventeenth century French, namely (30), is from La Fontaine's *Contes*, which are known for their archaistic style. The most robust construction type is substitution by *faire* in comparatives, with *faire* clearly keeping its auxiliary status, inheriting the complement types of its antecedent, and without semantic restrictions on the latter. Haase (1930 [1898]: 170) describes this construction as 'd'un usage courant'.[4] A classic example is (32).

(28) Si le plaisir *me fuit*, aussi **fait** le sommeil
(Malherbe, quoted in Lerch 1925: 130)
'If pleasure flees from me, so does sleep'

(29) N'ai-je *jamais vu personne qui se soit tué soi-même*? Si **ai**
(Malherbe, quoted in Haase 1930 [1898]: 237)
'Have I never seen someone who has killed himself? I have indeed'

(30) Serait-il *dit que vous m'eussiez vaincu/D'honnêteté*? non **sera**, sur mon âme (La Fontaine, quoted in Haase 1930 [1898]: 248)
'Would it be said that you had conquered me with honesty? It shall not, by my soul'

(31) On pensera peut-être que je *craigne les antagonistes*. Non **fais**
(Malherbe, quoted in Haase 1930 [1898]: 248)
'One may think that I fear opponents. I do not'

(32) On *regarde* une femme savante comme on **fait** une belle arme: elle est ciselée artistement d'une polissure admirable
(La Bruyère, quoted in Haase 1930 [1898]: 170)
'One looks at a blue stocking as one does a beautiful weapon: [...]'

As for the construction with *mon*, it is rare in the seventeenth century (see Haase 1930 [1898]: 237).

The result of the evolution just sketched is the disappearance of the syntactic class of auxiliaries in seventeenth-century French, resulting in the loss of grammatical morpheme status as pro-predicate for *faire* as well as for *être* and *avoir*. This led to the modern situation where *avoir* and *être* no longer function as pro-predicates and where all the remaining substitutive constructions involving *faire* are based on main verb *faire*, to which we turn in the next section.

5 Auxiliary versus main verb *faire*

In this section, I argue that main verb *faire* has functioned as a substitute verb since the OFr period. I show that such constructions are quite similar to *do so/it/that* in ModE, which similarly involve main verb *do*, rather than the auxiliary. Until the sixteenth to seventeenth centuries, this usage was paralleled by substitutive uses of auxiliary *faire*, just as ModE has both auxiliary *do* (VPE, PG) and main verb *do* (*do so/it/that*) in substitutive uses. After the seventeenth century, only main verb *faire* remains as a substitute.

Two main properties distinguish substitution by main verbs *faire* and *do* from substitution by auxiliaries. The first is that there are semantic restrictions on possible antecedents. Substitution by main verbs *faire* and *do* is based on their very general semantic content: they can substitute for any verb of which they are a hyperonym, that is, any verb with a more specific but compatible meaning. This leads to a semantic constraint on predicates for which *faire* and *do* can substitute, which can be broadly characterized as requiring agentivity (a detailed lexical semantic analysis of this constraint remains to be carried out). Thus, substitution by main verbs *faire* and *do* is based on the same type of semantic relation as that which allows one to use *the animal* to refer back to the entity designated by *the cat* in a discourse like *The cat ran into the attic. The animal was in a furious rage.* (see Miller 1992: 96).[5] These properties are illustrated in the following examples where the parallelism between French and English is evident.

(33) a. Marie regarde Paul et Anne le fait aussi/fait de même/en fait autant
   b. Marie is looking at Paul and Anne is doing it too/is doing so too/is doing the same

(34) a.##Marie voit Paul et Anne le fait aussi/fait de même/en fait autant
   b.##Marie sees Paul and Anne is doing it too/is doing so too/is doing the same

This situation contrasts clearly with that of auxiliaries *faire* and *do*, which, as pointed out in examples above, can substitute for such non-agentive predicates as *connaître/savoir/know* and *souffrir/suffer*.

The second property which distinguishes substitutive uses of main verbs *faire* and *do* from substitution by auxiliaries is that they do not allow certain types of complementation, notably direct objects. When these verbs must be followed by an argument corresponding semantically to the direct object of the antecedent verb, the latter appears as an indirect object, with the prepositions *à*, *de*, *pour* or *avec* in French, and *to*, *with* or *for* in English. It should be noted that the choice of the preposition is related to the type of semantic role assigned to the corresponding complements with those prepositions in nonsubstitutive uses of main verbs *faire* and *do* (cf. Miller 1990, 1992). This is illustrated in the following examples.

(35) Elle admire Paul comme on (le) ferait d'un/pour un frère aîné
   'She admires Paul as one would do (it) of one's older brother'

(36) Mary covered Ann with sunscreen and then Ann did it to/for her.

A preliminary investigation of the history of the substitutive uses of main verb *faire*, based principally on the data of Moignet (1974 [1960]), and on T&L shows the following. The expressions *le faire, faire ce, faire autel, faire autretel, faire autretant* all involve main verb *faire*. What these expressions have in common is that they include a direct object (*le, ce, autel, autretel, autretant*). An immediate consequence of this is that they are never followed by a second direct object, corresponding to the direct object of the antecedent. In such cases these expressions either are not used, or are used with a prepositional object similarly to (35) in ModFr (cf. Moignet 1974 [1960]: 27, note 9, for examples of this type with *faire autel* and *faire ce*). Further evidence that we are dealing with main verb *faire* comes from the fact that the examples in Moignet and in T&L (under *autel, autretel, autretant, faire*) satisfy the semantic constraints on substitution by main verb *faire*, and sound fine when translated into ModFr with a substitutive use of main verb *faire*. Among these expressions, *le faire* subsists into ModFr, and expressions like *en faire autant* and *faire de même* (cf. (33)) appear, replacing the others.

6 Conclusion

The study reported in this chapter of the substitutive uses of *faire* in the history of French, and of the related constructions involving the auxiliaries *avoir* and *estre*, leads us to the conclusion that there has been a complete reanalysis in the status of these three verbs during the sixteenth and seventeenth centuries. Specifically, before then, *avoir, estre* and *faire* formed a syntactically distinct subcategory of auxiliary verbs, which could function as pro-predicates. Subsequently, these possibilities disappear, and only the substitutive uses of *faire* as a main verb remain.

As discussed above, the syntax and semantics of the auxiliaries *avoir, estre* and *faire* in OFr and MFr had much in common with that of the ModE auxiliaries, namely with respect to the VP-Ellipsis and Pseudogapping constructions. The fact that these two constructions coexist in OFr and MFr and disappear simultaneously indirectly supports the idea that they are in fact both dependent on a single property of auxiliaries, namely their ability to function as pro-predicates with translations involving a variable which is a function to a VP type. As discussed in section 1, the common properties exhibited here between the OFr and MFr auxiliaries and those of ModE could be accounted for under a more GB-like analysis involving an empty category verbal complement of the auxiliaries.

One property which distinguishes auxiliary *do* in ModE from its counterpart in OFr is the absence of *do*-support in questions and negatives. However, this follows immediately from other well established syntactic differences between English and French, namely the fact that all verbs can be inverted in French (can move to Infl and then to Comp in the terminology of Chomsky 1986 and Pollock 1989), contrary to what is the case in

English where this is only possible for the auxiliaries. Under the assumption that *do/faire*-support occurs whenever there is no verb in a required position to support inflectional marking, then we automatically account for the complete set of data. In OFr and MFr, this only happens in cases of verbal ellipsis, namely the VPE and PG type constructions discussed here. But in ModE, the impossibility of movement for main verbs triggers *do*-support in questions and negatives.

Finally, to the extent that the data discussed here support the position that VPE and PG are in fact the same construction, they argue against a difference in the constituent structure attachment of subcategorized complements and adjuncts, as discussed in Miller (1992: 63ff). Indeed, the most central criterion for this distinction, namely the impossibility for a subcategorized complement to appear after a VPE site turns out not to be valid since clearly subcategorized complements can appear in that position, as shown by the PG examples.

Notes

*   I would like to thank Annick Englebert for her help in interpreting OFr examples, and for comments on a preliminary draft of parts of this chapter. She is obviously in no way responsible for any remaining misinterpretations. I would also like to thank Danièle Godard, Dan Hardt, Ans van Kemenade and Nigel Vincent for discussion. This chapter was presented as a paper at the 24th LSRL, Los Angeles, 1994. I would like to thank Rich Janda and Nigel Vincent for comments following the presentation.
1. As pointed out to me by Nigel Vincent (p.c.), Orr (1962: 19, 61–3) notes the parallelism between uses of *faire* as 'verbum vicarium' in OFr and ModE uses of *do*. However, Orr does not point out that the properties he discusses extend to the whole class of OFr auxiliaries. In any case, it is clear that the consequences of these data are not established in standard grammars of OFr and MFr, e.g. Foulet (1972 [1919]), Moignet (1973), Ménard (1973), Marchello-Nizia (1979), Martin & Wilmet (1980).
2. '[...] when you want to accept or reject what another person has said, you must listen for his verb, checking whether it is *estre*, *avoir* or any other verb. If it is *estre* or *avoir*, you will respond by the same verb. But if it is any other verb, you will respond with the verb *faire*. In all cases, you are to put the word *ce* before the verb and the word *mon* after the verb as in the following examples: The teacher is in the school / he is indeed / he is not; The students are with the teacher / they are indeed / they are not; The teacher has a lot of money / he has indeed / he has not; We have good rules / you have indeed / you have not; The teacher teaches us well / he does indeed / he does not; My schoolmates learn well / they do indeed / they do not...'
3. I have no definite proposal to make here as to the exact nature of the change that took place, specifically as to whether it was essentially a semantic change (the loss of the predicate-variable semantics for the auxiliaries discussed in section 1) or whether this change in fact depends on a syntactic reanalysis. One hypothesis in the latter perspective is that the change is related to the absence of the VP constituent in ModFr, as evidenced in Abeillé & Godard (1994a, b). In order to establish the validity of this hypothesis, it would be necessary to show that the set of data they present supporting the absence of VP in ModFr did in fact first appear at the time of the disappearance of the propredicate uses of *avoir* and *être*, and that earlier states of the language did in fact show evidence of the existence of a VP according to their tests.
4. For reasons that are not clear, after the disappearance of all the other constructions discussed, substitutive *faire* in comparative clauses followed by a direct object continues

to appear even into the twentieth century (qualified correctly by Moignet 1974 [1960]: 27 as 'une élégance archaïsante'). However, it appears that under these conditions *faire* is no longer capable of substituting for verbs which are non-agentive, leading me to believe that these examples are a marked remnant of the preceding system with *faire* reanalysed as the main verb (cf. section 5), rather than a real usage of auxiliary *faire*. Specifically, among eighteen literary examples quoted by Eriksson (1985: 151–2), all the antecedents satisfy the semantic constraints on substitution by main verb *faire*. A detailed study of the evolution of this construction between the seventeenth and twentieth century remains to be carried out, in order to verify this hypothesis.

5. Main verb and auxiliary *do* in English are further distinguished by their behaviour with respect to *do*-support, and in certain dialects by differences in their inflectional paradigms, as pointed out to me by Rich Janda (p.c.) (cf., for instance, Trudgill 1994: 47). It would be interesting to see if there are any similar distinctions in the inflectional paradigms of auxiliary and main verb *faire* in dialects of OFr or MFr.

5 Commentary on part 1: aspect, argument structure and case selection

Alessandra Tomaselli

This part consists of four contributions, two of which deal with the rise of the article in the Germanic (Gmc) languages, the other two with the morpho-syntactic status of 'functional' verbs. Even if the authors start from different perspectives and arrive at partially different results, it is possible to compare and contrast them on the basis of two facts: the data discussed are homogeneous, the theoretical framework which the authors explicitly refer to is that of generative grammar. The only exception is represented by Philip Miller's work on auxiliary verbs in Old and Middle French, which is developed in the framework of Head Driven Phrase Structure Grammar. Nevertheless, as Miller notes, the results arrived at within an explicit and formal model of grammar are in principle 'translatable in generative terms' with mutual interest.

In order to arrive at a comparative and contrastive discussion of how the papers deal with analytic and diachronic issues, let us start with a brief synthesis of the first two contributions both dealing with the rise of the definite (/indefinite) article in Gmc languages.

W. Abraham's paper represents an interesting and successful proposal to explain Leiss' (1991) observations within a specific module of generative grammar, i.e. Case Theory. Following Leiss, Abraham assumes that the rise of the definite article correlates on the one hand with the decay of overt aspectual morphology, on the other hand with the process of nominal deflection and the consequent loss of the opposition between accusative and verbal genitive. First of all, Abraham observes that the [±definite] character of the object NP in Old High German (OHG) was the result of the mutual interplay between aspectual morphology and case morphology in a way similar to the system of Russian and other modern Slavic languages:

(1)   a. the genitive NP governed by a terminative/perfective verb always had a [−definite] reading;
     b. the accusative NP governed by a terminative/perfective verb always had a [+definite] reading;

c. the accusative NP governed by an imperfective/durative verb allowed both a [−definite] and a [+definite] reading (contrary to Russian where just the [−definite] reading is allowed).

This allows the following correlations:

(2) a. the accusative-genitive opposition was crucial for the [±definite] reading of the NP governed by the class of terminative/perfective verbs.
   b. the accusative-genitive opposition presented a double asymmetry: only accusative NPs combined with both perfective and durative verbs; only accusative morphology allowed both a [+definite] and a [−definite] reading of the NP. In contrast, verbal genitive never combined with durative verbs and never allowed a [+definite] reading of the object NP.

It is important to note that Abraham's analysis does not take into account the possessive genitive; hence, the crucial opposition that he draws between the notion of 'verbal' versus 'partitive' genitive always refers to the verbal argument. Verbal genitive is selected by the verbal subcategorization, partitive genitive is assigned according to a selectional feature, i.e. [−countable], provided by the head of the NP.

In order to analyse this complex case system, Abraham adopts an articulated structure of DP which allows for two different Case positions (much in the spirit of Uriagereka 1992b and Philippi & Weerman 1993) — cf. diagram (45) on p. 52:

(3)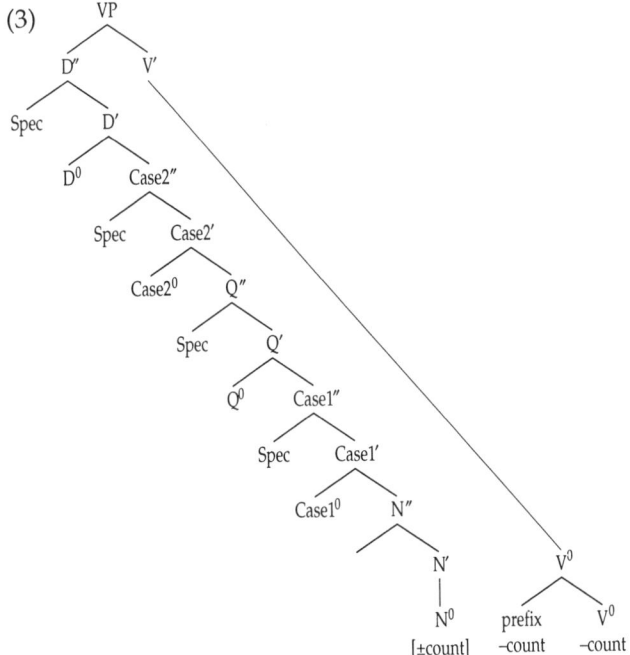

The [−count] feature of N^0 selects partitive genitive which is realized in the lower case Projection (Case1). The V-governed cases (such as the accusative and the verbal genitive??) are realized in the higher case Projection (Case2).

In MHG and pre-Modern German the higher case position emerged as the [+definite] position reserved for accusative NPs and the lower case position emerged as a [−definite] position reserved for both partitive and verbal genitive. The former selected by a feature of the nominal head, the latter obtained through a copy(/transfer) mechanism which crucially involved the aspectual prefix — cf. XP in (41).

After aspectual marking disappeared, genitive lost its status as opposed to the accusative (and prepositionally) marked objects. The loss of the accusative–genitive opposition had the following results in the case system:

(4) a. verbal genitive marking 'disappeared' (i.e. it was no longer a productive mechanism);
 b. genitive 'survived' as the case selected by the [−countable] nominal head (partitive genitive);
 c. accusative case marking acquired structural status, i.e. it implied movement to the specifier position of an Agreement Phrase.

Furthermore, the definite/indefinite reading of the object NP could no longer be obtained through the interplay between case opposition and aspectual conditions. This interplay weakened and finally disappeared completely; in its place, the determiner category was lexically filled, first with the definite and later with the indefinite article.

Abraham's analysis of the rise of the article in the Gmc languages is based on two fundamentally speculative assumptions.

First of all he assumes that the rise of two different article forms (definite versus indefinite) is 'foreseen' by the specialization of two functional case Projections: a higher one which qualifies for [+def] objects and a lower one which qualifies for [−def] objects. Second, he explains the delay which characterizes the rise of the indefinite article in the following terms: (a) the definite article arising from the demonstrative use of the homonymic determiner never changed its structural position (i.e. Spec,DP); (b) the indefinite article arose from a process of lexical disambiguation between the cardinal 'one' and an independent lexeme 'a(n)'. This process crucially involved both a categorial and structural change: the cardinal 'one' is an XP in the domain of QP (cf. (1)) while the indefinite article qualifies as the lexical head of DP.

Julia Philippi's analysis of 'The rise of the article in the Germanic languages' attributes a central role to the definite/indefinite (or specific/non-specific) distinction which she directly relates to the notion of referentiality. Given the hypothesis that the article acts as a reference marker for the NP, its rise (/evolution) in the history of Gmc languages is explained in the following terms:

(5) a. in the older Gmc languages the definite/indefinite distinction relies on case opposition. Genitive case identifies indefinite/predicative (existential) NPs, accusative case identifies definite/referential objects;
b. in the late MHG and ME periods the verbal genitive decays and is gradually replaced by accusative NP and PP. It is therefore no longer possible to identify the reference of the object NP by different case markings;
c. the demonstrative, formerly a purely emphatic element severely restricted by context, spreads considerably and is finally reanalysed as the new referential marker for the noun phrase. Referring to Uriagereka (1992b), Philippi assumes the following analysis (her (74)):

(6) a. Pre-article stage   b. Modern Germanic languages

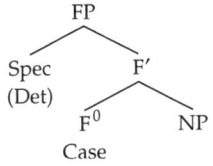
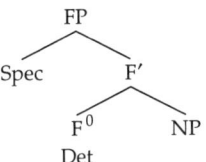

In (6a) F^0 is occupied by case such that the determiner in Spec,FP may only act as a redundant reference marker which is only allowed in emphatic contexts. In (6b) the emphatic determiner is reanalysed as the functional head of FP. In this position it takes over the function of specifying the referential interpretation of the noun phrase.

While Philippi's notion of definite object directly corresponds to referential or strong NP, the notion of indefinite object directly corresponds to predicative (existential) or weak NP. The opposition between strong and weak NP is first defined in logical–semantic terms by the author (who refers, among others, to Barwise & Cooper 1981, Higginbotham 1987 and Diesing 1992) and then translated in syntactic terms as follows:

Strong objects are always DPs. The function of specifying the referential interpretation of the NP is carried out either by the definite article in D^0 or by a strong quantifier (such as *all* and *most*) in Spec,DP, which is co-indexed by Spec–head agreement with an abstract feature in D^0 (cf. her (9)):

(7) a.   b.

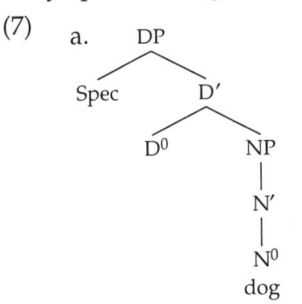
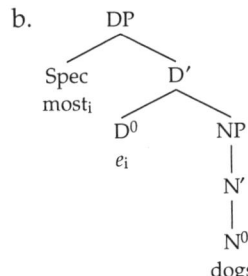

Weak objects are always NPs in that weak determiners such as *some* and *many* (including the indefinite article) are not realized in D^0, but rather occupy an adjective-like position, namely Spec,NP (with reference to Hudson 1989; Zwart 1992):

(8)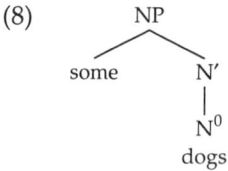

The hypothesis that strong and weak objects have radically different structures correlates with their differential syntactic behaviour. Philippi observes that only strong objects may be scrambled (moved to Spec,Agr_OP). In contrast, weak objects must remain *in situ* (i.e. within VP). This difference is accounted for by a revised version of the 'Mapping hypothesis' (cf. Diesing 1992).

The preceding brief and (needless to say) incomplete summaries have already implicitly brought to light both the main differences and the common assumptions of the first two contributions of this part. Let us start with the results on which the two analyses converge:

(9) a. both authors assume that the loss of the genitive–accusative opposition was crucial for the rise of the definite article;
   b. the referential status of the object NP plays a relevant role in both analyses even if the two authors start from different perspectives. Philippi takes the notion of referentiality as a kind of primitive; Abraham considers the [±definite] reading of the object NPs as the result of the interplay of different factors (i.e. aspectual and case morphology);
   c. the structural position of indefinite NP is lower than that reserved for definite NP. Abraham assumes that genitive NP occurs in the lower case Projection (CaseP1, cf. (3) above); Philippi assumes that the structure of weak objects (including indefinite NPs) lacks a DP projection (cf. (7a) versus (8)). In any case both authors assume that genitive is assigned *in situ* either as a lexical process (Abraham) or as a default case (Philippi). Genitive NP occupies a position 'close to the verbal head' and movement out of VP (to Spec,AgrP) is explicitly excluded.

The main differences between the two analyses in question emerge with respect to the following points: the attention attributed to the evolution of the indefinite article form and the role assigned to aspectual morphology.

(10) a. Abraham explicitly assumes that the indefinite article qualifies as a lexical head which occurs in D^0 and attributes the delay in its evolution to a process of lexical and categorial disambiguation. Philippi's position is rather different in that she assumes that weak

determiners occupy an adjective-like position, namely Spec,NP (cf. (8) above). The fact that the indefinite article emerged later than the definite one does not play any role in her account.

b. The decay of aspectual morphology is analysed in radically different terms by the two authors. Abraham assumes that it is the verbal aspectual morphology (as well as the object preposition) that triggers referential definiteness on the governed object-NP. In this respect aspectual morphology directly correlates with case morphology. Recall that in Abraham's system the accusative–genitive opposition is characterized by a double asymmetry (2b). In particular he observes that:

c. accusative case implied a definite reading of the object NP only if it was governed by a perfective verb;

d. the accusative object governed by a durative/imperfective verb in OHG allowed both an indefinite and a definite reading.

Contrary to Abraham, Philippi regards the role played by verbal aspect as incidental (cf. section 3.2 in her contribution). First of all Philippi suggests a theory of aspect which is purely semantic in nature. In fact the case–aspect correlation in OHG is explained in the following terms:

(11) a. genitive objects, which refer to noncountable entities, cannot measure out the event denoted by VP. As a consequence, VP acquires an atelic interpretation even if the verb itself denotes a telic event;

b. accusative objects refer to countable entities. A VP containing an accusative object is delimited as a whole and therefore is interpreted as a telic event.

In the second place her account is in contradistinction with Abraham's assumption that accusative NP governed by a durative (atelic) verb allowed both a definite and an indefinite reading. This contradiction could only be resolved by considering the primary data in detail. Unfortunately the only pertinent example I was able to find in Abraham's contribution is not conclusive; cf. his (13), here reported as (12):

(12) ne mornont an iuuuomu môde, *huuat* gi eft an
 not worry in your spirit what-ACC you then in (the)
 morgan sculin etan eftho drinkan
 morning shall eat or drink

(OS, Heliand 1663)

Note that the indeterminate accusative object is a *wh*-pronoun rather than an 'ordinary' NP.

This inconclusiveness relates to a common feature of both Abraham's and Philippi's contributions. Neither of them has considered the primary data of Old Gmc. The data are taken either from traditional historical grammars (such as Behaghel, Delbrück, Erdmann) or from recent studies on the specific topic such as Donnhauser, Elst and Leiss. This fact leads to a specific choice among older Gmc pieces of literature. As for OHG, for example, it is interesting to note the large number of examples taken from Otfrid compared to the quite marginal role of Isidor, whose translation nevertheless represents the first original example of OHG prose (as already noted by Fourquet 1938 and confirmed in Tomaselli 1990). This observation should not be interpreted as a criticism but rather as a suggestion for further research.

Some final remarks are reserved for the relevance of these two diachronic studies with respect to the general theory of grammar. Note first of all that in both Abraham's and Philippi's analyses it is assumed that a genitive NP receives case *in situ* and may not move out of VP to Spec,AgrP. This assumption poses an interesting question with respect to the Kayne/Zwart hypothesis of a universal VO order (cf. Kayne 1994 and Zwart 1992). In the data discussed by Abraham and Philippi, a genitive NP always shows up to the left of the finite verb in the relevant contexts. This fact, together with their common assumption that genitive NPs are assigned case *in situ* and never leave VP immediately suggests a head-final analysis of VP. Does this analysis of older Gmc languages present a potential counterargument to the hypothesis of a fixed head–complement order? In any case these results should be taken into account in the current debate (cf. Roberts, this volume; Donati-Tomaselli 1994).

A second question concerns the structural position of the definite article in Gmc languages. Philippi makes the orthodox assumption that the definite article occupies the head of DP (cf. (7a)); Abraham on the other hand assumes that the definite article occurs in Spec,DP. Is it possible to provide any argument in favour of Abraham's strong hypothesis? Is it reasonable to relate this potential peculiarity of German(ic) determiners to the diachronic evolution of lexical Comp V-2 languages? The subordinating conjunction also evolved out of the lexical and categorial disambiguation of the demonstrative pronoun.

Regardless of possible answers, these questions show beyond any doubt the relevance of the results emerging from diachronic studies within the generative framework.

Let us now turn to the two contributions concerned with the morphosyntactic status of functional verbs and their diachronic evolution.

Benincà & Poletto successfully show how the diachronic development of Italian *bisogna* (a modal verb of necessity) can be taken as an argument in favour of their fundamental hypothesis that verb syntax and morphology are determined in some of their aspects by the presence of a thematic grid. Their investigation through the history of Italian is based on the following texts:

(13) a. Boccaccio's *Decameron* (second half of the fourteenth century) and *Il Principe* by Macchiavelli (1513) for the first stage in the development of the Italian verb under investigation.

b. Galileo Galilei's *Dialogo sui massimi sistemi* (1632) represents the second intermediate stage.
c. Collodi's *Pinocchio* (1883) represents the modern stage.

The diachronic development of *bisogna* from a 'full' verb with a θ-grid to a modal verb of necessity can be sketched as follows:

(14) In the first stage *bisogna* has the following characteristics:
  a. it is a 'full' verb with two arguments: an experiencer and a theme;
  b. *bisogna* always agrees in person and number with the nominative NP (i.e., either the experiencer or the theme depending on specific conditions on case alternation);
  c. it can be inflected for all tenses;
  d. non-finite forms (past participle, gerund, infinitive) are attested.

Examples of impersonal *bisogna* (parallel to the modern usage) are also present in the corpus.

(15) In the second stage the impersonal/modal status of the verb is attested in the majority of examples. However, in a small group of examples *bisogna* still shows a behaviour which overlaps in part with the older usage. In this group *bisogna* takes a dative experiencer (always realized as a dative) and a nominative theme and we also find some instances of past participle.

(16) In the third stage *bisogna* always behaves as the modern modal verb of necessity:
  a. it lacks a θ-grid (i.e, no thematic role is assigned);
  b. it is always inflected for the third person singular;
  c. it selects either a CP with a subjunctive complement clause or an infinitival clause;
  d. it cannot be inflected for all tenses (simple past is not a possible form);
  e. non-finite forms are impossible;
  f. it cannot host clitics;
  g. subject raising out of the selected CP is barred.

Benincà & Poletto take the following fact as an argument in favour of their initial hypothesis: whenever *bisogna* occurred as an impersonal verb (i.e. in constructions without experiencer and theme), its morphosyntactic behaviour was parallel to the modern modal verb of necessity (cf. (16b–g) above).

In the final section of their contribution, the authors explain the morphosyntactic restrictions of modern *bisogna* on the basis of recent hypotheses proposed by Cinque (1993, 1994) which imply three distinct modal phrases in the structure of the sentence. More precisely the authors assume that:

(17) a. modal verbs of necessity like *bisogna* are directly inserted in the head of the lowest modal phrase (RootModP) — cf. their (20):

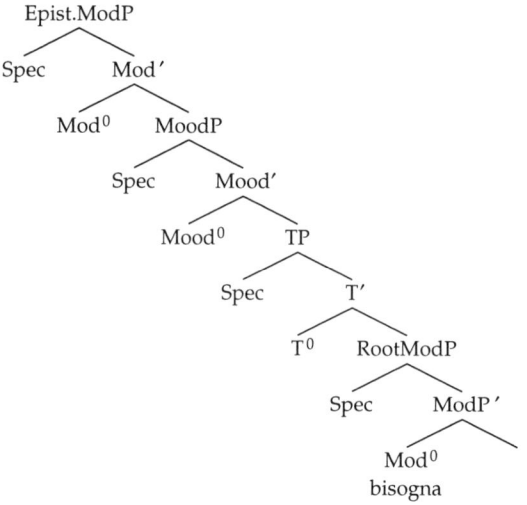

b. the lexicalization of this functional head is forced by a [+strong] feature which can only be satisfied by modal auxiliaries characterized by a 'deontic reading' of pure necessity; functional projections below (lower than) RootModP are 'inert'.
c. the lexicalization of the Root Modality head correlates with strong features in Mood^0;
d. the fact that *bisogna* does not assign any θ-role implies that no VP is projected in the structure.

The first three assumptions determine precise limitations in the temporal and aspectual paradigm (cf. (16d) and (16e) above).

The last assumption implies important consequences for both clitic and subject syntax. In fact Benincà & Poletto propose first of all the following descriptive generalization:

(18) A raising verb must have a θ-grid (cf. their (23)).

In other words, the lack of an internal argument (explicit or implicit) inhibits subject-raising in the *bisogna*-constructions. In the second place, the authors hypothesize that lack of a VP implies the lack of all Agr-Projections usually connected with VP. This should directly explain the fact that *bisogna* cannot host either a subject or an object clitic.

This short synthesis of Benincà & Poletto's contribution has underlined several aspects of their work that deserve some comment.

First of all it should be noted that this is the only contribution in this part that is based on an original diachronic investigation. The correlations established by the authors receive clear and systematic exemplification.

This fact allows an easier and more perspicuous interaction between the results of specific diachronic analyses and the theory of grammar.

If on the one hand the originality of the diachronic investigation leads to important, explicit generalizations, on the other hand the synchronic analysis of *bisogna* is strongly dependent on Cinque's theory and leaves some questions open. In fact, as Benincà & Poletto note (see their footnote 13), Cinque's approach to the functional structure of the sentence is essentially based on adverbial syntax and takes no account of the interaction between modal projections and agreement projections. This interaction plays an important role in the account of some morphosyntactic properties of Italian *bisogna*, first of all the fact that it is always inflected for the third person singular. Where is Agr_SP in *bisogna*-constructions? Benincà & Poletto suggest 'in a highly speculative vein' that an inactive Agr_SP must be located higher than VoiceP but lower than the Root Modality head. Does this exclude the assumption of an Agr_SP higher than RootModP?

A second question concerns the structural relation between *bisogna* and the selected CP. Since adverbs like *mica, più, già*, may intervene between *bisogna* and its clausal complement, Benincà & Poletto exclude the possibility that the selected CP occurs as the structural complement of the Root Modal head. Which kind of 'inert' lower functional head should then structurally govern the CP complement?

A third, final question concerns the generalization in (18). As we have already noted, Benincà & Poletto propose to derive the difference between *bisogna* and impersonal *sembra* 'it seems' in the following terms: *bisogna* lacks a θ-grid and thus disallows raising of the subject out of the selected CP:

(19) *Mario$_i$ bisogna t_i leggere
    Mario is-necessary to read

Impersonal *sembra* always assigns an (explicit or implicit) experiencer θ-role and thus subject-raising is allowed:

(20) Mario$_i$ (mi) sembra t_i leggere
    Mario (to me) seems   to read
    'It seems (to me) that Mario is reading'

If on the one hand the generalization in (18) seems to hold in the comparison between *bisogna* and impersonal *sembra*, on the other hand this generalization fails if we compare *bisogna* with copular constructions. In these constructions 'be' doesn't assign any θ-role (it lacks a θ-grid on a par with the Italian modal verb of necessity); nevertheless it allows subject-raising out of its small clause-complement (cf. Moro 1993, in press, and literature cited there):

(21) Mario$_i$ è [$_{SC}$ t_i intelligente]

The comparison between *bisogna* and copular constructions raises other interesting questions which deserve further research.

A final comment is reserved for the initial hypothesis on which Benincà & Poletto's contribution is based (cf. their Introduction, first paragraph):

... the loss of forms in a verbal paradigm is connected to the loss of certain semantic properties of the verb. The idea we have put forth is that a verb's syntax and morphology are determined in some respects by its thematic grid.

In their approach 'semantic properties' means 'θ-grid' and, in the specific case of *bisogna*, the lack of one. The authors' hypothesis that semantic properties determine morpho-syntactic properties should then be interpreted in the following terms (cf. their §5.3, last paragraph): 'functional and argumental structure go together: when there are arguments, all [verbal] forms are possible, when no argument appears to be selected by *bisogna*, only modal forms are found'. Note that, while this formulation is absolutely reasonable, the hypothesis of a causal relationship between semantics and syntax is simply beyond the scope of current generative theory. This contradiction relies on a general tendency within some recent generative studies to relate 'semantics' on the one hand with θ-grid/argument structure, on the other hand with the notion of 'referentiality' and its possible interpretation in the logical component of grammar (see, for example, the discussion of Philippi's contribution).

Note, however, that the notion 'θ-grid' is no more a semantic notion than θ-theory is a semantic theory. In other words, while the relationship between argument structure and morphology (i.e. the functional status of the verb) is illuminated by Benincà & Poletto, it is not obvious to me that argument structure/θ-grid is semantics.

As for the notion of 'referentiality' the situation is even more complex. Referentiality is indeed a purely semantic notion but its role in a syntactic theory is far from obvious and neither is its redefinition in terms of definiteness.

These observations raise major questions within the framework of generative grammar which go beyond the level of terminological correctness and deserve further reflection than this comment can offer (but see, for example, Chomsky 1993 and Graffi 1995).

Miller's contribution on auxiliary verbs in Old and Middle French focusses on the development of the verb *faire*. This development perfectly mirrors the history of Italian *bisogna*: *bisogna* develops from a 'full'/lexical verb to a functional verb (i.e. a modal verb of necessity), substitutive *faire* was a functional verb (i.e. an auxiliary verb) which 'survives' as a lexical verb.

In order to argue in favour of the hypothesis that Old and Middle French *faire* belonged to a distinct syntactic class of auxiliary verbs together with *avoir* and *estre*, Miller bases his analysis on the following pieces of evidence.

(22) a. In Old and Middle French *faire*, *avoir* and *estre* all allowed both VP-Ellipsis and Pseudogapping. When the ellipsed VP had no auxiliary verb, supportive *faire* appeared just as supportive *do* does in English; on the other hand, when the understood VP had an auxiliary *avoir* or *estre*, that auxiliary appeared.

b. In Old and Middle French *faire* together with *estre* and *avoir* could enter into two specific constructions, which the author defines as the *si/non* + AUX and *ce* + AUX + *mon* constructions.

All the constructions mentioned in (a) and (b) above seem to disappear together during the sixteenth and seventeenth centuries, leading to the Modern French situation where substitutive *faire* is no longer an auxiliary, and where *avoir* and *être* have differential syntactic behaviour: in particular, they no longer license VP-Ellipsis. This observation is adduced by Miller as a clear further argument in favour of his hypothesis.

It is important to remember that Miller bases the opposition between Old and Middle French AUXILIARY *faire* and the modern LEXICAL substitutive *faire* on the following facts.

On the one hand, contrary to Moignet, Miller shows that:

(23) a. Old and Middle French *faire* could substitute both agentive and NON-AGENTIVE verbs such as *souffrir*, *savoir* and *connaître*;
b. substitutive *faire* without *le* was not limited to comparative and *si/non faire* constructions.

On the other hand modern substitutive *faire* is subject to clear 'semantic' constraints (it expresses activity in the most general way and thus substitution of non-agentive verbs is disallowed). Furthermore, the expressions *le faire, faire ce, faire autel, faire autretel, faire autretant* all involve main verb *faire* and all include a direct object.

This last observation leads in the same direction as that pointed by Benincà & Poletto: when substitutive *faire* was a functional verb, it lacked a θ-grid of its own (it eventually took up the θ-grid of the ellipsed verb). On the contrary, modern substitutive *faire* is a lexical verb which always selects a direct object.

However, the possibility to extend Benincà & Poletto's analysis to the development of French *faire* has to be determined by further research. In particular, two points should be elaborated. First, the comparison with the English modal system has to be developed. While Miller establishes a clear correspondence between auxiliary *faire* in earlier French and auxiliary *do* in Modern English, Benincà & Poletto note some important differences between the Italian modal verb of necessity and English modal verbs. For example, English modals (parallel to Old and Middle French auxiliaries) seem to imply a monoclausal structure while Italian *bisogna* always selects a clausal complement (either a CP with a subjunctive complement clause or an infinitival clause). Second, the auxiliary status of Old and Middle French substitutive *faire* should be better defined with respect to the modern system of French auxiliaries. In fact, Miller does not provide any analysis for modern French *avoir* and *être*.

There are many topics to be put on the research agenda as the questions raised in the preceding discussion show. I do not want to repeat them here but a general comment is due. The mutual interplay between the results of diachronic investigations and the theory of grammar is of great interest. The relevance of this interplay strongly depends, at least for me, on two factors.

First of all, diachronic studies should provide clear and systematic collections of data. In this respect the interaction with philology is crucial.

Second, a specific theory of grammar can be tested on the basis of diachronic data only if that theory is taken holistically, with all its implications and consequences for synchronic analysis.

It is clear that these *desiderata* can be achieved only on the basis of specific research programmes, which should involve both 'general' and 'diachronically specialized' linguists.

Part 2
Clitics

6 The emergence of the D-system in Romance

Nigel Vincent

1 Introduction*

The close focus on functional categories which has characterized much recent research in generative grammar inevitably brings to mind, in a historical context, the traditional concern with so-called 'analytic' and 'synthetic' grammar and the diachronic relations between the two.[1] The categories that are of particular interest in the current generative work — notably D(eterminer), C(omplementizer) and I(nflection) and eventual splits thereof — are precisely the ones that are amply instantiated in all the modern Romance languages, but which play a limited role or are simply absent in Latin. The emergence of articles and clitic pronouns, the considerable extension in the use of verbal auxiliaries of various types and the changes in the complement system are all phenomena that are brought under the heading of 'analytic' innovations in Romance in the traditional grammars and manuals. In the present chapter, therefore, I wish to focus on one of these changes — the development of articles and clitic pronouns — and consider it in the light of the recent theoretical developments. The result will, I believe, be of relevance both to students of syntactic change in general and to Romance specialists in particular. I will argue, pretty uncontroversially it must be said (cf. Harris 1980b), that the developments in Romance of the two categories of article and clitic pronoun, neither of which were attested in Latin, are linked and that the assignment of both to the category D provides a natural way to incorporate this change into current thinking. More originally, I will argue that the different patterns of morphological realization of the third-person clitics (which always derive from Latin *ille*)[2] and the articles (sometimes from *ille* and sometimes from *ipse*) reflect two independent and convergent developments, one involving the verb–object relation and one the clause–subject relation. I will argue that these changes show the emergence in the historical period of a subject–object asymmetry that was not present in Latin. In other words, I will suggest that in the transition from Latin to Romance we are able to observe the evolution of a pattern of configurationality, and that the differential developments of *ille* and *ipse* constitute one of the overt signals of a typological re-organization of Latin into Romance syntax.

Before proceeding further a caveat is in order concerning the term 'clitic'. Throughout this paper it will be used to refer exclusively to the Romance elements such as French *me, te, se, le, la, lui, leur, en, y*, etc. and comparable items in the other languages of the family. These have the well-known properties of not being able to bear contrastive stress,[3] not being able to appear in isolation and not being co-ordinable (cf. Kayne 1975). It is a moot point whether on the basis of these and other properties a general category of clitic, exhibiting a consistent crosslinguistic phenomenology, can be identified (cf. in this connection the scepticism of Zwicky 1994, which I share). However, all that matters for the present study is the recognition that the Latin elements whose distribution is traditionally characterized by the labels *proclitic* and *enclitic* are not clitics in the sense of the abovementioned Romance elements but rather weak pronouns (cf. Introduction pp. 20–1, and Fontana, this volume). We will return to these questions below but for the moment the reader is warned not to jump to the conclusion that a Latin element whose distribution is stated in terms of *proclisis* or *enclisis* is a clitic in the (in my view unfortunate) categorial sense of that term which has become widespread in the recent generative literature (though cf. now Cardinaletti & Starke 1994).

The organization of this chapter is as follows. In section 2 we review some relevant background properties of Latin and outline the aspects of Latin syntactic structure that we will be taking for granted. In section 3 we set out the historical case for DP as an emerging category in Romance when compared with Latin, based on the formal parallells between clitics and articles and their co-evolution from Latin *ille*. We then complicate the traditional picture in section 4 by introducing the emphatic pronominal *ipse* and considering its relation to *ille* in terms of syntax, semantics, discourse function, geographical distribution and historical profile. Sections 5 and 6 then return to look in renewed detail at *ille* before examining the relation between the two. Once we have clarified the synchronic and diachronic situation, we will be in a position to offer an integrated theoretical account of the changes (section 7) before concluding with a brief reflection on the model of grammatical change that our data and their interpretation here presuppose (section 8).

2 *Ipse* and *ille*: the Latin background

By way of introduction then it will be useful to review the system of pronominals in Latin. The first and second persons and the third person reflexive pronouns are relatively unproblematic; the forms are set out in Table I. These could occur in both stressed and unstressed positions in the clause, could occur as independent elements and could be co-ordinated with each other and with full NPs.

Table 1. *Latin personal pronouns*

	1SG	2SG	3REFL SG/PL	1PL	2PL
nominative	ego	tu	—	nos	vos
accusative	me	te	se	nos	vos
genitive	mei	tui	sui	nostrum, –i	vestrum, –i
dative	mihi	tibi	sibi	nobis	vobis
ablative	me	te	se	nobis	vobis

When it comes to third-person non-reflexive pronouns, the situation is rather more complex. In addition to being, as is well known, a null subject language, Latin also permits object *pro*-drop (cf. van der Wurff 1993 for a recent discussion). Where a minimally marked, anaphoric element is required,[4] the pronoun *is* is used. Gildersleeve & Lodge (1895: §308) comment that *is* 'serves as the lacking pronoun of the Third Person'. However, the existence of widespread *pro*-drop virtually guarantees that when a third-person argument is overtly expressed, it will be associated with some degree of contrast, emphasis or other textual salience. Latin had four pronouns which could in different ways fulfil this function of giving overt expression to a textually or contextually highlighted item: (a) *hic*, conventionally translated as 'this', and more precisely a marker of proximal deixis, i.e. 'near the speaker'; (b) *iste*, a deictic associated with the second person, i.e. 'near the addressee'; (c) *ille*, a marker of distal deixis, i.e. 'distant from both the speaker and the addressee'; (d) *ipse*, which marks emphasis or contrast (cf. Harris 1978: ch. 4) for an integrated historical account of these elements). *Hic* and *iste* will figure minimally in what follows, where the focus will rather be on the evolving historical relations between *ille* and *ipse* and the emergence of overt DPs in Romance.

3 Latin *ille* and the category D in Romance

Looked at from a purely synchronic perspective, most of the Romance languages seem to offer a particularly direct argument in favour of the DP hypothesis in that there is more or less total morphological overlap in the forms of the article and the object clitics.

Table 2.

		MASC SG	FEM SG	MASC PL	FEM PL
Italian	article	i	la	i	le
	clitic object	l'	la	l'	le
French	article	le	la	les	les
	clitic object	le	la	les	les
Portuguese	article	o	a	os	as
	clitic object	o	a	os	as

The parallelism is less complete for those dialects which exhibit subject clitics, but even so there is a considerable degree of correspondence:[5]

Table 3.

		MASC SG	FEM SG	MASC PL	FEM PL
Florentino	article	il/lo*	la	i/li*	le
	subject clitic		la	li	le
Trentino	article	le	la	les	les
	subject clitic	le	la	les	les

(data from Brandi & Cordin 1989 and Renzi 1983)
*In Italian the forms *lo/li* represent an earlier stage of the language.

As we have said, Latin had neither articles nor clitics (in the modern Romance sense), while all the Romance languages have both, suggesting first that their historical emergence is linked and second that the change should be located in the transition from Classical Latin to Proto-Romance.[6] There are of course many, and sometimes quite profound, developments within the histories of the individual Romance languages but the basic shift that gives rise to articles and object, or better internal-argument, clitics is attested in all the Romance dialects and therefore must be presumed to be early enough to belong to a common phase of development.[7]

The formal overlaps noted in Tables 2 and 3 above are due to the fact that the articles and clitics derive from the same source, namely the Latin pronoun/demonstrative adjective *ille*. In seeking to account for the historical genesis of this situation, most treatments have followed what we may call the direct route and concentrated on the analysis of the changing role of *ille*. Thus, for instance (Harris 1980a: 146):

> In essence, then, *ille* maintained in Vulgar Latin its value as a marker of [+ definite, 3 proximity] [3 proximity = distal: NBV] and came to mark also [+definite, −proximity]. As a result of this change, *ille*, while retaining at first at least its demonstrative functions, was also used both as a 'personal' and an 'anaphoric' pronoun (these both also being [+definite, −proximity]), and additionally came to be used more and more prenominally (in Romanian, post-nominally) as the appropriate determiner to mark a particular nominal unspecified in respect of proximity. It is from this starting point that the systems of the modern Romance languages all derive.

Just prior to this paragraph, Harris does note what he calls the 'important complication' that *ille* in its non-pronominal function is 'significantly rivalled by *ipse*', but he then puts the questions posed by the presence of *ipse* on one side and returns to the analysis of the forms that derive from *ille*. Other scholars have also tended to downplay the role of *ipse*, as for example Renzi (1976). However, as Nocentini (1990: 140) observes in commenting on Renzi's treatment, 'l'esame delle fasi intermedie ... ci convinc[e] che lo sviluppo dell'articolo determinativo nelle lingue romanze non è stato così semplice e lineare' (the examination of the intermediate phases convinces us that the development of the definite article in the Romance languages was not so simple and linear). It is precisely such a non-linear development, in which we find the convergence of two structurally separate patterns, which I seek to elaborate here.

Another ingredient of the traditional view has been that the rise of the articles is related in some way to the loss of Latin nominal case inflection. Thus, Tekavčić (1980: §452) writes: 'L'articolo nasce dunque in stretto rapporto con la perdita della flessione nominale, come uno dei suoi sostituti' (the article emerges therefore in step with the loss of noun inflection and as one of the substitutes for it). What Tekavčić does not make clear is how the two phenomena are connected. One possibility might be that the case marking survives longer on the demonstratives that are the precursors of the article than on the nouns themselves. This is not intrinsically implausible. It is well known that pronominal elements often retain case marking where the corresponding nouns do not, English being a very clear instance in point. Similarly, in German, determiners exhibit a wider range of case markings than do nouns, with the consequence that in most NPs the morphological case is signalled on the determiner or adjective rather than the noun. The problem however is that there is very little clear evidence that these Germanic parallels are replicated in Romance. As Selig (1992: 86) observes in the course of a valuable review of earlier approaches:

> Als Fazit der Textanalysen kann festgehalten werden: die Determinanten vollziehen weitestgehend parallel zu den Nomina alle Phasen des Abbaus der Kasusunterscheidungen mit. (As a result of the text analysis we may conclude: determiners undergo every stage of the breakdown of the system of case marking in a way almost exactly parallel to nouns.)

Renzi (1992, 1993) has recently re-examined the Romance evidence and comes to a similar if rather more nuanced conclusion. In particular, he suggests the alternative possibility that the structural differences between subject and object are crucially involved in determining both the remodelling and differential survival of the case system and the selection of articles. It is this latter, indirect, view of the relation between grammatical function, case marking and the rise of articles that I will attempt to develop in the present study; our theoretical perspective will differ to some degree, though probably not to the point of incompatibility, from that espoused by Renzi. Once again the fate of *ipse* as one of the candidates for articlehood in the Romance family will be crucial to our argument.[8]

4 The problem of *ipse*

The questions that the presence of *ipse* poses for the traditional treatment, and therefore for what we may label the 'unified D' view of the emergence of articles and clitics, may be listed as follows: (a) what was the relation between *ille* and *ipse* in Latin, both in its classical and post-classical (sometimes called 'Vulgar' — see note 6) stages? (b) how did the uses of *ille* and *ipse* interact in the phase which leads up to the emergence of Romance articles and pronouns? In particular, given that in some parts of the Romance territory, *ipse* survives as the article, did *ipse* predominate in one area and *ille* elsewhere right from the beginning, or was there an initial preference for one followed by a historical generalization of the other? (c) how are we to explain the fact that while continuers of *ipse* function as both articles and independent subject pronouns, they are never attested as unstressed pronominals or clitics?

In his detailed survey of the philological data, Aebischer (1948) identifies two large areas in which there either is or has been evidence of *ipse* functioning as an article or something very akin to it (what he calls an 'articloid'). The first, 'western', area includes Catalonia and Gascony and much if not all of Provence (Aebischer 1948: 189ff.). Although an *ipse*-derived article survives today only in Balearic Catalan, 'les textes anciens laissent entrevoir un moment de l'histoire où l'article *ipse* régnait, incontesté, de la Gascogne à travers le Languedoc, le Quercy, le Rouergue, la Catalogne au sud, et à l'est jusqu'aux Alpes de Provence' (The old texts allow us a glimpse of a period in which the article *ipse* reigned unchallenged from Gascony through Languedoc, Quercy, Rouergue and Catalonia to the South, and to the East as far as the Alps of Provence) (Aebischer 1948: 193). The second, 'southern', area includes many sporadic places in southern Italy, Sicily and in particular Sardinia, the last-mentioned location being one in which an *ipse*-derived article was already firmly established in the earliest texts and survives unaltered to this day (Jones 1993: 34). Aebischer specifically rejects attempts to see any larger continuity between the two areas and is critical of suggestions that *ipse* served an article-like function in African Latin. Nor do we wish to develop any geolinguistic speculations here. Suffice it to note that the modern intermittent attestation of articles deriving from *ipse* reflects an earlier distribution over a rather significant portion of the Romance-speaking territory. The evidence for the early geographical spread of *ipse* is paralleled by its high textual fequency in late Latin documents. Traditional accounts often note the latter point but put it side by side with the modern limited geographical range of *ipse* as article and thereby deduce a paradox.[9] If instead we see both the earlier high textual frequency and the earlier wide geographical distribution as mutually supportive evidence of the centrality of *ipse* in the evolving morphosyntax of Romance, we need to address more closely the nature of that role.

In the classical language the difference between *ipse* and *ille* is clear (cf. section 2 above). *Ille* has both a distal and an anaphoric role. In the latter capacity it overlaps with *is*, which however falls out of the language, presumably for phonetic reasons. *Ipse* serves instead to emphasize and contrast the relevant items in the discourse.

Scholars have often assumed that at the point when the articles were about to develop, this earlier difference between *ille* and *ipse* had disappeared and the two items had virtually merged, perhaps differing only in register. Thus Aebischer (1948: 203): 'Il a donc existé, sans doute, un moment où toute la Romania a connu *ille* et *ipse* comme presque synonymes.' (There therefore undoubtedly existed a period when *ille* and *ipse* were almost synonymous throughout the whole of Romania.) Later studies, for example Renzi (1976), Nocentini (1990) and most recently and most extensively Selig (1992), have however shown incontrovertibly that the two items had distinct though overlapping functions. Thus, in her recent and richly documented monograph Selig offers the following characterizations of the different uses. For *ille*, 'Der Bereich der definiten Erstnennung ist die eigentliche Funktionsdomäne von *ille* in den hier analysierten Texten' (the realm of definite first mention is the real functional domain of *ille* in the texts analysed here) (Selig 1992: 165). On the other hand, '*ipse* wird in fast allen hier analysierten Texten in erster Linie zur Kennzeichnung anaphorisch definiter NPs verwendet' (in almost all the texts analysed here *ipse* was used in the first place as a marker of definite anaphoric NPs) (Selig 1992: 153). This conclusion closely parallels that reached by Nocentini (1990: 146): 'ILLE e IPSE si sono specializzati, il primo nella funzione cataforica, il secondo in quella anaforica' (ILLE and IPSE have become specialized, the former in a cataphoric function, the latter in an anaphoric one). Renzi (1976: 29) makes a similar point but makes the crucial observation of the partial overlap between the two items: 'Si sarà notato che gli usi di *ille* e di *ipse* non si sovrappongono, ma che *ipse* occupa solo una parte della referenza testuale (l'uscita [3]), che invece *ille* occupa interamente (uscite [2] e [3])' (the reader will have noted that the uses of *ille* and *ipse* do not completely overlap, but that *ipse* occupies only a part of textual reference (outcome [3]) while *ille* occupies the whole domain (outcomes [2] and [3])). (NB: The numbers 2 and 3 refer to Renzi's classification of the functions of the article. Number 2 means textually given by virtue of the syntactic structure and identifies the use of *ille* in restrictive relatives; this corresponds to Nocentini's label 'cataphoric' and Selig's 'definite Erstnennung'. Number 3 means second mention and equates to Nocentini's and Selig's use of the term 'anaphoric'.)[10]

The functions of *ille* and *ipse* identified here follow naturally from their earlier uses in the classical language. In the case of *ille*, it is a simple move from distal deixis to definiteness and the earlier contrastive–identitive function of *ipse* sits well with its later role of singling out the topic of a discourse. These textual functions are not always easy to see in the absence of long stretches of text. Consider therefore the following passage from the *Peregrinatio Aegeriae*, an account by a Spanish nun of a visit to the Holy Land in the late fourth century AD. The author is describing the topography of the region around Mount Sinai (*Mons Dei*) and in particular the vast valley (*vallis ingens*) which leads up to the mountain. (For ease of identification I have highlighted the occurrences of the relevant nouns *vallis* and *mons* in small capitals and the proto-articles *ipse* and *ille* in italics. No particular textual or phonetic emphasis is intended by these typographic devices.)

I.1. … ubi se tamen MONTES *illi*, inter quos ibamus, aperiebant et faciebant VALLEM infinitam ingens, planissima et valde pulchram, et trans VALLEM apparebat MONS sanctus Dei Syna.
[… 7 lines …]
2. … Habebat autem de eo loco ad MONTEM Dei forsitan quattuor milia totum per VALLE *illa*, quam dixi ingens.

II.1. VALLIS autem *ipsa* ingens est valde, iacens subter latus MONTIS Dei, quae habet forsitan, quantum potuimus videntes estimare aut *ipsi* dicebant, in longo milia passos forsitan sedecim, in lato autem quattuor milia esse appellabant. *Ipsam* ergo VALLEM nos traversare habebamus, ut possimus MONTEM ingredi. 2. Haec est autem VALLIS ingens et planissima, in qua filii Israhel commorati sunt his diebus, quod sanctus Moyses ascendit in MONTEM Domini et fuit ibi quadraginta diebus et quadraginta noctibus. Haec est autem VALLIS, in qua factus est vitulus, qui locus usque in hodie ostenditur; nam lapis grandis ibi fixus stat in *ipso* loco. Haec ergo VALLIS *ipsa* est, in cuius capite *ille* locus est, ubi sanctus Moyses cum pasceret pecora soceri sui, iterum locutus est ei Deus de rubo in igne. 3. Et quoniam nobis ita erat iter, ut prius MONTEM Dei ascenderemus, qui hinc paret, quia unde veniebamus melior ascensus erat, et illinc denuo ad *illud* caput VALLIS descenderemus, id est rubus erat, quia melior descensus MONTIS Dei erat inde: itaque ergo hoc placuit, ut visis omnibus, quae desiderabamus, descendentes a MONTE Dei, ubi est rubus veniremus, et inde totum per mediam VALLEM *ipsam*, qua iacet in longo, rediremus ad iter cum hominibus Dei, qui nobis singula loca, quae scripta sunt, per *ipsam* VALLEM ostendebant, sicut et factum est. 4. Nobis ergo euntibus ab eo loco, ubi venientes a Faran feceramus orationem, iter sic fuit, ut per medium transversaremus caput *ipsius* VALLIS et sic plecaremus nos ad MONTEM Dei. 5. MONS autem *ipse* per giro quidem unus esse videtur …

[I.1 … where in the meantime the mountains, between which we were going, opened out and formed an endless valley — huge, very flat and very beautiful — and across the valley there appeared Sinai, the holy mountain of God.
…
I.2 … It was however perhaps four miles from that place to the mountain of God right through that valley, which I have said was huge.

II.1 The valley is indeed truly huge, lying under the side of the mountain of God. It is, as far as we could guess from looking at it or as they said, perhaps sixteen miles long and, they said, four miles wide. This valley then we had to cross in order to approach the mountain. 2. This is the huge, very flat valley in which the children of Israel stayed in those days, because holy Moses went up into the mountain of God and remained there for forty days and forty nights. This is the valley in which the calf was made; this place is still pointed out to this day for a large stone stands on the spot. This then is the valley at whose head is the place where God spoke twice to holy Moses from the burning bush while he was grazing his father-in-law's cattle. 3. And it was in this direction that our route lay for us to first ascend the mountain of God, which can be seen from here, because the better way up is from the side from which we were coming; and thence we would descend again to head of the valley — that is where the bush was — because the better way down from the mountain of God is there. Thus it was agreed that, when we had seen everything that we wanted, we would come down from the mountain of God and would come to the place where the bush is, and then we would return to the road along the whole length of the valley with the men of God, who would show us each of the places along the valley which are mentioned in the scriptures. And thus it was done. 4. For us as we went from that place where, when we came from Faran, we had said a prayer, the route was such that we crossed the head of that valley and turned towards the mountain of God. 5. That mountain however, when you go round it, seems to be one ...]

In paragraph I.1 the two entities are introduced into the discourse without any accompanying item. Subsequently, *vallis* in particular usually co-occurs with either *ille* or *ipse*; *Mons Dei* is a proper noun and is therefore less likely to be modified in this way. After brief digression, *vallis* re-appears marked with *ille* and an accompanying relative clause that overtly refers to the previous mention (*quam dixi ingens* 'which I have called vast'). At that point in the narrative the valley is subordinated to the mountain, which is the principal goal of the visit. In paragraph II.1, however, the valley itself becomes the focus of attention, a fact which is marked by its first, topic, position and by the accompanying *ipsa*. Its topic-hood is reiterated at the beginning of the next sentence in the same way, the difference in this instance being that *ipsam...vallem* is marked accusative as object of the verb *traversare*. Attention remains on the valley until II.5, when it switches to the mountain. The new topic is established in exactly the same way, namely by initial position and the presence of *ipse*.

The patterns I have been describing here could be expanded on considerably and the analysis refined if space permitted. Enough has been seen however to indicate the semantic and pragmatic functions of the elements that concern us here.

Looked at distributionally rather than semantically, *ipse* occurs in a recurrent though not at first sight unified set of contexts:

— in those dialects in which it yields the etymon of the article it is also the source of subject pronouns (e.g. Sardinian *isso/a/os/as* — Jones 1993: 199);

— more generally, it provides the disjunctive pronouns, which occur contrastively and after prepositions (Jones 1993: 201 ff.);

— it forms part of a three-term deictic series in which the second person or middle member is derived from *ipse* reinforced with the exclamative *eccu* or *accu*. Thus, again in Sardinian, we have (Jones 1993: 34):

'this'	custu	< eccu+istum
'that by you'	cussu	< eccu+ipsum
'that'	cuddu	< eccu+illum

The distribution of three-term deictic systems of this kind in Romance is more extensive and historically more robust than that of the *ipse*-based article, but interestingly relates very closely to the western and southern groupings identified by Aebischer. Thus we have three-term deictic systems throughout the Iberian peninsula, not just in its eastern fringe where the articles from *ipse* survive. Similarly, virtually all Italian dialects from Rome south have forms that exactly parallel, phonetic differences aside, the Sardinian series cited here (Rohlfs 1966–68: §494).

— Sardinian also has a form *issoro* < IPSORUM, which functions as third-person plural possessive (cf. *loro, leur*). The dative plural clitic is however *lis* < ILLIS, again consistent with the generalization that clitics always derive from *ille* (contrast in this connection the dual function of Ital. *loro*, Fr. *leur* < ILLORUM).

The task now is to unite this set of contexts with the function of *ipse* as (proto-)article and with the semantic value attributed to it by Selig, Nocentini and others. The first stage is not too difficult. The two semantic ingredients which *ipse* retains from its earliest usage are contrast and identity. Via the contrast function *ipse* is able to mark changes of topic, and already did so in the classical language. Gildersleeve & Lodge (1895: §311) cite the following example: [*Camillus*] *ex Volscis in Aequos transiit et ipsos bellum molientes* (Livy VI.2.14) 'Camillus went across from the Volscians to the Aequians, who were likewise (as well as the Volscians) getting up war.' The identity function ensures continuity with a previously mentioned item. Hence the very frequent use in the classical language of *ipse* 'to lay stress on the reflexive relation' (Gildersleeve & Lodge 1895: §311). It is natural therefore that *ipse* should come to mark topics in the way (Selig 1992) in particular documents. The passage from topic marking to definiteness is also easily understood since definiteness is an intrinsic property of topics; topics too are commonly claimed to be in a relation of grammaticalization to subjects (Li & Thompson 1976) so *ipse* as the source of (tonic) subject pronouns is not hard to explain.

What then is the connection between *ipse* in its function as proto-article and its use in the (reinforced) deictic system to mark second person or 'middle' ground deixis? Consider first what is commonly agreed to be the Latin ancestor system in which deictics correlate with person in a neatly symmetrical fashion (Harris 1980a):

PERSON	PRONOUN	DEICTIC
1	ego	hic
2	tu	iste
3	ille	ille

Assume also Benveniste's interpretation that the primary split here is between the third or non-person and the first and second as the persons referring to participants in the discourse (Benveniste 1946). Diagrammatically:

The loss of *hic*, usually and not implausibly attributed to the effects of phonetic erosion, would leave *iste* as the only marker of person vs non-person and we would predict a two-term system such as is attested in Old French *cist* vs *cil* and Italian *questo* vs *quello*. We will assume that subsequent to the loss of *hic* and the shift of *iste* to the centre of the deictic system, *ipse* becomes interpolated to mark second person via an intrinsic pragmatic connection with the interpersonal function of topic marking as a means whereby the speaker sets out for the addressee the topic of the next portion of the discourse.[11]

To sum up this section, we can say that *ipse*'s etymological value determined its spread to a range of contexts all characterized by the core notions of contrast and continuity: it singles out an item that has been previously mentioned but has lapsed into the background of the discourse and brings it back into focus. It may perform this function for an item regardless of the syntactic role that item has in the clause, including, as we have seen in the passage quoted above, objects as well as subjects and adjuncts. Such objects will however typically be dislocated to a clause-initial topic position. What, given this etymology and these changes, we would not expect and do not find is *ipse* marking de-accented, second-mention but not informationally prominent, items. Yet it is precisely the latter value which is associated with clitic objects, and hence the absence of *ipse* as the etymon of clitics. It is time, therefore, to turn our attention to the source of clitics.

5 The distribution of *ille*

We have already briefly alluded to the role of *ille* in section 2 above, noting the argument of Harris (1980a) that it developed via the loss of its original deictic function and its increasing restriction to 'anaphoric' contexts.[12] Classical Latin, of course, also had a purely anaphoric item, *is*, which had a relation of partial overlap with *ille*, in that both items could pick up reference to an antecedent element, but only *ille* also had a demonstrative value. The forms of *is* were not likely to survive the various phonetic changes that affect Latin as it develops into Romance, so it is no surprise that this item is lost. However, the loss of *is* merely determines that *ille* should inherit what were already shared functions. Thus, Renzi (1976: 24): 'Si può considerare che *ille* diventi l'erede di *is* pronome, che rappresenta sempre quello che è solo qualche volta *is* aggettivo: il richiamo a un elemento testualmente nuovo' (We may conclude that *ille* is the heir of pronominal *is*, which always has the function only sometimes shared by adjectival *is*, namely that of pointing to a textually new item). At the same time, the loss of *is* does not in and of itself predict the new uses represented by the modern Romance clitic pronouns or articles. Let us therefore consider the development of each of these categories, starting with the pronouns.

As far as the pronouns are concerned there are two predisposing factors: first, the existing rules for weak pronoun placement and second the movement of the verb to first position in the clause. Thus, Wanner (1987: 451) writes: 'The essential force identified for the change affecting the position of the verb in the clause is the grammaticalization of the marked verb-initial arrangement pattern VXY.' The unmarking of verb-fronting combined with the occurrence of weak pronouns in so-called Wackernagel position created the context for a reanalysis whereby the pronoun is taken to follow the verb.[13] Even so, the interaction of these independent principles will explain how we get clitics but still not why. For this latter point the crucial additional circumstance is the gradual erosion of the Latin system of morphological case-marking. In a system which permits fronting of topicalized elements such as the uses of *vallis autem ipsa* and *ipsam ergo vallem* in section II.1 of the above-cited passage from the *Peregrinatio*, case marking will be important to distinguish grammatical function. If that is lost, the use of a pronominal copy of at least one will serve to maintain the distinction. An example in point is from the eighth-century parody of the *Lex Salica*, where we find: *ipsa cuppa frangantla tota* 'the cup, let them break it all'.

Examples parallel to the one just cited are also found in the earliest attested stages of the Romance vernaculars. Thus, what is generally acknowledged to be the first Italian text, a tenth century AD legal declaration reads as follows: *sao ko kelle terre, per kelle fini que ki contene trenta anni le possette parte Sancti Benedicti* 'I know that those lands, within those bounds which contain them, for thirty years were owned by the monastery of Saint Benedict.' Remarkably, this seventeen-word text provides all the evidence we need to identify the construction as what Cinque (1990) calls 'Clitic Left Dislocation'. According to his diagnostic properties (Cinque 1990: 57ff.):

i. the dislocated element can be any maximal phrase, and this example contains a fronted DP (*kelle terre* 'those lands'), a fronted PP (*per kelle fini* 'within those bounds') and a fronted time adverbial (*trenta anni* 'thirty years');
ii. the relevant type of dislocation is not, like topicalization proper, limited to root clauses, as evidenced here by the presence of these fronted elements in a complement to the verb *sao* 'I know';
iii. there is no upper limit to dislocated elements, as the presence of three in the same clause in our example demonstrates;
iv. the resumptive element is a pronoun (*le*, third-person plural to agree with *kelle terre*).

This demonstration is important in the present context, since Cinque goes on to show that the CLLD construction is base-generated and not the result of movement. The clitic occupies a position that would otherwise not be licensed by the theory of empty categories (Cinque 1990: 71 ff.), in effect spelling out what would have been a possible context for *pro* under the more generous identification conditions for that element in Latin (van der Wurff 1993). In sum, then, clitics provide an alternative strategy from morphological case for argument marking.

Yet, although morphological case and pronominal resumption may be functionally equivalent, they reflect very different types of syntactic system (dependent marking and head marking respectively in the terminology of Nichols 1986). Note then that in the above scenario what matters is, paradoxically, not the case form of the pronoun, since its case value can be derived from its post-verbal position, but its agreement properties; it must be able to encode the same properties as are marked on its antecedent in order to ensure recoverability. On the account offered here, therefore, the origin of clitic pronouns is to be found in contexts involving pronominal resumption of a focal and dislocated argument. From these contexts it generalizes to others in which the co-referential or antecedent item is elsewhere in the discourse or extra-linguistic context. We return to the consequences of these developments in the next section, but first a brief mention of the article function of *ille*.

For the article, there is a rather less complex story to tell. We have already noted the inherent definiteness associated with *ille*'s demonstrative function and its complementary distribution with *ipse*. The move from distal deictic to article is a diachronic pathway well familiar to students of grammaticalization — cf. Greenberg (1991). One peculiarity that should be noted for both *ipse* and *ille* is their relative infrequency with objects. In other words, the use of *ille*-derived pronouns to substitute for object arguments is not matched when *ille* accompanies the object NP. Thus, a brief count of the occurrences of these items in the first five chapters of the *Peregrinatio Aegeriae* yields the following results (the category Other includes both arguments of prepositions and free-standing genitives and ablatives):

Table 4.

	subject	object	other	total
ipse	16	3	27	46
ille	19	9	15	43
total	35	12	42	89

Of the three uses of *ipse* with an object, one is the topicalized example from II.1 quoted above (*ipsam ergo vallem nos trasversare habebamus*) and another also shows clear evidence of dislocation to the right beyond the final verb: *et ad directum descendi necesse est* [*singulos ipsos montes*] (III.1) 'and it is necessary to come straight down each individual mountain'. Of the object occurrences of *ille*, one is an unaccompanied pronominal, and all but one of the remainder co-occur with relative clauses — e.g. *videramus rubum illum, de quo locutus est Deus sancto Moysi in igne* (V.2) 'we had seen the burning bush from which God spoke to the blessed Moses'.

This limitation in the distribution of *ille* and *ipse* is matched in the earlier stages of the Romance languages by a similar absence of the article, which is not found in origin with objects and arguments of prepositions. Meyer-Lübke (1890–6 III: §178) observes: 'le cas régime s'employait originairement sans article'.[14] Indeed, we can cite examples from the modern languages where the traces of the pattern remain. Thus, in Italian, objects and unaccusative subjects in internal position may be found without article while the corresponding pre-verbal subjects require the article: *è venuta gente/*gente è venuta* 'people came'; *hanno mangiato carne cruda* 'they ate raw meat' vs **(la) carne cruda fa male allo stomaco* 'raw meat upsets the stomach'. A very similar pattern of distribution is found in Old French though not in the modern language (Harris 1978a: 74ff.).[15]

6 *Ille* and *ipse* summed up

We can sum up the situation we have described as follows. *Ipse* and *ille* converge on the function as markers of definiteness by two different and complementary routes. *Ipse* is used when an item is mentioned for the second time and is therefore given but is also implicitly contrasted with other items beside which it is singled out. It is thus appropriate as a topic marker and as a tonic form; from the latter come the subject uses and the 'strong' form after prepositions. The implicit value of focus and contrast make it inappropriate for use as a (proto-)clitic. *Ille*, on the other hand, is used when an item is repeated in discourse, is taken as given and therefore definite, but with no necessary implication of topic-hood. It may thus occur either as stressed or unstressed; the former provides the tonic or strong pronouns that derive from *ille*, the latter circumstance leads to (proto-)clitic uses. Notice in all this that, although the functions and values of these elements change, the asymmetric relation between *ipse* and *ille* noted by many commentators — (Nocentini 1990: 148; Renzi 1976: 29) — is preserved. We have here a nice though rather abstract instance of what Hopper (1991: 22) calls 'persistence': the properties of the earlier stages condition the distribution of elements at a later grammaticalized stage. In this instance what persists is the semantic relation of hyponymy though the semantic features over which it is defined have changed. The way in which *ille* and *ipse* converge from different directions on the marking of definiteness is also reminiscent of other examples from the literature on grammaticalization such as the multiple sources of future auxiliaries (Heine, Claudi *et al.* 1991: ch. 7.1.1) or conditional particles (Traugott 1985).

Once *ipse* and *ille* have attained the proto-article status — what Aebischer calls 'articloid' — the developments may go in two directions. Either *ipse* remains and shares the exponence of the general category D with *ille* (as in Sardinian) or *ille* generalizes over both article and clitic roles. The latter is of course the only possibility in the central Gallo-Romance territory, where there is no evidence of *ipse* having ever achieved the proto-article stage (Aebischer 1948), but it also seems that *ille* has been able to roll back the frontiers of *ipse* in many other regions where the latter was once dominant, thereby achieving a more general correlation between category and exponent.

7 Argument marking

On the traditional view the loss of morphological case marking in Latin is compensated for by the fixing of word order in an SVO pattern. This view treats subjects and objects in Latin as of equivalent status, each marked by its own case, nominative and accusative respectively. Though it is not usually expressed in this way, a further assumption of the traditional view is that the freedom of word order in Latin argues against the postulation of a VP constituent. The Romance languages on the other hand seem pretty incontrovertibly to have a VP. Thus, we might take the traditional view to imply a shift from non-configurational to configurational structure. There are other pieces of evidence that argue in favour of this conclusion. For example, there are instances in which the Latin reflexive may precede its antecedent — e.g. *suus rex reginae placet* (Plautus *St*, 133) 'her king is pleasing to the queen'.[16] The issue of configurationality is a complex and controversial one and there is not room to address it properly here. What is clear however from the evidence of the previous sections is that there is an asymmetry in the way the elements *ipse* and *ille* relate to subjects and objects. There is another asymmetry in that articles appear to originate with subjects (via the grammaticalization of topics) while clitics clearly start as a means of marking objects or more generally internal arguments; so-called subject clitics are demonstrably later and belong to the history of the individual Romance languages (Wanner 1987: 16). Whether this is taken as evidence of the emergence of configurational syntax in Romance from a non-configurational ancestor or the shaping of one configurational pattern into a new one, the underlying asymmetry in the development of articles and (object) pronouns is important to an understanding of the way the D-system in Romance has come into being.

One, paradoxical, conclusion of the previous argument is that the preservation of case marking for subject and object is not relevant in the pronominal system any more than in the nominal one; the configurational difference between subject and object takes the place of overt case marking. What is by contrast essential is an agreement system which allows the tracking of the relevant arguments. This explains the at first sight rather strange fact that the Italian masculine plural object pronoun *li* derives from the nominative form *illi* and not the accusative *illos* (Vincent 1995). The pressure for the coding of other internal arguments leads to three further developments:

— the marking of the distinction between direct and indirect object, even at the price of redeploying other forms. It is in this light that one should interpret developments such as French dative *leur*, whose etymon is the genitive plural *illorum*.

— the development of two new pro-elements corresponding to the prepositionally marked arguments, cf. French *y, en* and Italian *ci, ne*.[17] Where necessary genitive arguments can be coded via the elements *en/ne*, thus ensuring that the redeployment of the Latin genitive alluded to in the last paragraph is not fatal. (See Vincent 1995 for further development of these points and the logic that underlies them.)

— the spelling out of object *pro*, which survives in only a restricted set of environments in the modern languages (Rizzi 1986b). This is at first sight a puzzling development. Whereas subject *pro* can be related to the presence of 'rich' inflection, object *pro* — in Latin at least — cannot, since there is no system of overt object agreement in the language. It is plausible therefore to connect the need to mark pronominal objects explicitly to the loss of the existing system of marking objects, namely morphological case. The details remain to be worked out.[18]

Before leaving the issue of argument marking, I would like to make some brief comments about the relation of the changes described here to the distinction between head-marking (HM) and dependent-marking (DM) languages (Nichols 1986, 1992). In so doing, I follow up the general programme of inquiry sketched in Vincent (1993). Latin is a prototypical example of a DM language, where the status of a verbal argument is encoded, via case morphology, on the argument itself. The developments we have been describing, whereby the case marking is eroded and cross-referencing is achieved through the clitic system, is a move in the direction of head marking. This is particularly clear in those Romance languages which have developed patterns of clitic doubling. Another phenomenon that can be brought under the same rubric has already been alluded to, namely the development of subject clitics. In the latter instance, however, there is a clear correlation with the loss of the previous agreement system, itself the most widespread kind of HM effect. Note too the differential status of subject and object *pro* from this point of view.

One consequence, traditionally noted, of either an HM or a DM system is (relative) freedom of word order for the very good reason that in either instance an argument's status is already identified independently of linear position. And indeed the position of the subject is relatively free in many Romance languages, say by comparison with English or Germanic more generally, since there are either inherited agreement morphemes or newly evolved subject-clitics to encode its presence. Why then is there not the same freedom of object position? The answer seems to be that parallel to the development of object clitics in the way described here is a parametric shift, independently motivated in the relative order of verb and object. In VO languages arguments can be licensed without the need for overt case, something which is in general not true for OV languages, as Greenberg noted in his original word universals. Thus, the word order change sets up another, complementary, way to license arguments, one which however only holds for internal arguments. Once again the subject–object asymmetry re-emerges.

8 *Envoi*: lessons for the theory of syntactic change

The overall sequence of events that I have sought to outline in this chapter may be summarized as follows:

STAGE 1: As the historical antecedent to the changes discussed in the present chapter, we may presume a stage, which we may for convenience label 'Classical Latin',[19] which is characterized by the following properties:

a) There are no articles in the modern sense of markers of definiteness forming a more or less obligatory constituent of DPs, but only the deictic and/or emphatic elements *ipse* and *ille*.

b) There are two classes of pronoun, corresponding to the distinction made both in the traditional literature and in more recent theoretical terms by Cardinaletti & Starke (1994) between 'weak' and 'strong', but no clitics in the sense of Kayne (1975).

c) The weak pronouns obey special distributional rules identified by Wackernagel and subsequent scholars such as Adams (1994a, b).

d) The front position in the clause is used for focus (Wanner 1987).[20]

STAGE 2: A variety of changes then take place which taken together typify 'Romance' as opposed to 'Latin' syntax.

a) The emergence of a class of items, etymologically derived from various forms of *ille*, which obey the diagnostics for clitichood identified in Kayne (1975) and much subsequent work. In the terms of Cardinaletti & Starke (1994) this represents a historical progression along their asymmetric scale: clitic < weak pronoun < strong pronoun.

b) The emergence of two further items, exemplified by French *y/en* and Italian *ne/ci*, which correspond to full PPs rather than DPs. The generalization linking the changes under (a) and (b) is that the clitic system can now encode any sub-categorized argument whatever its syntactic category.

c) This new clitic-based (internal) argument marking system, centred around reflexes of *ille*, comes into being in parallel with the loss of morphological case, whose function it in part replaces.

d) Whereas *ille* (along with the first and second person pronouns) is the only appropriate candidate for the change from weak pronoun to clitic, it is in competition with *ipse* as part of an emergent system of markers of the discourse status of clause-initial arguments (*ipse* marks topicalized information and *ille* given information).

The overall consequence of the above changes is to create a Proto-Romance clause structure in which there is a pre-verbal 'focus/topic field' and a V-initial residue in which all internal arguments are encoded on the verbal head[21] by clitics while the external argument is signalled by the inherited subject–verb agreement (replaced in its turn by a new and historically later series of subject clitics in those dialects where the inherited person/number inflection is lost). Constituents in the pre-verbal field are marked by either *ille* or *ipse*, which have now attained the status labelled 'articloid' by Aebischer (1948).

STAGE 3: Two possibilities now arise, both leading to full article status for the reflexes of *ipse/ille*.

Either a) *ille* generalizes at the expense of *ipse*, thereby creating a single source for the exponents of the emergent category D made up of articles and pronouns. This is the pattern found today in all the 'standard' Romance languages.

or b) *ipse* generalizes at the expense of *ille* for all 'full' DPs thereby establishing two different lexical bases for the articles and clitics. This is the situation now only attested in Balearic Catalan and Sardinian but formerly more widespread (Aebischer 1948).

Whichever of these routes is followed in this last stage of the development, it is clear that both require the postulation of an earlier stage in which proto-article and proto-clitic functions are structurally distinct and to that extent the 'unified D' view of Harris (1980a, b) can be seen to oversimplify the actual historical picture.

What general lessons for the student of grammatical change can be learned from this sequence of events? We can begin by noting the variety of mechanisms at work here:

i) GRAMMATICALIZATION: as we have already noted, the development of both *ipse* and *ille* to their article functions follows a classic path already identified by grammaticalization theorists in several languages. Grammaticalization is also involved in the development of the pro-PP clitics *en/ne* and *y/ci* touched on in section 7.

ii) RE-ANALYSIS: what were in origin independent effects — the fronting of verbs (let us assume to C) and the attraction of weak pronouns to second position pronoun — permitted a re-analysis whereby clitics are associated with verbs and verbal projections. This in due course leads to the shift identifed by Rivero from C-oriented to I-oriented clitics.

iii) PARAMETRIC SHIFT: between Latin and Romance, as between OE and PDE, there is a word order change: OV > VO, which may be interpreted either as a canonical shift in the directionality parameter or, along the lines proposed by Roberts (this vol.), as a reversion to Kayne's (1994) universal base VO triggered by loss of morphology.

iv) ANALOGICAL SPREAD (GENERALIZATION): if the scenario envisaged here is right, then articles originate with a particular sub-class of DPs, namely topics, and generalize to other positions/relations.

v) EXAPTATION: within the clitic system overt agreement usurps the role of overt case in the marking of dependencies between verbs and their arguments.

None of these types of change is perhaps particularly remarkable in itself; certainly all have been noted at work in the histories of a number of languages. What is of rather more interest is the way, in the case study presented here, all these changes interact to produce a type of syntax in Romance very different from that of Latin. Some of these types of changes have figured centrally within generative debates about the nature of syntactic change — most notably re-analysis and parameter resetting — where others have been ignored or actively denied. Thus, it has long been a cornerstone of generative theorizing that analogical change (and the mechanism of analogy more generally) should not be admitted as an explanatory part of a model of change. Similarly, work within the grammaticalization tradition has all too often — and by participants on both sides of the debate — been seen as contradictory to, rather than complementary with, changes in syntactic structure. The aim here therefore has been to elucidate, for one particular exemplum, how changes of different types work together over long spans of time to produce a restructuring of the grammatical system. The next phase of research must then be a broader investigation of the way different categories of change interact and in what ways they can be reduced to more general principles.

Notes

* An earlier version of this chapter was presented at the Third Diachronic Generative Syntax Conference in Amsterdam, 30 March to 1 April 1994. Some of the material was also presented in classes at the Australian Linguistic Institute, La Trobe University, July 1994, where I profited from the encouragement and criticism of Elizabeth Traugott and Marianne Mithun. I would particularly like to thank Martin Harris, Lorenzo Renzi, three anonymous referees and my co-editor, Ans van Kemenade, for their invaluable help in revising the manuscript.
1. See Schwegler (1990) for the historical background to the ideas and a modern, non-generative treatment; cf. too Vincent (1996) for further discussion. For a valuable perspective from another language family and much fascinating material and argumentation, see now Steever (1993).
2. For the moment I exclude from consideration the pro-PP clitics such as French *y, en*; Italian *ci, ne*. I will return briefly to their role in section 7 below.
3. This property is sometimes mis-stated as the inability to bear stress at all. This is clearly false as an example such as Campidanese *neri-mí-ddu* 'tell-me-it' (Blasco-Ferrer 1984: 254) shows. The point is that the stress assigned here is word stress and not contrastive or focal stress.
4. A terminological note may be useful at this juncture. In much of the traditional and philological literature the term 'anaphoric' is used — e.g. by Harris, Renzi, Nocentini, Selig and others whose work will be cited below — to mean 'referring back to a textually present antecedent', though Harris also uses it to cover the use of *ille* in restrictive relatives, where a better term might be 'cataphoric' (cf. also Nocentini 1990: 138). In any case, it should be clear that the elements *is, ipse* and *ille* are not 'anaphors' in the technical sense of that term, but rather pronominals.

5. For details of subject clitics, see the important survey in Vanelli (1987). At this point our only concern is to exemplify the formal parallelism of clitics and articles; we return in §7 to the differences between subject and object clitics.
6. I do not wish to enter here into the voluminous discussion of the levels and strata of Latin. In particular, I wish to avoid the traditional hypostatization of 'Vulgar Latin' as an independent language different and temporally discrete from the classical language. For the most part, therefore, I will simply refer to Latin, giving details of date and geographical region as and when appropriate. I will also from time to time use the term Proto-Romance to identify phenomena which have to be reconstructed to some ancestor stage of the whole Romance family, but for which I wish to abstain from more precise location in time and space. Whatever one's views on these various questions of nomenclature, I do not believe that the essentially structural arguments I shall deploy here will be greatly affected one way or the other. The stance I adopt here is essentially the same as in Vincent (1988). For a recent critique of that position, see De Dardel (1993).
7. See also the recent treatment by Uriagereka (1995).
8. Another alternative would be to see the rise of articles as related to the loss of case as a means of signalling distinctions of count/mass and definiteness. This view is plausibly developed for Germanic in the work of Abraham and of Philippi reported in this volume, but there is, to my knowledge, no evidence for an interaction of case and aspect in Latin parallel to that postulated by these scholars as a precursor to the rise of the article in Germanic.
9. Put another way, earlier scholars raise, often implicitly, the question of why/how *ipse* was lost as article but neglect the logically prior question of how it came to assume that function in the first place. An honourable exception in this respect is Aebischer, whose work however is widely cited but rarely discussed in detail.
10. Harris (1980a) classifies these elements as [±definite, ±proximity]. *Ille* evolves from [+def, 3 prox] to [+def, -prox]. Subsequently, in what Harris identifies as the Vulgar Latin system, *ipse* and *ille* are set against each other as both being [+ def] but [3 prox] and [-prox] respectively — cf. p. 52. However, he is here concerned with the role of *ipse* in the evolving demonstrative system and, as we have noted, largely ignores the role of *ipse* as proto-article.
11. That there are certain intrinsic connections between person-related categories of deixis and the given/new status of discourse participants is also implied by Anderson & Keenan (1985: 284–5) in their discussion of Japanese, for which language see also Shibatani (1990: 387–8). The question is clearly a large and complex one that cannot be properly addressed in the present context.
12. See note 4 on the sense of 'anaphoric' here.
13. There are two essential modifications of this scenario which follow from the recent work of Adams (1994a). First we need to pay attention to smaller units than the clause, in particular the colon (cf. in this connection the fundamental works of Fraenkel 1932–3, 1965). Second, there is a distinction to be drawn between 'Wackernagel' clitics, non-Wackernagel elements (e.g. *quidem*, forms of *esse*) and the behaviour of weak pronouns. The situation is clearly a good deal more complex than Wanner and others would have us believe, and more research and analysis is called for. Nonetheless, the assumptions made in the text are, I believe, a sufficiently good approximation to provide a basis for the general scenario sketched in this chapter.
14. Renzi (1976: 19–20) expresses reservations about Meyer-Lübke's hypothesis, citing in particular the difficulty of reconciling the role of the article in PPs and the frequency of Late Latin examples such as *ad illum locum*, etc. We can reconcile Renzi's objections with Meyer-Lübke's original and attractive insight if we note the ambivalent role of PPs. On the one hand as the typical exponents of adjuncts they form a natural class with subjects; on the other both prepositional and verbal objects are governed by (theta-marking) case assigners. The latter property accounts for the absence of the article and the former for

15. the possibility of the disjunctive pronoun (cf. in this respect the ambivalence of PPs with respect to the distribution of pronominals and anaphors).
15. In a recent study, Rosén (1994) has challenged Meyer-Lübke's generalization concerning the relation between articles and syntactic function and suggests an alternative scenario. She argues that in the classical language elements in sentence-initial position are inherently definite, and that logically therefore a definiteness marker would only be required if an item was displaced from initial position. She then reports the results of an analysis of displaced (or in her terminology 'inverted') subjects in narrative prose from Cicero (first century BC) though to Augustine (fourth century AD), and shows that the expected effect only arises in the last-named author. 'Augustinus' *Confessiones* still preserve on the whole the tendency of the subject to be occupied by definite constituents (which are also subjects). If inversion takes place, a definite subject, unless inherently determinated (as is often the case), is accompanied by demonstrative pronouns, with a considerable number of occurrences of demonstrably diminished demonstrative force ... Significantly, *ille* is the pronoun found in this function of definitizing inverted subjects' (Rosén 1994: 143).
Rosén's findings are of considerable interest, and coincide with the argument developed here to the extent that they associate the origin of the article with elements displaced from their canonical syntactic position, in her case 'inverted' or postposed subjects and in mine topicalized subjects and objects.
16. For recent discussion of (non-)configurationality in relation to the marking of definiteness, see Lyons (in prep). I am grateful to Chris Lyons for letting me see part of his draft manuscript.
17. To this extent we would disagree with the decision by Wanner (1987: 16) to exclude the pro-PP clitics, which he sees as not part of 'the potential Late Latin clitic domain'. His argument rests on the fact these elements do not occur across the whole Romance domain and show more or less large etymological differences. We would interpret these facts as evidence that PP-arguments are less 'nuclear' than nominal ones and their marking is therefore less uniform and less rigid. Certainly their distribution throughout the family is more consistent than that of subject clitics and to that extent suggests an earlier dating. However, the issue is an interesting and understudied one that deserves further investigation. We have by contrast already acknowledged the wisdom of Wanner's decision to separate the treatment of subject and object clitics.
18. A valuable contribution in this direction, reaching the conclusion in fact that Latin unexpressed pronominal objects are variables and not instances of *pro*, is van der Wurff (1993).
19. With all the provisos about that term already mentioned in note 6.
20. Exactly what functional structure it is appopriate to assume at the front/top of the clause in Latin remains to be determined. The least controversial assumption is that the fronted verb is in C, where it may, but need not, be preceded by a phrasal constituent in Spec,CP. What we are calling weak pronouns will then be attracted into a post-C, Wackernagel, position. This is clearly the precursor of the C-oriented clitic system identified for earlier Romance by Rivero (this vol.).
21. Or some associated functional projection, I, Agr$_S$ or whatever. I do not wish to prejudge this issue, whose precise technical resolution is not germane to my overall argument.

7 On two locations for complement clitic pronouns: Serbo-Croatian, Bulgarian and Old Spanish

María Luisa Rivero

1 Introduction*

In this chapter, I argue that UG makes available two different functional projections in the clause where complement clitic pronouns may surface by PF, or Spell-Out (Chomsky 1993a): a Complementizer or *C-oriented position*, and an Inflection or *I-oriented position*. More precisely, I adopt the idea that the I-system is L-related to V, while the C-system is not (Chomsky & Lasnik 1993), and argue that clitics can surface in a functional position that is L-related to V, or in a position related to C and not to V. Languages with clitics in only one of these positions represent pure types, while languages with clitics in both of them represent mixed types. Pure type languages include Bulgarian (B), which has an I-oriented system, and Serbo-Croatian (SC), which has a C-oriented system with Wackernagel properties. Old Spanish (OSp) is interesting in that it represents a mixed type because it uses both of these systems. The mixed character of OSp and its syntactic consequences are lost in the course of its diachronic evolution; the C-oriented or Wackernagel-like system OSp shares with SC disappears, while the I-oriented system OSp shares with B survives, with the following change. The OSp and B I-oriented systems are sensitive to a first position prohibition; by contrast, after the seventeenth century, the Spanish I-oriented system is no longer sensitive to such a prohibition, resembling in this respect the I-oriented Modern Greek system.

I also argue that B, OSp and SC are *symmetric* languages as to clitic structure, with C- or I-orientation in root and non-root clauses. Without exception, all types of clauses display I-properties in B, while SC shows exceptionless C-properties. By contrast, OSp has the mixed characteristics which derive from the combination of its I- and C-systems in embedded clauses, but seldom in main clauses. In main clauses, OSp shows an overwhelming preference for the I-system that survives in later stages, and exhibits restrictions in its use of the C-system, which provides the basis for the diachronic evolution that eliminates it in later periods.

In section 2, I characterize I- and C-systems in embedded clauses, establishing how OSp combines the two systems which exist in pure form in SC and B. In Section 3, I argue that these systems are symmetric and found without restrictions in main clauses in B and SC, but with important restrictions in OSp main clauses. In section 4, I discuss the effect of this assumed symmetry on root Verb + Clitic order or 'enclisis' in these languages, coming to three typological conclusions, and one specific conclusion for OSp, with consequences for the evolution of this language. First, since V + CL order is found in both SC and B, I conclude that it cannot be essentially connected to the C- or I-orientation of clitics; by contrast, CL + V order is sometimes seen as a symptom of C-orientation in the literature on Old Romance. Second, SC and B are not V2 languages, and I contend that OSp is not V2. Thus, I conclude that V+ CL order cannot be intrinsically connected to V2; by contrast, this order is sometimes seen as a clear symptom of V2 in the literature on Old Romance. Third, since SC and OSp have C-oriented, or Wackernagel-like, clitics and are not V2 languages, I conclude that Wackernagel phenomena must be independent from V2 phenomena as well. Fourth, for OSp, I show that V + CL order in this period has properties compatible with an analysis where clitics are I-oriented, but incompatible with the analysis where clitics are C-oriented as in SC. Thus, OSp structures with V+ CL order can only be analysed as resulting from the I-system, not the C-system, so in the period where the two systems coexist, enclitics reinforce the I-system.

2 I-oriented vs C-oriented clitic systems in embedded clauses

In this section, I examine complement clitic pronouns in embedded clauses to determine the essential differences between the I-system and the C-system, and contrast the mixed characteristics of OSp with the pure characteristics of B and SC. In 2.1, I present the data, and in 2.2 and 2.3, the analyses for the C- and I-systems respectively. In 2.4, I discuss some OSp patterns that appear problematic for the specific C- and I-systems set out in 2.2–2.3, and propose that they fall under an alternative C-system absent in SC, but present in Ancient Greek and German.

2.1 Clitic position in I- and C-oriented systems

OSp clitics are documented in two different locations in subordinate clauses, as in the *if*-clauses in (1) and (2):

(1) a. E si él mejor *lo* faze — dixo el rey —, ¿en qué lo
and if he better it does — said the king — in what him
podremos nos castigar?   Z154
can   we advise
'And if he does it better — said the king— in which way will we be able to advise him?'

b. Seméjame   que vos tienen en estrechura, si Dios non *vos* ayuda
seems.to.methat you have   in difficulties, if God not you helps
'It seems to me that if God does not help you, they have you in a
difficult position'   Z91

(2) a. Si *lo* el   rey   por bien toviere, mándeme quemar   CD243
         if it the king for good had,   order.me burn
         'If the king considered it good, let him order that they burn me'
     b. E   grant derecho sería   que me matases ..., si *me* de   ti
         and big   right   would.be that me kill ...,   if me from you
         non guardase   Z238
         not protect
         'And it would be your right to kill me ..., if I did not protect myself
         from you'

On the one hand, in the *if*-clauses of (1) clitics precede and are adjacent to the inflected V, and follow but are not adjacent to the complementizer *si* 'if'; descriptively speaking, clitics in such clauses are *I-oriented*, and are not in second position (2P). On the other hand, clitics in (2) are in 2P, follow and are strictly adjacent to *si*, and precede but are not adjacent to V. In (2a), a NP and a PP separate clitic and V; in (2b) PP and Neg stand between the two. Descriptively speaking, the clitics in (2) are *C-oriented*, as opposed to those in (1). By contrast with (1), the order in the *if*-clauses of (2) is now ungrammatical. In many OSp texts, these alternations are found under parallel syntactic conditions, as in (3). In my view, they are grammatical because two systems based on the I- vs C-oriented dichotomy apply to complement clitics:

(3) a. E   el arçobispo dixo que *se*   non trabajase ende ...,
         and the archbishop said that himself not work   of.it
         ca   non *ge-*   *lo* darían   Z53
         since not to.him-it would.give
         'And the archbishop said not to get excited about it ..., since they
         would not give it to him'
     b. Fue a la   corte a demandar el palio   e   non lo pudo
         went to the court to ask   the pennant and not it could
         acabar, ..., que *ge-*   *lo* non darían   en ninguna manera Z53
         obtain   that to.him-it not would.give in no   manner
         'He went to court to ask for the pennant and could not get it, ...,
         since they would not give it to him at all'

C- and I-oriented clitics are documented in structures that disallow CP-recursion, like the adjunct and *if*-clauses in (2)–(3), or in contexts where CP-recursion may exist, as in the complement of the bridge V *dixo* 'said' in (3a). Thus, clitic position in embedded clauses is independent from, and unrelated to, the sites that result from OSp CP-recursion. As discussed next, the I-oriented system is shared with B, while the C-oriented system is shared with SC, which contrasts with OSp in that it lacks CP-recursion.

In Modern Standard B, clitic pronouns in subordinate clauses must be adjacent to V, as in (4), corresponding to the *if*-clauses in (1): the clitic is fourth after C, NP and AdvP, and V ends the clause, like in OSp. However, (5) shows that B tolerates no variation as to clitic position, and is exclusively I-oriented, which OSp is not. In B, I-orientation appears to be an innovation, with (5) being found in some dialects, and in religious texts early this century. Thus, it seems as if B and Sp have experienced parallel evolutions.

(4) a. Ako toj burzo *go* napravi, ... B
       if he fast   it does
       'If he does it fast, ...'
    b. Ako bog ne *ti* pomogne, ...
       if God not you helps
       'If God does not help you, ...'
(5) a. *Ako *go* toj burzo napravi, ...
    b. *Ako *ti* bog ne pomogne, ...

In SC subordinate clauses, clitic pronouns must be adjacent to C, as in (6), similar to the OSp *if*-clauses in (2), not to those in (1):

(6) a. Ako *to* on bolje radi, ... SC
       if it he better does
       'If he does it better, ...'
    b. Ako *ti* bog ne pomogne, ...
       if you God not helps
       'If God does not help you, ...'

As (7) illustrates, SC contrasts with standard B, but is not identical to OSp, as it tolerates no variation in clitic position, being exclusively C-oriented, which OSp is not. In Slavic, C-orientation seems to be shared by Czech, Slovak and Slovenian:

(7) a. *Ako on bolje *to* radi, ...
    b. *Ako bog ne *ti* pomogne, ...

I propose that the contrasts between B and SC, and the similarities OSp shares with both of them derive from the idea that C-oriented and I-oriented clitics surface in different functional projections in the clause.[1] This could be because they are base-generated in that position, or move to it out of the VP, an independent issue I do not discuss.

2.2 C-oriented clitics and Spec,WP

For the C-oriented system, I assume a functional projection that complements C, in tune with Cardinaletti & Roberts' AgrP (1991), Halpern's CleftP (1992), Rouveret's WP (1992) and Uriagereka's FP (1992b, 1995), among others. With Rouveret, I label this projection WP, suggesting Wackernagel (1892). I also adopt the idea that C-oriented clitics may occupy the Spec of this projection, following a proposal of Shlonsky (1994) for West Flemish subject clitics. This results in the structure in (8), which, as stated, is independent of CP-recursion.

(8)   [$_{CP}$ C [$_{WP}$ CL [$_{W'}$ W YP]]]

If WP belongs to the C-system, as Shlonsky argues, in (8) the clitic is in a position related to C. In §2.4, I discuss a second alternative in OSp, with the clitic in W, not Spec,WP.

Together with (8), I adopt Kayne's system (1994), which disallows multiple adjuncts/specifiers in one X^{max}. This means that WP does not allow further adjunction, since it already contains one specifier = adjunct. These assumptions correctly predict what I consider the most salient and exceptionless feature of clitics in the pure C-system of SC: namely, the clitic must always be strictly adjacent to an overt C, as in (6) and (9a), an exceptionless situation given the absence of CP-recursion.[2] As illustrated by (9b) from Haegeman (1992: 62), the distribution of SC complement clitics and West Flemish subject clitics in embedded clauses is identical, which follows if both types are in Spec,WP.

(9) a. Ivan kaze [$_{CP}$ da $_{WP}$[*nam* $_{YP}$[Olga ništa   ne dovikuje]]]   SC
       Ivan says   that   us   Olga nothing not tells
       'Ivan says that Olga is not telling us anything'
    b. [$_{CP}$ da [$_{WP}$ *se* $_{YP}$[zie da   kleed gisteren   gekocht eed]]]
       that   she   she that dress yesterday bought has
       'that she bought that dress yesterday'   West Flemish

OSp shares clitic structure with SC. In the medieval period, clitics that precede V need not be adjacent to it, as in (10a). This word order is dubbed *Interpolation* (Gessner 1893; Meyer-Lübke 1897; Chenery 1905; Ramsden 1963; Rivero 1986, 1992; Wanner 1987, 1992a, 1993b). In my view, Interpolation exists because clitics can occupy a position in WP that is related to C, and they almost always appear in Spec,WP, like SC clitics. Thus, as traditionally observed, the great majority of instances of Interpolation show clitics that are strictly adjacent to C. On this view, (2a) (*si lo el rey por bien toviere*) and (10a), from Wanner (1992a: 345), receive analyses as in (10b):[3]

(10) a. Ca   sy*la*   yo avn non veo yo morre.   SME 494
        then if.her I   still not see I   will.die
        'Then, if I still do not see her, I will die'
     b. [$_{CP}$ sy [$_{WP}$ *la* [$_{YP}$ yo avn non veo]]]

OSp differs from SC in allowing CP-recursion with bridge Vs (Lema & Rivero 1991), but this is immaterial for WP, a projection unrelated to CP-recursion.

Word-order motivates the clitic's being in a Spec in (10); in addition, Rivero (1992) argues that OSp clitic pronouns and ordinary NPs undergo an identical process of 'clitic' climbing with Vs like *querer* 'want'. Ordinary NPs are X^{max} and must 'clitic climb' to a Spec position; thus, OSp clitics also share this option. In brief, X^{max} movement phenomena provide a second type of motivation for the idea that clitics can surface in the Spec of a projection, as opposed to its head. This argument cannot be used for SC, which lacks *bona fide* clitic climbing. However, we saw in note 2 that, under a movement view, SC clitic pronouns also exhibit X^{max} properties.

On conceptual grounds, Kayne's system (1994) disallows right-adjunction, so C-oriented clitics cannot be right-adjoined to C, but are unproblematic if in WP, as in (8)–(10). An empirical argument that such clitics are not in C is based on OSp relatives with the clitic after the *wh*-phrase and before the subject, as in (11):

(11) a. Puede ser por la ventura de que se ninguno non puede
       can be because the luck   of which REFL no one not can
       amparar   CD157
       obtain
       'It can be because of the good luck that nobody can obtain'
   b. la ventura [$_{CP}$ de que [$_{C'}$ [$_{C_0}$ Ø] [$_{WP}$ se [$_{YP}$ ninguno non ...]]]]

In Rivero (1984), I argue that OSp relatives display 'doubly-filled Comp effects', like their counterparts in Modern Spanish. Then, in (11) C must be phonologically null, because *de que* 'of which' is in Spec,CP. However, if C-oriented clitics were right-adjoined to C, both Spec,CP and C would be phonologically filled in (11). Thus, I conclude that these clitics are strictly adjacent to C because they are in Spec,WP. The relative in (12) is like OSp (11), so this conclusion applies to SC (contra Cavar & Wilder 1994), which right-adjoins the clitic to C, as also advocated for Czech (Toman 1986), and for Slovak (Saez 1991):

(12) a. Sve bi   to moglo biti zbog   istine koje se   niko   ne
       all COND it can   be because truth which REFL no-one not
       moze setiti
       can remember
       'It could all be because of the truth which no one can remember'
   b. istine [$_{CP}$ koje [$_{C'}$ [$_{C_0}$ Ø] [$_{WP}$ se [$_{YP}$ niko ne moze setiti]]]]

This analysis implies that C cannot contain overt material if Spec,CP is filled. This interpretation of 'doubly-filled Comp' effects seems correct, since order in questions is *wh*-phrase–Subject–Verb as in *Sta Ivan kupuje?* 'What is John buying?'. In these questions, V-to-C does not apply, and Spec and C are not both filled, as required.

To conclude, SC clitics are C-oriented and in the Spec of the WP projection which complements C as part of the C-system, and is independent from CP-recursion. Strict adjacency between the clitic and the right edge of C follows if adjunction to the right and multiple specifiers are disallowed (Kayne 1994). The OSp patterns of this section conform to the SC situation, suggesting participation in a C-system with identical properties. However, I show in §2.4 that OSp exhibits a flexibility absent in SC: clitics may sometimes occupy W, not just Spec,WP.

2.3 I-oriented clitics and TM

Clitics in the I-system are in a functional projection whose defining characteristic is to take the Agreement(s)/Tense complex, for short IP, as complement. I label this projection TMP, suggesting Tobler (1875), and Mussafia (1886, 1888). In contrast with W-clitics, the core descriptive characteristic of TM-clitics is that they surface adjacent to the inflected V, that is, they are 'adverbal' in the sense of Renzi (1989), who also distinguishes two types of clitics based on location. In addition, in some languages and/or historical stages of a given language, TM-clitics cannot appear first in the clause, a restriction Romance philologists label the 'Tobler–Mussafia law'. This restriction is shared by B, and by TM-clitics in OSp. However, roughly after the seventeenth century, it is lost for the surviving TM-clitics of Spanish. In this chapter, I maintain that the core contrast between W and TM clitics is their assumed location, that is C- vs I-orientation. Both types can be sensitive to a first position prohibition (W: Serbo-Croatian; TM: Bulgarian), or escape it (W: Slovenian; TM: Modern Spanish), so this cannot be the crucial difference. From my perspective, Tobler and Mussafia discussed the first position prohibition of TM-clitics exclusively, because the languages they examined (Old French and Old Italian) lack productive W-clitics with the characteristics of the SC and OSp type discussed above, but show TM clitics that cannot be first like B.

If I-oriented clitics are adjoined to the head of TMP, as in Kayne (1989) and later work on Romance, these assumptions result in the structure in (13a). If I-oriented clitics are in Spec, as in Rivero (1994a) for Balkan languages including B, the structure is as in (13b).[4]

(13) a. $[_{CP} C [_{YP} Y ... [_{TMP} [_{TM'} CL IP]]]]$
    b. $[_{CP} C [_{YP} Y ... [_{TMP} CL [_{TM} \emptyset [IP]]]]]$

If TMP belongs to the V-system like IP, in (13) the clitic occupies a position which is L-related to V, as opposed to SC clitics, which are related to C.

A first difference between the C and I systems motivating the different analyses of clitics comes from negative clauses, as in the contrast illustrated by B (4b) and SC (6b). In subordinate negative clauses, clitics falling under the C-system must precede Neg but need not be adjacent to it, as in SC *Ako ti bog ne pomogne*: CL–NP–Neg–V. By contrast, clitics falling under the I-system must follow Neg, as in B *Ako bog ne ti pomogne*: Neg–CL–V. As we saw, variation in these orders leads to clear ungrammaticality in both SC and B. In my view, the contrast between the two languages derives from the structure of Neg, and the presence or absence of WP. In both B and SC (Rivero 1991, 1994a), Neg heads an X^{max}, and must complement the C-system. Thus, when the WP part of this C-system is projected for the SC clitics, NegP must be below WP, and Neg^0 will always follow the clitic. Thus, the structure of the SC negative conditional is (14):

(14) $[_{CP} $ ako $ [_{WP} $ ti $ [_{NegP} $ bog $ [_{Neg'} $ ne $ [_{IP} $ pomogne$]]]]]$ C-system

Word order eliminates a series of alternative analyses. First, the clitic cannot be an X^0 that adjoins to Neg as X^0. Second, the clitic cannot be an X^0 that adjoins to NegP, as this violates structure-preservation. Third, the clitic cannot be an X^{max} that adjoins to NegP, since this implies a double adjunction (of the clitic and the NP-subject). Fourth, right-adjunction of the clitic to C is impossible on conceptual and empirical grounds. The analysis in (14) does not face any of these problems.

In B, clitics must surface in TMP, and WP is not projected. Then, NegP must appear directly below CP, as its complement. Under these assumptions, (4b) corresponds to (15), and the contrast between B and SC follows from the effect of WP in the last case:

(15)   [$_{CP}$ ako [$_{NegP}$ bog [$_{Neg'}$ ne [$_{TMP}$ *ti* [$_{IP}$ pomogne]]]]]   I-system

That the TMP position is also unrelated to CP-recursion is suggested by the fact that (15) is an embedded context disallowing such recursion.

I contend that OSp shares the C-system of SC, and the I-system of B. Thus, since OSp Neg also heads a X^{max} complement of the C-system, the two orders of *non* and clitics documented in this period correspond to the two options making SC and B differ. From this perspective, the OSp clitics preceding Neg in (2b), (3b), (10) and (11b) are as in (16a–d), and signal participation in the C-system:

(16)   a.   [$_{CP}$ si [$_{WP}$ *me* [$_{NegP}$ de ti [$_{Neg'}$ non [$_{IP}$ guardase]]]]]
       b.   [$_{CP}$ que [$_{WP}$ *gelo* [$_{NegP}$ [$_{Neg'}$ non [$_{IP}$ darían]]]]]
       c.   [$_{CP}$ sy [$_{WP}$ *la* [$_{XP?}$ yo [$_{NegP}$ avn [$_{Neg'}$ non [$_{IP}$ veo]]]]]]
       d.   [$_{CP}$ de que [$_{C'}$ [$_{C0}$ Ø] [$_{WP}$ *se* [$_{NegP}$ ninguno [$_{Neg'}$ non IP]]]]]

The order with *non* preceding clitics in (1b), (3a) or the complement clause in (17) signals that the OSp clitic is operating in the I-system shared with B schematized in (18), as opposed to the C-system of SC.[5]

(17)   Entendió   que el   su   saber   non le   tenía pro   CD 93
         he.understood that the his knowledge NEG him had benefit
         'He realized that his knowledge did not benefit him'

(18)   a.   [$_{CP}$ si [$_{NegP}$ Dios [$_{Neg'}$ non [$_{TMP}$ *vos* [$_{IP}$ ayuda]]]]]
       b.   [$_{CP}$ ca [$_{NegP}$ non [$_{TMP}$ *gelo* [$_{IP}$ darían]]]]
       c.   [$_{CP}$ que [$_{NegP}$ el su saber [$_{Neg'}$ non [$_{TMP}$ *le* [$_{IP}$ tenía pro]]]]]

Several arguments motivate the above analysis of OSp Neg. First, (19) illustrates that OSp Long Head Movement (LHM) constructions with an untensed V moved to C across a tensed Aux are always affirmative (Lema & Rivero 1991: §2.4):

(19)   a.   Dezir-vos he   cosa   CD146
           tell- you   will.1SG thing
           'I will tell you something'
       b.   [$_C V^0_i$] – [$_I$ Aux^0] – [$_V$ t$_i$]

The same holds in SC (Rivero 1991: §4) and B (Rivero 1994a: §3.1). In all three languages, Neg blocks LHM for the same reason. Namely, Neg is an

X^0 that c-commands the untensed V, and Neg and C are the same type of head (Rivero 1994a), based on Roberts (1992), so when V crosses Neg to move to C, it violates Relativized Minimality.

Second, OSp Imperative Vs can only appear in affirmative sentences. In this respect OSp is like Modern Spanish. For Modern Spanish, two recent proposals exist to account for this restriction, based on Neg being an X^0 that takes as complement the remainder of the clause. Since these solutions entail that OSp Neg must also be a head as in (18), I just mention them. Rivero proposes (1994a) that Imperative Vs must raise to C to check a strong feature with illocutionary force, and cannot cross Neg because this would violate Relativized Minimality, like raising the untensed V to C across Neg in the LHM construction in (19). For Laka (1990) and Zanuttini (1994), Neg and Imperative Vs must head the same ΣP-projection, so they are in complementary distribution. In brief, LHM and Imperative constructions motivate the view that OSp Neg must be the head of a X^{max} that c-commands V and I, and cannot be an Adverb in a Spec position.[6]

Third, OSp Neg counts as the first constituent for items in the clitic cluster, which clitic pronouns cannot do; in this way OSp Neg resembles B Neg. Fourth, OSp Neg can be split from the cluster, which clitics cannot be; in this way it resembles SC Neg. These two factors indicate that even though B, SC and OSp Neg are X^0, as shown above, they differ importantly from clitic pronouns, whether those behave like X^0 or X^{max}.

In my analysis, functional heads like the B and OSp Neg head a X^{max}, and clearly establish that the clitic which necessarily follows them is not in the projection that complements C. This same conclusion can be reached in view of any X^{max} that intervene between C and CL, as in (20):

(20) a. A esta cosa non ay sufrimiento, ..., que   nunca estas dos cosas
         in this thing no is suffering   because never these two things
         se   allegaron a ome que non lo   llegasen a punto de muerte
         REFL arrived   to man that not him put   to point of death
         'In this there is no suffering, ..., because these two things never happened to someone in a way that they would not practically kill him' CD97
    b. [$_{CP}$ que [$_{XP?}$ nunca [$_{TMP}$ estas dos cosas [$_{TM'}$ se [$_{IP}$ allegaron ...]]]]]
    c. ..., porque con ellos Dios *nos* guarde de las maneras de ellos
         because with them God us protect of the manners of them
         'Because God should protect us from their actions with them' Z81
    d. [$_{CP}$ porque [$_{XP?}$ con ellos [$_{TMP}$ Dios [$_{TM'}$ *nos* [$_{IP}$ guarde ...]]]]]

If multiple adjunctions to one X^{max} are not possible, (20) strongly suggests that I-oriented clitics need not be in the complement of C, unlike C-oriented clitics; this is because the item in CP is separated from the clitic by two different phrases.[7] If the OSp *if*-clause in (1a) is as in (21a), and the B *if*-clause in (4a) is as in (21b), the same conclusion applies:

(21) a. [$_{CP}$ si [$_{XP?}$ él [$_{TMP}$ mejor [$_{TM'}$ lo [$_{IP}$ faze]]]]]
'If he does it better'
b. [$_{CP}$ ako [$_{XP?}$ toj [$_{TMP}$ burzo [$_{TM'}$ go [$_{IP}$ napravi]]]]]
'If he does it fast'

In brief, two kinds of evidence support the view that I-oriented clitics need not be in the structural complement of C: (a) X^0s that intervene between C and clitic, and (b) two or more X^{max} between the two (or a combination of both types).

A salient word-order difference is that C-oriented clitics must necessarily be in 2P, or after C, while I-oriented clitics escape 2P requirements altogether. This is because the essential factor for clitics in the 'I-mode' is to be in the projection which takes IP as complement, while the essential factor for clitics in the 'C-mode' is to appear in the complement of C. This difference is lost in embedded contexts like affirmative clauses with null subjects. To exemplify, if subject and Neg are removed, the B and SC *if*-clauses in (14-15) become identical and are asymptomatic as to the clitic system they represent, resulting in the C—CL—V sequences of (22):

(22) a. [$_{CP}$ ako [$_{WP}$ *ti* [$_{IP}$ pomogne]]]   C-system
b. [$_{CP}$ ako [$_{TMP}$ *ti* [$_{IP}$ pomogne]]]   I-system
'If he helps you, ...'

In OSp, similar sequences to (23) contribute to uncertainty as to the appropiate analysis, since two systems coexist. Thus, the clitic could be in the 'essential' 2P-position defined as Spec,WP in (23b), or in the TM-position second 'by accident', as in (23c). This means that the analysis of proclitic structures need not be uniform, even in one language (also Rouveret 1992: 104):

(23) a. Creo   que si *lo*   desçercasedes, que faríedes   mesura e bondat
believe that if him unsurrounded,that would.do good
'I think that if you ceased to surround him, you would do a good and appropiate thing'   Z155
b. [$_{CP}$ si [$_{WP}$ *lo* [$_{IP}$ desçercases]]]   C-system
c. [$_{CP}$ si [$_{TMP}$ *lo* [$_{IP}$ desçercases]]]   I-system

Summarizing, I propose two structures for clitics on the basis of non-recursive embedded clauses. I-oriented clitics are in the functional projection TMP which is above IP, and is part of the V-system L-related to V. By contrast, C-oriented clitics are in the WP part of the C-system. Identical C–CL–V sequences may result from either system, and since OSp combines the two systems, in this language they are structurally ambiguous.

2.4 Variation in the OSp C-system: clitics in W

OSp clitics are like SC clitics and can be located in Spec,WP, but they are also like B clitics and can be located in TMP. If in Spec,WP, they are strictly adjacent to C. If in TMP, clitics are strictly adjacent to V. However, a small number of OSp examples appear problematic for these systems. They are not numerous, but recur in different centuries, texts and styles. Consider (24) with examples from my previous work (except for (24c)). This paradigm shares a problematic characteristic: the lack of adjacency between clitic and C, and between clitic and V.

(24) a. Se de   nos *te*   non partes ...   A133d (O)
　　　　if from us yourself not depart
　　　　'If you do not leave us, ...'
　　b. Que ellos *te* non digan en que puede finar ...   A2842c (O)
　　　　that they you not tell in what can   end
　　　　'Let them not tell you how it can end'
　　c. Si dios *lo* non fizies ...   (GE-1.3r) (Fontana 1993: 36)
　　　　if god it not did
　　　　'If God did not do it ...'
　　d. Sy el físico   *la* bien connosçe ...   Set 36
　　　　if the physician it well knows
　　　　'If the physician knows it well'
　　e. Si buen entendimiento *le*   Dios quiso   dar para entender ...
　　　　if good understanding him God wanted give to   understand
　　　　'If God wanted to give him a good mind to understand...'   Z335
　　f. So cierto que tan buen entendimiento *vos* Dios dió ...   Est 16
　　　　am sure that so good understanding you God gave
　　　　'I am sure that God gave you such a good mind ...'

In each case, one constituent separates C and clitic (a PP, a subject NP, or an object NP) and another separates clitic from V (Neg, Adv, or a subject NP), in environments excluding CP-recursion. Paradigm (24) does not include the result from the I- and C-systems discussed above since parallel orders are ungrammatical both in SC and Standard B: *Ako bog ti ne pomogne*. In SC, the clitic must follow C: *Ako ti bog ne pomogne*. In Standard B, the clitic must precede V: *Ako bog ne ti pomogne*.

I propose that (24) results from a different option of the C-system, as in (25): the clitic fills W, and Spec,WP is filled by a phrase. Thus, the core aspect of WP-clitics is not that they are X^{max} (Spec) or X^0 (head), but the height of the projection where they surface in the clause. As we shall see, this is exceptional in OSp, but regular in other languages:

(25) a. [$_{CP}$ se [$_{WP}$ de nos [$_{W'}$ *te* [$_{NegP}$ non partes]]]]
　　b. [$_{CP}$ que [$_{WP}$ ellos [$_{W'}$ *te* [$_{NegP}$ non digan]]]]
　　c. [$_{CP}$ si [$_{WP}$ dios [$_{W'}$ *lo* [$_{NegP}$ non fizies]]]]
　　d. [$_{CP}$ sy [$_{WP}$ el físico [$_{W'}$ *la* [$_{IP}$ bien connosçe]]]]
　　e. [$_{CP}$ si [$_{WP}$ buen entendimiento [$_{W'}$ *le* [$_{IP}$ Dios quiso dar]]]]
　　f. [$_{CP}$ que [$_{WP}$ tan buen entendimiento [$_{W'}$ *vos* [$_{IP}$ Dios dió]]]]

I attribute (25) to the co-existence of the I-oriented and C-oriented systems. In section 4 on enclisis I provide evidence that the OSp I-oriented clitic is in

TM⁰, or in a head-position; if this aspect is extended to the C-system, then the clitic can head WP as well.[8]

The C-system sketched in (25) is not unique, and applies to Ancient Greek clitic pronouns and pronouns in the German Wackernagel position, as interpreted by Cardinaletti & Roberts (1991). First, in Ancient Greek, various discourse particles (PCL) such as *de* 'but' must, without exception, appear in strict 2P in all types of clauses. In non-root clauses, these particles follow C, as illustrated by the conditional sentence in (26):

(26) a. Ei *de* duo eks enos agoonos gegeneesthon ouk egoo aitios
 if PCL two from one trial have.been.made not I responsible
 'But if two trials have been made out of one, I am not responsible' Ant. 5.85 (Smyth 1920: 2300.b)
 b. [$_{CP}$ ei [$_{WP}$ *de* [$_{IP}$ duo eks enos agoonos gegeneesthon]]]

In my view, the Ancient Greek particles are in Spec,WP, and roughly speaking encode point of view (and see note 5). Their location derives the strict adjacency to the left edge of C, and gives them, in embedded clauses, the same overall distribution as the SC clitic pronouns, the West Flemish subject clitics, and the OSp clitic pronouns in 2.3. When a particle co-occurs with a clitic pronoun, the pronoun follows the particle, and is strictly adjacent to it in many cases. In her important study of second position and clitic pronouns, Taylor (1990) observes this situation, but discounts particles when computing positions. My proposal differs from Taylor's in that I consider particles, which occupy Spec,WP, the crucial factor in defining 2P in Ancient Greek. Clitic pronouns are less symptomatic than particles, and offer more variation in their position, as Taylor points out, but I will assume that when they are adjacent to the left edge of the particle, they have been attracted to the head of W. Under this analysis, the structure of the conditional clause in (27a), borrowed from Taylor (1990: 45), is as in (27b):

(27) a. Ei *de* moi ouk epeess' epipeisetai, ... Il. 15. 162
 if PCL my not words obey
 'If he will not obey my words, ...'
 b. [$_{CP}$ ei [$_{WP}$ *de* [$_{W'}$ moi [$_{NegP}$ ouk [$_{IP}$ epeess' epipeisetai]]]]]

As shown in (27b), clause structure in Ancient Greek is identical to the one in SC, as argued in Rivero & Terzi (1995): CP takes WP as complement, and NegP takes IP as complement. Under this analysis, the difference is that Ancient Greek clitic pronouns are in W, while SC clitics are in Spec,WP. This treatment correctly entails that, in the presence of particles, Ancient Greek clitic pronouns are not second, but third.[9]

Under the C-system, OSp and SC share identical clause structures, namely [$_{CP}$ C [$_{WP}$ W [$_{NegP}$ Neg IP]]]. Thus, the analysis in (27b) also captures the parallelism between the (exceptional) C-system of OSp in (24–26), and the distribution of Ancient Greek clitic pronouns when adjacent to particles. The difference is that the Ancient Greek Spec,WP must be occupied by the discourse particle, while the OSp Spec,WP in (24) can hold an ordinary phrase such as a NP or PP, if it does not hold a clitic.

The second case concerns pronouns in the German Wackernagel position, as in Cardinaletti & Roberts (1991: 2.1):

(28) a. ... dass *es ihm* der Johann gestern gegeben hat
 that it him the John yesterday given has
 b. ... dass der Johann *es ihm* gestern gegeben hat
 '... that John gave it to him yesterday'

For Cardinaletti & Roberts, *es ihm* is in the equivalent of W. In (28a), Spec,WP is empty; in (28b) it is filled by the subject NP. Under this analysis, OSp (24b, c) and German (28b) are parallel. The difference is that in OSp Spec,WP can be filled by a phrase that is not a subject, which is not possible in German.

In conclusion, in 2.2 I argued that OSp C-clitics almost always distribute like SC clitics: they occupy Spec,WP, so are adjacent to C and in strict 2P. In 2.3 I showed that OSp and B I-clitics are in TM adjacent to V, and escape 2P constraints. In this section, I have shown that some OSp clitics depart from this characterization, because they are adjacent neither to C nor to V, and proposed that they belong to a C-system where they fill W, as opposed to Spec,WP, resembling Ancient Greek clitic pronouns, also in W, and those German pronouns that follow the subject. By contrast with OSp clitics, SC clitics have a homogeneous 2P-distribution, which follows if they always occupy Spec,WP, like West Flemish subject clitics.

3 I-oriented clitic systems and C-oriented clitic systems in main clauses

This section has three aims. The first is to argue that complement clitic structure in B, SC and OSp is *symmetric*, because clitics in main clauses are in the same structural position they occupy in embedded clauses. The second aim is to establish that even though OSp displays two symmetric systems, the C-system is seldom displayed in root clauses, which is important for diachronic evolution. The third aim is to establish that V + CL order or 'enclisis' is not homogeneous, because it arises in the C-oriented system of SC and the I-oriented system of B, and is also found in OSp, which combines both types. From this, I also conclude that the restriction about clitics in first position these languages share is independent of the structural position of the clitics: WP or TM.[10]

This section motivates the symmetry hypothesis, beginning with SC, and concluding with OSp, and does not exhaustively survey clitic position in main clauses (and see Ewen 1979; Hauge 1976 for B; Browne 1974, 1975; Cavar & Wilder 1994; Halpern 1992; Radanovic-Kocic 1988 for SC; Dimitrova-Vulchanova 1993 for various Slavic languages; and the cited references for OSp).

3.1 C-oriented clitics in main clauses: Serbo-Croatian

SC clitics are always C-oriented, and in Spec,WP. In main clauses, this is motivated by questions. Compare (29a) and (29b): *da li* opens the clause, followed by clitic *nam*, which must necessarily precede all other constituents.

(29) a. Pita da li   nam Olga nešto   dovikuje
       asks whether us   Olga something tells
       'He asks whether Olga is telling us something'
    b. Da li *nam* Olga nešto   dovikuje
       Q   us Olga something tells
       'Is Olga telling us something?'

(30)   (Pita) [$_{CP}$ da li [$_{WP}$ *nam* $_{W'}$[W [$_{YP}$ Olga nešto dovikuje]]]]

I propose that (29a, b) share the structure in (30), with *da li* as [+*wh*]-item in CP, and clitic always in Spec,WP, which is the essential point. Thus, in SC there is no difference in the position of clitics in main vs subordinate clauses.

With several *wh*-phrases, the pronominal clitic must follow the first *wh*-phrase, which Rudin (1988) argues is in Spec,CP, and must precede all others, which she assumes are adjoined to IP, as in (31a). In my approach, (31a) has the initial *wh*-phrase also in Spec,CP, the clitic in Spec,WP, and the second *wh*-phrase adjoined to the complement of WP, as schematized in (31b):

(31) a. Koliko   im   ko   daje?
       how.much to.them who gives
       'Who gives how much to them?'
    b. [$_{CP}$ koliko [$_{WP}$ *im* [$_{YP}$ ko daje]]]

In brief, questions motivate that in root clauses the clitic is strictly adjacent to the left edge of C, with no X^0 or X^{max} separating the two, like in embedded clauses. Thus, clitic structure is *symmetric*.

Constituents other than *wh*-phrases can also front to Spec,CP, as in (32):

(32) a. Ništa *nam* Olga ne dovikuje
       'Olga is not telling us anything'
    b. [$_{CP}$ Ništa$_i$ [$_{WP}$ *nam* [$_{YP}$ Olga t$_i$ ne dovikuje]]]
    c. Olga *nam* ništa ne dovikuje
       'Olga is not telling us anything'
    d. [$_{CP}$ Olga$_i$ [$_{WP}$ *nam* [$_{W'}$ W [$_{YP}$ t$_i$ ništa ne dovikuje]]]]

These examples cannot result from the alternative C-system in §2.4 for OSp, Ancient Greek and German. Namely, in SC the initial X^{max} is not in Spec,WP, with the clitic in W, because questions exclude this option. If the clitic was in W, two *wh*-phrases could precede it: one in Spec,CP, and another in Spec,WP. However, this word order is ungrammatical in SC.

If a X^{max} precedes the clitic in a negative clause, a root sentence is similar to an embedded clause: the clitic must precede Neg, but need not be adjacent to it, as in (32). This makes clitic position *symmetric*. However, root clauses where no X^{max} has fronted past the clitic differ from embedded negative clauses: they must have Neg+ V + CL order, as in (33), which is excluded in embedded clauses. Here clitic position remains symmetric with the analysis in Rivero (1991) futher justified in Rivero (1994b): V raises to Neg, and the two form the complex head that moves to C and precedes the Spec,WP clitic, as in (33b). The V-to-C analysis in (33b) also serves for V + CL order in affirmative clauses: V raises without Neg, as in (34):

(33) a. Ne dovikuje *nam* ništa
'(He/she) is not telling us anything'
b. [$_{CP}$ [$_{C^0}$ ne+dovikuje$_i$] [$_{WP}$ *nam* [$_{NegP}$ t$_i$ [$_{IP}$ t$_i$ nista]]]]
(34) a. Kaze *mu* da je kukavica
tells him that is coward
'He tells him that he is a coward'
b. [$_{CP}$ [$_C$ V$_i$] [$_{WP}$ *CL* [$_{W'}$ W [$_{IP}$ t$_i$]]]]
c. *Mu* kaze da je kukavica

Under the symmetry hypothesis, the clitic in (34a, b) must be in Spec,WP like in embedded clauses, and V must then be in C, since current assumptions forbid V^0 to adjoin to Spec,WP, or WP. Thus, V^0 must move to the immediate superordinate head C^0.

The same treatment serves for affirmative and negative questions with V preceding *li*, which in turn precedes the complement clitic, as in (35). For Rivero (1993b), *li* is an alternative to *dali* in C, and (Neg) + V adjoins to it, as shown in (35b) and (35d):

(35) a. Ne govori li *nam* istinu?
'Is he not telling us the truth?'
b. [$_{CP}$ [$_{C^0}$ ne+govori$_i$ [$_{C^0}$ li]][$_{WP}$ *nam* [$_{NegP}$ t$_i$ [$_{IP}$ t$_i$ istinu]]]]
c. Govori li *nam* istinu?
'Is he telling us the truth?'
d. [$_{CP}$ [$_{C^0}$ govori$_i$ [$_{C^0}$ li]][$_{WP}$ *nam* [$_{IP}$ t$_i$ istinu]]]

Finally, left-dislocations are external to the CP-node of the above diagrams, so in such constructions, clitics in WP can be third, or fourth (see Radanovic-Kocic 1988 for examples). That left-dislocated phrases do not 'count' when determining 2P has been documented in many languages, including my work on OSp, so I will not reiterate this point for SC.

To summarize, complement clitics are always in Spec,WP, so SC displays a *symmetric* C-oriented system. With clitics in Spec,WP, our formal system entails that SC enclisis necessarily involves movement of V to C. In declaratives, (Neg) + V + CL order results when (Neg) + V raises. In questions, (Neg) + V + *li* + CL order arises when (Neg) + V adjoins to *li* in C.

3.2 I-oriented clitics in main clauses: Bulgarian

Clitics in B are consistently I-oriented or in the V-related projection identified as TMP in section 2. Thus, B is also symmetric.

B direct questions with a modal layer like (36) provide conclusive evidence that complement clitics in root clauses are in TMP. The clitic must immediately precede V, and can be separated from *dali*, as in (36a), but cannot be separated from V, and precede NP, as in (36c). Recall that SC *da li* must immediately precede the clitic, as in *Da li **nam** Olga nešto dovikuje* 'Is Olga telling us something?':

(36) a. Dali Olga šte *ti* dade knigata?
 Q Olga FUT you give book.the?
 'Will Olga give you the book?'
 b. [$_{CP}$ dali [$_{MP}$ Olga [$_{M'}$ šte [$_{TMP}$ *ti* dade knigata]]]
 c. *Dali *ti* Olga šte dade knigata?

If multiple specifiers/adjuncts are disallowed, (37a) suggests that the clitic is not in the X^{max} complement of C^0. Two phrases separate *dali* in C^0 from the clitic, so these phrases are adjoined to each other, which is unlikely, or the adverb is in a Spec that is higher than the subject, as in (37b):

(37) a. Dali vinagi Olga *ti* dava knigata?
 Q always Olga you gives book.the
 'Does Olga always give you the book?'
 b. [$_{CP}$ dali [$_{XP?}$ vinagi [$_{TMP}$ Olga [$_{TM'}$ *ti* dava knigata]]]]

Rizzi (1986a: 395ff.) proposes that quantified NPs do not function as left-dislocated phrases, which can be used to motivate the position of B clitics. In (38a), the clitic must be in TMP, because if the subject is not left-dislocated, it must be CP-internal. For the sake of the argument, if this NP is as high as Spec,CP, the following adverb strongly suggests the TM-analysis sketched in (38b). Clauses embedded under verbs that disallow recursion, such as factives, may exhibit parallel word orders, as in (38c):

(38) a. Nikoj nikoga ne *go* čete
 no.one never not it reads
 'No one ever reads it'
 b. $_{XP}$ [nikoj [$_{NegP}$ nikoga [$_{Neg'}$ ne [$_{TMP}$ go čete]]]]
 c. Sužaljavam če nikoj nikoga ne *go* čete
 regret.1SG that no.one never not it reads
 'I regret that no one ever reads it'

The examples in (38) show that in B negative clauses, Neg always precedes CL in root and embedded environments, in contrast with SC. Under my approach, B and SC differ because the prohibition against first position clitics discussed in 4 has a different effect on Neg, due to clitic structure. On the one hand, in SC WP takes NegP as complement, so the clitic precedes Neg^0. Since the clitic cannot be first, the two movement options discussed in the previous section arise: (a) an XP fronts to Spec,CP, giving XP–CL–Neg order, or (b) Neg and V form a complex that raises to C, giving Neg–V–CL order. Thus, Neg–CL–V order, which is the only option in B, is excluded in SC. On the other hand, B NegP takes TMP as complement, so

Neg precedes the clitic and provides the required first constituent in the absence of fronting rules, as in *Ne go čete* 'He does not read it.' A consequence of this situation is that B *ne* cannot be considered a 'clitic' for two reasons. As shown, it escapes first position restrictions on pronouns, which are clitics, and can count as the initial constituent for those pronouns.

Clitic structure in Modern Greek is like in B: clitics are in TMP in an I-oriented symmetric system. Thus, in root and non-root clauses alike, the clitic follows Neg and M like in B, as illustrated by the root clause in (39):

(39) a. I María den tha *to* girísi anápoda Modern Greek
   the Mary NEG FUT it turn upside.down
   'Mary will not turn it upside down'
  b. [$_{NegP}$ I María [$_{Neg'}$ den [$_{MP}$ [$_{M'}$ tha [$_{TMP}$ *to* girísi anapoda]]]]]

In brief, questions, quantifiers, and negation show that B root clauses differ from SC as to the structure of clitics: TMP vs WP. However, the systems of both languages are symmetric. In addition, the above sentences indicate that B like SC lacks V2-characteristics in main clauses.

Now let us consider the orders with V before CL found in two types of B affirmative constructions. The first type is illustrated by declaratives like (40a), which cannot be embedded, as shown in (40b, c):

(40) a. Pomaga *im*
   helps them
   'He is helping them'
  b. Znam če *im* pomaga
   'I know that he is helping them'
  c. *Znam če pomaga *im*

Earlier, I concluded that the apparently identical SC order always involves movement of V to C, since CL is in Spec,WP and V precedes it: [$_{CP}$ V$_i$ [$_{WP}$ CL [$_{IP}$ t$_i$]]]. However, B V + CL sequences like (40a) have the clitic in TMP, so nothing forces the landing site of V to be C. Minimalist principles like Shortest Movement, and Procrastinate, suggest other options. First, if clause structure in B is [$_{CP}$ C [$_{NegP}$ Neg [$_{MP}$ M [$_{TMP}$ CL [$_{IP}$ ... V...]]]]] (Rivero 1994a [1988]), the landing site of V could be M^0, as in (41a). This is 'long' head movement of V past CL, and the only option under the assumption that CL is in Spec,TM. Second, if CL is in TM^0, the landing site of V could be adjunction to CL, as in (41b):[11]

(41) a. [$_{MP}$ [$_{M^0}$ pomaga$_i$] [$_{TMP}$ *im* [$_{IP}$ t$_i$]]]
  b. [$_{TMP}$ [$_{TM^0}$ pomaga$_i$ [$_{TM_0}$ *im*]] [$_{IP}$ t$_i$]]

Option (41a) makes enclisis with I-oriented clitics similar to enclisis with C-oriented clitics in SC, with a different projection holding the raised V: the higher C for SC vs the lower M for B. Analysis (41b) resembles the treatment for Romance Infinitive + CL in Kayne (1991), and the analysis in Rouveret (1992: 108) for V + CL in European Portuguese. In section 4, I provide an empirical argument favouring (41a) over (41b) in B. By contrast the formal characteristics of enclisis in OSp seem to favour a structure like (41b), which is important in explaining diachronic evolution. Thus, the two options for the analyses of TMP-clitics mirror those of WP-clitics: namely, Spec vs Head.

Modern Greek lacks the restriction against initial clitics ensuring V-raising in B (40a), so word-order is always CL + V, as in (42):

(42)   To girízi anápoda
        it turns upside.down
        'He turns it upside down'

The second type of B enclisis is found in questions with *li* like (43a), and can be embedded under a question V, as in (43b). Rivero (1993b) argues that B *li* is in C, like its SC counterpart. Then V in (43a, b) raises to C and adjoins to *li*, as shown in (43c):

(43) a. Dava li *ti*   knigata?
        gives Q you book.the
        'Does (s)he give you the book?'
     b. Pitam se   dava li *ti*   knigata
        ask   REFL gives Q you book.the
        'I wonder if (s)he gives you the book'
     c. (Pitam se) [$_{CP}$ [$_{C0}$ dava$_i$ [$_{C0}$ li]] [$_{TMP}$ *ti* t$_i$ knigata]]

In section 4 I argue that this V-raising occurs to check the features of *li* in both main or embedded clauses. This forces 'enclisis' in indirect questions, an option always absent in Old Romance, including OSp. Notice, however, that the requirement imposed by *li* does not affect the symmetric position of the complement clitic: CL is in TMP in all clauses, including (43). *Li* and the complement clitic need not be adjacent, as in *Koj li šte im pomogne*? (Who Q M him help) 'Who on earth will help him?'; lack of adjacency follows if CL is in TMP, *li* is in C, and M separates the two.

In brief, B 'enclisis' is of two types. One type is for root clauses, and consists of affirmative declaratives with V strictly adjacent to the clitic pronoun. In this case, I argue in §4 that V raises to M so as to license the complement clitic. The second type is found in root and non-root interrogatives with V before *li*, and *li* before the clitic pronoun. In this case, I show in §4 that V adjoins to *li* in C, so as to license this item, and not the clitic pronoun. We shall see that licensing conditions for clitic pronouns and for *li* differ, and this accounts for the fact that enclisis is possible in non-root environments only in the presence of *li*. Since OSp lacks a lexical item with the language-specific properties of B *li*, enclisis in embedded questions is impossible, which is general across Old Romance.

Other than XPs in Spec,CP (focus for Rudin 1986, 1993) and those attached to the highest functional projection of the I-system (a second focus for Rudin), B allows XPs external to CP (left-dislocated phrases and topics for Rudin), but those are not indicative of clitic structure. As a consequence, I have argued that B clitic pronouns are in TMP and not WP on the basis of

CP-internal XPs, avoiding affirmative left-dislocations, topicalizations and focalizations, where B and SC may look alike.

To summarize, B complement clitics are always in TMP, so this language displays a symmetric I-oriented system like Modern Greek or Modern Spanish, but is subject to an additional first position prohibition. The order with V before CL arises in two types of affirmative clauses: (a) in root declaratives, V raises to M to license the clitic pronoun that cannot be first; (b) in root and non-root questions with *li*, V raises to *li* in C in order to license this item and not the pronoun that follows it when both are present.

3.3 C- and I-oriented clitics in Old Spanish main clauses

In this section, I argue that OSp is symmetric, and exploits the I- and C-oriented systems of embedded clauses also in main clauses. However, in main clauses, the C-system is seldom used, and the I-system is overwhelmingly favoured. This quantitative factor is important for the subsequent evolution that abandons the C-system, since ambiguous main clause patterns open in principle to either the C- or the I-analysis are more likely to receive the I-analysis which will fit in an unproblematic way almost all the evidence found in main clauses.

In addition, I show in §4 that the OSp V + CL order found in root clauses shows characteristics that are compatible with the analysis with CL as head in TM, and incompatible with analyses with CL as Spec in WP. This means that OSp enclisis in main clauses has an I-analysis as its only option, which constitutes an important qualitative factor in the subsequent death of the C-system. In brief, clitics in OSp main clauses provide the quantitative and qualitative basis for the subsequent changes Spanish undergoes, while clitics in embedded clauses offer less crucial properties for the abandonment of the C-system.

Positive evidence for the C-system in main clauses is limited, consisting of isolated examples, which nevertheless recur in different styles and authors. They belong to two main types. First, questions with clitics adjacent to *wh*-phrases and separated from V by Neg, as in (44a, b) from Rivero (1992: 245), look like SC questions, and correspond to deviant structures in B. This type is documented in Gonzalo de Berceo, *Mio Cid*, and *Calila e Dimna*, among others:

(44) a. Por qé *me* non recudes? B Milg 293c
     why me NEG answers
     'Why don't you answer me?'
   b. [$_{CP}$ Por qé [$_{WP}$ *me* [$_{NegP}$ non [$_{IP}$ recudes]]]]

The second type in (45)–(47) consists of declaratives with clitics separated from V by the NP-subject, like SC but unlike B. In (45), the adverb is in Spec,CP, and the clitic in WP in strict 2P. Example (46) has a left-dislocated phrase external to CP in TopP, an adverb in Spec,CP, and the resumptive clitic in WP, so not in strict 2P. Example (47) contains a hanging topic with no resumptive item, and a vocative, both outside Spec,CP, and an adverb in Spec,CP, with the clitic in WP in 'fourth' position:

(45) a. Nin   *me* yo pornía   en tan grandes grandías   Z156
       and.not.even me I would.put in such big   bigness
       'And even I would not consider myself so great'
    b. [$_{CP}$ nin [$_{WP}$ *me* [$_{IP}$ yo pornía en tan grandes grandías]]]

(46) a. Elo   que yo quis   nunca *lo* uos contradixiestes   A 2284c, d (O)
       and.the that I wanted never it you contradicted
       'What I wanted, you were never opposed to it'
    b. [$_{TOPP}$ lo que yo quis [$_{CP}$ nunca [$_{WP}$ *lo* [$_{IP}$ uos contradixiestes]]]]

(47) a. Et alo   que cosa son los angeles, fijo, ya   uos yo dixe
       and to.the which thing are the angels, son, already you I told
       quelas preguntas que me fazedes son de muchas sçiencias
       that.the questions that me make are of many   sciences
       'And as to what angels are, son, I already told you that the questions you ask me pertain to many sciences'   (from Chenery 1905)
    b. ... [$_{CP}$ ya [$_{WP}$ *uos* [$_{IP}$ yo dixe ...]]]

In embedded clauses these two patterns are the most frequent instances of Interpolation, so it does not seem unusual that they establish that the C-system is also found in root clauses. In addition, these patterns show that OSp lacks V2-characteristics in those cases where clitic structures resemble SC, another language that is not V2.

Now consider clitics in the I-system. If quantified NPs are not left-dislocated phrases (Rizzi 1986a: 395ff.), (48a) illustrates a clitic in TMP, because the subject of this sentence must be CP-internal. As in parallel patterns in B, the position of the adverb strongly suggests the TM-analysis shown in (48b):

(48) a. Mas, mal pecado, algunos de los señores grandes mas aina *se*
       and bad sin   some   of the lords big   more now REFL
       inclinan a creer las palabras falagueras de los mentirosos   Z61
       tend   to believe the words flattering of the liers
       'And, unluckily, some of the nobles now tend to lend more credibility to the flattering words of those who lie'
    b. Mas, mal pecado, [$_{XP}$ algunos de los señores grandes $_{TMP}$ [mas aina [$_{TM'}$ *se* inclinan ...]]]

In addition, (48) shows that when OSp is like B as to clitic structure, it lacks V2-characteristics, and is similar to Modern Spanish: *Algunos incluso todavía se inclinan a creer esas mentiras* 'Even now, some tend to believe those lies.'[12]

Let us now see how Neg in root clauses impinges on the I- vs C-systems. In negative sentences, OSp shows two word orders. It shares with B the order Neg CL V, absent in SC, and it shares with SC the order XP CL... Neg V, absent in B. OSp, however, lacks the root Neg V CL order also found in SC, which would be the third word order option in root negative clauses if OSp is mixed, as I claim. This absence follows if OSp Neg is a head that c-commands I, as assumed, but in contrast with SC Neg disallows Incorporation of the inflected V. Recall that SC Neg V CL order results in root clauses when V incorporates to Neg and the two move to C to licence CL in WP. If this incorporation is absent in OSp, in root clauses Neg + V will never precede CL. Under these assumptions, when *non* precedes the clitic, as in (49a, b), it must be in TMP, like in B, which gives Neg CL V order:

(49) a. Ninguno de los otros   non *lo* osavan al   Papa demandar   Z54
         none   of the others NEG it dare   to.the Pope ask
         'None of the others dared ask the Pope for it'
     b. [NegP Ninguno de los otros [Neg' non [TMP *lo* osavan ...]]]

The OSp alternative option CL... Neg V must be similar to SC in its analysis, so it indicates that the clitic is in WP, as in *Por qé me non recudes*? Thus one of the OSp orders for Neg and clitics is symptomatic of the I-system (Neg-CL), while the other one is symptomatic of the C-system (CL-Neg).

Qualitatively speaking, OSp root negative sentences are like embedded negative clauses in providing clear evidence as to the structural position of clitics. However, if we consider main clause evidence quantitatively, a difference picture emerges. As stated, negative root sentences almost always are of the Neg CL V type, including cases where a phrase precedes Neg, as in (49). Recall that in this last situation, SC shows CL...Neg order, given that clitics are always in WP in this language. Thus, quantitatively, the presence of *non* in main clauses favours the clitic-in-TM option in (49) over the clitic-in-WP option in (44). Thus OSp favours I-oriented clitics in main clauses, to the detriment of C-oriented clitics, even though the two systems in principle coexist. This preference opens the door to the disappearance of the C-oriented system, since it must be concluded that WP is very seldom projected in main clauses even in the period when examples with Interpolation are at their peak in frequency. In addition, I argue in section 4 that WP cannot be projected in cases that involve V + CL orders.

Neg also provides evidence that root negative sentences lack V2-characteristics. When *non* precedes clitic and V in (49), it indicates that the finite V has not raised past IP in main (or embedded) clauses; when *non* precedes V but follows the clitic in Interpolation in (44), it also shows a V not in C. Thus, we must conclude that both I and W-orientation are independent of V2 properties, as B and SC clearly suggest.

OSp root clauses that look like both B and SC sentences should in principle be open to two analyses under the two systems approach, and I will exemplify this point with only one case. The affirmative *wh*-question with obligatory CL + V order in (50a) looks like a question in B, SC or Modern Spanish. Cliticwise, it could be analysed as in (50b), or as in (50c), (traces are omitted):

(50) a. E   quién *lo*   mató?   Z85
         and who   him   killed?
         'And who killed him?'

b. [$_{CP}$ quién [$_{WP}$ *lo* [$_{IP}$ mató]]]
c. [$_{CP}$ quién [$_{TMP}$ *lo* [$_{IP}$ mató]]]

However, if unambigous root W clitics are rare, and Neg quantitatively favours an I-analysis in main clauses, analysis (50c) will be compatible with the great majority of patterns found in main clauses, and is likely to be preferred on these grounds.

Now, let us consider V+CL orders. In OSp, enclisis is restricted to OSp affirmative root declaratives like (51), affirmative direct *yes–no* questions, and a few cases of CP-recursion (neither of which is exemplified):

(51)   Dígo-*vos* -dixo el   capellán- que este vuestro amigo muere   Z70
       tell-you   -said the priest-   that this your   friend dies
       'The priest said: "I am telling you that your friend is dying"'

If V + CL order is found both within the C and the I-system, and OSp uses both systems, (51) should in principle be an ambiguous pattern. However, my contention is that it was analysed along the lines where the clitic is a head in the I-system, which is the second factor, this time qualitative, that contributed to the disappearance of the C-system.

Under this perspective let us consider the different analyses available for enclisis. For reasons given for SC, in the C-system clitics are in Spec,WP, and enclisis in (51) should be as in (52). The defining characteristic of a clitic in this system is its strict adjacency to C in main and subordinate clauses alike, so enclisis indicates that V is in C.

(52)   [$_{CP}$ [$_C$ V$_i$] [$_{WP}$ *CL* [$_{W'}$ W [$_{IP}$ t$_i$ ....]]]]   C-system

In the I-system, however, enclisis is open to several analyses, as in (53a–c). The first two options represent Long Head Movement of V to a higher head than TM, with V and CL retaining their independence from each other, and the third option is Incorporation of V as X^0 to CL in TM^0, with the two forming a complex head:

(53)   a. [$_{XP}$ [$_X$ V$_i$] [$_{TMP}$ *CL* [$_{TM'}$ [$_{TM}$ ø] [$_{IP}$ t$_i$]]]]
       b. [$_{XP}$ [$_X$ V$_i$] [$_{TMP}$ [$_{TM0}$ *CL*] [$_{IP}$ t$_i$]]]
       c. [$_{TMP}$ [$_{TM'}$ [$_{TM0}$ V$_i$ [$_{TM0}$ *CL*]] [$_{IP}$ t$_i$]]]

If OSp contrasts with B in lacking M (but see Pollock (1993) for M in French), in (53a, b) the landing site of V labelled X is likely to be Σ, for negation and affirmation (Laka 1990).

Thus, if OSp is mixed, it should exhibit several possibilities for the analysis of enclisis in root clauses. However, on the basis of coordination facts, I contend in §4 that this ambiguous situation appears to be missing, because the analysis of enclisis in the medieval period reduces to (53c) exclusively, with the verb and the clitic functioning as a morphological complex. This shows that my earlier contention (Rivero 1986) that OSp clitics behave exclusively as X^{max}, and Halpern & Fontana's idea (1993) that V + CL order signals X^{max} status for clitics unambiguously cannot be right.

The status of enclisis in Spanish is important for diachronic purposes. It means that while the first position prohibition for clitics survives roughly until the seventeenth century, enclitic structures provide positive evidence for the hypothesis that clitics in main clauses are heads in TM. As a result, enclitic structures are also instrumental in eliminating the three other alternatives, where clitic and V do not form a morphological complex, and in particular WP-analyses as in (52). Thus, the properties of enclisis in OSp appear to contribute to the survival of the I-system, and to the demise of the C-system which involves the projection of WP to hold clitics in its Spec, like in SC.

To summarize, OSp authors like thirteenth-century Gonzalo de Berceo and fourteenth-century Juan Manuel, among others, symmetrically employ both the C- and the I-systems in embedded and main clauses. In this sense, their language is doubly symmetric, with clitics in either WP or TMP in all types of clauses. However, it has traditionally been observed that Interpolation — the order symptomatic of C-orientation — is not usually found in root clauses in OSp. In my system, this means that even though OSp combines two options to locate clitics, TMP and WP, WP is seldom projected in main clauses, and is more often projected in subordinate clauses. By contrast, TMP shows no restrictions and is frequently and systematically projected in both main and subordinate clauses, and is the almost exclusive choice in main clauses. Neg has a clear symptomatic value as to the structure of clitics in this period, and quantitatively speaking, the presence of *non* also favours the TMP option in root clauses. In addition, in §4 I discuss in more detail the qualitative factor which eliminates the WP-analysis for enclitics. Namely, root V CL orders show properties incompatible with a WP analysis for clitics, but compatible with a TMP-analysis where the clitic is a head. Thus the enclisis resulting from the first position prohibition all clitics share during this period irrespective of WP or TMP orientation creates difficulties for the diachronic survival of the C-system, and favours a head analysis under the I-system, paving the way for the later I-system that treats clitics as heads but, after the seventeenth century, lacks the first position restriction.

4 On V + CL order

I just suggested that enclisis in OSp is instrumental in the demise of the C-system and the survival of the I-system. In this section, I substantiate this idea and its effect on the diachronic evolution of Spanish, while examining aspects of V + CL order that are relevant to B, OSp and SC at the same time. In 4.1 I begin by motivating the idea that V + CL orders are not intrinsic to a specific clitic system, so they can receive non-unitary analyses, and I establish properties of enclisis in SC and B vs OSp, motivating this idea. At this point I also show that, against what can be expected due to its mixed character, enclisis in OSp root clauses shows properties that are only compatible with the system with clitics as heads in TM. This is important for the later disappearance of the WP system. I continue in §4.2 with the discussion of the general first position prohibition for complement clitics shared by B, SC and OSp, which induce enclisis in root environments. I then conclude this section with the first position restriction on B *li* which induces a language-specific enclisis in root and non-root questions absent in SC and Old Romance, including OSp.

4.1 WP, TMP and first position

We already saw that V + CL order is found in languages such as B and SC that differ in clitic structure, if they share a prohibition against first position clitics. Thus, it must be concluded that this prohibition cannot be essentially tied to either the WP or the TMP location of the complement clitic. In addition, we now see that WP clitics and TMP clitics may escape first position prohibitions, which reinforces the same conclusion.

WP clitics displaying no first position restrictions are West Flemish subject clitics. Recall that West Flemish and SC clitics have identical distributions in embedded clauses. In main clauses, however, a difference emerges. SC clitics must follow a constituent. By contrast, West Flemish clitics satisfy V2 (Haegeman 1992: 96), as in (54a), and cannot follow a phrase, as in (54b):

(54) a. Z'   ee gewerkt   West Flemish
       she-CL has worked
       'She worked'
   b. *Gisteren z'   ee gewerkt
       yesterday she-CL has worked

For Shlonsky (1994), the subject clitic *z* in (54a) is in Spec,WP and satisfies the V2 requirement of the auxiliary *ee* in W. Here, then, we have a WP clitic insensitive to the factor triggering V-raising in V + CL orders in SC. A second case of a first position WP clitic is found in Slovenian. In this language, complement clitics in embedded clauses distribute like SC clitics, so they are in Spec,WP. Some root clauses like *yes–no* questions, however, allow initial clitics. As pointed out by Kudra (1993), the question particle *ali* can be absent, no V-raising applies, and the clitic opens the sentence, as in (55b):[13]

(55) a. Ali *ga* je pustila?   Slovenian
       Q   him has left
       'Has she left him?'
   b. *Ga* je pustila?
   c. [$_{CP}$ (ali) [$_{WP}$ *ga* je pustila]]

Recall that, in my view, the core characteristic of TMP-clitics is adjacency to the inflected V. Thus, most Modern Romance clitics are of this type, even though they escape first position prohibitions in that they can open the clause: MSp *Lo lees* 'You are reading it.' In addition, Modern Greek has CL + V order where B must display V + CL order, because in the first language clitics must be adjacent to the inflected V, or in TMP, but can be first in the clause, while in the second clitics also in TMP and adjacent to the inflected V must be protected by an initial constituent.

Now consider V2. SC is not V2 and displays V + CL, while West Flemish is V2 and lacks the V + CL orders characteristic of SC; thus, V + CL is also independent of V2. However, V + CL orders are found in V2 languages such as Old French, whose clitics are sensitive to a first position restriction like B and SC.

In brief, enclisis arises if a first position restriction exists, irrespective of the structural location of the clitic, and I will discuss the nature of this restriction in §4.3.

4.2 Structures for V + CL

A consequence of the various systems underlying V + CL orders stressed in the above sections is that enclisis need not have a homogeneous analysis from the perspective of the landing site of V, or the structural slot for CL, as in the analyses summarized in (56):

(56) a. $[_{CP} [_C V_i] [_{WP} CL [_{W'} W [_{IP} t_i \dots]]]]$ C-system
 b. $[_{XP} [_X V_i] [_{TMP} CL [_{TM} \emptyset] [_{IP} t_i]]]$ (LHM) I-system
 c. $[_{XP} [_X V_i] [_{TMP} [_{TM} CL] [_{IP} t_i]]]$ (LHM) I-system
 d. $[_{TMP} [_{TM'} [_{TM} V_i [_{TM} CL]] [_{IP} t_i]]$ (Incorporation) I-system

Empirical evidence showing that enclisis is not homogeneous comes from coordination. It has been noticed that in some Romance languages, clitics and Vs are in a tight relation when Vs precede clitics, but not when Vs follow clitics (Bosque 1987, §2 for Spanish; Benincà & Cinque 1993 for Italian; Rouveret 1992 for European Portuguese). This is shown by the fact that coordinated Vs may share a proclitic pronoun, as in European Portuguese (57a) from Rouveret, but enclitic pronouns must be repeated with each V, as in (57b):

(57) a. Que livro a Maria *lhe* deu e pediu de novo?
    which book the Mary him gave and asked of new
    'Which book did Mary give him and ask to be returned?'
 b. Ele viu-*me* e cumprimentou-*me*
    She saw me and complimented me
 c. *Ele viu-*me* e cumprimentou

The idea is that in these languages V + CL sequences form a morphological complex. The analysis Benincà & Cinque propose for Italian enclitics is that they incorporate to V; enclitics must appear on each V in cases like (57b) so as not to violate the Coordinate Structure Constraint: Incorporation cannot affect just one of the conjuncts.

SC and B CL + V and V + CL orders escape the above contrast. Like in

European Portuguese, coordinated finite Vs share proclitic pronouns, as in (58a) and (59a). Unlike European Portuguese, however, an enclitic with just the first finite V is grammatical, as in (58b) and (59b). These intuitions are more secure in SC than in B (this could indicate that SC and B clitics differ as to X-bar status, contrary to what I conclude next):

(58) a. Svaki dan *je* kupuje i čita   SC
       every day it buys   and reads
       'Every day he buys it and reads it'
    b. Kupuje *je* i čita svaki dan
       '(He) buys it and reads it every day'

(59) a. Maria *ja* kupi   i   pročete   B
       Mary it bought and read
       'Mary bought it and read it'
    b. Kupi *ja* i pročete
       '(He) bought it and read it'

In view of this, I extend to B the conclusion Radanovic-Kocic (1988: 62) offers for SC: (58) and (59) show that enclitics behave 'as independent words syntactically'. Without giving an analysis of coordination, I suggest that (58b) and (59b) show that the clitic as a syntactic constituent in the first conjunct identifies an empty category functioning as syntactic constituent in the second conjunct, similar to Spanish examples like *Yo como y tú no* 'I eat and you (do) not', with the second V missing. Under this view, (58) motivates that enclisis in SC is as in (52), since V must bypass the clitic in Spec,WP in order to precede it. Under the Shortest Movement principle, B enclisis in (59b) is as in (53a) or (53b), since V must raise to bypass the clitic, but must remain independent from it. In both (52) and (53a, b), V and clitic are separate syntactic constituents, as required by (58) and (59), but the landing site of V differs, as it must be C in SC, which is not the case in B.

The situation in OSp is less clear, as we must rely on the presence/absence of certain patterns and not grammaticality judgments. Nevertheless, I come to a tentative conclusion with important diachronic consequences. Cases with one proclitic with two coordinated finite Vs like (57a), (58a) and (59a) are documented since Gessner (1893), and exist in Modern Spanish (Bosque 1987). Cases with one enclitic on each coordinated finite V like (57b) are found, and Gessner lists several examples. One case I have mentioned in the past is (60):

(60)   Et el padre firio- *l*   et maltrexo *lo*   Por 45
        and the father wounded-him and mistreated him

However, Gessner does not cite a single case of one enclitic just on the first of two coordinated finite Vs, like (58b) and (59b). To my knowledge, this type has not been documented in later work, but since I have not surveyed texts as to missing clitics, I have no information to add. This absence does not appear accidental, and the likely conclusion is that the pattern was ungrammatical, like (57c). Thus, the properties of enclisis in finite coordination in OSp appear to be like those of European Portuguese today. I suggest that this is because (a) OSp clitics in main clauses are analysed as in the I-system, and not the C-system, and (b) V-raising in OSp enclisis is incorporation of V to the clitic functioning as the head of TM in the I-system, resulting in the structure in (53c). In this analysis, V and CL form a complex X^0, so the clitic cannot serve as the independent syntactic constituent that identifies the 'clitic'-like empty category in the second conjunct. Under this view, OSp V + CL + *et* + V orders are deviant, so the absence of examples of this type is principled and not accidental.

In brief, the mixed system of OSp should in principle allow for several analyses of enclisis, with one of them identical to what is found in SC enclisis. However, those various analyses are in fact not exploited, and with one exception seem impossible. Coordination properties suggest that OSp enclisis is compatible only with a head-analysis of CL in TM, and incompatible with the clitic system OSp shares with SC. If this is correct, we have evidence that in OSp, WP is never projected in structures which show enclisis, with TM being exclusively involved in such cases. In conclusion, OSp enclisis cannot be the result of V in C and CL in Spec,WP, in contrast with the situation in SC. Nevertheless, OSp exhibits clitics in Spec,WP in other syntactic patterns, and particularly embedded clauses.

Summarizing, TMP and WP systems may share a prohibition against initial clitics that triggers V-raising. This results in V + CL or enclitic word orders, as in SC and B, which receive different analyses depending on the structural position of CL. Even though the WP system is seldom used in main clauses, OSp nevertheless has TMP and WP clitic systems, and resembles both B and SC. In addition, OSp is parallel to B and SC in being sensitive to a first position prohibition that survives until approximately the seventeenth century, giving rise in root clauses to the V + CL orders found with finite Vs. As stated, OSp offers two systems of clitics, but the analysis of its V + CL orders appears unambiguous, as these sequences belong to the TM system with CL as head exclusively, and not the WP system.

As to the later diachronic evolution of Spanish, the situation is as follows. On the one hand, the OSp Interpolation phenomena that unambiguously signal the existence of the C-system with CL in WP begin to disappear in the fifteenth century. This quantitative change affects mainly embedded clauses, since in main clauses Interpolation is always scarce in all existing documents. On the other hand, the prohibition against initial clitics responsible for V + CL orders that we saw can in principle arise from either the C or the I-systems continues for a longer period, until roughly the seventeenth century. However, in OSp they are treated as the result of the I-system. This means that as Interpolation declines, positive evidence for WP disappears, while V + CL sequences in main clauses continue to constitute a clear obstacle to the projection of WP, and provide positive evidence for the projection of TMP with CL as head. In brief, if these proposals are correct, the first position restriction that led to enclisis in root clauses constituted in the history of Spanish a major qualitative factor both in the disappearance of the WP system OSp shared with SC, and in the growth of the TMP system with CL as head that survives up to present, a period where the first position restriction no longer exists, but the location of CL is still TM.

The conclusion of this section is that enclisis of pronouns on V is not a unitary phenomenon; thus it can arise from various clitic systems, such as the ones found in B and SC. The specific conclusion about OSp is that it mixes two clitic systems, so that its enclisis should in principle be open to several analyses, but this does not seem to happen. Rather, the properties of OSp enclisis in coordination appear to be such that they favour the I-system, and are incompatible with the C-system OSp shared with SC. This is an important analytical clue for the subsequent demise of the C-system, and the survival of the I-system no longer sensitive to the first position prohibition topic of the next section.

4.3 On first position prohibitions

Let us begin with clitic pronouns. Discussing first position restrictions in B and SC, I previously proposed (Rivero 1994b) that clitic pronouns are sensitive to two licensing requirements, as in (61), which are reminiscent of the split ECP (Jaeggli 1982 and later work), and conditions for little *pro* proposed by Rizzi (1986b).

(61) *Licensing principles for clitic pronouns*:
   a. A clitic must have its features identified by H^0 = a head.
   b. A clitic must be formally licensed by H^0 = a head.

The core idea is that clitics are functional categories, so fall under licensing systems designed in UG for such categories. For instance, Rivero (1993c) discusses in detail how the first position prohibition applying to all finite Vs in Breton is the result of a licensing system for Tense that relies on a formal principle like (61b), in addition to the familiar V-raising procedure that checks (some of) the features of Tense. Under this view, clitic pronouns and Tense exhibit positional restrictions because they fall under similar licensing principles for functional categories.

When a clitic cannot be first, the core idea is that its identifier and its formal licenser are different items, and that formal licensing derives from precedence. The identifier of the clitic in (61a) must be V, which contains the appropiate features to establish the role of the clitic as complement. The formal licenser in (61b) is, roughly speaking, the preceding constituent. Rephrasing this idea in minimalist terms, I propose that clitics as functional categories have two types of features: one type serves for identification, the other serves for formal licensing. I assume that the identification feature is consistently weak, and satisfied/checked in LF, perhaps because V raises at that point to the projection where the clitic is scoped out of the VP in overt syntax, and I do not discuss it further. The formal feature, however, is open to parametric variation. In SC, B and OSp, this feature is strong and triggers the first position restriction, because it must be licensed before Spell-Out, and, as stated, the licensing mode involves precedence. In view of the structural position of clitics in SC, B and OSp, let us see how their shared strong formal feature is licensed in each case.

Clitics subject to the first position restriction must always be preceded by a constituent. Within the formal sytem adopted in this chapter, this word order aspect has different consequences for clitics that are Specs and clitics that are heads. In my analysis, this salient fact follows in SC from the idea that the Spec,WP clitic must appear in the Internal Domain or minimal complement domain (Chomsky 1993a) of C in order to have its strong formal feature licensed, as in (62). In other words, this type of licensing involves a Head–Complement relation, similar to Uriagereka (1988), not a Spec–head relation.[14] This mechanism also licenses Tense in Breton (Rivero 1993c), a language whose clitic pronouns escape positional restrictions:

(62) $[_{CP}$ C $[_{WP}$ CL W']]
        Licenser   Internal Domain of C

That the clitic appears in the internal domain of C follows from Kayne's system (1994) without stipulation. The internal domain is overtly established when V raises to C past the clitic in Spec,WP, as in (63a), or when a phrase raises to Spec,CP and is coindexed with C by Spec–head Agreement, as in (63b). These movements never combine, as overt V-raising is last resort (Cardinaletti & Roberts 1991; Rivero 1993a; Wilder & Cavar 1993), and applies to support the clitic only when that is necessary, and not to check V-features (Rivero & Terzi 1995). Thus, (63c) is deviant:[15]

(63)   a. $[_{CP} [_C V_i] [_{WP} CL_{W'} [W [_{IP} t_i]]]]$
       b. $[_{CP} YP_i [_C \emptyset_i] [_{WP} CL_{W'} [W [_{IP} V t_i]]]]$
       c.   *$[_{CP} YP_i [_C V_j] [_{WP} CL_{W'} [W [_{IP} t_j t_i]]]]$

Now consider B. If the B clitic is in Spec,TMP, its strong formal feature is always licensed in an internal domain, like in SC. The difference between the two languages resides in the nature of the domain: in view of the structural position of the B clitic, it need not be the complement of C. For instance, the B structure corresponding to (63a) is (64), and the domain where the clitic is contained is internal to M and not to C. However, the idea that clitics are licensed in a Head–Complement relation remains unchanged:

(64) $[_{MP} [_M V_i] [_{TMP} CL [_{IP} t_i]]]$

V-raising to M in (64) is last recourse like in SC: it will only apply if no item such as *ste* in a filled M formally licenses the clitic in syntax, which for Rivero & Terzi (1995) means that it complies with Enlightened Self-Interest (Lasnik 1993) and not Greed (Chomsky 1993a). Thus, no differences arise between movement to C in SC, and movement to M in B, even though the assumed landing site of V differs.

However, under the assumption that the clitic is in TM^0, as opposed to Spec,TMP, licensing relations may be more complex. The Head–Complement relation of SC is required in questions with *dali* and *wh*-phrases in

(65a), negative sentences in (65b), future sentences in (65c), and enclisis in (64). Thus, licensing through the Internal Domain Condition must obtain when the clitic is a Spec or a head in TM:

(65) a. [$_{CP}$ {*dali*/*wh*-phrase} [$_{TMP}$ CL [$_{IP}$ V]]]
 b. [$_{NegP}$ Neg [$_{TMP}$ CL [$_{IP}$ V]]]
 c. [$_{MP}$ M [$_{TMP}$ CL [$_{IP}$ V]]]

In addition, the salient factor of a first position restriction is a preceding constituent, so a head clitic could have a licensing option not available to the Spec clitic. Namely, the TM^0 clitic could allow as formal licenser an X^{max} in Spec,TMP, as in (66) (a subject or an adverb with no focus characteristics):

(66)   [$_{TMP}$ XP [$_{TM'}$ CL [$_{IP}$ V]]]

In (66), CL is not licensed in an internal domain, but through a different formal relation: the Spec–head configuration where the X^{max} in the Checking Domain of CL licenses its strong formal feature, and is the 'first' constituent. Under this view, the Head–Complement relation to license pronominal clitics in (65) could be supplemented with the Checking Domain Condition used for the Spec–head relation of (66). In the system of this chapter, Spec,XP clitics sensitive to first position restrictions do not have a Checking Domain, so this licensing mode using a Y^{max} as opposed to a Y^0 is not available to them. However, if TMP does not project a Spec, and (66) is not generated, then licensing relations must be limited to the Internal Domain Condition like SC. Under this view, subjects preceding clitics would be higher than TMP, and occupy a topic-like position in a projection that is superior to the one holding the clitic, similar to subjects preceding clitics in SC, which in my analysis must be higher than WP. That is, clitics that are not in strict 2P, but cannot be first, are open to more analyses than 2P clitics; more formally, in the system adopted in this chapter, C-oriented clitics like those of SC offer a clearer analytical situation than the I-oriented clitics B and OSp share, which becomes relevant in OSp as the following discussion illustrates.

Like SC and B, OSp must appeal to the Head–Complement relation, or an Internal Domain, to license clitics sensitive to first position at least in *wh*-questions, equivalent to (65a) or, less often in Interpolation, (63b), and in negative sentences. In negative sentences, the clitic infrequently before *no* is in Spec,WP, so the first constituent licenses it through the Internal Domain Condition, projecting CP: [$_{CP}$ XP [$_{WP}$ CL [$_{NegP}$ *no* [IP]]]]. The clitic frequently after *no* is in TMP, so Neg as dominating head defines the internal domain for the clitic to be formally licensed: [$_{NegP}$ *no* [$_{TMP}$ CL [IP]]]. In the last case, it is immaterial to the licensing relation whether the clitic is seen as in Spec,TM or as in TM^0.

OSp shares with B and SC a licensing mechanism based on an Internal Domain, but the properties of OSp enclisis have an important effect on the licensing systems of this period. We saw that OSp enclisis in coordination suggests that V incorporates to CL, producing a morphological complex, which means that in enclisis CL functions as a head, as in [$_{TMP}$ [$_{TM'}$ [$_{TM}$ V$_i$ [$_{TM}$ CL]] [$_{IP}$ t$_i$]]]. This has consequences for the licensing of clitics, because it implies that this period does not have a homogeneous system for this purpose. Rather, OSp must appeal to a Checking Domain Condition in enclisis, and thus cannot exclusively rely on the Internal Domain Condition used in SC, whose system of clitics OSp nevertheless shares. That is, in OSp V + CL orders, V is in the Checking Domain of CL in TM, and this relation formally licenses the strong feature of the clitic, much like the Internal Domain relation does in the other cases. In SC licensing is homogeneous, in that all clitics are licensed in an Internal Domain, and the same could be maintained for B, where V and CL can function as independent constituents in a way that makes an internal domain approach for the licensing of enclitics a viable alternative. By contrast, in OSp, licensing of clitics that precede finite Vs involves an Internal Domain, but this environment cannot be used by clitics that follow finite Vs, since those have V in their Checking Domain for licensing purposes. This has two consequences. First, as discussed in section 3 from a somewhat different perspective, this situation hurts the chances of survival of Spec,WP clitics, because enclitics can never belong to this type in OSp. Second, as opposed to enclisis in B, the properties of enclisis in OSp also eliminate the analysis where TMP clitics occupy Spec,TMP, as Spec-clitics can never appeal to a Checking Domain in order to be licensed. This is because, in our formal system based on Kayne (1994), Spec-clitics do not have a checking domain, so can only be licensed in an internal domain. The result of this is that OSp TM^0 clitics can survive unscathed, as we know they do, while the Spec,WP type should be seen as an endangered species that eventually disappears. Under this view, the logically possible Spec,TMP clitic is equally at danger in OSp, but remains an option in B, because enclitic structures in this language contrast with those of OSp in not showing incorporation properties. In brief, enclisis in OSp indicates that CL is licensed in a Checking Domain. This unambiguously establishes the existence of CL as a head, in a period when CL also behaves like a Spec.

Other environments where the Checking Domain Condition of OSp could be at work are less decisive. As a case in point, consider the well-known alternation between enclisis and proclisis with preverbal NP-subjects most recently discussed by Wanner (1992b), who cites the following examples (and see (60) above).

(67) a. E el respondió*l*   (EE §316,184b22)
   and he answered.him
   'And he said to him'
  b. Et el *te* mostrará una albuhera   (EE §316,184b7)
   and he you will.show a pond
   'And he will show you a pond'

If my proposals are correct, (67a) is unproblematic: we are dealing with an enclitic, so it must involve the Checking Domain Condition. Thus, CL must be in TM⁰ and the licenser is V. Furthermore, if V-raising is last recourse, and applies only if it becomes absolutely necessary to license CL, as I assume, the subject in (67a) is in a distant projection as in Left Dislocations, and thus not used to license CL, which triggers V-raising. What about (67b)? The situation involves proclisis and is less clear. Here, we could assume that the subject is in the projection immediately superior to CL; then, CL is licensed by appearing in the internal domain of the projection holding the subject, which prevents last recourse V-raising. Alternatively, the Checking Domain Condition available to license CL in OSp in view of enclisis could be generalized. Namely, it could be assumed that since CL in TM can be licensed by the V in its Checking Domain in enclisis, CL can also be licensed by the phrase in its Spec as another item in the the Checking Domain of CL. Under this assumption, the subject could be in Spec,TMP, and be the licenser or 'first position' item, and this would also prevent last recourse V-raising. Since this generalization is based on the notion of Checking Domain, it is compatible with the analysis that treats CL as head, but not as Spec, and would in my approach contribute to reinforce the analysis independently required by enclitics, which function as heads and not Specs.

Under the view just developed, the loss of first position prohibitions for CL in later Spanish implies that CL no longer exhibits the strong feature which needs to be licensed in either a Checking Domain or an Internal Domain. This loss is independent of the abandonment of the C-system, since C-clitics disappear much earlier than the first position restriction. This again shows that the first position prohibition is independent from C- and I-orientation. We have seen that it can exist in both systems, or be absent in both, and I have now suggested that this prohibition disappears from Spanish after it abandons its C-system, but retains the I-system in existence today.

Now let us consider enclisis with B *li*, which differs from enclisis with clitic pronouns. Recall that in questions with *li*, V may precede *li*, and the clitic pronoun in main and embedded questions alike, as in (43) repeated now as (68).[16] In OSp, clitics are not preceded by V in non-root environments such as an embedded *yes–no* question; rather, only CL + V order is found in such constructions. From this Romance perspective, (68b) is surprising:

(68) a. Dava *li ti* knigata?
       'Does (s)he give you the book?'
     b. Pitam se [dava *li ti* knigata]
       'I wonder if (s)he gives you the book'

To account for (68) I propose that clitic pronouns and clitic *li* are sensitive to first position restrictions deriving from different licensing requirements, which is of interest in view of the systems discussed above. In brief, as I now show, *li* appeals to a Checking Domain condition exclusively, while we saw above that clitic pronouns can always use an Internal Domain Condition.

Recall that in (68a, b), V adjoins to *li* in C (Rivero 1993b; Rudin 1993), see (69):

(69)   (V) [$_{CP}$ [$_{C0}$ V$_i$ [$_{C0}$ li]][$_{TMP}$ [$_{TM'}$ CL [$_{IP}$ t$_i$ ....]]]]]

In (69), V-raising is triggered by *li*, and not the pronoun, which accounts for the root/non-root symmetry, and V + CL order in a *bona fide* embedded context. If *li* heads a higher projection, as assumed, the pronoun in (69) is in the complement domain of *li*; that is, it is in a configuration where its strong formal feature can be satisfied. Thus, V-raising in (68a) cannot be for the pronoun, and must be for *li*. As to (68b), in non-root clauses the pronoun is in the internal domain of C, so from this perspective, V-raising to C is unnecessary, and not usually found; thus, V-raising in (68b) must be triggered by *li*, not by the pronoun. Pronouns and the *li* particle are alike in requiring a preceding constituent, being subject to a first position restriction. However, in non-root clauses, pronouns cannot be preceded by the raised V, unless *li* is present. Thus pronouns and *li* differ. Let us see what the difference is by looking at the licensing requirements of *li*. With Rudin (1993), I assume that *li* has a focus feature (see King 1993 for Russian). In minimalist terms, the focus feature is strong, so must be licensed by PF in the Checking Domain of *li*. Recall that I argued that pronouns subject to the first position restriction can always satisfy their strong feature by appearing in an Internal Domain, and often do not have a Checking Domain. However, *li* differs from pronouns, and can only be licensed in a Checking Domain. In the absence of a Checking Domain, *li* is not licit. As a consequence, V raises and adjoins to C to provide the Checking Domain for *li* in two environments: when *li* appears within a complement, as in the embedded question in (68b), or when the CP containing *li* is not a complement, as in the main question in (68a). In this way, when *li* is involved no asymmetry arises between root and non-root clauses: V raises and precedes *li* and clitic pronouns in both cases. However, if *li* is absent, and the pronouns are present, B displays same asymmetry for V + CL orders as OSp. This is because both the B and the OSp pronouns can satisfy their first position restriction by appealing to the Internal Domain Condition, which B *li* can never do.

5 Conclusion

Old Spanish offers two alternative systems for its clitic pronouns. The first system shared with Serbo-Croatian leads to Wackernagel effects, as is observed mainly in non-root clauses. In such clauses, Old Spanish clitics that are not adjacent to the Verb are almost always in 2P. I argue that such clitics are C-oriented, occupying a functional projection that is the complement of C, and takes NegP as complement; clitics in this projection are usually in the Spec, so they are X^{max}. The second system shared with Standard Bulgarian leads in root clauses to Tobler–Mussafia effects. Clitics that are adjacent to the Verb can never be first in such clauses, but may appear in positions other than 2P in root and non-root clauses. I argue that such clitics are I-oriented, occupying a functional projection that is the complement of NegP, if present, and takes IP as complement. Through diachronic evolution, Spanish loses the medieval C-oriented system, and preserves as the only alternative the I-oriented system. In Old Spanish, two characteristics of root clauses already favour this change. Clear cases of C-oriented clitics are never too numerous, but in root clauses evidence to postulate such clitics is extremely limited. Second, formal properties of V + CL sequences, found only in root clauses, suggest Incorporation of the Verb to the Clitic for this word order. Since a head cannot incorporate to a phrase, root enclisis disfavours the analysis of the C-system with the Clitic as X^{max}. Thus, while non-root clauses display evidence for I-clitics and some clear but quantitatively limited evidence for C-clitics, root clause properties in the medieval period combine to favour a treatment of CL as I-oriented and in a head position, and against an analysis of CL as C-oriented and in a Spec position.

Notes

* Research for this chapter has been carried out under SSHRCC Grants 410-91-0178 and 410-94-0401, and the Eurotyp Project of the ESF. I owe many thanks to Danijela Kudra for help with SC, and to Galina Alexandrova and Olga Arnaudova for B. In addition, I must thank Danijela and Galina for constructing SC and B examples in a way that resembled the OSp sentences at my disposal. I also thank Arhonto Terzi for joint work, which has inspired this chapter in many points, and Ans van Kemenade and Nigel Vincent for many useful comments on a previous version. Usual disclaimers apply.
1. My proposal contrasts with that of Dimitrova-Vulchanova (1993), who places clitics in B, Macedonian, SC and Czech in a shared position labelled FRONT.
2. On this view, in syntax clitic pronouns can behave as X^{max}, as in SC, or as either X^{max} or X^0 at different points of the derivation, as suggested for Modern Romance since Kayne (1989). Chomsky (1994) states that clitic pronouns may be indeterminate as to X^0/X^{max} status, which the proposals in this chapter seem to confirm. Word order suggests that SC clitics occupy Spec,WP, as in (9a). In addition, SC clitic pronouns can precede Neg, which under a movement analysis may indicate that they encounter no problems in bypassing Neg as intervening X^0, when they raise as X^{max}. This contrasts with SC auxiliaries that in negative clauses must follow Neg, which may indicate that they move as X^0 and not X^{max}, so cannot cross Neg. Finally, SC li is an *in situ* clitic in C^0 (Rivero 1993b). Thus, clitic clusters with li, auxiliaries and pronouns must be formed postsyntactically, as in the model of distributed morphology of Halle & Marantz (1993), which also allows permutations and mergers.
3. This analysis updates ideas in Rivero (1986, 1992). There I argued that OSp clitics are X^{max} and adjoin to IP by a movement I called 'topicalization', which probably resembles scrambling. More recently, Halpern & Fontana (1993) also adopt the view that OSp clitics are X^{max}. My new proposal with OSp clitics in Spec,WP captures both the maximal and 'adjunct' nature of my early analysis, since the distinction between specifiers and adjuncts is obliterated in Kayne's system (1994). In previous work, I did not contemplate that OSp clitics could receive a double analysis, which does not depend as much on the X^{max} vs X^0 distinction as on the surface location of clitics in the clause. Halpern & Fontana (1993) and Fontana (1993) also see OSp clitics as homogeneous, so the new distinction I make here concerns their proposals as well.
4. The dichotomy I propose differs from the division between X^{max} and X^0 clitics in Halpern & Fontana (1993). For them, the equivalent of my C-oriented clitics must necessarily be X^{max}, so in a Spec-position, while I envision C-oriented clitics that are X^0s

and head WP. In addition, Halpern & Fontana propose that V + CL order necessarily results from clitics that are C-oriented, while I argue later that this order can arise with different types of clitics, irrespective of C- and I-orientation, and X^{max} or X^0 status. As suggested in note 2, the X^{max}/X^0 distinction for CL appears tangential, since one and the same clitic may show a double behaviour. In my view, the crucial issue seems to be the relative height where clitics surface in the clause.

5. B future clauses like (i) also motivate the properties of the I-system:
    (i) a. Znam če šte *im*   pomogne   B
            I.know that will them help
            'I know that he will help them'
        b. Znam $[_{CP} [_{C°}$ Ce$] [_{MP} [_{M_0}$ Šte$] [_{TMP}$ *im* $[_{IP}$ pomogne$]]]]$
    Their Modal Phrase complements C (Rivero 1994a [1988]), so the clitic must follow this projection. CL + M orders are disallowed (*im* Šte). Negative futures like *če ne šte im pomogne* 'that he will not help them' are obsolete, but show clitics after Neg and M.

6. Under this analysis, several differences emerge between the WP in the text and parallel projections for clitics in the literature, and I mention a few of them. Cardinaletti & Roberts (1991) consider their AgrP1 part of a recursive AgrP; the WP in the text is not in a recursive AgrP, since NegP stands between the two, and is not part of the V-system (in this, it differs from Rouveret's WP as well). In addition, Cardinaletti & Robert's AgrP1 participates in Nominative assignment, while WP resembles the AgrcP projection proposed by Shlonsky (1994), and need not. WP may be the site of 2P-particles in Ancient Greek (Rivero & Terzi 1995); this differs from Cardinaletti & Roberts and Shlonsky since their projections always make reference to Agr. The use of WP for clitic pronouns and discourse particles can be unified using Uriagereka's views on his FP (1995); roughly, he proposes that clitics as old/specific information move to FP, because this slot encodes point of view, an idea resembling informational approaches like Renzi's (most recently 1989). In my approach Ancient Greek particles encode point of view, and are in Spec,WP (=FP), while the head of this projection may attract the Ancient Greek pronouns as old information. In OSp, W is available, but clitics may move not only there, but also to the I-oriented position, in contrast with both Uriagereka and Rouveret. Perhaps this is because C-structure encodes illocutionary force and point of view, and I-structure tense and modality, so when clitics are scoped out of the VP, they can be attracted to either structure. WP is different and independent from Culicover's PolP (1991) and Laka's ΣP for Neg (1990); as seen in the text, WP is above NegP. Finally, WP is not to be confused with the Modal Phrase (MP) in Rivero (1994a, 1988) for Balkan languages: MP stands below NegP. It seems reasonable to assume that these different functional phrases are projected in view of positive evidence. On this view, B projects CP, NegP, MP, and TMP, but not WP. In SC, there is evidence for CP, WP, NegP, but not MP or TMP. In OSp, the status of MP is unclear, but there is positive evidence for CP, WP, NegP and TMP, but WP and TMP are not projected in the same clause.

7. The OSp patterns in section 2 are not unusual, but problematic for the idea in Fontana (1993) that OSp, like Yiddish, is a symmetric V2-language, with V2 in main and embedded clauses. In this analysis, V2 means that the inflected V is in I, with Spec,IP holding any type of constituent. Examples making this hypothesis untenable for non-root clauses include *if*-clauses with V-final order, cases of two XPs standing between C and V, and all negative sentences, since OSp *no* heads its own X^{max}, as argued in this chapter. This type of 'V2' must involve (a) V-to-I in an IP complementing NegP, (b) multiple X^{max} adjunctions to either IP or NegP, (c) the X^{max} for the C-oriented clitic, and (d) the C-layer.
    As to root clauses, I have argued elsewhere (Rivero 1993a) that OSp does not have the 'V2'-characteristics resulting from the obligatory V-to-C of German *wh*-questions and topicalizations. Here, I differ from Benincà (most recently, 1995), who does not discuss OSp, but suggests that medieval Romance languages are all V2. The reasons to conclude that OSp is not of this type of V2 are: (a) V1 is frequent, and null subjects unrestricted,

(b) V need not raise past I, so is not always second *within CP*, as argued in 3 here, (c) if the Long Head Movement construction like *Dar te he* 'I will give you' has the non-finite V in C, C cannot be reserved for finite items; and (d) if V + CL order results from finite V-to-C (but see section 4), this fronting has a last resort and altruistic nature absent in Germanic V2. SC and B are not V2 languages, and share with OSp characteristics (a) through (d); I will exemplify some of them in passing in section 3.

8. Earlier (Rivero 1992), I analysed (24) through multiple adjunctions/scramblings to IP or NegP. However, under such an analysis these patterns should be as frequent as the C–CL–XP alternatives, but they are not. The new analysis captures Chenery's idea (1905) that (24) departs from what is the norm in OSp Interpolation, or the situation identical to SC. In (24), the clitic could raise from TM^0 to W^0 by X^0-movement. This resembles the clitic movement from I^0 to C^0, with right-adjunction to C^0, for all interpolated clitics in Wanner (1992a: 352). My analysis captures the third position of clitics non-adjacent to V; OSp 2P clitics are in Spec,WP, like in SC.

   A restricted Interpolation of type (24), only with Neg, is also found in contemporary northern dialects of European Portuguese (Rouveret 1992: 110):
   (i)   Se a memória me nào falha ...
         'If my memory does not fail me ...'

9. As discussed by Haegeman (1992: 63ff.), the West Flemish focus marker *tet* follows subject clitic pronouns, as in (i):
   (i)   da-*me* tet wunder die   boeken gekocht een
         that-we FOC we   those books bought   have
         'that we have bought those books'
   This order could suggest that clitic *me* is in Spec,WP while *tet* heads W, filling one of the logical possibilities of the C-system I discuss. For Shlonsky (1994), however, the equivalent of my W is headed by an Agr^0 that raises to C^0 and produces the agreeing complementizer effect; under this analysis, WP cannot be headed by *tet*, so is not the focus phrase in West Flemish.

10. Here, I differ from Cardinaletti & Roberts (1991) and Uriagereka (1992b, 1995), who connect V + CL orders to the equivalent of my WP exclusively, and Halpern & Fontana (1993), who reserve this order for X^{max} clitics.

11. For Kayne (1989, 1994), clitics cannot adjoin to traces. If the clitic is in TM^0, and V is in I^0, V-raising past the clitic is unproblematic ; if V and clitic are adjoined to the same X^0, V-raising without the clitic is problematic from Kayne's perspective.

12. Under this approach, (i) from (Rivero 1986: 46a) has a NP containing a universal quantifier, but which functions as a definite description; alternatively, this NP is not left-dislocated, strictly speaking:
    (i)   Todas las animalias, ellas se   gobiernan que no   an   mester que
          all   the animals   they   themselves   govern   that not have   need   that
          ninguno ge-lo   aparege
          no.one them-it organize   Luc 318
          'All the animals, they govern themselves in a way that they need no organizer'

13. A third case appears to be Czech. This language has Spec,WP clitics; however, as Toman (1993: 113) points out, 'the first constituent of the clause can under certain conditions be truncated, leaving the clitic in the clause initial position', as in *Se uvidi* vs *To se uvid'* 'One will see.' Truncation is restricted to two or three lexical items.

14. By contrast, reformulating his earlier proposals, Roberts (1994) derives 2P effects from a Spec–head configuration, and assumes the existence of an AgrcP as part of the C-system and above CP, where the required agreement relation can be established. For Roberts, an additional projection like WP in the text complements C and holds clitics.

15. Wilder & Cavar (1994) offer an important discussion of the last recourse nature of this V-movement, which, as they show, is a challenging process for the Minimalist Programme. In their view, Vs necessarily raise to C by LF to check features; for instance, finite Vs must check the finite feature in C. In the enclisis case at hand, V raises early to

license the clitic and not to satisfy its own needs, but it lands in the target required by LF. Wilder & Cavar consider this early altruism, minimally departing from the principle of Greed, as in Chomsky (1993a). For Rivero (1994b) and Rivero & Terzi (1995), C in languages like SC does not hold specific features, and all Vs, including non-finite imperatives, may raise overtly to C in order to license clitics. As Rivero & Terzi argue, under this approach, V-raising is an instance of what Lasnik (1993: 12ff.) terms 'enlightened self-interest': roughly, a category A raises to satisfy the requirements of B as associate; this position is coherent with the view that Vs may move just to M in B. In Modern Spanish, clitics must follow imperative Vs: *cantadlo* 'Sing it !' (Rooryck 1992 for recent discussion). In OSp, however, clitics in imperatives distribute like in other root clauses, motivating Rivero & Terzi's approach:

(i) E quando demandáredes consejo a Dios, mucho orgullosamente
and when you.will.ask advice to God very proudly
ge-lo demandat   Z280
to.him-it ask.IMP.2PL
'And when you ask God for advice, ask him very proudly'

16. Similar phenomena may exist in some varieties of Serbian. For D. Kudra, from northern Bosnia, *li* is for main clauses, and *dali* is for main and embedded clauses; thus, the situation reported for B embedded clauses is excluded for her. However, a Zagreb speaker Kudra questioned on my behalf considered sentences similar to (68b) grammatical, suggesting a geographical difference.

Primary sources for OSp examples cited in the text
A = *El libro de Alexandre*, ed. R.S. Willis, New York, Kraus Reprint, 1965.
B Milg = Gonzalo de Berceo. *Milagros de Nuestra Señora*, ed. B.Dutton, London, Tamesis, 1971.
CD = *Calila e Dimna*, ed. J. M. Cacho Blecua and M.J. Lacarra. Madrid, Castalia, 1984.
Est = Juan Manuel. *Libro de los Estados*, ed. R.B. Tate and I.R. Macpherson. Oxford, Clarendon Press, 1974.
Luc = Juan Manuel. *El conde Lucanor*, ed. J.M. Blecua. Madrid, Castalia, 1984.
Por = *Poridat de las Poridades*, ed. L.D. Kasten. Madrid, CSIC, 1957.
Z = *Libro del caballero Zifar*, ed. J. González Muela. Madrid, Castalia, 1982.

8 On the integration of second position phenomena

Josep M. Fontana

1 Introduction*

For quite some time, philologists and linguists have observed that there are a number of languages in the world that impose some restrictions on the types of linguistic expressions that can appear as the second constituent in a root clause. For the most part, these languages do not seem to impose the same kinds of restrictions on the type of categories that can appear in sentence initial position. The two most well-known types of this second position phenomenon are *Second Position Clitics* (2P clitics) and the *Verb Second Constraint* (V2). The purpose of this chapter is to evaluate some of the recent attempts to provide unified accounts of a variety of 'second position' facts. The three proposals that will be compared in this work are those in Cardinaletti & Roberts (1991), Rivero (this volume), and Fontana (1993, in press).[1]

Since the term 'second position' is a non-technical term, not universally agreed upon and often used only in a loose sense, and, furthermore, since the three proposals to be compared here do not entirely coincide in their intended empirical coverage, I will begin by outlining some of the basic descriptive observations which have served as the impetus for these proposals. The core set of data that will be used as a testing ground for the comparison between them will be further delimited later on.

2 Second position phenomena

2.1 Second position clitics

The data below exemplify the distributional characteristics of a number of systems of clitic categories across the languages of the world that have been called second position clitics. Descriptively, 2P clitic phenomena are characterized by the following core traits. In matrix clauses, clitic elements do not appear in sentence initial position, but instead tend to appear after a non-clitic element occupying the first position. In subordinate environments, however, they tend to appear clause initially, immediately following the complementizer, and they can precede the same range of categories that usually appear in first position in matrix clauses. This is illustrated by the examples in (1) and (2) below, from Serbo-Croatian (from Halpern & Fontana 1994) and Homeric Greek (from Taylor 1990). The (a) and (b) examples illustrate the typical contrasts in clitic distribution between root and subordinate environments. Clitics are in bold-italic throughout this chapter.

(1) a. Sada *ga* Nada gleda (SCr)
 now him Nada watch
 'Nada is watching him now'
 b. da *ga* sada kupi Nada (SCr)
 that it now buys Nada
 'that Nada is buying now'

(2) a. Tudeidēi *min* egoge daiphroni panta eiskō, (HG)
 son-of-T. him I valiant in-all-ways liken
 'I liken him in all ways to the valiant son of Tudeus'
 b. hote *hoi* Zeus kudos edōken; (HG)
 when him Zeus glory gave
 'when Zeus gave him glory'

The orthographic conventions used in many of these languages often obscure the fact that 2P clitics are almost invariably enclitic, i.e. they attach phonologically to whatever lexical item precedes them independently of its category, forming a single phonological word with it. We must be careful to distinguish this original meaning of terms such as 'enclitic' or 'proclitic' from different usages also found in the literature. In some of the traditional work in Romance philology, for instance, we find that these terms are used sometimes to refer exclusively to the linear position clitics occupy relative to the verb. If they precede the verb, they are labelled *proclitic,* and if they follow it, *enclitic.* No crucial distinction is made, however, between those preverbal clitics that attach phonologically to the verb (proclitic, in our terms) and those that instead form a phonological word with a preceding lexical item (which would be enclitic, according to the definition adopted here). Much current work in syntax, e.g. Cardinaletti & Roberts (1991) and Rivero (this volume), has inherited this particular usage of the terms.

It is also necessary to emphasize at this point that the distribution illustrated by the above examples can be stated only as a tendency. As noted by a number of authors who have studied this phenomenon (e.g. Klavans 1982; Taylor 1990; Halpern 1992), most, if not all, languages said to have 2P clitics display some patterns which are exceptions to what is otherwise a fairly robust generalization. Specially relevant in this respect is Taylor's (1990) detailed discussion of the exceptions to the second position rule found in the Homeric Greek texts, since this is one of the prototypical languages on which the nineteenth-century Swiss scholar Jacob Wackernagel based his well-known observation that clitic elements generally appeared in second position in early Indo-European languages. Thus, the degree to which the generalizations stated above are accurate descriptions of the general state of affairs obtaining in particular languages can differ considerably from language to language.

More significantly, deviations from the general patterns illustrated in (1)–(2) have been observed to have become more frequent across time in some languages (e.g. Taylor 1990; Fontana 1993). For instance, in the Homeric Greek corpora used by Taylor (1990), the configuration in (2b) is found in 93 per cent of the relevant environments, against 7 per cent of the pattern in (3); however, the relative frequencies in which patterns such as (3) are found in the texts increases notably in later periods (Taylor, p.c). The significance of this kind of steady increase in the relative frequencies of counterexamples to a particular rule, generalization or hypothesis along a chronological axis will be discussed in sections 4.2.3 and 4.3.3.

(3) oud'   ei mala   *min* kholos hikoi·
    not-even if very-much her anger come
    'not even if anger should come upon her very strongly'

Finally, languages with 2P clitics differ according to whether clitics can appear following the first word (even in cases where they would appear to split a sentence initial constituent), the first phrase, or either, in a root environment. As noted by Halpern (1992), 2P is really a cover term for (at least) two different distributions: 2W (Second Word), and 2D (Second Daughter). Halpern observes that in some languages, e.g. Serbo-Croatian, Walpiri, Luiseño and Ngiyambaa, clitics can follow either the first word or the first syntactic daughter; in others, e.g. Czech, clitics can only appear after a complete first constituent; in still others, e.g. Alsea, Shuswap, they always follow the first word (complete references in Halpern 1992).[2]

To conclude, it should be clear that the term 'second position clitic' is simply a loose descriptive term and cannot be taken to describe any fundamental characteristic of these clitic categories. In this respect, we should be equally careful in handling and interpreting labels such as the Wackernagel's Law (WL) or the Tobler–Mussafia Law (TML). Rather than viewing these as linguistic laws that need to be formalized, with the result that exceptions will have to be explained, I will view these simply as rough descriptive generalizations which should follow (as should their putative exceptions) from a proper analysis of the syntax of clitics and of word order more generally. This analysis, I claim, need not and should not make explicit reference to notions such as 'second position', or to the above-mentioned 'laws'. As I will presently argue, the same caveats should apply to the use of the term 'verb second'.

2.2 Verb second phenomena

Since the basic set of facts related to the V2 constraint are much better known than those associated with 2P clitics, this section will be brief. A few observations, however, are in order.

First, as more knowledge of a wider range of data becomes available to researchers, it is becoming more clear that a homogeneous formal treatment for all the languages usually associated with the V2 label is not well supported. The suggestion recently made by a number of researchers that V2 languages fall into at least two major groups is becoming widely accepted among syntacticians. Specifically, a subset of the Germanic languages, including Yiddish and Icelandic, appear to manifest V2 in both main and subordinate clauses. They have been argued to obtain V2 effects by movement of the tensed verb to I^0, and topicalization of a constituent to Spec,IP (Diesing 1990; Santorini 1989; Rögnvaldsson & Thráinsson 1990). I will refer to such languages as *I-V2 languages*. These contrast with languages such as German and Dutch, which manifest V2 generally only in root clauses. On the analysis widely adopted for these languages, following den Besten (1978), V2 effects are achieved via movement of the tensed verb to C^0 and topicalization to Spec,CP. Such languages may be called *C-V2 languages*.

Second, as noted above in reference to 2P clitics, the label 'V2' understood as a strict requirement that the tensed verb appear always in absolute second position in a root environment is highly problematic. Exceptions such as the declarative V1 constructions found in, e.g., Old Norse, Old English, Yiddish and Icelandic, or the licensing of a restricted group of adverbials that can appear between the topicalized constituent and the tensed verb in some Scandinavian languages, are well known and have been the object of numerous discussions in the field of Germanic syntax. What is not as well known, however, or at least has received much less attention in the literature, is the fact that the rigid verb-second configurations which are often cited in support of certain accounts of the V2 constraint are only a very recent innovation in the Germanic family. Moreover, if we go beyond the narrow range of facts and dialectal varieties usually covered by most theory-building articles, we become aware that this innovation is restricted to a very small subset of the modern Germanic varieties, and that even in the most well-behaved standard dialects this restriction cannot be taken as an absolute (see Fontana 1993, sections 3.4.3 and 4.2.1.1, and references therein for examples and discussion).

Thus, independently of how one may choose to reconcile the exceptions to the strict V2 pattern with standard analyses of this phenomenon, it should be apparent that a unified treatment of the phrase structures of all the languages up to now associated with this label is only possible if 'V2' is considered simply as a descriptive, pre-theoretical term. To do otherwise would be to fail to relate languages which are historically and areally connected, and which display remarkable structural similarities, despite manifesting some superficial differences in their relative degree of adherence to a strict V2 word order. All languages referred to as V2 in this chapter — whether I-V2 or C-V2 — share the following basic traits: (a) the tensed verb must obligatorily undergo movement from its canonical position and land in a position to the left of the VP (within the GB framework, this position is arguably the head of a functional projection); (b) there is a position preceding the position where the tensed verb is found at S-structure which can host all kinds of phrasal constituents besides the subject (again, within the view of phrase structure of GB, this position would be the specifier position of a functional projection, arguably the same maximal projection hosting the tensed verb); and (c) whenever a constituent other than the subject appears in first position, and a phonologically expressed subject is available in the clause, there is a very strong tendency for the subject to appear in a position immediately following the tensed verb.

Beyond this, the various 'V2' languages can differ from each other in a number of respects. For instance, they can differ in whether the maximal projection hosting topicalized constituents and tensed verb is CP or a projection below CP; in whether adjunction of certain constituents above the relevant maximal projection (i.e. the domain where V2 effects are computed) is allowed or not, and with respect to the specific constituents allowed to appear (presumably adjoined) above this projection in each given language. They can also differ in terms of the availability of specific constructions where the tensed verb can appear superficially as the first element in the sentence (i.e. *yes/no* questions and imperatives vs declarative V1).

Of interest here is the fact that there appear to be languages where both V2 and 2P clitic properties are displayed. The present investigation is an attempt to achieve a better understanding of the interaction between a V2 phrase structure and a 2P clitic system. Obviously, this will necessarily limit the scope of our examination of the behaviour of 2P clitics crosslinguistically, since some relevant aspects of the syntax of these elements will have to be left unexplored. A comprehensive account of the behaviour of this class of clitics universally would require us to examine also how they interact with many other types of constructions available in non-V2 languages. In other words, determining how the available mechanisms of verb-movement or other general syntactic operations interact with systems of 2P clitics in the different languages is crucial if we are to account for some differences in superficial arrangements observed among them.

For instance, a similar type of V1 declarative structure to the one discussed above is found in some Slavic languages (languages exhibiting so-called 'Long Head Movement' phenomena, adopting the terminology used in Rivero, this volume, and in some of her previous work) under certain restricted conditions. Thus, one would also want to investigate exactly how the basic distribution of clitics is altered in the context of different constructions involving some modality of verb fronting in these languages and contrast it with the effects similar kinds of syntactic operations have on 2P clitics in V2 languages.

However, since the syntax of general word order in V2 languages is an area that has been much more extensively studied, it is arguably more profitable to use this as the starting point to try to understand how verb-movement and other general syntactic operations interact to affect the basic distributions of these categories crosslinguistically. I turn now to discuss the core set of facts that will be the main focus of the following discussion.

2.3 Second position clitics in verb-second languages

The limitations of the descriptive labels 2P and V2 become even more conspicuous when we study languages exhibiting both phenomena. Obviously, there is an essential incompatibility between a 2P clitic system and a V2 language, if we take strict linear order to be the essential component of the definition of these phenomena. Only one element can be second in the clause: either the tensed verb or the clitic.

As it turns out, however, some significant generalizations emerge if we restrict the term 'second position' to refer not to a specific linear position, but rather to a general and vaguely defined area towards which both clitics and tensed verbs tend to gravitate. The task of the linguist is then to determine whether a principled account can be secured that explains the patterns of alternation observed in the relative orders of clitics and tensed verbs in this general syntactic region, both in particular languages as well as crosslinguistically. Let us now review the basic facts for which a unified treatment is being sought.

Old English (OE) and Old French (OFr) are two languages that have been argued to be characterized by a V2 phrase structure (e.g. van Kemenade 1987 and Pintzuk 1991 for OE, and Adams 1987 and Vance 1989 for OFr). Thus, in spite of the fact that these languages differ from each other in a number of respects, both have in common the syntactic patterns discussed above in our informal characterization of the V2 constraint, namely, the initial position in root environments can be occupied by virtually any constituent besides the subject, and there is a marked tendency for the tensed verb to appear immediately following the category occupying the first position. The subject tends to appear right after the tensed verb whenever it has not been fronted to the sentence initial position.

OE and OFr share another important trait: the distributions of their clitic pronouns are remarkably similar. Moreover, these pronouns have several of the properties of 2P clitics.[3] First, there is a general restriction against clitic initial arrangements in root environments. Object clitics in OE and OFr tend to appear immediately following the first element in the sentence.[4] Second, as is also typical of 2P clitic systems, philological evidence suggests that clitics in these two languages also tend to attach to the preceding lexical item in the phonology. Note especially that the spelling of the OFr examples (4a) and (6a) reveals that clitics in this language do precisely this. There is, however, evidence of phonological cliticization to the following verb already in the earliest OFr texts. This contrasts with other medieval

Romance languages such as OSp, where encliticization is the norm in the earliest texts, and evidence of phonological procliticization is extremely rare until well into the fourteenth century (see Adams 1987; and Fontana 1994, for discussions of the implications of the change from phonological encliticization to phonological procliticization).

(4) a. Ge*l* *te* rendi a Paris ... (OFr)
I-him to-you delivered at Paris
'I delivered it to you in Paris' (Ch.N. 7,199, cited in Adams 1987)
b. and þæt hors *hine* bær forð (OE)
and that horse him carried forth
'...and that horse carried him forth...'
(ÆLS 265.54–5, cited in Pintzuk, in press)

(5) a. Toutes ces choses *te* presta Nostre Sires (OFr)
all these things you lent our Lord
'Our Lord lent all these things to you'
(de Kok, 1985: 74, cited in Cardinaletti & Roberts 1991)
b. Fela spella *him* sædon þa Beormas, ægþer ge of hiera
many stories him told the Permians, both of their own
agnum lande,... (OE)
country,...
'The Permians told him many stories, both about their own country...' (from van Kemenade 1987)

(6) a. .C. mil humes i plurent, ki*s* esguarderent (OFr)
one hundred thousand men there weep, who-them regard
'One hundred thousand men who see them are weeping.'
(Rol.3882, cited in Adams 1987)
b. thaet *him* irenna ecge mihton helpan aet hilde (OE)
that him swords' edges might help in battle
'that the swords' edges might help him in battle'
(from Pintzuk 1991)

The patterns illustrated in (4)–(6) above do not exhaust all the possible arrangements in which clitics appear in the medieval English and French texts, but they are representative.

Finally, although the clitic is typically found between the fronted constituent and the tensed verb in root environments, there are some root environments in which no constituent appears to be fronted to the initial position, and hence the tensed verb appears linearly in sentence initial position. When a clitic is also involved, it appears immediately after the tensed verb, as illustrated in (7).

(7) a. Voit *le* li rois (OFr)
sees him the king
'The king sees him'
(*Le Charroi de Nîmes*, 1. 58, cited in Cardinaletti & Roberts 1991)

b. het   *hine* mid þæm "lacum "leode "swæse "secean on
ordered him with those gifts   people his-own seek   in
"gesyntum   (OE)
safety

'He ordered him to seek in safety his own people with those
gifts'   (*Beo* 2518, cited in Pintzuk 1991)

This configuration is never found in subordinate clauses.

Thus, a rough description of the most distinctive distributional patterns of object clitics in these two V2 languages would be as follows: in a typical root V2 configuration, if a clitic is involved, it tends to appear between the constituent topicalized in the first position and the tensed verb. In certain root environments which are exceptions to the V2 constraint in these and other languages (i.e. *yes/no* questions, imperatives and V1 declaratives), the clitic appears immediately following the tensed verb. In subordinate environments, clitics can appear as the first constituent in the clause, and they always precede the tensed verb.

This description contrasts in a very interesting way with that of certain Germanic languages. Take Middle Dutch (MDu), for instance. Middle Dutch texts typically display the kinds of root/subordinate asymmetries exhibited by Modern Dutch with respect to the position of the tensed verb, and which served as the basis for the formulation of standard analyses of the V2 constraint in this language: the tensed verb generally follows a constituent fronted to the sentence initial position in root environments, but in subordinate environments it tends to appear in clause final position (van der Horst 1981; Weerman 1987).

What makes this language interesting in the context of the present investigation is its system of clitics. Pronominal object clitics in Middle Dutch are also phonologically enclitic, attaching to a host on their left independently of its category. However, contrary to what we have seen to be the typical situation in OE or OFr, object clitics are invariably found immediately following the tensed verb in root environments. In other words, as a number of authors have pointed out, we never find an object clitic preceding a tensed verb (i.e. a configuration of the form: XP Cl $V_{[+finite]}$) in root environments.

As the examples in (8) illustrate, Middle Dutch exhibits the characteristic V2 arrangements in root environments, with the fronting of a wide range of categories to the preverbal position. In contrast with the patterns in (4) above, however, whenever an object clitic is involved in a typical V2 structure, it does not appear between the topicalized constituent in sentence initial position and the tensed verb, but rather in the position immediately following the tensed verb.

(8) a. nu   moet*ene*   onse vrouwe bewaren   (MDu)
now must-him our   lady   save
'our lady must save him now'   (from van der Horst 1981)

   b. soe   troest*se*   de hope vander goetheit Gods   (MDu)
      in-this-way consoles-her the hope of   God's   goodness
      'in this way, the hope of God's goodness consoles her'
                                                                 (from Weerman 1987)
   c. Si hadde*t* wel verdient   (MDu)
      she had-it well earned/deserved
      'She had earned it well'   (from Weerman 1987)
   d. dat seg*gic u*   (MDu)
      this say-I you
      'I say this to you'   (from van der Horst 1981)
   e. Volmaect had*se*   die nature   (MDu)
      perfected had-her the nature
      'Nature had perfected her'   (from van der Horst 1981)

The patterns in subordinate environments differ from those in main clauses in significant and interesting ways. Object clitics in embedded clauses are almost invariably found in a position immediately following the complementizer, as in (9a, b). Full NPs are found occupying positions after the object clitic, with subjects preceding objects.

(9) a. datt=*en* God niet en   spaert   (MDu)
     that-him God not NEG-PART saves
     'that God does not save him'   (from van der Horst 1981)
   b. dat=*se*   onse here troest   (MDu)
     that-her our lord consoles
     'that our lord consoles her'   (from van der Horst 1981)

Middle Dutch, as far as I am able to determine, adheres rather strictly to these basic patterns (although see (12) below). However, there are other V2 languages that exhibit the same basic clitic system yet allow for some other possibilities not typical of Middle Dutch. The examples below are from the Bernese dialect of Swiss German.[5] As illustrated in (10) with a subordinate clause, clitics in this language can appear in the same basic positions discussed above for Middle Dutch. As illustrated in (11), however, Bernese German clitics can appear in a slightly wider range of positions than their Middle Dutch counterparts. Thus, both in embedded and subordinate environments, clitics can appear either preceding the subject NP or following it. With some minor differences, the distribution of clitics in High German is very similar to that of Bernese German. Other languages that also exhibit clitic distributions similar to Middle Dutch are, e.g., West Flemish (see Haverkort 1994).

(10) I weiss wo*s*-dr   Vater verloore het   (Bernese)
     I know where=it=the father lost   has
     'I know where father has lost it'

(11) I weiss wo   dr Vater*s*   verloore het   (Bernese)
     I know where the father=it lost   has
     'I know where father has lost it'

It seems desirable to try to unify our accounts of the clitic systems of Middle Dutch and those of the other Germanic languages discussed here in view of the fact that the differences between the two appear relatively minor. Note that, in spite of the fact that most of the available descriptions of Middle Dutch emphasize the almost categorical nature of the patterns in (8) and (9), instances of configurations such as those in (11), although extremely rare, can also be found in some of the Middle Dutch texts. This is illustrated in (12) below. The availability of such configurations in Middle Dutch, together with the situation in Modern Dutch (where only the kinds of patterns illustrated in (11) but not those in (8)–(9) are available), and with the variation observed in different Germanic languages mentioned above, strongly suggest that these patterns could be the reflection of various stages in some diachronic development affecting the same original system of clitics. The facts of Middle Dutch could thus reflect the situation at the earliest stages of this development, with the different varieties of German and West Flemish representing some intermediate stages, and modern Dutch manifesting a still further stage of development (see Fontana, in press, for additional discussion of these facts).

(12) Dat al mijn vrienden'*t* horen (MDu)
that all my friends=it hear (Heer Halewijn balad)
'that all my friends hear it'

The patterns illustrated in (8)–(10) bear some resemblance to those observed in (4)–(7) in connection with OE and OFr: from a strictly descriptive standpoint, tensed verbs and object clitics in root environments typically appear in the same general area which follows the sentence initial position occupied by a fronted constituent in a typical V2 configuration. The two groups of languages differ, however, with respect to the relative orders in which object clitics and tensed verbs are allowed to occur in root environments. Whereas in the former group, the Cl $V_{[+finite]}$ configuration is the norm in a V2 structure (with $V_{[+finite]}$ Cl strings showing up only in some restricted environments), this configuration is not available in the latter group of languages.

It may seem that, for languages such as Middle Dutch or Bernese German, the descriptive label '2P clitic' is rather inappropriate. However, the existence in OE and OFr of the configuration shown in (7) suggests we might establish a link between the systems of clitics in the two types of V2 languages. Since, in turn, we have also established similarities between the clitic systems of OE and OFr and the general class of 2P clitics found in, e.g., Homeric Greek and Serbo-Croatian, by extension we should consider the possibility that languages such as Middle Dutch and Bernese German might have 2P clitics as well.

An ideal analysis of second position phenomena should be able to provide a principled account not only of the contrasts between the two basic groups of V2 languages established above, but also of the differences between these languages and the languages that have 2P clitics but which are not characterized by a V2 phrase structure.

In the next section I will compare the analysis of second position phenomena suggested in Fontana (1993, in press) with those in Cardinaletti & Roberts (1991), and Rivero (this volume). I will argue that the approach outlined in Fontana (1993) is better positioned to provide an analysis that can cover the whole range of phenomena discussed above.

3 Three alternative treatments of second position phenomena

I begin by summarizing briefly the relationship between the three analyses considered here. Cardinaletti & Roberts (1991) seek to integrate the analysis of general second position phenomena in medieval Romance and Germanic, but are silent on the possible formal relationship between the clitic distribution in those two groups of languages and the systems of clitics traditionally studied under the rubric of 2P clitics. Rivero (this volume) sees no correlation between the syntactic mechanisms assumed to be responsible for the formation of V2 and related word order patterns and the distinctive distribution of clitics in the Old Romance languages (more specifically in Old Spanish), seeking instead to integrate the analysis of Old Spanish with the analyses of clitic facts and general word order in Serbo-Croatian and Bulgarian. Thus, the set of facts that determine the final make-up of her proposal are considerably different from those considered in Cardinaletti & Roberts (1991) and Fontana (1993, in press), and hence cannot be said to have much bearing on the analysis of word order and clitic facts in the Germanic languages. Finally, the proposal advanced in Fontana (1993, in press) takes the position that both Romance and Germanic families and those languages previously investigated within general research on 2P clitics share essentially similar clitic systems, but also sees a relationship between the phrase structure of the medieval Romance languages and that of the V2 languages. This approach also diverges from the other two in at least two other important respects.

First, unlike the analyses in both Cardinaletti & Roberts and Rivero, that in Fontana (1993) reflects the position that the TML and WL are simple descriptive generalizations that crudely reflect the interaction of the same basic type of clitic category with different syntactic/phonological systems which are ultimately responsible for the few but conspicuous differences in the distributions of these clitics across the relevant groups of languages. This is a significant point of departure from the other two proposals, since it does not entail any substantial complications of current grammatical models by rendering the syntax of specific languages sensitive in one way or another to those descriptive generalizations. In Fontana (1993, in press), I argue that both verb movement solely motivated as a last resort to prevent clitics from appearing in first position, as well as functional projections designed specifically to host clitics, are superfluous. Both are fundamental components of the other two analyses considered here. Instead, the differences and similarities observed in the relative positions that clitics can occupy with respect to the verb are accounted for in terms of the independently motivated differences and similarities in the syntax of verb movement and general phrase structure of the languages involved.

Second, the approach in Fontana (1993, in press) differs fundamentally from the other two in that it assumes a dynamic approach to the study of syntactic change (see, e.g., Kroch 1989, 1994; Santorini 1989; Pintzuk 1991; and also Miller 1991). This perspective can offer a principled explanation of how some of the properties of the OSp clitic system (and also, by extension, those of OFr and Old Italian) resemble those of clitics in Germanic, Serbo-Croatian and Homeric Greek, while others can be more adequately modelled after the clitic systems found in Modern Standard Bulgarian, or in the modern Romance languages.

3.1 Cardinaletti & Roberts (1991)

It is necessary to emphasize once again at the outset of this summary of the analysis in Cardinaletti & Roberts (1991) (henceforth the Agr1/Agr2P analysis) that their solution is explicitly restricted in its coverage to the second position phenomena observed in the Germanic and medieval Romance languages. Thus, no attempt is made to extend their general treatment to the analysis of 2P clitics crosslinguistically.

Cardinaletti & Roberts propose to account for a subset of the facts illustrated above through the postulation of a new phrasal projection within the IP complex. Specifically, they propose a further break-up of IP by positing, at least in the languages they consider, the existence of another functional projection, which they label Agr1P, in addition to TP, NegP and AgrP projections, assumed by many syntacticians working within the GB framework after Pollock (1989). Very roughly, the phrase structure they envision is that in (13).

(13)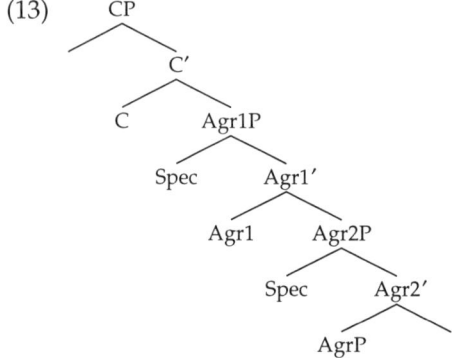

They propose that $Agr1^0$ is responsible for nominative case assignment, which, depending on the language, can be realized via government, via

Spec–head agreement, or both. These parameterized differences will permit subjects in some languages to occur only in the specifier position of Agr2P, where they would be assigned nominative case by $Agr1^0$ under government, while in other languages, those where nominative case can only be assigned via Spec–head agreement, subjects will be allowed to appear only in Spec,Agr1P. Finally, in languages where the two modalities of case assignment are operative, subjects can appear either in Spec,Agr1P or Spec,Agr2P. The other crucial assumption Cardinaletti & Roberts make is that $Agr1^0$ is the position for clitics in all these languages. One of the more attractive aspects of this analysis is that it tries to provide a unified account of a range of phenomena involving the interaction of verb-movement and clitic-placement on the basis of a small number of assumptions about the similarities between the phrase structures of the languages involved.

There are a number of facts that appear to be straightforwardly derived from the adoption of structures of the type illustrated in (2) and the ancillary assumptions about nominative case assignment and clitic placement. Among these, the most relevant for the present discussion are the following.

The first is the pattern of embedded verb-second observed in languages such as Yiddish and Icelandic. Cardinaletti & Roberts account for the word order patterns in these languages by assuming that Spec,Agr1 is the landing site for topicalized XPs, and Spec,Agr2, the position for subjects. The tensed verb is assumed to climb to $Agr1^0$ in sequences of the form *XP V[+fin] Subj (XP)*, and only to $Agr2^0$ in sequences of the form *Subj V[+fin] (XP)*. Subjects are assumed to receive nominative case from $Agr1^0$ under government. They further assume that in some exceptional environments, mainly questions and declarative V1, the tensed verb can move further up to C^0.

Since $Agr1^0$ is also argued to be the position occupied by object clitics in all the languages examined by Cardinaletti & Roberts, they derive the patterns in the German sentences in (14) below (their 25) by assuming that the subject is occupying Spec,Agr2, and the clitics are in $Agr1^0$.

(14) a. ... daß *es ihm*   der Johann gestern   gegeben hat
         that it him-DAT   John yesterday given   has
     b. Gestern   hat *es ihm*   der Johann gegeben
        yesterday has it him-DAT   John given

One of the advantages of the Agr1/Agr2P analysis is that it contains an additional position to host the subject between C^0 and the fixed position they assume clitics occupy. Thus it can account for sequences such as the ones illustrated in (15), which differ from (14) in terms of the relative positions occupied by subject and clitic. This particular arrangement, which is also possible in German, is the only option in Dutch. To account for these contrasts in a principled manner, Cardinaletti & Roberts propose that in Dutch the only position that receives nominative case is Spec,Agr1 (via

Spec–head agreement), whereas German additionally allows $Agr1^0$ to assign nominative case to the Spec,Agr2 position under government.

(15) a. ... daß der Johann *es ihm* gestern gegeben hat
    that John it him-DAT yesterday given has
b. Gestern hat der Johann *es ihm* gegeben
    yesterday has John it him-DAT given

Second, the Agr1/Agr2P analysis is designed to provide an account of the so-called TML effects. The following OFr examples (their (33a) and (33b)) are representative of these effects. Traditional Romance philologists as well as some authors working on the medieval Romance languages from a generative perspective, including Cardinaletti & Roberts, co-incide in correlating the relative positions occupied by clitic and tensed verb with a putative prohibition against clitic-first strings operative in these languages. Thus, the examples below reflect, in their own words, 'a ban on clitic-first orders; [hence] in constructions where a proclitic would appear in first position, enclisis is obligatory and proclisis is excluded (Mussafia 1893)'. The issue of the proper characterization of the TML facts is addressed in detail in Fontana (in press). For the moment, let us concentrate on how the Agr1/Agr2P analysis accommodates these facts.

(16) a. Toutes ces choses *te* presta Nostre Sires
    all these things you lent our Lord (de Kok 1985: 74)
b. Voit *le* li rois
    sees him the king (*Le Charroi de Nîmes*, 1. 58))

The contrasts observed in (16) are argued to follow from the assumption that the following underlying structures are assigned to the relevant examples. (17a) corresponds to (16a), and (17b) to (16b). (17a) is a slightly modified version of their (47a); (17b) is reconstructed from the discussion of sentences such as (16b) in section 2.2 of their chapter.

(17) a. $[_{CP}$ Top $[_{C'}$ Cl+V^0 [$[_{Agr1P}$(Subj) $[_{Agr1'}$ t $[_{Agr2P}$ (Subj) [...]]]]]]
b. $[_{CP}$ $[_{C'}$ V^0+Cl [$[_{Agr1P}$(Subj) $[_{Agr1'}$ t $[_{Agr2P}$ (Subj) [...]]]]]]

The different orders between tensed verb and clitic in the structures above are a consequence of their account of TML effects in medieval Romance. In (16a), the verb is said to have moved through $Agr2^0$ to pick up inflection, then to $Agr1^0$ to combine with the clitic, and, finally, the complex formed by the clitic and the verb is assumed to move to C^0. In (16b), however, the tensed verb is posited to have 'skipped' the $Agr1^0$ position and moved directly to C^0 in order to prevent the violation of the TML prohibiting clitic-first sequences. Cardinaletti & Roberts view this latter operation as a 'last-resort' operation of the sort contemplated in Chomsky (1989). Since they also assume, at least for the medieval Romance languages, that clitics must combine with the inflected verb, they further suggest that the clitic left-adjoins to V in C^0, possibly at PF.

Finally, this analysis is also claimed to provide a straightforward account of certain contrasts observed between OE and Old High German on the one hand and the medieval Romance languages on the other. The account of the patterns illustrated in (18)–(20) below (their (40a), (41a) and (42a) respectively, borrowed in turn from van Kemenade (1987)) is as follows. In the case of the OE example in (18), where they concur with both van Kemenade (1987) and Pintzuk (1991) in assuming that the inflected verb is in C^0, Cardinaletti & Roberts suggest that the clitic *hine* occupies $Agr1^0$.

(18) Ne geseah *hine* nan man nates-hown yrre
 not saw him so little angry
 'No one ever saw him so little angry'

This contrasts with the structure assumed for the example in (19), where they argue that the tensed verb shares the $Agr1^0$ position with the clitic. Note that, if we exclude the clitic, this would be a typical instance of a verb-second clause. Thus, this analysis of verb-second effects in OE coincides in some basic respects with the analysis suggested in Pintzuk (1991), contra van Kemenade (1987). While the former author proposes that in these types of configurations the tensed verb remains within IP, the latter argues for the extension of the standard analysis of V2 effects, following den Besten (1978), to OE; that is, she takes the position of the tensed verb in (18) to be the same as in (19).

(19) Fela spella *him* sœdon þa Beormas, œgþer ge of hiera agnum lande,
 many stories him told the Permians, both of their own country,...
 'The Permians told him many stories, both about their own country.'
 (van Kemenade 1987)

Finally, since the Agr1/Agr2P analysis provides additional landing sites for the tensed verb, Cardinaletti & Roberts propose that their system provides a more straightforward account of configurations such as that illustrated in (20). In these constructions, the clitic immediately follows a complementizer, and the tensed verb appears separated from the clitic by an intervening constituent.

(20) þæt *him* his fiend wæren æfterfylgende
 that him his enemies were following
 '...that his enemies were chasing him' (van Kemenade 1987)

In this case, they assume that the tensed verb has remained in the head of $Agr2^0$. Different restrictions concerning the possible landing sites for the tensed verb in root and subordinate environments, they argue, account for the existence of patterns such as (20) and their unavailability in the medieval Romance languages. While in the latter languages the verb moves to $Agr1^0$ in both matrix and subordinate clauses, in OE and OHG the verb moves to $Agr1^0$ only in matrix declaratives. The structures proposed to account for the patterns in (19) and (20) are those in (21a) and (21b), respectively.

(21) a. $[_{Agr1P}$ TOP $[_{Agr1'}$ Cl+V^0 $[$ $[_{Agr2P}$ Subj $[_{Agr2'}$ *t* $[...]$ $]]]]$
 b. $[_{Agr1P}$ Subj $[_{Agr1'}$ Cl $[$ $[_{Agr2P}$ Subj $[_{Agr2'}$ V^0 $[...]$ $]]]]$

3.2 Rivero (this volume)

As noted above, Rivero's proposal differs substantially from the Agr1/Agr2P analysis both in terms of the treatment suggested for some of the clitic categories typically studied in the context of second position phenomena and in terms of its intended empirical coverage. The analysis in Rivero (1993, this volume) (henceforth the TMP/WP analysis) explicitly rejects relating the behaviour of OSp phrase structure and clitics to that in the Germanic languages and OFr, in contrast to what is advocated by Cardinaletti & Roberts. Rivero seeks instead to formulate a unified account for clitic distribution in OSp, Homeric Greek and in several Balkan languages, including Serbo-Croatian and Bulgarian. Since her proposal is fully developed in this volume, I will not provide a detailed account of it here. I will, however, mention aspects of it that are most relevant for comparison with the other analyses considered here.

One of the most important contrasts between the TMP/WP and Agr1/Agr2P analyses is the former's departure from the notion that clitics are invariably head categories. Building on her earlier work (Rivero 1986, 1992), Rivero suggests that at least some of the clitic-like elements found in the OSp texts have the status of maximal projections (X^{max} categories) in the grammar. She specifically claims that OSp has what she calls a 'mixed system' of I-oriented clitics related to the TMP projection she posits (for Tobler–Mussafia Law effects) and characteristic of Bulgarian — and C-oriented clitics, related to the WP projection she posits (for Wackernagel effects) and characteristic of languages such as Serbo-Croatian. While C-oriented clitics are typically X^{max} categories, I-oriented clitics must be considered heads, i.e. X^0 categories. The two structures posited for I-oriented and C-oriented systems are illustrated in (22).

(22) a. [$_{CP}$ C [$_{NegP}$ Y [$_{Neg'}$ [$_{TMP}$ [$_{TM'}$ **CL** [$_{IP}$]]]]]]   I-system
    b. [$_{CP}$ C [$_{WP}$ **CL** [$_{W'}$ [$_{NegP}$ Y [$_{Neg'}$ [$_{IP}$]]]]]]   C-system

Thus, what characterizes clitics in I-systems is that they must be adjacent to a verb, presumably (although this is not explicitly said) because there is something forcing the tensed verb to move to the TM^0 position. Clitics in C-systems, in contrast, are characterized by the fact that they must be adjacent to the complementizer in subordinate environments, and can be separated from the tensed verb by one or more constituents. These differences are illustrated in (23) ((4b) and (6b) from Rivero, this volume):

(23) a. Ako bog ne *ti* pomogne,...   Bulgarian
      if   God not you helps
      'If God does not help you,...'
   b. Ako *ti* bog ne pomogne,...   Serbo-Croatian
      if   you God not helps,
      'If God does not help you,...'

OSp is classified as a mixed system because it exhibits both of the configurations illustrated in (23), as we can see in the examples in (24) below ((1a) and (2a) from Rivero, this volume).

(24) a. E   si él mejor *lo* faze...   (OSp)
         and if he better it does
         'And if he does it better...'   Z154
     b. Si *lo* el   rey   por bien toviere,   mándeme quemar   (OSp)
         if it the king for good   had   order+me burn
         'If the king considered it good, let him order that they burn me'
                                                                                CD243

3.3 Fontana (1993, in press)

3.3.1 Some methodological differences with other studies

3.3.1.1 Going outside Romance to understand medieval Romance clitics. The last proposal considered here is the one advanced in Fontana (1993) and further developed in Fontana (in press) (henceforth the V2/2P analysis). Perhaps the simplest way to characterize this analysis is to say that it is a deliberate attempt to incorporate the study of OSp clitics within the general framework developed for the analysis of 2P clitics. 2P clitic systems exhibit properties crucially different from those of the clitic systems found in most modern Romance languages (see, e.g., Zwicky 1977; Klavans 1982; Taylor 1990; Miller 1991; and Halpern 1992 for general typologies, discussions and additional references). The basic conclusion of my investigation is that OSp clitics should be excluded from any of the models currently considered for the analysis of so-called clitics in modern Romance (earlier suggestions that clitics in some of the medieval Romance languages should be studied as members of the 2P clitic class can also be found in, e.g., Klavans 1982).

This line of research goes in a rather different direction from recent work by, e.g., van Kemenade (1987), Cardinaletti & Roberts (1991) and Cardinaletti (1992). The latter presuppose that the models developed for modern Romance (based mainly on Kayne's (1975), initial study of French clitics and on further developments in the same spirit) can extend to virtually all categories called clitics, a presupposition which is highly problematic (see, e.g., Miller 1991 and Zwicky 1994, who concludes that clitics are 'unlikely to constitute a unified class for the purposes of theorizing about the nature of grammar').

Thus, whereas the latter strategy involves studying the behaviour of Germanic clitics in terms of the already developed models used to study modern Romance clitics, my strategy is to seek out instead a unified treatment of Germanic and Old Romance clitics, and to distinguish modern Romance clitics as an outgrowth of these categories, with fundamentally different properties. The basic idea behind this claim is that clitics in Romance went from being syntactically autonomous but prosodically dependent words to being verbal inflectional morphology or, to put it differently, from being X^{max}- to X^0-related categories. Although a much closer examination of clitic phenomena across the different modern Germanic dialects is needed before these matters can be resolved with total confidence, I will suggest that, for the most part, pronominal clitics are still better treated as X^{max} categories in the Germanic languages as well.[6] Additional justification for this claim will be provided throughout this chapter (see also Halpern & Fontana (1994); and Haverkort (1994) for further argumentation in support of this position).

3.3.1.2 Different approaches to the study of diachronic data.

I assume it to be rather uncontroversial that grammars of no longer existing languages are not substantially different, either qualitatively or in degrees of complexity, from the grammars posited for existing languages. Consequently, whenever possible, we should seek to relate patterns found in any given set of texts to established treatments of similar phenomena in living languages.

This is extremely difficult, if not impossible, if we adopt the view that a single and fully deterministic grammar is responsible for the generation of each and every string in a given text or set of texts, often ranging over several centuries. Instead, it is arguably much more fruitful to posit simple, well-motivated analyses which can cover the most substantial and representative subsets of the data. Data which do not fit the primary analysis must be then reconciled to the greatest extent possible by means of principled alternative analyses compatible with a well-worked-out theory of linguistic change.

Specifically, I have adopted a dynamic approach to the study of diachronic syntax often referred to as the *variationist approach* or the *double base hypothesis* (see, e.g., Kroch 1989, 1994; Pintzuk 1991; and Santorini 1989, 1992).[7] The central premise behind this approach, according to Kroch, is that syntactic change is gradual, and that, more often than not, a particular generation of speakers will differ from the previous generation in terms of the relative frequencies with which they use certain forms rather than in whether those forms are possible at all. Thus, proponents of this view of historical syntax assume that syntactic change has two distinct aspects: 'a discontinuous aspect involving the coexistence of (sets of) discrete linguistic forms in alternation, but also a continuous, dynamic aspect characterized by fluctuations in the frequency of these forms' (Santorini 1989: 4). Moreover, as research within this framework has shown, during processes of change languages display variation in specific areas of grammar where we do not usually observe optionality when stable systems are involved. To handle this kind of situation, which is the typical situation most diachronic studies have to face, these researchers have proposed a model which is based on the assumption that 'syntactic change proceeds via competition between grammatically incompatible options which substitute for one another in usage' (Kroch 1994).

A dynamic perspective is not the only one we could bring to bear on diachronic facts. A second option, which is the one implicit in both Cardinaletti & Roberts' and Rivero's work, is to attempt to describe the data in static terms, not taking into account factors such as contact with other languages or geographic, social, and stylistic variation. On such a view, one would accord what amounts to exceptional data on the dynamic view an equal status with all other data in the language. As implicit in the comments above, the principal reason for rejecting this perspective is that the complexity of the data is likely to lead us to posit a syntax which is considerably more cumbersome than the syntax of living languages is usually assumed to be. Additional and perhaps more important reasons to be wary of any static approach are: (a) the fact that most diachronic investigations must be based on written corpora, entailing familiar idiosyncracies and tendencies to linguistic unnaturalness; and (b) the fact that the traditional boundaries for the periods known as OSp, OE, OFr etc. encompass several centuries, a period which more than stretches the limits of true synchronic analysis.

As noted in Kroch (1994), the variation which is characteristically observed in written texts can be either interpreted as the reflex of competing grammatical systems in the linguistic community of which the author was a member, or of the competition between the grammar of the spoken language and an archaic but still influential literary standard at a given time. In the latter case, he points out, the competition between grammatical systems could not be said to have a purely linguistic significance, but it would still be crucial for the appropriate interpretation of the texts.

I bring up these issues because it is extremely important to distinguish the methodological assumptions that separate the different proposals in order to conduct a productive comparison, and more specifically to achieve a proper understanding of the kinds of predictions made by each analysis. In addition, the previous comments clarify how statements such as 'OSp can be described as a V2 language' or 'OSp has 2P clitics' should be interpreted in subsequent discussion. It should be obvious, given what has just been said, that such claims, in the present context, must be understood simply as an abstraction based on the patterns found to be more representative of the period by means of a careful qualitative and quantitative study of a sample of texts ranging from the XIIth to the XVIth centuries. Although we lack crucial data from the period in which the hypothesized V2 phrase structure and 2P clitic system of OSp must have manifested themselves in their most 'pure' state, Fontana (1993) shows that the relative frequencies of counterexamples to the idealized analysis rise steadily over time, with exceptions becoming remarkably more noticeable towards the end of the fourteenth century, thus providing further support for the hypothesis that conflicting data reflect the competition between different grammatical systems.

I now turn to the details of Fontana's (1993) proposal for OSp, leaving discussion of its extension to other languages and of the solutions suggested to deal with potential counterexamples for section 4.

3.3.2 Old Spanish as an I-V2 language with 2P clitics

OSp manifests the distinctive second position effects discussed above, both with respect to its clitics and with respect to the distribution of the tensed verb. As illustrated in (25), the initial position in OSp main clauses can be occupied by virtually any kind of constituent. When the fronted constituent is not a subject, and a phonologically expressed subject is available, it typically appears immediately following the verb (which is indicated in bold; the subject is underlined).

(25) a. este logar **mostro** <u>dios</u> a abraam
     this place showed God to Abraham
     'God showed Abraham this place'   (GE-I.62v)
  b. Grande duelo **avien** <u>las yentes christianas</u>
     great grief had the peoples christian
     'The christian people experienced great grief'   (PMC.29)
  c. dalli **fueron** <u>ellas</u> Sennoras luengo tiempo
     of-there were they ladies long time
     'they were the rulers of those lands for a long time'   (EE-I.137)
  d. tanto **fueron** <u>los godos</u> nobles de coraçon. &
     so-much were the goths noble of heart and
     sabidores & atreuudos [...]
     knowledgeable and daring   (EE-I.127v)
     'the Goths were so noble, and skilled and brave [in war that....]'

As illustrated in (26), V2 effects are found in subordinate contexts as well.

(26) a. Cuenta la estoria que nueue meses **touo** <u>el</u> çercada la noble
     says the history that nine months had he sieged the noble
     çibdat de valencia
     city of Valencia
     'History says that he had the city of Valencia under siege for nine months'   (EE-II.218v)
  c. Quando esta falssedad **dizien** <u>los de carrion</u>
     when this falsity said the of carrion
     'When the ones from Carrion told this lie'   PMC
  d. por que en agua **mataron** <u>ellos</u> los njnnos delos ebreos
     because in water killed they the children of-the Hebrew
     'Because they drowned the Hebrew children'   GEI.3

Finally, as also observed for languages discussed in relation to the data illustrated in (7), OSp manifests declarative V1 constructions, in addition to *yes/no* questions and imperatives, as in (27). This specific type of exception to the V2 constraint in root environments has been discussed in the Germanic syntax literature on Yiddish, Icelandic, Old English and Old Norse. The construction illustrated by (27) is an instance of Narrative Inversion (see Sigurðsson 1990 and references therein; see also Fontana 1993, for discussion of additional structures involving this basic configuration). The examples in (28) illustrate some instances of declarative V1 in Old Norse; (28b) is typical of Narrative Inversion structures frequently found in the Old Norse sagas.

(27) & **fizo** el papa penitencia & **dixo** Sant Antidio la missa
& did the pope penance & said sant Antidio the mass
en su lugar & **consagro** la crisma
in his place & consecrated the host
'And the pope did penance and Saint Antidio said the mass in his place and consecrated the host' (EE-I.126r)

(28) a. **Vil** ek, at þér brøðr farit þessa ferð
want I that you brothers go this trip
'I want you brothers to make this trip'
(*Ólafs saga helga*, cited from Faarlund 1990: 120)

b. Bjorn **nam** Þóru á brott ok hafði heim með sér á Aurland; **váru** Bjorn took Þóru away and had home with self in Aurland; were
þau þar um vetrinn, ok **vildi** Bjorn gera brúðlaup til hennar
they there in the winter, and wanted Bjorn make wedding to her
'Bjorn took Þóru away to his home in Aurland. They stayed there during the winter, and then Bjorn decided he wanted to marry her'

My account of the basic clausal structure of OSp is as follows. First, OSp is taken to have a phrase structure which, at least in its most basic attributes, is essentially like those posited to characterize languages such as Icelandic and Yiddish (Rögnvaldsson & Thráinsson 1990; Diesing 1990; Santorini 1989). Of course, these patterns could be amenable to various alternative solutions, and possibly one would want to revise the initial assumptions of these authors in light of new findings. However, the basic idea behind those proposals can still be maintained, and I will claim that it applies to the OSp data as well. Adopting the standard approaches to phrase structure in the GB framework, the patterns discussed here are most adequately accounted for by assuming that V2 effects in these languages are generally obtained via verb movement to one functional projection between VP and CP, and topicalization of a constituent to the specifier position in the same maximal projection. Within the rather conservative view of phrase structure adopted in Fontana (1993) (conservative at least relative to the split-Infl hypothesis of Pollock 1989 and its outgrowths), the landing sites for the topicalized XP and the tensed verb are Spec,IP and I^0, respectively, except in examples such as those in (27), where the landing site of the verb is argued to be C^0.[8] Positing verb movement to C^0 in these latter cases accounts for both the well-known fact that this specific class of constructions is restricted to root environments, and the distribution of clitics in these types of structures, as will shortly be shown.

OSp also manifests second position effects in its clitic system. As illustrated in (29), clitics in OSp tend to appear immediately following the constituent that has been fronted to initial position, preceding the tensed verb. As noted above in reference to OE and OFr, the appearance of a clitic constitutes an exception to what would otherwise be a typical manifestation of the V2 word order pattern.

(29) a. esto *les* mandaua el rey cuydando que...
 this them ordered the king thinking that
 'The king bade them to do this, thinking that...' GEI.002
 b. Tu *lo* otorgaras
 you-it admit.FUT
 'You will admit it' (PMC)

Clitics in OSp can also follow the tensed verb in verb initial sentences, as in (30). Interestingly, configurations of the form $V_{[+\text{finite}]}$ *Cl* are found in OSp precisely in the same types of constructions where they are found in OE and OFr, i.e. in environments where I to C verb movement can be independently motivated even in languages that are assumed to achieve verb-second effects via single verb movement from V to I (see, e.g., Santorini 1989; Sigurðsson 1990; or Fontana 1993, for justification of an I-to-C analysis of V1 declaratives). In (7) above, we saw instances of V1 declaratives from OE and OFr; (31) below contains a *yes/no* question and a counterfactual conditional from OFr. This situation clearly contrasts with the situation observed for the Germanic languages discussed above. Recall that in the latter languages, post-verbal object clitics are mandatory in all root clauses, including V2 structures, which is expected if in these languages verb movement is always to C^0 in these environments.

(30) a. rogaron*le* que *les* diesse la llaue
 begged.3P-him that them gave.3s the key
 Respondio*les* el que lo non farie;
 answered-them he it not would-do
 'They asked him to give them the key. He answered that he would not do it'
 b. ?Miembra*t* quando lidiamos çerca Valençia la grant?
 reminds-to-you when fought.we near Valencia the great
 'Do you remember when we fought around Valencia the great?'
 (PMC 3315)

(31) a. Oserai *le vous* demander?
 dare.1SG it you ask
 'Do I dare ask it of you?' (R.Gr.21, cited in Adams 1987)
 b. Fust *i* li reis, n'*i* oüssum damage
 were here the king not here had.1PL damage
 'If the king were here, we wouldn't suffer any damage'
 (Harris 1978: 240, cited in Cardinaletti & Roberts 1991)

As examples such as (32) show, V1 declaratives occur in OFr independently of the presence of a clitic as well.

(32) Plurent Franceis   pur pitet de Rollant
     weep   the French for pity of Roland
     'The French weep for Roland'   (Rol. 3120, cited in Adams 1987)

As was noted in the discussion of the TMP/WP analysis, clitics can also be found in subordinate environments immediately following the complementizer and preceding the subject or the topicalized XP (33a). The two patterns illustrated in (33) can be found in variable proportions, depending on the specific texts, until the fifteenth century. After the fifteenth century only the configuration in (33b) is found. The example in (33a) then, illustrates the fact that in OSp, as in OE or, in general, in the Germanic languages discussed here, object clitics can appear separated from the verb by intervening constituents. This phenomenon is known as *Interpolation* in the Romance philological literature.

(33) a. otro dia [que*les*   este buen mandado **dixo** Moysen]. fizieron
        other day that-them this good order   told Moses.   made.3PL
        muy grand fiesta
        very big   party
        'The day after Moses had given them directions, they organized a
        big celebration'   (GE-I.216v)
     b. ... dixo les [que esto *les*   fiziera el_ por mostrar ...]
        told them that this to-them did   he for show
        'He told them that he did that to them just to show ...'   E-I.324v

OSp clitics also had the phonological attributes of 2P clitics. While it is commonly agreed that in Modern Spanish clitics are part of the same phonological word as the verb, the spelling of the medieval texts provides ample evidence that this was not the case in OSp. The examples below illustrate the fact that phonological attachment of the clitic to the preceding word, independently of its category, was the unmarked case in this language. In other words, they were predominantly enclitic, although there are several attested cases of phonological cliticization to the following word (i.e. procliticization) found mainly in poetic texts.[9] It is interesting to point out in this respect that, although there are abundant instances of proclitic elements in the Homeric Greek data that served as the basis for Wackernagel's central observations, he noted that only enclitics are found in the distinctive second position that has come to bear his name. As these examples illustrate, this process of phonological merger frequently results in vowel reduction within the clitic. As noted above, this striking promiscuity of phonological attachment of clitic categories to virtually any type of category linearly preceding them is a typical trait of 2P clitic systems.

(34) a. Amigo Aynart, yos   prometo que oy...
        friend Aynart I-to-you promise that today
        'My friend Aynart, I promise you that today ...'   (EE-II.12v)

b. Esto*t* lidiare aqui antel Rey don alfonsso
   this-you dispute.1SG here before-the King don alfonsso
   'I will challenge you on this before King don Alfonso' (PMC.3344)
c. ... quien era el qui*l* llamara y*l* aquello dixiera
   who was the who-him called and-him that said
   '[he would see] who was the one who called him and told him
   that' (EEII.62r)

Building on a previous proposal by Taylor (1990) to account for the distribution of 2P clitics in Homeric Greek, in Fontana (1993) I advanced the hypothesis that OSp clitics are a special type of phrasal constituent (arguably NPs) which the syntax places at the left edge of the sentence by default. Taylor's analysis was in turn an adaptation to the GB phrase structure framework of Klavans' (1982) model to treat clitics universally. The V2/2P analysis has also benefitted from some of the central insights of the treatments of clitic phenomena found in Marantz (1988), Anderson (1992); and Halpern (1992), among others.

The basic idea behind this approach, as in most previous treatments of 2P clitic phenomena, is that syntactic cliticization (the process by which the clitic is placed in a position in the left edge of the sentence) and phonological cliticization (the process by which the clitic attaches to a phonological host on its left) operate independently of one another. Thus, there is a crucial distinction between being preverbal and being proclitic, one which, as we noticed earlier, is not always properly recognized in recent treatments of this phenomenon. In addition, 2P clitics are generally assumed to be categories which, due to their prosodically deficient nature, will typically have to lean on a lexical element to their left (i.e. they are enclitic by default).

As in other analyses of 2P clitic phenomena (e.g. Taylor (1990); Pintzuk (1991); Halpern (1992) or Halpern & Fontana (1994)), the V2/2P analysis takes this class of clitics to occupy a position below CP, and to be syntactically and morphologically independent of C^0. That is, the phrasal projection that serves as the syntactic domain for cliticization is argued to be S (i.e. IP or the Tense/Agr complex). The analysis of OSp clitics I defended in Fontana (1993) and, more specifically, in Fontana (in press), crucially differs from other analyses of this distinctive class of clitics in positing no syntactic constraint or last resort mechanism to govern their relative orders with respect to other constituents appearing in the general area which, for the moment, we can loosely characterize as the left edge of IP.

Rather, sequences involving sentence initial clitics, i.e. those typically found in subordinate environments in 'pure' 2P clitic systems, are syntactically acceptable, and could in principle arise in matrix environments as a result of the operation of those syntactic mechanisms ultimately responsible for clitic and non-clitic constituent arrangements.[10] These strings, however, would generally be ruled out at PF, because they conflict with a phonological constraint requiring clitics to attach to a lexical host on their left. A detailed justification of this analysis can be found in Fontana (in press).

While most of the previous analyses of 2P clitic phenomena, including this one, attempt to account for the relative positioning of the clitic with respect to other elements occupying the left edge of the sentence, they are silent with respect to the motivation of the syntactic mechanisms by which these special kinds of constituents gravitate toward the left edge of the sentence in the first place. See Anderson (1993) for an interesting and challenging proposal where morphologically based requirements are assumed to play a key role in the determination of second position phenomena, not only with regards to the account of 2P clitic distribution, but also with regards to the interpretation of the V2 constraint.

As far as I am able to determine, there are no totally unproblematic answers to deal with this rather puzzling aspect of clitic placement. Under the other two proposals being discussed here, and in general under any treatment positing a specific phrasal projection or head status for clitics, one could possibly attempt an explanation in terms of some kind of Spec–head agreement requirement or the need to lexicalize some feature present in the relevant functional head position. But these kinds of solutions are rather stipulative at this stage, and they appear to describe the problem more than solve it. Hence, they cannot be claimed to be truly explanatory unless they are more explicitly formulated and tested. A more promising direction of research could be to attempt to relate these patterns to the syntactic strategies used by the languages involved to encode the information structure of the sentence.

Suppose, for instance, that all the languages with 2P clitics share a strategy that we could call, for lack of a better term, *focus flight*, by which elements not being part of the sentential focus would be fronted so as to remove them from a specific domain in the sentence restricted to the presence of constituents that must be assigned a focal interpretation.[11] Pronominal clitics, unstressed by definition, would have a different distribution from stressed pronouns to signal their different role in the encoding of the information structure of the sentence. In other words, they would be the ones that undergo focus flight, in case such a strategy turned out to be motivated. Some specific attempts to relate the distribution of medieval Romance clitics to informational considerations can be found, e.g. in Renzi (1992) or Uriagereka (1992b). Such an approach seems rather promising in the case of OSp. However, I have not carried out extensive research on the OSp data to confirm or disconfirm this hypothesis, nor do I currently have enough information at my disposal to determine whether the data from the other languages with 2P clitics could bear this kind of approximation. Thus, this suggestion will have to remain speculative for the moment.[12]

3.3.2.1 The V2/2P analysis. The observations discussed above, taken in tandem with the claim that OSp has the general type of phrase structure found in I-V2 languages, suggest the following treatment of the syntax of 2P clitics. First, a basic syntactic operation displaces the object clitic from its canonical position within VP to a position below CP available for the landing of phrasal constituents (given standard GB assumptions, this would be an A' position). Within the view of phrase structure adopted in Fontana (1993), AGR is taken to be simply a feature of INFL instead of heading its own projection; thus the wide range of possibilities allowed by the richer systems inspired by Pollock's (1989) split-Infl hypothesis and subsequent developments are not available.

Nothing would prevent us, however, from integrating the basic insights of the analysis adopted there within these alternative frameworks if we so desired. Thus, the contrasts between examples in which the clitic follows vs precedes the fronted XP could be argued to follow from either adjunction or substitution in whatever maximal projection is posited immediately below CP, or in the maximal functional projection two projections below CP.[13] Note that the only aspect of the claim that is really crucial to preserve the integrity of this proposal is that 2P clitics, unlike modern Romance clitic-like elements, are phrasal categories, i.e. X^{max}, and that their default syntactic position is the left-most A-bar position within the minimal sentential domain, or IP.

Note also that this particular view of the syntax of 2P clitics bears an extraordinary resemblance to proposals advanced to treat a very similar set of facts, namely multiple *wh*-fronting in some Balkan languages. Rudin (1988) has proposed an account of the facts illustrated in (35) in terms of multiple adjunction of *wh*-phrases to the Spec,CP position. As shown by these examples from Bulgarian, whenever we have a question involving more than one *wh*-phrase, all are fronted to the sentence initial position. Furthermore, fronted *wh*-phrases must be positioned following a strict order: if one of the *wh*-phrases is the subject, it must appear as first in the sequence of *wh*-words, followed by the accusative *wh*-phrase and then by the dative *wh*-phrase. Similar facts obtain also in Rumanian. Other Slavic languages different from Bulgarian, such as Polish or Serbo-Croatian, allow for multiple *wh*-fronting as well, but the order of the fronted *wh*-phrases is not restricted.

(35) a. **Koj kakvo na kogo** e dal?
  who what to whom has given
  'Who gave what to whom?' (from Rudin 1988: 29a)
 b. ***Kogo koj** vižda?
  whom who sees (from Rudin 1988: 54b)

Rudin convincingly argues that the best hypothesis to account for these and other differences between these groups of languages is to assume that in 'Bulgarian, but not Serbo-Croatian, [...] *wh*-words [are] in the same structural position and [bear] the same relation to their traces at S-structure as English has at LF'. She proposes the phrase marker in (36) as the correct representation for the underlying structure of sentences such as those in

(35a). In this structure, a single *wh*-phrase is substituted into the Spec,CP position, and then additional *wh*-phrase or phrases may be adjoined to Spec,CP. As Rudin observes, nothing in standard models of phrase structure following Chomsky (1986a) would prevent adjunction of *wh*-phrases to Spec,CP, since this is an XP and is not an argument position, so it would be a permissible adjunction site.

(36)

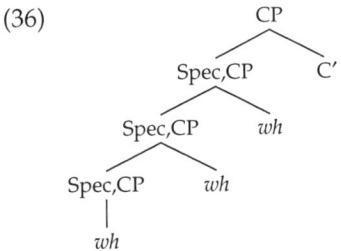

The analysis suggested above for 2P clitics in OSp is then essentially comparable to Rudin's treatment of multiple *wh*-movement in these Balkan languages and captures a similar set of facts. Like the *wh*-phrases in Bulgarian and Rumanian, 2P clitics move to an A' position at the left periphery of the sentence and must always appear in a particular order whenever more than one clitic is involved.

Given these assumptions, the A' positions where clitics are placed by the syntax could be: (a) adjunction to the left of IP; (b) substitution of the Spec,IP position (taken to be an A' position in I-V2 languages following Santorini 1989; Thráinsson 1994) in case no other constituent is found occupying this position; or (c) adjunction to the left or to the right of a maximal projection already occupying the Spec,IP position.

If this restricted set of possibilities is maintained, then, the only option available for the clitic in matrix contexts such as (29) would be the adjunction to the right of the XP occupying the Spec,IP position. This is sketched in (37a). For subordinate environments and for matrix clauses involving I^0-to-C^0, both option a) and c), as in (37b) or (37c) are available. Option b) would also be possible, in principle, in subordinate environments where no constituent has been topicalized to the Spec,IP position, as in (37d).

(37) a. [$_{IP}$ [$_{XP}$[XP]=*Cl* $_{XP}$] [$_{I'}$ V^0 [...]]]
   b. [$_{CP}$ que/si [$_{IP}$ =*Cl* [$_{IP}$ XP [$_{I'}$ V^0 [...]]]]]
   c. [$_{CP}$ que/si [$_{IP}$ [$_{XP}$=*Cl* [$_{XP}$ XP]] [$_{I'}$ V^0 [...]]]]
   d. [$_{CP}$ que/si [$_{IP}$ =*Cl* [$_{I'}$ V^0 [...]]]]

In addition, the V2/P2 analysis straightforwardly predicts that clitics will always follow the tensed verb in all and only those contexts in which the verb is demonstrably in C^0, namely in *yes/no* questions, imperatives and declarative V1. The two ways in which this configuration can be realized according to the analysis outlined above appear in (38). This prediction is in fact correct, as shown in the discussion of the examples in (30).[14] See also

Fontana (1993); and Fontana (in press) where these issues are discussed in more detail.

(38) a. $[_{CP} V^0 [_{IP} =Cl [_{IP} \text{Subj} [_{I'} ...]]]]$
 b. $[_{CP} V^0 [_{IP} [_{XP}=Cl [_{XP} \text{Subj}]] [_{I'} ...]]]$

To conclude this section, in the V2/2P analysis no mechanism in the syntax is triggered exclusively to prevent the violation of a phonological constraint. Rather, the syntax can license in principle more structures than are actually attested. That is, from a strictly syntactic standpoint, configurations in which the clitic is adjoined to IP or to the left of the constituent in Spec,IP are admissible. Representations in which the clitic lacks a host, however, conflict with restrictions imposed by the phonological component, and hence are generally filtered out at PF.

4 Comparisons

4.1 Basic descriptive coverage

I turn now to compare the three analyses that have been presented in the previous sections. As observed earlier, however, there some significant differences among them in terms of the range of data they aim to account for. The Agr1/Agr2P and V2/2P analyses are similar in that they attempt to provide a unified account of the distribution of clitics in the medieval Romance languages and in some of the Germanic languages; in addition, both of these proposals aim to explain the general constraints on the distribution of clitics in terms of the overall distribution of tensed verbs in the V2 languages. The Agr1/Agr2P analysis, however, does not consider the clitics in these languages to be 2P clitics in the sense used here, and therefore does not draw on the insights of the work on 2P clitics in languages outside the Romance and Germanic families. Crucially, according to this view, the medieval Romance and Germanic clitics are invariably analysed as heads, not as X^{max} categories.

Rivero, in contrast, does attempt to relate OSp clitics to the system of clitics in a language that is generally considered to have 2P clitics in the relevant sense (i.e. Serbo-Croatian); she takes clitics to be (at least in some cases) X^{max} categories rather than heads. However, Rivero does not consider OSp to be a V2 language and therefore does not attempt to illuminate the distribution of clitics in terms of the general phrase structure of V2 languages. Thus, the V2/2P is the only analysis that attempts to explain the general distribution of clitics in the medieval Romance languages in terms of independently motivated facts about the syntax of general word order and the specific syntax of 2P clitics, eliminating the need to build generalizations like WL or the TML directly into the grammar. As we will presently see, this feature of the analysis allows for a more successful, less stipulative account of the facts.

Before starting a detailed comparison, let us recall the patterns we are trying to explain. From what we have seen so far, two different groups of languages can be distinguished according to the relative positions clitics occupy with respect to the tensed verb in a typical V2 clause in a root environment. The first group of languages, including, e.g., Middle Dutch, Bernese German, and also German and Dutch, do not allow for sequences where the object clitic would appear in a position preceding the tensed verb in main clauses. This is illustrated by the schemata in (39) representing possible root environments involving the presence of clitics. As observed in section 2.3, some of these languages are more restricted than others in the range of positions clitics can occupy. Whereas the clitic appears almost categorically preceding the subject in Middle Dutch, it can appear only after the subject in Modern Dutch. Different varieties of German exhibit different degrees of variation in the distribution of their clitics, with preferences for one or the other sequencing.

(39) a. XP V[+finite] Subj *Cl* ...
 b. XP V[+finite] *Cl* Subj ...

The other group of languages includes, e.g., OSp, OE and OFr. In this group, clitics can appear either preceding or following the tensed verb in root environments. In sentences exhibiting distinctive V2 properties, clitics appear in sequences such as the one illustrated in (40a); in sentences with SVO word order, we obtain the similar pattern in (40b). Yet in some specific syntactic environments, where no constituent has been fronted to a preverbal position (including *yes/no* questions, imperatives and declarative V1 constructions), or where the preverbal constituent is a member of a restricted class of elements (e.g. certain adverbials such as those equivalent to English *then*, or certain types of negative words in OE alone — see van Kemenade 1987, 1992; and Pintzuk 1991, 1993, for discussion), clitics in all these languages appear following the tensed verb. Thus we obtain the sequences schematized in (40c).

(40) a. XP *Cl* V[+finite] Subj ...
 b. Subj *Cl* V[+finite] (XP) ...
 c. V[+finite] *Cl* Subj (XP) ...

Under the V2/2P analysis, the contrasts between OE and OSp on the one hand, and Middle Dutch and Bernese German on the other, can be made to follow quite simply from independently motivated differences between the basic phrase structures of these languages. Together with the hypothesis that OFr was also an I-V2 language (Dupuis 1989), this proposal would also correctly predict that the patterns in (40), rather than those in (39), will hold for this language as well. If the kinds of clitic categories we are discussing can be posited to be phrasal constituents situated in an A' position below CP, these contrasts are precisely what we would expect given the different mechanisms involved in the achievement of V2 effects in the two groups of languages. Positing a 2P clitic system such as the one outlined earlier, in combination with standard assumptions about the phrase structure of C-V2 languages such as Middle Dutch or Bernese German, would also yield the configurations illustrated in (39) for these languages, rather than those in (40a, b): again, a correct prediction.

Of course, the Agr1/Agr2P analysis can also account for a significant subset of these facts, thus achieving superficially similar results to those achieved by the V2/2P analysis. However, it only does so at a considerably higher cost. Under this view, verb movement over $Agr1^0$ must be invoked to account for the observed differences in the relative positions occupied by clitics and tensed verbs in V2 structures in OFr and German. Thus, sequences of the type XP Cl V[+finite] in OFr main clauses are accounted for by proposing that the tensed verb joins the clitic in $Agr1^0$, and the complex formed by the clitic and the tensed verb subsequently moves to C^0. In German, the tensed verb will always jump over $Agr1^0$, leaving the clitic in that position. The tensed verb in OFr, however, is also assumed to be able to skip over $Agr1^0$ when the TML ban on clitic-first sentences would otherwise be violated, thus creating a V[+finite] Cl sequence. OE and German are also expected to differ from each other. The postulated phrase structures for these languages in tandem with the assumption that clitics remain in $Agr1^0$ will yield the structures in (41). OFr will in turn differ from both of these languages in that the complex Cl-V[+finite] is able to move to C^0 (42).

This creates a paradoxical situation. Cardinaletti & Roberts classify OFr as a C-V2 language, and OE as an I-V2 language. Yet we have observed that the basic distribution of OFr clitics resembles that of clitics in OE more than those of C-V2 languages such as German, Middle Dutch and Bernese German, represented by (39) — a rather unexpected result. Cardinaletti & Roberts propose that this be attributed to some fundamental differences between the Romance family and the Germanic family. Recall that, according to this proposal, only the medieval Romance languages would be subject to the TML. The TML is then defined as a double requirement imposed by the clitics in these languages: '(a) [the clitic] cannot appear first, (b) it must combine with the inflected verb'.

(41) a. $[_{Agr1P}$ TOP $[_{Agr1'}$ Cl+V^0 [$[_{Agr2P}$Subj $[_{Agr2'}$ t [...]]]]] OE
 b. $[_{CP}$ TOP $[_{C'}$ V^0 [$[_{Agr1P}$(Subj) $[_{Agr1'}$ Cl $[_{Agr2P}$ (Subj) [...]]]]]] Ger
(42) $[_{CP}$ TOP $[_{C'}$ Cl+V^0 [$[_{Agr1P}$(Subj) $[_{Agr1'}$ t $[_{Agr2P}$ (Subj) [...]]]]]] OFr

4.2 Empirical and theoretical problems for the Agr1/Agr2-analysis

The basic differences between the V2/2P analysis and the Agr1/Agr2P analysis discussed above can be summarized as follows. While the former would classify V2 languages with 2P clitics in two main groups according to whether they display the basic patterns in (39) or those in (40), the Agr1/Agr2P analysis proposes what amounts to a tripartite division between OE, OFr and German, and is totally silent about the OSp facts. Although OSp was not considered in the investigation which resulted in the

Agr1/Agr2 analysis, were we to adopt the premises on which it is based, we would be logically forced to posit a considerably different syntax for OSp, thus resulting in a four-way classification. This is so because, on the one hand, OSp, like OFr, must be taken to be subject to whatever grammatical constraints are putatively embodied by the TML. On the other hand, however, OSp clitics share with those in OE and the other Germanic languages the property of being able to appear independently of the verb, cf. (33), (14a), and (20). However, as we have noted, the basic distributional patterns displayed by clitics and tensed verbs in this language closely resemble those in OE and OFr (40), and thus can be equally distinguishable from those displayed by German (39). The Agr1/Agr2P analysis is then in essence claiming that languages such as OFr, OE, OSp and German have fundamentally distinct phrase structures, at least with respect to the specific relationship conjectured between the syntax of clitics and the syntax of verb movement.

It may well turn out to be the case that we need to posit the existence of some differences in a number of areas of the syntax of all these languages. However, I would like to argue that the particular classification the Agr1/Agr2P analysis forces us to adopt is built on the basis of fundamentally flawed reasoning and it misses some important generalizations about the syntax of these languages. Furthermore, it can also be shown that this particular account of the facts introduces a significant amount of stipulation and additional machinery into grammatical theorization which are unnecessary under the V2/2P account.

4.2.1 Different types of 'last resort' mechanisms

First, recall that this analysis takes clitics to be in the head position of Agr1P. In addition, it crucially assumes that, whenever we find a sequence of the form V[+finite]-Cl, the tensed verb has moved to C^0, 'skipping' the $Agr1^0$ position containing the clitic. What this entails is that the Head Movement Constraint (HMC) (Travis 1984; Chomsky 1986b) is routinely violated in every root sentence for the languages represented by the patterns in (39), since the verb is always assumed to be in C^0 and the clitic is always assumed to be in $Agr1^0$. We saw that Cardinaletti & Roberts explicitly justify the violation of the HMC in the contexts traditionally related to the operation of the TML, which prohibits the formation of clitic initial sequences in root environments.

They also argue, however, that only the medieval Romance languages, and not the Germanic languages, are subject to this specific constraint; sequences such as (40c) in the medieval Romance languages are taken to be derived via verb-movement to the C^0 position, 'skipping' the $Agr1^0$ containing the clitic. It is further assumed that the clitic left-adjoins to V, arguably at PF. Thus, the HMC, a principle which is otherwise considered operative in UG, is allowed to be transgressed on the grounds that the TML is a 'last-resort' operation in the sense of Chomsky (1989). Again, according to

Cardinaletti & Roberts, 'the two requirements imposed by the clitic [namely that it cannot appear first and that it must combine with the inflected verb], are satisfied most economically if V moves to C^0, skipping $Agr1^{0}$'.

But this leads to some undesirable complications. First, notice that if the HMC can only be assumed to be dispensable in exceptional circumstances, such as to prevent the generation of clitic first sentences in languages subject to the TML, we must have an alternative explanation for the fact that it is routinely violated in all root environments in the relevant Germanic languages, given that the tensed verb is taken to always land in C^0. Note that these complications are easily avoided if we take clitics in these languages to be phrasal categories (i.e. X^{max}).[15]

Of course, one could argue that obligatory movement of the tensed verb to C^0 in root environments in these languages is in itself some kind of last-resort mechanism. But this leaves us with no explanation for the fact that clitics in the relevant Germanic languages appear in the configuration in (39) in a V2 sentence, while in OFr, which, on the Agr1/Agr2P analysis, obtains V2 effects in the same fashion as German, they must appear in the configurations in (40a, b).

This, in turn, raises an even more general and serious question: is this unified treatment of second position clitic phenomena compatible with previous unified accounts of verb second phenomena in the two language families?

4.2.2 Romance X-second vs Germanic X-second

A rather undesirable result of the particular view of things adopted in the Agr1/Agr2P analysis is that it creates unnecessary complications for a general unified account of V2 phenomena, since it obscures some well-established distinctions between basic types of syntactic mechanisms available in V2 languages. Thus, even though this is not explicitly said, this analysis claims in effect that there is an important subset of configurations, otherwise handled rather easily under an adequate general theory of V2 phenomena, which now must be taken to have been derived via substantially different syntactic mechanisms: namely, those structures in OFr (and, presumably, also in OSp, unless the TML-based distinction between Germanic and Romance is omitted for this language) which, except for the presence of a clitic, display all the basic distinguishing characteristics of the constructions known in the literature as V2 clauses and V1 declaratives.

Recall that the TML plays a crucial role in the specific account proposed to handle the unexpected differences in clitic distribution between OFr and German. However, resorting to putative grammatical constraints such as the TML is not only unwarranted but irreparably vitiates any attempt to arrive at a unified and principled account of second position phenomena. Upon some reflection, I can find absolutely no basis for positing that medieval Romance and Germanic languages diverge so fundamentally from one another by obeying such different sets of grammatical principles or constraints.[16] It is not difficult to see that the traditional association of the TML with the medieval Romance languages is the product of a mere coincidence; the consequence of a historical accident which has little to do with any putative intrinsic linguistic differences between the languages we are discussing. In other words, the traditional restriction in the use of this term to the domain of this specific language family has to do largely with the simple fact that Tobler and Mussafia were Romance philologists and, as such, devoted a great deal of their time to the study of medieval Romance texts. Hence, their observations happen to be based on the examination of a fairly restricted set of languages such as Old Italian, OFr or Provençal. It is not at all unreasonable to conclude, then, that if these two scholars had extended the scope of their investigations to texts in languages such as, say, OE, the 'law' that bears their name (which is no more than a simple descriptive label) would now be said to 'apply' in this language as well. If we follow this reasoning, then, most languages exhibiting the kinds of patterns illustrated in (40), that is, a considerable subset of the languages with 2P clitics, should be said to be also 'subject to' the TML.

Since a number of problems arise because of the assumption that OFr was a C-V2 language, we might wonder whether analysing OFr in this way is the right move, especially since Cardinaletti & Roberts themselves claim that just a century prior to the period they discuss, OFr *was* an I-V2 language. Their main motivation for positing a C-V2 structure is the absence of embedded V2 structures during this latter period. However, from this we cannot conclude that OFr was C-V2. Note that embedded topicalization of arguments is rare or nonexistent in OE, and infrequent in Modern Icelandic, and yet Cardinaletti & Roberts are willing to classify these languages as I-V2.[17]

Instead, we can rationalize the rarity of embedded topicalization in OFr (as opposed to OSp) by recognizing that OFr was already losing V2 and becoming SVO during the period under discussion. Given the extensive similarities between OFr and OSp, it seems more productive to view the differences in the availability of embedded topicalization as a consequence of the fact that OFr was in a more advanced stage of development away from a more 'pure' I-V2 phrase structure than was OSp during the relevant time period. This seems at least more justified than simply claiming that OFr had become a C-V2 language without providing any further motivation. Otherwise we are led to posit fundamentally different grammars for the two languages, a move that leaves their deep similarities unexplained. While embedded topicalization is attested in OSp, in many embedded environments we also find that no constituent has been fronted to preverbal position (or only a clitic is found in that position). Such variation cannot be given an elegant synchronic analysis, but can be rationalized on the double base hypothesis discussed in section 3.3.

Maintaining this hypothesis allows us to account for the enormous similarities between the two languages since, overall, OSp and OFr would still be I-V2 languages in the relevant sense, while also avoiding the difficult problem of explaining how the latter language could have so suddenly changed from having an I-V2 phrase structure to having a C-V2 phrase structure. Especially if, as we noted, OFr appears to have already been on the way to losing its V2 syntax altogether precisely during this time period (M. P. Adams 1987; Vance 1989).

A further problem for the Agr1/Agr2P analysis in this respect is posed by the underlying structures illustrated in (43a) and (43b) and proposed for OE and OFr respectively. The basic claim presupposed in these structures is that the subject will invariably precede the verb in embedded clauses in OE, in contrast to OFr, which is predicted to allow subjects either preverbally or postverbally.

(43) a. [Agr1P Subj [Agr1' Cl [[Agr2P Subj [Agr2' V [...]]]]]]   OE
     b. [Agr1P Subj [Agr1' Cl+V [[Agr2P Subj [Agr2' *t* [...]]]]]]   OFr

This analysis is intended to account for the existence of configurations such as those illustrated in (44a, b) in OE subordinate clauses, together with the observation that, in the period they discuss, embedded contexts in OFr display the configurations illustrated in (44b, c, d) but not that in (44a). These patterns are argued to follow from the assumption that the underlying structures of embedded clauses for the two languages are as in (43).

(44) a. Comp Cl Subj V
     b. Comp Subj Cl V
     c. Comp Cl V Subj
     d. Comp V Subj

However, evidence can be found which shows that OE and OFr do not differ so radically in this respect, either. This can be seen in the following OE examples taken from Higgins (1992). In (45) we can see instances of the Comp V Subj configuration, and in (46), instances of Comp XP V Subj. We cannot establish with certainty whether the pronominal object in (46) is a clitic, as opposed to a non-clitic object pronoun which has been topicalized; however, this is irrelevant for the issue we are trying to resolve here. What is important to notice, as pointed out by Higgins, is that the subject can appear following the finite verb in a wide range of subordinate contexts. This strongly suggests, he argues, that these sequences are not likely to have been derived via an operation of Verb Projection Raising, since it is widely assumed that this type of operation cannot yield these types of sequences.

(45) a. man sceal witan mid deopðanclum móde [hwær **beo**
        one shall know with deep-thinking spirit where be.OPT
       se mona týn nihta eald]
       the moon ten nights old
       'You must very thoughtfully observe when the moon is ten days old'   (ByrM 164.28–166.1)

b. [Ða   herde Ægelric biscop   þet   gesecgon], þa
when heard Ægelric bishop.NOM that.ACC say.INF then
amansumede   he ealle þa men
excommunicated he all   the men
'When bishop Ægelric heard tell of this, he excommunicated all those men that [...]'   (ChronE 1070 207.26-7)

(46) a. [hwilce hwile hine **wille** Drihten her on worolde lætan]
which-while him will Lord   here in world   leave
'the time which the Lord will grant him here in the world'
(HomS 46 [BlHom 11] 125.8-9)

b. He geseah ða [þæt hine ne **mihte** nan læce   gehælen...]
he saw   then that him NEG might no leech.NOM heal.INF
'He saw then that no doctor could heal him...'
(Æ Chom II, 32 279.213)

The fact that OFr and OE do not differ in this way further weakens the motivation for positing such a significant distinction between the phrase structures of these languages.

4.2.3 The Agr1/Agr2P analysis and the theory of language change

We have seen that there seems to be no justification for positing that OFr and OE differ so fundamentally in their phrase structures. Earlier, we saw that the distributional patterns exhibited by clitics in these two languages coincide in the relevant respects with those found in OSp. However, if we want to group OFr with OE and OSp, that is, as a language with an I-V2 basic phrase structure and a system of 2P clitics, we still need to account for one significant property which, as observed in the Agr1/Agr2P analysis, distinguishes OFr from all the other languages being discussed: namely, the fact that in this language clitics do not appear independently of the verb.

We saw that one of the distinguishing characteristics of 2P clitics is precisely the fact that their syntax exhibits a remarkable independence of the syntax of the verb. OFr clitics, in spite of sharing most of the other distinctive features of 2P clitic systems, lack this one. However, since a number of difficulties faced by the Agr1/Agr2P analysis in its handling of second position phenomena in the other languages arise only because clitics are taken to be invariably X^0 categories, we might ask ourselves whether maintaining this particular treatment of clitic facts in all these languages is still a productive strategy even in the case of OFr. This is especially the case if we bear in mind that an adequate analysis of second position phenomena should be able to provide a reasonable account of the similarities among these languages as well as of their differences.

At this point, the significant methodological disparities between the Agr1/Agr2P and the V2/2P analyses discussed in sections 3.3.1.1 and 3.3.1.2 must be emphasized once again. Specifically, recall that the latter builds on a dynamic theory of syntactic change such as the double base hypothesis, while the former does not. We noted that, by adopting a dynamic approach to the study of diachronic corpora, we can abstract away from certain apparent discrepancies in the data, in order to achieve a more principled and elegant analysis of the synchronic facts, while making more accurate predictions about syntactic change. I would like to argue that this is also the most productive strategy to solve the apparent problem posed by the lack of interpolation phenomena in the OFr texts being considered.

First, independently of whether OFr clitics can appear separated from the verb by other intervening constituents, a number of authors have noted that phonological attachment to a preceding lexical item different from the verb is not infrequent in the OFr texts. Treating each and every instance of a clitic-like category in the texts as an X^0 category incorporated to the verbal head forces us to maintain that, in these cases, a partial constituent of a complex word is prosodically dependent on a constituent external to that complex, a counterintuitive claim at best. Yet this is what the Agr1/Agr2P analysis entails in view of the structure in (17a), above. In contrast, if we allow for the possibility that these clitics were still, at least in some cases, syntactically independent of the verb, as on the V2/2P analysis, the phonological encliticization occasionally manifested in the texts can be straightforwardly accounted for.

Second, unless we can define a bit more precisely the time boundaries of what constitutes OFr, the basic empirical claim the Agr1/Agr2P analysis uses to justify its particular characterization of clitic facts in this language can be shown to be false. Not surprisingly, it turns out that OSp is not the only medieval Romance language where clitics can appear independently of the verb. As illustrated by the examples in (47), cases of interpolation such as the ones we are discussing are in fact attested in OFr (47a), as well as in Old Italian (47b) or Old Portuguese (47c).

(47) a. qu'*il vous* en mal averra   (Balain, 8.9–10, cited in Ramsden 1963)
     b. Ke *ce* non abbi quella dilectione   (DG 7.12, cited in Ramsden 1963)
     c. pois *m'*assy desenparades   (Lapa 15.13–14, cited in Ramsden 1963)

These kinds of examples, admittedly rare in OFr and Old Italian, and much less rare in Old Portuguese, do lend significant additional support to the hypothesis that the clitic systems of other medieval Romance languages were at some stage essentially the same as that of OSp, namely 2P clitic systems. Given that Old Portuguese and OSp are widely assumed to be more conservative than OFr in many respects, the scarcity of patterns such as those illustrated in (47) in a specific subset of the medieval Romance languages can be interpreted simply as the reflection of a divergence in the particular chronologies of the specific syntactic changes which arguably affected most of the languages in this group. The contrasts between OFr and OSp (only contrasts of degree, as we have seen) would then imply that OFr was at a substantially more advanced stage in the hypothesized evolution from a 'pure' 2P clitic system (i.e a system of X^{max} categories) toward a modern Romance-type system of clitic-like categories (i.e., a system of X^0-related categories).

On the view that a fully deterministic grammar is responsible for the generation of all the strings found in the texts ordinarily labelled 'OFr', the degree of complexity of the syntactic analysis postulated for this language would have to be increased even further, or else these patterns of data would have to be left unaccounted for. In addition, this kind of analysis would still have to account for the fact that these patterns cease to appear in the OFr texts at a certain point. But this is just the partial manifestation of a more general problem. Under this particular view of things, it becomes rather difficult to see how and why the distinctive properties of clitic systems in OFr and the other medieval Romance varieties could have disappeared altogether, allowing for the emergence of the systems typical of most modern Romance languages at the present time.

4.3 Empirical and theoretical problems for the TMP/WP analysis

While the Agr1/Agr2P analysis has trouble accounting for these various facts, it does succeed in relating the variations in the distribution of clitics to variations in the phrase structures of the languages studied. In contrast, the TMP/WP analysis does not relate the distribution of clitics in the Romance and Germanic languages at all. However, this cannot be considered a defect of the analysis until Rivero's claim that OSp was not a V2 language is refuted. Since the refutation of her claim grows out, once again, of the adoption of a fundamentally different approach to the study of diachronic data, I will postpone comparing the V2/2P and TMP/WP analyses until section 4.3.2, where additional implications of a dynamic approach to diachronic syntax are considered.

4.3.1 Theoretical considerations

The V2/2P analysis has arguably two costs in theoretical terms. The first is that it posits adjunction both to the left and to the right of a maximal projection. Some theoreticians have argued recently that adjunction should be only to the left. The second cost is that it requires that not all of the data analysed in any given period should be covered by a single grammar as it is generally assumed in most synchronic analyses of a given language.

The principal theoretical problem with the TMP/WP analysis is that it crucially posits two new types of maximal projections, TMP and WP, which are designated exclusively as the landing site for clitics in Serbo-Croatian and Bulgarian, respectively. But this raises the question of what the fundamental features of these categories are, since Rivero also assumes the full range of Agr and Tense projections widely posited in the GB literature. This approach thus seems to explain the TML and WL by building them directly into the theory.

I want to show that the V2/2P analysis is certainly no more costly in theoretical terms than the other analyses, and indeed would appear to involve the fewest complications. The cost of positing left and right adjunction, for instance, seems rather small in contrast to the theoretical complications entailed by the other two analyses, some of which we have discussed in the previous sections, especially since other linguists have argued that both adjunction options should be available (Rohrbacher 1994). In addition, the V2/2P analysis has the advantage of avoiding building the TML or WL into the grammar either via fundamental constraints or new phrasal projections, treating them instead as the simple descriptive generalizations that they really are and explaining them in terms of independently identifiable characteristics of the clitic systems and syntax of word order.

4.3.2 Methodological differences

As noted earlier, the V2/2P analysis builds on a specific dynamic theory of syntactic change, i.e. the double base hypothesis, while the others do not. I have just suggested how this difference allows for an analysis of OFr on the V2/2P analysis which captures the demonstrable similarities between OFr, OSp and OE. Here, we will see that, in adopting the double base hypothesis, one can also avoid certain weaknesses of the TML/WP analysis which arise simply because Rivero assumes that all sentences in the corpus should be subsumed under a single fully deterministic grammar. More specifically, Rivero disputes the claim that OSp was V2. Consequently, she claims that the OSp facts cannot be related to the Germanic and OFr facts as suggested by both the Agr1/Agr2P analysis and the V2/2P analysis. Since it has been argued that this would result in a significant loss of generalization, we should therefore examine Rivero's objections to the claim that OSp was V2.

Rivero points out putative counterexamples to the claim that OSp was V2 in the historical texts. For instance, she mentions that V1 is frequent. However, we have already discussed the fact that declarative V1 and many other exceptions to superficial verb second order exists in languages for which the V2 label is not in dispute. The conclusion we drew on the basis of such examples was that V2 should be considered only a rough descriptive label for these languages, reflecting deeper facts about their syntax (as developed in the various works cited in this chapter). Ironically, then, if OSp did not manifest such exceptions to superficial verb second order, we would have even less reason to classify it as an I-V2 language. Such putative counterexamples are discussed at length in Fontana (1993, in press).

A different sort of counterexample is the variable occurrence of V-final order attested in conditional clauses and other subordinate environments (see, e.g., (24) above); modern V2 languages show more internal consistency in the positioning of the finite verb (whether clause-initial or final). Again, however, we should not conclude from such examples that OSp was not V2. There are indeed a number of good reasons to want to preserve the term V2, at least in the sense this term is used in reference to languages such as OE, OFr, OIc, etc., to describe the basic phrase structure of OSp. First, this kind of V-final word order occurs only in a rather small percentage of embedded clauses (a total of 4 out of more than 800 embedded clauses, i.e. less than 0.5 per cent of the embedded clauses in the corpora used in the quantitative study carried out in Fontana 1993). Although more research is needed to determine why such examples exist, there are several plausible alternative explanations.

For example, these could be remnants of a V-final word order earlier in the history of OSp; Pintzuk (1991) has argued that such an analysis can explain the variable presence of V-final clauses in OE. Similar problems arise in the study of the phrase structure in other medieval languages such as Old Norse (Faarlund 1990), which, as OE, displays a considerable variation between verb-final and non-verb-final word order patterns in subordinate environments. In this respect, Rögnvaldsson (1992) has suggested a similar approach to that proposed in Pintzuk (1991) to handle the difficulties posed by this kind of variation for the analysis of the Old Icelandic syntax. In connection with the configurations in (24), we notice that the word order patterns in examples such as that in (48) below, where the auxiliary (in bold) appears to the right of the non-finite verb, which is, in turn, preceded by the subject (underlined), could suggest that this is a possibility at least in some of the cases.

(48) o en qual   guisa quier [que *lo* el auer   **podie**]
     or in which way want that it he have.INF could
     'or in whichever way he could have it'   (EEII)

Verb-final order could also reflect the influence of conventional syntactic patterns associated with the Latin stylistic tradition on writers during this period, since Latin was a V-final language. Philologists have long observed the influences of Latin in certain texts of this and later periods.

Finally, some cases of verb-final order arguably arise because of adjunction of one or more constituents to the left of the maximal projection which constitutes the domain for which V2 effects are computed. The 'mirror image' of this suggestion has been made by van Kemenade and Pintzuk, who argue that some cases of non-verb-final order in OE can be made consistent with positing verb-final syntax if we assume that some NPs extrapose to the right. In fact, the gradual replacement of structures involving substitution into a specifier position with ones involving adjunction of this sort to the left has been argued by, e.g., Kroch (1989), Vance (1989); and by Fontana (1993) to have played a central role in triggering the loss of V2 in OFr and OSp. This sort of adjunction, which is not usually assumed to be characteristic of V2 languages, must have already been an option, albeit limited, even at earlier stages in the development of OSp, and started to become more and more noticeable during the period under consideration here.

The data illustrated in (49) provide support for the assumption that some constituents, including subject NPs, can appear in adjunction structures, presumably base-generated in this position. Examples (49a–c) show an adverbial, an object and a subject, in the construction known as *recomplementation* (Higgins 1988). It is important to bear in mind that the only constituents that can appear between the two overt complementizers in these distinctive constructions are sentence-modifying adverbials such as *if/because/when* clauses; direct or indirect objects with a coindexed pronominal in the lower clause, as in (49b); and subjects. Note that although there is no overt doubling of the subject within the embedded clause, since OSp was a pro-drop language we can posit a null resumptive *pro* subject (see also Fontana 1994 and references therein for further justification of the adjunct status of subject NPs in Spanish). It is also important to observe that recomplementation structures appear as sentential objects of the types of predicates that have been argued to license CP recursion, i.e. bridge verbs (McCloskey 1992; Iatridou & Kroch 1992). The analysis suggested for these structures is that outlined in (50).

(49) a. ...dize que si a omne del mundo *lo* digo que toda mi
     says that if to man of-the world it say.1sg that all my
     fazienda et aun la mi vida es en grand periglo
     property and even my life is in great danger
     'He says that, if I tell anybody, all my property and my very life
     will be in great danger' (Lucan.144)

b. ...cuenta Maestre pedro... que aquel cordero$_i$ [...] que*l*$_i$
   tells Master pedro that that sheep that-it
   ponien en ell altar
   put.3P in the altar
   'apostle Peter [talks later on about the other reasons, and] says that
   they placed the sheep [which they sacrificed in the morning,] on
   the altar'

c. Dixome quel' dixeran que aquella muger, que era la
   told-me.he that-him told.3PL that that woman that was the
   mas fuerte et mas brava cosa del mundo
   most strong and most vicious thing of-the world
   'He told me that somebody told him that this woman was the
   strongest and meanest woman in the world' (Lucan.154)

(50) dize [$_{CP}$ [$_C$ que [$_{CP}$ si a omne del mundo ....[$_{CP}$ [$_C$ que toda mi fazienda..]]]]]

Support for the positing of a null resumptive *pro* comes from comparison of (49c) with a similar example from OE, which contains an overt resumptive subject pronoun:

(51) Hit is awriten þœtte David$_i$, þa he þone læppan
     it is written that David when he the corner
     forcorfenne hæfde, þœt he$_i$ sloge on his heortan,...
     (of Saul's coat) cut-off had that he struck in his heart
     'Therefore it is written that David, when he had cut off the corner (of
     Saul's coat), struck his heart...' (CP, 199,16, from Gorrell 1985)

Invariably when dealing with diachronic data, it will not be possible to account for all counterexamples without an unusually cumbersome and theoretically problematic grammar. It seems more productive to assume that the grammars of languages like OSp were not fundamentally different in degree of complexity from those of modern languages, and to attribute the observed degrees of variation to factors such as language change or influences related to specific literary traditions. More specifically, it can be shown that whatever problems face the hypothesis that OSp was V2 will arise for other languages for which the V2 label is not in dispute; even more so if the analysis is based over a corpus of similar dimensions and characteristics as the one considered here. Consequently, given the noted similarities between OSp and these other languages, there seems to be little reason to treat them differently, even if we eventually should decide that the label 'V2' is inadequate.

Another benefit of adopting a dynamic approach to the study of diachronic syntax has to do with the characterization of the clitic system of OSp. Rivero correctly notes that OSp clitics behave like heads in some cases and like X^{max} in others. From this she concludes that OSp had a 'mixed' clitic system. This conclusion is compatible with the argument advanced in Fontana (1993, in press) that OSp clitics gradually evolved from being X^{max} to being heads. Again, these facts can be viewed either as something to be accounted for under a single fully deterministic grammar or as a consequence of 'grammars' in competition. If we take the former view, then a principled explanation is needed to account for the contexts in which clitics function as heads vs phrases (i.e., where TMPs vs WPs are licensed). Another problem is that positing a mixed system of this sort fails to make any connection to the fact that this system represents an intermediate stage in the transition from a system in which all clitics are uniformly X^{max} to one in which they are uniformly (or close to uniformly) part of verbal inflection.

The V2/2P analysis, building on the double base hypothesis, is integrated into a theory of the interaction of the loss of V2 with the change in the clitic system from 2P to verbal inflection, and is supported by quantitative analysis on texts over a 500-year period. While an account of the language change may be compatible with either the TMP/WP analysis (or for that matter, the Agr1/Agr2P analysis), the burden is on the proponents of such analyses to explain the diachronic development of languages like OSp in an elegant fashion. For a much more extensive discussion of the implications these analyses have for an appropiate explanation of the changes which took place in the syntax of Spanish, I refer the reader to Fontana (in press).

5 Conclusion

I have argued that languages can manifest both V2 and 2P phenomena, and that OSp, OFr and a subset of the Germanic languages are such languages.

I have also argued that the V2/2P analysis in conjunction with a dynamic view of linguistic change can provide a more principled account of the basic differences in the distribution of clitic categories across these languages. Finally, I have also shown that this analysis represents the intersection of ideas in Cardinaletti & Roberts (1991) and Rivero (this volume), thus capturing the insights of both while improving on the descriptive and theoretical adequacy of their individual analyses.

Notes

* I wish to thank Ans van Kemenade, Louise McNally, Nigel Vincent and two anonymous reviewers for useful comments and discussion. The usual disclaimers apply.
1. See also Anderson (1993) for a rather different approach to second position phenomena which will not be included in this discussion.
2. Some authors have sought a unified analysis of 2P clitics by attempting to correlate the appearance of clitics following the first word with the general availability of split constituents in the relevant languages. In other words, according to this general view, 2W clitics would be underlyingly 2D clitics. For some of these authors (e.g. Klavans 1982), the status of the first word as a syntactic constituent would be masked by the fact that these languages are non-configurational (as defined in Hale 1982). For others (e.g. Taylor 1990; Progovac, in press), the first position in the sentence immediately preceding the clitic would be occupied by an element that has moved out of the maximal category containing it. This alternative approach to non-configurationality (Saito 1985; Webelhuth 1989) builds on the assumption that it is possible to derive all possible word orders from a fixed base order by movement, usually 'scrambling'. Halpern (1992) argues for an alternative approach to unify the analysis of 2D and 2W configurations.
3. Note that OE allows constituents to intervene between the clitic and the verb in certain contexts. This appears not to be an option in OFr. See section 4 for discussion.
4. Again, this can only be stated as a strong tendency, since various types of exceptions are attested in both languages. In one of the earliest poetic texts in OE, namely *Beowulf*, for instance, several instances of clitic-first arrangements have been observed to exist (Pintzuk 1991). While in the earliest available OFr texts clitic-first arrangements are also extremely rare, some instances are already attested in twelfth-century texts (Adams 1987), and they start to be fairly noticeable in the thirteenth-century texts, with their frequency increasing over time. See Fontana (in press) for a discussion of clitic-first configurations in OSp.
5. I wish to thank Marco Haverkort for providing me with these data he borrowed from Penner (1991).
6. Some possible exceptions to this general claim could be for instance the Dutch subject clitics discussed by Zwart (1991). A number of authors have observed that the distributional patterns of subject and object clitics markedly differ from each other in some of the Germanic languages. Since not all the languages examined here have subject clitics, I leave aside the discussion of whether a unified treatment of subject and object clitics is justified for all the languages that have these two kinds of pronominal clitics, and shall restrict the present comparative study to the syntactic distribution of object clitics. It is also important to recall, as noted in section 2.2 above, that there have been also some notable changes in the basic distributional patterns of object clitics in some of the Germanic languages.
7. See also Hankamer (1976) and Miller (1991) for similar claims that the linguistic competence of (some) speakers cannot always be modelled by positing a single, discrete grammar. And, for a radically different view of syntactic and morphological change, see also Tabor (1994). This latter theory of change, which is also dynamic in nature, is based on connectionist models of language learning.

8. This analysis could be made compatible with approaches to phrase structure that follow Pollock (1989) in splitting IP into various functional projections. The problem would be to formulate the appropriate set of principles and restrictions that would make such a rich system sufficiently constrained and disallow the generation of more configurations than are actually possible in the languages in question. This is the object of much ongoing research and does not fundamentally affect the basic observations made above.
9. See Fontana (in press) for a detailed discussion of the implications of this restriction in the direction of phonological attachment. For an interesting discussion of variation in the phonological attachment of clitics in *Beowulf* see Pintzuk (1991, in press).
10. As Pintzuk (1991) and other authors have observed, several instances of clitic initial strings are attested in *Beowulf*. Interestingly enough, some clitic initial strings are also found in *Poema de Mio Cid*, one of the first extant OSp literary texts. This has lead some philologists to claim that this segment of the poem was not part of the original text.
11. I would like to thank Enric Vallduví (p.c.) for this suggestion.
12. An anonymous reviewer notes, for instance, that there are some languages such as Serbo-Croatian where members of this general class of clitics can appear 'in the middle of emphatic constituents'. As Vallduví (forthcoming) points out, informational focus and contrastive 'focus' are distinct phenomena and are encoded differently in different languages. Consequently, without a better understanding of the particular functions of these 'emphatic' constituents, the connection between the reviewer's observation and the proposal concerning focus flight remains unclear.
13. This type of solution is proposed in Halpern (1992) and suggested as a possibility in Halpern & Fontana (1994). Halpern (1992) claims that cliticization always involves syntactic adjunction to the left of a constituent; I will leave this as an open question.
14. OSp *wh*-questions might at first appear to be a counterexample to this claim, since clitics always precede tensed verbs in this environment. However, there is strong independent evidence suggesting that *wh*-fronting is to a position below CP, arguably Spec,IP, in both OSp and Modern Spanish, hence implying that verb movement is to I^0. It is then unsurprising on the analysis advocated here that the clitic should precede the verb in *wh*-questions but not in *yes/no* questions. See Fontana (1994) and references cited there for a detailed discussion of these issues.
15. Additional arguments of an empirical as well as a theoretical nature in favour of considering Germanic clitics phrasal projections can be found in Haverkort (1994). See also the same work for an extensive critique of other recent attempts to unify the treatment of Romance and Germanic clitics similar to the one proposed in Cardinaletti & Roberts (1991).
16. See Fontana (in press) for an extensive critique of the use of notions such as the Tobler–Mussafia Law or the Wackernagel's Law in recent generative literature.
17. See van Kemenade (1992) and Pintzuk (in press) for similar discussions concerning the implications of these kinds of facts for the appropriate analysis of OE phrase structure.

Part 3

Verb second and Comp

9 Shifting triggers and diachronic reanalyses

David Lightfoot

In this chapter I want to address an old question: what is it appropriate for historians to explain in the domain of language change?* I shall defend the idea that much of language change is contingent and should not be explained by any theory of grammar, nor by what is sometimes called a theory of change. I argued for this idea in Lightfoot (1979) and here I shall discuss three new case studies; then I shall compare the idea with some more ambitious and more deterministic approaches which have emerged recently.

1 The nature of parameters

I make the now standard assumption that language acquisition includes the setting of genetically given parameters. If those parameters are binary, then 11 will suffice to generate 4,096 grammars and 32 will generate 8–9 billion grammars, enough for 2 for every inhabitant of the planet. So 30–40 structural parameters should provide more than enough scope to account for the range of variation that one finds among human languages. Restricting grammatical parameters along those lines would also help us meet the challenge posed by neuroscientists like Changeux (1983). Changeux discusses the simplicity of the genome and the complexity of the brain, arguing that the genome is very limited in the richness of information that can be carried, dramatically so when compared with the extreme diversity and complexity of the anatomy of the brain. The total quantity of chromosomal DNA limits the maximum number of genes. Estimates of the maximum number of structural genes are still very approximate, but in the mouse it seems to be *c.* 150,000. If we ask how the total DNA content per cell nucleus has evolved from bacteria to man, we find that there is a real increase from bacteria to mice: the egg of the fruitfly contains 24 times more DNA than *E.coli* and the mouse 25 times more than the fruitfly. Correspondingly, the nervous system of the fruitfly contains *c.* 100,000 neurons and that of the mouse 50–60 times more. However, when we pass from the mouse to humans, we encounter a paradox: the number of cerebral cells jumps from 5–6 million to several tens of billions; the level of organization and performance of the brain increases spectacularly, while the total quantity of DNA in the nucleus of the fertilized egg does not change significantly. Within 10 per cent, it is the same in mouse, cow, chimpanzee and human, pointing to a remarkable non-linearity between the DNA content and the complexity of the brain. The paradox is quite striking when one looks at humans: 200,000 or even a million genes are very little compared with the number of synapses in the human brain or even the number of different types of neurons in the cerebral cortex. So there is no simple relationship between the complexity of the genome and that of the central nervous system. Of course, complexity can emerge through *epigenetic* development, particularly in the case of the human brain, which grows enormously *after* birth; and so-called 'maturation' theories of language acquisition might exploit that kind of physiological development. But let's continue to take our notions seriously about a set of genetically prescribed parameters and to accept that we cannot let them proliferate arbitrarily.

Postulating 30–40 parameters does not allow much scope for analysis; they would need to be more general, more simple and very different from what one sees in the literature — sometimes a single issue of *Linguistic Inquiry* contains 30–40 proposed parameters. Some linguists have come to equate parameters with superficial 'differences' among languages. This runs the risk of allowing parameters to proliferate and run out of control, and in fact parameters have become more and more fine-grained, each one capturing smaller ranges of phenomena. So the '*pro*-drop parameter' fragmented as research progressed and linguists analysed languages/dialects showing some but not all of the early diagnostic '*pro*-drop properties'. Baker (1992) argues that this fragmentation results from research strategies comparing closely related languages or dialects.

The problem can be seen in the approach to 'exceptional' structures like (1a), which occur in English but not in other European languages. Linguists readily identify a parameter, 'S' Deletion' or 'Exceptional Case Marking', which is set positively on exposure to sentences corresponding to (1a). Postulating a parameter in response to such a small range of data opens the sluice gates. Latin and Irish also allow infinitives with accusative subjects in contexts in which English does not (1c, d), while Irish disallows anaphoric subjects, unlike Latin (1e). Postulating parametric differences simply to account for contrasts like these explodes the number of parameters far beyond 30–40. See Clark (1989) for discussion of this logic, and for a more abstract approach to Exceptional Case Marking see Lightfoot (1991: 87–90).

(1) a. I expect [her to win]
    b. spero [eam vincere]
       I-hope her to-win
    c. [eam vincere] mihi semper libet
       her to-win me always pleases
    d. is   cuimhneach leo   [iad a bheith ar seachran]
       [COPULA] mindful   with-them [they to-be lost]
       'they remember being lost'

e. *shil siad [a cheile a bheith breoite]
'they thought each other to be ill'
sperat   [se   vincere]
she-hopes herself to-win

Given these considerations, it is remarkable how little discussion there is on the nature of parameters and on their plausibility. There is some: Chomsky (1991) reanalysed a parameter postulated by Hilda Koopman (1992), ±Case Chain. Chomsky reformulated that parameter in terms of the notion (sometimes attributed to Borer 1984) that parameters are lexical, stated in terms of X^0 elements and X^0 categories: +C elements enter into case relations, not −C elements. X^0 elements with lexical content are always +C; languages differ with respect to whether other X^0 elements are ±C; i.e. the parameter is restricted to non-lexical elements. French and English are +C; Bambara is −C: so in Bambara, intransitive verbs raise to I and raise to a higher causative, but transitive verbs do not, because the trace of the verb, being non-lexical and −C in Bambara, cannot assign case to its complement (2a). Also Bambara has only *wh-in-situ* because the trace of an operator, being −C in Bambara, cannot receive case (2b), and there are no overt expletives, because expletives cannot receive case if Bambara is −C (2c).

(2) a. *V ... t, where V assigns case.
    b. *O ... t, where O is an operator and *t* the variable it binds.
    c. *E ... NP, where E is an expletive and NP its associate.

Chomsky raised no empirical issue here, just the matter of how parameters could plausibly be stated.

2 The settability of parameters

One condition that parameters must meet is that they must be settable on the basis of normal childhood experience; learning something about the ways in which parameters are set tells us something about the nature of the parameters themselves.

I have argued (Lightfoot 1991, 1993b, etc.) that parameters are set on the basis of structurally simple data that are robust in children's experience. There are various ways of defining 'structurally simple' and I will not discuss this matter here, but I would like to reflect for a moment on the central notion of triggers needing to be structurally simple and that complex structures have no long-term effects on the development of a child's linguistic capacity.

Consider the distinction drawn by Emonds (1976) between root and structure-preserving transformations. He distinguished transformations which yielded constituent structures which could in principle have been derived directly by the phrase structure rules without the application of transformations; these were structure-preserving. In contrast, other transformations, like 'Subject–auxiliary inversion', yielded outputs which could not have been derived directly by phrase structure rules and therefore 'deformed' structures in a way that structure-preserving transformations did not; these transformations applied only to root domains. A similar idea lay behind Ross' (1973) Penthouse Principle, which said that what goes on downstairs may also go on upstairs, but not vice versa. The insight that operations in embedded clauses constitute some subset of operations in matrix clauses is now well established. However, current theories which do not permit transformational operations like 'Subject–auxiliary inversion' and restrict us to 'Move something' or 'Affect something' cannot state the distinction of rule-types drawn by Emonds. If the insight cannot be captured by grammatical theory, it must follow from something else that embedded clauses manifest only a subset of the operations seen in matrix clauses. A natural candidate would be the acquisition theory which characterizes how parameters are set.

There are two approaches to this in the literature. One is degree-0 learnability. If parameters are set on the basis of data from unembedded binding domains, it follows that whatever affects embedded domains is a by-product of what is seen in matrix domains. So, for example, there is good reason to believe that Dutch and German children 'learn' that their grammars have underlying object–verb order (which is manifested superficially in embedded clauses) from data from matrix domains (which typically show the finite verb in second position). Lightfoot (1991: ch. 3) shows how this happens, how Dutch children endowed with a version of X-bar theory which requires verbs and their complements to be adjacent at D-structure must conclude that verbs move in Dutch, how sentences like (3a–c) show from where the verb moves (3b'); furthermore (3d) are instances of simple colloquial expressions manifesting the verb in its base-generated position.

(3)   a. Jan belt de hoogleraar op
         'John calls the professor up'
     b. Jan moet de hoogleraar opbellen
     b'. $_{CP}$[Jan$_i$ moet$_j$ $_{IP}$[e_j $_{IP}$[PRO de hoogleraar e_k] e_j opbellen$_k$]]
     c. Jan bezoekt de hoogleraar niet/soms/morgen/vaak
     d. en ik maar fietsen repareren
         'I ended up repairing bicycles'
         hand uitsteken
         'hand outstretch' [= signal]
         Jantje koekje hebben?
         'Johnnie wants a cookie?'
         ik de vuilnisbak buiten zetten? Nooit
         'me put the garbage out? Never'

Acquisition studies (Clahsen & Smolka 1986; Wexler 1994 and many others) show that Dutch and German children acquire the right verb positions early in their development. Children go through various stages, including Wexler's 'optional infinitive' stage, but there are two big facts which are salient for our hypothesis: First, after a brief period of experimentation, children place all and only finite verbs in second position in matrix clauses. Second, as soon as embedded clauses are attested, finite and nonfinite verbs occur only in final position and there is no period of experimentation. These facts alone suggest that children acquire verbal syntax in the manner indicated, and that relevant learning is based exclusively on matrix clause structures (Lightfoot 1991: ch. 3).

There are several *prima facie* counterexamples to the hypothesis of degree-0 learnability; of those, several (but not all) have been analysed away quite straightforwardly, for example, long-distance anaphors, variation in bounding nodes, and others. And a productive research programme has developed. I provide one illustration. Andersson & Dahl (1974) offered the facts of (4a–c) as a counterexample to Ross' Penthouse Principle and, *prima facie*, the facts would be problematic for degree-0 learnability. They pointed out that the Swedish verb *ha* is deletable in embedded clauses (4c) but not in matrix clauses (4a, b). However, Platzack (1986) shows that the generalization is not quite right and that *ha* may be deleted in matrix clauses if the 'second' position to which it would ordinarily move is already occupied by an adverb like *kanske* 'perhaps' (4d). This suggests that the correct generalization is that *ha* may be deleted quite generally, but in fact it fails to be deleted when moved to C (recall that Swedish is a V2 language, in which finite verbs typically move to C in matrix clauses). The restriction that it may not be deleted in C can then be understood in terms of the Empty Category Principle: if *ha* were deleted in that position, its trace would fail to be properly governed. This suggests that *ha* may only be deleted in its base-generated position, where it is not needed in order to properly govern a trace. This would also explain the non-deletability of a moved *do* or modal in English (5a); compare the non-moved *can* in (5b). Under this view the Swedish facts are not as peculiar as one might have thought, and there are certainly no special conditions that have to be learned.

(4) a. han hade sett henne
     'he had seen her'
  b. *han *e* sett henne
  c. ... att han (hade) sett henne
     'that he had seen her'
  d. Allan kanske redan (har) skrivit sin bok?
     'Allan perhaps already has written his book'

(5) a. *who did Ray greet and who Ray treat?
     *who can Jay visit and who Ray eat with?
  b. Jay can visit Fay and Ray eat with Kay

The other existing approach to capturing Emonds' distinction through acquisition theory instead of through grammatical theory is sketched by Roeper & Weissenborn (1990), who argue that children follow a 'subordinate clause strategy' and set their parameters on the basis of data from embedded clauses (6), in fact *only* from embedded clauses, when matrix and embedded clauses show contrasting properties.

(6) 'Parametric decisions have no local exceptions in subordinate clauses. Therefore subordinate clauses provide the locus for unique triggers which can set the primary parameter ... children will not get conflicting input involving tensed embedded clauses'

Roeper & Weissenborn (1990)

They point to discrepancies between matrix and embedded clauses and argue that in the case of such discrepancies it is the embedded clause which manifests the true generalization. For example, they point to (7) and claim that the alternation in (7a) gives contradictory data with reference to the presence/absence of null subjects in English, whereas embedded clauses uniformly manifest the correct generalization that null subjects are generally not possible.

(7) a. (it is) raining out today
    b. *I think that raining out today

Degree-0 learnability and Roeper & Weissenborn's subordinate clause strategy represent starkly contrasting approaches to capturing Emonds' distinction through acquisition theory, and I have argued elsewhere (1993b) that data from very different empirical domains militate in favour of degree-0 learnability and against the subordinate clause strategy. My point here is that under current conceptions of UG, Emonds' insight cannot be captured through grammatical theory and must therefore be captured differently, presumably through acquisition theory. Properties of one's acquisition theory will impose limits on how parameters can be defined.

With this in mind, I shall consider now some different issues concerning the settability of parameters, dealing with some changes in parameter settings. It is not difficult to determine when a parameter has come to be set differently; Lightfoot (1991: 167–69) provides some diagnostics for changes which must be due to parametric shifts. It is much harder to determine precisely what the parameter is that has been reset. In this chapter I shall discuss three parametric changes, but in no case do I know what precisely the parameter is; for each one, we do know some of its surface realizations and that is what I shall discuss.

3 Triggers and language change: three case studies

3.1 The emergence of ergative systems

I shall consider some cases of syntactic change, where we can see that a parameter has come to be set differently at some point and where we can see what changes in available trigger experiences led to the new setting, while not yet knowing what the true form of the parameter is. For me it is cases like these which provide the real interest in language change, where we can learn something about what it takes to set a parameter and therefore something about the form of the parameter which gets set.

It is sometimes argued that ergative–absolutive languages are fundamentally different from nominative–accusative languages, but S. R. Anderson (1988) has a very nice discussion of the emergence of ergative case systems and shows that this can not be true. He notes two fundamental facts about almost all ergative languages: (a) genuinely syntactic principles systematically treat the NPs we expect to be subjects as constituting a unitary category regardless of the transitivity of the V: regardless of their case, they are possible antecedents for reflexives, positions for controlled PRO, etc.; (b) so-called ergative languages are almost always 'split' systems, showing ergative case systems only under certain circumstances (e.g. with perfect aspect or past tenses), with nominative–accusative elsewhere. Anderson treats ergative–absolutive languages as cut from the same cloth as nominative–accusative languages but with a superficial discrepancy between syntactic and morphological categories. He takes agreement to be a syntactic operation which copies features of a NP on to the morpho-syntactic representation of the verb, first the object NP then the subject NP, yielding representations like (8). Then in an ergative language a NP which is co-indexed with the *outer layer* of a two(or more)-layer structure (i.e. a transitive subject — (8b)) is marked ergative. So he treats ergativity as a morphological phenomenon, not syntactic. The question then is: what would force a child into an ergative analysis? That is, what would trigger the relevant parameter setting? Anderson deals with the closely related question of how such a system might arise historically.

(8) a. [$_V$ V np$_i$]
    b. [$_V$ [V np$_i$] np$_j$]

One scenario is that a VSO language has a rule marking subjects with a -*s* ending, leaving objects unmarked (9). If such a language undergoes a phonological change whereby final obstruents are lost before a pause, this might affect many final -*s* markers on intransitive subjects (because they would be sentence-final) but not transitive subjects. So the emergent system would have only transitive subjects marked with -*s*, which would so become an ergative marker rather than nominative. Anderson suggests that the emergence of ergativity in Chinook comes close to this scenario.

(9) VSO:
    a. V NPs   b. V NPs NP

A well-attested source for ergative morphology is the reanalysis of earlier passive constructions. (10) has a notional object with the same case as that of the subject of an intransitive verb and the notional subject has a special marker *by*; and the verb agrees with the notional object. Hence all the characteristics of ergative morphology. We do not analyse passive sentences this way because they are *derived* from underlying actives. But if that derivation were to lose its motivation, sentences like (10) would be indistinguishable from ergatives.

(10) they were accosted by him on the way to the subway

Anderson argues that this is essentially what happened in several unrelated languages: originally passive constructions have lost their relation to the putative underlying active forms, and as a result their surface form has been reanalysed as ergative morphology rather than passive syntax. He cites work by Sandy Chung showing such a development in Tongan (Chung 1978). The passive construction in Polynesian nominative–accusative languages has a much wider distribution than in English: it is much more common, obligatory in certain contexts. If passives became still more common in Tongan, effectively obligatory in many structures, the corresponding active bases from which these passives were derived would simply have ceased to exist as surface forms. So the syntactically derived status of the 'passives' became opaque and the formal markers were reinterpreted. This represents a new parameter setting and the evidence suggests that it was triggered by increasingly common passives; that, in turn, was a change in the triggering experience, reflecting not a prior change in available grammars but rather a change in the ways that the old grammars were used, a change in the frequency of certain constructions. Anderson goes on to consider instances of 'split' ergative systems, ergative case markings being used only with, say, perfect aspect; in each instance he shows that existing structures, e.g. past tenses or possessives, are reanalysed as a result of shifts, sometimes minor shifts, in grammar use.

Parametric changes of this type are incomprehensible if one views ergative languages as fundamentally different from nominative–accusative languages. On the other hand, if one views ergative systems, or at least a significant class of ergative systems, as involving a parameter setting for case assignment along the lines of what we discussed in connection with (8), it is straightforward to understand how such systems emerged and why split systems are so common. Specifically, if this is the shape of the parameter, then it is easy to see how trigger experiences might have changed in such a way as to give rise to such grammars. That in turn enables us to postulate a plausible trigger experience for (split) ergative systems, and I take it that that is a major goal of our enterprise. So we have learned something about the parameter underlying ergative case systems and we have seen how morphological ergative systems might emerge historically as a result of haphazard shifts in a language's PLD.

3.2 V-to-I raising and triggers

Operations which associate inflectional features with the appropriate verb appear to be parameterized and we can learn about the shape of the parameter(s) by considering how the relevant grammars could be attained. In this case, I appeal not to any notion of the simplicity of the trigger, but

Shifting triggers and diachronic reanalyses 261

rather to the availability of any positive data at all which will have the desired effects. Again, I remain agnostic on the precise nature of the parameter involved, discussing some surface reflexes.

Most grammars raise their verbs to the position containing the inflectional elements (11c, d), but English grammars, unusually, have an operation which lowers I on to an adjacent verb ((11a) but not (11b)). We know this because English finite verbs do not occur in some initial C-like position (12a) and cannot be separated from their complements by intervening material (12b).

(11) a. Jill $_{VP}$[leave+PAST]
 b. Jill $_I$[leave$_i$+PAST] $_{VP}$[e$_i$]
 c. Jeanne $_I$[lit$_i$] $_{VP}$[toujours e$_i$ les journaux]
 d. lit$_i$ $_{IP}$[elle e$_i$ $_{VP}$[toujours e$_i$ les journaux]]

(12) a. *visited you Utrecht last week?
 b. *the women visited not/all/frequently Utrecht last week

What is it that forces French children to have the V-to-I operation and what forces English children to lack the operation and to lower their Is? This question has been a central focus of recent work, particularly Chomsky (1991, 1993a) but I shall sketch a somewhat different account.

It seems reasonable to construe the English lowering operation as a morphological phenomenon: in general, lowering operations are unusual in the syntax, and a lowering operation here would leave behind a trace which would not be bound or properly governed, and one would expect a morphological operation but not a syntactic operation to be subject to a condition of adjacency. Therefore the representation in (11a), reflecting a morphological operation, contains no trace of the lowered I. In any case, the English lowering needs to be taken as the default setting; there is, as far as I can see, no non-negative evidence available to the child which would force her to select an I-lowering analysis over a V-raising analysis (11b) for English, if both operations could be syntactic and subject to an adjacency requirement (which would itself raise learnability questions; how could an adjacency requirement be learned?). In that case, let us take the morphological I-lowering analysis as the default setting, always available to children and requiring no particular triggering experience. Specifically, this means that a French speaker is free to analyse a simple sentence like *Jean lit les journaux* in the English fashion, with morphological lowering: *Jean* $_{VP}$[*lit*+PAST *les journaux*].

Now one can ask what triggers a syntactic V-to-I raising operation in grammars where it may apply. Some generalizations have emerged over the last several years. One is that languages with rich inflection may have V-to-I operations in their grammars, and rich inflection could be part of the trigger. So Standard English has one verb which is richly inflected, the verb *be*, and this element raises to I (and may therefore move on to C, as in *is Bill President now?*, and may occur to the left of *not*, *Bill is not President now*).

Some forms of the language show no inflection here and use *be* uniformly and invariantly regardless of context (13b). These forms of English (Black English Vernacular and some forms of children's speech) use negatives and interrogatives like (13c, d) and not (13e); (13e) is what would be expected if the uninflected *be* raised to I.

(13) a. Bill is President now
 b. Bill be President now
 c. Bill don't be President now
 do Bill be President now?
 what do Bill be?
 d. did it be funny?
 do clowns be boys or girls?
 I don't be angry
 e. Bill ben't President now
 be Bill President now?
 what be Bill?

The contrast between these forms of the language strongly suggests that the inflected *be* raises to I, whereas the uninflected form does not raise. So rich inflection and V-to-I raising are linked in some way.

However, we cannot simply link the presence of V-to-I raising with rich inflection in a one-to-one fashion. It may be the case that if a language (or, as we have just seen, part of a language) has rich inflection, it has V-to-I raising. If there is no rich inflection, a grammar may have the raising operation (Swedish)[1] or may lack it (English). In that case, there will need to be a *syntactic* triggering experience. So, for example, a finite verb occurring in C, i.e. to the left of the subject NP (as in a V2 language or in interrogatives), could only get there by raising first to I, and therefore inversion forms like (11d) in French could be syntactic triggers for V-to-I. This suggests to me that the V-to-I operation applies only where necessary; otherwise the morphological operation may suffice to link inflectional elements with the appropriate verb, including for French. This is quite contrary to the way that Chomsky (1991) implements his economy notions in this domain, but more consistent with his (1992) Minimalist approach (differing in allowing morphological lowering for French finite verbs). However, one could dispense with the strong/weak morphological distinction, which has proven so problematic; under this view, verbs would raise to I only where there is *syntactic* evidence for the raising. In that case one can ask how robustly the parameter setting raising V to I is 'expressed'; it is *expressed* robustly if there are many simple utterances which can be analysed by the child only by applying the V-to-I operation. So, for example, the sentences of (11c, d) can only be analysed by the French child if the V *lit* raises to I;[2] a simple sentence like *Jeanne lit les journaux* 'Jeanne reads the newspapers', on the other hand, could be analysed with *lit* raised to I or with the I lowered down into the VP in the English fashion and therefore it does not express the V-to-I parameter setting.

By quantifying the *expression* of a parameter, we can understand why English grammars lost the V-to-I operation and why they lost it as the periphrastic *do* became increasingly common. We can reconstruct a plausible history for the loss of V-to-I in English. What we are doing here is identifying when a parameter came to be reset and how the available triggering experience seems to have shifted in critical ways prior to that parameter resetting.

As the periphrastic *do* came to be used in negatives like *John did not leave* and interrogatives like *did John leave?*, so the V-to-I operation was expressed less and less. Lightfoot (1993a) shows that V-to-I finally disappeared from English grammars in the early seventeenth century. The inflectional changes, simplifying verb morphology, were effectively complete by 1400, well before the eventual loss of V-to-I. Periphrastic *do*, on the other hand, began to occur in significant numbers at the beginning of the fifteenth century and steadily increased in frequency until it stabilized into its modern usage by the mid seventeenth century. Ellegård (1953) shows that the sharpest increase came in the period 1475–1550. The historical facts, then, suggest that lack of strong subject–verb agreement cannot be a sufficient condition for absence of V-to-I, but it may be a necessary condition. That is, if a language has strong verbal inflection, it will have V-to-I. Under this view the *possibility* of V-to-I not being triggered first arose in the history of English with the loss of rich verbal inflection; similarly in Swedish. That possibility never arose in Dutch, French, German, etc., where verbal inflections remained relatively robust. Despite this possibility, V-to-I continued to be triggered and it occurred in grammars well after verbal inflection had been reduced to its present-day level. However, with the increasing frequency of periphrastic *do* V-to-I was expressed less and less in the PLD, to the point that it eventually ceased to be triggered. That is, with the rise of periphrastic *do* there was no longer anything very robust in the PLD which *required* V-to-I, given that the morphological operation was always available. In particular, post-verbal adverbs and quantifiers (12b) were not triggers for V-to-I; they were too subtle, not robust enough, and they simply disappeared quietly, a by-product of the loss of V-to-I.[3]

We are led here to analyses of English verbal syntax which differ from those postulated under current versions of Minimalism. However, current versions of Minimalism have great difficulty with this area and Lasnik (1994) has argued that the fundamental notions of Weakness and Greed need to be changed in significant ways in order to deal with the properties of English verbs and the parameters involved; he advocates a 'hybrid Minimalism'. At this stage it is premature to specify the parameter(s) involved and it is unwise to postulate 'parameters' for the various surface differences that one observes among small sets of languages. Meanwhile we can learn something about those parameters by considering the conditions under which structural change took place historically, presumably resulting from a resetting of the relevant parameter(s). We can identify shifts in the PLD, mostly relating to morphological erosion and the rise of periphrastic *do*, which would plausibly help to reset the parameter manifested by the presence/absence of the V-to-I operation.

3.3 The loss of verb second

With this perspective, consider now V2 languages. A structure along the lines of (14), first proposed by den Besten (1983), represents the standard analysis.

(14) $_{CP}$[Spec C $_{IP}$[Spec $_{VP}$[...V...] I]]

But this standard analysis provides (a) no relation between XP-to-Spec movement and V-to-I-to-C movement, and (b) no explanation for the obligatory character of the phenomenon (positing an attractive feature in C merely restates the problem). It is because of negative data, i.e. *un*grammaticality judgments, that linguists know that an inflected verb *must* move to C if an XP moves to Spec,CP. Therefore the explanation cannot be data-driven for the child and must come from UG. Similarly for the obligatory character of the V2 phenomenon.

But OE-ME *appears* to have optional V2, which became more frequent during the OE-ME period. If the appearance were real, this would be highly problematic, because one could now not invoke UG to explain the obligatoriness of the movement in Dutch and German. Happily, Kroch & Taylor (this volume; henceforth K&T) have now provided arguments for the existence of two dialects in Middle English; if they are right, then there is no homogeneous language with optional V2. First, there is a northern, Scandinavian-based V2 grammar (15a). Note that the verb moves through I, which K&T take as different from the modern Scandinavian languages. However, despite claims by Platzack, Vikner and others in favour of analyses like (15b), there are good arguments that V moves through I in Modern Swedish too (15c, with adverbs left-adjacent to I); see note 1. In matrix clauses the finite verb moves from I to C, moving across the intervening negative (15d).

(15) a. Spec C [Spec I [V NP]]
     b. ... om [Jan I inte $_{VP}$[köpte boken]]
         'if John didn't buy the book'
     c. ... om [Jan inte $_I$köpte$_i$ [e_i boken]]
     d. Jan köpte inte boken

Second, there is a southern, indigenous grammar which lacks V+I-to-C. K&T's analysis, taken over from Susan Pintzuk's treatment of Old English, is (16), where the finite verb moves only to I and some phrasal category moves to Spec,IP.

(16) a. $_{CP}$[Spec C $_{IP}$[Spec I $_{VP}$[NP V NP]]]
     b. $_{IP}$[se cyning$_i$ eode$_j$ $_{VP}$[e_i inn e_j]]

This analysis cannot be right, for reasons discussed in the appendix to this chapter (see also van Kemenade, this volume; Kiparsky 1994a), and I take Spec,IP to be the initial position of the subject NP. There is an alternative analysis. Early English shows three major alternations (17) (not necessarily three distinct parameters, of course). This leads us to expect the initial structures of (18) with/without V-to-I raising. This is enough to generate what one finds in the texts. Therefore, at least (19) exists alongside (15a).

(17) a. VO/OV
  b. I-medial/I-final
  c. V+I to C

(18) a. $_{CP}$[Spec C $_{IP}$[Spec I $_{VP}$[V NP]]]
  b. $_{CP}$[Spec C $_{IP}$[Spec I $_{VP}$[NP V]]]
  c. $_{CP}$[Spec C $_{IP}$[Spec $_{VP}$[NP V] I]]
  d. $_{CP}$[Spec C $_{IP}$[Spec $_{VP}$[V NP] I]]

(19) ... $_{IP}$[Spec I $_{VP}$[...V...]]

There is much to be said about the various grammars manifested by the ME texts and I am not going to enter into that debate here. If there were multiple grammars along the lines suggested by K&T, then the problem concerning the loss of an optional V2 system is reconstrued: there were (at least) two coexisting grammars, one obligatory V2 (15a) and one with no obligatory V+I-to-C movement, i.e. (19), not V2 in the usual sense. The first of these grammars was lost, ceased to be attained. The problem now is to find why this grammar died out.

To tackle this question, let us back up for a moment and ask what V2 children have to learn? Lightfoot 1991 argued that they learn that utterances begin with an arbitrary XP with no particular grammatical or thematic role, therefore in the Spec of some functional category above I, i.e. Spec,CP (20).

(20) XP – Vf

UG says that lexical material in Spec,CP needs to be licensed by a lexically filled C.

Although the initial XP is in principle of arbitrary grammatical function, statistical counts for Dutch, German, Norwegian and Swedish show that it is a subject about 70 per cent of the time (see Lightfoot 1993b for details). Presumably it is those 30 per cent non-subjects which are a crucial trigger for inducing children to postulate that the XP is in Spec,CP and not in Spec,IP or whatever position is associated with subjecthood.

Now we can identify what is likely to have militated against the survival of the V2 grammar. Children in Lincolnshire and Yorkshire, as they mingled with southerners, would have heard sentences whose initial elements were non-subjects followed by a finite verb less frequently than the required threshold; if we take seriously the statistics from the modern V2 languages and take the threshold to be about 30 per cent non-subject-Vf, then southern XP–Vf forms, where the Vf is not I-final and where the initial element is not a *wh* item or negative, are too consistently subject-V to trigger a V2 grammar. Ans van Kemenade has given me some statistics from Sawles Warde, an early thirteenth-century, Southwest Midlands text. She counted 152 matrix clauses, excluding coordinate clauses with missing subjects, dislocated structures (i.e. with resumptive pronouns), and initial *þah*. She found non-subject-Vf (where the initial element is not a *wh* element, of course) in 26 cases, i.e. 17 per cent.[4] Second, as those northern children came into contact with southerners, they would have heard forms like (21), because southerners treated pronouns as clitics, according to most current analyses. But, K&T argue that pronouns are not clitics in northern grammars; therefore forms like (21) would not have been consistent with the V2 grammars of their parents and would have militated against V2 analyses, making such an analysis harder to attain, more opaque.

(21) XP – subject pronoun – Vf
      subject pronoun – XP – Vf

Obviously there are many questions glossed over here, but my point is that we can tell a plausible story about the development of English, about how its partial V2 character was lost, under the assumptions sketched. And this is an old puzzle.

4 More contingency and less determinism

I have shown how, given K&T's striking new analysis, it is plausible to assume that the trigger experience that northern children had came to differ in critical ways from the trigger experiences that their parents and ancestors had had as there was more contact with the south. With an appropriate kind of theory of parameters one can then show how different grammars came to be attained. Trigger experiences, i.e. sets of PLD, are always changing; that is the nature of the world and there is no reason to assume that any two people would ever have identical trigger experiences. Furthermore, we know from acquisition studies that children are sensitive to statistical shifts. For example, Newport, Gleitman & Gleitman (1977) showed that the ability of English-speaking children to use auxiliaries appropriately results from exposure to non-contracted, stressed forms in initial position in *yes–no* questions: the greater the exposure to these subject–auxiliary inversion forms, the earlier the use of auxiliaries in medial position. Also Richards (1990) demonstrated a good deal of individual variation in the acquisition of English auxiliaries as a result of exposure to slightly different trigger experiences. The issue is when trigger experiences differ critically, i.e. in such a way as to set some parameter differently. That is where work on historical change is so illuminating: sometimes we can identify points at which there have been clear shifts in parameter settings and sometimes we can also identify prior changes in the PLD. By hypothesis, this shows us changes in PLD having critical effects. In fact, for the immediate future, work on language change is likely to be the major source of insight into what triggers particular parameter settings.

There is no incoherence or paradox in this kind of account, nor do we need to postulate rules or formal operations which account for the changes in trigger experiences or relate sets of PLD (22).

(22) $PLD_1 \rightarrow PLD_2$

In fact, it is a fallacy to think that there could be formal operations that relate sets of PLD, the adaptive rules of Henning Andersen (1973) or the 'peripheral rules' of Weerman (1993). This fallacy is part of a more widespread problem, the view that for any 'language' there must be some recursive device or a grammar which will generate its sentences. Chomsky has discussed this problem in the introduction to the published version of his dissertation (Chomsky 1975) and in *Knowledge of Language* (Chomsky 1986b) and elsewhere but the distinction between E-language and I-language has not been properly absorbed. There need not be any single recursive device which generates a given set of PLD and sometimes there cannot be, as we have seen in our case studies here: as the V2 system was lost in northern England there was no single recursive device to generate what children were hearing, namely the output of their parents' grammar plus more expressions from people with southern, non-V2 grammars; similarly the statistical shifts which seem to have given rise to split ergative systems could not have been represented in any recursive device.

The notion of a formal device operating on sets of PLD seems to have reappeared in the recent work of Ian Roberts and it is linked to an attempt to explain some changes entirely through UG, independently of changes in trigger experiences. The idea of changes being motivated entirely by UG (i.e. in the absence of changes in the PLD) also seems to occur in Kiparsky's (1994a) notion of 'endogenous optimization' as a motivating force for changes. It also occurred in Keyser & O'Neil (1985; see Lightfoot 1987), and in a strikingly strong form in the work on 'drift' undertaken by the 'typologists' in the 1970s (see Lightfoot 1979 for discussion). I believe that there is some confusion here which is worth unpacking.

Roberts (1993a) developed a theory whereby English children ceased to postulate what he called Agr^{-1} (a 'negative projection' which yields a position for an affixal morpheme) because the morphological distinctions had been simplified appropriately. This links to changes affecting the modals, because only with the loss of Agr^{-1} could modals (or other free morphemes) be inserted into Agr, as opposed to V, and thus have the distribution of non-verbs (Roberts' section 3.3). The link with the new periphrastic *do*, which emerged in the Middle English period and spread enormously during the sixteenth century, is less obvious. Roberts (section 3.2) analyses *do* and makes its introduction *a result of* the loss of V-to-Agr rather than a precondition for it, unlike what we did above. Here he invokes a new technical device, what he calls a Diachronic Reanalysis (DR) (23), taking place in the sixteenth century (295, 315). Modal verbs and periphrastic *do* originally moved to T (23a) but came to be base-generated there, as in (23b).

(23) a. NP_i [$_T$ do/M_j T^{-1}] t_j [t_i VP] ⇒
 b. NP [$_T$ did/M] VP

This is the clearest invocation of a DR, although they are alluded to at several points in the book. Roberts distinguishes three notions in what he calls a theory of language change (158ff.): (a) a step, which might be the appearance or change in frequency of a new construction, (b) a new parameter setting as discussed above, and (c) a DR. Roberts (1993b) is devoted to explicating the notion of a DR; he puts it forward as the 'formal correlate of the informal notion of grammaticalisation'. There he describes DRs as relations between the E-language of one generation and the I-language of a subsequent generation. DRs are seen as the causes of parametric shifts and for any given phenomenological change one needs to ask whether it manifests a new parameter setting or a DR. He also says that 'Parametric Changes can trigger DR' and that 'Parametric Changes are usually observable as clusters of DRs' (1993b: 253).

This is where the confusion lies. DRs are said to be provoked by principles of acquisition, often by the 'Least Effort Strategy' (LES); the LES led children to reanalyse (23a) as (23b) in the sixteenth century. So early grammars had structures like (23a) and later grammars had structures like (23b). But then what is the role of a DR? Roberts clearly thinks of DRs as formal devices, but what do they relate? (23a), containing structures and indexed empty elements, is not a piece of E-language but a *grammatical* representation. So DRs relate 'the grammars of successive generations', as he notes in Roberts (1993a: 154) they, in fact, do not relate the E-language of one generation to a later grammar. If DRs relate grammars of successive generations, then they occur where parametric shifts have taken place. Roberts notes that 'the notion DR may also prove to be epiphenomenal. All DRs may turn out to be instances of Parametric Change' (159) and therefore to have no reality of their own, but he insists that the notion has real utility and is necessary for a theory of syntactic change.

But why? Apart from the notion of parameter setting needed to account for language acquisition and therefore needed independent of an account of change, Roberts' 'theory' of change consists of two things: steps and DRs. He calls a 'step' the traditional, 'observationally adequate' notion of change, and a DR is an epiphenomenon, really a particular type of parametric shift which involves different analyses for given strings of morphemes. This is not a theory and DRs gain no credibility for being part of a coherent theory of change.

It has always seemed to me that historical linguistics is more concerned with explanations than our other subdisciplines. But sometimes the concern with explanation is excessive and seeking a theory of change shows the downside of the pedigree. There is no theory which accounts for why people speak French in France and Japanese in Japan, and no theory of grammar or acquisition will predict that people in a certain location talk somewhat differently from the way people there spoke a generation previously. Such things happen for various reasons which often are of no particular interest to grammarians. The facts, where they can be established, are crucial, for without these shifts there would be no systematic change, no parametric shifts, no changes in grammars. This is the point of connection between traditional work on change and work on parametric shifts in grammars; the traditional work is describing changes in trigger experiences which in turn entail the parametric shifts. The parametrist needs the descriptivist.

The reality is that Roberts' DRs and parametric shifts more generally are *not* provoked by the LES, nor by the Transparency Principle (Lightfoot 1979), nor by any 'endogenous' tendency toward 'optimization'. Specifically, the LES cannot be 'the sufficient condition for the move from one step to the next' (Roberts 1993a: 159). If there were no change in trigger experiences, there would be no changes in grammars. If representations like (23a) disappeared, it was because they ceased to be triggered; the children who did not acquire them must have had different experiences from earlier generations — it was not because they were more sensitive to the demands of the LES or the Transparency Principle.

In the case studies I have examined here, one can plausibly reconstruct shifts in the available trigger experiences such that the relevant parametric changes were forced. These shifts consisted in changes in frequencies, i.e. changes resulting from the way that grammars were used rather than changes in the grammars themselves, and changes in trigger experiences resulting from population movements. For these cases the notion of a DR with the formal properties of (23) is irrelevant and, in fact, inadequate; the relevant changes cannot be represented in schemata like (23). Therefore the burden of proof lies on the one who argues for a new mechanism of change.

Irrespective of the validity and usefulness of DRs, I have not yet seen a persuasive argument for a change motivated entirely by internal factors, by economy or another element of UG. It seems to me to be axiomatic that there can be no change in grammars without change in trigger experiences. Similarly, there will be no variation in grammars independent of variation in triggers, ... apart perhaps from possible cases of indeterminacy. In cases of indeterminacy, the variation would be random and could not be systematic enough to be manifested in a new parameter setting.

Language change is fascinating because it represents an interaction between chance oscillations in the trigger experience and the biological necessities of the human language acquisition device. I have tried to suggest here that if one looks in the right places, one can show with some plausibility that shifting trigger experiences caused some of the parametric shifts that have interested us. To explain language change it seems to me that one needs nothing more than (a) an account of how trigger experiences shifted and (b) a theory of language acquisition that matches PLD with grammars in a deterministic way. People seeking a substantive theory of change are too ambitious, too principled and seeking to explain too much, and they fail to come to grips with the essentially contingent nature of language change.

Appendix

If (16) were the correct analysis, with subjects base-generated in VP-internal position in Old English but not in a genuine V2 language, then the OE child would have to learn that Spec,IP is not necessarily a subject position, unlike in Modern Dutch and German. If one asks how this could be learned, it turns out that there are no simple or robust data which would trigger the analysis. For example, one does not find finite verbs preceded by two XPs in matrix clauses (one in Spec,CP and one in Spec,IP: *who_i John saw e_i?), with the exception of those involving subject pronouns: XP–subject pronoun–Vf and subject pronoun–XP–Vf. But these subject pronoun sentences do not provide evidence for I-medial structures because K&T (again following Pintzuk) analyse the pronouns as cliticized on to the adjacent 'topic' XP and so the Vf is preceded by only one constituent. There does seem to be evidence for I-medial in subordinate clauses. Pintzuk (1991) assumes various rightward movement operations (V-raising, V-projection raising and postposition) so many apparent I-medial structures can in fact be derived by those movement operations from underlying I-final structures (24).

(24) a. þæt se eorðlica man e_j e_i sceolde$_i$ geþeon$_j$
'... so that the earthly man should prosper'
b. þe god e_j e_i worhte$_i$ þurh hine$_j$
'... which God wrought through him'

She points, however, to three types of embedded phenomena which do 'express' the I-medial analysis.

i. She finds 36 cases (out of a potential 134: 27%) of Vf-particle and these occur with the verb in second position. Since particles do not postpose (so post-verbal particles do not occur with infinitives or clause-final finite verbs) and since Vf cannot move to C in an embedded clause, these must manifest underlying I-medial with movement of the verb to I (25).

(25) a. hu he $_i$siðode$_i$ up e_i
'... how he went up' ÆLS 18.291
b. þæt he $_i$wearp$_i$ þæt sweord onweg e_i
'... so that he threw away the sword' Bede 38.20

ii. Pronominal objects and monosyllabic adverbs always preceded a Vf which is unambiguously I-final, therefore they are base-generated preverbally and do not postpose. However, with embedded clauses which *could* be I-medial they occur post-verbally in 7 of 123 potential instances (5.7%: (26)).

(26) a. swa þæt hy ₁asettan_i him upp on ænne sið e_i
'so that they transported themselves inland in one journey'
ChronA 132.19 (1001)

b. þæt martinus ₁come_i þa into þære byrig e_i
'... that Martin then came into the town' ÆLS 31.490–91

One wonders why the percentage is so low, and so much lower than the percentage for post-verbal particles; one also wonders why the percentage does not rise over time as I-medial structures become more common.

iii. Comparative evidence from the relevant modern languages suggests that V-projection raising does not take place with pronominal objects, but Old English manifests structures like (27) with apparent V-projection raising with a pronominal object. If the constraint shown by Zurich German, West Flemish and early Yiddish also holds for OE (*and if there is no cliticization on to the verb*), these are plausibly I-medial.

(27) ... þæt heo wolde hine læran
'... that she would teach him'

None of these data are robust and none are degree-0, so it is very questionable that there is any trigger experience for an I-medial analysis of the type that K&T assume. In any case it is evidence only for I-medial order and not for Spec,IP being a position for non-subjects; that is, it is not evidence for the 'IP-V2' analysis that K&T adopt. Furthermore, that analysis makes some big false predictions: if Spec,IP is not necessarily reserved for subjects, then there should be many instances of structures like (28a) and there should be many subordinate clauses like (28b). Neither of these patterns is attested.

(28) a. _CP_[wh/adverb Vf _IP_[non-subject ...]]
b. ... _IP_[XP Vf _VP_[subject ...]]

In addition, neither Pintzuk nor K&T have anything much to say about how Spec,IP might have changed to become exclusively a subject position in later forms of English.

Notes

* This chapter was conceived in a seminar on language change given by Ian Roberts at the University of Maryland in the spring of 1994. It was nurtured through discussions with Ian, Juan Uriagereka, Mark Arnold and Norbert Hornstein. The current version reflects changes to an earlier version suggested by Mark Arnold, Ans van Kemenade and Nigel Vincent.
1. Swedish is sometimes analysed as lacking the V-to-I operation. So Vikner (1994a) has verbs moving directly to C, because negatives precede finite verbs in embedded clauses: ... *om Jan inte kopte boken* 'if John didn't buy the book'. But this indicates that *inte* 'not' and other such adverbs occur to the *left* of I and does not provide evidence against the application of V-to-I. Occurrence of verbs in C is strong evidence of movement through I, given almost any version of the proper government condition on traces.

2. I ignore here the very plausible suggestion of Iatridou (1990) that infinitival counterparts to (11c) may not be direct evidence for movement of V across an intervening adverb, if French allows complex verbs of the form [V Adv].
3. Some readers balk at the notion that sentences like (12b) were too subtle and not robust enough to trigger a V-to-I operation. However, the fact of the matter is these forms did not trigger V-to-I or anything else, because they dropped out of the language — compelling evidence, it seems to me. They also dropped out of the language at the same time as other putative reflexes of the V-to-I operation. This shows not only that they had no triggering effect, but also that they were incompatible with the grammatical operations that *were* being triggered. Hence their disappearance. I know of no alternative account of this particular change.

   Furthermore, it also seems reasonable to take the periphrastic *do* forms as robust enough to act as a trigger for grammatical development. They appear in interrogative and negative statements and imperatives. There are several statistical studies showing that *most* of the speech directed at young children consists of interrogatives and imperatives (see Newport, Gleitman & Gleitman 1977).
4. Van Kemenade (personal communication) reported 73 instances of subject-initial clauses, where the subject was followed by a finite verb, 32 instances of V3 (i.e. XP–subject–Vf), 6 *wh*-questions and 23 instances of Vf preceded only by *þa* or the negative particle *ne*. Of the 26 cases of XP–Vf–subject, 19 involved a full noun in subject position and 7 a subject pronoun.

   Van Kemenade's figures suffice for my point here, but if K&T are right to postulate the two dialects, then one must take account of a significant amount of dialect mixture and there are several puzzles. For example, the Anglo-Saxon Chronicle shows a much lower rate of subject–Vf than one finds in even the modern V2 languages; Bean's (1983) statistics show that subject–Vf becomes more frequent over the period covered by the Chronicle, but the percentage rises only from 28 per cent in the initial sections (written in 891) to 41 per cent toward the end (in sections written in 1048–1140), way below what one finds in a modern strict V2 language, mysteriously.

10 Viewing change in progress: the loss of V2 in Hiberno-English imperatives

Alison Henry

Introduction

There is a strong tradition in sociolinguistics of studying the nature of language change by looking at changes currently in progress (for an outline of this, see Milroy 1992). However, this method of understanding change has been less frequently exploited in studies within the generative framework. Such study can, it will be argued, contribute significantly to the understanding of the mechanisms of change by enabling the study of the grammars of speakers which represent various stages of the change, rather than being restricted to written records.

One of the changes that is often argued to have taken place in the history of English is the loss of Verb second (V2) order in most sentence types (see for example Roberts 1993a; van Kemenade 1987) with a few exceptions, such as in questions and sentences with initial negative-type elements (Rizzi 1991).

In this chapter, I argue that Belfast English, a variety of Hiberno-English, has retained V2 in imperatives, but that this possibility is disappearing; we can therefore observe the loss of V2 in progress in this construction. I show that, between the stage where V2 is widespread and that where it is impossible, is an intermediate stage where it appears that certain verbs permit V2, but where speakers have in fact developed grammars which, although they allow verb–subject order in certain circumstances, do not in fact involve verb raising.

The fact that the Belfast speech community contains speakers with grammars representing the various stages of the change allows us to observe the mechanisms of change, and in particular the role of language acquisition in language change. I show that possible grammars are strongly constrained by UG, and do not admit language-particular rules; the acquisition process, I argue, is governed by a simplicity metric which disfavours statements about individual functional elements in favour of statements about the functional category as a whole; and I show how the interaction of changes in another structure with that in imperatives favours a change in the latter.

Viewing change in progress allows us to examine change at the level of individual grammars in a way which is not possible when study is restricted to examining surviving historical texts. I note that studying a pool of examples recorded from a variety of different speakers would give a misleading impression of the nature of the change — it would appear that the dialect was going through a stage where inversion was still possible with all verbs, but statistically more frequent with certain types of verb, such as unaccusatives; if sampled over time, on the basis of the output of a variety of different speakers, the change would appear to proceed by a gradual reduction in the frequency of inversion with certain types of verbs, and eventually its loss with all verbs; but the study of individual grammars shows us that, in this case at least, grammars are categorical. Speakers have grammars of one of three distinct types, and the pattern is one of radical inter-generational shift triggered by the language acquisition process, rather than gradual change in different linguistic environments. The findings presented here, then, may present a serious challenge to the validity of drawing conclusions about the gradualness of historical change and the nature of its spread across environments by applying variationist methodology to the study of texts from a range of different speakers.

Before we consider the historical changes however, we need to look in some detail at the facts of imperatives in Belfast English. For many of the youngest generation of speakers, inversion is impossible in imperatives; as in Standard English, an overt subject must precede the verb:

(1)   You come here

However, for many speakers, the subject may occur after the verb:

(2)   Come you here
(3)   Bring you that with you

In relation to inverted imperatives, two possible grammars can be identified. In one of these, now more or less restricted to older speakers, inversion is possible with any verb in imperatives; this I have termed the Unrestricted Inversion dialect. A second dialect, spoken mainly by young and middle-aged adults, permits the inverted structure only with a subset of verbs — unaccusatives and passives — but not with transitives or unergatives (see section 2 below); speakers of this dialect judge (2) to be grammatical, but not (3). This I will call the Restricted Inversion dialect. A detailed discussion of the syntax of these dialects is given in Henry (1995); an outline is given below of the facts of these varieties, and the syntactic analysis of the structures, before we proceed to discuss the implications of this for language change.

1 The Unrestricted Inversion dialect

1.1 Introduction

As I noted above, Belfast English possesses not only the Standard English imperative strategies, but also an alternative strategy, involving a post-verbal subject: as with Standard English, the overt subject is most frequently second person (in Belfast English this can be *you* or its plurals *youse* and *yousuns*) but, as in Standard English, can be one of a limited range of other items:

(4)   a. Sit you down
       b. Sit everybody down

(5)   a. Get youse the coats
       b. Get somebody the coats

The effect of including the subject is roughly the same as that of including a preverbal subject in Standard English imperatives; it has a slightly emphatic or contrastive effect.

Inversion of full verbs and subjects occurs only in imperatives. As in Standard English, full verbs cannot invert with subjects in questions, but must have do-support.

(6)   a. *Sat you down?
       b. Did you sit down?

(7)   a. *Got somebody the coats?
       b. Did somebody get the coats?

Nor can such verbs raise to I (=Agr_s); as in Standard English this is ungrammatical with verbs other than *be* and *have*, as shown by the fact that full verbs cannot raise above negation or adverbs.

(8)   a. *I like not coffee
       b. I do not like coffee

(9)   a. *I read often books
       b. I often read books

Belfast English (BE), then, in general patterns like Standard English (SE) in relation to verb position. Apart from imperatives, the only major difference between the varieties in relation to verb raising is that inversion is available in embedded questions in Belfast English (McCloskey 1992; Henry 1995).

(10)   BE/*SE They asked me was I going to the party

However, it seems unlikely that this is directly related to imperative inversion, for a number of reasons. First, while almost all speakers of Hiberno-English use inversion in embedded questions, and it shows no signs of disappearing from the language, imperative inversion is restricted to speakers in certain areas — roughly northern and Eastern Ireland — and is, as we have noted, becoming obsolete; the two features do not therefore necessarily co-occur in the grammar of speakers and do not seem to be subject to the same changes. Secondly, although inversion is available in embedded questions in Belfast English, that inversion is, as in matrix questions, restricted to auxiliaries, *have* and *be*; inversion is not possible with main verbs:

(11)   *They asked me went I to the party

Finally, this difference concerns embedded clauses, whereas imperatives are a wholly root phenomenon. It does not look likely therefore that, in terms either of syntactic analysis or of historical change, we can establish a link between inversion in embedded questions and inversion in imperatives.

Returning to imperatives, then, let us consider the position of the verb in imperatives in the Unrestricted Inversion dialect. Clearly, if we accept the standard view that the subject originates in the Spec,VP position, preceding the verb, the verb–subject order must be derived by movement of the verb out of the verb phrase. We will consider here the position to which the verb moves.

1.2 Verb position in relation to adverbs

Let us begin by looking at the position of the verb and subject in relation to adverbs. Where there is an adverb, it generally occurs after the subject.

(12)   Talk you always to your mother
(13)   Write you carefully your homework

but is also possible after the verb but before the subject.

(14)   Talk always you to your mother
(15)   Write carefully you your homework

Thus, it appears that the verb moves in these imperatives to a position in front of adverbs, and that the subject may either move to a position in front of these adverbials, or may stay *in situ*.

That the subject may stay *in situ* is also indicated by the positioning of the subject after unaccusative and passive verbs. In general, where an auxiliary is present, the subject must occur between the auxiliary and the lexical verb; but where the verb is unaccusative (the precise class of verbs involved, and the reason why the subject may stay *in situ*, is discussed in detail in the section on the Restricted Inversion dialect below) or passive, it may occur after the verb, in what would be its base position according to most analyses of unaccusatives and passives.

(16)   a. Be you reading that book when I get back
       b. *Be reading you that book when I get back
(17)   a. Be you going out of the door when they arrive
       b. Be going you out of the door when they arrive
(18)   a. Be you picked for the team before the end of term
       b. Be picked you for the team before the end of term

Imperatives with aspectual markers, or in the passive, are somewhat unnatural in English, but the examples below are no worse than their Standard English counterparts:

(19) You be going out of the door when they arrive
(20) You be picked for the team before the end of term

1.3 Weak object pronouns

The position of weak object pronouns in imperatives is particularly interesting. In imperatives only, these pronouns seem to raise out of the VP, in a process similar to object shift in the Scandinavian languages, which raises such objects if and only if the main verb has raised out of VP.

In general in both Belfast English and Standard English, such pronouns appear in the normal object position after the verb where non-pronominal DPs also occur.

(21) a. I bought the book
    b. I bought it
(22) a. A student was reading the books
    b. A student was reading them

However, in imperatives, weak object pronouns, unlike full DPs, may occur before the subject, whereas full DPs may only appear after the subject.

(23) a. Send them you to your friends
    b. Send you them to your friends
(24) a. Give me you that letter
    b. Give you me that letter

The pre-subject position is not possible for non-pronominal DPs.

(25) a. *Send the books you to your friends
    b. Send you the books to your friends
(26) a. *Give the teacher you that letter
    b. Give you the teacher that letter

We noted that a weak object pronoun may either precede or follow the subject. In relation to sentential adverbs however the position of a weak object pronoun is fixed; it must precede such adverbs.

(27) a. Give you them always your seat
    b. *Give you always them your seat
    c. Give them always you your seat

However, where the object is a full DP, it must occur after the adverb.

(28) a. *Give you your grandparents always your seat
    b. Give you always your grandparents your seat

Note, incidentally, that sentences like (28b) show that there is in fact no surface adjacency requirement between the verb and its object in English, at least in this variety.

Stressed pronouns, coordinated pronouns and the '-*uns*' pronouns such as *yousuns* and *themuns*, which refer to groups (Henry 1995: ch. 2) behave like full DPs; they occur after the subject and after adverbs.

(29) a. Tell you HIM the truth
b. *Tell HIM you the truth
(30) a. Tell you him and her the truth
b. *Tell him and her you the truth
(31) a. Tell you themuns the truth
b. *Tell themuns you the truth

Whatever is responsible for the particular placing of weak object pronouns singles out the same class of items as do other processes (object shift in the Scandinavian languages; pronoun placement in verb-particle constructions in English) where, as here, certain pronouns behave like full DPs; in these cases, stressed or coordinated pronouns behave like full DPs rather than weak pronouns.

In the Scandinavian languages, raising of the lexical verb triggers leftward movement of weak object pronouns (see, for example, Holmberg 1986, 1992; Vikner 1990), and it seems that this is also what is happening in Belfast English imperatives. The following example (from Vikner 1990) shows how object shift operates in Danish; where the verb raises out of the verb phrase, a weak pronoun object also moves to the left.

(32) a. I gar   laeste Peter den uden   tvivl ikke
Yesterday read   Peter it   without doubt not
b. *I gar laeste Peter uden tvivl den ikke
c. *I gar laeste Peter uden tvivl ikke den

Before we can conclude that it is object shift that is responsible for the placement of weak pronoun objects in Belfast English imperatives, we need to exclude the possibility that the object pronoun is simply cliticizing to the verb and raising with it. There are two arguments against this. First, weak pronoun objects do not necessarily appear immediately after the raised verb in inverted imperatives. Although they must precede adverbs, they may appear either before or after the subject; the fact that they do not necessarily tag on to the verb seems to indicate that they are not clitics which must attach to the verb. Note that the subject itself may be a non-pronominal, so that attachment to the subject cannot be analysed as attachment to an array of clitics attached to the verb.

(33) a. Read it everybody quickly
b. Read everybody it quickly

Moreover, where the subject is a pronoun, it is always in its stressed rather than reduced form in imperatives

(34) a. *Read [jə] it to me
b. Read [juː] it to me

so that it does not seem that the subject could be considered a clitic even where it is pronominal.

Secondly, there is evidence that weak pronouns are not clitics which attach to verbs in the behaviour of such pronouns with the verb *have* when it raises in English.

In both Belfast English and other varieties, *have* as a main verb may raise to Agr_s (and thence to C), as shown by its position in relation to negatives and adverbs, and its ability to raise to C in questions.

(35) a. I haven't any money
 b. They have always a lot of things to do
 c. Has anybody the answers?

If weak object pronouns could cliticize to V, one would expect them to be able to raise to C with *have*. But this is absolutely ungrammatical:

(36) a. *Has them John?
 b. Has John them?

Likewise, it seems impossible for pronouns to occur above *not*, though here the findings are complicated by the fact that it seems more or less obligatory for *have+not* to appear as the contracted form *haven't*:

(37) a.??I have not the ingredients
 b. I haven't the ingredients
(38) a.??I have not them
 b. I haven't them
 c. *I have them not

(38c) is somewhat worse than (38a), although neither is particularly good, seeming to show that weak pronouns cannot cliticize to the verb in negatives either, though the evidence is not as clear as with questions.

Like object shift in the Scandinavian languages, movement of the weak object pronoun in Belfast imperatives is dependent on raising of the main verb. The object cannot raise unless the main verb does.

(39) a. Tell you her always the truth
 b. Tell her always you the truth
(40) a. *Her always you tell the truth
 b. *You her always tell the truth
(41) a. *Be you her helping when I get back
 b. *Be her you helping when I get back
 c. *Be you helping her when I get back

In the Scandinavian languages, object shift moves the object in front of negation and adverbs. In Belfast English, as we have seen, it moves the object in front of adverbs; as regards negatives, negative imperatives have as we shall see below a special marker *don't* which always occurs sentence-initially, and does not seem to be in the usual NegP position, so that it is not a good diagnostic of the position to which the object moves. Negative imperatives are considered in some detail below.

Object shift is obligatory for weak pronouns, again as in the Scandinavian languages. As we noted above, weak pronouns must precede sentential adverbs.

It is interesting that object shift, which occurs in the Scandinavian languages when the main verb raises out of VP, also comes into operation in English, a language which in general does not have main verb raising, where a dialect has a construction which involves the movement of the verb out of VP. Speakers who allow inversion with all verbs all seem to have object shift; I have been unable to find any speakers of the Unrestricted Inversion dialect who do not have obligatory movement of weak object pronouns. It could be said that English has 'latent' object shift, which in most varieties does not show up because of lack of main verb raising, but surfaces when a dialect contains a construction where main verb raising occurs.

The fact that the verb in the Unrestricted Inversion dialect occurs in front of adverbs and the subject, and appears to trigger object shift, presumably to Spec,Agr_O, seems to be evidence that the verb has raised out of the verb phrase, at least as high as the head position above Agr_O. Before we conclude that this is so, however, we need to exclude a possible alternative explanation.

1.4 Imperatives as *pro*-drop sentences

Imperatives differ from other sentences in both Belfast English and Standard English in that the presence of an overt subject is optional. Thus, imperatives like the following are possible.

(42)   Sit down

(43)   Go away

It might be suggested that imperatives then are a type of *pro*-drop construction, and that the post-verbal subject possible in Belfast English is similar to that found in many *pro*-drop languages, where the subject may occur post-verbally, apparently adjoined to VP, as in the following examples from Italian.

(44)   *pro* mangia le   mele Gianni
        pro eats   the apple Gianni
        'Gianni eats the apple'

(45)   *pro* ha telefonato Gianni
        pro has telephoned Gianni
        'Gianni has telephoned'

It would not be surprising to find that in some variety of English, post-verbal subjects were permitted in the imperative structure, which exceptionally allows null subjects, whereas in other varieties post-verbal subjects were not permitted. *Pro*-drop languages also appear to differ among themselves in this way, with many, such as Italian (Rizzi 1982, 1986b), allowing post-verbal subjects, but some others, such as Brazilian Portuguese, lacking these (Chao 1980). A plausible analysis could be provided by arguing that some characteristic of imperatives (perhaps a strong Agr, necessarily marked as second person singular) allowed them to be *pro*-drop, and that while Belfast English belonged to the group of *pro*-drop languages which permits post-verbal subjects, Standard English belonged to the group which does not.

Unfortunately, however, this analysis does not appear to be the correct one, for positions available for subjects in Belfast English imperatives differ from those available to post-verbal DPs in *pro*-drop languages. Thus in Belfast English imperatives the VP-final position, in which these post-verbal DPs characteristically occur in *pro*-drop languages, is not generally available. Although an inverted subject can occur VP-finally if there are no other constituents in VP, it cannot follow an object or other constituent in the VP. Of course, a vocative can occur after the VP, as in Standard English, but a true subject cannot; thus *you* can occur after the object of the verb only if there is an intonation break between the verb and *you*, showing that it is a vocative rather than a true subject.

(46) a. Eat your dinner, you
 b. *Eat your dinner you
 c. Eat you your dinner

It may be objected that the presence of an obligatory intonation break is difficult to perceive, and therefore the argument is not conclusive. However, there is a clearer difference between post-verbal DPs in the *pro*-drop languages and those in Belfast English imperatives, which shows that they cannot be *pro*-drop type structures.

In *pro*-drop languages, the subject may appear in a variety of positions within the VP — a fact often attributed to restructuring at PF (see, for example, Burzio 1981; Bouchard 1983); in particular, the subject can occur between the direct object and a prepositional phrase. However, this subject position is not available in Belfast English.

(47) Scrivera   una lunga lettra Gianni a Paolo
 will write a   long letter Gianni to Paolo

(48) a. Write you a long letter to Paolo
 b. *Write a long letter you to Paolo

(49) a. Write everybody a long letter to Paolo
 b. *Write a long letter everybody to Paolo

The only case where the subject can occur after the object is where the object is a weak pronoun, when we find verb–object–subject order.

(50) a. Do it you now
 b. Do you it now

This ordering cannot simply be a consequence of low-level reordering of elements within VP, putting weak pronouns first. The order found is not necessarily weak pronouns followed by other DPs; thus both orders in (50) are possible, with the stressed pronoun *you* in (b) preceding the weak object pronoun, and indeed even a non-pronominal subject can also precede a weak pronoun.

(51) Take everybody them home

Moreover, note that, if the possibility of low-level reordering within VP existed in general in English, we would expect examples like the following to be grammatical.

(52) *The teacher gave it the pupils
  (='The teacher gave the pupils it')

but such reordering is impossible in most varieties, and certainly does not occur in Belfast English.

Thus, the post-verbal subject in Belfast imperatives does not seem to be similar to the post-verbal subjects found in *pro*-drop languages, and an explanation for post-verbal subjects in Belfast imperatives in terms of *pro*-drop does not seem to be correct.

It seems then that we can conclude that the verb has moved out of VP, and the subject has either remained *in situ*, or raised to a node lower than that to which the verb has moved (for example, the verb could be in C and the subject in Spec,Agr$_S$ (as in English questions), or the verb might be in Agr$_S$ and the subject in Spec,TP (as proposed by Bobaljik & Jonas 1992 for Irish) or the verb could be in some sort of Mood projection and the subject in a lower specifier. Let us now consider where the verb has moved to.

1.5 Negation in imperatives

A key indicator of verb and subject position is generally taken to be the position of these elements in relation to negatives. However as we noted above, this is complicated in relation to imperatives because they do not use the normal negative marker *not*, but rather have an invariant sentence-initial negative marker *don't*. This marker precedes the subject, which is then followed by the main verb. It is ungrammatical to have inversion after *don't*, unless that inversion is with an unaccusative or passive verb. In other words, verbs cannot raise above the subject where *don't* is present; apparent cases of inversion only arise where the subject is *in situ* after the verb.

(53) a. Don't you touch that
  b. *Don't touch you that
(54) a. Don't you go away
  b. Don't go you away
(55) a. Don't everybody run home
  b. Don't run everybody home

This does not appear to be the familiar *do* of *do*-support; in Belfast English, as in Standard English, only the form *don't* is available in negative imperatives, and the full form *do not* does not occur. This contrasts with the situation in other negatives, where *don't* and *do not* are both available:

(56) a. They don't like coffee
  b. They do not like coffee

In questions, where, as in imperatives, *don't* occurs sentence-initially, it is also possible to have a negative form with *do* sentence-initially in C, and *not* left lower in the sentence in NEG. But this possibility is not available in imperatives which have overt subjects, either in Standard English or in Belfast English.

(57) a. Don't you like coffee?
   b. Do you not like coffee?
(58) a. Don't you read that
   b. *Do you not read that
   c. *Do not you read that

Note also that emphatic *do*, although it can occur in subjectless imperatives, never appears in overt-subject imperatives.

(59) a. *Do you eat your dinner
   b. *Do you read that book soon

Thus it appears that what we have here may not be a combination of *not* and *do*-support, but rather, as proposed by Beukema & Coopmans (1989) and Zhang (1991), an invariant negative imperative marker, *don't*.

Note that *don't* always precedes the subject; in a negative imperative, the subject cannot precede *don't*:

(60) a. Don't you touch that
   b. *You don't touch that

Although in Belfast English the subject can as we have seen remain in VP, in Standard English, where the facts of negative imperatives are the same in relation to the behaviour of *don't*, the subject seems to be uniformly in Spec,Agr$_S$P; *don't* must therefore be in a higher node, presumably C.

There is evidence that the inverted verb in Belfast English occupies the same position as *don't* from the fact that inversion is incompatible with *don't*; negative imperatives cannot have inversion, unless they are unaccusative or passive and the apparent inversion does not involve verb movement but rather lack of subject raising.

(61) a. *Don't throw you that stone
   b. Don't you throw that stone
(62) a. Don't stand you up
   b. Don't you stand up

Verb movement to C is of course generally excluded where there is another element in C. For example in the Verb second languages, such as German, the verb cannot move to C where the complementizer position is filled, for example by a complementizer. If *don't* is in C, then the movement of an imperative verb to C will be blocked, thus accounting for the incompatibility of verb raising in imperatives with the presence of *don't*.

There is also evidence that the inverted verb in the Unrestricted Inversion dialect is in C, from the interaction of imperative inversion with the NEG criterion (Rizzi 1991), that is, the requirement that where certain negative elements are in Spec,CP, C must be filled by a verb.

In Standard English overt-subject imperatives cannot co-occur with those sentence-initial negative elements which are subject to the NEG criterion.

(63) *Under no circumstances you go there again

(64) *On no account you let that book out of your sight

Note that in non-imperatives such expressions trigger obligatory inversion, with *do*-support as required.

(65) Under no circumstances do they go there

(66) On no account do they let that book out of their sight

Do-support is however impossible in imperatives.

(67) *Under no circumstances do you go there

(68) *On no account do you let that book out of your sight

These are of course grammatical if they are not imperatives; to be sure that they are ungrammatical as imperatives, we need to look at cases where the verb in imperatives and indicatives differs.

(69) SE* Under no circumstances do everybody go there

(70) SE* On no account do anybody let that book out of their sight

Moreover, *have, be* and auxiliaries cannot raise, even when an element is required in C because of the presence of an inversion-triggering element in Spec,CP. This suggests that in Standard English there is some element in C already which blocks the raising of verbs into C, but which, because it is not overt, is insufficient to satisfy the requirement that an element appear in C.

(71) SE* Under no circumstances be you impertinent

(72) SE* On no account have you another day off

1.6 The imperative verb *away*

There exists in Belfast English a verb[1] which can only be used in imperatives, and that is *away*; it is possible only in the Unrestricted Inversion dialect.

(73) Away you and get an ice-cream

(74) Away you to your bed

This verb has approximately the same meaning as *go*. It cannot occur as a verb unless it is imperative.

(75) *They away to work early in the mornings

(76) *We away to France for our holidays

Unlike other verbs, with which inversion is optional, where this verb occurs with an overt subject it obligatorily precedes the subject.

(77) a. Away you on
     b. *You away on

(78) a. Away youse to your beds
     b. *Youse away to your beds

(79) a. Away you kids and play outside
     b. *You children away and play outside

Unlike other verbs which do not inflect (such as *come, go*, preceding a verb: see Jaeggli & Hyams 1993), *away* does not occur in other contexts which do not have overt inflection.

(80) *She asked them to away on

(81) *I told the children to away to their beds

(82) *I away home after work

Compare:

(83) She asked them to come see her

(84) I told the children to go ask him

(85) I go see my tutor every week

Thus it is not simply the case that the verb *away* occurs in uninflected contexts; rather, it is entirely restricted to occurring in imperatives.

Away cannot occur with a negative, suggesting that this verb obligatorily raises for checking to some 'imperative' position, and that this raising is blocked by the presence of the negative imperative marker *don't* in that position.

(86) *Don't away you to bed

(87) *Don't away everybody to school

There are two possible explanations for this blocking; either the presence of negation blocks raising of the verb, as in English negatives, but there is no *do*-support available to rescue the structure; or the place into which the imperative moves is the same node in which the negation is located. We consider this issue in more detail later.

1.7 Verb position in the Unrestricted Inversion dialect: conclusion

It is clear from the facts discussed above that the verb is moving out of the verb phrase. Note, on the other hand, that the subject does not appear to have to move obligatorily to Spec,Agr$_S$P; it may move to the position immediately after the verb, but this is optional; it can also stay *in situ*, so that it can follow a raised weak pronoun object, and can occur after the main verb rather than the auxiliary in an unaccusative or passive:

(88) Give me you that book

(89) Be picked you for the team

We will consider the subject-*in-situ* option in more detail below, when we look at the Restricted Inversion dialect, where the facts are clearer, since it is only in unaccusatives and passives that the subject can occur post-verbally in that dialect; for the present let us consider the position to which the verb moves.

The verb moves to a position which precedes that of moved weak object pronouns. If movement is triggered by a checking requirement, as envisaged in Chomsky (1993a), then the only position an object is likely to move to is Spec,Agr$_O$P, the position in which it checks case. The verb, then, must move to a position in front of this. Possible candidates are C, Agr$_s$, Tense, or another node such as the Mood/Modality node proposed by den Dikken (1992) among others.

1.7.1 Imperative positions in the history of English

At certain stages in the history of English, imperatives have patterned with questions in having inversion of the I-to-C type; thus Pintzuk (1991) points out that imperatives pattern with questions in Old English, in that pronouns, which generally appear before the finite verb, appear following the verb in negatives and questions; she uses this to argue that, in imperatives and questions, the verb is in C.

(90) beo ðu on ofeste
 be you in haste
 'Be quick' (*Beowulf* 386)

(91) hwi sciole we oþres mannes niman
 why should we another man's take
 'Why should we take those of another man?' (ÆLS 24.188)

And in the King James Bible, there is inversion in imperatives, for example:

(92) Be ye not proud

A possible analysis of the Unrestricted dialect imperatives might be that Belfast English has retained the possibility of verb movement to C in imperatives which was available in earlier stages of the standard language. There are some apparent problems with this analysis that we need to consider, however. First, note that in general in English, most verbs cannot raise out of VP; where a verb is required in a higher position, *do*-support is needed. Raising is restricted to auxiliaries and the verbs *be* and *have*:

(93) *Went he away?

(94) Did he go away?

(95) Are they happy?

(96) Have they any books?

Verb raising in Belfast English imperatives, however, applies to all verbs, not only *be* and *have*, and *do*-support does not occur with any verbs.

A further problem arises in relation to negation. Whereas in the example from the King James Bible quoted above, the verb does indeed precede the negative, this is not possible in Belfast English:

(97) a. *Be you not proud
 b. *Be not you proud

(98) a. *Go you not there
 b. *Go not you there

Rather as we noted above, there is an invariant sentence-initial negative marker in imperatives, *don't*, which does not appear to occur in the normal negative position. We can see this from the fact that even *be* and *have*, which can normally raise over negation, nevertheless still occur after *don't* in imperatives.

(99) a. *Be not you silly
b. *Be don't you silly
c. Don't you be silly

Don't, then, appears to be a marker which occurs above the normal negative position; it is also in complementary distribution with verb raising, suggesting that it is in the same position to which verbs raise in imperatives. The question then is what this position is. It is above Agr_O and negation, and can hold a feature which is exclusive to imperatives, since it is only in imperatives that the verb raises out of the verb phrase.

It seems unlikely that this is Tense (since imperatives are not marked for tense) nor Agr, since they are unmarked for agreement. This leaves C. We noted above that if the imperative is in C, this can explain why in Belfast English, inverted imperatives containing 'Neg criterion' adverbials are grammatical; these negative elements require to be followed by a filled C, and this requirement appears to be met by the movement of the imperative verb in Belfast English.

(100) a. *On no account you sit down
b. On no account sit you down

It has been suggested, from studies on other languages, that C contains an illocutionary force marker in sentences such as imperatives (see, for example, Rivero & Terzi 1994). It seems that this marker is overt in its negative form, *don't*, but not in its affirmative form, and that in Belfast English it is strong, triggering raising of the verb to C, whereas in Standard English it is weak, so that raising does not occur in the overt syntax.

One problem that we noted, if this analysis is correct, is why main verbs can raise here, but not in questions, where only *be* and *have* raise, other verbs requiring *do*-support. One would expect that if main verbs cannot raise to C in questions, they should equally be unable to raise in imperatives; it would be expected that as *do*-support is required in questions with verbs other than *have* and *be*, it would also be required in imperatives. But we have noted that *do*-support is impossible in imperatives. A possible reason for the lack of *do*-support is that *do* is inserted under Tense, and Tense may not be instantiated in imperatives. We will see in the following section, on the Restricted Inversion dialect, that the lack of a subject raising requirement in Belfast English imperatives also points to the non-instantiation of Tense in imperatives, so that there is no strong NP-feature forcing the subject to raise. As to why the verb raises in imperatives, but not for example in statements, it must be the case that the V-feature of C is strong in imperatives but weak in other types of structure. This makes imperatives exceptional in Belfast English, because they have a marker in C which is strong, whereas other morphemes which occur in C are weak; we can see why therefore the structure is vulnerable in terms of change; it is exceptional in the language, and in acquisition terms, is likely only to be acquired if there is overwhelming evidence in its favour. We return to this issue later.

The Unrestricted Inversion dialect, then, involves verb raising out of the VP of a type restricted to imperatives, and therefore marked. This dialect is as we noted earlier disappearing, being used mainly by older speakers. Middle-aged speakers, in fact in general those of about age 20 or above, are usually speakers of the Restricted Inversion dialect, where verb–subject order is restricted to a subset of verbs. We now turn to look at the structure of that dialect.

2 The Restricted Inversion dialect

In the Restricted Inversion dialect, inversion is not available with all verbs. In this variety

(101)   Go you away

is grammatical but

(102)   *Eat you those vegetables

with a transitive verb is not. The only verbs which permit post-verbal subjects in this variety are motion verbs which are telic (that is, whose meaning includes an end-point for the action), or are part of a verb phrase which is telic.

(103)   Arrive you on time

(104)   Go you home

Note that a verb which is not telic when used alone, and therefore does not permit a post-verbal subject, may acquire telicity through the addition of other elements to the verb phrase, such as an indication of destination; it may then have a post-verbal subject:

(105)   *Run you

(106)   *Run you around the room

(107)   Run you away

(108)   Run you home

(109)   Run you into the classroom

It is telicity which determines unaccusativity in some languages, for example Dutch (see van Hout et al. 1993; Van Valin 1990; Zaenen 1993), and this suggests that the class of verbs which takes imperative inversion in the restricted inversion dialect is the unaccusative class (on unaccusativity in general, see Burzio 1986; Levin & Rappaport Hovav 1992, 1995; Rappaport Hovav & Levin 1992).

Note that it is precisely those verb phrases which allow imperative inversion that also allow inversion of the following type, generally considered to be a characteristic of unaccusatives, showing that there are cases in Standard English also where the verb in unaccusatives may remain in the

VP. These 'locative inversion' constructions also have the appearance of verb second structures, with an element other than the subject in sentence-initial position followed by the verb, and the subject appearing post-verbally. But the fact that they only occur with unaccusative verbs suggests that here, too, we have a case, not of V2, but of an unaccusative with the subject *in situ* in VP.

(110)   Out of the hole ran a mouse
(111)   *Around the house ran a mouse
(112)   Run youse out of the door
(113)   *Run youse around the house
(114)   Into the room walked three students
(115)   *In the room walked three students
(116)   Walk you into the room
(117)   *Walk you in the room

In the Restricted Inversion dialect, 'inversion' is also possible in passive imperatives

(118)   Be picked you for the team
(119)   Be elected you president

But the corresponding actives cannot have inversion

(120)   a.   *Pick you Bill for the team
        b.   *Elect youse Jill president

Incidentally, note that similar facts apply in the other inversion structures mentioned above. Here, the subject can occur post-verbally in passives also, confirming the suggestion that here also we have a case of the subject remaining *in situ*.

(121)   a.   In the garden were found three coins
        b.   Out of the door were pushed two cats

We have seen that in the Restricted Inversion dialect of Belfast English, the only structures where the verb can precede the subject are those where the subject is, according to most analyses, assumed to be generated in post-verbal position, that is, in unaccusatives and passives. There is thus no movement involved; the subject and the verb remain *in situ*.[2]

Thus, the underlying structure of imperatives like

(122)   Go you to class

would be

(123)   — go you to class

and of

(124)   Be picked you for the team

would be

(125)   — be picked you for the team

Nothing moves in the structure, so that the apparent inversion does not in fact involve movement.

That the verb does not move out of the verb phrase in imperatives in the Restricted variety can be seen from the fact that the subject always occurs directly following the verb; the verb clearly does not move over adverbs.

(126)   a.   *Go always you home on time
         b.   Always go you home on time

That the subject remains *in situ* can be seen from the position of the subject in imperatives containing an auxiliary; it is always after the main verb, rather than after the auxiliary. Affirmative imperatives with auxiliaries are somewhat marginal in English in general; but for speakers of the Restricted Inversion dialect, sentences like (127a) and (128a) are much better than (127b) and (128b), which are wholly ungrammatical.

(127)   a.   Be going you out of the door when he arrives
         b.   *Be you going out of the door when he arrives
(128)   a.   Have been picked you for the team before the end of term
         b.   *Have you been picked for the team before the end of term

Negative imperatives in this the Restricted Inversion dialect are formed, as in all the dialects, with a sentence-initial *don't*, and they may be inverted, with the verb preceding the subject, only where the verb is unaccusative or passive.

(129)   Don't go you on
(130)   Don't stand you up

Under the Minimalist Programme the way in which languages may differ from one another is in whether movement occurs before or after Spell-Out. It is therefore not surprising to find a variety where the internal argument DP in unaccusatives is not raised into subject position before Spell-Out, although of course the question arises as to why this is a possibility specifically in imperatives.

According to the Minimalist Programme, whether or not the subject raises in the overt syntax is determined by the strength or weakness of the NP-features of the node to which raising takes place. I argue in Henry (1995) that Belfast English differs from Standard English in that the NP feature of Agr_S can be weak in Belfast English; raising as far as Spec,Agr_S is not always required. This is reflected in a construction known as 'singular concord', in which subject–verb agreement does not occur, the verb appearing in a default form:

(131)   The eggs is cracked
(132)   Yousuns was late

But I argue that the NP-feature of Tense is strong, so that the subject is forced to move out of the VP into Spec,Tense. It seems plausible that in imperatives, which have no overt Tense marking, the Tense node is not instantiated, so that there is nothing to force the subject to raise where Agr$_S$ has weak NP features. A further argument for this is that it is impossible to have *do* as an auxiliary in overt-subject imperatives, and Henry (1995) argues that *do* is inserted under Tense.

(133)   a.   *Do you come in
           b.   *Do come you in

Note, incidentally, that there is nothing to assign case to the subject in imperatives such as

(134)   Sit you down

(135)   Run you home

providing an argument for an approach along Minimalist lines, where case can be checked at any stage during the derivation, including LF and against the traditional Case Filter approach where a DP had to be in a case position or part of a case-marked chain by S-structure.

Thus, the Restricted Inversion dialect appears to have lost the possibility of verb raising; otherwise, it is identical to the Unrestricted Inversion dialect; for we noted above that the possibility of not raising the subject exists in the Unrestricted Inversion dialect also. This was shown by the fact that the subject could occur after the main verb in imperatives containing an auxiliary, only where the verb was unaccusative or passive.

(136)   Be going you out of the door when they arrive

(137)   Be elected you president before the end of the year

Where the verb is not of this type, i.e. where the subject does not originate post-verbally, the subject must occur after the auxiliary rather than after the main verb:

(138)   *Be eating you your dinner when I get back

(139)   Be you eating your dinner when I get back

Similarly, we noted that in negative imperatives, where verb raising could not occur because of the presence of *don't*, the subject could still occur after the verb, again only if the verb was unaccusative or passive.

(140)   Don't go you away

(141)   Don't be picked you for Saturday's team

Compare:

(142)   *Don't touch you that machine

(143)   Don't you touch that machine

Therefore, it seems that the Unrestricted Inversion dialect allows non-raised subjects also; the difference between it and the newer, Restricted Inversion dialect is that in the former, verb movement to C is also possible. The change between the Unrestricted Inversion dialect, and the Restricted Inversion one, is, then, the loss of the possibility of moving the verb to C: in other words, the imperative morpheme in C has been recategorized as weak, so that the dialect has C as consistently weak, rather than requiring a special statement about the status of the imperative morpheme.

3 The no-inversion dialect

We noted that the youngest speakers, mainly under-20s, in the majority do not use inverted imperatives. Neither verb raising to C, nor subject-*in-situ* in imperatives, is possible. Imperatives are thus as in Standard English, with overt subjects necessarily preverbal (for an analysis of imperatives in Standard English, see Beukema & Coopmans 1989).

(144)   You sit down

(145)   *Sit you down

(146)   You read that

(147)   *Read you that

These speakers do not allow inversion in imperatives with any type of verbs, even unaccusatives. They appear to have lost both the possibility of verb raising in imperatives, and the possibility of leaving the subject *in situ* in the verb phrase. These, generally younger, speakers also do not have the possibility of non-agreement between subject and verb, which, as argued in Henry (1995), is another structure where the verb does not raise to Agr_S though, as these structures have, unlike imperatives, got Tense, the subject is required to move out of VP as far as Spec,Tense.

(148)   *The eggs is cracked

(149)   *The papers is useful

It is important to note that included in this group of speakers are many who have retained other non-standard features in their dialect, such as inversion in embedded questions and non-standard irregular past tense verbs.

(150)   They asked me was I going to the meeting

It is thus not the case that they are generally shifting to Standard English.

4 The change in progress from Unrestricted Inversion dialect, to Restricted Inversion dialect, to uninverted imperatives

We have seen that there are three possible grammars in relation to imperatives. There is a dialect in which the verb can raise to C in imperatives, the Unrestricted Inversion dialect, now largely found in older speakers. There is a variety in which the verb does not raise, but the subject may remain *in situ* in VP in imperatives, the Restricted Inversion dialect, found mainly in middle-aged and younger adult speakers. And there is a dialect in which imperatives, as in Standard English, do not show inversion — found most frequently in children and teenagers.

The question arises as to why and how Belfast English is changing: why there is a movement from the Unrestricted Inversion dialect, which has verb movement to C in imperatives, to the Restricted Inversion dialect which allows a much more restricted range of inverted structures, to a variety which like Standard English does not have post-verbal subjects in imperatives.

It might be thought that the last part of the shift — to a dialect without inversion — is simply a shift from the use of Belfast English toward the use of Standard English. This might indeed be regarded as the motivation if we observed that the change took place after the first language acquisition stage, and we observed speakers shifting their usage toward Standard English. Although this undoubtedly happens in some cases, there are two problems with this as an explanation for the shift. First, one would expect to see other aspects of the dialect disappearing together with imperative inversion, whereas in fact many aspects of it, from inversion in embedded questions to the use of different forms of past tense verbs from those found in Standard English, are very robust and show none of the signs of disappearing that imperative inversion does. At the very least, we would need to explain why this feature, but not other features, of the dialect is particularly susceptible to standardization. Second, we have observed a radical shift in the language acquisition process, with children of inverted-imperative users adopting a grammar which does not permit inversion; in their input to the acquisition process, these children have heard inverted imperatives, and even if their parents, attempting to be 'more standard' in their speech, have reduced the number of inversions, the children will have had input which contained inversions; we need to explain why, even at the earliest stages of acquisition when presumably sociolinguistic choices were not involved, they abandoned the possibility of inversion and adopted grammars which did not permit it.

Rather what seems to have happened is that non-agreement between subject and verb, as in sentences like

(151)   The books is interesting

is disappearing; we noted above that it is absent from the grammar of no-inversion speakers. Exploring why this structure is disappearing would require another chapter, but the important point for present purposes is that it means that an analysis involving the subject not being required to raise to Spec,Agr$_S$ is not available to these learners; the possible analysis of inverted imperatives as involving subject-*in-situ* then is no longer possible; the only possibility is to analyse such imperatives as involving verb movement, and this, although they undoubtedly hear some inverted imperatives, learners do not seem to do.

As regards the change from the Unrestricted Inversion dialect to the Restricted one, there are two reasons why the former would seem to be vulnerable to change through the process of language acquisition. First, because negative imperatives have a negative marker in C rather than in NegP, the position of the verb in relation to negatives, arguably an important trigger for the realization by the learner that the verb has moved out of VP, is not available. Secondly, although the possibility of leaving the subject *in situ* can be seen to relate to the general optionality of movement to Spec,Agr$_S$P in Belfast English, the availability of verb raising is restricted to imperatives, thus essentially construction-specific; it involves a statement about the strength of the V-feature of a particular morpheme in C, the imperative morpheme, rather than about C in general. Although it is clear from Belfast English imperatives that grammars must be able to include statements about the strength or weakness of individual functional elements which may occupy a node, as well as general statements about that node, such statements are presumably avoided by the learner on simplicity grounds unless there is overwhelming evidence in their favour in the input data.

Envisage how a child, endowed with an innately specified universal grammar, acquires Belfast English imperatives. The child has set the parameters affecting the position of the subject and verb in the general case, that is, that the NP feature of Tense is strong (forcing subject raising), but the V-feature of Tense is weak, so that the verb generally remains within VP. The child then realizes that inverted imperatives do not fit into the current grammar. If the data on these is too frequent to ignore, there appear to be only a small number of possible ways for the child to change its grammar to accommodate them. Either the subject does not raise (thus the NP-feature of some element must be weak in imperatives) or the verb does raise (thus the V-feature of some element is strong in imperatives). There is a very restricted choice of possible grammars.

Now, if acquisition of a different grammar from that of the speakers who provide the input to language acquisition is a significant element in language change, we would expect to be able to observe this in progress in Belfast; and it is particularly noteworthy that children learning Belfast English, and whose parents are users of inverted imperatives, often have grammars which do not admit inversion, and judge it ungrammatical. It is well known that parents address a significant number of imperatives to their children, so that, even though inversion is optional, the input to the language faculty on which learning was based must have included many inverted imperatives. Nevertheless, many children have established grammars which do not permit inversion; not only do the children not use inversion themselves, they reject imperative sentences in grammaticality judgment tasks where they are asked to give a puppet a sweet if it says a sentence correctly, but not do so if it says it incorrectly. Although these children have undoubtedly heard many inverted imperatives, they do not reward the puppet for inverted imperatives. We have tested children from ages 3;6 to as old as 9, to allow for the fact that inversion may be a characteristic which is acquired late, but have found them in general to reject inverted imperatives at all age ranges, with the exception of two children of Unrestricted Inversion dialect-speaking parents who accepted those structures which would be grammatical in the Restricted Inversion dialect. It appears that here, the evidence of inversion was too strong to ignore, and the children have therefore adopted a grammar which permits it, but have done so in a way which has not required a morpheme-particular statement about the strength of a functional category to be included. We have studied a number of families where the grandmother speaks the Unrestricted Inversion dialect, her daughter the dialect with Restricted Inversion and the grandchildren a dialect without inversion.

It is noteworthy that the range of possible grammars is highly constrained: there are only three possibilities, a grammar allowing verb raising to C, the Unrestricted Inversion dialect; one permitting the subject to remain *in situ* in VP, the Restricted Inversion dialect; and one with obligatory subject raising as in Standard English. We have obtained grammaticality judgments from over 200 native speakers, and there appear to be only these three possible grammars. If speakers were hypothesizing rules, rather than selecting from a small number of possible grammars made available by UG, one would expect to find a wider range of possibilities; for example, learners who had input from both Restricted Inversion dialect speakers and Unrestricted Inversion dialect speakers might hypothesize that inversion was possible in any sentence where the verb has no overt object, having observed that the majority of inversion was happening with such verbs; such a conclusion on the part of a learner is likely because inversion occurs with verbs without surface objects in both the Restricted Inversion dialect and the unRestricted Inversion dialect, but with verbs which have objects only in the Restricted Inversion dialect; such a hypothesis would cover a large proportion of the data. Similarly, although in most Unrestricted Inversion dialect imperatives the subject follows the lexical verb, there is not a possible grammar in which the subject always follows the lexical verb, even when *don't* or an auxiliary is present. Again, such a grammar would fit most of the data, but would not accord with UG which offers no way of deriving the order auxiliary–lexical verb–subject–object, as in (152).

(152)   *Be doing you your homework when I get back

Thus, it seems that language learners do not work out rules, but rather check the possibilities offered by UG against the data. They do not have to adopt a grammar which covers all the input data, but rather consider the limited range of possible grammars made available by UG, and select one which can accommodate the majority of the data in the input. They also preferentially select the simplest possible grammar; a grammar where the V feature of C is uniformly weak is preferred over one where C is usually weak but a specific element which can appear in C is strong, and the learner will select the former unless there is very strong counterevidence. Thus the learner can develop a grammar without inversion, despite receiving input containing examples of inverted imperatives. Language learning appears to be more strongly driven by UG than by the need to cover all the data; thus children can adopt grammars different from their parents, and be major contributors to language change.

Note that if we could not study individual grammars, through obtaining intuitions from a variety of speakers, as in this case, but rather had to work from data recorded from a variety of speakers, we would have a misleading picture of the progress of the change. As we have seen, this change is progressing by means of a radical shift in grammars. But a study of a selection of examples at various time periods would have given the impression of a gradual shift, with the use of inverted imperatives gradually declining with certain verbs, but remaining with others (unaccusatives), and gradually declining with those also. However, as we have seen, as an indicator of the mechanism of the change, this would be misleading. Individual grammars are categorically one of three types, and change is radical, apparently driven by the acquisition process, rather than gradually moving through various verb types. It seems important, therefore, to look at change in progress in order to better understand the mechanisms by which change takes place.

Notes

1. I have termed *away* a verb because it occurs in the same position as raised verbs in imperatives; clearly, since we are concerned with imperatives, which show no inflection, we cannot test whether it is a verb by considering whether it takes verb inflections. It is of course possible that it is in fact a particle which takes on verb-like status in certain imperatives.
2. If this approach is correct, it suggests that the correct analysis of unaccusatives is the classic one, as proposed for example in Burzio (1986), where the subject originates in object position in the underlying structure and moves to the subject position. Some recent approaches, such as Jackendoff (1990), have suggested an account for unaccusatives in terms of 'linking rules', which link lexical conceptual structure to syntax by placing the elements in their correct syntactic positions; under such an account, there is no point in the syntax at which the surface subject occurs post-verbally.

11 Verb movement in Old and Middle English: dialect variation and language contact

Anthony Kroch and Ann Taylor

1 Introduction*

Our goal in this chapter is to show that the northern and southern dialects[1] of Middle English (ME) differ significantly in their verb-movement syntax. In particular, we will give evidence that these dialects exemplify a recently discovered typological distinction within the Germanic language family in the landing sites of verb movement. Several studies have indicated that the Verb second (V2) constraint characteristic of the Germanic languages involves movement to either of two different positions, depending on the language investigated. In the better-known languages (German, Dutch and Mainland Scandinavian), verb second word order results from movement of the tensed verb to the Comp (C^0) position and concomitant movement of some maximal projection to the specifier of CP. In other Germanic languages (Yiddish and Icelandic), however, V2 word order can reflect movement of the tensed verb to a lower position. In studies using the phrase structure of Chomsky (1986a), that position is I (I^0) (Diesing 1990; Santorini 1992; Pintzuk 1991). Under current assumptions, where the I projection has been decomposed into a varying number of functional projections with simpler feature content, the verb in this second type of language seems to move to the highest projection below C^0. As there is no consensus on the label or precise character of this projection, we will distinguish the two types of languages terminologically as 'CP-V2' versus 'IP-V2' languages, with the understanding that 'IP' here stands for the highest projection below C^0, whatever that may be.[2] In section 7, we will give reason to believe that a split-I analysis is, in fact, useful in understanding the character of ME V2; but for most of this chapter we will, for the sake of simplicity, assume a unitary I^0.

The difference in the position to which the verb moves in different languages leads to subtle but clearly observable differences in the shape and distribution of verb second clauses. Most strikingly, while all V2 languages exhibit verb second word order in main clauses, the two subtypes differ in the availability of this word order in subordinate clauses. The CP-V2 languages allow verb second order only in those embedded clauses that in some way have the structure of matrix clauses, either because the complementizer position is empty or because there is an additional complementizer position embedded below the one that introduces the subordinate clause (the so-called 'CP-recursion' structure discussed in de Haan & Weerman 1986 and Iatridou & Kroch 1992). As the cited authors show, instances of these exceptional subordinate clauses are largely confined to the complements of bridge verbs. The IP-V2 languages, on the other hand, show V2 word order in a broad range of subordinate clauses (Diesing 1990; Santorini 1989, 1992; Rögnvaldsson & Thráinsson 1990). Pintzuk (1991, 1993) has recently shown that the verb in Old English (OE) V2 clauses surfaces in the I^0 position; and despite the empirical difficulties pointed out by van Kemenade (this volume), we will support her conclusion. We will further see that the southern dialect of ME preserves the V2 syntax of OE, despite having become, unlike OE, overwhelmingly I-medial and VO in basic word order (see also van Kemenade 1987). In striking contrast to the southern dialect, however, the northern dialect of ME appears to have developed the verb-movement syntax of a standard CP-V2 language and hence to be similar in its syntax to the modern Mainland Scandinavian languages. In the following pages, after a brief discussion of the historical context of dialect differentiation between North and South in OE and ME, we will lay out the complex V2 syntax of OE. With this background, we will proceed to describe the syntax of V2 in the southern and northern dialects of ME respectively, and will show that V2 clauses in the two dialects differ in the landing site of the verb. Given the strong and well-known linguistic influence of Scandinavian on northern ME, we are immediately led to ask whether the CP-V2 character of northern ME could reflect contact with Scandinavian. We give evidence in support of this possibility and suggest what the nature of the contact effect might have been.

2 The sociolinguistic background

Although we are here not primarily concerned with the historical and sociolinguistic dynamics that established the ME dialects, the sociolinguistic history of population contact and diffusion which underlie them is a matter of considerable interest, and it sheds light on why the dialect difference we have uncovered should exist. Specifically, we will see that the northern dialect of English most likely became a CP-V2 language under the extensive contact it had with medieval Scandinavian, contact that resulted from the Danish and Norwegian population influx into the North of England during the late OE period. In the course of its history, English has been more heavily influenced by Scandinavian than by any other language. The only comparable influence was the effect of French and Latin on the literary and learned vocabulary, but these languages influenced English grammar hardly at all. The strength of Scandinavian influence resulted from the large numbers of Norwegians and Danes who settled in England in the three centuries before the Norman Conquest (Stenton 1967; Geipel 1971). The Viking seafarers that harassed the British Isles from the ninth to the eleventh centuries came at first to plunder but eventually stayed permanently. For long periods in the ninth and tenth centuries, the Danes or Norwegians ruled extensive kingdoms in England, and place name evidence indicates that the population of several shires was predominantly Scandinavian (Darby 1936; Ekwall 1936; Geipel 1971). Since the first settlers were soldiers of the Danish armies that plundered the English coastline, there must have been a great deal of intermarriage and intimate language mixture; but there were also substantial numbers of immigrants who came later, after areas of foreign control were established. Among these were substantial numbers of women as well as men (Stenton 1967: 513). In the Northwest of England, the major focus of Norwegian settlement, the settler-invaders came from already established Norse settlements in Ireland and may often have come as families. Moreover, in that region the density of Anglo-Saxon settlement was low and the newcomers necessarily formed a majority of the population in many places (Ekwall 1936). The linguistic effect of this combination of population movement and population mixture was extensive, comparable in some ways to the pidginization/creolization phenomena of more recent centuries, though not as extreme (see, however, Thomason & Kaufman 1988 for a more conservative assessment).

It is well known that many originally Scandinavian vocabulary items were borrowed into northern English; for example, Scandinavian *egg* for OE (and general West Germanic) *ey*, Scandinavian *sister* for OE *swuster*, and so forth. Most significantly for our purposes, several of the borrowings from Scandinavian were of closed-class items which functioned mainly as morphosyntactic signals of grammatical relations. For example, the third-person plural pronoun *they* was borrowed into northern English from Scandinavian and spread over time into other dialects (Morse-Gagné 1992, 1993, and the references cited there). Similarly, the anaphoric noun *same* is Scandinavian in origin. Other grammatical forms remained restricted to the North and never became general. The Middle Scots demonstrative system, for instance, contains an important Scandinavian element (Morse-Gagné 1993). Also, northern texts often show *till* for *to* as a preposition and *at* as a complementizer introducing both tensed clauses and infinitives (McIntosh et al. 1986). These features are clearly borrowed from Scandinavian, and so may be the use of an empty complementizer to introduce relative clauses and object complement clauses (Jespersen 1938). Another important effect of Scandinavian contact on northern English, which will play an important role in our discussion (see section 7), was to reduce the number of distinct person/number agreement endings on the finite verb.

Regarding the grammar of V2, the situation is quite complex. Unfortunately, we have no direct evidence regarding the syntax of the Scandinavian languages of the contact period. However, the extensive grammatical influence of Scandinavian on northern English indicates that the V2 grammar of the dialect could also have been affected by contact; and there is certainly no other apparent reason for the grammar of V2 in the North to differ from that in the South. The main difficulty with this hypothesis is that it is likely that Old Norse was an IP-V2 language, since Modern Icelandic is of that type and is very close in its syntax to that of Old Norse in the period for which we have records (from the twelfth century onward). If so, the influence of Scandinavian in producing the CP-V2 system of the North could only have been indirect. We will give evidence of just such an indirect effect; but to do so we must first develop an analysis of the V2 phenomenon in OE, out of which the northern system evolved. We now turn to this matter, which is a difficult one and will require extensive discussion.

3 The V2 syntax of Old English

OE is a West Germanic language with a syntax similar to that of Modern Germanand Dutch. In several ways, however, its word order exhibits more complex variation than do the modern West Germanic languages. For instance, it freely allows postposition of complements and adjuncts, both nominal and prepositional, to the right of the uninflected, VP-final verb.[3] This postposition leads to superficially free word order in texts, which misled some traditional scholars (though not all) into thinking that OE was a 'free word order' language. Recent studies have demonstrated, however, that the apparent freedom of order of the verb in OE with respect to its complements or adjuncts results almost entirely from the greater freedom of rightward extraposition in that language relative to its modern West Germanic cousins (van Kemenade 1987; Pintzuk & Kroch 1989). In addition, and of more immediate relevance to the present discussion, there is work by van Kemenade, Pintzuk and others on the V2 pattern in OE; and they have shown that it too is highly patterned and rule governed (van Kemenade 1987; Pintzuk 1991, 1993). Here too, the superficial behaviour of sentences is highly variable, leading earlier scholars to say that V2 was only a tendency, not a rule, in OE; but the cited studies have substantially reduced the amount of variability that must be postulated.

Pintzuk (1991) and Haeberli & Haegeman (1995) do demonstrate, however, that OE texts manifest competition between two underlying phrase structures for clauses, one I-final and the other I-medial.[4] Both main and subordinate clauses exhibit this variation, though main clauses are more often I-medial and subordinate clauses more often I-final. Examples of I-final and I-medial sentences from both main and subordinate clauses are given in (1) and (2) respectively. See Pintzuk's discussions (1991, 1993) for detailed analysis of these cases:

(1) a. ... ðeah   hit ær   upahæfen wære   (CP 34.6)
         although it before up-raised was
    b. Se manfulla gast þa   martine gehyrsumode   (AELS 31.1050)
         the evil   spirit then Martin obeyed

(2) a. ... þæt he ahof upp þa   earcan   (GC(C) 42.6)
       that he lifted up   the chest
    b. þa sundor-halgan eodun þa   ut   soþlice
       the Pharisees   went   then out certainly   (WSCp, Matt. 12.14)

The relative frequency of these two phrase structures changes over time, with the number of I-medial sentences increasing steadily in both main and subordinate clauses. By the end of the OE period, the language has become entirely I-medial, though the character of the reanalysis which leads to this outcome is obscured by the collapse of OE as a written language in the early twelfth century and the paucity of ME documents in the earliest period (see Lightfoot 1991; Pintzuk 1991, 1993, for further discussion). The existence of I-final main clauses in OE indicates that, at some point before the period documented by texts, its grammar must have been consistently SOV and I-final, a configuration presumably inherited from Proto-Germanic and ultimately from Proto-Indo-European (Kiparsky 1995). V2 word order, as far as one can tell, arose and spread along with I-medial phrase structure; and by the time of the earliest texts, it was dominant in main clauses. In subordinate clauses, the I-medial structure also became increasingly common during the course of the historic OE period. Significantly, only underlyingly I-medial clauses seem to be V2, showing that, unlike in German or Dutch, V2 sentences in OE do not derive from an underlying I-final phrase structure. Instead, I-final phrase structure is a feature of the declining Proto-Germanic grammar, whether it appears in main or subordinate clauses; and it is driven out of use by the competing I-medial *cum* V2 option. Pintzuk argues that the association in OE between I-medial underlying structure and V2, and the corresponding absence of the German/Dutch derivational relationship between I-final and V2 can be explained only if we suppose that OE is an IP-V2 language like Yiddish or Icelandic and not a CP-V2 language such as German or Dutch. We agree that only this perspective permits an adequate explanation of the occurrence of I-final main clauses in a V2 language while also accounting in detail for the word order patterning in the V2 sentences of the language.

The range of superficially distinct word orders in OE V2 sentences is broad and has been difficult to account for in a principled way. Pintzuk's IP-V2 analysis, however, accounts quite simply for the different word orders, without the postulation of numerous special rules or principles. We list here the types of V2 sentences found in OE and explain how the analysis accounts for them. Subsequently, we will propose a modification of the analysis to relate it more closely from a theoretical perspective to standard treatments of Germanic syntax and to improve somewhat its descriptive adequacy.

3.1 Subject-initial sentences

The single most common sentence type in OE is the subject-initial sentence, in which the first constituent is the subject and the second is the tensed verb. The subject is a nominative case noun phrase or pronoun which moves to the specifier of a functional projection in the C/I system, while the tensed verb also moves to the head of a functional projection. Subject-initial matrix clauses are not SVO sentences but just V2 sentences in which the topic happens to be the subject.[5] In the case of embedded clauses, the correct analysis of subject-initial sentences is trickier and will be discussed further in section 4.

3.2 Sentences with non-subject topics

The second sentence type consists of those sentences in which the first constituent is a topicalized non-subject, either a non-pronominal NP complement, a prepositional argument or adjunct, or an adverb. In this type, word order depends on whether the subject is a pronoun or a non-pronominal NP. In the latter case, the tensed verb appears immediately after the first constituent—that is, in second position; hence, it is inverted with respect to the subject. Some examples, taken from Pintzuk (1991) and van Kemenade (1987), are listed in (3):

(3)   a. & of heom twam is eall manncynn cumen   (WHom 6.52)
       and of them two is all   mankind   come

    b. þæt hus   hæfdon Romane to   ðæm anum tacne geworht
       that building had   Romane with the   one   feature constructed
                                                                            (Or 59.3)

    c. þær wearþ se cyning Bagsecg ofslægen
       there was   the king   Bagsecg slain
                                                        (Anglo-Saxon Chron., Parker, 871)

When the subject is a pronoun, however, it ordinarily appears before rather than after the tensed verb, yielding superficial verb-third word order. This special behaviour of pronoun subjects is due to their clitic-like character (van Kemenade 1987; Pintzuk 1991) and is not evidence of variability or irregularity in the adherence of OE to the V2 constraint. Here are some examples of the use of pronoun subjects yielding verb-third word order, taken from Pintzuk (1991):

(4)   a. Ælc yfel he mæg don   (WHom 4.62)
       each evil he can do

    b. scortlice ic hæbbe nu   gesæd ymb þa þrie dælas ...   (Or 9.18)
       briefly   I have now spoken about the three parts

    c. æfter his gebede he ahof þæt cild up ...   (AEChom. 2.28)
       after his prayer he lifted the child up

Under Pintzuk's analysis of OE as an IP-V2 language, the word order in (4) reflects movement of the verb to I^0 and movement of a topic to Spec,IP. Clitic pronouns in OE, like pronouns in the other verb-final West Germanic languages, move to the boundary between CP and IP and so should appear sentence-initially. However, because sentence-initial position is not available for clitics (perhaps for reasons of prosodic phonology), Pintzuk proposes a special rule to postpose clitic pronouns to the immediate right of the first constituent. Hence, when the verb moves to I^0, the pronominal subject appears immediately before it, between the topic and the verb. Full NP subjects, as in (3), remain in their underlying position in Spec,VP and are assigned nominative case under government, as has been proposed for the modern IP-V2 languages (see Hulk & van Kemenade 1988, 1993; Santorini 1992). With pronominal objects of verbs and prepositions, as in the examples from Pintzuk in (5) below, the same verb-third effect appears, and for the same reason, since they too generally behave as clitics.

(5)   a.   þin   agen geleafa þe   hæfþ gehæledne   (BlHom 15)
         thine own faith   thee has   healed
    b.   &   seofon ærendracan he him hæfde to asend   (ASC, Parker, 905)
        and seven   messengers he him had   to sent

Example (5b) shows that the verb appears in fourth position when a sentence contains both a subject and an object clitic. In addition to pronouns, certain monosyllabic adverbs (for example, *so*) may also move to this position, suggesting that the clitic behaviour of OE pronouns is a grammaticized form of the leftward scrambling of constituents commonly found in Germanic.

3.3 Sentences with verb movement to C^0

The third V2 sentence type of OE comprises four exceptional cases in which subject pronouns regularly invert with the tensed verb. These are: non-subject *wh*-questions, sentences introduced by *þa* and *þonne*[6] (when they are equivalent to Modern English *then*), sentences with preposed negated or subjunctive verbs, and certain verb-initial sentence types (principally so-called 'Narrative Inversions'). Examples of these four cases are given in (6):

(6)   a.   hwi sceole we oþres   mannes niman?   (AELS 24.188)
         why should we another man's   take
    b.   þa   ge-mette he sceaðan   (AELS 31.151)
         then met   he robbers
    c.   ne mihton hi   nænigne fultum æt   him begitan   (Bede 48.9–10)
         not could   they not-any help   from him get
    d.   hæfdon hi   hiora onfangen ær   Hæsten to Beamfleote come
         had   they them received   before Hæsten to Beamfleote came
                                                                                   (ASC, Parker, 894)

Under Pintzuk's analysis, the exceptionality in (6) arises because in these cases the verb moves further leftward than it does in ordinary declaratives, thereby passing the position of the clitic pronoun subject. Specifically, the verb moves to C^0, perhaps because it must pick up certain morphosyntactic features there. Crucially, the structural position of the verb in *wh*-questions is not the same as in topicalized sentences, in contrast to the situation in CP-V2 languages, where the verb is always found in the higher functional projection. The split between questions and topicalizations helps to explain why, when English lost the V2 constraint, word order in questions was unaffected. Like OE, the other IP-V2 languages also exhibit movement to C^0 in questions and certain other sentence types;[7] but these languages do not show the verb-third effect with pronominal clitics, because they do not have clitic pronouns that move to the CP/IP boundary.

3.4 Sentences with true verb-third order

While most adverbs behave as described above, temporal adverbs functioning as 'scene setters' may fail to trigger subject–verb inversion of either pronoun or full NP subjects. These are cases of adjunction to CP to the left of the specifier position and are true exceptions to the V2 constraint as it is known from the Modern Germanic languages.[8] Here are some examples from the Anglo-Saxon Chronicles:

(7) a. ða   þy ylcan gere onforan winter þa Deniscan þe on
       then the same year before   winter the Deniscan that on
       Meresige sæton tugon hira scipu up on Temese   (ASC, Parker, 895)
       Meresige sat   pulled their ships up on Temese
   b. On þisum geare Willelm cyng geaf Raulfe eorle Willelmes
       in this   year Willelm king gave Raulfe earl Willelme's
       dohtor   Osbearnes sunu   (ASC, Laud 1075)
       daughter Osbearne's son
       'In this year King William gave William FitzOsborn's daughter in marriage to Earl Ralph'
   c. Her   Oswald se eadiga arceb   forlet   þis lif
       in-this-year Oswald the blessed archbishop forsook this life
                                                      (ASC, Laud, 992)

We should note that, even in Modern German, extremely strict in its expression of the V2 constraint, there are sentences with verb-third word order. These are of two types, *if-then* sentences and left-dislocations, as illustrated in (8):

(8) a. Wenn du   kommst, dann amüsieren wir uns
       if   you come   then amuse   we ourselves
   b. Diesen Mann, den kenne ich nicht
       this   man   him know I   not

Significantly, however, verb-third word order in German is limited to cases where the adjoined sentence-initial constituent is a constituent coindexed with the sentence topic. (We assume that such a coindexation relation obtains between the *if* clause and *then* in conditionals.) Examples such as (8) with correlative conjunctions also occur in OE (for example, the þa ... þa construction), but the range of constituents that can adjoin to CP goes beyond these cases to sentences without correlative syntax. There are even rare cases where adverbs other than scene-setting temporals adjoin to CP to generate verb-third word orders. The examples given in (9) are cases from the last OE portion of the Peterborough Chronicle:[9]

(9) a. eac þis land wæs swiðe afylled   mid munecan   (ASC, Laud 1087)
       also this land was very   filled-up with monks
    b. þeahhweðer   his hiredmen   ferdon ut   mid feawe mannan
       nevertheless his household-men went   out with few   men
       of   þam castele   (ASC, Laud 1088)
       from the castle
    c. &   syððan   litlan & litlan his leoht wanode   (ASC, Laud 1107)
       and afterwards little by little his light waned

The possibility of verb-third word order in OE gives additional evidence for Pintzuk's IP-V2 analysis. Though we do not know exactly how to formalize the constraint, the CP-V2 phenomenon in languages like German involves a prohibition against adjunction to CP; for if it did not, there would be no constraint against adverb-initial verb-third sentences. In an IP-V2 language, therefore, we might expect the prohibition against adjunction to apply at the IP level, leaving open the possibility of adjunction to CP. Determining the precise conditions under which such adjunction can occur requires further investigation and is beyond the scope of this chapter, but we will see it again in our ME data.

4 Revising Pintzuk's analysis

While Pintzuk's analysis of OE V2 yields an economical description of many relevant facts of the language, it faces two significant problems. First, it is not clear how to make the analysis consistent with the fact that, CP-recursion environments apart, OE texts do not freely exhibit subordinate clauses with non-subject topics and V2 word order. Van Kemenade (this volume) states that V2 order with non-subjects in first position occurs only in limited types of subordinate clause in the texts, and Pintzuk's observations (personal communication) confirm this finding. Pintzuk's analysis, however, does not predict this limitation. Second, the special clitic movement rule needed by Pintzuk to account for the placement of pronouns between topic and verb in V2 clauses has no counterpart elsewhere among the Germanic languages and does not have clear theoretical justification. In this section, therefore, we will propose a modification of Pintzuk's approach which preserves its essential claim—that OE is an IP-V2 language—while mitigating these two difficulties. Suppose that, while the tensed verb in an OE V2 sentence moves to I^0, the topic moves not to Spec,IP but to Spec,CP. In that case, the clitic pronoun can move straightforwardly to the CP/IP boundary and the correct word order will result, without Pintzuk's special clitic-inversion rule. The result of changing the landing site of the topic is that V2 in OE seems to become a hybrid between the CP-V2 and the IP-V2 types. The tensed verb moves as in an IP-V2 language while the topic moves as in a CP-V2 language. We will see below, however, that the other IP-V2 languages are more like OE than they first appear to be and that the analysis of the IP-V2 phenomenon itself must be changed. Once this change is made, OE again falls together with the other IP-V2 languages.

Clearly, our proposal permits a standard treatment of OE pronouns as Germanic-type clitics, which Pintzuk's account does not;[10] but to make the proposal viable, we must explain why both C^0 and Spec,IP can, and indeed must, remain empty in OE main clauses. If either contained phonetically overt material, OE would not exhibit V2 word order in sentences with non-subject topics. We begin with the question of C^0. We have already seen (section 3.3) that OE reserves the C^0 position for verbs with special morpho-syntactic features, suggesting that ordinary indicative verbs do not belong in that position, at least on the surface. In line with recent proposals regarding economy (Chomsky 1993a, 1995), we can say that the ordinary indicative tensed verb in OE carries only a weak feature driving its movement to C^0 and so moves there only at LF. In questions and the other environments discussed above, on the other hand, the feature driving movement to C^0 will be strong, making movement visible on the surface. In either case, movement to C^0 will occur by LF; and, therefore, the topic will have to be in Spec,CP in order to be properly licensed. Cross-linguistically, topicalized constituents are always the leftmost elements of their clauses; and it seems reasonable to assume that they hold this position because they are the surface 'subjects' of the clause's topmost predication level (Heycock 1994). Given the phrase structure we are using, this requirement implies that topics in matrix clauses must occupy Spec,CP, making our requirement on topics analogous to the *wh*-criterion of Rizzi (1990a). In subordinate clauses with topicalization, this leftmost position seems to vary between Spec,IP and Spec,CP depending on the language, dialect and sentence type involved (see immediately below, also section 6).

We move on now to explaining why Spec,IP is empty, a more difficult question. The simplest treatment would be to say that the features driving movement of the subject to Spec,IP, which are strong in Modern English, are weak in OE. By economy then, this feature assignment would force movement of the subject to occur only at LF, leaving Spec,IP empty on the surface. However, while this solution is adequate for simple sentences like those in (3) above, it fails when more cases are considered. To start with, it predicts that in I-medial subordinate clauses the verb should come first, since Spec,IP will be empty; but the fact is, of course, that OE subordinate clauses are predominantly subject-initial, not verb-first. There is no reason to question the standard line that these subjects are in Spec,IP. A second and extremely important consideration is that, as described by van Kemenade (this volume), OE subordinate clauses do sometimes exhibit V2 word order with a topicalized non-subject outside CP-recursion environments. Such subordinate V2 order occurs in clauses where the nominative subject is absent or is licensed to appear in a position other than Spec,IP, as in passive sentences or in sentences with experiencer dative 'subjects'. In such cases there is often no nominative NP, and agreement on the verb is the default third-person singular. Otherwise, the nominative NP which agrees with the verb remains inside VP, while some other constituent, often but not always an experiencer dative, appears in Spec,IP. These possibilities are illustrated in the following examples from van Kemenade (this volume):

(10) a. þæt eallum folce   sy   gedemed beforan ðe
       that all   people(DAT SG) be(SG) judged before thee
                                                          (Paris Ps. 9.18)
     b. þonne ælce dæge beoð manega   acennede þurh hys
        when each day are(PL) many(NOM PL) given-birth through his
        mihte on woruld   (AEHP.VI. 120)
        power on world

Significantly, it turns out that in Icelandic and Yiddish, both IP-V2 languages,[11] examples of subordinate clause topicalization outside CP-recursion contexts are similarly limited to (or are more acceptable in) contexts where the subject is missing or appears in a VP-internal or a postposed position (Magnússon 1990; Sigurðsson 1991; Thráinsson 1994; Beatrice Santorini, personal communication). The facts thus suggest very strongly that in the IP-V2 type of language, Spec,IP ordinarily hosts a subject and can only be a topic position in sentences where the subject is either absent or licensed to surface elsewhere. This marked use of Spec,IP in subordinate clauses must be made to harmonize with the emptiness of the position in main clauses.

It is difficult under current assumptions to account for the occurrence of topics in Spec,IP (or Spec,Agr$_S$) because that is the locus where Spec–head agreement between the finite verb and the subject is checked. Even if the subject in a certain sentence type does not appear there on the surface, checking theory of a Minimalist sort requires an expletive in Spec,IP, which forms a chain with the subject and is replaced by it at LF. The expletive may be phonetically null, but even so it will prevent a fronted topic from landing in Spec,IP. Thus, the presence of the empty expletive forces us to say that the topic lands in a higher specifier than Spec,IP, somewhere between I^0 (or Agr$_S^0$) and C^0, as in Cardinaletti & Roberts (1991). If we follow this line, however, we will have no simple explanation for the complementarity that van Kemenade has found in subordinate clauses between the appearance of an overt subject in Spec,IP and the possibility of a fronted topic. To avoid this consequence, we propose that the checking mechanism for subject–verb agreement in sentences with empty expletives be changed so as to free up Spec,IP as a landing site for topics. What we have in mind is similar to proposals that have been made many times to the effect that it is the agreement morpheme on the tensed verb rather than an expletive in Spec,IP that serves as the binder of a postposed or VP-internal subject (cf. den

Besten 1985). Such a subject forms a chain not with an empty expletive but directly with the agreement morpheme on the finite verb, with which it is co-indexed. The index on the agreement morpheme can be taken to reflect incorporation of the empty expletive into the feature complex of I^0. Such incorporation satisfies (that is, checks off) the agreement features in I^0 and also the nominative case feature. The chain between agreement and the subject thereby case-licenses the subject, rendering expletive replacement unnecessary. If we assume that incorporation frees up Spec,IP or that it occurs without movement through Spec,IP, topics will be able to move to that position, as desired. The proposed treatment applies in the obvious way to impersonal sentences with empty expletives, where no nominative case noun phrase occurs. In these sentences, there is, of course, no chain; but the empty expletive will check off agreement and nominative case by incorporation. The existence of such sentences (illustrated by the OE and the German examples of (11) below) demonstrates, in any case, that expletive replacement cannot be the general mechanism by which the existence of expletives is reconciled with the Principle of Full Interpretation (Chomsky 1986b) and suggests that we may be better off without the device.[12]

(11) a. ... sua sua be   sumum monnum cueden is
         as   about some men   said   is
                                              (van Kemenade, this volume)
    b. ... daß gelacht wurde
         that laughed was

Our analysis of Spec,IP in subordinate clauses now allows us to understand why the position is empty in main clauses in OE. V2 languages are universally defined by a requirement that topics be in a Spec–head relationship with the finite verb. While much discussed, this striking requirement has never been reduced to anything more fundamental. We assume that OE, as a V2 language, is subject, like the others, to this 'V2 constraint'. However, under our analysis the V2 constraint cannot apply directly to the topic and verb themselves in OE, because these are not in a Spec–head relationship on the surface. The topic is necessarily in Spec,CP because that is the specifier of the highest projection of its clause; and the verb, due to its feature content, raises only as far as I^0. To establish the required relationship, therefore, the topic must move through Spec,IP on its way to Spec,CP, leaving its trace to fulfil the V2 constraint. That traces may serve this function is shown by the following German and Yiddish examples of extraction out of complementizer-less subordinate clauses, where the verb in C^0 is in a Spec–head relationship with the trace of the extracted topic:[13]

(12) das Museum$_i$ hat er gesagt [$_{CP}$ e_i dürfen [$_{IP}$ wir e_i besuchen]]
     the museum has he said   may   we   visit
(13) dvorem-beteylem$_i$ vilst du [$_{CP}$ e_i zol [$_{IP}$ ikh mit dir redn e_i]]?
     simple words   wantyou   shall   I   with you speak

Because Spec,IP is the intermediate landing site for the topic in an OE main clause, it can never contain anything but the trace of the topic and so will always appear empty.

If the topic is to move through Spec,IP, that position must not be needed to establish a Spec–head relationship between the subject and the agreement morpheme. We must assume, therefore, that, as in subordinate clauses in OE, matrix sentences with non-subject topics contain incorporated empty expletives to check off the agreement features of I^0 and to chain-license the subject in a lower position (Spec,VP or, assuming a split I, Spec,TP). Since the licensing of topics in main and subordinate clauses is identical, we are now without a simple syntactic explanation for the greatly reduced range of topicalizations in subordinate as opposed to matrix clauses; but this difference may, indeed, not be a syntactic fact. The difference between main and subordinate clauses seems to reflect discourse-based information-structure considerations. In matrix clauses, topicalization is often highly favoured, or even required, by the discourse context; and in order for the needed topicalized sentences to surface in OE, empty-expletive chains must be used across a wide range of cases. In (non-CP-recursion) subordinate clauses, by contrast, topicalization has very weak discourse motivation and so expletive chains are used only where information-structure considerations favour them—that is, in the classical environments in which subjects prefer not to appear in Spec,IP. The use of the expletive chain then frees up Spec,IP for a non-subject to appear as topic even if the topicalization is only weakly motivated. The correctness of attributing the differences in the range and frequency of main and subordinate clause topicalization to discourse considerations cannot be demonstrated in the current state of our knowledge of discourse structure; but it is consistent with the facts as we know them, including the uncertainty of native speaker judgments on the acceptability of subordinate clause topicalization in living IP-V2 languages like Icelandic and Yiddish. In both of these languages, speakers differ on whether the full range of topicalization is available in subordinate clauses; and text corpora show only cases such as those found in OE, for which the expletive chain analysis is plausible (Eiríkur Rögnvaldsson, personal communication; Beatrice Santorini, personal communication). The variability in judgments and the difference between what is judged acceptable and what actually occurs in connected discourse point to the plausibility of a discourse constraint (and speakers' differential sensitivity to discourse factors in giving judgments) as the source of the main/subordinate difference in the range of topicalization.

To summarize a complex discussion, we have provided in our modified version of Pintzuk's analysis a treatment of OE V2 with the following virtues:

i. It explains how OE can both be a V2 language and exhibit I-final main clauses. Since the landing site for the verb in a V2 sentence is a medial I rather than Comp, as it is in German or Dutch, we do not expect underlyingly I-final clauses to exhibit V2 word order.

ii. The position of OE clitic pronouns, subject and non-subject alike, requires no special treatment. Pronouns simply move to the CP/IP boundary, as in Modern German.
iii. The existence of true verb-third sentences with sentence-initial adverbial adjuncts is accommodated because the V2 constraint is imposed at the IP level instead of at the CP level.
iv. The grammatical and historical relationship between declaratives and questions is straightforwardly expressed. Questions belong to the class of sentence types in which features in C^0 force movement to that position, while the C^0 of ordinary declaratives lacks the appropriate feature content to force movement. Historically, Modern English simply preserves the OE distinction between questions and declaratives; but while it has kept V-to-C movement in the former, it has lost V2 in the latter.
v. The possibility of V2 word order in non-CP-recursion subordinate clauses is accommodated, and its limitation to contexts where the subject does not appear in Spec,IP is accounted for.

Although the proposed analysis leaves us with an important open question, namely how exactly discourse effects produce the different distribution of main and subordinate clause topicalization, we can conclude that Pintzuk's claim that, in OE, V2 sentences involve finite verb movement to I^0 rather than to C^0 is defensible.[14]

5 The V2 syntax of the ME dialects

The V2 pattern we have described for OE is largely maintained in the earliest ME of the West Midlands and southern dialects, except for the complete loss of the I-final phrase structure option. This loss occurs in all dialects but is irrelevant to the I-medial *cum* V2 pattern, which persists into the fourteenth century. From the beginning, however, there are a certain number of exceptions to expected word order, and these grow in number with time. Except in Kentish, a particularly archaic southern dialect, we find by the mid fourteenth century that the V2 constraint is clearly being lost. The analysis of the exceptions and how they increase is a matter of considerable interest, but it lies beyond the scope of this chapter (see Kroch, Taylor & Ringe 1995 for further discussion). We believe that the loss of V2 is the result of competition between the grammars of the northern and southern dialects. This competition, however, can only be studied once we have a reasonable picture of the competing systems, which is our goal in the present discussion. The texts we investigate in this chapter are as close to pure representations of single grammatical systems as the surviving ME data affords.

In the North and in the Northeast Midlands, the areas of greatest Scandinavian settlement and linguistic influence, the history of the V2 pattern is different from the history in the South. Unfortunately, there are no manuscripts of northern prose before 1400, which makes direct comparison with southern dialects impossible; but evidence from poetry indicates a pattern unlike the OE one. A recent investigation of the *Ormulum* (Morse-Gagné 1992), a very early ME poem written in Lincolnshire, an area of dense Scandinavian population, reveals that pronoun and full NP subjects are more alike than different in their behaviour. Both exhibit nearly categorical subject–verb inversion in sentences with NP objects in topic position. In sentences with adverbs in topic position, inversion is categorical with full NP subjects and variable with pronominal subjects. While we do not understand this variability, it is sufficient for present purposes to note that it does not follow the pattern described above for OE, but is rather more random. We believe that the variability of inversion with pronouns in the *Ormulum* and other northern texts reflects contact of the OE V2 system with a Scandinavian-influenced one and hope to show this in future work. For the present, however, we have fortunately found material, to be described below, in which this variability is minimized and which allows us relatively direct access to a single, coherent northern grammar.

5.1 The southern dialects

As we have remarked, the early southern texts of ME exhibit the same basic patterning of the V2 constraint as is found in OE. Table 1 shows this clearly. It combines data on positive declarative sentences from seven Midlands texts of the early to mid thirteenth century: the Trinity Homilies, Lambeth Homilies, *Sawles Warde*, *Hali Meiðhad*, *Vices and Virtues*, St. Katherine, and Ancrene Riwle. The sample consists of a total of 3,064 matrix clauses, an exhaustive sample of the text excerpts in the Penn-Helsinki Parsed Corpus of ME (1994) (PPCME), the source of all our ME data.[15] The contributions of the individual texts in this early southern group range from 230 to 689 clauses. They have been grouped together to increase the size and reliability of the figures in the table, since there is no evidence of any difference in the V2 syntax of these texts.

Table 1. *V2 in seven early Midlands texts*

preposed element	NP subjects			pronoun subjects		
	number inverted	number uninverted	% inverted	number inverted	number uninverted	% inverted
NP complement	50	4	93	4	84	05
PP complement	12	4	75	0	11	00
Adj. complement	20	1	95	7	14	33
þa/then	37	2	95	26	10	72
now	12	1	92	8	22	27
PP adjunct	56	19	75	2	99	02
any other adverb	79	59	57	1	181	01

We see above, with exceptions as noted, the expected OE pattern. Preposed complements generally trigger inversion of subject and verb with full NP subjects but almost never do so with pronoun subjects. The temporal adverbs *þa* and *then* trigger inversion with both NP and pronoun subjects, though not as regularly with pronoun subjects as in OE, an indication that these adverbs are losing their special status. The adverb *now* is included in the table because in OE it sometimes behaves like *þa* and sometimes like other adverbs; and as in OE, it here behaves variably.

If we look at a sample of approximately 200 clauses from a text of the Kentish dialect, the 'Ayenbite of Inwit', we see the pattern repeated:

Table 2. *V2 in the 'Ayenbite of Inwit' (Kentish)*

preposed element	NP subjects			pronoun subjects		
	number inverted	number uninverted	% inverted	number inverted	number uninverted	% inverted
NP complement	14	3	82	1	11	08
PP complement	2	0	100	0	1	00
Adj. complement	5	0	100	0	1	00
then (no *þa* in text)	4	12	25	7	5	58
now	1	0	100	7	7	50
PP adjunct	5	9	36	1	30	03
any other adverb	19	15	56	5	52	10

The data in Table 2 is interesting because the 'Ayenbite' text is from a holograph manuscript of the mid fourteenth century, at least 100 years later than the Southwest Midlands texts. By this time, the language of most of England was well on its way to losing the V2 constraint; but Kentish, an isolated dialect that eventually died out, still preserved the OE pattern of V2 nearly intact. The only difference between the Kentish data and the earlier texts is a further erosion in the exceptional status of *then* and *now* and a generally freer attachment of adjuncts to CP, reflected in the lower rates of inversion of full NP subjects after PP adjuncts and adverbs.

5.2 The northern dialect

Because of the gap in the surviving record mentioned earlier, the syntax of the northern dialect is not easy to investigate. Nevertheless, there is sufficient evidence to support our claim that northern ME was a CP-V2 language. Well before 1400, the date of the first prose texts from the North, northern texts (for example, the writings of Richard Rolle) as well as texts from the Midlands (for example, the works of John Wycliffe) show less than half of appropriate sentences inverting subject and verb in order to obey the V2 constraint (van Kemenade 1987). The mixture of V2 and non-V2 sentences in these texts indicates competition between V2 and non-V2 grammars (see the references cited in note 4), and, therefore, these texts cannot be treated as grammatically uniform.[16]

In surveying for descriptive purposes the syntax of all the text samples in the PPCME, however, we unexpectedly found that one northern text, the *Northern Prose Rule of St Benet* (Kock 1902), exhibits word orders in V2 contexts that are not variable in the way that other late texts are. The Benet text is the first surviving prose document in the northern dialect and it comes from central west Yorkshire, hence either within or directly bordering the major area of Norwegian settlement in the North (McIntosh et al. 1986; Wells 1916). Until the rise of the cloth industry in the late fourteenth century, the area was thinly populated and isolated, due in part to the famous devastation of the region wrought by William the Conqueror. Hence, like Kent in the South, it is a plausible relic area in which a dialect once spoken more widely might have survived longer than elsewhere. Indeed, the linguistic evidence is clear. In sentences with non-subject topics, the text exhibits almost categorical subject–verb inversion, in accordance with the V2 constraint. Crucially, this inversion occurs whether the subject is a full NP or a pronoun and also independently of the grammatical function or lexical identity of the topic. In other words, the complex conditioning found in OE and in the Early ME of the South is absent. The sharp distinction between the two dialects of ME is clearly revealed in the Table 3.[17]

Table 3. *V2 in the 'Northern Prose Rule of Saint Benet'*

preposed element	NP subjects			pronoun subjects		
	number inverted	number uninverted	% inverted	number inverted	number uninverted	% inverted
NP complement	7	0	100	58	3	95
PP complement	18	0	100	10	0	100
Adj. complement	1	0	100	4	2	67
then (no *þa* in text)	15	0	100	28	1	97
now	—	—	—	2	0	100
PP adjunct	42	5	89	73	7	91
any other adverb	25	1	96	51	5	91

As is evident, there are two major differences between the frequencies of V2 in Benet and in the Midlands and southern texts. First, pronominal subjects, instead of failing to invert in most environments, invert nearly as frequently as full NP subjects do. Second, there is no tendency for preposed adverbs and PPs to adjoin to CP; that is, not to trigger inversion. These differences show that the V2 pattern of the northern dialect differs sharply from that of the southern dialect and give us an indication as to how it does. One possible analysis that we have discussed (Kroch 1989a; Morse-Gagné 1992) is that the grammar of pronouns has changed in the North. Instead of being clitics of the OE sort, they might have become like the pronouns of Modern English , behaving syntactically more or less like full NPs. The plausibility of such a change occurring in the North is supported by the fact that it was into the northern dialect that the Scandinavian pronoun 'they', a demonstrative in origin, was first borrowed (Morse-Gagné 1992). That borrowing could well have altered the syntactic character of the entire pronominal system. As we will see, however, the syntax of pronouns in Benet does not appear to differ from that of pronouns in the southern texts, apart from those environments where the grammar of V2 is at issue. Pronouns do eventually change character in ME, losing their tendency to move leftward, but this change is common to North and South and is not responsible for the differences in V2 patterning between the dialects.

The most evident defect of an appeal to pronominal syntax as the source of the differences in the V2 patterns of Benet and the southern texts is that it accounts for only one of the two major differences between those texts that are apparent from Table 3. As noted, in addition to what happens in sentences with pronominal subjects, the table shows nearly categorical inversion of full NP subjects in sentences introduced by adverbs or adjunct PPs. The character of pronouns is irrelevant to this distribution; hence, even if the pronouns in the North had changed character and so had come to invert in V2 environments, some additional difference with the South would have to be invoked to account fully for the V2 pattern of the Benet text. The obvious candidate is the difference between verb movement to I^0 and to C^0. If the language of Benet were CP-V2, then, like German or modern Mainland Scandinavian, it should exhibit inversion nearly categorically when preposed adverbial and prepositional phrase adjuncts were attached at the CP level, where they regularly fail to trigger inversion in OE or southern ME. Of course, as in German, there would be cases of verb-third word order as well; but, in general, we would expect elements that adjoin to CP in OE to move to Spec,CP in Benet and to trigger inversion from that position. Under this analysis, categorical inversion with pronoun subjects would have to occur even if the pronouns did not lose their clitic status, because the verb would always move beyond the CP/IP boundary to C^0, and so appear to the left of any subject, NP or pronoun. Thus, a single difference between the grammars of Benet and the southern texts would account for both of the differences revealed by our table.

Another problem with reducing the differences between northern and southern V2 to a difference in the clitic status of pronouns is that there is positive evidence for treating subject pronouns in Benet as clitics of the OE sort. Consider the following examples:

(14)   þat   *erin* hauis, herkins wat þe haly spirt sais in haly writ
        whoever ears has   harkens what the holy spirit says in Holy Writ

        (Benet 2.4)

(15) a. Bot yef it *sua* bi-tide, þat any falle in mis-trouz; þan sal
         but if it so betide that any fall into mistruth then shall
         scho pray gerne   to god   (Benet 19.30)
         she pray earnestly to God

b. Yef yt *sua* may be, alle sal   lie in a hus,   þat ilkain wite of
    if   it   so may be all   shall lie in a house that each   know of
    oþir   (*Benet* 20.18)
    (the) other

Example (14) is an instance of stylistic fronting, a process known from the Scandinavian languages (Maling 1990) and found in all dialects of ME. It is possible only where the subject position is empty (Maling's 'subject gap condition'). The examples in (15) might also be analysed as instances of stylistic fronting (and are not easily amenable to any other analysis), but in these cases there is a preverbal subject present. Such examples, however, are limited to sentences with pronominal subjects; and if the pronouns are analysed as clitics which move leftward out of Spec,IP, then these examples too conform to the subject gap condition. Indeed, just such an analysis has been proposed for entirely parallel cases in Old Swedish (Platzack 1988). The application of Platzack's analysis to northern ME is clearly incompatible with the claim that pronouns in the North have lost their clitic status.

6 Further grammatical comparisons of North and South

6.1 'Doubly filled Comp' sentences

Certain additional pieces of grammatical evidence support the hypothesis that *Benet* and the southern texts differ in the syntactic domain of V2. The first is provided by the presence of 'doubly-filled Comp' sentences of a type also attested in the Modern Germanic languages, as well as in other languages, including Latin and modern dialects of Spanish (Iatridou & Kroch 1992). These are subordinate clauses introduced by an overt complementizer, in which a constituent has been preposed to the immediate left of C^0, as in (16):

(16) a. I sal   yu lere   þe dute of god, *his wille* þat ȝe may do
        I shall you teach the duty of God, his will that ye may do
                                                                        (*Benet* 2.5)
     b. ilkain   sal   take discipline at oþir,   als *hir mastiresse*
        each-one shall take discipline of the-other, as her mistress
        þoz   scho ware   (*Benet* 10.7)
        though she   were
     c. Lauerd, we prai þe   for þi   misericorde þat we mai sua
        Lord   we pray thee for thy mercy   that we may so
        yeme þis reul o mekenes, *In þe felazscap   of þin   angels*
        take this rule of meekness in the fellowship of thine angels
        þat we may be   (*Benet* 11.25)
        that we may be

There are ten examples of this sort in *Benet*, while in the much more extensive Midlands and southern material in our corpus, there are only two possible cases, one of which is doubtful. The *Benet* examples are all cases where the clause in which the topicalization occurs is ungoverned—hence, not a CP-recursion environment. Indeed, the examples look very much like certain cases in Bavarian described by Bayer (1983) and Fanselow (1987).[18] The following examples, quoted by Santorini (1989) in her discussion of these cases, illustrate the Bavarian construction:

(17) a. *Die Franca* daß du kennst glaube ich nicht
the Franca that you know believe I not
'I don't believe that you know Franca'
b. *Die Franca* daß geheiratet hat ist nicht wahrscheinlich
the Franca that married has is not likely
'It's unlikely that Franca has married'

The most straightforward analysis of the *Benet* examples is the one given by Fanselow for Bavarian, under which the italicized constituent has been preposed into the specifier position of the complementizer of its clause.[19] The fact that movement to Spec,CP occurs in non-CP-recursion subordinate clauses with filled complementizers in this text makes it unlikely that Spec,IP could be a subordinate clause topic position in this dialect in the way that it is in OE. We would not expect two topic positions to coexist for a single clause type. Hence the *Benet* dialect must be strictly CP-V2.

Since the *Benet* text is the translation of a Latin original and since Latin allowed doubly filled Comps, we might think that the presence of the construction in *Benet* reflected the literary influence of Latin.[20] If so, its occurrence would tell us little or nothing about the nature of V2 in the indigenous northern language. However, it is unlikely that the construction reflects Latin influence, and for two reasons. First, the conditions on the preposing are not the same in Latin as they are in *Benet*. In Latin, unlike in *Benet* or in Bavarian but just as in certain modern Romance dialects, the preposing may occur in governed subordinate clauses rather than being limited to ungoverned ones. Second, none of the examples in *Benet* is a translation of a Latin doubly filled Comp sentence. Indeed, the *Benet* text is a very free rendering of *St Benedict's Rule*, with much omitted and with considerable commentary, not identified as such, that is absent from both the Latin original and the OE version. As it happens, almost all of our examples come from such sections of commentary and, therefore, are not translations of any material in the originals. None of the examples corresponds to any sentence in the Latin or OE versions that could have served as a model for its syntax.[21]

6.2 A comparative idiom

Another source of evidence on the difference between the V2 syntax of the North and South lies in the syntax of a common but marked construction of English, the 'more ... more' construction, a modern example of which is given in (18):

(18)   The more (that) he drinks, the drunker he gets

This construction also occurs in *Benet*, as the following example shows:

(19)   for þe   mare þat sho est heȝid ouir toþir   þe mare aȝh
       for the more that she is   raised over the-other the more ought
       sho at halde þe cumandement of þe reule   (Benet 44.4)
       she to hold   the commandment of the rule

Tellingly, the first clause of the construction is introduced by a 'that' complementizer and does not exhibit inversion of the subject and verb, while the second clause has no introductory complementizer and does exhibit inversion. Given the close parallelism between the two clauses in this construction, it seems reasonable to suppose that the phrase 'the more' occurs in the same position in both. If so, that position must be Spec,CP, given that the phrase occurs to the left of a complementizer in the first clause. It is instructive to compare the construction in (19) to a corresponding construction found in the southern texts,[22] illustrated by the example in (20):

(20)   for eauer se   ȝe nu   her mearred me mare se mi
       for ever   so (= as) ye now here damage me more so my
       crune schal beon brihttre ba   & fehere   (St. Juliene 101.19)
       crown shall be   brighter both and fairer

Here the comparative particle *so* that introduces the parallel clauses does not trigger inversion of subject and verb in either. If we assume that *so* is in C^0 in both cases, we correctly expect no inversion after it. Compare, moreover, the sentence in (21):

(21)   & eauer se þu   mare hauest se þe   schal mare trukien
       and ever so thou more has   so to-thee shall more fail
                                                  (Hali Meiðhad 131.11)

In this sentence, in which a dative pronoun has moved to Spec,IP, the subject and verb are inverted within IP inside the second clause. This case, where the dative acts as a subject of predication, is of just the type which in OE exhibits IP-V2 structure.

7 The effect of Scandinavian contact on V2 in the North

It is well known that northern ME had a reduced set of agreement endings on its verbs (Brunner 1938; Mossé 1968; Roberts 1993a). Indeed, in the present tense in all persons and numbers but the first singular, which had -*e*, the ending was -(*e*)*s*; and in Scotland even the first person singular was occasionally -*s* (Brunner 1938). This system represents a simplification compared to the OE and southern ME pattern, which had -*e*, -(*e*)*s*(*t*), -(*e*)*th* in the three persons of the singular and -(*a*)*th* (-(*e*)*n* in the Midlands) in all persons of the plural. Since the Old Norse system of endings was richer even than OE, it has not been clear where the northern simplification came from. However, if we follow modern sociolinguistic approaches to the relationship between language change and second-language acquisition (see Appel & Muysken 1987), we are led to suggest that the simplification is the result of imperfect second-language learning of English by the Norse invaders of the ninth to eleventh centuries. The appearance of Norse-origin grammatical markers in the northern dialect (see section 2 above) is clear evidence that second-language learners with an imperfect command of English grammar were a sufficiently large fraction of the population in the North to pass on their mixed language to succeeding generations, what is traditionally known as a substratum effect. One feature of imperfect learning, as is well known, is the imperfect acquisition of inflectional endings; and the northern ME endings seem to have originated in this way. The simple replacement of the marked anterior fricative /θ/ by the unmarked anterior fricative /s/ is nearly all that is needed to transform the OE paradigm into the northern ME one, and there is evidence of confusion between the two sounds in ninth-century Northumbrian (that is, the northern dialect of OE). Scribes, in addition to writing /s/ for /θ/, occasionally wrote a hypercorrect /θ/ for /s/ in verbal endings (Brunner 1965).[23] We propose, therefore, that imperfect learning in a language contact situation was responsible for this morphological change (see Kroch, Taylor & Ringe 1995 for further discussion).

Now we have the basis for understanding the origin of the northern V2 grammar. According to the most straightforward interpretation of the idea that V-to-I movement depends on rich agreement, the northern system of endings does not make enough distinctions to support movement (Platzack & Holmberg 1989; Roberts 1993a; Rohrbacher 1994a); if there is no V-to-I movement, it is clear why the northern dialect must be a CP-V2 language. With the verb not appearing in I^0, IP could not be the locus where the V2 constraint (see section 4 above) was satisfied, since no Spec–head relationship between topic and verb could be established in overt syntax. Therefore, the reduction of the verbal agreement system would force the reanalysis of an IP-V2 grammar into a CP-V2 one.[24] There is, however, one substantial obstacle to the scenario we have sketched. As Roberts (1993a) points out, sentences like (22) indicate that, contrary to our hypothesis, northern ME did exhibit V-to-I movement:

(22) þe barnis   þat ere yunge þat vnderstandis noht what
      the children that are young that understand   not what
      paine   fallis til cursing   (Benet 23.101)
      punishment falls to cursing

Since the negation in (22) is in a relative clause (not a domain for CP-recursion), the order of tensed verb and *not* must be due to movement of the verb to a lower functional head than C^0; that is, to I^0 under the phrase structure we have been assuming. Not only is the word order in (22) possible, it is obligatory for all verbs, as one would expect if it reflected V-to-I movement. Further effects of this movement are exemplified in a sentence like (23), in which the order of pronoun object and *not* reflect Mainland Scandinavian-type object shift of pronominal objects, which is also obligatory:

(23) rennes fast do wilis ye haue liht þat   þe mirkenes o
     run   fast while ye have light so-that the murkiness of
     ded   our-take þe   noht   (Benet 2.6)
     death overtake thee not

These data make it clear that the northern dialect does not share the apparent lack of verb movement characteristic of modern Mainland Scandinavian, despite its relatively impoverished verbal inflections (see Roberts 1993a for further discussion).

If we accept the conclusion that northern ME had verb movement, we cannot maintain our scenario for the history of the dialect in the simple form outlined above. There is, however, a modified version that can be maintained, provided that we adopt the split-I hypothesis of Pollock (1989). We assume, as is usual, that Agr_S is the highest projection below Comp and that T(ense) is the next highest. Let us further suppose (following a suggestion by Næss cited in Thráinsson 1994) that the modern Mainland Scandinavian languages have verb movement to T, though not to Agr_S. This proposal has the virtue of maintaining a strict relationship between overt morphology and verb movement.[25] Since Scandinavian has overt tense marking in both the present and the past, it has verb movement to T. By the same logic, so does northern ME; and if so, then raising only as far as T could explain why we see movement across negation and object shift. If northern ME *not* is an adverb adjoining to VP, as it certainly was in OE and earliest ME (see Frisch 1994 for detailed discussion), then verb movement to T will produce the attested order of V_{finite} > *not*. Further, if object shift is movement to any functional specifier above VP (see note 26), the order pro_{object} > *not* found in examples like (23) will also be correctly generated. The remaining question is why the order of *not* and tensed verb should be different in northern ME than in modern Mainland Scandinavian, given that we take the verb movement facts to be the same in the two cases. But the answer here is straightforward: northern ME inherited the OE double negative construction '*ne... not*', in which *ne* is the negative head and *not* is a VP-adjoined adverb, as Frisch shows. Hence, we expect to find *not* below and to the right of T. In modern Mainland Scandinavian, on the other hand, there is no counterpart to *ne*, so that the single negative *inte/ikke* must be either a negative head or the specifier of NegP, which is located above T in both English and Scandinavian. Therefore, movement of the verb out of VP to T does not change its relative order with respect to negation.[26]

Using a split IP forces us to reformulate slightly our account of the role of the V2 constraint in the reanalysis in the northern dialect. We have argued that the constraint is met in OE by a surface Spec–head agreement relation between the trace of the fronted topic in Spec,IP and the verb in I^0;

and this relationship requires overt verb movement to I^0. Once I has been split, we must ask again where the V2 constraint will be satisfied. The obvious answer is Agr_S; and if that is the locus of the constraint, our analysis of the northern dialect remains viable, since we claim that the verb in the northern dialect does not move as high as that position. If, however, the constraint could be met at the level of T, our analysis would fail, since we have claimed that the verb in the northern dialect does move to T. Notice, however, that using T as the locus of the constraint implies empty expletive incorporation into T to free up Spec,TP as an intermediate landing site for the topic. But for conceptual reasons such incorporation is not possible. Expletive incorporation must entail the merger of the expletive, a pronominal, with the agreement features of a verbal functional head; and the whole point of the split-I analysis is to put these features in a different functional head from the one that bears tense.

8 Dating the CP-V2 grammar

If, as we have supposed, the difference in V2 syntax between *Benet* and our southern texts is due to contact with Scandinavian in the North, the language of the North must have acquired its properties much earlier than 1400. Indeed, we would expect such a contact effect to date to the tenth century or earlier, the time of the mixing of the Scandinavian and Anglo-Saxon populations. Unfortunately, there are no OE texts from Northumbria, the area of contact at the appropriate time, except for two glosses of the Latin Vulgate Bible. These texts, the Lindisfarne and Rushworth glosses, do, however, turn out to be informative. They consist of interlinear OE glosses added above a previously written Latin text. The Lindisfarne gloss is in Northumbrian dialect spelling and was added to the Latin manuscript around 950 by the priest Aldred, probably in Durham. The Rushworth gloss is in two (contemporary) hands. All of Matthew and up to Mark 2:16, as well as John 18:1–3, are written by a priest named Farman in a spelling which differs little from the West Saxon standard and is probably Mercian, while the rest is written by Owun in the Northumbrian dialect. The Rushworth gloss depends on the Lindisfarne to some extent and dates from the latter half of the same century.

The first interesting fact about these glosses is that they exhibit variability in the verbal agreement endings. Alongside the expected OE endings are found the later northern ME ones (Brunner 1938). In the admittedly fragmentary Northumbrian texts which predate the arrival of the Scandinavians, on the other hand, no such deviations from the expected OE forms are found (Whitelock 1967).[27] These facts point clearly to the the period between the eighth and the tenth centuries as the time of origin of the northern ME endings and thus support the postulation of Scandinavian contact as a causal factor in their development.

As for the dating of the northern V2 grammar itself, the glosses are also helpful. Although we might not expect word-for-word glosses to yield evidence on word order, there was one particular context in which the glossers of the Vulgate had to make word order choices; and in this context we see a pattern that gives evidence for the existence of CP-V2 in the North at an early date. The relevant context is the tensed sentence with a preposed sentence-initial constituent and a pronoun subject. Because Latin is a *pro-drop* language and OE is not, the glossers routinely added subject pronouns in the gloss which were absent in the original. While most added pronouns occur in the canonical position before the verb, there are a significant number of cases where the Latin word order places a constituent in sentence-initial position, with the verb immediately following, thereby suggesting to a Germanic speaker an interpretation of the sentence as a topicalization with V2. In such cases, the northern glossers sometimes wrote the subject pronoun after the verb. By contrast, in the Early West Saxon translation of the gospels, the standard OE pattern with the pronoun in preverbal position always obtains. Below are some examples from Skeat (1881–7) with the relevant verbs indicated in boldface and their pronoun subjects in italics.[28] For comparison we give the corresponding sentences in the Early West Saxon full translation:

(24) Latin: dominum deum tuum adorabis
 Lindisfarne: drihten god ðin **worða** *ðu*
 Rushworth: drihten god ðinne **wearða** *ðu*
 West Saxon: drihten þinne god *ðu* **geead-metst**
 'You will worship the Lord your God' (Luke 4.8)

(25) a. Latin: oculos habentes non uidetis
 Lindisfarne: ego **habbað***gie* ne geseað gie
 Rushworth: ego **habbas** *ge* ne gi-seas ge
 West Saxon: Eagan *ge* **habbað** & ne ge-seoð
 'Having eyes, do you not see?' (Mark 8.18)
 b. Latin: aures habentes non auditis nec recordamini
 Lindisfarne: & earo *gie* **habbað** ne geherað gie ne eft ðohto gie
 Rushworth: earu **habbas** *ge* ne gi-heras ne eft ðohtun ge
 West Saxon: & earan & ne gehyraðne ge ne þencaþ
 'And having ears, do you not hear? And do you not remember?' (Mark 8.18)

The following table summarizes our findings on the inversion of pronouns in the Lindisfarne and Rushworth glosses and compares them to the Early West Saxon translation:

Table 4. *Pronoun subject inversions in the Northumbrian glosses and West Saxon gospels*

	Topic appears in both Northumbrian and West Saxon texts	Topic appears in Northumbrian only
Inversions in Northumbrian	5 out of 58	14 out of 82
Inversions in West Saxon	0 out of 58	—

We see from the table that in 10–20 per cent of the cases where the Latin text can be interpreted as having a preposed topic, the pronoun subject inverts with the verb in the Northumbrian glosses. In contrast, the West Saxon text follows the standard OE pattern, and so inversion of pronoun subjects never occurs following a topic. As the glosses date from late in the period of Scandinavian settlement, it appears that the CP-V2 grammar of the North is old enough to have arisen out of contact with Scandinavian. Of course, an early date for the North's CP-V2 grammar does not guarantee that contact brought it into being. It might, for one thing, actually antedate the arrival of the Scandinavians. Unfortunately, the fragmentary pre-contact Northumbrian texts contain no contexts relevant to the CP/IP-V2 contrast, so this possibility cannot be directly ruled out. Thus, in its present state, the syntactic evidence by itself supports the possibility that contact with Scandinavian was responsible for the northern CP-V2 grammar but is consistent with an earlier date as well. This latter possibility is, however, extremely unlikely in light of the evidence from the verbal endings outlined above. We feel confident, therefore, in claiming, on grounds of dating as well as of grammatical analysis, that the characteristic features of the V2 syntax of northern ME arose out of contact with Scandinavian. More specifically, the trigger for the change was the reduction of the relatively rich OE agreement system to one with almost no person distinctions, due to imperfect learning of OE by the large number of Scandinavian invaders and immigrants of the ninth century and later.

Notes

* An earlier version of this chapter was presented at the International Conference on Historical Linguistics at UCLA in August 1993 and appeared in the University of Pennsylvania *Working Papers in Linguistics*, volume 1. The work reported here was supported by a research grant from the NSF (BNS 89-19701), with supplementary support from the University of Pennsylvania Research Foundation and the Institute for Research in Cognitive Science. We would especially like to thank Donald Ringe for numerous helpful suggestions and for help in the interpretation of various OE and Latin documents. We are also indebted to Robin Clark, Caroline Heycock, Jack Hoeksema, Sabine Iatridou, Ans van Kemenade, Susan Pintzuk, Bernhard Rohrbacher, Beatrice Santorini and an anonymous reviewer for their helpful comments on various aspects of this chapter. We have not in every case been able to do justice to their observations and suggestions, but they have materially improved the work.
1. The dialect divisions of ME are complex and controversial. Divisions based on phonology recognize three to five major dialect areas. In this chapter, however, we will be concerned only to show that there was at least one northern dialect and one southern dialect with the characteristics that we describe. Roughly, the two syntactic dialects at issue were found in the North and in the (North)east Midlands, on the one hand, and the South and (South)west Midlands on the other. Within these areas further distinctions can be made that are beyond the scope of this chapter.
2. Vikner (1990) calls the IP-V2 languages 'generalized V2' languages because the two he considers, Yiddish and Icelandic, are said to exhibit V2 word order in all types of main and subordinate clauses rather than in the more limited set of environments where it is found in German, Dutch and Mainland Scandinavian. This terminology has the advantage of theoretical neutrality; but, as we will see, it is inaccurate. IP-V2 languages do not

allow V2 word order as freely in subordinate clauses as in main clauses (see also van Kemenade, this volume).

3. Our chapter does not take account of recent proposals by Kayne (1994), Zwart (1993), and Roberts (this volume) that treat OV languages as underlyingly VO. If that proposal proves viable, the analyses presented here should be straightforwardly translatable into the new framework.
4. For further discussion of the notion of competition between grammars see Kroch (1991, 1994), Pintzuk (1991), Santorini (1992), Taylor (1990, 1994).
5. See, however, Heycock & Kroch (1994) for a more nuanced analysis of V2 sentences with subjects in topic position.
6. Other narrative sequencing adverbs (for example, *nu* 'now') sometimes behaves like *þa*, and sometimes like ordinary adverbs.
7. This statement is not entirely uncontroversial. See Diesing (1990).
8. Examples similar to those found in OE are apparently found in all older West Germanic dialects. Medieval German (Ebert 1986; Behaghel 1932: 15) appears to have been intermediate between OE and Modern German in its tolerance for this kind of adjunction. Further work on the V2 syntax of the medieval Germanic languages is needed to determine the proper analysis of these cases.
9. The differences between Modern German and the older Germanic languages may be exaggerated by differences in the conventions of the written language at different times. Jack Hoeksema has pointed out to us that the Modern German and Dutch counterparts of (9b) are perfectly acceptable with a pause after the initial adverb:
   (i) a. Nichtsdestotrotz, wir müssen weiter
       b. Desalniettemin   we moeten verder
          nevertheless   we must   further (go)
   Without the comma as an indicator of the pause, V2 order is obligatory in the written language. In medieval texts punctuation was much less regular than now, so the absence of commas in (9) does not mean that there were not obligatory pauses after the sentence-initial adverbs.
10. The account in van Kemenade (1987), which takes OE to be a CP-V2 language, also fails to unify OE clitics with the general Germanic pattern.
11. Though we do not have the space to enter into the matter here, our analysis of the IP-V2 phenomenon has as one of its consequences that main clauses in Icelandic and Yiddish are most likely CP-V2 structures, with IP-V2 limited to non-CP-recursion subordinate clauses.
12. It is worth noting that empty expletive incorporation has as one of its virtues that it provides a mechanism for the agreement relation between finite verbs and nominative objects in Icelandic, a phenomenon not easily treated if all agreement relations are checked in Spec–head configurations.
13. We thank Beatrice Santorini for these examples.
14. Beatrice Santorini points out to us that one interesting feature of our analysis here is that it relates topicalization in Modern English more closely to the OE construction than is usual. In Modern English, where V2 does not obtain, the order topic > subject > verb is the only one allowed, and one might ask what licenses the topic position. Our analysis gives an obvious answer: verb-movement to C^0 at LF, just as in OE. The difference between the two languages is simply that Modern English has lost the V2 requirement, perhaps because it lost expletive incorporation, forcing agreement and case to be checked with an overt subject in Spec,IP. The difference between the two languages proposed here would most plausibly have arisen because Modern English lost empty expletive incorporation in connection with its loss of empty expletives.
15. The Penn-Helsinki Parsed Corpus of ME is a syntactically annotated and somewhat extended version of the prose ME section of the Helsinki Corpus of English Texts originally assembled under the direction of Matti Rissanen at the University of Helsinki (see Kytö 1993). The annotation work was done under the direction of Anthony Kroch

at the University of Pennsylvania with the support of the National Science Foundation (Grant #BNS89-19701) and with supplementary support from the University of Pennsylvania Research Foundation. The annotation scheme was designed by Anthony Kroch and Ann Taylor and implemented by Taylor. The PPCME is available to scholars without fee for educational and research purposes via anonymous ftp from babel.ling.upenn.edu and over the World-Wide Web (http//ling.upenn.edu).
16. The works of Chaucer show a higher rate of inversion in topicalized sentences than other well-known late fourteenth century texts (van Kemenade 1987; Kroch 1989). Chaucer was also as likely to invert a pronominal subject with the tensed verb as a non-pronominal one, unlike other authors. If the argument presented below linking inversion with pronoun subjects to Scandinavian influence is correct, Chaucer's syntax may be of a piece with his East Midlands phonology, since the East Midlands were part of the Danelaw. His language may, therefore, indicate a certain conservative regionalism compared to the developing London standard.
17. The discussion in this section is based on an exhaustive sample of the *Benet* text, which has been entered in its entirety into PPCME.
18. Constructions similar to the one we have found in *Benet* are not hard to find in the Germanic dialects. Thus, in Modern Dutch such sentences are found as exclamatives:
    (i) a. Gelachen dat we hebben!
    laughed that we have
    'How we laughed!'
    b. Een boeken dat ik gelezen heb!
    a books that I read have
    'What a lot of books I have read!'
    The singular article with plural import in (i-b) is characteristic of exclamatives. We thank Jack Hoeksema for drawing our attention to these cases.
19. Santorini gives reasons to modify Fanselow's analysis, but in a way that does not affect our reasoning here.
20. We thank Harm Pinkster for bringing this possibility to our attention.
21. We thank Donald Ringe for checking our examples against the Latin and OE texts in Logeman's (1888) edition of *St Benedict's Rule*.
22. Examples such as (19) are almost non-existent in the southern text samples in our corpus. We have found only three, of which two are from the 'Ayenbite of Inwit' and so are quite late.
23. It might seem odd that Norse speakers should fail to acquire the word-final /θ/ of OE, since their native language contained the sound. In support of our proposal, however, are two facts. First, the distribution of the voiced and voiceless allophones of the phoneme differed in the two languages. Norse had the voiced allophone everywhere but word-initially, while OE had only the voiceless allophone in word-final position (Noreen 1923; Brunner 1965). Thus, speakers of Norse apparently heard final /θ/ as the phonetically similar /s/ because in their language /s/ but not /θ/ could occur in word-final position. Furthermore, /s/ in Norse was always voiceless. Second, verbal endings in OE must have been weakly articulated, hence perceptually unsalient and prone to being misheard by non-native speakers. Evidence for the phonetic weakness of the endings appears in the phonologically unmotivated syncope of the vowel in the endings, though this syncope is characteristic of the southern (West Saxon and Kentish) dialects of OE and occurs only rarely in Mercian and Northumbrian (Brunner 1965). We thank Donald Ringe for guidance through the philological literature on the points made here.
24. From the usage patterns in Orm and Chaucer (see above), it seems that, besides arising in the North, the CP-V2 grammar also took hold to some extent in the East Midlands, although the morphology of verbal endings in Midlands ME was rich enough to support the original OE syntax. Further investigation will be needed to uncover why the CP-V2 grammar appears in the East Midlands. One possibility is that the collapse of agreement in that area, one of extensive Scandinavian settlement at the time of the

25. ninth- and tenth-century Danish invasions, is subsequently reversed, due to contact with and population influx from adjacent dialect areas that maintained the native English morphology. This reversal could easily have happened without reversing the syntactic change from IP-V2 to CP-V2.
25. There is one major problem with saying that finite verbs in Mainland Scandinavian move to T: we would expect on such a proposal to find the verb moving across left-adjoined VP adverbs, but such movement seems never to occur. It is unclear how to interpret this fact, however, because it is hard to show that the languages allow left-adjunction to VP, and without such adjunction we cannot test whether the verb has moved out of VP to T. Evidence exists, in fact, that the Scandinavian languages resist the left-adjunction of adverbs to VP. Thus, in English certain aspectual adverbs, *completely*, *entirely* and so forth, always occur VP-adjoined, either to the left or the right, and can never occur adjoined to higher projections. This is clear from the contrast between (i-a) and (i-b):
(i) a. Mary has completely finished her work
     b.*Mary completely has finished her work
In Swedish, by contrast, the word order corresponding to (i-a) is impossible, while that in (i-b) can occur, though the sentence is less acceptable than one where the adverb is right-adjoined to VP. Here are illustrative examples from Anders Holmberg (personal communication to Bernhard Rohrbacher). The context is a non-CP-recursion subordinate clause to avoid interfering V2 effects on word order:
(ii) a.*Jag beklagar att du har helt   misslyckats i testet
         I am sorry that you have wholly failed   on the test
     b.?Jag beklagar att du helt har misslyckats i testet
         I am sorry that you wholly have failed   on the test
The contrast between English and Swedish is striking. We take it to show that left-adjunction to VP is blocked for some reason in Scandinavian, so that the adverb facts cannot be used to argue against movement to T.
26. If Mainland Scandinavian has verb movement to T and the negative particle is generated in a NegP above T, then we cannot maintain the widely known analysis of object shift as movement to Spec,Agr$_O$. The problem is that movement of the direct object to Spec,Agr$_O$ will always be string vacuous with respect to negation and adverbs adjoined above T. We assume that some other analysis will prove viable, perhaps one based on cliticization (see Bobaljik & Jonas 1993 and the references cited there). The clitic position would have to be higher than T in Scandinavian and lower than T in northern ME. Then when the verb moves to T in Scandinavian it will still be in a position that blocks object shift, while in ME it will have moved far enough to permit the object to move. This difference presumably reflects a general prohibition against overt material between TP and VP that Scandinavian seems to have, of which the prohibition against left-adjunction to VP discussed in note 25 is another manifestation.
27. The texts do, of course, exhibit phonological differences from West Saxon in their person endings, but no morphological differences. See Kroch, Taylor & Ringe (1995) for further discussion.
28. The negated verbs in these examples are not relevant, as they would have moved to C^0 even in the southern dialect. The example from Luke is equivocal because the verb is interpretable as an imperative, though the Latin original has second person future.

12 V2 and embedded topicalization in Old and Middle English

Ans van Kemenade

1 Introduction*

In recent years, considerable debate has arisen as to the proper grammatical representation of the position of the finite verb (Vf) in early English. Van Kemenade (1987) argues that the position of the finite verb in Old English (OE) is asymmetric: in root clauses Vf is preposed to Comp; in non-root clauses it remains in sentence-final position. Pintzuk (1991, 1993) takes issue with this and argues that that the position of Vf is symmetric between root and non-root clauses: movement is always to the position of Infl which is variable. The specifier position of Infl is then a topic position rather than a subject position.

In this chapter, we will examine some of the evidence for the position of the finite verb in OE and early ME, and for the nature of the specifier position of IP. We will come to the conclusion that there is no independent evidence for the topic status of this position. The only instances where it is occupied by a non-nominative element is when the verb heading the VP of the clause is one that assigns no thematic role to a subject. It will be argued that such constructions are in several ways special and cannot be advanced as evidence for the 'topic' status of the position in question. We must therefore conclude that V movement is asymmetric.

The analysis defended for OE provides an interesting perspective on the changes that take place in the course of the Middle English (ME) period. The evidence for the CV2 character is, as of the earliest ME period, even clearer than in OE, in all dialects and texts. The V2 character is in decline as of the middle of the fourteenth century.

This article is organized as follows: in section 2, the theoretical assumptions underlying my analysis are outlined. Section 3 deals with V2 and embedded topicalization in Old English. Section 4 discusses the same phenomena in Middle English, and the changes that take place in the Middle English period.

2 Theoretical assumptions

2.1 Verb second, the issue: CV2 vs IV2

We assume, following Hulk & van Kemenade (1993), a typology of languages in which they are either C-oriented or I-oriented.[1] We take the nature of the position of the finite verb (Vf) to be the diagnostic for C- vs I-orientation. One of the heads C or I is dominant. The starting point is (1) as a general sentence structure, adapted on the basis of Chomsky (1986a) and Sportiche (1988). The result of this section will be that Spec,IP in (1) is not exclusively a position for subjects.[2]

(1)
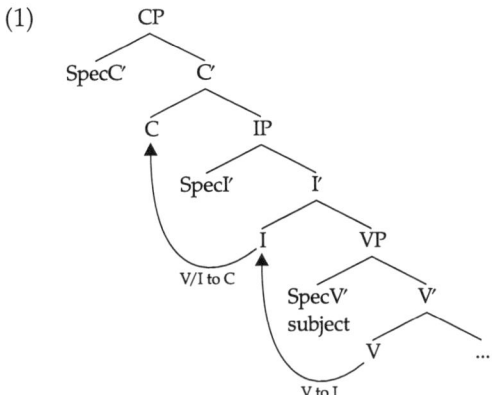

Let us first consider how we view V2 in the classical sense. We assume, following much current work, that V2 is a process that takes place regardless of the basic sentence structure, and fronts Vf to presentential position in all types of root clause; declarative, interrogative, imperative. One of the core characteristics of V2 in this sense is the asymmetry between root and non-root clauses with respect to V-fronting. Fronting of Vf/I to C is found in root clauses only, cf. early work on V2 in den Besten (1983). This is the main reason why V2 is widely analysed as movement of Vf/I to Comp, which is blocked in non-root clauses by a base-generated complementizer, as shown in the German examples in (2). In (2a) and (2b), Vf is fronted from its VP-final base position. (2c) shows that in the presence of a base-generated complementizer *daß*, Vf remains in its VP-final position. (2d) and (2e) show that fronting of Vf is ungrammatical in the presence of a complementizer. Hence, it is assumed that lexical material in the C-position blocks fronting of Vf to that position.

(2) a. Er hat ihm gestern gesehen
      he has him yesterday seen
   b. Gestern hat er ihm gesehen
      yesterday has he him seen
   c. ... daß er ihm gestern gesehen habe
        that he him yesterday seen has

d *... daß gestern   hat er ihm gesehen
         that yesterday has he him seen
 e *... daß hat er ihm gestern   gesehen
         that has he him yesterday seen
      '... he saw him yesterday'

The V2 phenomenon is not entirely restricted to main clauses. V2 in embedded clauses is essentially of two types. The first type is represented by languages like Dutch, German, Frisian Continental Scandinavian, Old French. These allow embedded V2 in the complements of bridge verbs, which are verbs that allow complementizer deletion (see, e.g., de Haan & Weerman 1986; Vikner 1990). This is illustrated with (3) from Danish:

(3) a. Vi ved   (at) denne bog   har Bo ikke læst
       we know that this   book has Bo not   read
    b. Vi ved   (at) Bo har ikke denne bog læst
       we know that Bo has not   this   book read
    c. Vi beklag *(at) Bo har ikke læst denne bog
       we regret   that Bo has not read this   book

I follow current work in analysing this type of embedded V2 as CP-recursion. In terms of the structure (1), this type of V2 language is analysed as follows: V2 in this type is movement of Vf to I, and subsequent movement of V/I to C in root clauses.[3] V/I-to-C movement is presumably triggered by the requirement that C be lexical. In root clauses this is satisfied by moving V/I; in non-root clauses by a base-generated complementizer. The requirement that C be lexical is found in various guises in recent proposals for the analysis of V2. We shall be referring to V2 languages of the sort discussed so far as *CV2 languages*. Crucial for this notion is a *root/non-root asymmetry* for V2. In this language type, Spec,IP is the canonical position for the nominative subject.

The second type of embedded V2 is represented by languages like Yiddish and Icelandic, as analysed in Santorini (1989), Diesing (1990), Rögnvaldsson & Thráinsson (1990). In these languages, embedded V2 occurs more or less freely and is compatible with a base-generated complementizer. This is illustrated in (4) with some examples for Icelandic from Rögnvaldsson & Thráinsson (1990):

(4) a. Jón efast um að   á morgun fari María snemma á fætur
       John doubts that tomorrow get Mary early   up
       'John doubts that Mary will get up early tomorrow'
    b. Jón harmað   þessa bók   skuli ég hafa lesið
       John regrets that this   book shall I   have read
       'John regrets that I have read this book'

Given the compatibility of lexical complementizers and V2 in such languages, there is *no root/non-root asymmetry* with respect to V-fronting. We shall be referring to this type of language as an *IV2 language*.[4] In such languages,

XP–Vf–subject sequences occur more or less freely in both root and non-root contexts. However, these are to be analysed as instances of V to I. The asymmetry between root and non-root contexts can only emerge in a CV2 language. An important consequence of this is that Spec,IP in these languages is a topic position, an Ā-position; it is not the canonical position for the nominative subject.

Non-V2 languages (ModE and ModFr) are characterized by movement of Vf to I (or vice versa, as appears to be the case in ModE), and no movement to C, except under restricted circumstances such as in Modern English interrogative contexts and Modern French subject–clitic inversion and complex-inversion constructions. Rizzi (1990a) calls them *residual V2* as opposed to *full V2*. Strikingly, V/I-to-C movement in the residual V2 contexts exhibits the same root/non-root asymmetry as verb movement in CV2 languages.

The essential difference between CV2 (CP) languages on the one hand and non-V2 and IV2 (IP) languages on the other then is that in CV2 languages C is always lexically realized, whereas this is not the case in IP languages. We consider this to be a reflection of the fact that in CP languages C has a number of crucial head properties that in IP languages are characteristic of I.

Under this view, the distinction C- vs I-oriented languages as drawn above reflects a deeper distinction. In CV2 languages, C is in some sense a more prominent head than I, whereas in non-V2 languages the reverse seems to be the case. We will henceforth call this C-orientation (CV2 languages) and I-orientation (non-V2 languages, and IV2 languages, i.e. languages that have no root/non-root asymmetry for V2) (cf. also Hulk & van Kemenade 1993; Tomaselli 1990). I suggest the licensing condition (5) for functional projections.

(5) The dominant functional head must be lexicalized.[5]

Lexicalization results from V to I in I-oriented languages; in C-oriented languages C is lexicalized by V/I to C in roots; by a base-generated complementizer in non-roots.[6]

2.2 Mixed languages

In the previous section, a distinction between C-orientation and I-orientation was suggested. In this typology, Modern English and Modern French are I-oriented languages, as they do not have I-to-C movement in declaratives. This suggests that under these conditions, the C-level is not involved. Interestingly, in precisely those contexts where the C-level is activated, viz. in interrogative contexts, and Modern English constructions with a preposed negative constituent, we find typical CV2 properties; I-to-C movement with *do*-support in English and complex inversion and subject–clitic inversion in French, both crucially with asymmetry between root and non-root clauses. It seems then, that once the C-level is activated, i.e. when there is an operator in Spec,C', C must be lexicalized.[7] We will come back to this below.

So far, we have not discussed why it should be that, in I-oriented languages like English, French (and Icelandic which I analyse as an IV2 language), an operator-type of first constituent, such as a *wh*-element or (in English) a negative constituent, should invoke the C-level. A possible answer to this question is suggested by the *wh-criterion* as formulated in Rizzi (1990a) to account for 'residual' V2 phenomena such as ModE subject–verb inversion and ModFr complex inversion and subject–clitic inversion:

(6) *Wh-criterion*:
 Principle A: each [+wh] X must be in a Specifier–Head relation with a *wh*-phrase.
 Principle B: each *wh*-phrase must be in a Specifier–Head relation with a [+wh] X.

Once a *wh*-phrase moves to Spec,C', the head C must be lexicalized in order to satisfy principle B of the *wh-criterion*.[8]

2.3 The nature of Spec,IP

The analysis presented here is motivated by a typological correlation between null subjects (both referential null subjects as in Italian, and expletive null subjects as they are typically found in a number of Germanic languages such as Dutch, Icelandic, German), preposed non-nominatives and nominatives occurring in the VP. I assume that the canonical configuration for nominative case marking is one of government by the dominant lexical head (C or I) into the specifier of the complement projection:

(7) NP → nominative iff it is governed by the dominant head C or I

Thus in the structure (1), C in a C-oriented language assigns nominative case to Spec,IP; I in an I-oriented language assigns nominative case to Spec,VP.

The presence and position of the nominative subject is in this analysis keyed to the agreement properties of I, elaborating on the analysis of *pro*-drop in Rizzi (1982, 1986b). Rizzi characterizes the properties crucial for *pro*-drop in the following way:

(8) *Pro*-licensing:
 a. *Pro* is formally licensed under government by a designated case-assigning head.
 b. The content of *pro* (morphological ɸ-features) must be identified.

It is assumed by Hulk & van Kemenade (1993) that each language has an inventory of Designated case-assigning heads (DCH) for the formal licensing of *pro*, and that it is also possible that languages lack such designated heads entirely. In languages with referential *pro*-drop such as Italian, (8a, b) are both met. Languages that allow expletive *pro*-drop have the possibility of formal licensing (8a) only. Crucial for the formal licensing of *pro* is that the dominant functional head be a DCH. The presence of overt φ-features then further determines the possibility of referential *pro*-drop. The properties of I (and C) thus allow or disallow some form of *pro*-drop. The reverse also holds true: it is claimed that the functional features of I need to be licensed and this is crucially determined by the same properties as those licensing *pro*-drop. The property of being a DCH acts as a formal licenser for I; and the φ-features of I must be visible as some form of syntactic or morphological agreement. With respect to *formal* licensing there are three types of I:

(9) a. I is not a DCH.
 b. I is not a DCH but can be related to C which is a DCH.
 c. I is a DCH.

The typology in (9) is complemented with the option for I to have morphologically overt φ-features. There are three ways of identifying the φ-features of I, if you will, three types of agreement relationship:[9]

(10) a. syntactic: Spec–head Agreement with NP in Spec,IP (I is not a DCH and not related to a DCH C).
 b. Agr-chain: I forms part of an agreement chain between a DCH and NP marked nominative (I is DCH or related to a DCH C).
 c. morphological: φ-features are morphologically realized (I is a DCH).

(10a) represents the 'ordinary' case of agreement between a preverbal subject and I, such as *John hits Mary*, where *John* is in Spec,IP and is a syntactic licenser of the φ-features of I. (10b) represents agreement between V/I and NP in Spec,VP or an internal argument marked nominative, as in the examples in (11). The crucial insight here is that I is formally licensed. However, its φ-features are not identified. Hence, an agreement relationship must be established between I and a nominative NP, but this relationship is not necessarily local as for (11a): the agreeing element may be more deeply embedded.

(11) a. dat mijn broer   jouw verhalen   niet   (Dutch)
   that my brother(DAT) your stories(NOM.PL) not
   bevielen/*beviel
   pleased(PL)(*SG)
 b. daß meinem Bruder(DAT) deine Geschichten (NOM.PL) (German)
   nicht gefielen/*gefiel(PL)(*SG)
   'that my brother was not pleased by your stories'

(11) are examples of the so-called nominative–dative inversion construction in which unaccusative verbs figure. This is discussed in detail in den Besten (1985). Den Besten shows that there is good reason to assume that in Dutch and German both the nominative and the dative NP are in the VP, since

they obey tests for objecthood. This is analysed as follows: in Dutch and German, which are C-oriented and where C is a DCH for formal licensing, I is not a DCH and has no morphological φ-features. I is, however, part of an agreement chain between the DCH C and the nominative NP in the VP. Spec,IP is presumably empty. The central insight here is that there is a typological correlation between such nominatives in the VP and the possibility of expletive *pro*-drop.

(9c) is the case of languages where φ-features are realized as I-morphology, also the case of full *pro*-drop as analysed by Rizzi (1982, 1986b) for Italian. Observe that this overlaps partly with languages ruled by (10b), since I in the relevant languages is a DCH *and* has overt φ-features. The cases (10b, c) are cases where one of the functional heads C or I is a DCH, hence an agreement chain can be formed with a nominative in the VP.

Nominative assignment to an NP in the VP proceeds through chain government. See definition (12) from Hulk & van Kemenade (1993), to which we refer for further motivation. This definition was adapted from den Besten (1985):

(12) a. α chain-governs β iff α governs γ^1, γ^1 governs γ^2, ..., γ^{n-1} governs γ^n, and γ^n governs β ($n \geq 1$).

b. If NP_i is governed by a category α which cannot or may not assign *structural* (addition H/vK) case, NP_i will acquire its case from the first structural case-assigner up by which it is chain-governed.

The result of chain government is that in those cases where Spec,VP (or Spec,IP) is occupied by NP bearing lexical case, and if V has a complement to which it cannot assign structural objective case (i.e. in unaccusative contexts), I (or C via I) transmits its nominative feature to V through chain government. Thus, an NP in object position will receive nominative case when V cannot assign accusative and the nominative cannot be assigned to a different element in its canonical government configuration.

3 Old English

In this section, I first give an initial characterization of the nature of V2 in OE as CV2 (section 3.1), and a characterization of the nature of Spec,IP as one that is the canonical position for the nominative subject, except in subjectless constructions (section 3.2). This is followed by discussion of the alternative proposal of Pintzuk (1991, 1993) who analyses OE as IV2 (section 3.3). Arguments will be given why this view cannot be correct. The conclusion will be that there is no independent evidence for general embedded topicalization in OE, and that an analysis of OE as CV2 is in order.

3.1 V2 in Old English

The history of V2 in English is treated in some detail in van Kemenade

(1987). Van Kemenade analyses OE as a CV2 language in the sense understood in this chapter. We assume for OE a basic structure as in (1) modulo VP-internal OV order and I-final IP.[10] OE is analysed as SOV with V-fronting in root clauses. The examples in (13) are an initial illustration:[11]

(13) a. hwi wolde God swa lytles þinges him forwyrnan   (ÆHTh.I.14.2)
         why would God so   small thing him deny
         'Why should God deny him such a small thing?'
     b. On twam þingum hæfde God þæs mannes sawle gegodod
         in two   things had God the man's soul endowed
         'With two things God had endowed man's soul'   (ÆHTh.I.20.1)

It seems clear that with respect to V2, there is a root/non-root asymmetry in OE; as far as we are aware, the pattern with XP first in embedded clauses occurs only in clauses after bridge verbs, i.e. in embedded root clauses as discussed above.[12] This is illustrated in (14):

(14) Gregorius se trahtnere cwæð þæt forði   wolde drihten
     Gregory   the interpreter said that therefore wanted God
     getrahtnian þurh   hine sylfne þæt bigspel ðe ...   (ÆHTh II.88.13)
     interpret   through himself   the parable that

Given this root/non-root asymmetry with respect to V2, we predict that OE is a C-oriented language.[13] A consequence of this is that the topic *forði* in (14) is in Spec,CP position in the structure (1), and the nominative subject *God* in Spec,IP. More generally, we analyse Spec,IP as the position for nominative subjects. Apart from occasional postposed heavy subjects as discussed in van Kemenade (1987), there is one set of contexts in which Spec,IP is apparently not the canonical position for the nominative NP and these can be broadly defined as unaccusative contexts. We come back to this in the next subsection.

The largest class of potential counterexamples to a V2 analysis of OE clause structure is in the positioning of pronouns with respect to the preposed Vf. OE personal pronouns, pronouns ending in -r, and perhaps also adverbs, are reasonably analysed as Wackernagel clitics.[14] Van Kemenade (1987) pursues such an analysis.[15] Subject pronouns and object pronouns cliticize on the left of the preposed Vf/I. There is a curious discrepancy between topic-initial V2 sentences (including subject-initial ones), where the clitic precedes Vf/I and sentences that have an initial operator constituent such as a *wh* constituent, an initial negative element, or initial adverb *þa*, where the clitic follows Vf/I. These are illustrated with subject pronouns in (15):

(15) a. Be ðæm we magon swiðe swutule oncnawan ðæt ...   (CP.181.16)
         by that we may very clearly perceive that
         'By that, we may very clearly perceive that ...'
     b. for hwam noldest   þu ðe sylfe me gecyðan   (ÆSL.XXXIII.307)
         for what not-wanted you yourself me make known
         'wherefore would you not make yourself known to me'

c. ne sceal he noht   unaliefedes don   (CP.60.15)
      not shall he nothing unlawful   do
      'he shall do nothing unlawful'
   d. þa   began he to modigenne   (ÆHTh.I.10.22)
      then began he to grow proud
      'then he began to grow proud'

In the analysis of van Kemenade (1987), this variable positioning is analysed as follows: in (15a) the clitic subject is cliticized on the left of V/I; in examples like (15b–d) such cliticization is blocked by the operator character of the first constituent (*hwi, þa, ne* contracted with the verb to *n*+Vf).[16]

3.2 Spec,IP in Old English

It was observed above that Spec,IP is the canonical position for the nominative subject in OE. There is one set of contexts where this is not the case and this can be broadly defined as unaccusative. By this term, we understand the classes of verbs that do not assign a thematic role to an external argument. This includes first of all the famous and much discussed impersonal verbs which can have a dative as the leftmost NP in embedded clauses, and a nominative that is presumably in the VP.[17] Some examples are given in (16):

(16) a. gif ðam gifran   angemetlicu spræc   ne eglde (CP.309.3)
        if the greedy(DAT) eloquent   speech(NOM) not afflicted
        'if the greedy are not afflicted by loquacity'
     b. Gif hwam   seo lar   oflicige, ...   (ÆHTh.II.216)
        if anyone(DAT)   the doctrine(NOM) dislike(SUBJUNCTIVE)
        'if the doctrine should be displeasing to anybody, ...'
     c. ac Gode   ne licode   na heora geleafleast   (ÆHP.XX.71)
        but God(DAT)   not pleased not their faithlessness(NOM)
        'but their faithlessness did not please God'

It is impossible to establish conclusively the precise position for the dative in the examples (16). Note that these examples are very similar to the Dutch and German ones in (11) above. For these, it was established by den Besten that both the dative and the nominative are in the VP, on the basis of language-specific tests involving extractability. These tests are not available for OE. What we can conclude is that the nominative cannot possibly be in Spec,IP, and that Spec,IP is either empty or, if the dative is in Spec,IP, filled by a non-nominative.

Some, though not all, of these impersonal verbs, allow omission of a nominative element altogether, as in (17), This phenomenon is restricted to nonthematic subjects. The verb then shows up in the default third person singular form. This is what we have termed above *expletive pro-drop*, and applies also to weather verbs as in (17d)[18]:

(17) a. hine   nanes þinges   ne lyste   on þisse worulde
       him(ACC.SG) nothing(GEN.SG) not pleased(3SG) in this   world
       'nothing in this world pleased him'   (Boeth.102.9)
   b. þonne ofþyncþ   him   þæs ilcan   þe he ær
      then regrets(3SG) him(DAT.SG) the same(GEN.SG) that he before
      forbær   (CP.225.19)
      endured
      'then he regrets what he endured before'
   c. gif us   ne lyst   ðæra ærrena yfela   ðe we
      if us(DAT.PL) not pleases(3SG) the earlier evils(GEN.PL) that we
      ær   worhton   (CP.445.29)
      earlier wrought
      'if the evil that we first wrought displeases us'
   d. and swa miclum sniwde   swelce micel flys   feolle
      and 0 so   heavily snowed(3SG) as if   much fleece fell
      'and it snowed so heavily, as if a lot of fleece were falling'
                                                     (Epist.Alex.159.538)

The second class of contexts relevant here is that of impersonal passives.
This involves quasi-passivization of an inherently case-marked NP. This
may, but need not, involve fronting of the NP. Example (18a) might involve
fronting, (18b) definitely does not. Nominatives do not feature in this
construction.

(18) a. þæt eallum folce   sy   gedemed beforan ðe (Paris Ps.9.18)
       that all   people(DAT.SG) be(SG) judged before   thee
       'that all the people be judged before you'
   b. ... ðætte forðy   to ungemetlice ne sie   gliðod
          that 0 therefore too greatly   not be(SG) mitigated
       ðæm scyldgan   (CP.151.2)
       the guilty(DAT.SG)
       'that therefore it must not be mitigated too greatly to the guilty'
   c. sua sua be   sumum monnum cueden is   (CP.71.01)
      as   about some   men   said   is

In passives that involve a nominative transform of an accusative object, the
nominative can remain in the VP:

(19) a. þonne ælce dæge beoð   manega   acennede þurh
       when each day are(PL) many(NOM.PL) given birth through
       hys mihte on worulde   (ÆHP.VI.120)
       his power on world
       'when every day many are given birth through his power on earth'
   b. for þan þe on me is   afunden ætforan Gode rihtwisnyss
      because that in me is(3SG) found   before God justice(NOM.SG)
      'because justice before God is found in me'   (ÆHP.XXI.331)

There is general agreement that the verbs belonging to the classes illustrated so far, have no external argument. We will now discuss a few

classes of verbs for which this is not so straightforward. One reasonable criterion for deciding whether a verb assigns no external thematic role is to show that it allows expletive *pro*-drop, as in the examples (18) above. This seems reasonable enough in the light of the fact that OE allows no referential *pro*-drop. The only other context in which subjects can be omitted is in conjoined sentences. Therefore, if a verb occurs without a subject in a non-conjoined sentence, there is good reason to assume that it assigns no external role there. A further class of verbs that meets this criterion are modal verbs. On the assumption that modals are largely main verbs in OE, the fact that they occur without a subject shows that they do not assign an external role.[19] This can be shown clearly on the basis of sentences that have an impersonal verb or a passive embedded under a modal. Such cases are discussed in detail in Warner (1990, 1993), Denison (1990b). Some of their examples are given in (20):

(20) a. Hwi ne *sceolde* me   swa þyncan   (Boeth.38.119.3)
       why not should me(DAT) so   seem
       'Why should it not seem so to me?'
   b. Hwam   ne *mæg* earmian swylcere tide? (ChronE.218.4.AD 1086)
      whom(DAT) not may pity   such   time(GEN)
      'Who can fail to feel pity for such a time?'

We can identify a further group of verbs by the fact that their surface nominative subject can show agreement in case and number with an adjective or participle. According to Mitchell (1985), this group includes *wesan* 'be'; *weorþan* 'become'; *cuman* 'come'; *hweorfan* 'return'; *licgan* 'lie'; *sittan* 'sit'; *standan* 'stand'; *gan* 'go'. Some examples in (21):

(21) a. þæt hie   gesunde   from eodon
       that they(NOM.PL) unharmed(NOM.PL) from went
       'that they should go away unharmed'   (ChronE.49.21.AD 755)
   b. ond ic   reotugu sæt   (Wulf, 10) (from Mitchell 1985)
      and I(NOM.SG) dejected sat
      'and I sat dejected'

I analyse the verbs in (21) as raising verbs followed by a small clause that has an adjectival participial predicate. The surface subjects are generated as the subject of the small clause and raised to the matrix subject position. These verbs then do not assign an external theta-role.

We also find presentative constructions with *there* as in PDE. I do not wish to go into the issue whether at this chronological stage of the language *þær* 'there' is already an expletive or whether it is purely locative. Nevertheless, the examples show that the nominative NP must be in the VP:

(22) a. swilce þær wære geworden sum sacu   betweoh
       as if there were become   a   conflict(NOM.SG) between
       þa   þe ...   (GD Hecht.msH.46.14)
       those who
       'as if a conflict had arisen (there) between those who ...'

b. þæt þær byþ ypped   &   gehyred seo wynsumnes &
     that there is disclosed and heard the loveliness and
     dream   þæs   heofonlican lofes   (GD Hecht.msC.281.5)
     joy(NOM.SG) of the heavenly   praise
     'that the loveliness and joy of the heavenly praise are disclosed and heard (there)'

This occurs also with verbs as exemplified by (21):

(23) a. forðam þe him burston ut butu his eagan   (ÆLS.19.120)
        because that him burst   out both his eyes(NOM)
        'because both his eyes burst out'
     b. þæt þær   eode fyr   ut   (GD Hecht.msC.123.27)
        that there went fire(NOM) out
        'that the fire went out there'

The examples in (22) and (23) again show that in these constructions, the nominative NP can be in the VP.

The above do not exhaust the contexts in which initial non-nominatives in embedded clauses occur. Other verbs occur in what look like contexts of nominative–dative inversion. A case in point is the verb *fremian* 'benefit'. It must be noted that this verb can occur without a nominative subject:

(24) þæt eow sylfum   fremað þæt ic fare   (ÆHP.VII.12)
     that you self(DAT.PL) benefits that I   go
     'that it benefits you yourselves that I go'

Note the default 3sg form of the verb. Another verb is *derian* 'harm' which occurs in both nominative–dative order and dative–nominative order. I haven't come across examples of subjectless usage of this verb. However, there are some interesting passages in the Pope edition of homilies of Ælfric where this verb is conjoined with a series of well-established impersonal verbs. See (25) (also XI, 560):

(25) He bið swaþeah   gehæled to ansundre
     he is   nevertheless healed   to health
     on Domes-dæg, þonne he of deaþe arist,
     on Doomsday   when he of death arises
     and syþ(ðan   ne swylt)   ne seoc ne gewyrð
     and afterwards not perishes nor sick not becomes
     ne him hyngrian ne mæg n(e) him þurst   ne deraþ
     nor him hunger   not may nor him thirst(NOM.SG) not harms
     'nevertheless he is healed to health on Doomsday, when he arises from death, and does not perish after, nor falls ill, nor goes hungry, or harmed by thirst'   (ÆHP.II.109)

Let us take stock at this point and see what properties of the verb classes we have established. In constructions with impersonal verbs, impersonal passives, and impersonals or passives embedded under a modal, it is possible to have no nominative element at all. When there is a nominative element in impersonal constructions as in (16), and in passives as in (19) and (22b), the nominative may be in the VP. In all such constructions, it is possible to have a non-nominative element as the first constituent in embedded clauses. This may be followed by nominative–Vf inversion, as in (16c), (19a) and (23b), thus yielding what looks like embedded V2. This is, however, not necessarily the case; in (16a, b) the nominative is in complement position; in (19b), (22) and (23a), the nominative follows the nonfinite verb or particle. And in all these cases, it cannot be shown conclusively that the 'topic' is in Spec,IP. It might be, but Spec,IP could also be empty.

Let us analyse this situation against the background of our theoretical assumptions in section 2. There is a root/non-root asymmetry with respect to V-movement in OE. Genuine embedded topicalization is restricted to clauses embedded under bridge verbs that allow CP-recursion, as was illustrated in (14). Furthermore, we come across what looks like embedded topicalization in clauses with a verb that assigns no external thematic role. These are typically potential expletive *pro*-drop contexts.

Given the fact that OE is CV2 and allows expletive *pro*-drop, our analysis predicts that C is the dominant head for (5) and the formal licenser for (expletive) null subjects. OE does not allow referential *pro*-drop of any kind, hence we assume that I does not have the phi-feature morphology to license referential *pro*. C can assign nominative case under government to Spec,IP, or under chain government to an NP in the VP if there is no external argument, i.e. in unaccusative contexts. Since C is a formal licenser, it can form an agreement chain for (10b) with a nominative NP that is not in Spec,IP, but further to the right, in the VP. I will always form part of this agreement chain. In such contexts, Spec,IP can remain unfilled, or is accessible for a non-nominative constituent.

The facts presented in this section and the analysis proposed, which draws on crosslinguistic correlations in the Germanic and Romance languages, underlines the importance of analysing the set of constructions discussed here as one with special behaviour. The fact that we can show that what may be analysed as embedded topicalization is a construction-specific phenomenon in OE reinforces the analysis of OE as a CV2 language.

3.3 An alternative analysis

The analysis of OE as CV2 goes against that in Pintzuk (1991, 1993). Pintzuk analyses OE as an IV2 language. She adduces three main arguments for this. Two of these touch on the character of Spec,IP position and only these are dealt with here.[20] The first argument that leads Pintzuk to assume that the topic position in root declaratives is not Spec,CP in OE is an indirect one, based on her analysis of the position of clitics. OE allows variable positioning of the pronominal subject with respect to the finite verb (Vf), as observed and analysed in van Kemenade (1987) and briefly summarized above. For convenience, the above examples (15) are recapitulated here:

(15) a. Be ðæm we magon swiðe swutule oncnawan ðæt ... (CP.181.16)
   by that we may   very clearly perceive   that
   'By that, we may very clearly perceive that ...'
 b. for hwam noldest   þu ðe sylfe me gecyðan   (ÆSL.XXXIII.307)
   for what not-wanted you yourself me make known
   'wherefore would you not make yourself known to me'
 c. ne sceal he noht   unaliefedes don   (CP.60.15)
   not shall he nothing unlawful   do
   'he shall do nothing unlawful'
 d. þa began he to modigenne   (ÆHTh.I.10.22)
   then began he to grow proud
   'then he began to grow proud'

In the analysis of van Kemenade (1987), this variable positioning is analysed as follows: in (15a) the clitic subject is cliticized on the left of V/I; in examples like (15b–d) such cliticization is blocked by the operator character of the first constituent (*hwi, þa, ne* contracted with the verb to *n*+Vf).[21] Pintzuk (1991) takes the position of the pronominal subject as a diagnostic for the position of Vf: sentences with the subject clitic preceding Vf reflect IP; (15a) is then analysed as having a topic in Spec,IP with the pronominal subject right-adjoined to Spec,IP. Sentences with the pronominal subject following Vf reflect CP: (15b–d) (with an initial *wh* constituent, *þa* or *ne*) are analysed as CPs, with the finite verb fronted to C and the pronominal subject left-adjoined to Spec,IP. Pintzuk analyses OE then as mixed between IV2 and CV2.

Pintzuk's second argument (Pintzuk 1993) is that topicalization in OE embedded clauses occurs at the same low but significant frequency as in languages like Modern Icelandic which are often analysed as IV2. However, the examples she gives for this all involve embedded clauses with a modal as finite verb. Given the fact that OE modals can be analysed as raising verbs, these fall under the general classes of verbs that do not assign a thematic role to an external argument, as in the previous section, and do not constitute evidence for the general availability of Spec,IP as a topic position in OE.

Pintzuk's analysis predicts that Spec,IP in embedded clauses is generally available as a topic position, and that this triggers subject–Vf inversion. We have seen in the previous section that both these predictions are disconfirmed by the facts. Embedded topicalization is only found in subjectless contexts and, given the analysis advanced, this supports the CV2 analysis for OE. The position of clitic pronouns therefore does not discriminate between contexts with V to I movement and those with V/I-to-C movement. Since there is a root/non-root asymmetry with respect to V movement, we have to assume that root clauses involve V/I movement to the C-domain. We leave open the possibility that the landing site for topic + Vf is a lower one than that of interrogatives, negatives, *þa* + Vf. This would imply a more articulate structure of the C system, as in van

Kemenade (1993b), following the spirit of Shlonsky (1994), Zwart (1993).

In conclusion, there is no independent evidence for the topic status of Spec,IP in Old English. Spec,IP is the position for the nominative subject, and is accessible for other constituents in subjectless contexts only. Given the fact that verb movement is asymmetric, a CV2 analysis for OE seems in order.

4 Middle English

The previous section was an apology for the CV2 character of Old English. This rests on two empirical arguments: the first is the asymmetry of verb movement: topic + Vf + subject generally appears in root clauses only; the second is the fact that embedded topicalization is restricted to subjectless contexts, where Spec,IP is allowed to be empty or filled by a non-nominative constituent, and where nominatives may be absent altogether, or occur in the VP.

The type of evidence adduced above for OE continues to be found in the early ME period. By this time, most texts give evidence of a VO character, although there are still quite a few OV orders and mixed orders. The position of I seems to be much more dominantly initial in the head domain than it is in OE. It is therefore easier to work out the position of Spec,IP, although with continued caution. We will first discuss in this section the asymmetry with respect to V-movement in a number of texts (§4.1). These texts do not abound in examples of subjectless constructions. Therefore, we will consider these in a separate section, drawing on data from a wider range of texts, and from secondary sources (§4.2). We will conclude by discussion of some criteria that are adduced by Kroch & Taylor (this volume) to decide between IV2 and CV2 patterns (§4.3).

4.1 The asymmetry of V2

From the earliest ME texts and in all dialects, the OE pattern continued in full force. We begin by looking at some texts that are recognized as the closest successors of the dialect of late Old English prose: West-Saxon. The twelfth-century 'Poema Morale' (Egerton ms., ed. Morris, whole text) is an immediate candidate for this. Illustrating the various patterns, (26) shows inversion of NP-subject with a topic; (27) shows the noninversion of pronominal subjects with a topic; (28) shows inversion of all types of subject in *wh*-initial and negative-initial sentences:

(26) Þer inne boð þa   þe   was to lof wreche men to swenchen   (PM.175.250)
    therein are those who delighted poor   men to prosecute
    'Therein shall be those who delighted to prosecute poor men'

(27) a. well late ich habbe me bi-þoht   (PM.161.8)
    full late I   have me repented
    'full late I have repented me'

b. Erȝe we beoð to done god (PM.161.17)
   slow we are to do good
   'we are slow to do good'

(28) a. Hwet sculen ordlinghes don þa swicen and ta forsworene
       what shall whoremongers do the traitors and the perjured
       hwi boð fole iclepede. and swa lut icorene
       why are many called and so few chosen
       wi hwi weren ho biȝeten to hwon weren ho iborene ...
       why were they conceived wherefore were they born
       (PM.165.103-5)
       'What shall whoremongers do, the traitors, and the perjured? Why are so many folk called and so few chosen? Why were they concei-ved-wherefore were they born ...'
    b. nolde he for al middenerd þe þerdde þer abiden
       not-would he for all middle earth the third there abide
       'He would not for all middle earth abide there the third' (PM.169.1)
    c. Ne lipnie wif to hire were (PM.161.31)
       not trust wife to her husband
       'let no wife trust to her husband'

There are no instances of embedded topicalization in this text. V2 is asymmetric. There is one example in this text that according to Kroch & Taylor (this volume) is diagnostic for topicalization to a C-oriented context. We give the example here, and will come back to this below:

(29) Ac drihte crist he ȝiue us strencþe. *stonde* þat we mote (PM.179.30)
     but lord Christ he give us strength stand that we may
     'but may Christ give us strength that we may stand'

The infinitive *stonde* must be assumed to be topicalized to the left of the C-position in its own clause, which is signalled by þat. This shows that the topic position is presumably Spec,CP.

In early ME, there is a further source of evidence for determining the topic position. If sentences with a negated Vf, followed by a subject pronoun, are to be analysed unequivocally as reflecting movement of V/I to C (recall that this is so even in Pintzuk's analysis), it is telling that this pattern is found preceded by a topic in all the texts examined.[22] Here are some examples from *Poema Morale*:

(30) For þer ne þerf he bon of-dred of fure ne of þoue (PM.163.43)
     for there not need he be afraid of fire nor of thief
     'for there he needn't be afraid of fire or of thief'

(31) þer ne þerf he habben kare of ȝefe ne of ȝelde (PM.163.45)
     there not need he have care of gifts nor of rewards
     'there he needn't be worried about gifts or rewards'

I now turn to examination of data from several other texts that are from areas closely related to the West-Saxon/southern Mercian dialect areas in

OE. The first of these is *Sawles Warde,* a prose treatise in the dialect of the SW Midlands in the early thirteenth century (ed. Morris, whole text). Example (32) illustrates the inversion pattern with a nominal subject; (33) the noninversion of pronominal subjects in topic-initial sentences; (34) shows inversion of subject in *wh*-initial and negative-initial sentences:

(32) þat ne mei na tunge tellen   (very few examples) (SW.249.35)
 that not can no tongue tell
 'noone can tell that'

(33) a. bi þis ȝe mahen seon ant witen ...   (SW.263.23)
 by this you may see and know
 b. i wis ich habbe þrin isehen a þusent siðe wurse   (SW.253.25)
 truly I have therein seen a thousand times worse
 'truly I have seen therein a thousand times worse'

(34) a. Hweonone cumest tu ...   (SW.249.29)
 whence comest thou
 'where do you come from ...'
 b. Ne mei ich he seið. nohwer speoken   (SW.249.12)
 not may I he says, nowhere speak
 'I may not, he says, speak anywhere'

In this text too, V2 is asymmetric. Example (35) is an example of embedded topicalization occuring after a bridge verb:

(35) ... as ha soð seið þat þurh unweotennesse ne mei ha
 as she truly says that through ignorance not can she
 nawt sunegin   (SW.255.33)
 not sin
 'as she truly says that through ignorance she may not sin'

Note that this is a CP-recursion environment. We will have to allow that in this text, CP-recursion is not entirely restricted to complements of bridge verbs. There are several examples of fronting of a negated Vf, with or without topic:

(36) a. he is warde ... þat onont him ne schal nan un-þeaw (SW.249.1)
 he is ward that anent them not-shall no vice
 cumen in
 come in
 'he keeps watch,..., so that no vice shall come in through them'
 b. þat ne mahte ich longe hwile elles hwider lokien (SW.261.5)
 that not could I long while else where look
 'that I was unable for a long while to look elsewhere'
 c. þat al is hare blisse. se muchel þat ne mei hit munne
 that all is their bliss so great that not may it mention
 na muð   (SW.263.20)
 no mouth
 'that all their bliss is so great that no mouth may mention it'

Note that the context with a negated Vf, followed by a pronominal subject, is uncontroversially analysed as a CV2 context. *Sawles Warde* further contains a number of examples of topic-initial negated sentences with a subject pronoun following Vf:

(37) a. for in þe   ne mei hit naneswis neomen in   (SW.263.35)
         for in thee not-can it in no way enter
         'for in thee may it in no wise enter'
     b. for of al his strengðe ne drede we nawiht   (SW.255.8)
         for of all his strength not dread we not
         'for of all his strength we don't have any dread'

Patterns such as those encountered in *Sawles Warde* are representative of all the southern Midlands texts from this period. Another example from the Southeast Midlands, from around 1200, is the *Book of Vices and Virtues* (ed. Holthausen, whole text). The patterns are the same as in the other texts. (38) illustrates inversion with a topic and a nominal subject; (39) the noninversion of pronominal subject with a topic; (40) the inversion of all types of subject with a *wh*, *þanne*, or negative first constituent:

(38) ȝewiss   hafð godd forworpen ðan ilche mann ...   (VV.13.31)
     certainly has God rejected   that sameman
     'certainly God has rejected that same man...'
(39) a. alle ðese bebodes   ic habbe ihealde fram childhade
         all these commandments I have   kept   from childhood
                                                              (VV.67.32)
     b. For hire we sculen alle deað þolien   (VV.7.23)
         for it   we shall all   death suffer
         'we shall suffer death for it'
(40) a. hwat hafst ðu swa lange idon on ðare woreld?   (VV.17.18)
         what have you so long done in the world
         'What have you done so long in this world?'
     b. Đanne wunest ðu   sikerliche on Gode   (VV.39.8)
         then abide you truly   in God
         'Then you abide truly in God'
     c. Ne cam   ic noht te bidden ȝew forbisne ...   (VV.15.9)
         not came I not to give   you example
         'I did not come to give you example...'

A topic can precede a negated Vf followed by a subject pronoun, showing that the topic position is Spec,CP:

(41) a. þis ne habbe ic nauht ofearned   (VV.17.9)
         this not have I not   earned
         'This I have not earned'
     b. for his ȝemeleste ne latt   he naht te donne (VV.63.9)
         for his carelessness not omitteth he nought to do

Another text from further south is the *Kentish sermons* (ms. C13, full text). The patterns are the same as in the other southern texts: (42) illustrates inversion with a topic and a nominal subject; (43) the non-inversion of pronominal subject with a topic; (44) the inversion of all types of subject with a *wh* first constituent, and illustrates that the differentiating factor between inversion and noninversion of pronominal subjects is the negation on Vf:

(42) Nu   loke euerich man toward himseluen   (KS.218.134)
      now look every   man to   himself
      'now it's for every man to look to himself'

(43) a. Nu   ye   habbeþ iherd þe miracle   (KS.217.116)
        now you have   heard the miracle
     b. þerefore we sollen habbe ure peni   (KS.221.237)
        for that we shall have our penny

(44) a. Wat   belongeth hit to me oþer to þe, wyman?   (KS.216.93)
        what matters   it to me or   to you woman
        'What does it matter to me or to you, woman?'
     b. þo   dede he somoni   alle þo wyse clerekes   (KS.214.16)
        then did he summon all the wise clerks
        'then he had summon all the wise clerks'
     c. ne solde   noman targi forto ...   (KS.222.257)
        not should noone delay to
        'Noone should delay to ...'

A topic can precede a negated Vf followed by a subject pronoun:

(45) a. þet ne seide he noht   (KS.214.25)
        that not said   he not
        'That he did not say'
     b. Nu ne dorste hi namore sigge   (KS.216.94)
        now not dared he nomore say
        'Now he did not dare say more'

Again, as in the other texts, no examples are found of embedded topicalization; V2 is asymmetric. We conclude that in all the early ME dialects of the south, V2 is asymmetric.

When we move further north, we still find V2 patterns similar to the southern ones. A major example is the *Peterborough chronicle*, from the Northeast Midlands, with noncopied continuations up to 1154 (ed. Clark, full text). The patterns are the same as in the southern texts: (46) illustrates inversion with a topic and a nominal subject; (47) the noninversion of pronominal subject with a topic; (48) the inversion of all types of subject with a *wh, þa* or negative first constituent:

(46) a. Ðus wæs se mynstre   of Burch   forbærnd (PC.AD 1070.56)
        thus was the monastery of Peterborough burnt down
        'Thus, the monastery of Peterborough was burnt down'

    b. On his dagan wæs þet mare mynster   on Cantwarbyrig getimbrad
       in his days was the big monastery in Canterbury built
       'In his days, the big monastery in Canterbury was built'
(PC.AD 1087.68)

(47) a. Ðas þing we habbað be   him gewritene   (PC.AD 1087.143)
       these things we have   about him written
       'these things we have written about him'
    b. Fela   þinga we magon writan þe ...   (PC.AD 1087.146)
       of many things we may   write that (happened during that year)
       'we can write about many things that ...'

(48) a. Hwæt magon we secgan?   (PC.AD 1083.23)
       what can   we say
    b. Ða   herde Ægelric biscop þet gesecgon   (PC.AD 1070.60)
       then heard Æ.   biscop that say
       'Then bishop Æ. heard this be said'
    c. ne mihte he beon ...   (PC.AD 1093.16)
       not could he be
       'he could not be ...'

A topic can precede a negated Vf, followed by a subject pronoun:

(49) a. of his utgang ne cunne we iett noht seggon   (PC.AD 1127.73)
       of his exit   not can   we yet not   say
       'we can't yet say anything of its exit' (i.e. how the year would end)
    b. on fif & twenti wintre ne biden hi   næfre an god dæi
       in five and twenty winters not had   they never a good day
       'they didn't have a single good day in twenty-five years'
(PC.AD 1131.25)

From areas more northern than Peterborough, there is an unfortunate sparsity of material in the early ME period. The only texts of any size from this area are the poetic *Cursor Mundi* and the northern prose version of the Benedictine Rule. The nature of the verse of *Cursor Mundi* is such that an investigation would need special consideration beyond the scope of this chapter.

In the northern *Rule of St Benet* (ed. Kock), we find an interesting and apparently systematic deviation from the pattern that we established for the other dialects, cf. also Kroch & Taylor (this volume). V2 inversion is systematic with all types of first constituent and with all types of subject. There is no discrepancy between the behaviour of nominal and pronominal subjects when the first constituent is a topic. This is illustrated in (50):

(50) a. Allekin   mekenes sal   man muster til þe gestis   (*Benet*.35.11)
       all manner of meekness shall man muster to the guests
       'all manner of meekness shall be shown to the guests'
    b. Oþir labur sal   þai do   (*Benet*.33.20)
       other labour shall they do
       'they must do other labour'

c. In þa dais sal we here sumþing of godes seruise (Benet.33.35)
in the days shall we hear something of God's service
'in the daytime we will hear something about the service of God'

4.2 Spec,IP in early ME

In the previous section, evidence was given that V2 in early ME is asymmetric. V2 with subject–Vf inversion is restricted to root contexts. Noninversion there is restricted to subject pronouns, for which a clitic analysis seems indicated. Let us now consider some instances of constructions with unaccusatives of the types that were exemplified in section 3.2. Recall that in OE constructions with impersonal verbs, impersonal passives, impersonals or passives embedded under a modal, it is possible to have no nominative element at all. When there is a nominative element in impersonal constructions and in passives, the nominative may be in the VP. In all such constructions, and in constructions with verbs like *go*, it is possible to have a non-nominative element as the first constituent in embedded clauses. It must be noted that examples do not come frequently. Exemplification is therefore not restricted to the texts examined for the previous section, and extended to data culled from other texts and from secondary sources like Elmer (1981) and Allen (1995). Let us first give some examples evidencing expletive *pro*-drop; (51) are root clauses, (52) non-root clauses:

(51) a. þenne *scheomeþ* me þerwiþ (St.Marh.352.53)
then shames me(OBJ) with that
'then I am ashamed of that'
b. him (OBJ) wile sone *longe* þarafter (Trin.148.19)
him wile soon long after that
'he will soon long for that'

(52) a. þat mare *bi-houis* hir studie for to auance hir cuuent,
that more behooves her study for to advance her convent
þan maistri for to haue (Benet.42.14)
than authority for to have
'that it is more fitting for her to study to advance her convent, than to have authority'
b. ðat me *nis* naht of alles woreldes blisse (VV.31.27)
that me not-is naught of all world's bliss
'that to me there is nothing to all the world's bliss'

We can observe on the basis of (52) that Spec,IP is either empty, or filled by a non-nominative. The conclusion that *mare* in (52a) and *me* in (52b) are in Spec,IP is not warranted. While this may seem plausible, there is nevertheless a possibility that they are scrambled, since scrambling to a position preceding the finite verb in embedded clauses is possible, as in Kroch & Taylor (this volume). They could then be remnants of the OE V-final pattern.

In embedded unaccusative constructions that do feature what is presumably a nominative NP (we can only tell if agreement is distinct and that is not the case in these examples), that NP can be in the VP, as in (53):

(53) a. ac ʒif ðar cumþ scip to hit tobrekð   (VV.45.19)
     but if there comes ship to it breaks up
     'but if a ship comes thereto it breaks up'
  b. swa ðat him baðe hit wel likede and ec teiþede   (VV.119.17)
     so that him both it well pleased and also yielded
     'so that it both pleased him well and yielded'
  c. þegg wisstenn þatt himm wass þatt daʒʒ summ unncuþ
     they knew that them was that day some unknown
     sihhþe shæwedd   (Orm.227)
     sight shown
     'they knew that some unknown sight was shown him that day'
  d. Forr whatt himm wass his spæche anan þurrh Drihhtin
     for which him was his speech anon through Lord
     all biræfedd   (Orm.2831)
     all bereaved
     'for which his speech was forthwith taken away completely from him by the Lord'

The last two examples (from Allen 1995) are interesting in that the position of Vf/I is distinct from that of the nonfinite verb. This makes it very plausible that the dative pronoun is in Spec,IP. We conclude that the syntactic properties of Spec,IP in early ME have not changed in any essential way since OE, and that the analysis advanced for OE in section 3 is still relevant at this stage.

4.3 Discussion: the nature of V2 in early Middle English

I have presented arguments for regarding both OE and early ME as an asymmetric V2 languages. The arguments are the lack of embedded topicalization, and, in early ME, the compatibility of a topic with a post-verbal subject pronoun. The latter shows that the topic position is Spec,CP. The evidence in early ME is quite uniform in all non-northern dialects. Divergent behaviour is shown in the northern dialect of the *Rule of St Benet*. This has uniform asymmetric V2, whether the subject is nominal or pronominal.

Kroch & Taylor (this volume) adapt Pintzuk's (1991) analysis of V2 in OE, and carry it over to such ME texts as exhibit the same patterns as in OE, i.e. all the non-northern texts. They analyse the evidence from the *Rule of St Benet* as characteristic of asymmetric V2 and hypothesize that the northern dialect of ME became CV2 under the influence of the extensive language contact situation with Scandinavian settlers.

The evidence I have quoted and the way we have analysed it suggests a different perspective on the nature of the dialect differences in ME. If our analysis of V2 in OE and early ME is correct and all V2 is asymmetric, the divergence in patterns between the southern and northern dialects is of a different nature: the southern dialects are CV2 and have a clitic position in the C-system, whereas the northern dialects are CV2 and do not have this clitic position. The absence of the clitic position in the northern dialect may be due to the contact situation with the Scandinavians, but we have no evidence for the Scandinavian languages at this stage.

Kroch & Taylor advance some further arguments for the difference between IV2 in the South and CV2 in the *Benet* text. The first is that the *Benet* text has a number of examples of topicalization over a complementizer, as in (54):

(54) I sal   yu   lere þe dute of God, his wille þat ʒe may do   (*Benet*.2.5)
    I shall you teach the duty of God his will that ye may do
    'I shall teach you the duty of God, that you may do his will'

However, such examples are not entirely nonexistent in the South, witness the example (29) above, from *Poema Morale*. The second argument they give is that in examples like (54), the second clause introducer should plausibly be in the same position as that of the first, which is to the left of a *that*-complementizer, hence in Spec,CP. There is no parallel inversion in such clauses in the South:

(57) for þe mare þat sho es heʒid ouir toþer,   þe mare aʒh   sho at
    for the more that she is raised over the-other the more ought she to
    halde þe cumandement of þe reule   (*Benet*.44.5)
    hold the commandment of the rule

This is hardly a conclusive argument, since these clause introducers in the South may well have different properties.

4.4 Late Middle English

From the middle of the fourteenth century, V2 declines. The reader will recall that in OE, there was an asymmetry with respect to the position of the pronominal subject between topic-initial sentences and operator-initial sentences, as discussed in section 2.3. Van Kemenade (1987) analyses this as a process of cliticization of the pronominal subject to V/I, Pintzuk (1991) as a difference between CV2 and IV2 patterns in OE. This asymmetry gradually disappears in the course of the second half of the fourteenth century and first quarter of the fifteenth century. I do not wish to go into the nature of this process here. For some discussion, see van Kemenade (1987: ch. 6). The loss of this asymmetry is, I claim, the main trigger for the loss of V2. Pronominal subjects regularly appeared on the left of V2 in root clauses, while nominal subject regularly 'inverted'. As this discrepancy between nominal and pronominal subjects got lost, nominal subjects adopted the pronominal pattern. This is subject to some dialectal variation, cf. van Kemenade (1987). In the dialect of Chaucer, pronouns adopted the nominal subject pattern. For instance, in one of Chaucer's prose works, the Treatise on the Astrolabe, V2 inversion is completely regular. This is in marked contrast to the dialect of Wycliffe, who is a near-contemporary of Chaucer. Interestingly, there is good reason to assume that the Wycliffite sermons represent an important literary standard, see Warner (1982). I illustrate this with some examples from the Wycliffite writings; the case is discussed in considerable detail in van Kemenade (forthcoming a):

(56) a. wiþ newe wenchis is Crist now weddid and
       with new wenches is Christ now wedded and
       on newe maner he kepte his furste matrimonye
       in new manner he kept his first matrimony
       (The Wyccliffite sermons.361.42)
   b. And by þis same skyle hope and sorwe schulle iugen us
      and by this same skill hope and sorrow shall judge us
      (The Wyccliffite sermons.372.97)
   c. for more ioyȝe þei myhte not haue
      for more joy they could not have (The Wyccliffite sermons.382.106)

In these texts, we regularly find these three patterns: non-inversion of a subject pronoun (50c), non-inversion of a subject noun (50b); and inversion of a subject noun (50a). There are very few examples of inverted subject pronouns, except with an operator type of first constituent like a *wh*-element. What these examples indicate is that in this dialect, which there is some reason to assume played an important role in the rise of the standard language, the nominal subjects tended to adopt the pattern of pronominal subjects. The result of this was that fronting of XP to Spec,CP no longer went hand in hand with V/I to C.

Hence V2 declined and English changed from a C-oriented language to an I-oriented language. Since Spec,IP was, from the earliest times, the canonical position for the nominative subject, and I was never itself a formal licenser for null subjects, the language did not become IV2, but lost its V2 character completely except in constructions with an operator in Spec,CP. Let us consider the relationship between the loss of V2 and the other constructions under consideration more closely.

The loss of V2 goes hand in hand with changes in the subject position as discussed here. This can be illustrated with several well-studied cases from the literature. Expletive *pro*-drop is lost in the last part of the fourteenth and the early fifteenth century, cf. van Kemenade (1993a). Van der Wurff (1990) shows that, in *easy to please* constructions, which in earlier stages could remain subjectless (*is hard to do this* rather than *it is hard to do this*), *it*-insertion becomes obligatory in the same period. Similarly, Butler (1980) shows that at the same stage, insertion of *there* became obligatory in existential sentences. With respect to preposed datives, Allen (1986, 1993) shows that in impersonal constructions with preposed dative experiencers and in dative-fronted passives, the preposed dative, were reinterpreted as nominative during the same span of time.

At the stage when English was still V2 with expletive *pro*-drop, say c. 1250, the basic sentence structure may be represented as in (1). C is the dominant head, hence it must be lexicalized, either by a complementizer or by a finite V. C is the DCH that acts as a formal licenser for *pro*. I does not have inherent ɸ-features, hence referential *pro*-drop is excluded; only expletive *pro*-drop is possible. The ɸ-features of I must therefore be licensed by movement of the nominative NP to Spec,IP to ensure licensing of I under Spec–head agreement in IP. In subjectless constructions, a DCH C may form a chain with the VP-internal nominative. As in the course of the latter half of the fourteenth century, subjects come to appear more and more frequently to the left of the finite verb, V2 declines; English changes from a C-oriented language to an I-oriented language. I is then the dominant head and must be lexicalized. V/I to C is lost, except in operator-first constructions. I was never a DCH for the licensing of *pro*-drop, hence expletive *pro*-drop is lost, and nominatives in the VP cease to occur. Since now the language becomes subject-NP initial rather than XP-initial, preposed dative experiencers come to be reanalysed as nominative subjects.[23] The loss of V2 and the loss of expletive *pro*-drop, or rather the emergence of obligatory nominative subjects, coincide historically.[24]

Notes

* I am grateful to Marcel den Dikken, Aafke Hulk, Willem Koopman, Nigel Vincent and two anonymous referees for very helpful discussion and comments on an earlier version of this chapter. Furthermore I thank the audiences of the Workshop on Null Subjects at the ICHL X (Amsterdam), the 7th ICEHL (Valencia), the second Diachronic Syntax Workshop (Philadelphia), the Autumn 1993 meeting of the LAGB (Bangor), where parts of the material discussed here were presented.

1. In this article, the labels C-oriented vs I-oriented refer primarily to the position for the finite verb in root clauses. But there is an obvious relationship between the functional orientation as employed here, and that advocated in Rivero (this volume) for the typology of clitics.
2. We leave open the possibility that the labels C and I should actually represent a more elaborate functional structure than the one presented here. While there is some evidence that this is the case, it is not of immediate relevance to the issue at hand.
3. Note, however, the argument in Vikner (1991, 1995) that Continental Scandinavian has no V to I movement.
4. The term IV2 is somewhat misleading here, since it suggests that, as in CV2 languages, the term V2 applies as an absolute word order constraint. This does not seem to be the case in IV2 languages. Crucial for our notion of IV2 language is that Spec,IP is an XP position rather than a NP subject position. This results in many XP–Vf sequences, but does not prohibit intervention of other elements between XP and Vf. For the sake of comparison with CV2 languages, however, we continue to use the term IV2.
5. Sometimes a non-root C position can remain lexically null in C dominant languages. This is restricted, however, to environments where the complementizer is selected by the matrix verb, cf. Rizzi & Roberts (1989). Also, in indirect questions, the C-position may count as lexical if Spec,C is filled by a *wh*-constituent, as in *I was wondering* [$_{Spec,C'}$ *who* [$_C$ e [$_{IP}$ *we should turn to*]]]. Presumably, Spec,C' and C are co-indexed here, in the vein of Pesetsky (1982).

V2 and embedded topicalization in Old and Middle English 351

6. Or in non-root clauses with a selected complementizer, C can remain empty, or be lexical by being coindexed with a *wh*-element in Spec,CP, cf. note 5.
7. Unless the operator is saturated by movement of the subject to Spec,CP and I to C is blocked, as in *Who saw John?* vs *Who did see John?* See Koopman (1984), Rizzi (1990a); for a treatment of this that is compatible with ours.
8. It must be noted that French differs from English (and Icelandic, as I see it) in that I to C movement is not obligatory when Spec,CP is filled in the syntax, cf. the grammaticality of (i) with non-inversion:
   (i) A qui tu as parlé?
       to who you have spoken
       'who did you speak to?'
   Rizzi (1990a) suggests that French has an additional way of licensing a [+wh] specification under agreement in CP. Hulk (1993) argues that the mechanism invoked by Rizzi (1990a) is redundant in French, and that French does not have I to C in interrogatives.
9. For further motivation and discussion of this analysis, the reader is referred to Hulk & Van Kemenade (1993).
10. Pintzuk (1991) gives evidence that IP is variable between I-final and I-initial order in the head domain. This does not affect the arguments presented here.
11. These examples are suggestive of a fairly homogeneous word order in OE, but in fact this is far from being the case. Van Kemenade (1987) analyses the core exceptions as (heavy) NP shift to post-verbal position; a relatively free process of verb raising as attested in various West Germanic languages; and a clitic analysis of personal pronouns. Pintzuk (1991) presents an analysis in terms of phrase structure variation between an I-medial and I-final IP and various types of rightward movement as in van Kemenade.
12. Only a pattern with a fronted XP is valid as evidence here, as examples with Subject–Vf–(XP)–V–(XP) occur quite frequently in non-root clauses. The latter may be analysed either as an instance of a variant pattern with I-medial order in OE (cf. Pintzuk 1991), or as an instance of verb-projection-raising (cf. van Kemenade 1987).
13. Pintzuk (1993) observes that embedded topicalization occurs at a low rate in the complements of non-bridge verbs. This will be discussed below.
14. Pintzuk (1991, 1994) analyses OE adverbs as clitics of roughly the same type as the personal pronouns. Koopman (1994) disputes this view.
15. There is another set of counterexamples that is not easily handled in this analysis: V/I to C is not entirely obligatory in OE. There are (infrequent) examples where V-fronting simply does not apply. In van Kemenade (forthcoming a) a refinement of this analysis is suggested that handles these cases.
16. An interesting alternative analysis fully compatible with the clitic facts and the CV2 analysis of OE is presented in Tomaselli (1995).
17. This set of verbs is discussed in detail in Elmer (1981), Allen (1993). I assume that this set is generally characterized by not assigning an external thematic role. Allen (1986a, 1995) analyses the preposed dative arguments of a number of these verbs as subjects in the sense that they control coordinate subject deletion. I do not wish to enter into this issue here. While I find her case convincing, it is not clear whether her argument would lead to the conclusion that these datives should be analysed as external arguments in our analysis. I merely wish to address the syntactic properties of the position Spec,IP here.
18. It must be noted that weather verbs in the vast majority of cases have an *it* subject in OE.
19. Denison (1990b) and Warner (1990) take the co-occurrence of modals with impersonals (and passives) to suggest that they could already be auxiliaries in OE. This is worked out considerably more fully in Warner (1993). Van Kemenade (1993a) suggests that these instances of modals are best analysed as raising verbs. The idea that they are not modals at this stage is supported by the fact that they occur in V-(projection) raising structures, as in van Kemenade (1987), since V-(projection) raising is a main-verb phenomenon.

20. The third argument is a quantitative comparison of V-position in root and non-root clauses. Her figures show a large discrepancy of Vf position between root and non-root clauses that in my opinion does not warrant an analysis of OE V-placement as symmetric between root and non-root clauses. This is discussed in detail in van Kemenade (forthcoming a).
21. An interesting alternative analysis fully compatible with the clitic facts and the CV2 analysis of OE is presented in Tomaselli (1995).
22. This pattern, though attested, is very rare in OE, for reasons that are not entirely clear to me. A suggestion might be that the preverbal negation *ne* was stronger in OE and acted itself as a topic. There is independent evidence that *ne* in OE is stronger than the same element in ME, in that in OE, it could occur as a single sentential negation element. In ME, it came to be reinforced by a second negation element. This is discussed in van Kemenade (forthcoming b).
23. This solves a dating puzzle in Allen's (1986a) analysis. I have always been puzzled by the fact that dative experiencers were reinterpreted as nominative late in the fourteenth century, if this is due to a large extent to the loss of inherent case, as Allen (1986) hypothesizes. There is clear evidence for the loss of inherent case from the early thirteenth century. One would therefore expect datives that already behaved like subjects to be reanalysed as nominative earlier. On the analysis here, we view the preposed datives as being in topic position. They were therefore generally reanalysed as nominative when the topic position was generally reanalysed as nominative.
24. At a later stage, even V to I is lost. This change does not concern us at present, but should be dated as later than the general loss of V2. Roberts (1985) dates the loss of V to I to the sixteenth century.

13 Qu'est-ce que *ce que*? The diachronic evolution of a French complementizer

Laurie Zaring and Paul Hirschbühler

1 Introduction*

In contemporary Modern French, the morpheme *ce* has a variety of uses:

(1) a. Nominal determiner: *ce beau lac* 'this beautiful lake'
    b. Subject pronoun:
        C' est dommage que tu partes
        it is too-bad that you leave
        'It's too bad that you're leaving'
    c. Clausal arguments preceded by *à, de*:
        Je m' attends à *ce* qu' il vienne
        I me wait to it that he come
        'I'm expecting that he will come'
    d. Heading relative clauses and indirect questions:
        Ce que tu as dit est ridicule
        it that you has said is ridiculous
        'What you said is ridiculous'
        Je me demande *ce* qu' il a fait
        I me ask it that he has done
        'I wonder what he did'

Our purpose here is to focus on *ce*'s use in association with non-*wh* clausal arguments, i.e. those illustrated by (1c), in order to understand how and why this construction evolved over time. In contemporary Modern French, this combination of *ce* plus a tensed clause (henceforth referred to as *ce que*) is limited for most speakers to occurring with the prepositions *à* and *de* (see Zaring 1992, 1993). In Old French (OF), however, *ce que* appeared not only with a wide variety of prepositions, but also as subject and direct object clauses. Our account of *ce que*'s evolution will propose that *ce* here is not a pronominal, but a determiner which selects for a clause rather than for a nominal, and whose use begins to become limited at the same time that another *ce*-morpheme, the masculine singular demonstrative determiner illustrated in (1a), begins to develop in the language. We propose the existence of a parameter based on Grimshaw's (1991) Extended Projection theory, and argue that strategies of first language acquisition, such as Roberts' (1993a) Least Effort Strategy and Berwick's (1985) Subset Principle, led to a shift in the setting for this parameter and to a reanalysis of *ce que* as a unitary complementizer. Thus, our analysis provides support for diachronic reanalysis and affirms the importance of the notion of parameter in an explanatory theory of grammar.

We begin in section 2 by examining the syntactic properties of pronominal *ce* in OF and Middle French (MF) in order to show that this pronominal and the one occurring in Extraposition structures are one and the same. In section 3, we discuss the properties of *ce que*, concluding that the behaviour of the *ce* occurring here is substantially different from that of pronominal *ce*, and is, in fact, that of a determiner. Section 4 details the evolution of *ce* into a clausal determiner, and examines the implications of its existence for Grimshaw's Extended Projection theory. We argue that a parameterized version of this theory provides the best explanation for the progressive limitation in the use of non-*wh ce que* in the history of the French language.

Historically speaking, scholars recognize three primary stages of the French language:

(2) a. Old French: spoken in an area around Paris (Ile de France) between the early eleventh and late thirteenth centuries;
 b. Middle French: spoken in north-central and north-eastern France between the early fourteenth and late sixteenth centuries;
 c. Modern French: the standardized language spoken from the early seventeenth century to the present.

In addition, as Hirschbühler (1990), Roberts (1993a) and others note, there is good evidence from the distribution of null subjects in OF that this period comprises two sub-stages of the language: conservative OF, represented by twelfth century verse and prose and thirteenth century verse, and innovative OF, represented by thirteenth century prose. Our present corpus, which is being progressively expanded, is drawn from the following texts representative of the OF and MF periods:[1]

(3) OF texts
 a. Conservative OF
 twelfth century:
 La chanson de Roland (*Ro*) (assonating verse, first half of the twelfth c.)
 Chrétien de Troyes (verse, second half of the twelfth c.):
  Cligès (C), *Yvain (ou le Chevalier au Lion)* (Y), *Le Chevalier de la Charrette (Lancelot)* (L), *Érec et Énide* (E), *Le Roman de Perceval* (P)
 Béroul (verse, second half of the twelfth c.): *Tristran* (Tr)
 thirteenth century:
 Jehan Renart (verse, first half of the thirteenth c.): *Le Lai de l'Ombre* (Om), *Le Roman de la Rose ou de Guillaume de Dole* (Do)
 Guillaume de Lorris (verse, first half of the thirteenth c.): *Le Roman dela Rose* (Lo)

b. Innovative OF
La Mort le Roi Artu (Ar) (prose, first half of the thirteenth c.)
(4) Middle French
Les Cent Nouvelles Nouvelles (CNNA) (anonymous; prose, second half of the fifteenth c.)
Philippe de Vigneulles (prose, very early sixteenth c.): Les Cent Nouvelles Nouvelles (CNNV)

2 The syntax of pronominal *ce*

2.1 Plain pronominal *ce*

As grammars of OF and MF attest (Foulet 1961; Brunot 1924; Martin & Wilmet 1980), the neuter pronoun *ce* was widely used in both OF and MF in all grammatical functions: subject, direct object (DO) and object of P:

(5) a. Morz est ses sires, *ce* li poise (Y2093)
    dead is her lord this to-her weighs
    'Her husband is dead, this grieves her'
  b. Le pouvre homme, oyant *ce* que son filz avoit dit, fut
    the poor man hearing that which his son had said was
    fort esbahis que *ce* voulloit dire, ... (CNNV93-185)
    very frightened what this wanted to-say
    'The poor man, hearing what his son had said, was very afraid of what this might mean ...'

(6) a. Li rois respont: '*Ce* sai ge bien;/ mes por ce n' an
    the king answers this know I well but for this NEG of-it
    lerai ge rien, ...' (E0059)
    will-leave I nothing
    'The king answers: "This know I well, but even for this will I not yield in any way ..."'
  b. ... et *ce* disoit il en les truffant et en soy mocquant d'eulx
    and this said he in them jeering-at and in self mocking of them
    (CNNV26-14)
    'And he said this while jeering at them and making fun of them'

(7) a. ... iert an mimoire/ tant con durra crestïantez;/de
    will-be in memory as-long as will-endure Christianity of
    ce s' est Crestïens vantez (E26)
    this self is Chrétien boasted
    '... (it) will be remembered as long as Christianity endures; of this Chrétien has boasted'
  b. Et pour *ce*, cedit seigneur pria à cellui sergent qu' il
    and for this the-said lord begged to that sergeant that he
    luy tint compaignie pour aller à la feste, ... (CNNV30-55)
    to-him hold company for to-go to the festival
    'And for this, the said lord begged the sergeant to keep him company in order to go to the festival...'

In OF, Foulet (1961: 167, 331) notes that *ce* is clearly a stressed, non-clitic pronoun, since it can (and regularly does) occupy the first position in a matrix clause, triggering inversion of the subject and verb, as required by the V2 status of OF (cf. (6) above). This claim is reinforced by the fact that *ce* can occur in isolation, can be separated from the verb and can be modified by adjectives such as *meïsmes* 'even', *tout* 'all', properties which are impossible for clitic pronouns:

(8) a. ... et   *ce,*   comant pot   avenir?   (P2377)
       and this how   was-able to-happen
       'And this, how was it able to happen?'
    b. *Ce,*   fet   la dame, ne   me poise   (Y6619)
       this makes the lady NEG me bother
       'That, says the lady, doesn't bother me'
    c. ... et   tout *ce*   fesoit Boorz et   Hestor qui   vouloient prendre
          and all   this   did   Boorz and Hestor who wanted   to-take
       le roi   (Ar112-49)
       the king
       'And Boorz and Hestor, who wanted to take the king, did all this'
    d. *Ce* meïsmes sachiez des   ialz,/ et   del   voirre et   de la
       this even   know   of-the eyes and of-the glass and of the
       lanterne ...   (C724)
       lantern
       'You can be sure of even this concerning the eyes and the glass and the lantern ...'

In early stages of OF, the form *ce* was unambiguously a pronoun, and not a demonstrative (nominal) determiner as well, as is the case in Modern French (cf. (1a)). Dees (1971) argues that nominal determiner *ce* does not begin to appear until late twelfth century and early thirteenth century OF, and is not the regular masculine singular form until the end of the MF period, when the OF two-way (proximate/distant) demonstrative system was fully replaced by the Modern French one-way system. Brunot (1924) states that the use of the particles *ci* and *la* to distinguish proximity began to appear with all demonstratives, including pronominal *ce*, in the fourteenth century; by the end of the fifteenth century, these forms were common, giving three possibilities for a neuter pronoun: *ce* (unmarked), *ceci* (proximate), *cela* (distant). Brunot notes that pronominal *ce* did not come to be restricted in use until the first half of the seventeenth century. By the end of the century, pronominal *ce* had essentially its Modern French limitations: as subject, it was restricted to *être* 'to be'+ NP/past participle; as direct object, its use was discouraged (notably, by Vaugelas); and its use as object of a preposition was rare and used to comic effect when it did appear. Even its use with participles (*et ce dit, en ce faisant* 'and this said', 'while doing this') and incises (*ce dit elle* 'she said') was discouraged.

The use of *ce* in our corpus brings to light other interesting characteristics.

The diachronic evolution of a French complementizer 357

In OF, subject *ce* occurs in the vast majority of cases with *être*; it is also found regularly as the subject of impersonal and psych-verbs, but only sporadically with other verbs (unergative or transitive verbs). The table below shows the percentages found in *Roland*, Chrétien, and *Artu*:

(9) Pronominal subject *ce*

	Roland (33 exx.)	Chrétien (227 exx.)	Artu (222 exx.)	Overall
être	94%	82%	88%	85.7%
imp./psych	3%	17.6%	11.5%	13.7%
other	3%	0.4%	0.4%	0.6%

Interestingly, subject *ce* is exceedingly rarely attested where it is inverted with the verb in non-interrogative contexts. This is surprising in that, given the strong V2 nature of OF and the optional V2 nature of MF, subjects in non-interrogative contexts often follow the verb, either at the end of the clause, in free inversion, or immediately following the verb, in simple inversion:[2]

(10) a. Sire, hui, nos a ce fet li nains, ... (L5154)
       lord today to-us has this done the dwarf
       'Lord, the dwarf has done this to us today'
   b. Einsi dist li rois son pleisir ... (C4703)
       thus said the king his pleasure
       'Thus, the king expressed his will ...'

Vance (1989), however, notes that pronominal subjects as a whole do not occur in free inversion, a fact which also explains the lack of subject *ce* in this context.[3] However, subject *ce* is distinct from other nominative pronouns in that it also does not readily occur in simple inversion (in non-interrogative contexts).[4]

DO occurrences of *ce* also display interesting characteristics. In OF, the position which DO *ce* occupies differs slightly in matrix and embedded clauses. In matrix clauses, *ce* virtually always precedes some type of verbal element, be it finite, infinitival or participial. The 189 examples of DO *ce* found in *Roland* and Chrétien (conservative OF) had the following distribution:[5]

(11) DO pronominal *ce* in *Roland* and Chrétien (matrix clauses)

ce V_I ... S	*ce* V_I ... S_{null}	S *ce* V_I	V_I *ce* V_{-fin}	post-V
53%	44.5%	1%	0.5%	1%
(100/189)	(84/249)	(2/189)	(1/189)	(2/189)[6]

In embedded clauses, DO *ce* also precedes some type of verbal element in the majority of cases, but not to the extent it does in matrix clauses. There appears to be a difference between conservative OF (Chrétien) and innovative OF (*Artu*) with respect to the frequency of post-V *ce*:

(12) DO pronominal *ce* in Chrétien and *Artu* (embedded clauses)

	ce V_I ... S	*ce* V_I ... S_{null}	S *ce* V_I	V_I *ce* V_{-fin}	post-V
Chrétien	16%	53%	21%	10%	0%
Artu	23%	10%	16%	32%	19%

In conservative OF, DO *ce* precedes a finite verbal element 90% of time, and never follows the main verb. On the other hand, in innovative OF, *ce* precedes the finite verb only 49% of the time, and precedes no verbal element 19% of the time. Thus, in conservative OF, there appears to be a strict pre-verbal requirement for DO *ce* (not unlike subject *ce*); in innovative OF, this requirement begins to be relaxed.

The MF evidence from the *CNNV* bears out this trend away from strictly pre-verbal DO *ce*. In matrix clauses, the proportion of post-verbal *ce* is identical to that found in innovative OF embedded clauses, and in MF embedded clauses, the instances of post-verbal *ce* are even more frequent:

(13) DO pronominal *ce* in *CNNV*

	ce V_I ... S	*ce* V_I ... S_{null}	S *ce* V_I	V_I *ce* V_{-fin}	post-V
matrix	62.5%	0%	6%	12.5%	19%
embedded	0%	43%	3%	17%	37%

The strict pre-verbal character of subject and DO *ce*, at least in conservative OF, suggests that there may very well be some general restriction on its position. An exploration of what this might be lies outside the scope of the present chapter, so we will simply note the fact and turn next to the properties of pronominal *ce* in Extraposition structures.

2.2 Extraposition and pronominal *ce*

In addition to its plain NP function, *ce* also plays a role in introducing clausal arguments in a sentence. *Ce*'s mediating function turns up in two forms: one is classic Extraposition, in which a pronoun functioning as an argument is associated with an extraposed clause (14a), and the other is our non-*wh* clausal-argument *ce que*, where *ce* and the *que*-clause are contiguous (14b):

(14) a. ... ne *ce* mie   ne li   greva /*qu'* il   ne luisoit
         and this not-at-all NEG to-him grieve that there NEG shone
         lune n' estoile ...   (L4560)
         moon nor star
         'And it did not grieve him at all that there shone neither moon nor star ...'
     b. Mes *ce que* li   cuens avoit tort / Li   grieve formant et
        but it that the count had   wrong to-him grieved strongly and
        anpire   (C1898)
        upset
        'But that the count was wrong grieved and upset him mightily'

In this section, we will limit our discussion to *ce* in Extraposition (14a), postponing the discussion of *ce que* (14b) until section 3.

The examples of Extraposition garnered from our corpus show that this construction is common and readily used from subject (14a), DO (15a) and object of P (15b) positions in OF:

(15) a. Ce dïent an cest païs   tuit /*que* il les deliverra toz ... (*L2300*)
    this say in this country all that he them will-deliver all
    'Everyone says this in this country, that he will deliver them all'
  b. mes *de ce* ai ge duel greignor/ *que* ge ne verrai mon
    but of this have I grief greater that I NEG will-see my
    seignor, ...   (*E2593*)
    lord
    'But I have greater grief from this, that I will not see my lord ...'

As Rouquier (1990) notes, the extraposed clause can take a variety of forms: a finite clause introduced by *que* (16a), by *quant* 'when' (16b), or by a *wh*-phrase (17); or an infinitival clause (18):

(16) a. Ce mout li desabeli *que il einsi l' avoit perdue*
    this much to-him displeased that he thus her had lost
    'It displeased him much that he had lost her thus'
    (*P7118*, Lecoy's edition; cited in Rouquier 1990: 61)
  b. Ce mout li desabeli *quant il l' avoit einsi perdue*
    this much to-him displeased when he her had thus lost
    'It displeased him much when he had lost her thus'
    (*P7369*, Roach's edition; cited in Rouquier 1990: 61)

(17) a. Mes ço ne set *quels abat ne quels chiét*   (*Ro2553*)
    but this NEG knows which fights nor which falls
    'But he doesn't know which one is fighting nor which one is falling'
  b. ... mes ce ne sei ge *se ce fu por l' amour la reïne ou por moi*
    but this NEG know I if it is for the love the queen or for me
    (*Ar52-49*)
    'But I do not know if it was for the love of the queen or for me'

(18) a. Ce fut folie, fet Lancelos, *de baer a moi en tel*
    this was folly makes Lancelot of to-yearn to me in such
    maniere, ...   (*Ar57-21*)
    manner
    'It was folly, says Lancelot, to yearn after me in such a manner'
  b. Et est à ce propos, comme j'ay dit devant, que *c' est*
    and is to this matter as I have said before that it is
    chose impossible de soy bien gouverner en ce monde icy ...
    thing impossible of self well to-govern in this world here
    'And it's in this regard, as I've said before, that it's impossible to govern oneself well in this world...'   (*CNNV 97-70*)

Common in OF, Extraposition becomes much rarer in MF. One indication that this construction was on the decline beginning in innovative OF comes from the type of separation found between *ce* and the extraposed clause. In conservative OF, the overwhelming tendency was to have *ce* (subject, DO or PP) be clause-initial, and the extraposed clause clause-final, although DO *ce* and *à* and *de* argument PPs could also occupy other pre-verbal positions. Adjunct PPs could also be separated from the extraposed clause by *se ... non* 'except' or incises:

(19) a. E! Dex! conme il fust ore liez/ Du retorner, se *por ce*
oh God how he was now happy of-the return if for this
non/ Qu' il estoit en grant soupeçon /Qu' el ne li
not that he was in great suspicion that she NEG to-him
veille l' anel rendre! (Om664–667)
want the ring to-give-back
'Oh! God! How overjoyed he was to return, except for this, that he
greatly feared that she might wish to return the ring to him'

b. Ne vostre hoste ne vostre hostiex/ N' avra ja s'
NEG your guest NEG your house NEG will-have ever 3SG
onor non par moi;/Non pas *por ce*, en moie foie, /Que il
honor not by me not at-all for this in my faith that it
ne m' ait molt bien esté/ conseillié et amonesté
NEG to-me has very well been counselled and warned (P5250–4)
'Neither your guest nor your house will have anything but honor
from me; not that, by my faith, I haven't been very well counseled
and warned to do the opposite'

Beginning with innovative OF, however, adjunct PP Extraposition is attested only in the two environments illustrated in (18). Thus, a limitation was placed even on how the Extraposition was realized.

Notably, the syntactic behaviour of *ce* in Extraposition conforms to that of plain pronominal *ce*, detailed in section 2.1 above. Whether functioning as subject, DO or object of P, *ce* occupies its canonical position, pre-verbally for subject and DO, and following the P for P-objects. There are no attestations of non-interrogative inverted subject *ce*, nor any attestations of post-verbal DO *ce*, in Extraposition.

With respect to subject Extraposition, it is interesting to note that this occurs significantly less frequently with *être* and more frequently with impersonal verbs, psych verbs and others than did plain pronominal subject *ce*. Compare (20) to (9) above:

(20)	conservative OF	innovative OF	MF
être	32.8% (21/64)	40% (2/5)	83.3% (10/12)
imp./psych	45.3% (29/64)	20% (1/5)	16.7% (2/12)
other	21.9% (14/64)	40% (2/5)	0%

The drop in frequency with *être* is no doubt due at least in part to the fact that only a subset of predicates possible with *être* accept clausal subjects (e.g., *m'être avis* 'to seem to me' does, *être ma suer* 'to be my sister' does not; plain pronominal *ce* is possible with both). However, the rise in frequency in OF with verbs other than *être*, impersonal and psych verbs is significant. In addition, it appears to be the case in MF that subject Extraposition becomes impossible with these other verbs, and limited to *être*, impersonal and psych verbs. In fact, the two examples of non-*être* Extraposition found in our MF corpus both occurred with impersonal, not psych, verbs, and both in CNNA. In the CNNV, the only examples of Extraposition attested occurred with *être*. Finally, it is important to note that the relative frequency of subject Extraposition also declines over time.[7] The number of examples attested in our corpus was distributed as follows:

(21)

	attested ex.	size relative to Chrétien	expected # of exx. relative to Chr.
conservative OF			
12th-c. verse (Chr. only)	45	—	—
13th-c. verse:	16	29.2%	13
innovative OF			
13th-c. prose:	5	40%	18
MF			
16th-c. prose:	5	58.6%	26

Roughly speaking, the thirteenth-century verse corpus constitutes 29.2% of the size of the Chrétien corpus, the thirteenth-century prose corpus, 40% and the sixteenth-century corpus, 58.6%. If Extraposition occurred at the same rate of frequency in these latter corpora as in the Chrétien corpus, we would expect to find approximately 13 examples for thirteenth-century verse, 18 examples for thirteenth-century prose and 26 examples for sixteenth-century prose. Thus, subject Extraposition occurs at about the same frequency in the conservative French corpora, but decreases dramatically in innovative OF and MF. Thus, it is safe to say that by the end of the MF period, subject Extraposition is severely restricted in its productivity.

DO and P-object Extraposition in OF and MF display the same characteristics as does subject Extraposition. In all of the examples from our corpus, DO *ce* appears pre-verbally:

(22)

	ce V_I ... S	*ce* V_I ... S_{null}	S *ce* V_I	V_I *ce* V_{-fin}	post-V
cons. OF	35 (58.3%)	14 (23.3%)	10 (16.7%)	1 (1.7%)	0
innov. OF	6 (85.7%)	0	0	1 (14.3%)	0
MF	2 (66.7%)	1 (33.3%)	0	0	0

Furthermore, the relative frequency of DO Extraposition declines beginning with innovative OF:

(23)

	attested ex.	size relative to Chrétien	expected # of exx. relative to Chr.
conservative O			
12th-c. verse (Chr. only)	29	—	—
13th-c. verse:	7	29.2%	8
innovative OF			
13th-c. prose:	7	40%	11
MF			
16th-c. prose:	3	58.6%	17

P-object Extraposition is attested in our corpus primarily with *à*, *de* and *pour*.[8] With *à*, the PP must be a complement; with *de*, the PP can be either complement or adjunct (the latter having a causal reading); *pour* can only be an adjunct, with either a causal ('because') or final ('so that') reading:

(24)

	à-compl.	de-compl.	à-adjunct	de-adjunct	pour
12th-c. verse	8	18	0	13	29
13th-c. verse	7	2	0	0	8
13th-c. prose	4	0	0	0	4
15th-c. prose	8	0	0	0	1
16th-c. prose	0	0	0	0	1

Again, it is clear that Extraposition is truly viable only in conservative OF; innovative OF loses the ability to extrapose with *de*, and finds Extraposition with *pour* severely restricted in frequency. In MF, P-object Extraposition has all but disappeared.[9]

To summarize, it is clear that Extraposition was regularly available only in conservative OF. Beginning with innovative OF, its use, independent of grammatical function—subject, DO, P-object—became severely limited, to the extent that in MF, only sporadic occurrences are found.

3 Contiguous *ce que*

3.1 The distribution of contiguous *ce que* in our corpus

Having established the characteristics of pronominal *ce*, both as an argument by itself and linked to Extraposed clauses, we turn next to contrast the behaviour of non-*wh* clausal argument *ce que* with pronominal *ce* in Extraposition. This is important in that most OF and MF grammarians consider these two constructions to be one and the same, namely, instances of Extraposition, which are string vacuous in the case of *ce que*. Indeed, *ce que* resembles Extraposition in OF in that it can serve all grammatical functions: subject (25a), DO (25b) and object of P (25c):

(25) a. Mes *ce que* li   cuens avoit tort / Li   grieve formant et
       but it that the count had   wrong to-him grieved strongly and
       anpire
       upset   (C1898)
       'But that the count was wrong grieved and upset him mightily'
    b. Ge li   dis *ce qu'* il s' en   alast, ...   (Tr435)
       I to-him told it that he self of-it go
       'I told him that he should leave ...'
    c. Et sa gent si   grant duel an   font/ de cequ' il ne
       and his people such great grief of-it do   of it that he NEG
       vient ne   repeire ...   (L5087)
       comes NEG returns
       'And his people greatly lament that he neither comes back nor returns ...'

Nonetheless, our corpus provides evidence that Extraposition and contiguous *ce que* are distinct structures. Notably, *ce* in *ce que* does not occur in the same types of positions as it does with Extraposition, nor with the same types of predicates, and it is significantly less frequently used than Extraposition.

3.1.1 Subject *ce que*

Consider first subject *ce que*. Unlike plain pronominal *ce* and Extraposition *ce*, *ce que* can appear either pre-verbally or post-verbally in non-interrogative contexts:

(26) a. ... et *ce que* je vos voi plorer / me   fet   grant mal et
       and it that I you see to-weep to-me makes great pain and
       grant enui   (E2758)
       great torment
       'And (the fact) that I see you weep gives me great pain and great torment'
   b. mes *ce que* il se   desguisa en semblance de nouvel chevalier
      but it that he self disguised in appearance of new   knight
      m'   en toli   la droite connoissance   (Ar30-38)
      to-me of-it took-away the true recognition
      'But (the fact) that he disguised himself as a new knight took away from me any true recognition'

(27) a. 'Biax niés, fet   il, pas ne m'   agree / *Ce que*
        fair nephew makes he at-all NEG to-me pleases it that
        partir volez de   moi'   (C4187)
        to-leave you-wish from me
        "Fair nephew, says he, it does not please me at all that you wish to leave me"
   b. Bien afferoit a sa hautece/ *ce qu'* il ert sages et   cortois
      well befitted to his greatness it that he was wise and courtly
      'It was quite befitting to his greatness that he was wise and courtly'
                                                                     (Do53)

However, there is a clear dichotomy between the two positions with respect to the type of matrix verb that occurs with them. With *être*, impersonal and psych verbs, subject *ce que* is usually post-verbal, while with other verbs (unergatives and transitives), it is usually pre-verbal:

(28)

	OF		MF	
	pre-V	post-V	pre-V	post-V
être/impers./psych	2	7	0	0
other V	6	1	2	0

Given the unaccusative character of at least impersonal and psych verbs, it is not surprising that *ce que* here is usually post-verbal, since this is its D-structure position. We believe it noteworthy, however, that *ce que* occurs in this position while other instances of subject *ce* do not, even with impersonal and psych verbs (but see note 2).

Another difference between subject *ce que* on the one hand and Extraposition *ce* and plain pronominal *ce* on the other is the type of verb they occur with. Recall that the latter two instances of *ce* occurred regularly with *être* and impersonal and psych verbs, and much less frequently with other types of verbs. Subject *ce que*, however, occurs extremely rarely with *être*, and with equal frequency (at least in OF) with impersonal/psych and other verbs. Only one example of *ce que* with *être* is attested in our corpus:

(29)   ... il ne poïssent pas durer si longuement comme il
        they NEG were-able not to-endure so long   as   they
        durerent, se ne fut *ce qu'* il se deffendoient si
        endured if NEG was it that they SELF defended so
        merveilleusement   (Ar168-6)
        wondrously
        'They would not have been able to endure as long as they endured, if it hadn't been (for the fact) that they defended themselves so wondrously'

Moreover, we saw that subject Extraposition became limited to *être* by the end of the MF period. As (28) shows, subject *ce que* also becomes limited, but to unergative and transitive verbs, not to *être*.

Given the relative rarity of subject *ce que* in our presently limited corpus, any claims with respect to changes in relative frequency from period to period can only be made cautiously. Nonetheless, there does appear to be a decline in the use of *ce que* beginning with the innovative OF period:

(30)

	attested ex.	size relative to Chrétien	expected # of exx. relative to Chr.
conservative OF			
12th-c. verse (Chr. only)	10	—	—
13th-c. verse:	4	29.2%	3
innovative OF			
13th-c. prose:	1	40%	4
MF			
16th-c. prose:	1	58.6%	6

3.1.2 DO *ce que*

Like subject *ce que*, DO *ce que* differs from its Extraposition and plain pronominal counterparts in occurring both pre- and post-verbally:

(31) a. Et, si m' aïst Dex, fet ele, *ce que* je li donnai
     and so me help God makes she it that I to-him gave
     avant le fruit a mengier ne fesoie ge se par grant
     beforehand the fruit to to-eat NEG did I if by great
     deboneretĕ non   (Ar62-84)
     kindness not
     'So help me God, says she, that I gave him the fruit to eat beforehand did I only do out of great kindness'

b. Je vos pri qu' a mal ne taigniez / ce qu' a vostre salu
I you beg that to evil NEG you-hold it that at your greeting
me toi (P941)
me remain-silent
'I beg you that you not hold it against me that at your greeting I remained silent'

Ce que occupies in (31a) what would be a canonical position for DO *ce*, but its position in (31b) is one which DO *ce* almost never occupies, at least in conservative OF. Nonetheless, it is this latter position in which most of the DO *ce que* attested in our corpus are found:

(32)
	OF		MF	
	pre-V	post-V	pre-V	post-V
DO *ce que*	2	4	0	1

Examples of DO *ce que* are even rarer in our corpus than were subject *ce que*; nonetheless, they do appear to decrease in frequency over time:

(33)
	attested ex.
conservative OF	
12th-c. verse:	4
13th-c. verse:	0
innovative OF	
13th-c. prose:	2
MF	
15th-c. prose:	1
16th-c. prose:	0

3.1.3 P-object *ce que*

The truly productive domain for *ce que* in both OF and MF is that of prepositional object. Like Extraposition, it occurs with *à* and *de* complements and adjuncts, and with *pour*; in addition, it occurs with a slew of other prepositions which increase in number during the MF period. The tables below give the number of occurrences found in our corpus:

(34) *à ce que, de ce que, pour ce que*

	à-compl.	de-compl.	à-adjunct	de-adjunct	pour
12th-c. verse	0	20	8	14	176
13th-c. verse	1	7	2	9	22
13th-c. prose	6	16	34	8	108
15th-c. prose	6	11	3	1	40
16th-c. prose	0	13	0	2	58

(35) other P
  12th-c. verse: après (5), sans (9), par (1), atot (1)
  13th-c. verse: sans (1), en (4), avec (1), selon (1), sur (1)
  13th-c. prose: après (4), sans (1), en (8), devant (2), encontre (1), ja soit (1)

15th-c. prose: après (6), sans (14), jasoit (8), jusqu'à (16), excepté (1)
16th-c. prose: après (17), sans (46), par (17), jasoit (20), jusqu'à (1), avec (4), selon (1), à cause de (3)

These tables show that adjunct P *ce que*, with Ps other than *à* and *de*, was quite possible and fairly common (especially with *pour*) from the early OF period, gaining ground with new Ps as the language progressed. *À ce que* and *de ce que* as adjuncts are also readily attested in OF, but appear to lose steam in MF, possibly because other Ps are assuming the role of expressing causal adjuncts. While *de ce que* complements are attested throughout the periods of OF and MF, *à ce que* complements are not attested with any regularity (at least in our corpus) until the innovative OF period.[10]

One of the clearest indications in our corpus that Extraposition and contiguous *ce que* are distinct structures is that the relative frequency with which each is used changes over time. The tables below compare the two for each type of P:

(36) Change in relative frequency: *ce que* and Extraposition

a. *à* complements

	Extrap.	ce que
cons. OF	94%	6%
innov. OF	40%	60%
MF	57%	43%

b. *de* complements

	Extrap.	ce que
cons. OF	42.5%	57.5%
innov. OF	0%	100%
MF	4%	96%

c. *à* adjuncts

	Extrap.	ce que
cons. OF	94%	6%
innov. OF	40%	60%
MF	57%	43%

d. *de* adjuncts

	Extrap.	ce que
cons. OF	42.5%	57.5%
innov. OF	0%	100%
MF	4%	96%

e. *pour*

	Extrap.	ce que
cons. OF	15.7%	84.3%
innov. OF	0.4%	99.6%
MF	2%	98%

f. Other

	Extrap.	ce que
cons. OF	7.4%	92.6%
innov. OF	0%	100%
MF	0.6%	99.4%

First, note that *à* complements and *à* adjuncts are virtually in complementary distribution in conservative OF: the vast majority of complements are extraposed, while all adjuncts use *ce que*. Second, conservative OF overwhelmingly prefers *ce que* for adjuncts of all types. This appears to indicate a division of labour: *ce que* for adjuncts and Extraposition for complements. The exception in both cases occurs with *de*, which has Extraposition with adjuncts in one out of three cases, and *ce que* for complements in two out of five. The reason for this may be the fact that the line between complement and adjunct is very difficult to draw for *de* PPs: the former most often supply a source for a psychological state, which is not far from the causal meaning of the adjunct phrases. In any case, it would be unexpected to find this division of labour between *ce que* and Extraposition if in fact they were one and the same construction. Moreover, the diachronic development of Extraposition and *ce que* differ markedly, in that by the end of the MF period, P-object Extraposition becomes limited essentially to *à* complements, while *ce que* becomes possible with more and more Ps.

3.2 Further contrasts between *ce que* and Extraposition

Rouquier (1990) also takes issue with the traditional assumption that *ce que* is simply string vacuous Extraposition, arguing, as we have done, that the two uses of *ce* represent different structures. She begins by examining both subject and DO instances of *ce que* which precede their verb, as in (26a) and (31), repeated here as (37a, b):

(37) a. ... et   ce que je vos voi plorer / me   fet   grant mal et
          and it that I you see to-weep to-me makes great pain and
          grant enui   (E2758)
          great torment
          'And (the fact) that I see you weep gives me great pain and great torment'
     b. Et, si m' aïst Dex, fet   ele, ce que je li   donnai
          and so me help God makes she it that I to-him gave
          avant   le fruit a mengier ne fesoie ge se par grant
          beforehand the fruit to to-eat   NEG did   I if by great
          debonereté non   (Ar62-84)
          kindness   not
          'So help me God, says she, that I gave him the fruit to eat beforehand did I only do out of great kindness'

Rouquier notes that, given V2 requirements, one must in these cases either analyse *ce* as a dislocated element, doubled by the clause in first position, or analyse *ce* as being in first position, with the clause a sort of appositive or parenthetical. In the second case, the clause is a type of adjunct, with essentially the same status as the clause in Extraposition. However, she notes that there are striking differences between Extraposition and *ce que* in the realization of the clause. As we noted earlier (cf. section 2.2, (16)–(18)), extraposed clauses can be introduced by *que*, by *quant*, by a *wh*-phrase, or be infinitival instead of finite. Rouquier notes that in her corpus, as in ours, the only type of clause to which *ce* occurs contiguously is a *que*-clause; the other types of clauses are unattested. Care must obviously be taken here to distinguish free relative clauses of the form *ce qui, ce que, ce dont*, etc., from true embedded interrogative clauses, since strings of the form *ce+wh*-clause do occur in the former:

(38) a. Et la reïne qui antant ce dom   eles se   vont vantant,
          and the queen who hears that of-which they SELF go   bragging
          /a soi meïsme an   rit ...   (L6008)
          to self same   about-it laughs
          'And the queen, who hears that which/what they are bragging about, laughs to herself about it'

b. Or   ot   Erec *ce* *qui*   li   siet   (E5399)
   now heard Erec that which to-him suited
   'Now Erec heard that which/what suited him'

A reliable means for doing so is to look for clauses in which the *wh*-phrase is capable of being interrogative only—i.e., *se* 'if', *quel* X 'which X', etc. While these phrases do occur in Extraposed clauses (cf. (17)), they do not occur contiguously to *ce* in our corpus.

Turning next to post-verbal instances of *ce que*, Rouquier notes that while neither subject nor DO *ce* occurs in this position by itself (as we indeed noted in section 2 above), *ce que* does so fairly regularly. If *ce* generally can't occur post-verbally, she asks, why should it be able to just in case it occurs in Extraposition (i.e. with an extraposed clause)? Moreover, she argues that *ce que* appears to form a unit. Take, for example, an instance of post-verbal subject *ce que*:

(39)   se   li   pesa   molt   et   desplot / *ce que* il n'   i
        and to-him bothered much   and   displeased it that   he NEG there
        avoit esté   (L0313)
        had   been
        'And it bothered and displeased him greatly that he hadn't been there'

Post-verbal subject pronouns in OF were clitics, and as such could not be separated from the verb by adverbial elements such as negation. If *ce* in *ce que* were a subject pronoun, and the *que*-clause extraposed, one would expect to find examples where the *ce* and the *que* were separated by negation or adverbs, but such examples do not occur. Furthermore, Rouquier notes that not even versification ever separates the *ce* and the *que*.

Our corpus confirms Rouquier's claim that *ce* and the *que*-clause form part of a larger constituent, since it is able to occur in isolation (as an answer to a question) and as the second conjunct in a conjunction:

(40) a. Qui   le   me   chalonge? *Ce que* je cuit   dire   mançonge
          what it   to-me   disputes   it that I believe to-tell lie
          'What disputes me concerning this? That I believe myself to be
          telling a lie'   (C1380)
      b. ... qu' Amors le   fet   molt grant aïe /et *ce que* il n'
                that Love him makes much great aid   and it that he NEG
          avoit haïe / rien   nule tant   come celui   qui se   conbat
          had   hated creature   any as-much as   the-one who SELF fights
          ancontre lui   (L3722)
          against him
          '...That Love gives him great aid and that he hadn't hated any
          creature as much as the one who was fighting against him'

c. Sa crualté, sa felenie, / la fet molt tainte et molt
    her cruelty her unkindness her makes very spotty and very
    nercie, / et *ce qu'* ele voille et geüne ... (L4193)
    blackened and it that she stays-awake and fasts
    'Her cruelty, her unkindness makes her very spotty and dark-complexioned, and (the fact) that she cannot sleep and fasts ...'

Rouquier concludes that the two instances of *ce*+clause cannot be the same construction. While Extraposition *ce* is indeed a pronoun linked to a postposed clause, Rouquier suggests that *ce que* represents a unitary conjunction. However, our corpus provides evidence that this is not the case, since the two morphemes can be minimally separated by an adverbial modifying the clause:[11]

(41) a. *Ce* seulement *que* je i pans /Me fet grant mal et si
         it only that I about-it think me makes great ill and so
         m' esmaie (C3026)
         me distresses
         'Just thinking about it makes me ill and distresses me'
     b. ... que à peine se pouvoit tenir qu' il ne fust ruez jus,
         that to pain SELF could to-hold that he NEG was thrown off
         avec *ceu* aussi *qu'* il avoit desja destendu ses cordes... (CNNV65-24)
         with it also that he had already loosened his strings
         '... that scarcely could he keep from being thrown off, considering also that he had already loosened his strings'

4 Analysis

4.1 Summary: *ce que* and Extraposition are different constructions

The previous two sections have detailed the syntactic characteristics of pronominal *ce*, Extraposition and *ce que* in OF and MF. By comparing the last of these entities with the first two, we have seen significantly distinct syntactic behaviours, supporting the idea that *ce* in *ce que* is not the pronominal, and the *que*-clause is not simply an extraposed clause. To begin with, the syntax of subject and DO pronominal *ce* is somewhat unusual: they must both precede a verbal element, although this requirement is relaxed somewhat for DO *ce* beginning with innovative OF. In contrast, subject *ce que* regularly occurs in post-verbal position, especially with impersonal and psych verbs. Likewise, DO *ce que* only rarely occurs in pre-verbal position, unlike plain pronominal and Extraposition *ce*. Finally, we noted that the position of subject *ce que*, whether pre- or post-verbal, depended on the matrix verb type: pre-verbal *ce que* predominated with unergatives and transitives, while post-verbal *ce que* predominated with *être*, impersonal and psych verbs. Significantly, pronominal and Extraposition *ce* showed no such variation in position.

Another characteristic separating *ce que* from Extraposition *ce* is the type of verb class with which each occurs. Subject Extraposition *ce* occurs readily with *être*, but much less readily with transitive and unergative verbs. On the other hand, subject *ce que* occurs with the unergative and transitive verb types more often than it does with *être*, impersonal and psych verb types.

Direction of diachronic change also distinguishes *ce que* from the other uses of *ce* which we have examined. Notably, the distributions of subject Extraposition and subject *ce que* with respect to verb class type develop in opposite directions in MF. Subject Extraposition in MF is lost with impersonal, psych, unergative and transitive verbs, becoming limited to *être* only. In contrast, subject *ce que* in MF is lost with impersonal, psych and *être* verb types, becoming limited to unergatives and transitives only. In addition, we noted that the relative frequencies of P-object Extraposition and P *ce que* also develop diachronically in different directions, in that Extraposition here becomes limited essentially to an occasional *à* complement in MF, while P *ce que* is used progressively more often and with a greater range of Ps as time goes by.

4.2 The analysis of *ce* and its diachronic evolution

4.2.1 From Extraposition to DP

The evidence reviewed above provides strong motivation for three conclusions concerning OF and MF *ce que*: (1) their syntactic structure is distinct from that of Extraposition, (2) *ce* and the *que*-clause are subconstituents of a larger phrase, and (3) the two words constitute separate lexical items of some sort. Given these facts, what might the structure of *ce que* be? To answer, we need to take a closer look at the origins of *ce que*. Herman (1963) notes that attestations of pronoun+complementizer sequences occur from the Classical Latin period, increasing in frequency in Vulgar Latin; very often, these take the form *pro/per eo quod*:

(42) a. neque se   *pro eo, quod* spondendo pacem
        nor   themselves-ACC for it   that arranging peace-ACC
        seruassent   exercitum populi   Romani,
        save-3PL-PLUPERF army-ACC people-GEN Roman-GEN
        poenam   ullam meritos   esse
        penalty-ACC any   deserved to-be   (Livy IX, 8, 15) (Herman 1963: 84)
        'Nor (did they think that) they deserved any penalty, since, having arranged peace, they had saved the Roman army'
   b. eorum   exercitum maximum   interficit,   terraque eorum
      3PL-GEN army-ACC largest-ACC destroy-3SG-PST land-and 3PL-GEN
      uastata, peruagans   totam Toringiam   ac
      ravaged wandering-through all-ACC Thoringia-ACC and
      depopulans, *pro eo quod* solacium   Saxonibus
      laying-waste for it that comfort-ACC Saxons-DAT
      prebuissent; ...   (*Liber Historiae Francorum*) (Herman 1963: 84–85)
      offered-3PL-PLUPERF
      '(He) destroyed their largest army, and their land having been ravaged, wandered through and laid waste to all of Thoringia, because they had offered comfort to the Saxons...'

Herman claims that this is the only type of (P+) pronoun+clause to occur in the early texts of all the Romance languages; occurrences with other Ps and without P arise in individual Romance languages, but not until after the Proto-Romance period, and with vastly varying results from language to language. He takes this as evidence that the only instantiation of pronoun+clause which existed in Proto-Romance was *pro/per eo quod*, and this gave reflexes in all of the Romance languages. Finally, Herman notes that both the contiguous form *pro/per eo quod* and the extraposed form *pro/per eo ... quod* existed in Vulgar Latin and in early Romance texts; as a result, he argues that neither one developed from the other.

In early Gallo-Romance, then, children acquiring the language had evidence that embedded clauses could be realized as a pronoun+clause string. What hypotheses might they have made concerning its structure? We noted above that contiguous *ce que* is not incompatible with an Extraposition analysis, since it could be that the Extraposition is simply string vacuous in this case; the same can be said of *pro/per eo quod* strings. Thus there is no necessity, at least in the early Proto-Romance period, for the child to posit a difference between contiguous *pro/per eo quod* and separated *pro/per eo ... quod*; both are possibly instances of Extraposition.

However, if we wish to account for the evidence that *ce* and the *que*-clause are subconstituents of a larger phrase in OF (and MF) *ce que*, it cannot be the case that children continued to analyse Proto-Galloromance *por/par ce que* uniquely as Extraposition, since in this case, the pronoun forms a constituent with the P, not the clause. At some point, reanalysis occurred, from a structure like that in (43a), to one like (43b):

(43) a. Extraposition: [[P *ce*] [*que* . . .]]
     b. Contiguous *ce que*: [P [*ce* [*que* . . .]]]

A priori, it is conceivable that *ce* in (43b) could still represent a pronominal, forming a sort of complex NP with the clause.[12] This would account for the fact that *ce* and *que* are separate lexical items, that they occur in a constituent apart from P, and that P and *ce* do not form a constituent. The difference in position between plain pronominal *ce* and *ce que* could then result from the former's being a 'lightweight' element, easily preposable, while the latter is a 'heavy' constituent, easily postposable.

Another possibility, and the one we ultimately adopt, is proposed and motivated by Zaring (1992) for Modern French, and suggested informally by Wunderli (1978) for MF: *ce* is reanalysed in very early OF as a clausal determiner, selecting for a *que*-clause complement.[13] This means that (43b) has the structure in (44):

(44) [$_{PP}$ por [$_{DP}$ ce [$_{CP}$ que ...]]]

Ce and *que* form separate lexical items, as required, and they participate in the formation of a single constituent, dominated by DP. This analysis seems more plausible from the point of view that complex NPs headed by a pronominal which takes the clause as a complement appear to be rare across languages. Be that as it may, the DP *ce que* is not constrained in the same way that instances of pronominal *ce* are, since pronominal *ce* is not present in this case; this accounts for the difference in the types of positions the two occupy. Finally, the determiner analysis of contiguous *ce que* in OF and MF enables us to account in section 4.2.3 for its diachronic evolution in terms of first-language acquisition strategies.

4.2.2 Extended Projection and the DP analysis

The idea just proposed, namely that OF and MF had a determiner which selected for a clause (henceforth CP), encounters no difficulty with principles of grammar in standard views of X-bar structure. However, it is potentially in conflict with the version of X-bar theory envisioned by Grimshaw (1991), and consequently deserves further scrutiny.

With the extensions of X-bar theory proposed by Abney (1986), Pollock (1989), Fukui & Speas (1986) (among many others) to include functional categories such as determiners, inflection, etc., the ways in which functional projections and lexical projections can *a priori* combine have multiplied dramatically. Nonetheless, intuitively and canonically, determiners are categories that belong to nominal projections, not verbal ones, just as tense specification belongs to verbal projections, not nominal ones. Grimshaw (1991) captures this intuition in her theory of extended projections (EP). She suggests that functional categories, like lexical categories, are of two basic types, nominal and verbal ([+N, –V], [–N, +V]). A feature F distinguishes lexical (F0) from functional (F1) categories.

As a limitation on the ways in which lexical and functional categories can combine, Grimshaw proposes as a principle of grammar that verbal functional heads (e.g. I^0, C^0) can only select verbal projections (e.g. VP) and nominal functional heads (e.g. D^0, P^0) can only select nominal projections (e.g. NP).[14] This captures the canonical relation between NP and D^0, but if absolute, it would rule out the possibility of D^0s, like *ce* in OF, which combine with CPs. Indeed, Grimshaw argues that combinations such as these are uniformly illicit; apparent exceptions, she suggests, are simply cases in which one of the categories involved is neutral—underspecified for one of the [±N, ±V] features. Extended projections can thus be formed as long as the categorial features of the functional head and its complement are non-distinct. For example, Abney (1986) analyses English gerunds as involving a D^0 selecting a VP; however, Grimshaw notes that gerunds have both verbal and nominal properties, and suggests that the nominalized verb in a gerund is unspecified for the feature [N], allowing its projection to be the complement of D^0.

If Grimshaw is correct, one of the categories in the D^0+CP structure that we have proposed for French must be neutral. The evidence available to us at this point to determine which, if any, categories are neutral is delicate and suggestive at best, but we would like to argue that no category neutrality is in fact involved here. Suppose first that D^0 is the neutral category. This would predict that determiner *ce* should be able to select either a nominal or a verbal complement. However, in OF, the point at which *ce que* is attested most frequently, *ce* occurs only with clauses, not with nominals (see below for further discussion of nominal determiner *ce*). Furthermore, as soon as nominal determiner *ce* begins to develop in innovative OF, clausal determiner *ce* starts to wane. This is surely unexpected if determiner *ce* is in fact neutral in category, since the rise of nominal determiner *ce* should simply reinforce *ce*'s neutrality and the availability of clausal *ce*, rather than marginalize it.

Another reason to believe that determiner *ce* is not neutral stems from the fact that, if it were neutral, the constituent dominated by DP should have essentially identical behaviour to ordinary CPs, since the features of this constituent would percolate up to the neutral DP (cf. Grimshaw 1991: 27). However, there is good evidence that ordinary CPs and *ce que* do not have the same behaviour. We noted above that tensed clauses are resistant to appearing in positions assigned case. While less true for OF than for Modern French, the combination [P [$_{CP}$ que ...]] is in general ruled out (cf. **à que, **de que in all stages of French), while *ce que* versions of this combination are fine (i.e. *à ce que, de ce que, pour ce que*, etc.). Furthermore, Rouquier (1990) cites Ritchie (1907: 113), who notes that CPs which follow the verb that selects them in OF can have either the *ce que* form, or the plain *que* form, while CPs which precede their selecting verb virtually always have the form *ce que*. Rouquier also notes that CPs in the pre-verbal position are indicative in mood if the form is *ce que*, but subjunctive if the form is plain *que*.

If D^0 is not category-neutral, could it be that CP is? One problem in going this route is that CP is itself an extended projection of VP, and any one of the functional categories in between (Agr$_O$, T, Agr$_S$) and including C^0 could be the site of the neutrality. Determining which it might be would be empirically extremely difficult, especially since regular CPs have so few overt functional category differences from those with *ce que*. If CP were neutral in category, we would expect *ce que* to have the same behaviour as any DP, as indeed is the case for English gerunds. This would lead us to expect that *ce que* would be much more widely attested in OF, since it would provide an easy way around the case resistance properties of tensed clauses. In fact, as we noted early, *ce que* occurs quite rarely when compared to ordinary *que* CPs. The only real evidence in favour of D^0 or CP neutrality is that fact that an apparent determiner and a CP form a constituent. As a result, we conclude that there is no convincing, independent evidence that either D^0 or CP is category-neutral in our *ce que* structures. Indeed, we will argue that it is precisely the hybrid character of the combination which explains *ce que*'s evolution, the matter to which we now turn.

4.2.3 Determiner *ce* and the parametrized Extended Projection theory

In section 4.2.1 above, we proposed that the development of OF (P) *ce que* from Latin *pro/per eo quod* involved a reanalysis from an Extraposition structure (43a) to a DP structure (44). As northern Gallo-Romance developed into early OF, the neuter pronoun inherited from Latin acquired mild deictic force and took on the form of demonstrative (*i*)*ço*, eventually *ce*. Although this pronoun itself functioned only as a pronoun, other members of the demonstrative paradigm were both pronoun and determiner. Thus, children acquiring very early OF had evidence that categories which looked like demonstratives could have the status of determiners, paving the way for an analysis of *ce* in *ce que* as a determiner in just this case. Indeed, if Roberts (1993a) is correct concerning strategies of language acquisition, then reanalysis of *ce* as a clausal determiner, instead of a pronoun in Extraposition, was the favoured analysis. Roberts argues that one strategy innately guiding acquirers is the Least Effort Strategy (LES):

(45) Least Effort Strategy (LES)
Representations assigned to sentences of the input to acquisition should be such that they contain the set of the shortest possible chains (consistent with (a) principles of grammar, (b) other aspects of the trigger experience).

In terms of chain positions, it is clear that *ce* and *que* in Extraposition comprise two such positions for one argument, since they are obligatorily co-indexed:

(46) [$_{IP}$ ... [$_{VP}$ [$_{VP}$ ... [$_{PP}$ por ce$_i$]][$_{CP}$ que ...]$_i$]]

In contrast, the DP *ce que* constitutes only one chain position, occupied by the DP itself, the argument:

(47) [$_{IP}$ ... [$_{VP}$ ... [$_{PP}$ por [$_{DP}$ ce [$_{CP}$ que ...]]]]]

Thus, the LES, which prompts reanalysis when the result contains fewer chain positions, would dictate the reanalysis of *ce* in *ce que* from pronoun in Extraposition to determiner in *ce que*. Once the reanalysis had occurred, acquirers of early OF had evidence that embedded clauses could be realized as DPs, and use of this DP generalized to other Ps and grammatical functions by the early OF period.

The above analysis of *ce* in *ce que* as a clausal determiner accounts nicely for the syntactic properties (constituency, syntactic position) of *ce que* in OF and MF, and is motivated from an acquisition perspective as well. Furthermore, this account provides the means for explaining the further diachronic development of *ce que* after the conservative OF period. We noted in section 3 that use of *ce que* becomes suddenly quite limited from the innovative OF period on, to the extent that it occurs regularly only as a prepositional object. Why did this limitation occur, and why in innovative OF? We would like to suggest that a simultaneous development in the OF and MF demonstrative system provided contradictory evidence as to the syntactic properties of determiner *ce*, resulting in the evidence for clausal *ce* being increasingly marginalized, and in eventual reanalysis of clausal *ce que*.

Note, to begin with, that the change in *ce que* in innovative OF cannot be attributed to a change in the syntax of pronominal *ce* at the same time. It is true that the syntax of pronominal *ce* changed fairly radically in the history of French, but as noted in section 2, this change did not begin to occur until the seventeenth century. This is another indication that we are on the right track in analysing *ce que* as not involving pronominal *ce*. To understand the change in *ce que*, we must first examine another change which began to occur in innovative Old French, namely the reduction of the demonstrative system from two paradigms to one. As documented by Harris (1978a) and Dees (1971), among others, the OF demonstrative system underwent a radical shift between the late OF and late MF periods. In conservative OF, there were two demonstrative paradigms, distinguishing proximate from distant:

(48) OF demonstrative paradigms

	proximate		distant	
	masculine	feminine	masculine	feminine
singular				
nominative	cist	ceste	cil	cele
oblique	cest	ceste	cel	cele
plural				
nominative	cist	cestes	cil	celes
oblique	cez	cestes	cels	celes

Beginning in the late twelfth and early thirteenth centuries, the oblique masculine plural forms *cez* (proximate) and *cels* (distant) collapsed into a single form, *ces*, in their use as determiners, creating a nominal demonstrative determiner unmarked for the proximity distinction. Soon, a masculine singular form *ce* appeared as well, innovated perhaps by analogy with the definite determiners *le, les*.[15] The appearance of *ce* extends the range of the unmarked demonstrative system, and with the loss of the nominative/oblique case system in early MF, this unmarked system becomes predominant, so that by the early sixteenth century, the forms which previously had marked a distinction in proximity now marked a distinction between determiner and pronoun.

The important development in this shift is that it creates, alongside the clausal determiner *ce*, a homophonous nominal determiner *ce*. Above, we noted that Grimshaw's (1991) theory of Extended Projection (EP) would allow the latter, but not the former, unless some sort of category neutrality were involved. We propose, however, that there is another way of conceiving of EP which captures Grimshaw's insights while allowing a certain amount of leeway in how functional categories combine with lexical ones. Suppose that, instead of category neutrality, the EP is couched in terms of a parameter consistent with Berwick's (1985) Subset Principle, so that the positive setting allows a smaller set of structures than the negative setting:

(49) Functional categories can only extend lexical projections of their same type (nominal or verbal)? yes/no

Given the Subset Principle, the 'yes' setting is the default one, since it is the setting which provides the most restricted grammar and the smallest set of structures. When chosen, the EP will hold absolutely, ruling out hybrid combinations like OF *ce que*. The 'no' setting will require unambiguous positive evidence in the trigger experience for acquisition, and once chosen will permit hybrids like clausal determiners insofar as there is positive evidence of their existence. In conservative OF, the evidence that *ce* in *ce que* was a D^0 that extended a verbal projection (CP) was robust and unambiguous; indeed, as we saw above, it is the only analysis consistent with the evidence available to the acquirer. As a result, the EP parameter was set in the negative, allowing this combination of nominal category plus verbal projection.

In innovative OF, however, evidence for both nominal determiner and clausal determiner *ce* is present in the trigger experience, and the evidence for which parameter setting to choose became contradictory. That is, there was abundant evidence for the positive setting in the frequent examples of *ce*+N to which our corpus attests. On the other hand, there was evidence for the negative setting, given the not-infrequent occurrences of P *ce que* and rarer instances of subject and DO *ce que*. Nonetheless, it is not so much the contradictory nature of the evidence, as the mere possibility of analysing *ce* in keeping with the positive default setting of the parameter, available for the first time in innovative OF because of the change underway in the demonstrative system, which caused the crucial evidence for the existence of clausal determiner *ce* to become marginalized. This meant that use of *ce que* decreased in scope (becoming rare as subject and DO), perhaps to the extent that learners posited a condition on its use, namely assignment of inherent case, by P. This would help to explain why *ce que* continued to be used regularly only as object of P.

Once the evidence for clausal *ce* was no longer robust, the theory predicts that at a certain point acquirers would choose the positive setting of the EP parameter, eliminating the D^0 analysis for *ce que*. We would cautiously like to suggest, pending further investigation, that this indeed did occur, after the MF period. Our corpus provides evidence that as late as the early sixteenth century, clausal *ce* still existed, since the *ce* and the *que* can still be minimally separated by a modifier in the CNNV (cf. (41b)). In Modern French, however, this separation of the two elements is impossible. We would like to suggest that the reason for this was that the negative setting for the EP parameter was indeed lost, making clausal *ce* an impossibility. Conceivably, acquirers of French after this point, confronted with the *ce que* which still existed, posited that these two words comprised not two morphemes, but one, given the normal pronunciation by that time of [skə]. As Wunderli (1978) suggests, the status of this item is reasonably C^0. We would add that it might be best conceived of as a complementizer with unusually nominal properties, in view of its current Modern French restriction. Namely, *ce que* in Modern French is restricted to occurring with *à* and *de*, which, if Zaring (1991) is correct, are the only overt instances of case-marking in Modern French. Modern French *ce que* would thus be a C^0 capable of bearing case, but limited to overt inherent case only. We leave for further research the precise mechanism to capture the nominal character of this complementizer.

5 Conclusion

In addition to accounting for the syntactic behaviour of *ce que* and for its evolution in the history of French, the analysis detailed above provides support for a number of ideas which have recently been proposed to play a part in the theory of grammar and how this interacts with language change. The idea that the ways in which a first language is acquired determine diachronic syntactic change is one that has received support in our analysis, since we make crucial use of strategies of first-language acquisition, namely the LES and the Subset Principle, to motivate the changes which occurred in the use of *ce que*. Notably, these strategies are ones based on the idea of economy of representation and derivation, which has been proposed (cf. Chomsky 1988) as an essential limitation on the form grammars take, and insofar as we have succeeded in showing that they play an integral role in the evolution of *ce que*, our analysis provides evidence in favour of the relevance of economy in grammatical theory. Furthermore, our analysis has highlighted once again the crucial role that the notion of parameter plays in grammatical variation, diachronic in this case, since the EP parameter is fundamental to understanding the development which *ce que* undergoes.

Although we do not have room to pursue it here, our analysis also makes predictions about the extent to which hybrid categories, such as D^0+CP, occur crosslinguistically. Specifically, we expect them to be relatively rare, and to arise via reanalysis of some other structure. Other occurrences of D^0+CP have been claimed to exist in Modern Greek, Lakhota and Squamish:

(50) a. Modern Greek (B. Joseph, pers. com.)
To oti o Janis ine enoxos ine fanero
DET that the John is guilty-MS is obvious-NS
'That John is guilty is obvious'
b. Lakhota (Comrie & Thompson 1985: 393)
El cihipi kin iyonicip´ipi
to I-came-you DET has-pleased-you
'That I came to you has pleased you'
c. Squamish (Noonan 1985: 61, citing Kuipers 1967)
Č-n čiws k^{w}i n-s-na wa
DECLAR-1SG tired-body DET 1SG POSS-NOM-fact PROG
c´aq´-an-umi
hit-TRANS-2SG OBJ
'I'm tired of hitting you'

In these examples, the characteristics of normal clauses have been retained; a determiner has simply been added, as in French. Another possibility for this combination might be those Romance languages in which an infinitival phrase follows a determiner. Clearly, it will be necessary to thoroughly examine each potential hybrid combination in each language to verify that they do involve a true determiner and a true verbal projection. Insofar as this is possible, we expect that they will resemble quite closely in diachronic evolution what we have seen for French *ce que*.

Finally, our analysis also provides indirect support for Chomsky's (1993) Minimalist view of language variation, since the vast majority of the changes discussed in connection with *ce que* revolve around the properties of functional categories and the ways in which these change. In this case at least, then, syntactic variation is indeed limited to non-substantive parts of the lexicon.

Notes

* We would like to acknowledge the following people for their helpful comments and insights: Jacqueline Guéron, Brian Joseph, Ans van Kemenade, Tony Kroch, Marie Labelle, Ian Roberts, Johan Rooryck and Nigel Vincent. All shortcomings, of course, remain our own. Research for this article was supported in part by Grant 410-89-1131 from the Social Sciences and Humanities Research Council of Canada, awarded to Paul Hirschbühler.

1. The examples we used were garnered from concordances based on these works; see the bibliography for references for the concordances and the editions of the above works on which the concordances were based. Given after the title of each work in (3) and (4) is an abbreviation which will be used to identify the text of origin in the examples we cite below.

2. An anonymous reviewer suggests that pragmatic properties of *ce*, namely its discourse anaphoric status, might account for the fact that it does not occur post-verbally. This suggestion is certainly well taken, since it reflects the importance of factoring out the various determinants of *ce*'s behaviour, so as not to impute to the syntactic component something which is easily explained in discourse terms. At this point, we can only note that personal pronominal subjects (e.g. *il* 'he', *elle* 'she'), which are also discourse anaphoric elements, do regularly appear in simple inversion in non-interrogative contexts, in contrast to subject *ce*. Thus, the discourse anaphoric status of *ce*, in and of itself, does not appear to be sufficient to account for the lack of post-verbal *ce*. Given the complexity of this matter, a thorough exploration must be left for future work targeting not only *ce* and personal pronouns, but also demonstrative pronouns such as *cil*, *cest* 'this, that', etc. See also the discussion following (10).

3. Roberts (1993a) suggests the following formalization of this constraint:
   (i) nominative pronouns must form a chain with a position governed by or in Spec–head agreement with Agr^0 (where Agr^0 is present) (Roberts 1993a: 121).

4. 3% of subject *ce* occur in simple inversion in *Roland* (1 out of 33 examples), 0.4% in Chrétien (1/227) and 2% in *Artu* (4/222); all are subjects of *être* +NP (X *être ce* NP). This fact might be taken to suggest that Roberts' condition on nominative pronouns (cf. note. 3) is even more restricted in the case of *ce*, to the effect that nominative *ce* can form a chain with a position governed by Agr^0 (i.e. where it occurs in free inversion, governed by $V+Agr^0$ in C^0) only in interrogative contexts; otherwise it must be in a Spec–head relation with Agr^0 (i.e. where it precedes $V+Agr^0$). We leave the proper analysis of this phenomenon for later work.

5. The first line of the table in (11) indicates the position of *ce* in the examples: *ce* V_I ... S means that *ce* is clause-initial, and that the subject is inverted; *ce* V_I ... S_{null} means that *ce* is clause-initial, but that the subject is either a trace or *pro*; S *ce* V_I means that *ce* occurs between the subject and the inflected verbal element (main verb, modal or auxiliary); V_I *ce* V_{-fin} means that *ce* occurs between an inflected modal or auxiliary and an infinitive or past participle, respectively; and post-V means that *ce* follows the main verb.

6. These two examples were both found in Chrétien; one was modified by *meïsmes*, the other was written *ceu*. These facts may indicate something special and exceptional occurring with this post-V *ce*.

7. Due in part, perhaps, but not wholly, to its becoming lexically restricted.
8. Apart from these Ps, our twelfth-century verse corpus has two examples of Extraposition with *par* and our fifteenth-century prose corpus has one example of Extraposition with *en*.
9. The eight examples of *à*-complement Extraposition in fifteenth-century prose (all from the CNNA) all occur with the verb *mener* 'to lead'. This restriction, along with the fact that no such examples are attested in the CNNV, may indicate that these extrapositions in MF had become formulaic and were not representative of the language at the time.
10. It may be an anomaly that none are found in the CNNV, since *à+ce* is rare in this text in any of the three contexts which we are studying. It provides only three examples of plain pronominal *ce* with *à* (vs 23 with *de*), and no examples of Extraposition *ce* with *à*.
11. We also found an example in our corpus in which the modifier separating the *ce* and the *que* is an adjective, rather than an adverb:
    (i) Et   elle ne donnoit nulle responce audit   curé, ne ne faisoit
        and she NEG gave   no   answer to-the-said curé and NEG made
        semblant   de luy ne des   sacremens, par *ce* possible *qu'* elle ne
        appearance of him nor of-the sacraments by   it possible that she NEG
        l' entendoit pas, ...   (CNNV63-22)
        him heard   at-all
        'And she gave no answer to the curé, and didn't notice him nor the sacraments, possibly because she didn't hear him ...'
    Given the relative rarity of contiguous *ce que* in our corpus and the even rarer occurrences of a modifier intervening between the two elements, we put this issue aside until further data can shed new light on it.
12. It is also possible that the complex NP structure existed instead of the string-vacuous Extraposition structure. Both alternatives are compatible with our analysis.
13. Wunderli offers a single argument against *ce* being a pronoun here, based on occurrences of P *ce que*: he notes that if *ce* is a pronoun coreferent to the clause, one ought to be able to substitute clause for the pronoun and have a licit structure (P+clause). Since this is generally impossible, especially following the Ps *à* and *de*, Wunderli concludes that *ce* must not be a pronoun. Unfortunately, this is not a necessary conclusion: as Stowell (1981) notes, tensed clauses are commonly illicit in positions assigned case, such as object of P position. The impossibility in French of P+clause sequences could be due to this Case Avoidance property, rather than to the nonpronominal character of *ce*. Thus, while we accept Wunderli's conclusion, we arrive at it for different reasons.
14. Specifically, she proposes the following:
    (i)   X is the extended head of Y, and Y is an extended projection of X iff:
        (a)   Y dominates X;
        (b)   Y and X share all categorial features ([±N, ±V]);
        (c)   all nodes intervening between X and Y share all categorial features;
        (d)   if X and Y are not in the same perfect projection (i.e. a maximal projection in the traditional sense), the F value of Y is higher that the F value of X.
    (ii) Generalized Theta Criterion
         Every maximal projection must either
        (a)   receive a role;
        (b)   be part of an extended projection that receives a role.
    This means that while lexical categories can select for an XP of a different categorial type, since they assign roles, a functional category must select only for the same category type in order for the complement to form part of an extended projection with it.
15. Dees (1971) proposes this analogy. Note also that *ce* and *cest/cel* are in complementary distribution, the former occurring before consonant-initial words, the latter before vowel-initial words.

14 The structure of parametric change, and V-movement in the history of English

Anthony Warner

Two particular topic areas arising from the chapters in this past section concern the structuring of parametric change and the interpretation of V-movement in the history of English.* In what follows, it will be argued from a reinterpretation of the loss of V-to-I in English that the possibility of competition between grammatical subsystems implies that parametric change may be structured, and that UG may be involved in such structuring. The notion of the structuring of change also has methodological implications for interpretation, and the question of the relationship between parameters and exception statements in the lexicon as ways of talking about change needs discussion. The first section of this epilogue will review these issues in commenting on the chapters by Lightfoot, Henry, and Zaring & Hirschbühler. The second section will turn to a series of problems involving V2 in the history of English, in particular the timing of the loss of V2, its relationship to processes of decliticization, and the interpretation of evidence for the typology of the northern dialect in ME. The chapters by van Kemenade and by Kroch & Taylor are discussed here.

Parametric change

In the most fully articulated of his three histories which interpret the relationship between parametric change and triggering shifts in PLD, Lightfoot (=L) makes a carefully argued case for the importance of changes in frequency as a cause of language change. He also notes that the loss of rich verbal inflection was necessary for the subsequent loss of V to I, and claims that the loss of V to I is late. But if we accept this claim, and take seriously the notion of variation between competing analyses, it is possible to reconceptualize the change as one with some structuring across time, and this has implications for his emphasis on the importance of contingent shifts in PLD for the causation of change.

Late loss of V-to-I

The starting point of my discussion must be L's claim that the loss of V-to-I in English was late. L places it 'in the early seventeenth century' (p. 263), distinctively later than suggested by other recent authors (Kroch 1989; Roberts 1993a); this might seem to cause some embarrassment, since he needs to claim that the continuing negative type *came not* is 'too subtle, not robust enough' (p. 263) to trigger V-to-I, and this is surely contrary to the general assumption. But if L's account is correct and it is inversion and not the position of *not* which provides salient data to learners,[1] then we might reasonably expect the decline of V-to-I in questions to lead to a rapid shift in negatives. L does not discuss this in detail, but the data does indeed seem to be consistent with his suggestion. Ellegård's written data shows 27% interrogative inversion with nonauxiliary in positive clauses for 1625–50; 26% for 1650–1700.[2] Tieken's (1987) figures for positive interrogatives in the eighteenth century average 13% overall (though this masks a wide range of variation). Compare with this the situation in negatives. The proportion of negative declaratives with nonauxiliary *V not* in Ellegård's data for 1625–50 is 68%; for 1650–1700 it is 54%. But Tieken's average for the eighteenth century is considerably lower at 20%, and this includes a high proportion of recurrent items (*know, doubt,* etc.) which Ellegård omitted from his figures. Thus in both construction types there is robust evidence for V-to-I throughout the seventeenth century, followed by a sharp drop in the eighteenth.[3] The question of what this means for the date of loss of V-to-I is complex, and may vary between types of language.[4] But the data is certainly consistent with L's proposal that *V not* is weak evidence for V-to-I, and that the loss of V-to-I is late; one might indeed want to place it later than he does.

The shape of parametric change

So L's view that the final loss of V-to-I is late is justified. L attributes this loss to the loss of evidence for it in PLD which is a consequence of the increasing frequency of *do*. But are there other less immediate reasons underlying the preceding decline of V-to-I? If so, then L's focus on the end point of a period of change and on changes in frequency as a trigger for change may tell us less than the whole story. In considering the progress of this loss, two points seem particularly important.

(i) The sequential weakening of the evidence for V-to-I: the morphological evidence is lost early, different types of syntactic evidence are lost subsequently at different times. L argues that loss of rich inflection may be a necessary condition but cannot be a sufficient one for loss of V-to-I, which may be maintained given sufficient other evidence of inversion.[5] A corollary is that different types of evidence in the PLD may have distinct consequences for acquisition and change.

(ii) The lengthy period of variation in the data, granted that the loss of V-to-I is late. This suggests that we should account explicitly for a period of competition. L supposes that I-to-V is generally available alongside V-to-I, and his account depends on the increasing incidence of *do*. But variation as such is not central to his account. Kroch also interprets variation in terms of competition between V-to-I and I-to-V but only until V-to-I is lost in 1550/1575.

Suppose (as Kroch and others assume) that an individual may internalize distinct subgrammars. Suppose, too, that these may involve the setting in distinct ways of some parameter with a 'marked' value (requiring positive evidence) and an 'unmarked' value (assigned in the absence of contrary evidence). Then a weakening of positive evidence for the marked value may, in some circumstances, result in a dual analysis in which both marked and unmarked values hold of different subgrammars. This is merely a logical consequence of the position that speakers may internalize more than one grammar, and it might be a rather general type of change.

Now, suppose that morphological evidence of rich inflection is positive evidence for V-to-I, but that when it is lost, the fact that the surviving syntactic evidence for V-to-I is characteristic of only a subset of the data allows also for the abduction of I-to-V (though at first perhaps only at the margin). Note that the typical presence of variation within texts implies that we need to account for variation within the individual. Then we can see the outline of a more structured account. Here I shall assume for concreteness (with Roberts 1993) that ME generates verbal affixes as I^{-1}, and that this requires V-to-I, but that in today's English they are I^0, and that this requires I-to-V.[6] Variation (or the dual parameter setting) may then be instantiated as selection of affixes from the lexicon as either I^{-1} or I^0. The account (which builds on work by Lightfoot, Kroch, Roberts) goes as follows.

1. The loss of rich inflection means the loss of morphological evidence for I^{-1} and V-to-I.[7] But the continuing syntactic evidence for V-to-I leads to an ambiguity in the data for parameter setting. There is syntactic evidence (inversion, negation) for V-to-I; the morphological evidence is consistent with the default setting, I^0 and I-to-V. The solution is to adopt both accounts. Does early Modern English have V-to-I? — Yes and no. The development of I^0 leads to the generation of modals and *do* as I^0, and the consequent loss of their nonfinites; cf. Roberts (1993: 295f., 315ff.).

2. *Do* makes progress, through successive acquisitions, perhaps (also) for reasons (of some abstractness, cf. Kroch 1989) connected with processing. There is a corresponding decline in syntactic evidence for V-to-I.

3. There is a change in the distribution of *do* 1550–75 from one which parallels that of modals, to one in which a movement toward the modern restrictions is apparent. This is identified by L (1991) as the point when the decline of V-to-I started, but by Kroch (1989) and Roberts (1993) as its final point of loss. But it must instead show some restructuring of the grammar

of *do* which gave I-to-V priority. One possibility is Roberts' suggestion that it was at this period that *do* became a 'last resort' expression of tense.[8] Another is that *do* was reanalysed as a member of the tense morpheme so that it began to compete directly with the affix instead of being a distinct lexical item (Warner 1993: 223ff.).

4. Loss of V-to-I in interrogative inversion means loss of V-to-I in other contexts, except with a residue of lexical items, hence the steep decline in *V not*.

5. Subsequently, from some point in the eighteenth century, V-to-I in interrogatives and with *not* is found only with a small number of exceptional lexically specified items.

On this account the change has a coherent shape, in that it is triggered by an initial morphological loss, which leads to the abduction of a doubly valued parameter. The marked (non-default) value is maintained by syntactic evidence, which itself declines, leaving the default value. The parameter ('For I^0 is there I^{-1}?'; see Roberts 1993: 244) requires positive evidence for the value 'yes' since the Subset Principle otherwise implies the value 'no'. The parametric change is structured as follows:

1. Yes (I^{-1}).[9]
2. Yes and no (I^{-1} and I^0). Modals and *do* are I^0
3. No, with lexical exceptions (I^0 with lexically controlled instances of I^{-1}).
4. No (I^0).

(To this we add the complication of the intermediate change in the grammar of *do*.)

So, if we take seriously the twin possibilities that speakers may internalize subgrammars with distinct parameter settings, and that morphological and syntactic evidence may point in different directions, we can see a coherent pattern over time in this instance of gradual change. In the relevant respects this is like longer term changes, and not like changes which apparently involve the simple resetting of a parameter, whose extension in time is a product of social and stylistic diffusion rather than of a centrally grammatical mechanism.[10]

This speculative account needs a rationale for the competition of the middle phase, since the question of why the change progresses remains open. If we can find a coherent and motivated account of this competition which involves abstract grammatical properties (interpreted in terms of their impact on acquisition by successive generations, or perhaps on processing), which are themselves appropriately related to the factors involved in the parametric change, then this sequence of events will appear as a whole rather than as a potentially accidental collection of separate bits. There is an example of such an interpretation in Warner (1993: ch. 9), which is worked out in Head-driven Phrase Structure Grammar. This proposes that the decline of inflectional mood (and the corresponding rise of lexicalized mood and tense in modals) results in the markedness of V2 structures with full verbs, which is avoided by the use of *do*.[11] This gives an account of the rise of *do* and the decline and loss of inversion with full verbs as motivated by fundamentally the same factors throughout; the preferences are built into the grammar as suggested in Kiparsky's chapter in this volume. Such an account attributes the progress of the long-term change to the continuing relevance of grammatically based factors, which structure the sequence of changes in frequency which bridge the initial and final stages of the parametric shift.

L discusses changes in frequency, changes in the way grammars are used (which may represent haphazard shifts in PLD), as motivation for parametric change. Now, it is clear that changes in frequency underlay the final abduction of grammars without V-to-I. But if the account I have sketched above stands up, and those changes were themselves motivated in some grammatically relevant way, then this case history points to the potential role of UG,[12] and away from a major role for 'chance oscillations in the trigger experience' (p. 269); it also implies that long-term change may involve more structuring across time than L apparently envisages. There is also an important methodological issue, since I would argue that it is necessary to attempt to devise such more structured accounts, if only so that accounts in which change is interpreted as more accidental in causation are not adopted without alternative. The best argument for contingent fluctuation in output as the cause of a change is surely the failure of alternative accounts.

The importance of UG in acquisition is clearly shown by Alison Henry (=H) in her careful and detailed description of imperative dialects in Belfast English, with its radical intergenerational shifts (see also Henry 1995). This looks initially like another case history which might support the proposition that UG may play a motivating role in change. But the methodological imperative to interpret close sequences of changes as structured undermines the case for this. H's account of the loss of inversion involves two apparently distinct processes. The first is the loss of V to C which results in the Restricted Inversion dialect. In discussing the motivation for this change, H points particularly to the importance of a preference for 'a grammar where the V feature of C is uniformly weak' (p. 295). This is clearly open to interpretation in terms of Kiparsky's inbuilt preferences, as a characteristic depending on UG which motivated the decline and loss of V to C, though it is not clear that H intends to go so far; her focus on acquisition leaves longer-term considerations obscure, though she sees language learning as strongly driven by UG. But it is not straightforwardly possible to see the change itself as motivated in this way, because this would leave us without a coherent account of its relationship to her second change: the loss of the Restricted Inversion dialect when movement of NP subject to Spec,Agr$_S$ became obligatory following the loss of 'singular concord'. This loss 'triggers' the obligatory movement, though H does not use this terminology. Since the two changes follow rapidly on one another, the lack of an interrelationship is a weakness, and the question of the timing of the first is left open (why now? why immediately before the loss of 'singular concord'?). It seems methodologically appropriate to seek a more unified account in which there are not two changes, with apparently distinct causes, but one in which the incidence of the Restricted Inversion dialect is an intermediate stage. Two other points support this suggestion.

(i) The transience of the Restricted Inversion dialect is striking. It is apparently found in the generation between speakers of the UnRestricted Inversion dialect, and speakers of the dialect without these inversions.

(ii) H's description identifies two inversion dialects, but offers no account of the apparent absence of an intermediate dialect which retains V to C, and requires NP to Spec,Agr$_S$. Such a dialect would have the following pattern of data:

Take you (now) the cake
Be you going home
*Be going you home
Go you home
Don't you go home
*Don't go you home

If the two changes are not grammatically interconnected, why are they ordered so that this option is excluded?

The general conclusions we can draw are (i) that we should look for a more structured account, in which the Restricted Inversion dialect is a transitional stage; (ii) that there is a potential 'simple and robust' trigger in the L tradition; (iii) that we have no evidence here for a distinctive role for UG as itself a motivation for change, and, for similar reasons, (iv) that we have none either for L's haphazard shifts in PLD as motivation for change.

What then might motivate a shift from the UnRestricted Inversion dialect to a dialect without inversion? The issue is clearly open to sociolinguistic as well as linguistic causation, and we may hope that H's ongoing survey of acquisition will provide clues, if not answers. But it is tempting to speculate that the loss of 'singular concord' is involved in the original loss of V to C.[13] If an account on such lines can indeed be constructed we might have a change with properties similar to those of the loss of V-to-I (and see L 1991 on the importance of morphology in parameter setting): a morphosyntactic change (weakening of 'singular concord') drives (or permits) syntactic change (loss of inversion); the weight of syntactic evidence leads to the survival of inversion for a period in an intermediate analysis, though in this instance it is too fragile to support its continuation more than briefly. Note that if this change is of this type, it is distinguished by its rapidity, and that H rules out the relevance of variation within the individual: here the situation is categorical. As a speculation this account is based simply on what H tells us in her chapter, and may be wide of the mark. But I suggest that it has appropriate external properties, in that it interrelates the three developments and provides a coherent rationale for the timing of the change in imperatives. More importantly this discussion reflects a general point made by L: that it must be good methodology to consider what type of historical accounts we might postulate to give us a coherent account of (sequences of) changes, even independently of particular grammatical formulations, turning subsequently to the question of how our theories of grammar can inform such speculation.

Parameters and the lexicon

If this is an appropriate account we have an instance of change located in the properties of functional categories, whose effects are more local than global within the grammar, but which is identifiable through a complex interrelationship between surface changes. H briefly refers this to 'parameter setting'. This contrasts with the use made of the notion 'parameter' by Zaring & Hirschbühler (=ZH) in their account of the history of French *ce que*. They develop a parametrization of Grimshaw's Extended Projection Principle to account both for the decline of *ce que* + clause except after a preposition, and for the later reinterpretation of *ce que* as a monomorphemic item.

The general rationale for their account is appealing. But it is worth considering just what is meant by 'parameter' here. Grimshaw's (1991) Extended Projection Principle requires that functional projections are necessarily nondistinct from the N, V category features of their complement, and for Grimshaw this holds absolutely. But ZH interpret it as a parameter whose marked value permits exceptions to the general principle. This is the case in conservative OF. Then in innovative OF and MF they suggest that the decline of *ce que* + clause except after a preposition occurs because the rise of *ce* + nominal (which did accord with the default value of the parameter) marginalized the evidence for *ce que* + clause, and that the parameter is eventually reset. This is clearly a very different matter from L's more abstract parametric changes, in which a wide range of consequences may follow the resetting of a parameter. Indeed it suggests the survival of a lexically encoded exception (a subinstance of a category, *ce* with inherent case), and this makes it worth considering whether Grimshaw's EPP could be taken to be not a parameter open to different settings, but a general principle to which exceptions might be stated in the lexicon. This might hold if the rise of *ce* + nominal was what led to the reclassification of *ce* as a determiner and functional category subject to the EPP, whereupon *ce que* became a violation with the consequence that it began to decline. This would provide a sharp rationale for the subsequent restriction of *ce que* and its later monomorphemicization, again in terms of preferences built into the grammar. In earlier conservative OF when *ce* occurred as a pronominal in case-marked positions and in *ce que*, this distribution (and notably the absence of the combinations typical of functional categories under the EPP) will have supported its analysis as N rather than D.[14] Thus there would have been no violation of the EPP, and no pressure for change at this period.

So perhaps EPP is not a parameter which may be differently set, but is a principle to which specific exceptions may be stated. The notion that a functional morpheme may be (lexically) exceptional is a simple and powerful one with which to extend a learnable account of irregularity and change.[15] It is directly relevant to L's general arguments that parameters should be restricted to a small number of (presumably) relatively abstract instances, and to Henry's (1995) referral of some parameter setting differences between English dialects to properties encoded within specific morphemes.

Reflections on V2 in English

A dominant theme of the chapters by van Kemenade (=K) and Kroch & Taylor (=KT) is the nature of English clause structure and the landing site for V in V2 clauses, together with the dialectal, historical and typological consequences of their views. K presents a new and important generalization about the positional syntax of OE, which implies strongly that OE was an 'asymmetric' language, and she also sketches an attractive account of the development of English into an I-oriented language as a consequence of the loss of V2 (which itself depends on the decliticization of subject pronouns: K 1987). Here, though, KT's early Middle English data is very suggestive for K's account, since their figures imply that the decliticization of pronouns may already have been under way.

In OE the order TopicPhr–SubjPrn–V was categorical in main clause declaratives with topicalized full phrases (not including *þa, nu, swa*, etc.) (Koopman 1992: 51; Pintzuk 1991: 203), but KT's Table 1 shows a different picture for early ME: here, in positive clauses with topicalized complements, the incidence of TopicPhr–V–SubjPrn is 9% (with NP topic, 5%). This can be plausibly interpreted as showing that the decliticization of subject pronouns has already made some progress, so that the selection of a clitic form is optional rather than obligatory.[16] Now, if decliticization did underlie the loss of V2, as in K's account, then we might reasonably suppose that the decline of V2 also started early. KT's data seems consistent with this, since in their eME texts inversion with NP subject fails in as many as 11% of instances after topicalized NP/PP complements. Unfortunately we lack relevant comparisons with the situation in OE, since published data does not draw the distinctions we require (cf. Minkova & Stockwell 1992: 149–50). But Kohonen's overall figures suggest that 'in main clauses with topicalization ... inversion was decreasing' in early Middle English (1978: 171). K puts the loss of V2 in the period 1350–1425; but perhaps it had already started over a century earlier. If so, then it might then be interpreted as another long-term change, starting slowly, potentially involving competition between different analyses over a period of time (and probably not completed until the early Modern period, see Warner 1993: 229).[17] This suggestion has been made on the basis of K's postulated interconnection between decliticization and loss of V2. But if loss of V2 did indeed start early, we might wonder about other possibilities for actuation, in particular whether it could depend on the loss of I-final structures.[18] Suppose that instances of 'V3' in OE may be underlyingly instances of I-final main clauses disguised by rightward movement of internal material, as Pintzuk (1993) suggests. Then when learners ceased to abstract I-final grammars, they may have accounted for some of this data as I-medial clauses which lacked inversion. The connection with cliticization may then have been that the decline of V2 provided a source for pronoun + V order which did not involve movement to a special position for clitics, so that this simply became optional and was lost.[19] Maybe then it is the decline of V2 which leads to decliticization, instead of the other way round. Note that on this interpretation, evidence for decliticization will still be suggestive evidence for the decline of V2.

The state of V2 in eME is an empirical question, and we need some careful and detailed unpicking of the interaction of various factors in the relevant texts to be confident of developments here. But at the moment it is not obvious that the facts of eME ordering will be better interpreted in terms of the continuation of I-final or other factors which do not represent the loss of V2, and it would seem worth investigating the possibility that the loss of V2 starts earlier than has been suggested.[20]

The syntax of verb movement in Middle English

KT reinterpret the structure of IP-V2 languages in a way which seems interestingly to imply that economy considerations operate relative to discourse properties (as suggested in recent work by Adger 1995a, b). Their reinterpretation underpins their analysis of OE as an IP-V2 language, and they go on to make the interesting claim that though the characteristics of OE V2 can be seen to continue in early southern (and midland) ME, there is a northerly dialect which is CP-V2 with V-to-C.

One major characteristic of OE is the distributional contrast between the inversion of full NP subjects and lack of inversion of pronominal subjects after a topicalized phrase, and essentially this contrast is found in southern early ME. In later midland ME V2 is declining, and NP and pronoun are not so sharply distinct in distribution as earlier (to the extent that we have information: but note Schmidt's comment on Mandeville that 'there is a strong tendency for pronominal subjects to have S V order' — 1980: 225 — and K's similar claim for Wycliffite writings). Then in the North in the first quarter of the fifteenth century KT have identified a text in which inversion

Parametric change and V-movement 389

with both NP and pronoun is virtually categorical: *The northern Prose Version of the Rule of St Benet* (in Kock 1902; hereafter referred to as *Ben.Rule*). In discussing this text KT focus on two facts.

i. 'Pronoun subjects ... invert nearly as frequently as full NP subjects do.' (p. 313) This is radically distinct from southern early ME.
ii. Inversion is 'nearly categorical' after topicalized adjuncts or adverbs (if we omit *then* and *now*, exceptions are in the range 4–11%), which contrasts with the early southern texts.

KT adopt V to C for inversion in general in the northern dialect represented by this text, since it gives a unitary account of the high degree of regularity of these contrasts between dialects.

The context of ME inversion

There are, however, some reasons for caution in accepting KT's conclusions. These depend on the general context of inversion in ME, and here my comments can only be preliminary, because relevant data for inversion in ME is hard to come by. There has not been much investigation, and published surveys do not normally yield just the types of figures useful to current research. But we have clearly to reckon with the possibility of a high degree of individual variation between texts. So, after a short list of initial adverbs occurring in prose (*then, now, there, yet*, etc.) Jacobsson (1951: 96–7) found 89% inversion in Chaucer (*c.* 1390) beside 39% in Mandeville (*c.* 1400); 86% inversion in Capgrave (1450) beside 10% in Fortescue (a1475). It is also instructive to see the figures MacLeish (1969) gives for inversion after an initial adverbial element in a series of prose texts from the second half of the fourteenth century: Usk's *Appeal* 17%, Wyclif 18%, *Petition to Parliament* 29%, Chaucer's *Melibee* 77%, *Astrolabe* 83%, *Parsons Tale* 84%. These figures compare with 92.5% inversion after an initial adverb or adjunct in *Ben.Rule*. After an initial complement NP or PP, inversion is found in a striking 97% of instances in *Ben.Rule*, and with all of the 25 instances with full NP subject. Set this beside MacLeish's figures for fronted direct and indirect object in all six texts, which show inversion in over 84% of instances.[21]

These figures must make us wonder whether we really have in *Ben.Rule* a radically different grammar or whether it could represent an idiosyncratic set of stylistic choices taken within the framework of a more generally available grammar. The difficulty is that of interpreting the significance of a type of distribution found in a single text: is the peculiarity a stylistic or a dialectal one? *Ben.Rule* was presumably intended to be read aloud to the monastic chapter, and it is possible that it was stylistically formal or elevated. It also contains some verse mixed in with its prose (Kock 1902: xii); and there is some incidence of movement to pre-verbal positions, of a type which is found in the (alliterative) verse of *Piers Plowman*, but (with objects at least) is absent in the prose of some contemporaneous ME sermons (Swieczkowski 1962). If the text were stylistically marked, this might provide some rationalization for the high incidence of inversion. It is clear that we need a better understanding of the stylistic implications of inversion in ME to make a confident decision here.[22]

Historical and dialectal considerations

KT make admirably ingenious use of the evidence of two glossed texts from the tenth century to show that there is some time depth to the development of inverted pronouns in the North. Their claim is that contact with Norse led to the loss of the agreement paradigm, which forced the loss of V-to-I and required reanalysis of the language as CP-V2. This accommodates the apparent oddity that contact between two IP-V2 languages led to the development of a CP-V2 language. But placing the development of CP-V2 in the North may leave a problem for the history of relevant midland dialects if KT's preliminary report of Orm as showing close identity of distribution of NP and pronoun is borne out, since this text retains a distinctive agreement paradigm. Since the development of CP-V2 is recessive in KT's interpretation, with *Ben.Rule* surviving in a 'relic area' (p. 313), this implies a separate development for Orm. But then, in search of a unitary development underlying both texts, we might return to K's suggestion that the decliticization of subject pronouns is central to the difference between early ME and *Ben.Rule*, despite the real difficulty implied by KT's analysis of Stylistic Fronting.[23] If decliticization preceded loss of V2 in the north, the simplest assumption (especially if the loss was gradual) is that pronouns would take on the distribution of NP, so that the development would have reinforced V2. This could account for the distribution in Orm and the northern glossed gospels (as described by KT), or for that in *Ben.Rule* if we assume that this was indeed a matter of dialect rather than style. Moreover, early decliticization in Norse-influenced areas seems rather plausible. KT note the demonstrative origin of *they, they/them* survive in modern dialect as demonstratives, and the origin of *sho* and *she* may also be referred to stressed forms.

KT have clearly shown that pronoun inversion was early in the North, and it may be that this is due to contact with Norse. Their careful account of the dialectal data raises a series of very interesting questions, and we need to know considerably more about the dialectal and stylistic incidence of inversion in ME before we can have confidence in answers. In particular it is not yet clear whether or not we should accept their argument that a northern dialect was typologically distinct from southern English.

Envoi

In reviewing these chapters I have discussed both theoretical issues and some specific topics in the history of English. The most important general theme has been the significance of interrelationships between changes, and between the parts of a change. This has methodological consequences, and I have also tried to work out some of the implications of adopting a view of change as potentially a relatively long-term matter involving competition between grammatical subsystems. This is very different from the reanalysis model, in which change is typically abrupt and social or stylistic complexity is appealed to when data which seems to show gradualness is to be accommodated. Instead the s-curve of change implies a gradual onset and termination, and a potentially lengthy period of competition, which fits some data sets rather well. It also implies that different types of data play different roles in parameter setting, and it seems to leave less room for truly accidental variation in usage as a cause of change.

Notes

* I am grateful to the editors for their very helpful comments on the chapter. But the blame for any mistakes or misunderstandings is mine. The five chapters are discussed as they stood in July 1995.
1. This may not involve an inherent weakness of *V not* as evidence, but the contrast between a situation with two (or more) mutually supportive pieces of evidence (inversion, *V not*) and one with a single isolated piece of evidence (*V not*).
2. See Ellegård (1953: 204). These figures include interrogatives with *wh*-object (which Ellegård omits from his general comparative figures on p. 161), because they give a truer comparison with Tieken's later figures. Figures for negatives are from Ellegård (1953: 161).
3. Ellegård himself investigated only one work written after 1700, Swift's *Journal to Stella* (1710), which has a proportion of 10% *do*-less positive interrogatives, and 13% *V not*. But this is likely to be closer to more informal and colloquial registers than most of Ellegård's texts, so it may be potentially misleading to take it in direct comparison with his earlier figures.
4. The question of dating is a tricky one; usage was subject to social and stylistic variation as is clear from Salmon (1965) and Tieken (1987), and there were plainly some strong lexical preferences in later usage.
5. Roberts (1993: 297) also distinguishes the date of loss of morphological evidence for Agr^{-1} (1500) from the date of its actual loss (1550/75), noting that 'we are forced to postulate an abstract Agr^{-1}' (p. 301) in the interim.
6. Roberts distinguishes projections of Agr and of T, which play different roles in his analysis; a single functional projection I is instead adopted here. Since (on Roberts' account) the loss of Agr^{-1} and T^{-1} depend on the loss of plural and infinitival morphology, which seem to be close in date, and the two developments involve the resetting of the same parameter for closely related verbal functional projections, the identification seems a reasonable one, even if it is interpreted as a matter of presentation rather than analysis.
7. L suggests that loss of 'rich verbal inflection' is 'effectively complete by 1400' (p. 21). If we adopt Roberts' interpretation that what is involved is loss of overt equipollent marking of number (Roberts 1993: 267; required for postulation of Agr^{-1}), this seems too early to me; the second half of the fifteenth century would be a preferable date.
8. So that *do* will no longer occur with *not* where *not* is Spec,Neg, hence the observed increase in *V not* at this period (cf. Roberts 1993: 304). It is probably necessary to assume a further double analysis: that *not* may be either Spec,Neg or the head of Neg.

9. With lexical exceptions in the case of modals earlier restricted to finites, if we assume these are already I^0 (i.e. T^0).
10. Contrast Roberts' interpretation of evidence for V-to-I after 1575 as reflecting archaistic usage, and his comment that evidence of change was 'blurred by extra-grammatical factors connected with literary style' (1993: 250).
11. This ends a period of competition dating from OE. The higher frequency of *do* in inversion than in other contexts follows, but the increase in frequency is passed on to other contexts with this lexeme. Hence the results are not necessarily inconsistent with Kroch (1989).
12. There is no need to suppose that a change could take place without some shift in PLD, since the sequence of changes in frequency will presumably itself depend on corresponding shifts in PLD.
13. Intuitively, it might work as a result of generalizing strong D features across functional categories when 'singular concord' nonagreement (weak D feature) is lost, from Agr_S to IMP (or from INDIC to IMP in a system without Agr). Subsequently D features on IMP are strong in positive imperatives, and V NP order ceases (perhaps with some further restructuring). *Don't* will specify the possibility of weak D features. Unaccusative 'inversions' provide a temporary bridge between old and new analyses, but are themselves marked, and disappear rapidly. Note that H reports a number of families with 'UnRestricted Inversion dialect' grandmother, 'Restricted Inversion dialect' mother, 'no Inversion dialect' children.
14. ZH discuss in their note 11 the possibility of adopting an analysis of early OF *ce que* in which *ce* is a pronominal heading a complex NP. ZH argue against this analysis on distributional grounds (§4.2.1), but the types of difference relevant here are partly discounted by discourse considerations as is recognized in their note.
15. For another example of this, see Warner (1995). Here it is proposed that a parametric change occurred in English in the eighteenth century when the properties of the class of auxiliaries altered (as modals ceased to show overt agreement morphology). But the form *being* was learned as irregular, and it is by virtue of this irregularity that English develops and retains the progressive passive.
16. The loss of verbal inflection could not, then, underlie this stage of decliticization as K suggests (1987: 204–5, 221) if the development is internal to the dialects, since verbal inflection maintains essentially the OE system in these texts, though admittedly we are dealing with traditional and in some cases partly standardized languages.
17. This should imply early development of the I-oriented characteristics listed by K, but presumably with a very low incidence, to match the gradual onset of the change; see Allen (1986: 399) for some evidence that oblique case of nominal experiencer subjects of impersonals is neutralized early. Relevant pronominal nominatives with impersonals and oblique passives are later (Elmer 1981), and this may count against the suggestion, unless the incoming grammar is initially restricted in its application to such contexts. This may mean that the change here is evidenced first when least salient; see Warner (1982: ch. 6), Fischer (1990: ch. 4) for this proposal in another context.
18. Could this (also) be associated with the decline of overt case, as suggested by Pintzuk (1991: 371–4) and (for a later period) by Kiparsky, this volume? V2 seems sometimes to survive the loss of nonpronominal case well, but perhaps this indicates that V2 syntax is robust (unless disturbed, say, by the reanalysis of I-final clauses). There are, however, problems of establishing what stage of morphological decline is relevant, and whether it meshes appropriately with the state of V2 across dialects, in so far as this can be separated from stylistic variation.
19. On some assumptions this would imply that the lack of inversion with NP (25%) should be in advance of the incidence of inversion with pronouns (10%) in KT's eME data, as is the case. But the possibility of the continuation of OE adjunction structures without inversion reduces the value of such comparisons.

20. I-final order was declining in eME, and its incidence in main clauses is likely to have been low at best. KT state categorically that I-final order is absent in their eME texts. Dahlstedt reported finding only three instances of infinitive preceding finite auxiliary in his account of the *Ancren Riwle* (1903: 43); but they are all in subordinate clauses and they all accord with KT's description of Stylistic Fronting, so they do not support the presence of I-final.
21. 87% if we set aside some apparent misclassifications. For MacLeish's data see especially his Tables I, III, VIII and IX for each text, and his appendix.
22. KT appeal to two specific constructions as evidence that *Ben.Rule* is CP-V2 and southern texts are IP-V2. But in both cases, they have to admit exceptions in the data to the generalizations they need, so support is not strong. The first construction involves fronting of a subordinate clause element before C. K gives a verse example from the early south; here is one I know from alliterative prose:
    (i) 'Pet liht   pba   Ich ne   mahte lengre pbolien, ...
        that light when I   could no   longer endure
                                    Sawles Warde, Bennett and Smithers (1966) 19.279
    For a few other examples (from alliterative verse of the Midlands and North) see Koziol (1932: 149).
23. KT reject decliticization as the motive for change here for two reasons. One is that their account also covers the difference between S and N distribution of inverted NPs after adjuncts and adverbs. But there is a basis for generalization in the range of variation found after adverbs (95% after *pba* in KT's early texts), and the difference to be bridged is not immense (75% versus 89% after PP adjuncts, and 57% versus 96% after adverbs). So, although a unitary account of differences between N and S dialects is attractive, it is more attractive to have an account which covers both *Ben.Rule* and Orm. Their other argument claims that N pronouns are shown to be clitics in a construction parallel to Icelandic Stylistic Fronting which requires a subject gap. If the ME construction does indeed turn out to require a subject gap or pronoun, this will be very suggestive, and it may sink an account based on decliticization. But it is not yet clear that it need imply that English shows just the same condition, or that more than a proportion of subject pronouns are clitics. One respect in which the construction is not straightforwardly parallel to the Icelandic Stylistic Fronting is worth noting: that in *Ben.Rule* phrases and not only words may be fronted (but see Rögnvaldsson & Thráinsson 1990 for the claim that this is also true for Icelandic).

Part 4

Scrambling and morphological case

15 Directionality and word order change in the history of English

Ian Roberts

1 Introduction*

A standard view of the historical development of English word order involves the idea that Old English (OE) was, like all other attested West Germanic varieties (with the possible exception of Yiddish — see Santorini 1990), head-final at least in VP and IP (see Stockwell 1977; Canale 1978; Lightfoot 1979, 1991; Bean 1983; van Kemenade 1987; Pintzuk 1991; Traugott 1992; Denison 1993; although not all of these authors assume an IP). In this respect, OE (and West Germanic generally) differs from Modern English (NE) (and North Germanic generally) in the value of the directionality parameter in (1), for at least some values of Y:

(1) Directionality parameter: Y' → Y XP
     Y' → XP Y

According to the standard view, at some point in the Middle English (ME) period — probably in the twelfth century — there was a change in the value of the directionality parameter (for the relevant categories). As a result of this change, the language became uniformly head-initial. This means that OV and V–Aux orders, formerly abundantly attested (see section 2), are no longer found.

Recently, Kayne (1994) has argued that UG cannot contain a parameter like (1). Kayne proposes a theory of phrase structure which derives many of the properties of X'-theory from the central idea that asymmetric c-command relations among non-terminals are intrinsically connected to linear order among terminals. We can phrase the central constraint as follows:[1]

(2) If A, a non-terminal, asymmetrically c-commands B, a non-terminal, then all terminals a dominated by A precede all terminals b dominated by B.

To see how (2) works in the case of head–complement order, consider the VP in (3):

(3) [$_{VP}$ [$_V$ see [$_{DP}$ [$_D$ him]]]]

Here V asymmetrically c-commands D (the definition of c-command is 'X c-commands Y iff X does not contain Y and every category dominating X dominates Y'). Hence, by (2), *see* must precede *him*. This conclusion would follow even if we chose to draw the phrase-marker the other way around. Thus there can be no parametric variation as regards head–complement order; (2) (or whatever it derives from, cf. note 3) requires that heads precede their complements. Hence, all languages are underlyingly head-initial.

In a system like Kayne's, superficial OV patterns, or, more generally, head-final typologies, must be derived by leftward-movement processes. Chomsky (1994) adopts a similar position. Zwart (1993) has shown that this approach yields positive results in the analysis of Dutch; in particular, one can dispense with the idea that Dutch is a mixed-branching language, with some categories (e.g. CP) right-branching and others (e.g. VP) left-branching. Zwart's proposal is that 'The SVO order of Dutch main clauses is derived from an "underlying" SOV order, visible in embedded clauses. However, this SOV order is derived from an underlying SVO order in the Dutch VP, still visible when the object is not a noun phrase but a clause' (p. 29). The proposal accounts for the following generalizations about Dutch: (i) 'top projections', e.g. C and D, are always head-initial; (ii) 'when a head allows its complement to appear on one side only, the complement always follows the head' — this is true of the complements of N, for example; (iii) 'when the head allows its complement to appear on both sides, the head and the complement are never adjacent when the complement precedes the head' — this is true of the complements of A, P and V. Zwart captures these generalizations by assuming that all categories are head-initial, and that some complements, in particular direct objects of V, move leftward during the derivation. In addition to accounting for these generalizations the proposal allows a simple treatment of verb raising (as in fact the absence of overt verb movement). Various other proposals made by Zwart will be discussed and adopted to OE below.

The purpose of this chapter is to explore the consequences of what we might call the Zwart/Kayne view for OE and, in particular, for the word-order changes that took place in ME. I will argue that the Zwart/Kayne view is at least as good as the more standard views as regards the synchronic analysis of OE, and that it permits a more natural and revealing account of the ME changes. One advantage can be identified straightaway. On the 'standard' view, OE is not a uniformly head-final language. For example, there is no doubt that CP and DP are both head-initial projections, as in Dutch. The projections that are usually regarded as head-final are IP and VP (we leave aside AP, NP and PP; these are usually regarded as either head-initial or mixed, and so they do not affect the point at hand). However, there is a fair amount of evidence for a medial IP of some kind (cf. in particular Pintzuk 1991), some of which I review below. If we split IP into various functional projections, then we may be able to claim that some of them are head-initial and some head-final. A claim like this is made in Cardinaletti & Roberts (1991), for example. However, this kind of analysis shares with the standard analysis the consequence that at some point in the functional system that makes up the clause there is a switch from head-initial to head-final patterning. Note also that this is the most restrictive view compatible with the mixed typology. Such mixed typologies look very suspect: clearly it would be better to opt for a uniform direction in head–complement ordering. In that case, the only possibility that is seriously workable is to assume that OE is uniformly head-initial.

More generally, the view I advocate is:

(4) Principle: Y' → Y XP
    Parameter: Morphosyntactic features causing leftward movement from VP.

What changed in ME could not, *ex hypothesi*, have been the base expansion of V' or I'.[2] Instead, leftward-movement possibilities are lost in ME. In this way, the word-order change becomes one of a type that is already very familiar: the loss of a movement dependency. It thus falls into the same general category of changes as the loss of V-to-I movement in early Modern English (cf. Roberts 1985, 1993a: ch. 3; Rohrbacher 1994a) or the loss of V2 in English (van Kemenade 1987; Platzack 1995) or French (Adams 1987; Roberts 1993a; Clark & Roberts 1993), etc. More precisely, in each case I take it that strong features of the relevant kind (I's V-feature in the case of V-to-I movement; the relevant feature of C in the case of V2) are lost, leading to the impossibility of movement thanks to UG-internal economy conditions (the Procrastinate Principle). In the case at hand, Agr_O loses strong N-features, and so DP-movement to Spec,Agr_OP is lost. Thus change in base expansion of X' is reduced to the more familiar loss of movement dependencies, itself caused by changes in abstract features of functional heads. This kind of change is well attested, and, if Clark & Roberts are right, can be understood in terms of the idea that the language-learning algorithm contains a simplicity metric which values the absence of overt movement, and therefore weak features of functional heads, more highly than overt movement, i.e. strong features of functional heads. Hence language acquirers will tend to assign representations without overt movement to parts of the input which involve movement in the adult grammar. I take this treatment of word-order change to be a positive move.

The chapter is organized as follows. In section 2, I review what I will call the 'standard' GB view of OE word order and describe the ME changes. The 'standard' view is a distillation of the work of many researchers, most notably van Kemenade (1987), although it probably does not correspond precisely to any one analysis that has been put forward. In section 3, I present an alternative view, arguing that OE can usefully be seen as a VO language. Section 4 deals with the word-order change in ME.

2 'Standard' GB accounts of OE word order

2.1 Introduction

In this section, we first discuss the evidence for head-final order in OE IPs and VPs. Then we discuss the various operations that must be postulated in order to account for the attested facts if this order is assumed. These fall into two groups: three rightward-movement operations (verb raising, verb-projection raising and extraposition) and two leftward-movement rules (scrambling and clitic placement). We will discuss each of these operations in turn. I should emphasize at the outset that throughout this section we are reporting a point of view that will be replaced by an alternative later in the chapter.

There is a consensus among scholars who have worked on OE syntax that the predominant word order in the clause is verb-final in subordinate clauses and verb-second in main clauses (see Stockwell 1977; Canale 1978; Lightfoot 1979; Bean 1983; Denison 1993; van Kemenade 1987; Traugott 1992). The situation is thus very similar to that in Modern Dutch or German.

The following examples illustrate OV order in subordinate clauses:

(5) a. ... þæt ic *þas boc* of Ledenum gereorde to Engliscre spræce
that I this book from Latin language to English tongue
awende (AHTh, I, pref, 6; van Kemenade 1987: 16)
translate
'... that I translate this book from the Latin language to the English tongue'

b. ... þæt he *his stefne* up *ahof* (Bede 154.28; Pintzuk 1991: 77)
that he his voice up raised
'.. that he raised up his voice'

c. ... forþon of Breotone *nædran* on scippe lædde *wæron*
because from Britain adders on ships brought were
'... because vipers were brought on ships from Britain'
(Bede 30.1-2; Pintzuk 1991: 117)

The example in (5b) shows that verb–particle complexes can appear in the order *Particle–V*, again as is typical in Modern Dutch and German subordinate clauses (see Koster 1975). The example in (5c) shows that auxiliaries can follow participles in subordinate clauses (auxiliaries also follow infinitives in embedded clauses where there is no verb (-projection) raising — see below). This is another trait shared with Modern Dutch and German (although verb raising interferes with this pattern in Dutch — see below), and is also a typological feature of 'OV' languages (see Greenberg 1963; Hawkins 1983). The usual assumption is that verb-second order is derived by an operation which fronts the verb from its final position to the second position (although the precise nature of the second position remains a matter of debate on which I will take no position here), see Koster (1975), den Besten (1983) on Dutch, and van Kemenade (1987) for a clear demonstration that the arguments applied to Dutch carry over to OE. Hence OV order is taken as underlyingly general to all clauses in OE.

Aside from verb second, various factors disguise the basic OV order. In the following subsections, I illustrate these, summarizing the standard analysis in each case.

2.2 Rightward movement rules

2.2.1 Verb raising

This phenomenon is well known from studies of Standard Dutch (see *inter alia* Evers 1975; den Besten & Edmonson 1983; Rutten 1991). As we mentioned above, finite auxiliaries usually follow non-finite participles or infinitives in languages conforming to the OV typology; (5c), where a finite auxiliary follows a participle in an embedded clause, illustrates this for OE. This is also generally the case in Standard German, for example. However, in Dutch a large class of finite auxiliaries and auxiliary-like verbs must or may precede the participle or infinitive. The following contrast (from van Kemenade 1987: 56) illustrates this:

(6) a. ... dat Jan het boekje *wilde hebben* (Dutch)
    that John the booklet wanted to-have
  b. ... daß der Johann das Büchlein *haben wollte* (German)
    that the John the booklet to-have wanted
   '... that John wanted to have the booklet'

The precise details of which Dutch verbs allow this, and under which conditions, are complex, and are treated in detail in the references just given. The essential point is that, alongside the expected order (given an assumed OV typology) of non-finite verb followed by finite verb (or aux), Dutch also allows the order in which the finite verb/aux followed non-finite verb.

Verb raising is found in OE, as the examples in (7) show:

(7) a. þe æfre on gefeohte his hande *wolde afylan*
    who ever in battle his hands would defile
   'who would ever defile his hands in battle'
                                            (ÆLS 25.858; Pintzuk 1991: 102)
  b. & from Offan kyninge Hygebryht *wæs gecoren*
    and by King O. H. was chosen
   'and H. was chosen by King O.'
                                            (ChronA 52.8-54.1 (785), Pintzuk 1991: 102)

Assuming an OV, I-final structure for OE (7) would involve verb raising as in (8):

(8) þe æfre on gefeohte [$_{VP}$ his hande t_i] *wolde afylan$_i$*

(8) shows that the infinitive *afylan* moves to the right. Most analyses (e.g. Rutten 1991) assume that it adjoins to the right of I, the position containing the inflected verb.

2.2.2 Verb-projection raising

This phenomenon is the counterpart of verb raising, with the extra complication that some further constituent, typically a complement of the non-finite verb, appears to the right of the finite auxiliary and (consistent with OV typology) preceding the non-finite verb. Although not attested in Standard Dutch or German, this phenomenon is found in many Continental West Germanic dialects, e.g. West Flemish (Haegeman & van Riemsdijk 1986; Haegeman 1992) and varieties of Swiss German (Haegeman & van Riemsdijk 1986). It is also found in OE, as the examples in (9) show:

(9) a. hwær ænegu þeod at oþerre mehte [*frið begietan*]
    where any people from other might peace obtain
    'where any people might obtain peace from another'
    (Or 31.14–15; Pintzuk 1991: 113)

   b. þæt nan man ne mihte [*ða meniu geniman*]
    that no man NEG could the multitude count
    'that no man could count the multitude'
    (ÆLS 25.418; Pintzuk 1991: 33)

Here the bracketing indicates the constituent that, on an OV analysis, must be assumed to move to the right of the finite auxiliary. This constituent is often thought of as a VP or other V-projection, whence the term 'verb-projection raising'. Although the issue of the category of the post-verbal constituent is clearly distinct from the issue of the underlying position of this constituent, we will suggest below that these constituents represent something larger than VP, and in fact may be clausal. In any case, this constituent is assumed by proponents of an OV analysis of OE word order to move from a position immediately preceding the inflected verb to the superficial position seen in (9).

2.2.3 Extraposition

If we assume an underlying OV order for OE, we must assume that this language, once again like Dutch and German, allows rightward extraposition of PPs and CPs. Unlike these languages, however, it also allows apparent rightward extraposition of DPs (cf. Stockwell 1977 on 'exbraciation'):

(10) a. drihten wæs acenned [$_{PP}$ *on þære byrig*]
    the lord was born in the city
    'The Lord was born in the city' (ÆCHom i.34.9; Pintzuk 1991: 69)

   b. þæt turonisce folc wilnigende wæs [$_{CP}$ *þæt Martinus wære to*
    the Tours people desiring was that M. were as
    biscope gehalgod to heora burh-scire] (ÆLS 31.254-6; Pintzuk 1991: 69)
    bishop consecrated of their city
    'the people of Tours wanted M. to be consecrated as bishop of their city'

c. ... þæt ænig mon atellan mæge [$_{DP}$ *ealne þone demm*]
 that any man relate can all the misery
 '... that any man can relate all the misery'

(Or 52.6–7; Pintzuk 1991: 36)

In each of these cases, the bracketed constituent is assumed to have moved from a VP-internal position to the left of the main predicate. We could schematize this operation as follows:

(11) [$_{VP}$ t_i V] XP$_i$ (where XP = CP, PP and, possibly, DP)

Clearly, the existence of examples like (10c) is superficially incompatible with the OV typology, although the facts can be accounted for by postulating an optional DP-extraposition rule. Pintzuk & Kroch (1989) show, on the basis of a metrical analysis of *Beowulf*, that whenever a DP is found in final position in that text, after the finite verb in a subordinate clause, it receives stress. They interpret this as indicating that these orders result from the application of an operation like Focus NP Shift (cf. Ross 1967; Stowell 1981). They also show that final PPs and CPs are not always subject to stress of this kind, hence these elements appear finally due to the operation of an extraposition rule just like that of Dutch or German (cf. Koster 1975). In this way, the basic 'OV' typology of OE can be maintained; the sole difference between OE and Modern Dutch or German is the existence in OE of Focus NP-Shift and the absence of a rule of this type in Dutch and German. However, it is not clear if this result can be maintained for OE in general, aside from *Beowulf*. In that case, we must postulate optional DP-extraposition for OE prose texts. OV analyses of OE word order have not properly solved this problem.

Verb raising, verb-projection raising and extraposition all involve rightward movements of various kinds. OE also had various leftward-movement operations that distorted the basic OV typology. We now turn to these.

2.3 Leftward movement rules

2.3.1 Scrambling

Originally discussed in Ross (1967), scrambling is an operation which, in West Germanic languages, moves definite DPs leftwards within the clause, to some position outside VP. In Dutch and German, a diagnostic for scrambling is the order of a definite complement with respect to clausal negation, since the marker of clausal negation is taken to be at the left margin of VP (cf. Bennis & Hoekstra 1986; den Besten & Webelhuth 1990; Deprez 1994; Fanselow 1990; Lee & Santorini 1994; Webelhuth 1991). The following examples illustrate scrambling in German; in both cases, the fact that the direct object *das Buch* precedes *nicht* is taken to show that it has left VP:

(12) Gestern kaufte$_V$ Peter ...
 yesterday bought Peter
 a. ... *das Buch*$_i$ ohne   Zweifel nicht [$_{VP}$ t_i t_V]
    the book without doubt not
 b. ... ohne   Zweifel *das Buch* nicht [$_{VP}$ t_i t_V]
    without doubt the book not
 'Yesterday John without doubt didn't buy the book'

(Vikner, to appear: 5)

Assuming the adverb *ohne Zweifel* to occupy a constant position (an assumption that is denied by Zwart 1993, for example), the object is clearly moved further in (12b) than in (12a). There is little consensus in the literature on West Germanic either as to the nature of the scrambling operation as A-movement or Ā-movement or as to the landing sites of the operation. For our present expository purposes, this is not important; what is crucial is that the different positions occupied by the direct object in (12), along with the possibility of it following negation (i.e. remaining in the putatively VP-internal position) show that it can be moved to the left out of VP.

In OE, clausal negation is signalled by pre-verbal *ne*, hence this diagnostic for scrambling is not available. Nevertheless, the following is a plausible instance of scrambling since the complement precedes an adjunct, and hence, given standard assumptions about the base positions of complements and adjuncts, must have moved leftward out of VP as indicated:

(13) ne mihton hi *nænige fultum*$_i$ æt him [$_{VP}$ t_i begitan]
 not could they any help from him get
 'They couldn't get any help from him'

(Bede 48.9–10; Pintzuk 1991: 144)

We can also see the effects of scrambling from interactions with verb-projection raising. On the standard view of OE word order, the following example involves scrambling of the direct object combined with rightward movement of the constituent containing the trace of the scrambled object:

(14) þæt he *þæt godes hus*$_i$ wolde [myd fyre t_i forbærnan]
 that he the god's house wanted with fire   to-burn
 'that he wanted to burn the god's house with fire'

(ÆLS 25.613–14; Pintzuk 1991: 39)

The above discussion does not take into account the possibility of movement to Spec,Agr$_O$P. Clearly, 'short' scrambling of the type in (12b) might be analysable in this way (if NegP is taken to be contained in Agr$_O$P). This possibility, which does not figure in 'standard' accounts of OE word order, will be considered in more detail below. If such an operation can be motivated, it adds a third case of leftward movement to the inventory of OE leftward movement rules (or, if it could be shown that there is only one position for leftward-moved complements outside VP, then it would substitute for scrambling on the view I am outlining here — however, we will see below that there are clearly two such positions). For our present exposition, we do not distinguish movement to Spec,Agr$_o$P from scrambling.

2.3.2 Cliticization

OE had a special position, or class of positions, for clitics. These elements preceded the main verb in ordinary matrix declaratives, followed the verb in matrix interrogatives, negative clauses and clauses beginning with a certain class of adverbs and followed the complementizer or the subject in embedded clauses. These positions are illustrated by the following examples:

(15) a. God *him worhte* þa reaf of fellum (clitic–verb)
God them made then garments of skin
'God then made them garments of skin'
(AHTh, I, 18; van Kemenade 1987: 114)

b. Hwæt *sægest þu*, yrþlincg? (verb–clitic)
'What sayest thou, ploughman?'
(AColl 22; van Kemenade 1987: 138)

c. ... þæt *him his fiend* wæren æfterfylgende (clitic–subject)
that him his enemies were following
'... that his enemies were following him'
(Oros., 48, 12; van Kemenade 1987: 113)

d. ... þæt þa Deniscan him ne mehton þæs ripes
that them the Danes NEG could the harvest
forwiernan (subject–clitic)
refuse
'... that the Danes could not refuse them the harvest'
(ChronA 89.10 (896); Pintzuk 1991: 188)

It is usually assumed that the clitic moves to its special position from an underlying position within VP. The precise nature of this movement rule, and of the alternating *cl–V* and *V–cl* orders, is not clear. It is likely that West Germanic cliticization processes are connected to scrambling — see for example Haegeman (1993) and below. On the relative order of verb and clitic, see van Kemenade (1987) and Tomaselli (1995).

The above paragraphs outline the kinds of assumptions and analyses that are typically proposed for OE, assuming that the language is head-final in VP and IP (although we should note that Pintzuk 1991 argues for a 'double-base' system where both IP and VP were subject to synchronic variation in OE with respect to the headedness parameter). In the next section, I will propose a head-initial analysis for OE VPs and IPs.

3 OE as a head-initial language

3.1 Introduction

The purpose of this section is to show that OE can plausibly be analysed as head-initial. Our goal is quite limited: I wish to show only that a head-initial analysis does no worse than a head-final one. In fact, a number of peculiar properties of OE have to be stipulated on a head-initial analysis, just as they do on a head-final analysis; it is interesting to observe that many of the same descriptive puzzles arise on both approaches, suggesting that they are not mere artifacts of a given approach.

I should also note that this section is compatible with a less restrictive theory of phrase structure than Kayne's, such as standard GB versions of X'-theory: I argue that there are no compelling empirical reasons to analyse OE as head-final. What we will see is that since OE can be analysed as VO, it does not pose a strong empirical challenge to a thesis such as Kayne's. To put it another way: there is a weak version and a strong version of the thesis being put forward here. The weak version states OE is not an OV language and hence that there are fewer underlyingly OV languages than previously thought. The strong version says that there are no OV languages, and hence OE is not an OV language. The facts do not decide between the weak and the strong version, and, in a sense, it is not crucial for the empirical claims of this chapter that Kayne's view be accepted. Either version, however, requires that our conception of the attested word-order changes in English be rethought. Moreover, if Kayne's view is accepted, then all cases of OV-to-VO change will have to be looked at in the terms proposed here, and so our argument has a more general scope (see note 11).

We begin by discussing the position of I, and then move to the position of V.

3.2 The position of I

Zwart (1993) points out that if we adopt the checking theory of Chomsky (1993a) there is no reason to assume that any verbal functional projection, i.e. any I-type element, is ever head-final. The basic motivation for this assumption in all the West Germanic languages has been that V-to-I movement creates an inflected verb. Hence, if inflected verbs are found in final position, I must be final. But if V is inserted fully inflected and raises to I to check its morphological features, it is possible to assume that its final position does not correspond to I but to V, with the possibility that the raising takes place covertly. Thus the final position of inflected verbs does not tell us anything about the position of I. (I will return to the question of V-movement below.)

Other properties can serve as diagnostics for the position of I-type elements, though. It has often been proposed (beginning with Kayne 1989) that clitics raise to I-type positions. It is clear that there are at least two types of 'clitic' elements crosslinguistically, and there are at least two types of positions that they raise to. On the first point, Cardinaletti (to appear) distinguishes between clitics and weak pronouns by saying that (a) the latter are homophonous with strong pronouns while the former are not, and (b) that latter only optionally move to 'special' positions while the former do so obligatorily. By criterion (a) OE 'clitics' are weak pronouns; by criterion (b), they are clitics since they are always found in special positions (although there are some examples where this is debatable — see (19) below). While it may be correct to view OE 'clitics' as weak pronouns, this does not affect the argument to be made here since the important point for our purposes is the nature of the special position that is moved into. The fact that this movement is obligatory in OE (examples like (19) notwithstanding) strongly suggests that these elements are clitics, and I will take this view in what follows. I will also follow Cardinaletti (to appear) in regarding movement of these pronouns as head-movement, although I will return to this point in section 4. Concerning the second point, clitics or weak pronouns seem to be attracted either to the inflected verb (as in Romance) or to a position after C (as in Germanic; possibly identifiable as the Wackernagel position). Rivero (this volume) distinguishes 'I-oriented' from 'C-oriented' clitics. In these terms, OE clitics are clearly C-oriented, like other West Germanic clitics. However, I will suggest directly that the 'C-oriented' position is a kind of Agr-position; in particular, although close to C, it cannot be identified with C at least in OE.

The OE clitic alternations in main clauses that are illustrated in (15) suggest strongly that clitics occupy a functional position lower than C. In the orders WH–V–CL (15b), V can be reasonably thought of as being in C (Rizzi 1991), in the order XP–CL–V (15a) either we must explain why the clitic selectively moves with V only in these cases (cf. Tomaselli 1995 for an attempt to do this for the comparable OHG data) or we must conclude that the verb and the clitic are in positions lower than C. Cardinaletti & Roberts (1991), Pintzuk (1991) and Kiparsky (1995) take the latter option. The alternative of regarding the clitics as consistently moving to C (with V left-adjoined to C in (15b) and not raising to C in (15a)) cannot be maintained for embedded clauses where clitics can follow the subject. Taking the weaker position that clitics always move to C in main clauses would (a) mean that there is no unified target for clitic placement and (b) posit an otherwise unmotivated root–embedded distinction in clitic placement which would be quite separate from that affecting verb placement. I thus conclude that clitics do not always move to C, and, since it is desirable to assume that there is the minimum possible number of targets for clitic placement, that they never move to C. The alternative, directly motivated by the position of the clitic in (15d) and indirectly by its position in (15a), is that clitics occupy 'medial' head-initial functional projections. These projections do not seem to form part of the complementizer system, since their nature does not seem to be determined by factors to do with complementation, and so I conclude that they are part of the I-system. This seems natural to the extent that it is plausible to consider that clitics move to special positions because they are subject to special checking requirements. The features to be checked are presumably ϕ-features (since the content of these elements is exhausted by such features), and hence the checking position is presumably an Agr-type position (cf. Sportiche 1995 and section 4 for a proposal along these lines). Note that this view of putatively 'C-oriented' clitics reduces the distinction between 'C-orientation' and 'I-orientation' either to orientation to different parts of the I-system or, perhaps, to orientation to the same position with independent differences in V- and subject-placement.

We thus have evidence for medial I-positions and, if we assume inflectional affixes are attached to verbs in the lexicon, no evidence for final I-positions. Following Zwart (1993) (as the above reasoning does, *modulo* certain differences between Dutch and OE), we can conclude that IP, or the IP-type projections, are head-initial. We will see further evidence that supports this conclusion below.

3.3 The position of V

The V-raising operation is proposed in order to regularize the head-final order. If inflected verbs are assumed to have raised to I, then we must assume that the non-finite V has raised to the right of I in an example like (7a), repeated here:

(7) a. þe æfre on gefeohte his hande *wolde afylan*
      who ever in battle   his hands would defile
      'who would ever defile his hands in battle'

(ÆLS 25.858; Pintzuk 1991: 102)

However, if the finite verb has not moved, we are not forced to conclude that the non-finite form is external to the VP headed by the finite verb. Hence it is possible that the non-finite verb is in a constituent that is a complement of the finite verb; in this case, it is likely that it is something larger than VP. Note that the position of the object is immaterial here; we must postulate leftward movement out of VP in any case, and so we could say that this element has moved here. In that case, the structure for (7a), rather than (8), would be (8'):

(8) þe æfre on gefeohte [$_{VP}$ his hande t_i] *wolde afylan$_i$*
(8') þe æfre on gefeohte his hande$_i$ *wolde* [$_{VP}$ *afylan* t_i]

Presumably, the object moves for case-checking purposes. It may be that 'verb-raising triggers' are verbs whose complements do not contain an (active) Agr$_O$, and so movement out of them is forced (cf. note 10). It is certainly well known that this class of verbs is close to the class of restructuring verbs in Romance (cf. Evers 1975; Rizzi 1982; Rutten 1991), and it may be correct to analyse the phenomena associated with restructuring as the reflex of the functional substitution of the matrix Agr$_O$ for the lower Agr$_O$ (cf. Roberts 1994).

Where the non-finite verb precedes the finite verb, I assume that the complement (or, in some cases, part of the complement — see the discussion around (29) below) is fronted for checking. It seems then that infinitival clauses are subject to a distinct checking requirement from finite clauses, which are able to remain final. Non-finite complements are subject to the same leftward-movement processes as DPs and other complements (e.g. small clauses). However, we must impose one restriction on them: material cannot intervene between a non-finite verb and a finite verb. This property is shared with Dutch small clauses, and implies, as in Zwart's (1993) analysis of the placement of these elements, that they can only be moved to a relatively 'low' position. Positions available to definite DP complements which are non-adjacent to V are not available for non-finite clauses (see note 4 for more on this). Given these assumptions, and an analysis of (7a) as in (8'), V-raising has no clear motivation in OE.

V-projection raising is also rather suspect. The same comments as were just made about verb raising apply: if we do not assume a final I it is not clear that we must treat a VP in post-finite-verb position as external to the VP headed by the finite verb. Zwart's position on this is that 'V-projection raising' is exactly like 'verb raising' with the single difference that Agr_O is available in the lower clause for checking the lower object (1993: 19, n. 14). We can adopt this view. This means that an example like (9a), repeated here for convenience, would involve only movement of the object *frið* internal to the complement, as illustrated in (9a'):

(9) a. hwær ænegu þeod at oþerre mehte [*frið begietan*]
      where any people from other might peace obtain
      'where any people might obtain peace from another'
                                      (Or 31.14–15; Pintzuk 1991: 113)
(9') a. hwær ænegu þeod at oþerre mehte [*frið*$_i$ *begietan* t$_i$]

One piece of evidence for this point of view for OE is discussed by Haeberli & Haegeman (1995). They show that OE contrasts minimally with West Flemish (WF) in that negative polarity items can appear in putatively raised VPs and form a single semantic negation with *ne* on the finite verb in OE, while this is impossible in WF:

(16) a. þæt heora nan ne mehte [*nanes wæpnes gewealdan*]   (OE)
       that of-them none NE might no   weapon wield
       'that none of them could use any weapon'
                             (Mitchell 1989: 660, cited in Haeberli & Haegeman 1995)
    b. *... dan-ze en-willen [*tegen niemand klapen*]
         that-they *en*-want   to   no-one talk
    c. ... dan-ze tegen niemand en-willen *klapen*
         that-they against no-one *en*-want talk

In (16b), the WF negative polarity item *niemand* cannot be licensed in a raised VP. This is unsurprising since it is a typical property of rightward-moved categories that they form islands of various kinds (cf. Haegeman & van Riemsdijk 1986 on this and other properties in both WF and Zurich German). However, (16a) indicates that the putatively rightward-moved VP in OE allows the negation to link up with the main negation NE (OE, like most varieties of English, has negative concord). Haeberli & Haegeman conclude that many instances of V-projection raising in OE should be analysed as involving verb movement to a medial I. This conclusion provides further evidence against a head-final IP, and partially undermines one of the rightward-movement rules that the standard account assumes. (If we are to adopt Kayne's general view, then we cannot account for the WF facts in terms of the islandhood of rightward-moved projections; for our purposes, it suffices to say that WF negative concord is subject to a restriction that OE negative concord is not subject to. I have no speculations to offer as to what that restriction might be. However, the important point for present purposes is that the absence of rightward movement makes this claim possible, while a theory that treats orders like those in (16) as derived from an island-creating rightward-movement rule has no recourse for accounting for the OE vs WF differences).

Haeberli & Haegeman nevertheless argue that V-projection raising is needed in some cases (where van Kemenade 1987 had proposed it). These are cases where there is both a non-subject and a subject before the inflected verb, creating a situation in which there is 'not enough space' for both constituents if the finite verb is in I (e.g., the bracketing here is what is implied by Haeberli & Haegeman's analysis):

(17) a. ... þæt [$_{IP}$ he [$_{??}$ þæs gewinnes$_i$ [$_I$ mehte$_j$] [$_{VP}$ mare t$_i$ gefremman t$_j$]
          that   he   the victory   could   better achieve
    '... that he could better achieve the victory'
                                              (van Kemenade 1987: 21, Oros 47, 14)

    b. ... þæt [$_{IP}$ mon [$_{??}$ ælcne ceap$_i$ [$_I$ mehte$_j$] [$_{VP}$ be *twiefealdan*
        that   people each commodity could   by twofold
    bet   t$_i$ *geceapian* t$_j$]   (van Kemenade 1987: 21, Oros 130, 23)
    better buy
    '... that people could buy each commodity twice as cheaply'

These examples are only problematic if one takes evidence of the type in (16a) as forcing a medial-I analysis. However, as mentioned above, another possibility is to treat the VPs (more precisely, the complement to *mehte*) as occupying the complement position of *mehte*. In that case, we are not forced to regard the finite verb as having raised to I, and we know that there must be landing sites for scrambling to its left.

Haeberli & Haegeman also note the following example with a negative polarity item in the putatively raised VP:

(18) þæt wæs ða   ða he *Iudeas* nolde   nan   wuht læran
    that was when he the Jews not-wanted nothing/not to-advise
    hwæt hi   don scolden   (Haeberli & Haegeman 1995, (31c), CP 58.433.3)
    what they do should
    'that was when he didn't want to advise the Jews what to do'

The authors note that *Iudeas* here must be in an adjoined position; presumably it would be adjoined to I'. In terms of the idea just sketched, we can regard this DP as occupying a scrambled position to the left of the category whose head contains the inflected verb, clearly a more satisfactory analysis (in fact the I'-adjunction possibility is ruled out on Kayne's 1994 assumptions). There may be a 'Pollockian' argument for V-movement here. If the second element of negation — *nan wuht* — is in a position comparable to NE *not* or French *pas*, then the inflected V is not in VP. However, if there is a scrambled position to its left the verb cannot be in the position that inflected verbs occupy in French (Agr$_S$). But the negative polarity evidence shows that the verb is not final with a raised VP following it. I conclude that it must be in a medial I-position (medial in the sense of being lower than Agr$_S$ but nevertheless VP-external). The natural candidates are T and Agr$_O$ (assuming the clause structure proposed in Belletti 1990 and Chomsky 1993 where Agr$_S$ is higher than T and T higher than Agr$_O$; Agr$_O$ is only a candidate to the extent that it is above NegP — see Roberts 1995).[3] For the sake of concreteness, we take this position to be Agr$_O$.

Another property that has been attributed to V-projection raising in WF and other contemporary West Germanic varieties is that pronouns cannot be part of 'raised' projections. However, Pintzuk (1991) gives examples where pronouns are in such positions in OE:

(19) ... þæt heo wolde *hine læran*   (Pintzuk 1991, ÆLS 18.291)
     that she wanted him to-teach
     '... that she wanted to teach him'

There are several ways to interpret examples like this. First, if we assume V-projection raising, then we are led to conclude that OE pronouns are different from those of WF and other Modern West Germanic varieties. In that case, (19) would be evidence that pronouns do not always move to a special position in OE on a 'V-projection raising' analysis, supporting the idea that OE 'clitics' are really weak pronouns in Cardinaletti's terms (and conversely that they are clitics in Cardinaletti's sense at least in WF). Second, we could deny that this example contains V-projection raising, and treat it as evidence for medial I. In principle, such a conclusion would not tell us anything about the existence of V-projection raising elsewhere in OE or about the position of V in VP. Third, if we consider that 'V-projection raising' reflects the presence of an *in situ* complement, then we must take it that the pronoun has moved within the complement in (19). This option is unavailable in WF, etc. On this view, we have no evidence that OE weak pronouns are anything other than clitics. The kind of variation in clitic positions between OE and WF that we posit is attested in Romance languages with the very similar operation of clitic climbing: in Standard Italian, clitics can climb (with the appropriate matrix verb) or cliticize to the lower verb, while in Sardinian and a number of southern Italian dialects climbing is obligatory wherever it is possible. This parallel can be maintained whether or not we consider clitic movement to be head movement, since West Germanic languages allow 'long' scrambling in contexts which can be plausibly regarded as restructuring contexts (Evers 1975; Rutten

1991; Zwart 1993). The third position is consistent with everything else we have said, and also indicates that OE weak pronouns are clitics in Cardinaletti's sense. I thus adopt this position.

The evidence from Haeberli & Haegeman combined with the general considerations regarding verb raising and the position of functional heads that we raised earlier combine to cast some doubt on the existence of V-projection raising in OE. If V-projection raising is not assumed, we have more cases of leftward movement than was previously thought: orders where VP precedes the finite verb might be derivable by leftward movement (again, not necessarily of VP, rather of a larger constituent). Since leftward movement is required in any case, this is not a problem. We also have *prima facie* cases of complements to the right of the verb. As in the case of verb raising we do not take these complements to be VPs. They must be at least IPs; more generally, they are complements that are 'transparent' rather in the manner of the complements to restructuring predicates in Romance languages (a similarity that was originally observed by Evers 1975), hence clitic climbing and scrambling can take place from within them. I thus suggest that V-projection raising, which has always been a highly problematic operation, does not exist. More specifically, I conclude that OE provides no cases of such an operation: the derived structure of putative examples of this construction is as in (9a').

I have now dispensed with two of the rightward-movement rules of OE that the standard analyses assume. The remaining one is extraposition. For CP- and PP-extraposition, I simply assume that the elements in question are able to remain in their complement positions (Zwart 1993 provides evidence from the fact that post-verbal CPs are not necessarily islands — which extraposed clauses always are — in favour of the idea that this is the situation in Dutch; I do not have comparable data in OE, unfortunately). DP-extraposition is more interesting. Here, one possibility is to adapt Pintzuk & Kroch's analysis in the obvious fashion: focussed DPs are able to remain in complement position. An alternative, at least for complements of non-finite verbs, is to say that final DPs are fronted inside the complement and the remainder of the complement undergoes the usual leftward movement operation for non-finite complements. The derived structure of an example like (10c) would then be as in (20):

(20) ... þæt ænig mon [$_{XP}$ atellan t_i] mæge [$_{YP}$[$_{DP}$ ealne þone demm]$_i$ t_{XP}]

We will discuss this kind of derivation in more detail below — cf. (29). Focussing and remnant fronting account for many cases of final DPs. The residue must be demonstrably unfocussed and in embedded clauses with a single finite verb which are demonstrably not V2; and note that even this kind of example could be handled by postulating V-raising higher than Agr$_O$ and object movement to Spec,Agr$_O$ (see Note 4). (Similarly, V-movement allows for cases where the final DP is not adjacent to the finite verb).

An important argument for V-final orders, originally due to Koster (1975), has to do with the positions occupied by particles belonging to separable verbs like *terug+geven* 'give back' in V2 clauses. Koster's observation was that the position of the particle always corresponds to the position of the verb+particle combination in a verb-final clause: it cannot be followed by a DP, cannot be preceded by a finite clause, and may be followed by a PP. Koster argued that this distribution of particles could be simply accounted for if one assumed that the particle was stranded by V-movement. Hence the underlying position was final (*modulo* the position of finite clauses and certain PPs).

Van Kemenade (1987: 29–39) applies Koster's criteria to OE. What emerges is that particle positions pattern fairly systematically with V-positions, although they can be more readily separated from V in OE than in Dutch and they are also able to move with V in V2 clauses in OE, unlike Dutch. It seems, then, that the rule attaching Prt to V applies more liberally in OE. Aside from this, however, the particle positions in OE differ from those in Dutch in three main respects.

i. Particles can be followed by complement DPs, as can finite embedded verbs:

(21) ... þa   ahof   Paulus *up his heafod*
      then raised P.   up his head
      '... then P. raised up his head'   (van Kemenade 1987: 33, AHTh, I, 96)

As van Kemenade notes, the 'postposing' of DP here is just a case of the general possibility of having post-finite-verb DPs in OE (here it seems clear that the post-verbal DPs are not necessarily focussed). Pintzuk (1991) shows that particles do not occur after a non-finite verb, and interprets this as an argument for a medial I. I concur in this view; this is consistent with the suggestion made above that finite V moves to Agr_O.

ii. In Dutch, predicate adjectives and participles have to precede the final V in embedded clauses and always precede the particle in V2 clauses. This is not the case for OE; (22a) shows that adjectives can follow V, and (22b) shows that an adjective can follow Prt:

(22) a. ... forðam ðe   hi   licettað hie   *unscyldige*
         because that they pretend   themselves   innocent
         '... because they pretend themselves to be innocent'
                                                   (van Kemenade 1987: 35, CP, 439, 19)

   b. ... he ahof   þæt cild   up *geedcucod   and   ansund*
         he raised the child up quickened   and   healthy
                                                   (van Kemenade 1987: 36, AHTh, II, 28)

These examples arguably involve small clauses. Zwart (1993) argues that small clauses have to move to a special checking position (which he calls Spec,PredP) in Dutch, this derives the fact that constituents of this type always precede V in embedded clauses. Suppose this is true; then the OE data indicate that V can raise to a higher position in that language. We thus have another piece of evidence for V-movement. We also arrive at an important difference between OE and Dutch.

iii. In Dutch, very few adverbs follow the finite V in embedded clauses, and very few follow Prt in main clauses. OE does not show the embedded pattern of Dutch, i.e. it allows post-verbal adverbs in embedded clauses:

(23) ... ðæt hie ðæt unaliefede doð *aliefedlice*
       that they the unlawful do lawfully
    '... that they do unlawful things as if they were lawful'
(van Kemenade 1987: 36, CP, 144, 10)

There is no data available with respect to the root pattern. Again, I take (20) as evidence for V-to-Agr_O movement in OE. The object has been moved to Spec,Agr_O, or perhaps higher.

More generally, I regard particles, following Kayne (1985), as small-clause predicates. They optionally adjoin to the left of V in OE. I also have to assume that V can 'excorporate' from Prt in OE, as in Dutch. When Prt does not adjoin to the left of V, it occupies the same positions as other small-clause predicates like those seen in (22). This gives the following possibilities:

(24) ... V ... Prt + *t* [DP *t*]:   (V-movement and Prt-movement)
    ... þæt he *ahof up the earcan*   (Pintzuk 1991: 78, GD(C) 42.6–7)
    that he lifted up the chest

(25) ... V [DP Prt]   (no movement)
    ... þæt he *wearp þæt sweord onweg*   (Pintzuk 1991: 91, Bede 38.20)
    that he threw the sword away

(26) ... Prt+V [DP t]   (Prt-movement)
    ... þæt *up arisað lease leogeras*   (Pintzuk 1991: 84; WHom 1b.16)
    that up arise false liars
    '... that false liars rise up'

(27) ... V X [DP Prt]   (V-movement)
    þa *ahof* Drihten *hie up*   (van Kemenade 1987: 33, Blick 157)
    then raised the-Lord them up
    'then the Lord raised them up'

The examples of 'V-movement' in (24)–(27) are cases where V moves beyond Agr_O. In some cases, e.g. (27), this is clearly movement to C; in others, e.g. (24), it may not be (note the different position of the verb with respect to the subject in (24) vs (27)). The DP subject of the small clauses in (24)–(27) may be moved out of the small clause to a checking position — this is very likely for the clitic *hie* in (27), and cannot be excluded in the other examples (this depends on what we assume about the position of V — see note 3). If V does not in fact move further than Agr_O in (25) and (26), then we must assume that the object can check for case inside the small clause; notice that on this view (26) becomes analogous to our proposal for final DP-complements of non-finite verbs in (20). It is striking that this order, like that in (20), is not found in contemporary West Germanic.

So far, we have seen that we can do without the three rightward-movement processes assumed by the standard analysis. We have seen that V moves to Agr$_O$, and that small clauses, non-finite complements and DP-complements move leftwards. We have suggested that finite CPs, some PPs and, possibly, focussed DPs can stay in complement position, and that DP can be 'stranded' in final position by remnant complement-movement. It is natural to relate the CP- and PP-positions to the idea that such categories are not required to check for case, although given that we assume small-clause predicates and non-finite complement clauses are also subject to a checking requirement the notion of 'case' here is much more abstract than in GB theory — we return to this point briefly in the next section. We are also assuming both scrambling and cliticization. At this point, we should make our general position clear regarding the leftward movement of complements.

I propose that the OE clause contains the following positions:

1. a topic position: active only in V2 clauses (although V is not always in C in such clauses, as the clitic evidence shows);
2. C;
3. a subject position, although, as in Dutch and German, the subject can and often does remain in a lower position;
4. the clitic position, again comparable to German;
5. a scrambling position, which can also be occupied by the subject;
6. a second scrambling position;
7. the checking position for objects, non-finite complements and small clauses: Spec,Agr$_O$P;
8. the position of the finite verb in non-V2 clauses: Agr$_O$;
9. the base position of V (which in certain examples it appears to stay in);
10. the complement position, occupied by CP, some PPs and (possibly) focussed DPs.

I distinguish two scrambling positions on the assumption that OE scrambling is parallel to that of German as seen in (12), although we have not seen any direct evidence of this. There are thus three possible positions for the direct object: 5, 6 and 7. For concreteness, we identify the second scrambled position (Position 6) as Spec,TP. If we take Position 3 to be Spec,Agr1P in the sense of Cardinaletti & Roberts, then the clitic position is Agr1 and the first scrambling position may be Spec,Agr$_S$ (following Kayne 1994 we do not structurally distinguish specifiers from adjoined positions and assume a given YP cannot simultaneously support a specifier and an XP adjunct, hence Position 5 is the position adjoined to Agr$_S$P and when the subject moves there it presumably checks with Agr$_S$, but a scrambled element may not).[4] These assumptions give us the following clause structure:

(28) [$_{CP}$1 [$_{C}$2 [$_{Agr1P}$3 [$_{Agr1}$4 [$_{Agr_SP}$5 [$_{Agr_S}$ [$_{TP}$6 [$_T$ [$_{Agr_O}$P7 [$_{Agr_O}$8 [$_{VP}$9 10]]]]]]]]]]]

The above proposal accounts for the word orders found in OE with little stipulation. Like all other analysts, we must allow for a certain optionality:

for example, V-movement is not always required, even in main clauses. Also, we may have to allow for focussed DP complements to have a special privilege with respect to Case Theory. It may be that the optionality in verb movement concerns the strength of features of functional heads which trigger movement (what this effectively means in a framework like that of Chomsky 1993a is that the optionality represents distinct parameter values; this view of OE is argued for by Pintzuk 1991, but there the idea is framed in terms of variation in the branching direction of I' and V'. The proposal in Kiparsky 1995 that C may be absent from OE main clauses reduces to the same idea in Minimalist terms — C cannot be absent, but may have weak features in some instances and strong in others).

To see how the system works, let us consider the principal subordinate-clause word orders, as discussed in van Kemenade (1987) and Kiparsky (1995), here I gloss over clitic positions, and use Aux to mean finite V:

(29) a. S V   Aux O   (standardly DP-extraposition)
     b. S O   Aux V   (standardly V-raising)
     c. S   Aux O V   (standardly V-projection raising)
     d. S O V Aux   (standardly underlying)
     e. S   Aux V O   (V-raising, DP-extraposition)
     f. *S V O Aux   (underivable)

In the head-initial system being advocated here, the grammatical orders are derived by combinations of object-movement and 'VP-movement' (here again, it is likely that the category being moved is larger than VP). I now outline the relevant derivations in detail.

On our account, (29a) must involve fronting of the non-finite verb. We can view this as a kind of VP-fronting if we can motivate moving the object out of VP. As sketched earlier (cf. (20)), I assume that this happens on the lower cycle, i.e. that the object moves out of the fronted constituent inside the lower clause, and the remnant of the lower clause is fronted. This analysis ties the existence of post-verbal DPs in OE to the existence of examples like (19) in terms of the idea that nominals, full DPs and pronouns, can be fronted for checking on the lower cycle (cf. also the discussion of (25)). Neither examples like (19) nor post-verbal DPs are found in Modern West Germanic; this then reduces to the same fact (but cf. the discussion of (29c) below). Recall again that similar variation is found in clitic-climbing constructions across Romance. On this view, the relevant parts of the S-structure for (29a) are as follows:

(30) ... [$_{AgrO}$P [$_{VP}$ V t_i] [$_{AgrO}$ Aux] [$_{XP}$ ... O$_i$ ...

We could capture the connection to focus observed by Pintzuk & Kroch in the following manner: at LF, the object must raise to a position c-commanding its trace. This can only happen where the object is focussed and undergoes LF raising. The well-known weak-crossover effects discussed in Chomsky (1977) show that LF raising places DPs in a position higher than the subject position. Therefore, this position is higher than the position of the fronted VP in (30), and the object c-commands its trace at LF. This idea has two disadvantages: first, the empirical status of Pintzuk & Kroch's result for texts other than *Beowulf* is uncertain, as we mentioned earlier; second, it is not clear that the fronted complement cannot be reconstructed (although if this is a kind of A-movement, we do not expect this possibility, unlike the Modern English VP-topicalization discussed in Huang 1993). We thus leave this question open.

The order in (29b) results straightforwardly from either object scrambling or object-movement to the higher Spec,Agr$_O$. (29c) involves raising of the object to Spec,Agr$_O$P for case-checking inside the complement clause without movement of the remnant category containing V. Since this kind of order is found in some contemporary West Germanic varieties (it is standardly analysed as V-projection raising, cf. section 2.2.2), we have to conclude that checking on the lower cycle is allowed in these varieties. What is not allowed in these varieties, however, is (i) clitic-placement on the lower cycle (cf. the discussion around (19)), and (ii) fronting of the remnant constituent into the higher clause (to give the order in (29a)). We can now derive the following prediction for West Germanic (other than English): a language in which non-finite complements are fronted has the order in (29a) only if it has V-projection raising, i.e. the order in (29c). This prediction is fulfilled; Old High German and Middle Dutch are like OE in having both orders, while no modern variety which has the order in (29c) has the order in (29a).

(29d) can be analysed as object scrambling combined with VP-fronting (note that the object c-commands its trace inside VP), or as fronting of the entire complement including the direct object. We could regard (29e) as not involving movement (except for Aux-to-Agr$_O$) and claim that the object must be focussed in order to escape the requirement that it move to Spec,Agr$_O$P. Once again, if this cannot be sustained empirically, we need an alternative analysis. To capture (29e) while ruling out (29f) and without assuming that the final DP is obligatorily focussed, we must invoke a variant of the standard verb raising idea (cf. section 2.2.1). We propose, then, that the infinitive attaches to the auxiliary in these cases (and, presumably, in (29b)). This captures the further fact that nothing can intervene between Aux and V in such cases. As in all analyses of verb raising in systems where the order in (29c) ('V-projection raising') is also found, we have to treat this infinitive-movement as optional.[5]

Consider now the illicit order (29f). There are several possible derivations to look at. First, we can rule out the possibility that V and O move as a constituent, since the object must leave VP in order to be licensed in the lower clause (and V does not move to Aux here, clearly). So we assume that the object and the VP are both fronted separately. Essentially, VP must front to a position lower than the object. We have already guaranteed this by assuming that VP must move to the same position as small-clause predicates (including particles): Position 7. Thus, the object would have to be in

VP to give the order in (29f), and we have just seen that this is impossible. (We also need to prevent the object from being focussed here; perhaps this can be achieved by requiring LF-raising of focussed categories and preventing raising out of a constituent on a left branch).

The above paragraphs give my account of OE word order. The account fares no worse than standard ones (which are highly stipulative; all the processes described in section 2 are motivated purely by the need to attain descriptive adequacy) and in some cases does better, e.g. regarding the crosslinguistic prediction about the relation between the orders in (29a) and (29c). Our approach also captures the observation that non-finite Vs always form a 'verbal cluster' with finite Vs in West Germanic (cf. Evers 1975; den Besten & Edmonson 1983; Prinzhorn 1990), except when they undergo remnant topicalization to the first position (cf. den Besten & Webelhuth 1990). Verbal clusters result either from fronting a non-finite complement to Position 7 or from V-raising out of the complement (note that this is not optionality in the sense of two parametric systems; the same checking operation takes place in each case, and, seemingly, equally economically).[6]

One final point: the ten positions of the OE clause carry over straightforwardly to Dutch and German. There are three properties which distinguish both Dutch and German from OE, all of them well known and all of them unaccounted for on this or any other analysis. First, V always precedes clitics in V2 clauses in both Dutch and German but not OE. We illustrate with German — this example should be contrasted with the grammatical OE (15a):

(31) *Gott ihnen werkte die Kleider
    God them made the clothes

We take this to indicate that V moves to C obligatorily in topic-initial V2 clauses in Dutch and German, but not in OE (cf. Kiparsky 1995), we take no position on the analysis of SV V2 clauses — cf. Zwart (1993), Vikner & Schwartz (to appear). Second, V does not raise to Agr_O in embedded clauses in either Dutch or German (but cf. note 3), hence we do not find post-verbal final adverbs or small-clauses in these contexts. Compare the following Dutch examples with (22) and (23) respectively:

(32) a. *... omdat hij ontving de wijnglazen gebroken
       because he received the wine-glasses broken
   b. *... omdat hij zijn werk deed ijverig
       because he his work did industriously

(van Kemenade 1987: 27)

Third, as we have seen, final (light) DPs are not allowed, as the following Dutch example shows:

(33) *... omdat hij kocht het boek
     because he bought the book

(van Kemenade 1987: 26)

Dutch also differs from both German and OE in not allowing complement clitics to precede the subject. We take this to indicate that the subject must appear in Position 3 (Spec,Agr1P) in Dutch — cf. Cardinaletti & Roberts (1991). These differences aside, Dutch and German pattern like OE.

4 Changes in ME

In this section will outline my account of how word-order change took place in the early ME period. This account can link the word-order change to three other important changes that took place at this time and can be embedded in a general approach to language change. These advantages follow naturally from the assumption of head-initial order in OE. It follows that if Kayne's theory of phrase structure forces us to assume that OE was head-initial, this theory has advantages in this particular domain over less restrictive theories such as the standard GB one.

At the same time as the word-order change, two other important syntactic changes took place:

(34) a. Loss of complement clitics (but cf. note 7)
     b. Loss of scrambling

Van Kemenade (1987) argues at length that the object cliticization was dramatically reduced in the twelfth century and completely extinct by 1400. On the other hand, subject clitics are found until *c.* 1400, especially in southern texts. The loss of the subject clitics was connected to the loss of V2 (cf. van Kemenade 1987). However, our main interest here is in complement clitics. It is often observed that English word order was 'rigidified' in ME.[7] Although the word order in ME (and indeed ENE) was freer in various ways than in NE (see note 7), we interpret this observation as meaning that scrambling disappears quite early on, around the time of the word-order change.

Another change that takes place in early ME is the loss of the morphological case declensions. OE had a system of case marking on nouns which distinguished four cases and two numbers, and up to seven declension classes (case marking on articles has a slightly different history — see note 9). Owing at least in part to phonological changes (the reduction of unstressed vowels to [ə] and the loss of final nasals) and in part to standard processes of morphological 'levelling', this system was reduced by EME to one where nominative–accusative distinctions were essentially no longer made, and only the dative ([-ə]) and genitive singular ([-(ə)s]) survived. Of these, the former did not last long, and so we arrive at essentially the modern system. These changes can be illustrated with the following paradigms for *stone*, which in OE was a representative of the masculine *a*-stem declension, the one to which all other declensions were apparently levelled:

(35) OE: nom: stan   stanas
         acc: stan   stanas
         gen: stanes   stana
         dat: stane   stanum
    12c.   ston   stones
                 ston   stones
                 stones   stone(s)
                 ston(e)   stonen/s
    14c.   stoon (sg) stoon(e)s (pl/gen sg)

For further details on the loss of the OE morphological case system, see Lass (1992: 103–12).

The 'standard' account of the development of English word order postulates a change in the directionality parameter in (1), taking place in the twelfth century (see van Kemenade 1987 and Lightfoot 1991). It is unclear how to connect this change to the loss of clitics and scrambling, and to the loss of morphological case (although van Kemenade posits a connection between the loss of clitics and the loss of case morphology). The account that I propose here has the merit of connecting the word-order change to the changes in (34). It is also possible, as we shall see, to regard the loss of morphological case as the trigger for all these changes.

The account of OE word order sketched in section 3 crucially involves object fronting to Spec,Agr_OP. Along with scrambling, this gives rise to many OV orders. Suppose in fact that these two processes are linked. For concreteness, I take scrambling (in West Germanic) to be Ā-movement. That is, scrambling is movement to a non-L-related position; the landing site of scrambling is adjoined to a maximal projection that has no lexical feature to assign to the scrambled element. However, scrambled DPs must check for case; thus, they move through Spec,Agr_OP en route to the scrambled position (I assume the same, or the analogous, for scrambled indirect objects and some PPs; the checking mechanism that is relevant here may correspond to the GB notion of inherent case, and so it is no surprise to see it extended to at least some PPs).

Movement to Spec,Agr_O is required because Agr_O has a strong N-feature (although, possibly, focussed DPs are exempt from this requirement, as we have seen). I take the general view that 'deep' syntactic changes such as word-order change arise through restructuring of grammars by language acquirers (see in particular Lightfoot 1979, 1991). In that case, if we are to understand the word-order change in early ME, we must understand what leads language acquirers to postulate a strong N-feature associated with Agr_O. On this point, I assume the following:

(36) a. Morphological trigger: if a head H has the relevant L-morphology, then H has strong L-features.
     b. Syntactic trigger: if a well-formed representation can be assigned to a given string by assuming that H has strong L-features, then H has strong L-features.

c. In general, weak features are the default value. These are assumed in the absence of clear evidence to the contrary of the type in (a) or (b).

(36a) states, in general terms, what the morphological trigger of a strong feature is. It is motivated by the attested facts involving the loss of V-to-I movement and the loss of agreement features in sixteenth-century English (see Roberts 1985, 1993a; Pollock 1989; Rohrbacher 1994a). Similarly, (36b) gives a rough statement of the syntactic trigger for a strong feature. The assumption in (36c) derives from the general idea that a preference for maximally simple representations of the input is a property of the learner (cf. Clark & Roberts 1993, in progress, for formalizations of this). The simplest representation compatible with the input is chosen, where representations lacking overt movement are defined as simpler than those featuring movement dependencies (arguably because overt movement always creates adjunction structures, while the lack of movement may not, and adjunction structures are more complex than non-adjunction structures). In this sense, we see that weak features give rise to simpler representations than strong features, and so robust positive evidence is required for strong features, while weak features represent the default (or unmarked) value (this conception of markedness is discussed and illustrated at greater length in Roberts, forthcoming).

In the case of the word-order change in early ME, the morphological trigger in the sense of (36a) is provided by nominal morphology, i.e. case marking. As we saw above, the OE morphological case system broke down in the early ME period. Once this happened, there was no morphological trigger for strong N-features on Agr_O. So we see that the loss of case marking in English removed part of the trigger for these features.[9]

However, the loss of part of the trigger for the strong value of the Agr_O parameter does not on its own change the value of that parameter; it simply means that the syntactic trigger became crucial for determining its value. To prevent the parameter defaulting to the weak value in the absence of morphology, OV orders must be robustly attested in the trigger experience, forcing the postulation of representations where Agr_O has a strong N-feature. In this respect, the crucial factor was the existence of post-verbal DPs, and a number of other post-verbal constituents (particles and other small-clause predicates) owing to the existence of V-to-Agr_O movement and stranding of final DPs by remnant movement of non-finite complements. As long as the morphology provided a clear trigger for a strong value of Agr_O, these constructions were assigned representations of the type seen in section 3. Once the morphological trigger for DP-movement to Spec,Agr_OP was lost, however, VO and other V–complement orders could be assigned simpler representations not involving DP-movement. In such representations, Agr_O has a weak N-feature. This kind of analysis is favoured by the preference for weak feature-values, (36c) (which in turn derives from a general preference for simpler representations wherever possible, as mentioned above). Hence the presence of these orders weakens the syntactic trigger for a strong feature on Agr_O, by making possible more highly valued representations in which Agr_O has a weak feature. Given this possible analysis of VO orders, the weak value of Agr_O is both the default value, and confirmed by part of the trigger experience. Hence there is no robust syntactic trigger for the strong value of the parameter, and the OV orders either die out or are reanalysed.[10] Thus the Agr_O-parameter changed: the formerly strong N-feature became weak. This entails the loss of the orders in (29b, c, d).

As I mentioned above, scrambling must move through Spec,Agr_OP in order for the scrambled DP to check its case. Once Spec,Agr_OP loses its strong case feature, there is no reason to move there overtly. Hence, by Economy, movement to this position becomes impossible, and scrambling is lost. Of course, *wh*-movement survives the loss of a strong N-feature on Spec,Agr_OP. We must assume that *wh*-movement can allow its trace to check for case, but that scrambling cannot. The reason for this might be that *wh*-traces are 'true variables' while the traces of scrambling are not, a fact which we can connect to the well-known fact that (Germanic) scrambling does not trigger weak crossover (cf. for example Lee & Santorini 1994; Vikner 1994b). Suppose further, following Sportiche (1990), that clitic-placement (in West Germanic) involves DP-movement followed by local D-movement. The only kind of DP-movement that can place D within range of the clitic position without violating the head-movement constraint is scrambling, given our analysis of OE clause structure. The loss of scrambling thus implies the loss of special positions for clitics. More precisely, it implies the loss of complement clitics; subject DPs can move within range of the clitic position by A-movement. As we saw above, complement clitics are essentially lost at the same time as the word order changes in early ME.

We are thus able to treat the principal cause of the word-order change as the loss of morphological case marking, and connect this change to the loss of scrambling and complement clitics. Notice that the loss of the latter two operations is guaranteed by central principles of the theory, in particular economy constraints on movement.

Linking the word-order change to the loss of morphological case raises two major objections from a comparative Germanic perspective. First, Icelandic is VO and has a rich morphological case system. Second, Dutch is OV and lacks morphological case (by and large). We can account for Dutch in terms of the idea that (36) provides: the morphological trigger for the strong N-feature of Agr_O. (36) states that Agr_O has a strong feature if the morphology is present. Hence, the lack of morphology implies nothing. In Dutch, the syntactic properties that facilitated the change in Agr_O's feature-value in English are missing: V-to-Agr_O movement and final DPs.[11] Hence the reanalysis has not taken place, and Dutch retains a strong N-feature on Agr_O despite the lack of a morphological trigger. For Icelandic, we must say that V always moves to a higher position than the object: here the issue of object shift comes up again. It is unclear, however, why Icelandic should lack scrambling. Again, though, our account simply says that there is a necessary condition for scrambling — a strong N-feature on Agr_O — we have nothing to say about what the sufficient condition might be.

5 Conclusion

I have argued that the facts of OE and ME word order, and the changes relating the two systems, can be accounted for in terms of the idea that OE was a head-initial language. Our argument concerning the synchronic analysis of OE was simply that such an analysis does no worse than many recent analyses which postulate a head-final order. Many descriptive problems remain for both approaches. The real motivation for our approach comes from the treatment of the word-order changes in early Middle English. I argued that the loss of OV orders was caused by the loss of a strong N-feature on Agr_O, a development which is related to the loss of morphological case on DPs by (36). In this way, the word-order change in English can be viewed as an instance of a typical kind of change: the loss of an overt movement rule caused by the loss of the morphological trigger for a strong feature of a functional head. The loss of overt movement of inflected verbs in early Modern English was arguably a change of a similar kind (cf. in particular Roberts 1993a). I further suggested that the loss of scrambling and of complement clitics was connected to the change in the value of this feature: once this feature had changed, economy constraints on movement prevented overt scrambling from taking place, and this in turn blocked cliticization of complements. In this way, our account connects four salient changes in early Middle English in terms of the loss of a single abstract feature, and the account of the causation of the change is embedded in a more general theory of language change, from which it follows that strong features may become weak when a morphological trigger for overt movement disappears from the input to language acquisition.[12]

Notes

*   Earlier versions of this material were presented at the University of Venice; University of Geneva; University of York; the Centre National pour la Recherche Scientifique, Paris; the School of Oriental and African Studies; London; the ninth Comparative Syntax Conference (Harvard University); Georgetown University; and the 3rd Diachronic Generative Syntax Conference (Free University of Amsterdam). I would like to thank the audiences at those presentations, and particularly Anthony Kroch and Giuseppe Longobardi, for their comments and criticisms. Thanks also to the editors of this collection and one anonymous reviewer for comments and suggestions. All errors are my own.

1.   This is not quite how Kayne puts it. Kayne proposes the Linear Correspondence Algorithm (LCA):
   (i)   For a given phrase marker P, with T the set of terminals, d(A) is a linear ordering on T

   where d(X), for X a non-terminal, is the set of terminals X dominates, and A is the set of pairs of non-terminals such that the first asymmetrically c-commands the second. These

notions formalize the relation between asymmetric c-command and linear order. However, as Chomsky (1994) and Rohrbacher (1994b) both point out, it is necessary to stipulate *precedence*, not just *ordering*, in order to derive the result that Specifier–Head–Complement is the only possible order within XP. To see this, take the VP in (3). Here, d(VP) is {⟨*see, him*⟩}. So the LCA requires that the terminals *see* and *him* be ordered, but not necessarily that *see* precede *him*. Moreover, where d(X) contains more than one ordered pair, say {⟨x, y⟩, ⟨y, z⟩}, nothing in Kayne's system prevents us from choosing 'precede' as the ordering among x and y and 'follow' as the ordering among y and z (giving xzy where y asymmetrically c-commands z).The fact that precedence has to be stipulated makes Kayne's system less elegant than it might have been.

2. Note that in a theory of the type advocated in Chomsky (1993), which lacks a single point in the derivation that can be defined as a base, it is not even clear that the notion 'base expansion of X' can be defined.

3. This conclusion depends on the assumption that there are no scrambling positions to the left of $Agr_S P$. This assumption is somewhat dubious, and has been explicitly denied by Haegeman (1994) and Sportiche (1995). If these authors are right in positing scrambling positions between C and Agr_S, then we could maintain that V raises to Agr_S in examples of this type (and more generally in OE and West Germanic). If there is a clear relation between the 'richness' of verbal inflection and verb movement to Agr_S of the type proposed by Roberts (1985, 1993a) and Rohrbacher (1994a), then we are forced to say this anyway for at least some of these languages. However, in that case superficial OV order is the result of obligatory scrambling to positions above Agr_S; it is not clear what causes this (although this does not affect the account of the word-order change given in section 4, which postulates a relation between the loss of scrambling and the loss of overt movement to $Spec, Agr_O P$; even if superficial OV derives from obligatory scrambling to positions above Agr_S, loss of movement to $Spec, Agr_O P$ will nevertheless account for the loss of scrambling). For the purposes of the present argument, however, we can maintain the slightly simpler assumption that the verb raises to T or Agr_O in OE.

4. Alternatively, given the discussion in note 3 of scrambling positions above Agr_S, both positions 5 and 6 may be above $Agr_S P$. This would entail a number of modifications to the tree in (28).

5. Put this way, V-raising might be thought to involve right-adjunction, another structural configuration ruled out by the proposals in Kayne (1994). We can avoid this consequence by positing that V left-adjoins to Aux (i.e. the higher V-position), and Aux then raises to Agr_O by excorporation. Note that any analysis of West Germanic verb raising must assume excorporation (cf. Roberts 1991; Rutten 1991). To get the correct orders in clusters of more than two verbs, we have to assume that non-finite verbs also move; in fact, this is exactly the same operation.

6. The reason for verb clustering might be that 'transparent' complements must be licensed by an external head. The licensing head would always be the finite verb, and the relationship either a Spec–head one (where the complement moves to Position 7) or a head–head one (motivating V-raising in (29b, d)). On this view, VPs can front to the specifier of a position occupied by the finite verb or its trace (e.g. $Spec, Agr_O P$ or, in V2 clauses, Spec,CP). A similar constraint holds for 'restructuring' complements in Romance languages — cf. Kayne (1989), Roberts (1994b).

7. Until the sixteenth century, pronoun object shift of the sort found in contemporary Mainland Scandinavian is attested:
   (i) They tell vs. not the worde of God

   (1565, T. Stapleton, *A Fortress of the Faith* (Antwerp 1565); Roberts 1995: 274)
   This is a different kind of pronoun movement from the type being considered in the text. It always places the pronoun in a position lower than the subject (i.e. below Agr_S), and it is dependent on verb movement to a higher position (cf. Holmberg 1986). On the other hand, clitic movement of the kind found in West Germanic and OE places the pronoun above Agr_S (but below C, we have argued) and is independent of V-movement.

The historical development of English strongly suggests that the latter system developed into the former. Here we propose an account of how the latter system was lost.

There are residual OV orders in ME with full DPs. These are mostly found with infinitives and participles, e.g. (thanks to Najib Jarad, p.c., for (ii-b,c)):

(ii) a. I may no rest haue a-mongys ʒow

(MKempe A 122.19–20; Fischer 1992: 373)

    b. and prattest hine to slayne and his cun to fordonne
       'and threaten to slay him and destroy his kin'

(CursM 12965; Visser 1963–73: §1039)

    c. She did him excite ... hir story for to write

(Lydgate Fall Pr. 9.518; Visser 1963–73: §2279)

These are reminiscent of similar orders found in Old French (cf. Pearce 1990). This construction is too restricted to be considered a case of scrambling. Perhaps it is a variant of Icelandic-style object shift, although to show this we would have to show that ME infinitives move (and note that (ii-a–c) illustrate the three main kinds of ME infinitive: bare, *to* and *for-to*). We have no detailed analysis along these lines to offer here, although it is tempting to consider such a movement as the diachronic residue of OE V-raising — see below.

8. In minimalist terms, this may seem strange, but one could claim that scrambling assigns an interpretive feature rather than a formal, morphosyntactic feature; probably the basis of the distinction between L-related and non-L-related movement/positions can be recast in these terms, with L-related positions being 'pure' checking positions and non-L-related ones being associated with an interpretive feature of some kind. On what the interpretive property of scrambled positions might be, cf. Diesing (1992).

9. Here the question which arises is what we should call the 'relevant' morphology in terms of (36). One possibility is that it concerns the existence of overt morphological nominative–accusative distinctions. However, only two out of seven noun declensions ever distinguished nominative from accusative in OE, and those only in the singular. A more promising proposal would be to attribute the crucial properties to determiners. Masculine and feminine singular forms of the proto-definite article (a demonstrative at the time — cf. note 13) distinguished Nominative from Accusative in OE (masc *se* (NOM), *þone* (ACC), fem *sēo* (NOM), *þā* (ACC)) but this distinction dies out around the same time as the word-order becomes VO. The correlation here seems quite close in that, for example, the Final Continuation of the *Peterborough Chronicle* (1132–55) shows an invariant *þe* as the singular definite article (Lass 1992: 112), and is usually thought to be VO (Mitchell 1964, cited in Fischer (1992: 372), shows that this text has 88% VO order). We might take it, then, that morphological case-marking on articles, in particular a nominative–accusative distinction, provides the 'relevant morphology'. This conclusion is consistent with the situation in Modern German, which provides a morphological trigger for a strong N-feature on Agr_O only if we regard case marking on articles as crucial. On Modern Dutch, see below.

10. As we saw in note 7, residual OV orders survive for some time after the twelfth century. We must assume that these orders neither depend on nor trigger a strong N-feature of Agr_O, although their analysis remains unclear. In this situation, we can only conclude that twelfth-century acquirers reanalysed OV orders as whatever construction the one seen in note 7 is.

11. Final DPs are found in Middle Dutch (Weerman 1989). Our expectation is then that these orders are lost before morphological case is lost. Weerman shows that Old and Middle High German also had final DPs. It is clear, then, that these properties can be lost independently of the English developments that we are discussing here. An intriguing possibility is suggested by our analysis of (29a). We suggested above that Modern West Germanic varieties with 'V-projection raising' and without final DPs lack the possibility of remnant fronting of non-finite clauses. A plausible speculation is that this is due to these complements having a more reduced functional structure than the

OE (or OHG and Middle Dutch) counterparts. If non-finite complements develop a more reduced functional structure then there are fewer landing sites for the object on the lower cycle and correspondingly less possibility of remnant complement fronting. Such a development, which is quite independent of anything discussed in the text, may have led to the loss of final DPs in all of Continental West Germanic. If this can be maintained, then we do not have to predict that final DPs were lost before morphological case-marking in Dutch.

12. In the highly restrictive view of parametrization imposed by the Minimalist framework, it is difficult to see what other properties might give rise to OV orders. It is then tempting to regard other cases of OV-to-VO change as being caused in the same way. This is a plausible speculation as regards the development from Latin to Romance. Latin was OV with free word order and morphological case; Modern Romance languages are all VO, have rigid word order and — with the possible exception of Rumanian — have no morphological case (outside the pronominal system). Taking Latin 'free word order' as indicative of scrambling (whether of a type precisely like that found in West Germanic or closer to what is found in Russian, Hindi or Japanese remains to be seen), and the Romance 'rigid' word order to indicate the absence of scrambling, it seems likely that an account of the sort given above would carry over. The obvious anomaly concerns clitics/weak pronouns: why has Romance retained such elements while English has lost them? Although I cannot give a full answer here, I speculate that this is connected to the fact that Romance clitics are essentially V-related elements that license *pro* (cf. Rizzi 1993 on the former and Sportiche 1995 on the latter), rather than being Wackernagel elements like their Germanic (and Late Latin) counterparts. The changes described in the text eliminate Wackernagel pronouns (or 'C-oriented' clitics in Rivero's terminology — cf. the discussion of this notion in section 3.2), they are not necessarily incompatible with clitics with the particular properties that the Modern Romance ones have. On this view, when the movement source for clitics described in the text was lost, Romance pronouns changed status. The question now becomes: why did this change not happen in English? One possible answer is that it did: I mentioned in note 8 that Middle and early Modern English show pronoun object-shift of the sort found in Mainland Scandinavian languages today — see Roberts (1995) for an analysis that is largely, but not entirely, compatible with the analysis of word-order change given here. However, English/Scandinavian pronoun object-shift is radically different from Romance cliticization, essentially in that the English and Scandinavian pronouns do not seem to be V-related. A more intriguing possibility is that English lacked a sufficiently rich agreement system to allow a new class of licensers of *pro*. The question for this approach is why the clitics themselves did not become an agreement system; to attempt an answer to this would take us too far afield here.

Giuseppe Longobardi (p.c.) points out another possible consequence of the account of word-order change given here. Suppose, as is often suggested, that scrambling is a way of marking the specificity of a DP. Then the loss of scrambling led to the loss of this mode of marking specificity, and may thereby have contributed to the development of the article system of Middle and Modern English, absent in Old English (sē, sēo, þæt was a demonstrative at this time). More generally, OV languages with rich morphological case and scrambling tend to lack article systems: cf. once again Latin. Here we see how changes in clausal functional categories can interact with developments inside DPs, another very rich area that we cannot begin to investigate adequately here.

16 On the relation between morphological and syntactic case

Fred Weerman

1 Introduction*

Many Germanic languages went through a period of deflection of case morphology. In the oldest sources of nearly all Germanic languages we can find evidence for the existence of an overt morphological case system. In many languages we can witness the disappearance of this overt case morphology. For instance, Middle Dutch (MDu) has a morphological paradigm as in (1), while Modern Dutch (ModDu) has only the overt form (2) for the Dutch phrase 'the man'.

(1) MDu
nominative die man 'the man'
genitive dies mans
dative dien manne
accusative dien man

(2) ModDu
de man 'the man'

For historical syntacticians, the question arises if and to what extent the loss of morphological case is connected with syntactic change. Basically, the following two views are possible.

In the first view, overt, morphological case is just a spell-out of abstract, syntactic case. In this view the difference between MDu and ModDu is that the former has an overt reflex of abstract case, while the latter does not. If the MDu paradigm is as in (1), the ModDu paradigm is not (2) but (3) (where '–Ø' indicates that there is no morphological reflex of case).

(3) ModDu
nominative de man-Ø 'the man'
genitive de man-Ø
dative de man-Ø
accusative de man-Ø

From a syntactic point of view, then, the case paradigms of MDu and ModDu are equivalent. If this is correct, one does not expect morphological deflection to lead to syntactic change.[1]

In the second view, there is a direct relation between overt, morphological case and abstract, syntactic case. In this view, alongside the MDu paradigm in (1), the abstract ModDu paradigm is (2), or at best (4):

(4) ModDu
     case   de man-Ø   'the man'

The implication is, of course, that there are syntactic differences between MDu and ModDu. Abstract notions like nominative, genitive, dative and accusative (henceforth, NOM, GEN, DAT and ACC, respectively) exist in the former but not in the latter, just like the morphological realization of these cases. Consequently, one expects morphological deflection to have syntactic effects.

The question which view is correct is central in the Minimalist Programme as introduced in Chomsky (1993a). If Chomsky's is correct in claiming that parametric differences must be reduced to morphological properties detectable at PF, we might expect the second view to be in the right direction.

Interestingly, however, Case Theory as introduced in the late seventies and early eighties (Rouveret & Vergnaud 1980; Chomsky 1981; Stowell 1981, among others) is more in line with the first view. In order to account for passive facts like in (5), this theory makes a three-way case distinction between NOM, ACC and DAT case:

(5) a. dat Jan   het meisje de boeken geeft
        that John the girl   the books gives
        'that John is giving the girl the books'
     b. dat de boeken het meisje gegeven worden
        that the books the girl given   are
        'that the books are given to the girl'
     c. *dat het meisje de boeken gegeven wordt
         that the girl   the books given   is

The standard explanation for this is that passive absorbs structural ACC case but not inherent DAT case. Therefore, the direct object has to move to subject position where it gets structural NOM case. If the indirect object moves to subject position, no case is available for the direct object, while the indirect object is in fact case-marked twice. Hence, the ungrammaticality of (5c). Since exactly the same passive facts are present both in ModDu and MDu, and indeed more generally, in languages with and without morphological case, we can conclude that the abstract three-way case distinction is not related to the presence or absence of morphological case. The loss of ACC and DAT are, then, only true from a morphological point of view. In syntax no change took place. There are no syntactic effects of morphological case.

It should be noted, though, that several linguists have tried to amend Case Theory in such a way that it might accommodate syntactic effects of the presence or absence of morphological case (among others: Stowell 1981; Manzini 1983; Holmberg 1985, 1986; Weerman 1987). Stowell (1981: 122), for instance, refers to the traditional observation that 'free word order' seems to correlate with rich case morphology and suggests that adjacency of V and its object does not hold for languages with rich case morphology, thereby bending Case Theory in the direction of the second view.

In this chapter I will suggest that both these amendments as well as the recent suggestions in the Minimalist Programme on the relation between morphological case and syntactic case do not suffice. I will argue instead that the second view is correct in a rather radical and direct way: the difference between a morphologically case-marked phrase 'the man' and one that is not is quite literally that the latter lacks lexicalized functional information. If there is no such information, there is a gap (as already indicated in (4)), in contrast to the phrase that is morphologically case-marked. Like other empty categories, this gap is subject to a general constraint on empty elements (for the sake of concreteness I will assume Rizzi's 1990b version of the ECP). This will allow us to reduce the effects of Case Theory to independently motivated principles, along lines first suggested by Lamontagne & Travis (1987).

This chapter is structured as follows. In section 2, I will discuss some (West Germanic) syntactic phenomena which, both from a comparative and diachronic perspective, seem to be related to the presence of morphological case. Next, I will argue in section 3 that these syntactic effects of morphological case cannot be properly accounted for from a Minimalist perspective, nor in the (amended) traditional Case Theory view on the relation between morphological and syntactic case. Section 4 contains the basic motivation for and exposition of my proposal. In section 5, I will discuss some remaining issues which are all related to the question: why does morphological case not always have (the same) syntactic effects? Section 6 evaluates the findings of this chapter.

2 Some syntactic effects of morphological case

For the most part it is not difficult to see that a language has morphological case. However, it is not so easy to see that syntactic phenomena are related to it. What kind of evidence might show that a syntactic phenomenon is an effect of morphological case? If some language L-A with a morphological case system has some syntactic construction C, this does not warrant the conclusion that C is there because L-A has morphological case. If, in addition, some language L-B has no morphological case and no C, this is not in conflict with the idea that C is an effect of morphological case, but it does not prove much either, since the absence of C might be due to some totally independent factor. The evidence becomes stronger if there are many languages like L-A and L-B. It seems to me that the above-mentioned traditional observation that there is a correlation between morphological case and 'free word order' has this character.

Evidence becomes more convincing if it can be shown that L-A and L-B are, apart from C and morphological case, in relevant respects comparable. Also, if a diachronic analysis of L-A shows stages in which there is morphological case as well as C, and C is absent in the stages in which morphological case has disappeared, we have suggestive evidence that C is an effect of morphological case. In this section I will review four syntactic effects of morphological case that are supported by this type of qualitative comparative and diachronic evidence. In order to reduce the chance that independent factors intervene, I will limit most of the discussion here to the West Germanic OV languages (that are characterized by V2 in root clauses and OV order in embedded clauses). The older stages of this group all have morphological case. At present, only Modern German has a morphological case system.

In the ultimate diachronic test one would like to show that C disappears precisely in the same period in which morphological case disappears. All (and only) texts showing morphological case should have C. For several reasons this precision is not attained below. First of all, I was not able to perform such a test for practical reasons. However, even if I were, it is not so clear whether this test will tell us much at this stage of research. If a language changes, there is always some diffusion. Moreover, it is not at all easy to date the loss of morphological case precisely. Sometimes overt markers may in fact no longer be signs of a productive system (as we will discuss in section 5), sometimes there are good reasons to assume that there is a morphological case marker even though it is not always phonologically overt. More research is needed to decide these issues. For these reasons the diachronic claims below in most cases rest on a less subtle division of stages.

2.1 The order of direct object and indirect object

As is well known, the West Germanic OV languages allow scrambling of their complements: (definite) objects do not have to appear adjacent to verb, but can appear in a variety of positions to the left of the verb (see Corver & van Riemsdijk 1994 and the references mentioned there). This is illustrated for ModDu in (6).

(6) a. dat de vrouw waarschijnlijk vaak *de mannen de film* toont
 that the woman probably often the men the picture shows
 'that the woman will probably often show the men the picture'
 b. dat de vrouw waarschijnlijk *de mannen* vaak *de film* toont
 that the woman probably the men often the picture shows
 c. dat de vrouw *de mannen* waarschijnlijk vaak *de film* toont
 that the woman the men probably often the picture shows
 d. dat de vrouw waarschijnlijk *de mannen de film* vaak toont
 that the woman probably the men the picture often shows
 e. dat de vrouw *de mannen* waarschijnlijk *de film* vaak toont
 that the woman the men probably the picture often shows

f. dat de vrouw *de mannen de film* waarschijnlijk vaak toont
   that the woman the men   the picture probably   often shows

The variants multiply, so to speak, when three, four or more adverbs appear instead of the two adverbs in (6). That is not to say that all these variants are in all respects equivalent. There are certainly subtle differences, having to do with the scope of adverbials and aspects of topicality of the arguments. However, all these variants can have an unmarked intonation. For our purpose the subtle differences between the variants of (6) are not relevant.

The term scrambling might perhaps suggest that every order is permitted. This, however, is clearly not the case. One restriction that is relevant here is that the word order between the DP direct object and indirect object has to remain constant in ModDu. Under neutral intonation the word order in (7) is ungrammatical (it improves if *de film* 'the picture' gets focus — but this is not the intended interpretation here).

(7)   *dat de vrouw waarschijnlijk *de film*   *de mannen* toont
      that the woman probably   the picture the men   shows

I conclude that the indirect object has to precede the direct object in ModDu, abstracting from cliticization and topicalization. The same restriction holds for Modern Frisian — and indeed for many other Germanic languages.

Interestingly, the restriction does not hold for the West Germanic OV languages that have morphological case. In Modern German (ModG), for instance, the direct object may precede the indirect object (cf. Lenerz 1977). The ModG sentences in (8) show the same scrambling pattern as the ModDu sentences in (6).

(8) a. dass die Frau   wahrscheinlich oft *den Männern den*
       that the woman-NOM probably   often the men-DAT the
       Film   zeigt
       picture-ACC shows
       'that the woman will probably often show the men the picture'
    b. dass die Frau   wahrscheinlich *den Männern* oft   *den*
       that the woman-NOM probably   the men-DAT   often the
       Film   zeigt
       picture-ACC shows
    c. dass die Frau   *den Männern* wahrscheinlich oft   *den*
       that the woman-NOM the men-DAT   probably   often the
       Film   zeigt
       picture-ACC shows
    d. dass die Frau   wahrscheinlich *den Männern den*
       that the woman-NOM probably   the men-DAT the
       Film   oft   zeigt
       picture-ACC often shows

e. dass die Frau   den Männern wahrscheinlich *den*
   that the woman-NOM the men-DAT probably   the
   Film   oft   zeigt
   picture-ACC often shows
f. dass die Frau   *den Männern den Film*
   that the woman-NOM the men-DAT the picture-ACC
   wahrscheinlich oft   zeigt
   probably   often shows

The sentences in (9) show that there are further possibilities. The direct objects can precede the indirect objects and they can both precede adverbials.

(9) a. dass die Frau   wahrscheinlich oft   *den Film*   *den*
       that the woman-NOM probably   often the picture-ACC the
       Männern zeigt
       men-DAT shows
    b. dass die Frau   wahrscheinlich *den Film*   oft   *den*
       that the woman-NOM probably   the picture often the
       Männern zeigt
       men-DAT shows
    etc.

The pattern where the direct object precedes the indirect object can also be found in MDu and Old English (OE). In (10) some examples from a MDu prose text around 1275 are presented, the 'Luikse Diatesseron' (de Bruin (ed.) 1970) (see van Gestel *et al.* 1992 for some discussion).

(10) a. om te geuene sinen volke   ene leeringe   van harre
        to give   his people-DAT a teaching-ACC of their
        salegheit
        salvation   (LD 12)
     b. sal dan v   vader ... nit gheuen goede ghichten den ghenen
        will then your father   not give good gifts-ACC those-DAT
        die hem bidden?   (LD 50)
        that him ask
        'Will not your father give good gifts to them that ask him?'
     c. so began si oc getugnesse   hem   te gheuene   (LD 20)
        so began she also testimony-ACC him-DAT to give
        'She also began to give him testimony'

The examples in (10b,c) show the order where the direct object precedes the indirect object, while (10a) shows the reverse order. To my knowledge, the strict order between the direct object and the indirect object appears when the morphological case system breaks down and the dative disappears. Note, moreover, that these sentences demonstrate that VO order instead of OV order was possible in MDu — we will return to this in the next subsection.

For OE the word order of dative and accusative objects has been described in much more detail than for MDu. In particular, two studies of Koopman (1990, 1993) are relevant here. Koopman went through the OE microfiche concordance looking at the different spellings for verbs taking a dative and accusative object. This procedure yielded over 4,000 sentences containing double objects. There are 340 sentences in this set where the objects are full DPs and where both objects appear before the verb in embedded clauses or in between the finite verb and an infinitival verb in root clauses. Both orders are present in this set. For instance, in (11a) the dative object precedes the accusative object, while we can observe the reverse in (11b).

(11) a. þæt ge *Ongolþeode* ætgædre mid us *Drihtnes word* bodige
that you the English together with us God's word preach
'that you will preach God's word together with us to the English'
b. Ac gif we þa *mirran gode* gastlice geoffriað
but if we then myrrh God spiritually offer
'but if we offer myrrh to God spiritually'
((25) and (22) in Koopman 1993)

In all, the objects show the following distribution:

(12) DAT-ACC   ACC-DAT
203 (60%)   137 (40%) 340 (=N)
((11) in Koopman 1993)

Apparently, for full DPs both orders were possible in OE — like in German and in MDu (the languages that have morphological case) and unlike ModDu (or more generally, the languages that have no morphological case). If morphological case is lost, only one order is possible in a neutral intonation.

To summarize, let me formulate the following descriptive generalization:[2]

(13) *Generalization 1*:
The order of indirect object and direct object has to remain constant unless there is a morphological case system.

2.2 The order of object and verb

In addition to the restriction just discussed, scrambling in ModDu is restricted in yet another way. The scrambled direct object or indirect object cannot appear to the right of the verb. It has to remain to the left of the verb. Compare, for instance, (6) with (14).

(14) a. *dat de vrouw waarschijnlijk vaak *de film* toont *de mannen*
that the woman probably often the picture shows the men
b. *dat de vrouw waarschijnlijk vaak *de mannen* toont *de film*
that the woman probably often the men shows the picture
c. *dat de vrouw waarschijnlijk vaak toont *de mannen de film*
that the woman probably often shows the men the picture

It should be noted that this word order improves if the object to the right of the verb is in some way extremely 'heavy', as in (15).

(15) a. dat de vrouw de film   toont de mannen, de jongens en
       that the woman the picture shows the men,   the boys   and
       de meisjes
       the girls
       'that the woman will show the picture to the men, the boys and the girls'
   b. dat wij heden hebben verloren onze lieve   dochter
      that we today have   lost   our beloved daughter
      (text on a funeral card)
      'that we lost today our beloved daughter'

Apart from this exception (and, as above, from V2 and topicalization), the general restriction is that DPs always precede the verb.

Again this restriction does not seem to hold for MDu. MDu, although an OV language, allows VO-orders. There is extensive literature on this construction in MDu (see Weerman 1989 and the references cited there). Some examples are given in (16).[3]

(16) a. Ic sal   senden *minen ingel* vor   dijn anschin
       I shall send   my   angel before your face
   b. so sagen si   liggen *kolen* op dat oeuer
      so saw   they lie   coals on the bank
      'they saw coals lying on the bank'
   c. hi soude dorbreken *den muur*
      he would break   the wall

Recently, Burridge (1993) observes, on the basis of an extensive Dutch corpus from 1300 to 1650, that not only word orders as in (16) gradually disappear, but that in addition the factor 'weight' gradually becomes more important in this period — resulting in the modern situation illustrated in (14) and (15). The morphological case system breaks down in precisely the same period.

A similar observation holds for OE. Several linguists have argued that objects in OE can appear to the right of the verb, although there is no complete agreement on the analysis of these facts (see, amongst others, Pintzuk & Kroch 1985; van Kemenade 1987; Pintzuk 1993). In addition to the 340 OV-sentences mentioned in section 2.1, Koopman's corpus also contains all sorts of VO-like sentences. In (17) absolute figures are given of several types of embedded clauses containing one or more full DP objects in a position to the right of the verb.

(17) a. C ... Vf DO IO   70
   b. C ... Vf IO DO   86
   c. C ... DO Vf IO   42
   d. C ... IO Vf DO   29
   e. C ... Vf DO V I O 11

f. C ... Vf IO V D O 6
g. C ... Vf V DO I O 22
h. C ... Vf V IO D O 38
i. C ... DO V Vf I O 2
j. C ... IO V Vf D O 5
(where C = complementizer, IO = full DP indirect (or dative) object,
DO = full DP direct (or accusative) object) (based on Koopman 1990)

Obviously, it depends on one's analysis of OE whether or not all this evidence should be looked upon as evidence against the restriction we are considering. For instance, if one allows some kind of V-to-I in embedded clauses, as in (18), (17a, b) do not count as evidence (although they do support Generalization 1 in (13)).

(18) C Subj $[V_i+I]$ $[_{VP}$ DO-IO/IO-DO $t_i]$

We can safely conclude, though, that the evidence as summarized in (18) contains violations of the OV-restriction in all current analyses of OE. As has been noted several times before (for instance by van Kemenade 1987), it is likely that the possibility to have both orders is related to the presence of morphological case.

So far, it seems we can formulate the following generalization:[4]

(19) *Generalization 2*:
The order of indirect object and direct object with respect to the verb has to remain constant unless there is a morphological case system.

The situation in Old High German (OHG) is very similar to the one in MDu and OE, which supports (19). I will not discuss the facts here, but simply refer to Lenerz (1984).

The situation in ModG, however, is not in accordance with Generalization 2. Although ModG has morphological case, the sentences in (20) are as ungrammatical as the ModDu sentences in (14).

(20) a. *dass die Frau   wahrscheinlich oft   den Film   zeigt den
       that the woman probably   often the picture-ACC shows the
       Männern
       men-DAT
    b. *dass die Frau   wahrscheinlich oft   den Männern zeigt den
       that the woman probably   often the men-DAT shows the
       Film
       picture-ACC
    c. *dass die Frau   wahrscheinlich oft   zeigt den Männern den
       that the woman probably   often shows the men-DAT the
       Film
       picture-ACC

If we stick to (19), we clearly need an explanation for this exception. The problem falls under the question, formulated in the introduction, why morphological case does not always have (the same) syntactic effects.

2.3 The complements of nouns

The next generalization is perhaps the most obvious one. In ModDu the complements of nouns have to be PPs and cannot be DPs, as illustrated in (21)–(22).

(21) a. het huis *van de buren*
       the house of the neighbours
   b. de vernietiging *van Carthago*
       the destruction of Carthago
   c. het draaien *van het wiel*
       the turning of the wheel

(22) a. *het huis *de buren*
       the house the neighbours
   b. *de vernietiging *Carthago*
       the destruction Carthago
   c. *het draaien *het wiel*
       the turning the wheel

To my knowledge, there are no languages without a morphological case system where the facts show a different pattern than in (21)–(22).

However, if a language does have morphological case, the construction of the type in (22) is grammatical. For instance, in the MDu examples in (23) the complements of the nouns are DPs that appear in the genitive (see for an extensive discussion, van Es 1938).[5]

(23) a. Derste *der werelt*
       the-first the world-GEN
       'the first of the world'
   b. 't drayen *des Fortuyns*
       the turning Fortune-GEN
       'the wheel of fortune'
   c. die versakinghe *des herten*
       the renouncement the heart-GEN
       'the betrayal of the heart'

Van Schayik (1995) observes that there is a sharp decline of the MDu genitive in the fourteenth century. In the same period there is a rise of postnominal complements that are introduced by the preposition *van* 'of'. In other words, the construction in (24a) is the oldest construction and (24b) is the younger one, although they do not seem to exclude each other in an intermediate stage. From a diachronic point of view it is remarkable, however, that there is no trace of (24c) in the intermediate stage. This construction is always ruled out.

(24) a. [$_{DP}$...N... [$_{DP<GEN>}$ ....]]
   b. [$_{DP}$...N... [$_{PP}$ ....]]
   c. *[$_{DP}$...N... [$_{DP}$ ....]]

OE and OHG pattern with MDu (see, for instance, Mitchell 1985 and Drosdowski *et al.* 1984 respectively), and also languages with a morphological case system that are not within the scope of this chapter, like Icelandic and Russian, show this pattern (see Holmberg 1985 and Franks 1981, respectively). Hence, we can formulate (25).

(25) *Generalization 3*:
The complement of N is a PP unless there is a morphological case system.

2.4 The complements of adjectives

The last generalization, though comparable to the third one, is more controversial. Van Riemsdijk (1983) argues that there is a correlation between the existence in a language of a morphological case system and the possibility for adjectives to have a DP complement (in 1983: NP complement). Van Riemsdijk's analysis is based on ModG facts. Some of his examples are given in (26) and (27). In (26) the adjective is used predicatively and in (27) it is used attributively. In the (a)-examples the adjective assigns genitive (the marked case, according to van Riemsdijk) and in the (b)-examples dative (the unmarked case).

(26) a. Der Hans is *seiner Freundin überdrüssig* geworden
Hans has his girl-friend-GEN weary become
'Hans has grown tired of his girl friend' (van Riemsdijk's (4))
b. Das Französische ist *ihm ungeläufig*
French is him-DAT not-fluent
'He is not fluent in French' (van Riemsdijk's (5))

(27) a. Der *seiner Freundin überdrüssige* Student
the his girl-friend-GEN weary student
'the student (who is) tired of his girl friend' (van Riemsdijk's (9))
b. Ein *ihm ungeläufiges* Wort
a him-DAT unfamiliar word
'a word (which is) unfamiliar to him' (van Riemsdijk's (7))

Van Kemenade (1987) argues that in OE adjectives can have DP complements that appear in the dative or the genitive. In MDu DP complements of adjectives tend to appear in the genitive (see van Gestel *et al.* 1992 for discussion). Some examples are given in (28).[6]

(28) a. Nochtan was hi onweger *sijns lijfs*
nevertheless was he indifferent his body-GEN
'Nevertheless he did not mind his body'
b. Herodes *des* harde toornich was
Herodes this-GEN very angry was
'Herodes was very angry about this'

To my knowledge, genitive complements as in (28) are replaced by PP complements when the genitive disappears. In ModDu, adjectives comparable to the MDu adjectives in (28) take a PP complement, and cannot take a DP, as the sentences in (29) show.

(29) a. Hij was onverschillig *over zijn lichaam*
    he was indifferent about his body
    'He did not mind his body'
  a′ *Hij was onverschillig *zijn lichaam*
    he was indifferent his body
  b. Hij was *hierover* zeer boos
    he was here-about very angry
    'he was very angry about this'
  b′ *Hij was *dit* zeer boos
    he was this very angry

So far, the facts suggest a parallel with the complementation of nouns that we can formulate as follows:

(30) *Generalization 4*:
  The complement of A is a PP unless there is a morphological case system.

Things are, however, not as clear-cut as they were for Generalization 3 in (25). Although ModDu adjectives tend to take PP complements, there are examples of adjectives that take a DP complement. See the examples in (31)-(32).

(31) a. Hij is *het Frans machtig*
    he is the French able
    'he is able to speak French'
  b. Hij is *dat gezeur beu*
    he is that moaning enough
    'he is tired of that moaning'

(32) a. ?De *het Frans machtige* man
    the the French able man
  b. *De *het gezeur beue* vrouw
    the the moaning enough woman

One might object that this set of adjectives is very limited. The predicative constructions in (31) have an idiomatic character and the attributive ones in (32) are rather odd or even ruled out for several speakers. Nevertheless, it is significant that this type of exception is absent (to my knowledge) for complements of N. Moreover, idiomatic as these adjectival constructions may be, the complement itself is not idiomatic and does not have any (relic of) morphological case. If we stick to (30), we need an explanation for the exceptions in (31)–(32).[7]

3 Case Theory and syntactic effects of morphological case

In section 2 I discussed four examples of a potential syntactic effect of morphological case. The descriptive generalizations are brought together in (33).

(33) a. The order of indirect object and direct object has to remain constant unless there is a morphological case system.
  b. The order of indirect object and direct object with respect to the verb has to remain constant unless there is a morphological case system.
  c. The complement of N is a PP unless there is a morphological case system.
  d. The complement of A is a PP unless there is a morphological case system.

If true — and from now on I will assume that they are correct in essence — these generalizations need an explanation. I will show in this section that Case Theory as we know it does not provide us with an explanation. The discussion will be split into two parts. In the final part I will examine Case Theory as it is incorporated in the Minimalist Programme. The first part will be devoted to the GB version of Case Theory.

3.1 GB Case Theory

At the relevant level a theory should make a distinction between languages that have and languages that do not have morphological case in order to be able to explain the observations in (33). If both types of languages are syntactically equivalent, that is, if morphological case is considered to be a phonological spell-out that takes place in some languages, but not others, we cannot make the proper distinction. Unless, of course, we take the position that word order and complementation are phonological phenomena. As already indicated in the introduction, many GB variants of Case Theory indeed consider morphological case to be an optional phonological spell-out of abstract case, but, as far as I can see, they do not and probably cannot accept the implication that word order and complementation are phonological phenomena. Since several GB syntacticians have noted (in some way or the other) the generalizations in (33), attempts have been made to incorporate syntactic effects of morphological case into the theory. I will briefly discuss three proposals here that illustrate the problem.

As noted already, van Riemsdijk (1983) argues that there is a correlation between the existence in a language of a morphological case system and the possibility for adjectives to have DP complements. Although he admits that he is not able to explain this correlation, it is illustrative to see why his attempt fails. Van Riemsdijk develops a system in which the Case Filter requires that a DP be marked for [± Subject] and [± Closest Argument]. Adjectives assign the features [−Subject] and [−Closest Argument] to their complements. Therefore, an adjective with a DP complement passes the Case Filter. Since the features [± Subject] and [± Closest Argument], as well as the rule that assigns features to complements of adjectives, are concepts that are not related to the presence or absence of morphological case, it is impossible to make a distinction as required.

Stowell (1982) discusses the effects of morphological case on word order: word order tends to be more free if a language has morphological case. The generalizations (33a, b) are instantiations of this tendency. Stowell argues as follows (his p. 123): If a verb has more than one case to assign, one of the cases can never be assigned under adjacency; therefore, case is not assigned in such a language, but instead the verb itself must subcategorize for nominal complements. Stowell's assumption here apparently is that a verb will only assign more than one case if there is a morphological case system. This does not follow from something else, and it is precisely this that needs an explanation.

Apart from this, the disadvantage of Stowell's proposal is that the difference between languages with and without morphological case becomes too extreme: the former obey Case Theory, the latter do not. However, both types of languages behave similarly in many ways. Passive facts, for instance, are in essence similar in all West Germanic OV languages, whether they have morphological case or not. Since Case Theory was designed to explain these passive facts, this is rather damaging for Stowell's idea.

Finally, Holmberg (1985, 1986) discusses contrasts between Icelandic and Swedish that support the generalizations in (33) in several ways. In order to explain the syntactic effects of morphological case, Holmberg proposes the following condition on chains (where 'm-case' is 'morphological case').

(34) A chain is visible iff
    a. it is structurally governed
    b. it has m-case
       ((10) in Holmberg 1985)

The difference between languages with and without morphological case is not as extreme as in Stowell's proposal. However, the mere stipulation that m-case is of an exceptional nature in (34) is still rather unsatisfactory. Why does m-case have this effect?

3.2 Minimalist Case Theory

In contrast with the GB version of Case Theory, syntactic effects of morphological case are to be expected in the Minimalist Programme. According to Chomsky (1993a), case features can be either 'strong' or 'weak'. If they are weak the result of movements is not visible at PF, since movement can and hence should be delayed until LF. If the case features are strong, movements have to take place before PF, since strong features should be eliminated before PF. The proposal is that the opposition strong/weak correlates with strong/weak morphological evidence. For instance, MDu might have strong features and visible movements, since it has a visible case paradigm. In ModDu the features might be weak, and therefore movements should be covert, since there is no visible case paradigm.

In Minimalist practice, however, the opposition between strong and weak case features is not used in accordance with a morphological distinction along these lines. For instance, if one combines Chomsky (1993a) and Kayne (1993) one is forced to use the weak/strong opposition to derive the difference between VO and OV surface orders, irrespective of whether or not there is case morphology (cf. Zwart 1993). Thus, given that both MDu and ModDu have OV-orders, the N-features of Agr_O should always have been strong, thereby causing movement of the object to the left of the verb, as depicted in (35).

(35) [.... [$_{AgrOP}$ DP_i[[$_{AgrO}$ V_j] [$_{VP}$ ... [t_i t_j]]]]]

Apparently, then, the fact that only MDu had morphological case is irrelevant. As in the GB version of Case Theory, the notion 'case' is exploited to explain syntactic effects that do not seem to be related to case morphology. As a result there is no easy way to accommodate the descriptive generalizations in (33) where case morphology seems to have a syntactic effect.

There is an additional reason for this. In particular generalizations (33a, b) express that a language without morphological case allows only one word order whereas a language with morphological case allows more orders. The generalizations suggest that a DP with morphological case is less dependent on an external head. It is not easy to fit this apparent freedom into the Minimalist Programme, since features are either strong or weak and there is no optional movement. The Minimalist Programme predicts that word order in languages with morphological case is different but just as strict as in languages without morphological case. As for this strictness, there is, again, no difference with the GB version of Case Theory.

4 The Gap Hypothesis

In order to come to a better understanding of the syntactic effects of morphological case I will take the difference between a morphologically case-marked phrase and one that is not to be a real one: the latter lacks lexicalized functional information — that is, it contains a gap, in contrast to the case-marked phrase. Therefore, if a language does not have morphological case a DP can be represented as (36a) and if it does, we get (36b).

(36) a. [$_{DP}$ ... Ø ......]
     b. [$_{DP}$ ... case....]

Like other empty categories, the gap in (36a) is subject to a general constraint on empty elements. Therefore the position of (36a) is, in general, more restricted than the position of (36b).

To see this point more clearly, let us take generalization (33b) (repeated here for convenience) as an example.

(33) b. The order of indirect object and direct object with respect to the verb has to remain constant unless there is a morphological case system.

Suppose that at some abstract level only hierarchy counts and that there is no ordering of complements with respect to the head (cf. Weerman 1987, 1989; Chomsky 1994). At this level a language has both VO and OV orders, as indicated in (37).

(37)

If no additional constraints apply, both orders can surface. However, if the DPs in (37) contain a gap, the gap should be licensed and only one order survives. For the sake of concreteness I will assume here a more or less 'traditional' licensing in terms of government. That is, if V governs to the right only the VO order will surface and if V governs to the left we get an OV order. Note that this line of argumentation not only allows us to incorporate quite naturally a syntactic effect of morphological case, but also allows us to reduce an effect of Case Theory to an independently motivated principle on the licensing of empty elements.[8] The idea that effects of Case Theory can be reduced to the ECP has been suggested before in Lamontagne & Travis (1987). Although they discuss a different class of facts, namely adjacency effects in case-drop in languages like Japanese and Turkish (and in Comp-drop in Japanese and English), my approach is reminiscent of theirs.

First I will now go somewhat deeper into this independently motivated principle, which I will take to be Rizzi's (1990b) version of the ECP (section 4.1). Then I will try to identify the gap in (36a) more precisely (section 4.2). Next, I will consider some of the implications for subjects and nominative case (section 4.3). Finally, we will return to the first generalization (section 4.4).

4.1 Rizzi's Empty Category Principle

The ECP is not designed to explain the facts that are central in this chapter, but rather an impressive list of extraction facts: Extraction (out) of subjects, objects and adjuncts. Rizzi (1990b) reduces the formulation of the ECP as in (38), the formulation of Chomsky (1986a) *Barriers*, in several stages to the formulation in (39).

(38) *ECP* (Chomsky 1986a)
A nonpronominal empty category must be
(i) lexically governed, or
(ii) antecedent-governed

(39) ECP (Rizzi 1990b)
A nonpronominal empty category must be properly head-governed

For our discussion at least three issues are immediately relevant. First of all, the gap in the DP should be in a position where it can be head-governed by an external head. This is taken up in the next subsection. Two other issues will be central here. Since I argued that the ECP is responsible for OV/VO contrasts, I have to show that head government as referred to in (39) is sensitive to direction. Also, we have to know whether the type of heads that are able to 'properly head-govern' matches what we need in order to account for the generalizations in (33). I will start with the latter issue.

The status of two lexical heads with respect to head government is hardly disputed. V clearly is a proper head governor, and Rizzi also shows that there are several arguments that show that N does not have this status. If we combine this with the Gap Hypothesis we predict that (40a) is grammatical, while (40b) should be wrong.

(40) a. ok [$_{VP}$ ... V [$_{DP}$ ... Ø ...]]
 b. * [$_{NP}$ ... N [$_{DP}$ ... Ø ...]]

If there is morphological case (and hence no gap), a DP complement of V and N should be possible:

(41) a. ok [$_{VP}$ ... V [$_{DP}$ ... ACC ...]]
 b. ok [$_{NP}$ ... N [$_{DP}$ ... GEN ...]]

Note that this matches rather precisely the complementation facts that we found in section 2. As expressed in (33c), it is not possible to have a DP complement of a N, unless there is morphological case. This follows now from the independently motivated assumption that N is not a proper head governor. Apparently something should happen as soon as the genitive disappears. The loss of the genitive will lead to a gap that N is not able to license. How the preposition *van* in Dutch (*of* in English) fills this gap is something we will discuss in the next subsection.

Disappearance of the accusative, on the other hand, does not have a similar effect on complements of V, since V is able to properly head govern the gap in the DP. It follows that insertion of an element like *van* 'of' is not required for verbal complements. Deflection of accusative does not affect the status of verbal complements, as predicted.

Generalization (33d) suggests that A patterns as N. That is, (42a) is ungrammatical, while (42b) is correct.

(42) a. * [$_{AP}$ ... A [$_{DP}$ ... Ø ...]]
 b. ok [$_{AP}$ ... A [$_{DP}$ ... GEN/DAT ...]]

In other words, A should be unable to properly head govern the gap in (42a), just like N in (40b). On this assumption generalization (33d) follows as well. However, in this case it is much more difficult to give independent support. Rizzi does not discuss the status of A, although his general conclusion that [−V] heads are no proper governors indicates that A is a proper governor in his view. It is not easy to construct convincing extraction evidence that might support (or contradict) this idea. In a way this is reminiscent of our finding in section 2 that there are a significant number of exceptions to (42a) as opposed to (40b). Let us assume here that there is some parametric variation with respect to the proper governor status of A, perhaps as a consequence of the fact that positive evidence is largely in accordance with both options (both 'no [–V]' as well as 'only V' do most of the job), but obviously more research is needed here.

Let us now turn to the directionality issue. In many cases it is impossible to show that the ECP is sensitive to direction. Obviously, if there is no remnant after extraction has taken place, we cannot prove whether the gap is to the left or to the right of the verb, since the gap is invisible (cf. (43)). But also if there is a remnant, the evidence is not conclusive. In (43), for instance, there is a remnant after the extraction of DP out of ZP. If ZP also has to appear to the right of V if there is no extraction at all, we do not show that the ECP is sensitive to direction, since the position of ZP in (43) might be due to some independent factor.

(43) DP_i ... [$_{VP}$ ... t_i ... V ... t_i]

DP_i ... [$_{VP}$ ... V ... [$_{ZP}$ t_i Z ...]]

In other words, what we need is a complement that is in principle able to appear on both sides of the head, but that can only appear on one side if subextraction takes place. This evidence would show that the ECP is sensitive to direction.

Fortunately, ModDu shows evidence of precisely this kind. The sentences in (44) show that PPs can appear on both sides of V:

(44) a. dat de vrouw de film *aan de mannen* toont
   that the woman the picture to the men shows
   'that the woman will show the picture to the men'
 b. dat de vrouw de film toont *aan de mannen*
   that the woman the picture shows to the men
 c. dat Jan Piet *van het bewijs* overtuigt
   that John Pete of the evidence convinces
   'that John will convince Pete of the evidence'
 d. dat Jan Piet overtuigt *van het bewijs*
   that John Pete convinces of the evidence

Generally, extraction out of PPs is impossible in standard ModDu. However, if the extracted constituent is a so-called R-pronoun extraction is allowed (cf. van Riemsdijk 1978), as the sentences in (45) show.

(45) a. (ik vraag mij af) *waar* de vrouw de film *aan* toont
      (I wonder)   where the woman the picture to shows
      'I wonder to whom the woman is showing the picture'
   b. (ik vraag mij af) *waar* Jan Piet *van* overtuigt
      (I wonder)   where John Pete of convinces
      'I wonder what John is convincing Pete of'

Some additional examples are presented in (46) (from Koster 1993).

(46) a. (ik vraag mij af) *waar* je *mee* aan je dissertatie hebt
      (I wonder)   where you with on your dissertation have
      gewerkt
      worked
      'I wonder with whom you have collaborated for your dissertation'
   b. (ik vraag me af) *waar* hij *mee* op zondag naar de kerk gaat
      (I wonder)   where he with on sunday to the church goes
      'I wonder with whom he goes to church on Sundays'

The crucial observation is that extraction out of PPs is only possible if the PP is to the left of the verb as in (45)–(46). The facts in (47) show that subextraction is impossible to the right of the verb.

(47) a. *(ik vraag mij af) *waar* de vrouw de film toont *aan*
      (I wonder)   where the woman the picture shows to
   b. *(ik vraag mij af) *waar* Jan Piet overtuigt *van*
      (I wonder)   where John Pete convinces of
   c. *(ik vraag mij af) *waar* je aan je dissertatie hebt gewerkt
      (I wonder)   where you on your dissertation have worked
      mee
      with
   d. *(ik vraag me af) *waar* hij op zondag naar de kerk gaat *mee*
      (I wonder)   where he on sunday to the church goes with

Apparently, a gap in the PP is at least also dependent on its linear position in the V-projection. More precisely, a gap can only be licensed in ModDu if it appears on the lefthand side of the V-projection. The conclusion is that the ECP is sensitive to direction, and precisely this implies that we can derive the OV character of ModDu from the ECP — under the assumption that DPs in ModDu contain a gap. Moreover, it follows that it is possible to escape directionality if there is no gap. The fact that MDu DPs are not subject to the same word order restriction as their ModDu counterparts follows from the fact that MDu still had morphological case. The diachronic fact that the VO order disappears, when the case system gets lost, follows as well. In other words, we derive generalization (33b).[9]

4.2 The position of the gap

Let us now try to find out exactly what the structural status of the gap is.

There are several considerations that point in the same direction. First of all, the gap in the DP should be in a position where it can be head governed by an external head. The easiest way to achieve this, is to assume that the gap is the head of the DP. Thus, in (48) the head X is empty in the sense of the ECP.

(48) $[_{XP}$ X $[_{DP}$ ... N ... $]]$

If we assume (48), the construction is parallel to one that has played a role in discussions on the ECP since the early eighties: several linguists argued that English complementizer deletion is also subject to the ECP (Stowell 1982; Aoun *et al.* 1987; Rizzi 1990b). It follows from the ECP that the complementizer in (49) can be deleted, because C is head governed by the main verb of the root clause.

(49) John said $[_{CP} [_C \emptyset]$ $[_{IP}$ he did not know it$]]$

Note that we predict that X is filled if a language has a morphological case system. In such a situation X contains (information that is relevant for) case. The implication is that these features head the DP. Interestingly, the proposal that case heads the nominal phrase in languages with a morphological case system has independently been made several times in the literature (Lamontagne & Travis 1987; Laughren 1989; Philippi, this volume, among others) for several reasons.

Let us see whether we can be more precise on the character of X in (48). At least some class of prepositions is very unlikely to have the status of a proper head governor. For instance, the preposition that is inserted in front of a DP complement of a noun (cf. generalization (33d)) does not seem to allow extraction. So, if X in (48) is a gap, it cannot be rescued by such prepositions, as indicated in (50).

(50) *$[_{PP}$ P $[_{XP}$ ... X $[_{DP}$ ... N ... $]]]$

Nevertheless we know that these prepositions can have DP complements. For this reason, standard Case Theory stipulates that not only V but also P is able to assign case. Under the present proposal a rather different solution presents itself: these Ps are a manifestation of X. In this case, (48) can be formalized as (51).

(51) $[_{PP}$ P $[_{DP}$ ... N ... $]]$

In one respect, however, (51) is still wrong. The formalization in (51) expresses that the top node is of a fundamentally different category (namely PP) than the complement (namely DP). Until now we assumed, however, that the constituent that contains the gap is a DP. The problem that a PP resembles a DP in some respects has been noticed before, and there is an interesting solution that I will adopt here.

Grimshaw (1991) assumes that a PP has to be regarded as an extended (functional) projection of DP, in much the same way as CP is in her terms an extended verbal projection. Grimshaw gives several arguments for this view. One of her arguments immediately ties in with our previous discussion on extraction out of ModDu PPs. If a non-R-pronoun contained in a PP is questioned, as in (52), Pied-Piping has to take place.

(52) a. (ik vraag mij af) *aan wie* de vrouw de film   toont
      (I wonder)   to who the woman the picture shows
      'I wonder to whom the woman will show the picture'
   b. *(ik vraag mij af) *wie* de vrouw de film   *aan* toont
      (I wonder)   who the woman the picture to   shows

Apparently, the whole constituent *aan wie* 'to whom' counts as ⟨+wh⟩, and is a source for *move* ⟨+wh⟩. It would be a mystery why this constituent is able to fulfil the requirement of the matrix clause if it was not marked ⟨+wh⟩. The sentences in (53) show that the matrix clause requires a ⟨+wh⟩ element introducing the embedded clause.

(53) a. (ik vraag mij af) of   de vrouw de mannen de film   toont
      (I wonder)   whether the woman the men   the picture shows
      'I wonder whether the woman will show the men the picture.'
   b. *(ik vraag mij af) dat de vrouw de mannen de film   toont
      (I wonder)   that the woman the men   the picture shows

Apparently, the PP is marked for ⟨+wh⟩, although the DP contained in it is questioned and is the source for the ⟨+wh⟩-feature. If the PP is marked for ⟨+wh⟩, then the PP is apparently on the same projection line, and is an extended nominal projection.

Obviously, if P is a proper head governor, the structure in (50) is correct and the problems that I just solved do not arise. For some prepositions this seems a good analysis. The actual status of prepositions might not only vary from language to language, but also within a language. In the proposal I am developing here, this would boil down to saying that prepositions might have the status of either a functional or a lexical element, correlating with the possibility of (not) assigning a theta role. This, again, should correlate with the possibility of (not) allowing extraction.

Interpreted in this way, the top node of (48) is indeed a DP and we can maintain that a ModDu DP contains a gap, while at the same time the gap heads the DP along the lines of (48). In general, we now have the following possibilities for the head in (51):

(54)
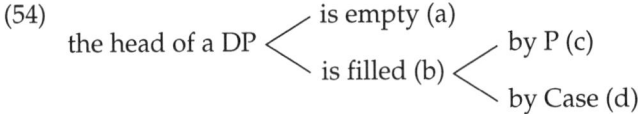

Note that the oppositions in (54) are well known for other functional markers. For instance, languages differ in whether or not they have a visible agreement system for subjects, which is an illustration of the opposition between (54a, b). Languages differ, to take another example, in whether or not they lexicalize modality as an affix or as an independent (auxiliary) verb, which is similar to the opposition between (54c, d), etc.

In the literature there are several ways to formalize these sorts of oppositions. For instance, we could assume that either (a functional) P or the case-affix heads the DP. Under this view, either the case-affix has to lower, or lower heads have to raise to pick up the affix. This view seems to predict that prepositions and morphological case are always in complementary distribution, which is, of course, wrong. Alternatively, we can assume that only the abstract information that controls the morphological realization downstairs heads the DP but that the affixes as such are base-generated in their surface position. This allows, at least in principle, the option that both Ps and case-affixes appear. For the time being I will adopt this view here, although it is difficult to decide the issue at this moment.[10]

Note that as for the complements of V in ModDu, we predict that the DP behaves like a DP with morphological case, as soon as the gap can be filled by a preposition, since it is not dependent on the ECP in that case.[11] Where DPs that contain a gap have to remain to the left of the verb, extraposition should be possible if the (extended) DP is headed by a preposition. This is precisely what happens, as we already saw in section 4.1. The relevant sentences are repeated in (55) (cf. (44)).[12]

(55) a. dat de vrouw de film   *aan de mannen* toont
       that the woman the picture to the men   shows
       'that the woman will show the picture to the men'
    b. dat de vrouw de film   toont *aan de mannen*
       that the woman the picture shows to the men
    c. dat Jan Piet *van het bewijs*   overtuigt
       that John Pete of the evidence convinces
       'that John will convince Pete of the evidence'
    d. dat Jan Piet overtuigt *van het bewijs*
       that John Pete convinces of the evidence

To conclude, there are several indications that the gap heads the extended DP and that it can be lexically realized by a functional element that is an affix or a word. If the head is empty, it is subject to the ECP.

4.3 Subjects and nominative case

The Gap Hypothesis has many consequences that fall outside the scope of the present chapter, but at least one cannot be ignored here. One of the central points in the ECP discussions is, of course, the subject–object asymmetry for extractions. The explanation for this asymmetry is that subjects are not properly head governed, as opposed to objects. If subjects are the specifiers of the functional head I, while objects are complements of V, as, for instance Rizzi (1990b) assumed, this is in accordance with the idea that V but not I is a proper head governor.

At first sight, it seems that the combination of the Gap Hypothesis and the ECP approach of Rizzi causes an insurmountable problem here. According to the Gap Hypothesis a DP in ModDu contains a gap. However, such a DP cannot surface in subject position since the gap cannot be properly head governed, cf. (56).

(56) [$_{CP}$ ... [$_{IP}$ ...[$_{DP}$ Ø ...] I ... [$_{VP}$ ... [$_{DP}$ Ø ...] V]]]
                *   ok

In other words, all sentences with a DP subject should be ungrammatical. In contrast, sentences where the subject gap is filled should be grammatical. Recall that there is only one way in ModDu to fill the gap, namely by inserting P. We thus predict PP subjects to exist. PP subjects are not excluded, as (57) illustrates, but it is quite clear that this is a marked phenomenon, as opposed to ordinary DP subjects.

(57) (ik denk) dat over Las Palmas korter is
     I think that over Las Palmas shorter is
     'I think it is shorter via Las Palmas'

It seems that we make the opposite prediction of what seems empirically justified.

There is a rather obvious solution to this problem, namely to assume that subjects are not headed by a gap. Of course, if we do not want this solution to destroy our above findings for objects, we have to know why the outer functional shell of a DP has to be present for objects but not for subjects. What triggers the outer functional shell?

My proposal is that this shell is triggered by Theta Theory. I will assume that a constituent can be interpreted at LF as an argument only through the intervention of functional structure. In the case of objects, the obligatory presence of an outer shell is derived in the following way: at LF the DP in (58a) cannot be interpreted as an argument of V, as opposed to (58b).

(58) a. [$_{VP}$ ...DP.... V]
            ↓
     no argument
   b. [$_{VP}$ ...[$_{XP}$ Ø [$_{DP}$ ...]] ...V]
            ↓
     argument

Note that an LF interpretation mechanism along these or similar lines becomes essential if one assumes, as in the Minimalist Programme, that there is no D-structure. If there cannot be D-structure theta-role assignment, the link with the theta grid of the verb is most plausibly made at LF.

The difference between subjects and objects can now be related to another asymmetry in the languages under discussion: Subjects show agreement with the verb. Subjects are similar to objects in the sense that also in the case of subjects functional structure has to intervene in order for the subject to be interpretable as an argument. The difference is that this functional structure is part of the extended V-projection itself: it is I, or Agr$_S$, with which the subject has to agree, as indicated in (59).

(59) [$_{CP}$ ... [$_{IP}$ ...[$_{DP}$ ...]$_i$ I$_i$ ... [$_{VP}$ ...[$_{DP}$ Ø ...] V]]]
          ↓   ↓   ↓
       argument   argument

As for objects, this analysis is reminiscent of the standard analysis since Chomsky (1981). Several linguists have argued before that the head I is involved in theta-role assignment; some have argued that the theta role for the subject is in fact assigned to I (see Evers 1986; Hoekstra 1986; Weerman 1989 for some discussion). Pertaining to objects, the present proposal differs both from the GB approach and the Minimalist Programme. The difference regarding the GB approach is that the intervention of functional structure for theta-role assignment is extended to objects. The difference with the Minimalist Programme is that the intervention of functional structure for objects is worked out in another way. In the Minimalist Programme the functional structure for objects (Agr$_O$) is part of the extended projection of V in the same way as Agr$_S$ is. In the present proposal, the functional structure for objects is in the outer shell of the objects, while the functional structure for the subject is part of the extended V-projection. The present approach concurs with the fact that there is no overt trace of object agreement on the verb in the languages under discussion (as opposed to subject agreement). If there is a rich morphological inflection system this is especially visible on the object itself (namely: case) — as predicted by the present approach.[13]

More generally, I predict that there are two types of licensing: either via functional information on the (extended) projection of the theta-role assigner, or via functional information on the argument itself. This concurs with the typology of Nichols (1986). In other words, languages may have object agreement, but the prediction is that morphological case affixes, if present at all, are not triggered here by Theta Theory.

The implication of the present proposal is that a DP does not have to (and hence: will not) project an outer functional shell with an empty head if it is in subject position, contrary to what will happen in a complement position. It follows that there are two abstract representations of a ModDu phrase like *de man* 'the man'. In one representation a functional shell headed by a gap has to be projected (in complement position); in an another representation a bare DP appears (in subject position). Note that this has an interesting consequence for NOM, which should now be considered as essentially different from GEN, DAT and ACC. Only the latter three correspond to an outer functional shell. NOM appears if no such shell has to be projected. This position is similar to what has been defended recently on independent grounds for a rather different set of languages by Bittner & Hale (1993). NOM is the default value in that it contains less information — a view that has been defended by many generative linguists since Franks (1981).[14]

4.4 The order of direct object and indirect object revisited

We now have an explanation for all the syntactic effects of morphological case that we discussed in section 2, with one exception. In section 2.1 we formulated generalization (13), repeated here as (60).

(60) The order of indirect object and direct object has to remain constant unless there is a morphological case system

As the reader may have noticed already, (60) does not follow directly from the Gap Hypothesis as it was formulated in the previous subsections. From the fact that both the direct object and the indirect object in ModDu have to appear to the left of the verb, we have to conclude that both contain a gap. However, if both indeed contain a gap, we predict that the order in (61b) is as grammatical as the order in (61a). Nevertheless, only (61a) is correct.

(61) a. dat de vrouw [$_{VP}$ [$_{DP'}$ ∅ [$_{DP}$ de mannen] [$_{DP'}$ ∅ [$_{DP}$ de film]] toont]]
     that the woman   the men   the picture
     shows
     'that the woman will show the picture to the men'
  b. *dat de vrouw [$_{VP}$ [$_{DP'}$ ∅ [$_{DP}$ de film] [$_{DP'}$ ∅ [$_{DP}$ de mannen] toont]]
     that the woman   the picture   the men
     shows

Another set of facts, though, suggests that our hypothesis is part of the answer. Recall that the gaps of DPs in ModDu can, at least in principle, be filled by a preposition. As a result these extended DPs can escape the ECP and they have a distribution that is comparable to DPs with morphological case, see (62).

(62) a. dat de vrouw *aan de mannen* de film   toont
     that the woman to the men   the picture shows
     'that the woman is showing the picture to the men'
  b. dat de vrouw de film   toont *aan de mannen*
     that the woman the picture shows to the men

As for generalization (60), we can observe once again that extended DPs that contain a preposition pattern with DPs with morphological case. That is, alongside the word order of the (a)-sentences in (61) and (62), the word order in (63), where the PP appears to the right of the object, is possible as well.

(63) dat de vrouw de film   *aan de mannen* toont
    that the woman the picture to the men   shows

In order to explain these facts, I will adopt and slightly reformulate a proposal by Neeleman (1994). Recall that I argued that the outer functional shell of the DP has to be present in order to make it possible to interpret the DP as an argument (which is vital if there cannot be theta-role assignment at D-structure). It is reasonable to go one step further here. Not only should we know at LF that a DP is an argument, we have to know as well which argument is to be connected with which theta role of the theta grid of the verb. Thus, the outer functional shells of the DPs in (63) make clear that these DPs should be interpreted as arguments. However, since the head is empty, there is no further information on the thematic role of the argument: there is no information to indicate which argument is the goal and which the theme. In order to solve this problem, we can make use of the idea that theta roles are hierarchically ordered. Neeleman bases the hierarchy in (64) on Grimshaw (1990).[15]

(64) *Thematic Hierarchy*
 AGENT > GOAL > THEME

Given the general hierarchy in (64), we can easily determine the roles of the arguments in (61a). The lowest argument has to be the theme, the next one the goal. Hence, the ungrammaticality of (61b).[16]

If the outer functional shell of the DP is not empty, and gives information on the status of the argument in a transparent way, one is not dependent on (64). This is what happens if the preposition *aan* 'to' appears: the argument is explicitly designated as a goal. Therefore interpretation is not dependent on (64) and consequently both orders in (62a) and (63) are allowed.

Precisely the same happens if the gap is filled by case. If there is, for instance, a transparent relation in a language between DAT and the goal-status of an argument, we predict that the direct object and the indirect object can be switched — which was claimed to be the case in generalization (60).[17]

5 Neutralizing case effects

As far as we can see, the disappearance of morphological case in West Germanic languages takes place rather gradually. This can only be possible if there is some overlap between a system with and without morphological case. For this reason, the theory should not only account for syntactic effects of morphological case, but in addition it should preferably make clear why these effects are not always visible, or not always in the same way.

In the preceding sections we already saw several phenomena that may cause overlap between a system with and one without morphological case. For instance, if it is parameterized whether or not A is a proper head governor (cf. section 4.1), the grammars that are characterized by (65a–c) will all allow (extended) DP complements for A.

(65) a. +Morphological case, +A as proper governor
 b. −Morphological case, +A as proper governor
 c. +Morphological case, −A as proper governor
 d. −Morphological case, −A as proper governor

Similarly, the intervention of movement may cause the word order in a language with morphological case to be as strict as the order in one without morphological case. According to the Gap Hypothesis, DPs in a language with morphological case do not have a gap and hence are not subject to the ECP. Consequently these languages are predicted to show both OV and VO orders, as indicated in (66) (cf. (37)).

(66) a. ... [$_{VP}$ [$_{DP}$ ...case ....] V]
     b. ... [$_{VP}$ V [$_{DP}$ ...case ....]]

However, if the verb has to move to some higher head position to the left, the surface result will always be a VO order. Similarly, if the DP for some reason has to move to a higher specifier position to the left, the surface result is OV, etc.

In the above examples the morphological case system is constant and some additional syntactic factor intervenes. Another logical possibility is that the morphological case of two separate stages is only similar at surface level, but has to be represented differently.

At this moment, I am not able to do more than suggest some possible directions to solve many of the intricate problems that surround this issue of overlap. However, I will try to discuss one problem that I think is illustrative.

As discussed in section 2.1, ModG is in accordance with generalization (60). The crucial facts are given in (67) (cf. (8) and (9)).

(67) a. dass die Frau   den Männern den Film   zeigt
        that the woman-NOM the men-DAT the picture-ACC shows
        'that the woman will show the picture to the men'
     b. dass die Frau   den Film   den Männern zeigt
        that the woman-NOM the picture-ACC the men-DAT shows

The problem arises when we turn to (68). Although OHG allows extraposition, ModG does not (cf. section 2.2, (20)).

(68) a. *dass die Frau   den Film   zeigt den Männern
        that the woman the picture-ACC shows the men-DAT
     b. *dass die Frau   den Männern zeigt den Film
        that the woman-NOM the men-DAT shows the picture-ACC

The facts in (67) show that morphological case in ModG has a syntactic effect. The facts in (68), however, suggest that morphological case in ModG does not fill the gap of the DP. Merely as an illustration, I will follow two different routes to solve this problem here.

In a first approach we could assume that morphological case in ModG does not have the same status as in the older stages of the Germanic languages. It would have become more of a peripheral surface phenomenon from the point of view of the grammar. This boils down to saying that at least the standard language makes use of rather artificial rules, or relics of some older system. It should be noted here that many German dialects indeed show more or less the same deflection history as Dutch with respect to morphological case.

If we try to formulate this in terms of the Gap Hypothesis, we have to assume that a ModG DP contains a gap just like a ModDu DP. The implication is that it is possible to have an empty extended head, while there is a morphological affix. Moreover, artificial as this morphological system might be, the dative is able to mark the DP as a goal such that identification of the argument is not dependent on the hierarchy in (64).

Evidence might come from language acquisition facts. Under the scenario just described, we expect that children acquiring ModG word order come to the conclusion that DPs contain a gap, that is, they first assume (69).

(69) L1: [$_{DP}$ Ø DP]

Only relatively late they acquire case morphology, but at this stage they cannot get rid of the gap, so they end up with something like (70).

(70) L1+: [[$_{DP}$ Ø DP] case]

The presence of the gap forces the DP to remain to the left of the verb, while at the same time the presence of case allows the DP to be interpreted independently of the thematic hierarchy.

Interestingly, there is some evidence for a development along these lines. Clahsen, Eissenbeiss & Vainikka (1994) show that German children acquire overt morphological case relatively late. Initially DPs occur in the form without overt case, even in contexts in which accusative or dative would have been required. Clahsen et al. cite examples of overgeneralizations made by children of over age 3;6. They assume that this late acquisition is due to the fact that morphological case is not visible (enough) on the nouns in ModG. Only when the determiners have been analysed, can the child come to the conclusion that ModG has morphological case. This is in contrast, for instance, with Finnish, where case is therefore acquired much earlier.

The other relevant observation is that, quite in contrast, children acquire the German OV order quite early (cf. Clahsen & Muysken 1986, among others). In terms of the present proposal this implies that they indeed start out with DPs like (69). The presence of the gap immediately explains the strict OV order. The observation that German children acquire morphological case at a relatively later stage suggests that the German children have to be satisfied with this structure for quite some time. The claim would be that they are no longer able to specify the gap as morphological case after this period.

A second approach departs from the observation that there seems to be another relevant difference between ModDu and ModG. In the above we have seen that PPs in ModDu can easily appear on both sides of the verb. Although the PP-V order is admitted in ModG, the reverse, V-PP, is rather controversial. At least in the standard language this order is ungrammatical according to many German speakers. These speakers disapprove of sentences like (71).[18]

(71) a. *dass er Peter überzeugt von dieser Tatsache
            that he Pete convinces of this fact
       b. *dass Julia immer spricht über Kasus
            that Julia always talks about case

c. *dass Werner nicht glaubt an diese Theorie
   that Werner not believes in this theory

We can interpret this as an indication that, quite independent of the status of morphological case, a word order like in (72) cannot surface in ModG.

(72) [$_{VP}$ ... XP .... V .... YP ...]

Suppose, for instance, that the head is moved to a higher head I to the right-hand side of VP, as indicated in (73).

(73) [$_{VP}$ ... XP .... t$_i$ .... YP ...] I$_i$

The implication is that the V–YP orders in ModG, although allowed if the head is filled by case or by P, are neutralized.

We can only maintain this position if the relation between I and V in ModDu is crucially different from (73), otherwise V–PP word orders are (wrongly) predicted to be ungrammatical in ModDu as well. That there is indeed a remarkable difference between Dutch and German has been well known in the generative literature since Evers (1975). In accordance with (73), standard ModG verb strings have a so-called 'OV order', while ModDu has a 'VO order', as the contrast between (74a) (German) and (74b) (Dutch) illustrates.

(74) a. dass wir Julia das Gebirge   zu besteigen versuchen sehen wollen
        that we Julia the mountains to climb   try   see   want
        'that we want to see that J. tries to climb the mountains'
     b. dat we Julia het gebergte willen zien proberen te beklimmen
        that we Julia the mountains want see try   to climb

There is a debate going on in the literature as to whether or not this difference between Dutch and German is related to the presence or absence of Verb Raising (cf. for instance Rutten 1991; Broekhuis 1992).[19]

The discussion whether the first or the second approach is correct will certainly take us too far afield within the context of the present chapter. Note, moreover, that they do not necessarily exclude each other. For now, the conclusion suffices that the effects of morphological case predicted by the present proposal can be neutralized in basically two different ways: either via some extra syntactic operation or alternatively via another representation of morphological case. Needless to say that whatever factor intervenes, we should give independent evidence for it.

6 Conclusion

In this chapter I argued that the difference between a morphologically case-marked phrase and one that is not is that the latter lacks lexicalized functional information — that is, it contains a gap, in contrast to the morphologically case-marked phrase. The DP with a gap is dependent on an ECP à la Rizzi (1990b) that is motivated on independent grounds. The presence of the outer functional shell of the DP is forced, I argued, by the necessity to interpret theta roles at LF.

As I hope to have made clear, my proposal gives more insight into a couple of syntactic effects of morphological case than its predecessors. Moreover, my proposal is in keeping with several observed subject–object asymmetries and is able to shed some light on the fact that morphologically case-marked DPs are to some extent syntactically comparable to PPs.

It is worthwhile to consider here not only what progress has been made, but also what losses we might have contracted. My proposal implies that there is no such thing as 'case assignment' or 'case checking' as in other theories. One might wonder then whether or not we have lost empirical ground that was covered for instance by GB Case Theory. GB Case Theory accounts for the following empirical phenomena:

(75) a. N and A do not take a DP but a PP complement (in languages without morphological case)
b. P and V take a DP complement
c. DP complements either precede or follow V
d. NP-raising

As for (75a–c) there is no empirical difference with the present approach. There is, however, for (75d). GB Case Theory accounts for the fact that in a structure like (76a) the object has to move to subject position, as in (76b), since it cannot be assigned case in its base position (cf. Chomsky 1981).

(76) a. [e [was killed [the man]]]
b. [the man$_i$ [was killed [t_i]]]

However, for several reasons independent of the present proposal, this explanation has never been entirely convincing.

First of all, one might wonder why it is not possible to insert some kind of semantically (and perhaps even phonologically) empty preposition in front of the object. Note that such a procedure is proposed in order to assign case to a complement of a noun in a DP as in (77).[20]

(77) a. *[the [destruction [Carthago]]]
b. [the [destruction [of [Carthago]]]]

Therefore, the construction in (78) is good for reasons of Case Theory.

(78) *[e [was killed [P [the man]]]]

The fact that (78) is nevertheless ungrammatical calls for an explanation. Such an explanation, however, threatens to make the original explanation of passive in terms of Case Theory redundant.[21]

In fact, as is well known, such an explanation is available. Both (76a) and (78) are excluded by the Extended Projection Principle (EPP): A sentence needs a subject (cf. Chomsky 1982). Hence, movement of the direct object to subject position in passives (and ergatives) could be a consequence of the EPP. As is well known, the EPP is needed for reasons independent of Case Theory: The ungrammaticality of (79a), for instance, cannot be due to Case

Theory, since the embedded clause does not need (and might even resist, cf. Stowell 1981) case; the ungrammaticality follows from the EPP. Since there is a dummy subject inserted in (79b), the sentence is saved.

(79) a. *[e [is said [$_S$ that he shot the man]]]
 b. [it [is said [$_S$ that he shot the man]]]

One might perhaps object that we now have to explain why (80) is ungrammatical, since the EPP is satisfied.

(80) *[it [was killed [the man]]]

As pointed out by Marantz (1992), however, the ungrammaticality of (80) might follow if the insertion of a dummy subject is a last resort option to satisfy the EPP.

A final reason to prefer an EPP explanation over an explanation in terms of Case Theory has to do with the notion of case absorption. As for passives, one could argue that ACC is used to somehow save the external argument, and therefore it is not available for the internal argument (cf. Roberts 1985a; Hoekstra 1986, among others). However, such an explanation is not available for ergative verbs, as in (81).

(81) a. [e [arrived [the man]]]
 b. [the man$_i$ [arrived [t_i]]]

Here it has to be stipulated ('Burzio's generalization') that the verb is not able to assign case (thereby causing movement of the internal argument to subject position). Languages with overt morphological case quite often show, however, that Burzio's generalization is not obeyed (see for some discussion Sigurðsson 1989). We can now simply skip this problematic stipulation under an EPP approach: movement is triggered in order to satisfy the EPP.[22]

Although many questions remain, the general conclusion of this chapter then seems to point in a clear direction: we can dispense with Case Theory.

Notes

* For suggestions and comments I would like to thank Peter Ackema, Denis Delfitto, Frank Drijkoningen, Arnold Evers, Kozo Kato, Ad Neeleman, Maaike Schoorlemmer, Josep Quer, Höskuldur Thráinsson, Jacqueline Vermeul, Petra de Wit and the editors and the reviewers of this volume. In addition many fruitful suggestions came from audiences at DIGS 3 in Amsterdam (March/April 1994), the Universität Stuttgart (November 1994) and CGSW in Brussels (January 1995).
1. Although here and below my phrasing is perhaps misleading, my central claim is not that the disappearance of morphological case (always) *causes* syntactic change and that the reverse cannot be true. The main concern in this chapter is that there is a relation between morphological case and syntactic change.
2. There is some evidence that this generalization is not only true for the West Germanic OV languages, cf. Kiparsky (this volume).
3. For (16a, b) cf. (20a, b) in Weerman (1989: 163), for (16c) cf. (18c) ibid., p. 162.
4. There is evidence that a generalization related to (19) holds for the North Germanic languages. See Holmberg (1985, 1986) for discussion.

5. For (23a, b) cf. (82b, c) in van Gestel et al. (1992: 63), (23c) ibid. (14), p. 80.
6. For (28) see (91a) and (91d) resp. in van Gestel et al. (1992: 65).
7. A similar problem for Generalization 4 appears if we turn from West to North Germanic: Platzack (1982) shows that Swedish has a group of adjectives that take a DP complement, although Swedish does not have a morphological case system. See also Holmberg (1985).
8. It is also possible to assume that empty elements are licensed if the DP is moved to some specifier position of a functional projection. The main reason for me to choose a more traditional formulation here is that there are many concrete proposals for the licensing of empty elements in pre-Minimalist work (such that I can show that indeed the same condition is relevant), while it is still unclear how these aspects are to be incorporated in the Minimalist Programme.
9. Note that the sensitivity of the ECP to directionality points in the direction of a PF character of this constraint. See Aoun et al. (1987) for discussion.
10. Note that a DP headed by a preposition is not necessarily predicted to be in all respects the same as a DP that is headed by case. As we will see more clearly in the next subsection, the essence is that both P and case are realizations of functional information that is necessary to interpret a DP as an argument, but these different realizations might very well have different side-effects. My expectation is that here one can find the explanation for asymmetries between case-marked DPs and PPs, apart from the possible differences between functional and lexical prepositions hinted at above (cf. Collins & Thráinsson 1993 for discussion).
11. The same is true if P is a proper governor.
12. Obviously, the VO or OV order may be excluded for some independent reason, even if the gap is filled. See section 5 for some discussion.
13. I consider this asymmetry (in the languages under discussion) between subjects and objects as rather problematical for proposals with Agr_S and Agr_O. The solution that Agr_O is lexicalized as morphological case on an object (whereas Agr_S is lexicalized by agreement on the verb) does not seem very satisfying to me.
14. Obviously, it can only be shown in a rather direct way that NOM is a default value if a language has (or loses) a morphological case system. The fact that a subject pronoun appears in ModDu construction as in (i) is at best indirectly related, since pronouns are in fact not representatives of full DPs.
    (i) a. Ik een feest bezoeken? Kom nou!
            I a party visit   come now
            'Me visiting a party? Come on!'
      b. Wie gaat dit doen? Ik!
            who goes this do   I
            'Who is going to do this? Me!'
    Several independent arguments for an asymmetry between NOM and ACC that show that NOM is the default in the sense of the present proposal are discussed in Weerman (1995).
15. In the past several other linguists have hinted at a hierarchy of theta roles. See, among others, Jackendoff (1972), Hale (1983), Bresnan & Kanerva (1989).
16. Recall that I am only discussing OV languages here. Neeleman (1994: ch. 5) discusses in detail how the hierarchy in (65) works out in VO languages.
17. Recall that not only the goal but also the theme can take the form of a PP (cf. section 4.2). However, in this case the preferred order for many Dutch speakers tends to be constant (as Mascha Damen brought to my attention; cf. Damen 1994 for some discussion).
    (i) a. dat Jan het meisje *van zijn onschuld* overtuigt
            that John the girl   of his innocence convinces
            'that John will convince the girl of his innocence'
      b.?dat Jan *van zijn onschuld* het meisje overtuigt
            that John of his innocence the girl   convinces

Note that in constructions like in (i) the preposition is lexically selected by the verb. The verb and the preposition form a fixed, idiomatic combination and it does not seem to be predictable which preposition a verb takes (for instance, *vertrouwen op* 'trust on', *houden van* 'love of', *geloven in* 'believe in', etc.). This is in contrast with what we observe for the goal, where there is a transparent relation with the preposition *aan* 'to'. If the prepositions in (i) indeed do not give transparent information on the theme status of the argument, one is dependent again on the hierarchy in (64). In this case, then, the preposition only formally fills the gap. Consequently, we correctly predict extraposition to be possible (cf. section 4.2):

(ii)   dat Jan   het meisje overtuigt *van zijn onschuld*
       that John the girl   convinces *of   his innocence*
       'that John will convince the girl of his innocence'

18. Werner Abraham and Julia Philippi, p.c. Julia Philippi informs me that the word order V–PP order is in use, nevertheless, in spoken German. In particular, the sentences improve when a special focus is added (but recall that this is not the interpretation that we aim at here). I have no idea whether or not dialect and standard rules interfere here.
19. For a detailed account of how the V–XP orders in ModDu interfere with possible analyses of the relation between V and I see Reuland (1990) and Ackema *et al.* (1993).
20. Note that it is claimed that *Carthago* receives the same theta role as it will receive if *destroy* is a verb, as in (i).
    (i) they will destroy Carthago
    In other words, the claim is that the presence of *of* in (77) has nothing to do with Theta Theory but with Case Theory.
21. Note that 'e' in (78) does not refer to *pro*. Therefore one cannot argue that (78) is excluded because English is no *pro*-drop language (as a reviewer suggested). Here 'e' means that there is no subject at all (even no *pro*).
22. Note that it does not follow directly from the EPP why indirect objects are not moved to subject position. Under the present approach it follows, however, if indirect objects are somehow inherently marked as a goal, under the assumption that 'double' interpretation, that is, via both a functional shell and the flexion of the verb is excluded (cf. the case clash). For ModDu, however, there is no inherent goal marker in a double object construction, so here, apparently, the restriction boils down to saying that an internal goal interpretation has to build on an outer functional shell of a DP. For a serious explanation we also have to take into account that sentences where the indirect object seems to have been moved to subject position are not unfamiliar in (modern) spoken Dutch (cf. the passive in English).

17 The rise of positional licensing

Paul Kiparsky

1 Introduction

The transition from Middle English to Modern English in the second half of the fourteenth century is a turning point in the syntax of the language. It is at once the point when several constraints on nominal arguments that had been gaining ground since Old English (OE) become categorical, and the point when a reorganization of the functional category I is initiated, whose completion over the next several centuries yields essentially the syntactic system of the present day. From this time on, subjects are obligatory, and they must be placed in Spec,IP position (Hulk & van Kemenade 1995). In the VP, the last traces of OV order disappear (Pintzuk 1991, 1992), the order of direct and indirect object becomes fixed, the first 'recipient passives' enter the language (Allen 1995: ch. 9), and objects cease to be separable from the verb by adverbs or adjuncts. The V2 constraint of Old and Middle English (ME) is lost, as topicalized constituents cease to trigger verb-fronting (Hulk & van Kemenade 1995). Concurrently, in the I system, the first instances of periphrastic *do*-support begin to replace fronting of the finite main verb (Kroch 1989), and, with the appearance of split infinitives and pro-infinitives, *to* starts to pattern as a non-finite Aux rather than, as in earlier stages, as a prefix marking the infinitive (van Gelderen 1993). All these changes have been dated to the second half of the fourteenth century, most of them specifically to the period between 1360 and 1380.

From the perspective of traditional grammar, the new syntax of subjects and objects reflects a shift from inflection to word order as the signal of grammatical relations, due to the loss of case and agreement endings through sound change and analogical levelling. As Allen (1986a, 1992, 1995) shows, the relation between the morphological and syntactic changes was rather more complex than such accounts tend to assume. Furthermore, they have nothing to say about the concurrent changes in I. There have been several recent attempts to bring these into the historical picture. Hulk & Kemenade (1995) suggest that the status of the functional categories changed in the second half of the fourteenth century, directly causing the loss of the V2 constraint, and indirectly causing the new requirement that there must be an obligatory nominative subject in Spec,IP. Van Gelderen (1993) attributes a series of changes, including the rise of *do*-support and the reanalysis of infinitival *to*, to the rise of I, which she thinks was not present at all as a syntactic category in OE and ME.

Each of these proposals is attractive and ties together several phenomena in an interesting way. They are however mutually incompatible in several respects, both with respect to what they assume about the nature and chronology of the changes, and with respect to the way they analyse and explain them. Moreover, they all fall short of providing a single structural motif for the whole complex of innovations that constitute the great syntactic shift of the late fourteenth century. None of them, in fact, connects the changes in I to the simultaneous internal reorganization of the VP.

I attempt the outline of such a unifying account here. It implements the traditional idea that inflectional morphology and positional constraints are functionally equivalent elements of grammatical structure, but using the framework of the more articulated conception of phrase structure that has emerged from recent syntactic research, as well as a theory of licensing and structural case that I have been developing for some years. I believe it offers a framework that does justice to each of the insightful conjectures and observations just summarized, though it differs on several points of historical fact, as will become clear in the course of the discussion.

That there is a relationship between the loss of inflectional morphology and the development of rigid positional constraints is clear from comparative syntax. The most important point about this relationship is that it is not a vague correlation or tendency, as often assumed, but an exceptionless implication, which however holds in one direction only: *lack of inflectional morphology implies fixed order of direct nominal arguments* (abstracting away from Ā-movement of operators.)[1] The converse is not true, and hardly even a tendency. The unclarity of traditional formulations on this point is probably to blame for the disrepute and neglect into which even the valid half of the implication has fallen in modern theorizing about syntax.

The Germanic languages illustrate both the implication and the failure of its converse. Every Germanic language which has lost case and agreement morphology, whether VO (English, Swedish, Danish, Norwegian) or OV (Dutch, West Flemish, Frisian, Afrikaans), has imposed a strict mutual ordering requirement on its nominal arguments, without changing the headedness of its VP. The order is always that subjects precede objects, and indirect objects (NPs, not PPs) precede direct objects:

(1) German:
    a. ... dass Jan seinem Vater das Buch gibt
          that Jan his   father the book gives
          'that Jan gives his father the book'
    b. *... dass Jan das Buch seinem Vater gibt
    c. *... dass seinem Vater Jan das Buch gibt
    d. *... dass seinem Vater das Buch Jan gibt

e. *... dass das Buch Jan seinem Vater gibt
f. *... dass das Buch seinem Vater Jan gibt

Dutch (Vikner 1990: ch. 4; Neeleman 1994; Zwart 1993: 303):
a. ... dat Jan zijn vader het boek geeft
b. *... dat Jan het boek zijn vader geeft
c. *... dat zijn vader Jan het boek geeft
d. *... dat zijn vader het boek Jan geeft
e. *... dat het boek Jan zijn vader geeft
f. *... dat het boek zijn vader Jan geeft

Swedish:
a. ... att Jan ger sin far boken
b. *... att Jan ger boken sin far
c. *... att sin far ger Jan boken
d. *... att sin far ger boken Jan
e. *... att boken ger Jan sin far
f. *... att boken ger sin far Jan

Showing that the converse implication does not hold, several Germanic languages with rich inflection require fixed word order anyway. Icelandic is the best-known case, but not the only one. Grisons Swiss German has the same four-case system as standard German, but allows no scrambling whatever. In Grisons it is neither possible to switch the direct object with the indirect object, as in (2b), nor to switch the subject with either object, as in (2c, d, e), though sentence (2c) could be acceptable as a case of focus scrambling in a context that puts the focus on *Bbuur*.[2]

(2) a. und den het dr dogdor S. em   Bbuur de   KB erklärt
       and then has the doctor S. the(DAT) farmer the(ACC) AI explained
       'and then Dr S. explained artificial insemination to the farmer'
    b. *und den het dr dogdor S. de KB em Bbuur erklärt
    c.?*und den het em Bbuur dr dogdor S. de KB erklärt
    d. *und den het de KB dr dogdor S. em Bbuur erklärt
    e. *und den het em Bbuur de KB dr dogdor S. erklärt

Closer investigation shows that the identical positional constraint plays a role in all Germanic languages, but relates to case in at least four different ways. In those languages which scramble freely (independently of whether they are VO, as in Yiddish, or OV, as in German) the contextually unmarked 'neutral' word order is the same as the fixed word order of non-scrambling languages (again whether VO, such as English and Swedish, or OV, such as Dutch and Grisons).[3] In Grisons, position must harmonize with case, so that the order of arguments is fixed as Agent/Recipient/Theme, as the data in (2) show. In Icelandic, position is fixed but is independent of case; hence the 'quirky subject' phenomenon. Finally, in OE, position and case interact in a complex and systematic way as partly joint, partly independent licensers (see section 5). In the account to be developed here, these systems follow from the respective licensing categories of the languages:

structural case is determined only by morphological case in German, by both morphological case and position in Grisons, only by position in Icelandic, and by either case or position in OE.

I begin by taking a closer look at the English syntactic innovations under discussion, and at how they might be explained and related to each other under various theoretical assumptions. I then summarize the licensing and case theory that I will be presupposing. At the end of the chapter I come back to the comparative and typological generalizations just outlined and sketch out how they can be explained in the proposed framework, and how they bring together the syntactic changes that took place in English in the second half of the fourteenth century.

2 The loss of V2 and the obligatoriness of subjects

Hulk & van Kemenade (1995) draw a connection between the loss of subject–verb inversion after topicalized constituents and the rise of obligatory nominative subjects in IP. They analyse the first change as analogical and the second as an indirect consequence of the first. They trace the loss of subject–verb inversion to a positional difference between pronominal and nominal objects in OE and ME. In main clauses, NP subjects followed the fronted verb in C, whereas pronominal subjects, being clitics, preceded the verb:

(3) a. $_{CP}$[XP V $_{IP}$[subject–NP ...
    b. $_{CP}$[XP subject–pronoun+V $_{IP}$[...

Hulk & van Kemenade assume that in the form of ME that gave rise to the modern language, that of such writers as Wyclif, nominal subjects began to adopt the pattern of pronominal subjects.[4] Of course NPs could not simply join pronouns in cliticizing to the verb according to the pattern in (3b). Rather, cliticized pronoun subjects would have had to be reinterpreted as being *in situ* in Spec,IP, an analysis which in turn implies that the verb then remains in I. In this way, (3b) is reanalysed as (4a). Subsequently, this reanalysis was analogically extended to nominal subjects, causing the verb to remain in I after any subject: (4a) is generalized to (4b).

(4) a. $_{CP}$[XP $_{IP}$ [subject–pronoun V ...
    b. $_{CP}$[XP $_{IP}$ [subject–NP V ...

After this change, V-to-C movement was restricted to *wh*-constructions, where there was an operator in Spec,CP (and where in any case pronouns had always followed the verb). In OE, when there was no external argument, C had assigned nominative case under chain government to an NP inside the VP, in which case Spec,IP could be filled by a non-nominative constituent. This chain-government mechanism was now lost, and henceforth Spec,IP had to have a lexicalized nominative subject to ensure licensing of I's φ-features under Spec–head agreement in IP. Consequently, preposed dative experiencers, formerly in Spec,VP, are reanalysed as nominative subjects in Spec,IP, and as another effect of this shift expletive *pro*-drop, which was already rare anyway, was completely lost.

Platzack (1995: 206) objects that the reanalysis of (3b) as (4a) is unmotivated: '... the language learner must have experienced a certain number of sentences which unambiguously indicated the presence of verb second, and a bulk of sentences which were structurally ambiguous between a verb-second interpretation and a basic SVO interpretation. It is unclear why the language learners should ignore these unambiguous cases in favour of a particular interpretation of the ambiguous ones.' We might add that the idea that learners could be simply confused about the position of pronouns versus NPs in (3) is implausible because the order of object pronouns and NPs has differed systematically at every stage in English and there is no evidence that these differences have been hard to learn or that they have triggered any reanalysis.[5] To make the reanalysis more plausible Platzack posits that not only derived X–subject V structures such as (3b) were reanalysed,[6] but also derived subject–verb–object structures such as (3a) where XP was the subject. Even if just one of these kinds of ambiguous structures would not have been enough to trigger reanalysis, both of them together were just too much for learners to handle. However, it is not clear exactly why this extra set of cases should tip the balance in favour of reanalysis. Platzack's objection that all the unambiguous evidence favoured the V2 analysis counts equally against his own proposal; in fact it counts equally against any pure reanalysis account of any change whatever. For prior to actual reanalysis, the data will always divide that way: some of it will be equally consistent with both analyses and some will positively support the old.

I am aware of three possible answers to this general objection to pure reanalysis as a mechanism of syntactic change. One is to posit some restriction on acquisition which makes the evidence for the old analysis inaccessible to learners. An example of such a restriction (which however is of no use in the case at hand) is Lightfoot's (1991) degree-0 learnability hypothesis, according to which only main-clause evidence is accessible to learners for parameter setting. It is not clear that there is a reasonable restriction of this kind that would give the desired results for the case at hand. We would need something like the assumption that only pronouns are part of the 'triggering experience', and that the syntax of NPs is projected from them, but this is obviously false.[7]

The second way to salvage the reanalysis story would be to posit a threshold of frequency which the evidence must exceed in order to be accessible to the learner. This seems to be the implicit assumption behind Platzack's proposal, in particular. For some evidence which tells against frequentistic threshold hypotheses (as well as against Lightfoot's degree-0 learnability hypothesis), see Kiparsky (to appear).

A third approach, to my mind the most promising, is to build the appropriate preferences (whether formal or substantive) into the theory, and to view acquisition and change in terms of a push–pull mechanism where preferences, if sufficiently strong, may override available evidence, if sufficiently weak. An example is the Subset Principle (Wexler & Manzini 1987), which posits, on learning-theoretic grounds, a preference for the most restrictive hypothesis. In Kiparsky (1996) I argue that a preference for uniform direction of θ-role assignment lies behind the shift from head-final to head-initial VP in English, Scandinavian and Yiddish.

Let us set aside for a moment the question why V2 was lost, and ask why that change then triggers the loss of expletive *pro*-drop. Hulk & van Kemenade, who suggest this causal connection, are careful not to speculate on what it might be, emphasizing that it is in any case not a direct one. Indeed, Chaucer, according to van Kemenade (1987), represents a dialect that extended the nominal V2 pattern to pronouns rather than the other way round, yet as far as obligatory subjects are concerned, his language appears to be similar to that of his contemporaries. As a factor contributing to the loss of expletive *pro*-drop, Hulk & van Kemenade point out that by the end of the ME period, it had already become so weak that the change in I was enough to trigger its complete loss. But then what made expletive *pro*-drop so weak in the first place that this 'last straw' was enough to finish it off somehow? One wonders whether the as yet unidentified factor which causes overt nominative subjects to become increasingly frequent in ME could not be the same factor that finally makes them obligatory around 1375. I will here put forward a candidate for that factor, which connects the obligatoriness of nominative subjects with the other changes under discussion.

3 The rise of I

Van Gelderen (1993) agrees with van Kemenade in adopting the Dutch/German-style V-to-C analysis for OE and ME, but differs in claiming that at this stage the language did not have the functional category I in overt syntax. She dates the introduction of this category — T(ense), in her terms — to *c.* 1380, and derives from it a series of changes in verb syntax that come into the language at this time. The appearance of split infinitives, *pro*-infinitives, accusative-and-infinitive constructions, periphrastic *do*, and modals are all analysed as structural reflexes of this new category.

Split infinitives are one indication that *to* has joined the auxiliaries as a non-finite element of I (e.g. *to perfectly know* on the pattern of *will perfectly know*). They first appear in the mid fourteenth century (Mustanoja 1960: 515; van Gelderen 1993: 41).[8] This citation from the *OED* is from *c.* 1400:

(5) to enserche sciences, and *to perfitly know*e alle manere of Naturels
     thinges   (*Secreta Secretorum*)

Stranded infinitival *to* conforms to the deletion pattern seen with auxiliaries (which, as Warner 1992 shows, occurs already in OE). The first instances are attested in the early fourteenth century (van Gelderen 1993:42; Visser 1963:73–1062). The *OED*'s earliest example is:

(6) þe soules of synners, ... þer to take and resseyue so As þei on eorthorne *deserueden to* ('Minor Poems from Vernon' ms. xxxiii.74) (14th c.)
'the souls of sinners, there to be taken and received as they on earth deserved to'

The accusative and infinitive construction with a bare infinitive, presumably a VP complement or small-clause construction, existed early with verbs of causation and perception. The *to*-infinitive begins to appear with verbs of saying and believing around the middle of the fourteenth century, and is widely used from the second half of the fourteenth century by Wyclif and others (Mustanoja 1960:527; van Gelderen 1993:61).

(7) Salomon ... expressith the gretter perel of synne to come bi begrie than to come bi richessis (Pecock, *Repressor* 305) (15th c.)
'Solomon says that poverty is more likely to lead to sin than wealth is'

The assumption is that these *to*-infinitive complements are IPs, with the subject in Spec,IP and *to* in I.

Periphrastic *do* appears in prose from about 1400 on, with isolated attestations earlier; in western and southwestern poetry it is attested as early as the late thirteenth century (Mustanoja 1960:603). The date for the emergence of modals is controversial. Lightfoot (1979) argued that they did not become a separate category until the late sixteenth century, but more recent research has pushed back the date at least to the second half of the fourteenth century (Warner 1982) and perhaps even to OE.[9]

Finally, van Gelderen (1993:67) interprets the decline of V2 as a reinterpretation of OE CPs with V-to-C movement as IPs without V-to-I movement (a reanalysis similar to the one proposed by van Kemenade). Since this again presupposes IP, it could be taken as evidence for the introduction of the category I at this time.

In this way van Gelderen brings together an impressive number of seemingly independent changes as instances of a single abstract modification of the grammatical system. The idea that languages differ in which functional categories they project in overt syntax is in tune with the Minimalist Programme, and is receiving some empirical support as work on comparative syntax progresses. Most significantly, perhaps, it opens up for investigation new kinds of causal connections between a language's word structure and its syntax.

However, van Gelderen's argument seems flawed in one important respect. The constructions she discusses show only that I is a category of overt syntax in the second half of the fourteenth century. We cannot conclude conversely from the absence of these constructions prior to that time that the language had no I yet. For example, even if we assume that accusative and infinitive constructions must be IPs (which is plausible but would have to be shown)[10] there is no reason why a language must have them just because it has IPs. Under the indicated assumptions, the presence of any of these diagnostic constructions can provide at most a *terminus ante quem* for the rise of the category I. The actual date of its introduction must be established by different evidence.

This evidence, while it does support van Gelderen's claim that English changed from an I-less language to one with I, shows that I actually came into the language much earlier. In Kiparsky (to appear) I argue that the introduction of I dates to OE already. For several centuries, English had competing phrase structures, with and without I. The decisive change of the second half of the fourteenth century is that I became an obligatory element. Since the point is crucial, I will first review the issue in comparative Germanic perspective here, before proceeding to present my case for OE.

Recent studies of the SOV languages German and Dutch have established that they have no overt syntactic V-to-I movement (Reuland 1990; Haider 1993; Zwart 1993:68; van Gelderen 1993; Ackema, Neeleman & Weerman 1993). This point was not obvious to begin with, since the finite verb comes in final position in these languages (except of course when it is fronted to C), and the VP is also head-final. In these languages V-to-I movement would therefore be a string-vacuous rightward movement, which was previously assumed to be simply undetectable (Vikner 1990; Rohrbacher 1994a). But subtler evidence shows that the verb in fact never moves to I in either Dutch or German. Zwart observes that, if complement clauses are generated in the same position as nominal complements (as would be expected since they bear the same kinds of thematic roles), V-to-I raising would require them to be extraposed to the right periphery of the IP. This extraposition would have to be obligatory, which creates a problem because extraposition is optional elsewhere.[11] Worse, as Haider notes, the assumption of obligatory extraposition is incompatible with coordination data:

(8)   Dass der Mann ihr [weder [sagte, [von wo er komme]], noch [verriet, [wohin er gehe]]]
        'that the man neither told her from where he came, nor disclosed where he was going'

Here the complements must be inside VP, and the V hence cannot have raised to I. Both Zwart and Haider also point out that the strict inseparability of the verb cluster and of the particle+verb combination in verb-final sentences tells against rightward verb-raising to I. Van Gelderen (1993) makes a similar point, and argues that it holds for OE as well. But perhaps the most striking argument comes from Reuland's observation that V-to-I raising predicts non-existing readings for adverbs, on the commonly accepted assumption that their scope is determined by constituent structure.[12]

In Dutch (as in Swedish), the absence of V-to-I movement is quite consistent with the existence of an IP projection in the overt syntax. The verbs of these languages are essentially uninflected, so they would not move to I in any case, according to the fairly well supported generalization that V-to-I movement presupposes rich person/number inflection.[13] For these languages, the evidence for or against a syntactic IP would therefore have to come from other facts than verb movement. And these facts show that both Dutch and the Mainland Scandinavian languages do have an IP (contrary to van Gelderen 1993: ch. 2). The most straightforward argument that Dutch and Mainland Scandinavian have an IP in spite of lacking V-to-I movement is that the subject position is obligatorily filled, by an expletive pronoun if necessary:[14]

(9) a. dat er/*Ø gedanst wordt (*Dutch*)
     that it   danced   was
     'that there was dancing'
   b. att det/*Ø dansades (*Swedish*)

As Haider (1993: 136, 189) also notes, Dutch and Swedish, like English, show the Definiteness Effect:

(10) a. dat er $\begin{Bmatrix} \text{iemand} \\ \text{een jongen} \\ \text{*Jan} \end{Bmatrix}$ werkt (*Dutch*)

   b. att det arbetar $\begin{Bmatrix} \text{någon} \\ \text{en pojke} \\ \text{*Jan} \end{Bmatrix}$ där (*Swedish*)

It is generally assumed that the Definiteness Effect is due to different interpretations being assigned to NPs in Spec,IP and Spec,VP position. In so far as this is correct, the presence and absence of the Definiteness Effect in a language would constitute evidence for the presence and absence of a distinct Spec,IP position, respectively.

Swedish has accusative and infinitive complements with some *verba sentiendi et dicendi* (most often with *anse* 'consider' and *påstå* 'claim'). These complements are demonstrably IPs. They cannot be CPs because they neither have a complementizer nor undergo verb fronting, and (under standard assumptions) they cannot be VPs with internal subjects because negation and other adverbs adjoined to VP can freely follow the subject.

In a language with full inflection such as German, though, the absence of V-to-I movement can only mean that there is no I at all. And this is confirmed by the fact that German, unlike Dutch and Swedish, does not require expletives in impersonal passives or in experiencer constructions, except as necessary to safeguard the V2 requirement (Haider 1993),

(11) a. dass (*es) getanzt wurde
    b. Mich friert (*es)

and does not observe the Definiteness Effect (Bennis 1987):

(12)   dass da {jemand / ein Junge / Jan} arbeitet (*German*)

The absence of accusative and infinitive complements with *verba sentiendi et dicendi* in German is consistent with this conclusion.

Haider (1993) concludes from such evidence that Dutch, English and the Scandinavian languages, but not German, have the syntactic category IP. In this respect, German falls in with other rigidly SOV or predominantly SOV languages with rich morphology (such as most of the older Indo-European languages). If it indeed turns out to be the case that SOV languages lack a syntactic I projection, this would support the conjecture that functional projections are always left-headed (a special case of Kayne's antisymmetry hypothesis).

4 IP as an optional category: competing grammars

How does OE fit in? In this section I will argue (in part summarizing earlier work) that I was introduced already in the course of the OE period, and that grammars with and without IP coexisted from the time V-fronting first become possible in embedded clauses up to the time when V-fronting and VO order became fully obligatory. In this account, the competition between a grammar with I and a grammar without I takes the place of Pintzuk's competition between an I-medial grammar and an I-final grammar. It is the change to obligatory I which I will argue is part of the major syntactic shift in the fourteenth century.

That IPs arose already during the OE period, and competed with I-less structures, is shown by several kinds of syntactic evidence.

OE and ME clearly have verb fronting both to I and to C (van Kemenade 1987, this volume; Pintzuk 1991; Kiparsky 1995, 1996; Kroch & Taylor, this volume). The finite verb moves to I, and to C after *wh*-words and demonstratives such as *þa*. Topicalization is adjunction to IP and to CP. For this reason, fronting of the finite verb in OE is obligatory only after *wh*-words and demonstratives (focus elements must be in Spec,CP, so their presence forces a C). Elsewhere the finite verb can remain in final position, a receding option which disappears altogether as the category I and VO order within the VP become obligatory. The evidence for V-to-I raising includes: (1) the possibility of V-fronting in subordinate clauses, (2) the position of the finite verb in relation to adverbs, and (3) the licensing of oblique subjects.

If OE main clauses were IPs unless CP was required by the presence of *wh* or some other focus element, then OE may never have been a strict V2 language in the Dutch/German/Scandinavian sense (Stockwell 1984; Swan 1994; Weerman 1989: 234; Pintzuk 1991; Kroch & Taylor, this volume). At any rate, it permits both V1 and V3 declarative main clauses, and V2 clauses arise in at least two distinct configurations: (1) a focussed element in Spec,CP, with the verb in C position after it, (2) a subject (or, in sentences without an external argument, some other constituent) in Spec,IP, with the verb in I position after it, a possibility clearly evinced in subordinate clauses (van Kemenade, this volume). Adjoining an adverbial or PP to these two structures in turn yields two distinct types of V3 order.

Another piece of evidence that OE had IP available as a category is that it had dative subjects, in the sense that oblique experiencers were structurally parallel with nominative subjects (Allen 1986a). On our assumptions this is at least a *prima facie* indication of Spec,IP positioning (as also assumed by van Kemenade 1992). These dative subjects, like nominative subjects, but unlike objects, trigger deletion of a following coordinated nominative subject:

(13) a. Ac gode   ne licode na heora geleafleast, ne heora
       but god-DAT not pleased not their lack of faith nor their
       ceorung,   ac   @   asende him   to fyr of   heofonum
       grumbling and (he) sent   them to fire from heavens
       'But God did not like their lack of faith, nor their grumbling, and
       sent them fire from the heavens.'   (ÆHom 21.68)
    b. þa   gelicode ðam gedwolum   ðas bisceopesdom,   and Ø
       then pleased the heretics-DAT the bishop's sentence and (they)
       wacodon ða   ðreo niht   (Æls Basil 338)
       waked-PL then three nights
       'Then the heretics were pleased with the bishop's sentence, and
       they stayed awake three nights'
    c. þa   scamode þone biscop   and Ø nolde   him   þa
       then shamed the bishop-ACC and (he) not-would him-DAT then
       his costunge   geandettan   (GD, Pref.)
       his temptation confess
       'Then the bishop was ashamed and did not want to confess his
       temptation to him'

Experiencer constructions very rarely have expletive *hit* as other types of 'subjectless sentences' do. Moreover, after 1200, the former subjects, *if postposed*, are regularly accusative,

(14)   for ðat him   ereowe   ow
        for that him-ACC/DAT pitied   you-ACC
        'Because he pitied you'

and it seems that they do not trigger subject–verb agreement (Allen 1995: 241–3):[15]

(15)   and ðat hem likede   here lodlice   sinnes
        and that them please-SG their loathsome sins
        'and that they liked their loathsome sins'

Another subject-like property of oblique experiencers of verbs such as *sceamian* is that they can be controlled, at least in conjoined structures such as (16) (Denison 1993: 94):

(16) oððe forhwy hi   ne mægen hiora   ma   scamian þanne
      or   why   they not may   them-GEN more be ashamed than
      fægnian (Bo 68.15)
      rejoice
      'or why they may not be more ashamed of those things/themselves than glad'

Allen shows that these oblique experiencers of *like* and similar verbs became nominative subjects in the second half of the fourteenth century, the point when nominative subjects became obligatory as already discussed.

Finally, if modals existed in OE already (see note 9), and we assume that verbs which are intrinsically finite and assign no θ-roles are to be assigned to the lexical category I, then I must have been a category of OE.

However, the I category cannot have been an obligatory constituent in OE. As in German, the Definiteness Effect seems to be not categorical, since definite NP subjects evidently occur within VP:

(17) Ond þa   æfter þon þe ðær wæron ða halgan lofsangas   &
      and then after it   that there were   the holy   praise-songs and
      mæssan gefyllede (Bl 207.28)
      masses finished
      'and then, after the holy psalms and masses were finished (there)'

As far as expletives are concerned, impersonal passives, such as experiencer constructions, hardly ever have *hit* if there is a preposed constituent. Compare (18) with (9) and with (11):

(18) Be ðæm   wæs swiðe ryhte   gecweden ðurh sumne wisne monn
      of which was very   rightly spoken   by   a certain wise man
      (CP 118.21)
      'About which a certain wise man spoke very truly'

Weather verbs usually have an expletive subject regardless of V2, but this is true even of German (see Falk 1993 for discussion). The same is true of verbs with extraposed sentential complements:

(19) a. ðonne hit daȝian   ongynneþ   (Bede 4.10)
         when it dawn-INF begins
         'when dawn comes'
     b. On sumre   tide hit haȝalade stanum   ofer ealle Romane
         in summer time it hailed   stones-DAT over all   Romans
         (Or 3.5.8)
         'In the summertime it hailed stones over all the Romans'
     c. norþan   sniwde   (Sea 31)
         from north snowed
         'it snowed from the North'

d. Swa hit gebyreð ðæt ... (CP 431.27)
   so it happens that
e. ðonon cymð oft ðætte ... (CP 437.27)
   whence happens often that

In sum, OE clearly had a syntactic I category, with clear syntactic evidence for V-to-I raising and a Spec,IP subject position, and possibly a few lexical members, the modals. On the other hand, I was not obligatory in OE. The possibility of V-final main clauses, the absence of an obligatory Definiteness Effect, and the absence of obligatory expletives converge to show that main clauses with no separate I projection were still allowed. Additional evidence for the claim that OE had competing syntactic systems, one with I and the other without, comes from the variability in the position of the verb in complex sentences (Kiparsky 1995). Pintzuk (1991) had argued that OE has competing right-headed and left-headed structures both at the IP level and at the VP level. However, she observed that only three out of the four possible combinations are attested, the missing one being what on her terms was left-headed VP with right-headed IP. Thus, '(that) the bishop wanted to lift up the child' has three, not four, possible renderings in OE, namely (20a–c). The fourth variant, (20d), is ungrammatical, an arbitrary gap under her syntactic analysis:

(20) a. (ðæt) se biscop wolde ðæt cild up aheafan
     b. (ðæt) se biscop ðæt cild up aheafan wolde
     c. (ðæt) se biscop wolde aheafan up ðæt cild
     d. *(ðæt) se biscop aheafan up ðæt cild wolde

The absence of the fourth combination is explained by the two assumptions already mentioned: (1) that OE has two competing grammars, one with IP, the other without IP, and (2) that functional categories are always left-headed. The first parameter of syntactic variation is still headedness of the VP, as for Pintzuk, but the second one is now whether IP is syntactically projected or not. In that case, the ungrammatical sentence (20d) would have a right-branching VP nested in a left-branching VP, requiring two grammars to be in force simultaneously. Since code-switching in mid-sentence is in many cases excluded,[16] the analysis offers a natural explanation for the gap.

(21) a. ... $I0_o$ [[... V]$_{VP}$t]$_{VP}$
     b. ... [[... V]$_{VP}$V]$_{VP}$
     c. ... I^0[t[V ...]$_{VP}$]$_{VP}$
        ... [V [V ...]$_{VP}$]$_{VP}$
     d. *... [[V ...]$_{VP}$V]$_{VP}$

Several strands of evidence thus converge to show that the category I played a role in the overt syntax of OE, but that it was not obligatory. The structural change in the second half of the fourteenth century is not that I was introduced, but that it became obligatory.

5 Case and licensing

After this review of the late ME syntactic shifts, let us return to the question that ties them all together. In the background is the perennial problem of the relation between inflectional morphology, word order and grammatical relations. Two very different conceptions of this relation can be found in the grammatical literature.

Typologically oriented grammatical theorizing at least since Humboldt has assumed that word order and inflectional morphology are alternative means of expressing grammatical relations. From this premise, Boas, Sapir, and Jespersen explicitly derive the interesting crosslinguistic prediction that richness of inflection should be correlated with freedom of word order. Traditional grammars reflect this assumption in their standard practice of identifying subject and object by nominative case and/or by verb agreement in languages which have them, and by word order otherwise. The complementarity of rich inflection and fixed word order is here interpreted not simply in general functional terms, but seen as a basic principle of grammatical structure.

For the empirical reasons outlined in the introductory section, this is an overly simplistic picture, which fails to do justice to the fact that the implication is unidirectional, and that languages can combine positional and morphological constraints in several different ways. However, this does not mean that we have to go the other extreme and adopt the view of contemporary formal theories of grammar that there is no intrinsic connection between overt morphology and overt syntax[17] (as opposed to covert morphology and covert syntax, where theoretical connections are made on every hand, but with unclear empirical import). This tradition privileges configurationality by positing a level of representation at which abstract case is assigned on the basis of structural adjacency and government relations between the governing head and its dependent. The picture is however clouded by the fact that the order of syntactic constituents relevant to case assignment is not necessarily identical to their actual order either at PF or at LF, and the abstract case of an argument is at best indirectly related to the morphological case which it bears at PF — mismatches which are accommodated under Scrambling and LF movement on the syntactic side, and under Spell-Out on the morphological side. The upshot is that nothing in this theory precludes a language with the morphology of English or Chinese from having the syntax of German or Japanese.

A more constrained approach can be developed along the following lines. I adopt the idea that syntactic argument structure is projected from semantic content (Dowty 1979; Givón 1984: ch. 5; Jackendoff 1983; Foley & Van Valin 1984). Following Bierwisch (1983, 1986; Bierwisch & Schreuder 1992), we assume a level of Semantic Form at which conceptual knowledge is articulated in terms of linguistically determined invariants. This level is distinct from, but interacts with, conceptual knowledge on the one hand,

and syntactic structure on the other. A lexical item is represented at Semantic Form by an expression in which θ-roles are represented by lambda-abstractors over the variables in the function denoted by the predicate. The semantic role of the variable over which the lambda operator abstracts determines the semantic content of the resulting θ-role, and the variable's depth of embedding in Semantic Form determines the θ-role's rank in the θ-hierarchy. For example, three θ-roles are projected in the Semantic Form of the verbs *show*, *paint* and *put*, of which the highest θ-role (the 'Agent', defined as the first argument of CAUSE) is saturated first:[18]

(22) a. show: λz λy λx [x CAUSE [CAN [y SEE z]]]
 b. paint: λz λy λx [x CAUSE [y HAVE-ON z] & PAINT (z)]
 c. put: λz λy λx [x CAUSE [BECOME [y AT z]]]

Mismatches between Semantic Form and syntactic argument structure occur in both directions. Elements in Semantic Form which are not projected as θ-roles are implicit roles, such as the Agent in a 'middle' construction:

(23) a. *show* (middle): λy [x CAUSE [CAN [y SEE z]]
 b. This house shows (*customers) well (*even by incompetent real estate agents)

Semantically, *show* remains a three-place predicate, but in its middle use it is syntactically a one-place predicate. Conversely, there are *improper θ-roles*, which correspond to nothing in semantic structure, but are associated with expletives such as *it* and *there* in syntactic structure:

(24) a. *rain:* λx [RAIN] It rained
 b. *come:* λyλx [y COME) There came a war

Argument structure and its articulation by abstract case features here does the work that is usually assigned to configurational properties at D-structure. Structural cases are relational entities defined by the two cross-classifying features [±H(ighest) R(ole)] and [±L(owest) R(ole)]. These case features play a role at all levels of grammatical structure. In morphology, they are features of case and agreement affixes which they pass on to their stems in accord with general morphological principles and lexicalist constraints. In morphosyntax, they are features of arguments, assigned to them by inflectional case and agreement morphemes and by the structural positions they occupy. At argument structure, they are features structurally assigned to the hierarchical representation of θ-roles, where they define grammatical relations (or equivalently, abstract case). The assigment of a θ-role to an argument must be licensed by unification of the θ-role's abstract case features with the argument's morphosyntactic case features. Thus, the main work of relating the levels is done without any case-specific correspondence rules. In particular, I reject the current practice of providing formally heterogeneous representations for abstract cases or grammatical

The rise of positional licensing 475

relations/functions on the one hand, and morphological case on the other, and associating them by 'spell-out' rules of the form 'arguments with abstract case x (or with grammatical function x) are assigned morphological case Y'. This results in a more restrictive theory of licensing, and a principled account of a range of typological generalizations. Abstract case is defined by the positive values [+H(ighest) R(ole)], [+L(owest) R(ole)], which are assigned to the θ-roles according to their relative position on the θ-role hierarchy (itself a projection of Semantic Form).

(25) a. [+HR] is assigned to the highest role.
     b. [+LR] is assigned to the lowest role.

Our notion of abstract case resembles GB's in that it is a syntactically assigned feature complex, but we construe it in a somewhat different way since abstract case is not by itself a licensing property, but a set of featurally expressed *constraints* on morphosyntactic case. The licensing property is rather the successful unification (compatibility) of the case features at the different levels, in particular the unification of abstract case and morphosyntactic case.

By (25), the three ordered θ-roles of the verb *show* projected in (22a) (shower, showee, thing shown) are assigned the abstract case features in (26).

(26) $\begin{bmatrix} \lambda z \\ [+LR] \end{bmatrix} \begin{bmatrix} \lambda y \\ [\ \ ] \end{bmatrix} \begin{bmatrix} \lambda x \\ [+HR] \end{bmatrix} [x \text{ CAUSE } [\text{CAN } [y \text{ SEE } z]]]$

The sole role of an intransitive verb gets both [+HR] and [+LR], and the middle role of a three-place predicate gets neither [+HR] nor [+LR]. The result is an inventory of four abstract structural cases, in Dixonian terms 'A', 'S', 'O', and 'D'.

(27) a. S: [+HR, +LR]
     b. O: [+LR]
     c. A: [+HR]
     d. D: [   ]

Not explicitly indicated in (26) is the fact that all three θ-roles bear a feature of abstract structural case (say [+SC]), which is subclassified by the features [LR, HR]. For typographical simplicity, this will be tacitly assumed to be present in every bracketed feature matrix that follows, with the absence of structural case thus symbolized by the absence of a bracket. Because the case features are intrinsically relational, there can be at most one [+HR] role and at most one [+LR] role per argument structure. On the other hand, a predicate without a syntactically visible role (i.e. an impersonal verb) obviously does not have either a [+HR] role or a [+LR] role. And there can be more than one [−HR] and [−LR] element in an argument structure, or none. Being assigned on a purely structural, hierarchical basis, structural cases cannot be idiosyncratic lexical properties of specific θ-roles, and cannot be specific to particular predicates. The abstract case feature [+HR] therefore defines the highest syntactically visible θ-role of a predicate, its 'subject'. In this way, θ-role reversals, such as a verb 'kill' with victim as subject and killer as object, are correctly excluded in principle. This follows from the assumption that the order of λ-abstraction reflects semantic depth.[19] Cases such as *like* and *please* are not instances of such reversal, since *please* obviously has the Semantic Form of a causative. At the level of abstract case, the proposed decomposition into features makes it possible to individuate exactly the class of grammatical relations which play a role in syntactic constraints (such as binding, control, and parallelism in coordination). For example, the feature (+HR) picks out 'A' and 'S' in any language, irrespective of its case system, and thus universally defines the relation of grammatical subject. The features also provide the appropriate representation on which valency-changing operations are defined, which I assume are triggered by verb morphology in the lexicon. Passive affixes demote [+HR], i.e. render them ineligible to bear structural case, in which case the next highest θ-role with structural case receives the feature [+HR].[20]

(28)

a. *show*: $\begin{bmatrix} \lambda x \\ [+HR] \end{bmatrix} \begin{bmatrix} \lambda y \\ [\ ] \end{bmatrix} \begin{bmatrix} \lambda z \\ [+LR] \end{bmatrix}$

b. *show* + *n*: $[\lambda x] \begin{bmatrix} \lambda y \\ [+HR] \end{bmatrix} \begin{bmatrix} \lambda z \\ [+HR] \end{bmatrix}$

In Kiparsky (to appear) I argue, primarily on the evidence of ergative languages, that the theory of grammatical relations provided by abstract case in this sense is superior to that of GB-style configurational theories as well as those of Relational Grammar and LFG.

Morphosyntactic case feature complexes are assigned to maximal projections (NPs or DPs) as follows. Case features percolate in the morphology from affixes to stems, and in the syntax from clitics to their hosts and from words to the phrases they head. Agreement morphology and structural licensing positions confer their case features upon the arguments which are respectively co-indexed with them and positioned in them. (These are not case-specific conventions, but special cases of general mechanisms by which featural information is distributed in structural representations.) Morphosyntactic case feature values are normally negative, viz. [−LR] and [−HR]. The effect of the feature values [−LR] and [−HR] is to prohibit the arguments that bear them from being assigned the lowest- and highest-ranked available θ-role, respectively. (Positive morphosyntactic case feature values would have the effect of restricting a case or position to a specific role.) The four possible combinations of negative feature specifications give the basic inventory of four structural cases:

(29) a. [ ]: nominative (including 'absolutive')

    b. [–HR]:   accusative
    c. [–LR]:   ergative, genitive
    d. [–HR,–LR]: dative, partitive

The same morphosyntactic case features induce a parallel intrinsic classification of agreement and position as well. The familiar type of subject agreement is unspecified (i.e. nominative), but ergative agreement [–LR], accusative agreement (normal 'object agreement'), [–HR] and dative agreement ([–LR], –HR]) also exist. As for position, the feature values are assigned to internal argument positions as follows:

(30) a. Complement positions are [–HR].
     b. Non-final complement positions are [–LR].

Specifier positions are then featureless, the positional equivalents of nominative case. I assume further that Spec,IP is the basic licensing position for subjects. Spec,VP can also license subjects, but seems to confer some additional feature specifications. For example, the Definiteness Effect could be descriptively accounted for by assigning Spec,VP the features [+HR, +LR, -SPECIFIC], restricting it to nonspecific indefinite subjects of intransitive verbs. Of course, this is merely a placeholder for the more principled and general account which is ultimately required.[21] Arguments case-marked in this way get associated with θ-roles case-marked by (25), in accord with the following conditions:

(31) a. *Unification:* associated feature matrices must be non-distinct (one must not have a plus value where the other has a minus value).
     b. *Specificity (Blocking, 'Elsewhere'):* specific rules and morphemes block general rules and morphemes in the shared contexts.

The combined effect of Unification and Specificity is that each θ-role is associated with argument bearing the most specific (most highly marked) morphosyntactic case that is compatible with the θ-role's abstract case. The distribution of morphosyntactic cases follows from their feature composition on the basis of the predicate's argument structure in accord with Unification and Specificity. Consider a three-place verb such as *show*. Abstract case is assigned to the θ-roles by rule (25). The morphosyntactic cases nominative, dative and accusative — whether derived morphologically from case or agreement, or syntactically by position as in (30) — have the respective feature specifications [ ], [–HR,–LR], and [–HR]. In a language that has all three of these morphosyntactic case licensers, the constraints in (31) enforce the following association of arguments with θ-roles:

(32) $\begin{bmatrix} \lambda x \\ [+HR] \end{bmatrix} \begin{bmatrix} \lambda y \\ [] \end{bmatrix} \begin{bmatrix} \lambda z \\ [+LR] \end{bmatrix}$ θ-roles with abstract Case

$\begin{bmatrix} \\ \end{bmatrix} \begin{bmatrix} -LR \\ -HR \end{bmatrix} \begin{bmatrix} -HR \\ \end{bmatrix}$ morphosyntactic Case selected

No other case assignment is consistent with (31). Given that the active morphosyntactic case features in English come from position, and in German from morphology, the basic clausal syntax follows: the highest θ-role unifies with Spec,IP position in English and with nominative case in German, the next highest with the second argument position and with dative case, respectively, and so on. Hence we get in English the order *John showed Bill a picture* (Agent–Recipient–Theme). Positional case features thus impose an argument order which is a linear projection of the thematic hierarchy.[22] Certain role types can be prespecified with the morphosyntactic case features [–LR] and/or [–HR], either idiosyncratically or by lexical rule. For example, many languages assign [–LR, –HR] to recipient and experiencer-type roles, with the consequence that they receive an 'inherent' dative case, invariant under passivization, which is not unifiable with [+HR] and therefore blocks subject status for them (unless that is specially licensed in the way discussed below). Thus in OE, Recipients were assigned dative case inherently, e.g. *bringan* 'bring':

(33)
a. *bringan*: $\begin{bmatrix} \lambda x \\ [+HR] \end{bmatrix} \begin{bmatrix} \lambda y \\ -HR \\ -LR \end{bmatrix} \begin{bmatrix} \lambda z \\ [+LR] \end{bmatrix}$

b. *broht*: $[\lambda x] \begin{bmatrix} \lambda y \\ -HR \\ -LR \end{bmatrix} \begin{bmatrix} \lambda z \\ +HR \\ +LR \end{bmatrix}$

Of course not all languages have the same case system. Crosslinguistic variation results from two factors: (1) languages have different inventories of morphological cases, and (2) languages allow different case feature mismatches. The abstract case features of an argument may fail to unify with the morphosyntactic case features assigned to it either by morphology ('quirky case'), or by position ('scrambling'). I will refer to such morphosyntactic case features as being recessive. Since every argument must be properly licensed, it follows that languages with no inflection do not scramble, and that subjects with quirky case must be licensed by position (or by agreement). Consider first how prespecification of case features can conflict with the abstract case features assigned by (25) (in which case the latter must of course be licensed in some other way, viz. by agreement or by position). The Icelandic dative experiencer verb *líka* 'like' would have the following Semantic Form:

(34) *líka*: $\lambda y \, \lambda x \, [x \text{ LIKE } y]$

$$\begin{bmatrix} -\text{LR} \\ -\text{HR} \end{bmatrix}$$

By (25), the logical subject λx (the Experiencer) is assigned the abstract case feature [+HR]. Being lexically marked with the dative features [−LR, −HR], it is assigned to an argument bearing dative case. But the case feature [−HR] cannot unify with (and thereby license) the abstract case feature [+HR] assigned to the logical subject. Because morphological case is recessive in Icelandic, the mismatch between the dative's feature [−HR] and the θ-role's feature [+HR] is allowed. The latter must still be licensed, however. This can be done by positional nominative case in subject (Spec,IP) position. Therefore, the sentence is grammatical, as long as the experiencer is in subject position (as in (35a)):

(35) a. Mér   líka   þessir bílar
     me-DAT like-PL these cars
     'I like these cars'
   b. *þessir bílar líka mér

German morphological case is not recessive, and so, in the corresponding verb *gefallen* (whose Semantic Form is identical to that of *líka*), the abstract case feature [+HR] fatally fails to unify with the prespecified case feature [−HR]. The same would be true if the Experiencer were assigned [+LR]. So the Experiencer can get no structural case, and the abstract case features [+HR] and [+LR] must instead be assigned to the only other θ-role, the thing-liked, or 'Theme'. That makes the Theme the subject and the verb intransitive. Since positional case is recessive in German, both orders are grammatical.

(36) a. Mir   gefallen diese Autos
     me-DAT like-PL   these cars
     'I like these cars'
   b. Diese Autos gefallen mir

Thus German has 'free word order' and only nominative subjects, whereas Icelandic has fixed word order, and allows dative subjects.

What would happen if a language allowed both these types of mismatches, that is, both morphological case and positional case were recessive? Both orders should occur but their grammatical relations would be different: if the dative Experiencer is in Spec position, it is positionally licensed as a subject, but if it is an internal argument, it cannot be licensed as a subject (since neither its morphological case nor its positional case features can unify with [+HR]). Exactly this configuration of data is attested in OE. Allen (1986a, 1995) observes that the subject properties of oblique experiencers mentioned above are found *only when the experiencer is the first argument of the clause*. The arguments can be reversed, but then the experiencer loses its subject properties and functions as a dative object. The fourth logical possibility is that neither morphological nor positional case are recessive, so that no mismatch at all is possible. In such a language, subjects and objects must bear the appropriate cases and at the same time stand in the appropriate licensing positions. Grisons seems to be an example of this type (see (2)). The resulting typology of languages with morphological case appears in (37):

(37)

Recessive case features	OE	German	Icelandic	Grisons
Morphological	+	–	+	–
Positional	+	+	–	–

The combined results of the licensing theory and its predictions are illustrated in the schematic licensing configurations in (38), representing situations that arise in languages with both case and positional licensing, with all possible combinations of recessivity and dominance. In the diagrams, an association line shows a successful unification and absence of an association line shows a failure of unification (feature incompatibility). The first case, (38a), is a nominative subject in external argument position. As can be seen from the diagram, this configuration can never fail to unify successfully regardless of recessivity. If positional case is recessive (as in German and OE), then the order of objects is not fixed, and nominative subjects may be placed outside Spec,IP, including VP-internally (see (38b)). If morphological case is recessive (as in Icelandic and OE), then 'quirky subjects', and consequently nominative objects, are allowed (provided of course they are properly licensed by position, see (38c)). Finally, the reason why scrambling of quirky subjects (*qua* subjects!) must lead to failure of licensing and therefore to ungrammaticality regardless of recessivity or dominance is evident from (38d). The subject can unify neither with the case features carried by its dative morphology nor with the case features carried by an internal argument position, and therefore remains unlicensed. Of course, the very same string is grammatical with the nominative argument as subject, as in German (see (38e)).

(38) a. Nominative subject in Spec of IP, accusative object in VP:

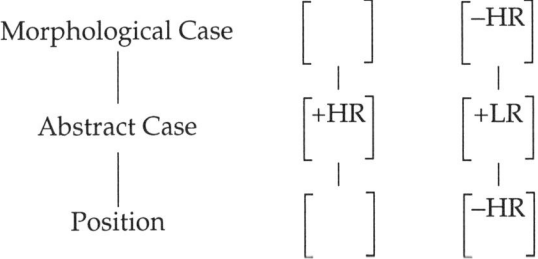

b. Scrambling (recessive positional Case):

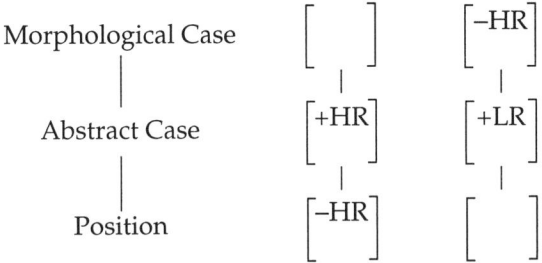

c. Dative subject, nominative objects (recessive morphological Case):

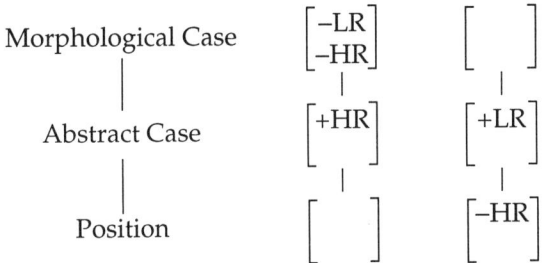

d. Scrambled dative subject (ungrammatical):

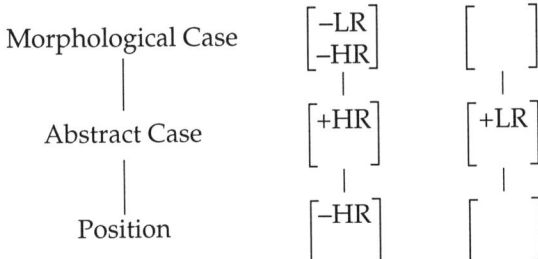

e. Dative nonsubject:

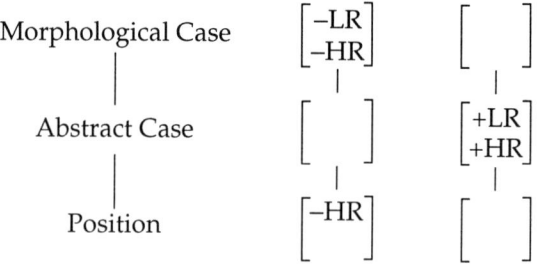

Of course, in languages that lack morphological licensing (such as Modern English, Dutch and Swedish), positional licensing must do the job. Since arguments must be licensed, there can be no question of recessivity of position in these languages. The fixed relative order of arguments seen in the Dutch and Swedish data in (1b, c) thus follows.

Implicit in this typology is the assumption that languages normally assign the same status to all licensing morphology (case and agreement inflections) and to all licensing positions (subject and object). I do not wish to claim that there can be no language in which agreement is recessive and case is dominant (or vice versa), or in which subject position is dominant and object position is recessive (or vice versa). However, convincing instances of this situation are hard to come by, which suggests that there is at least a tendency to avoid it; I will refer to this tendency as Uniform Licensing. Let us posit it as a descriptive generalization for now; a deeper explanation would of course be required. Uniform Licensing also makes sense of the fact that, while arguments with quirky case are commonly licensed as subjects by position, they are generally not licensed as subjects by agreement. This would involve recessive case and dominant agreement, contrary to Uniform Licensing. Note finally that Uniform Licensing conforms to the expectations of a parametric model of grammatical organization. The historical changes to be examined below will offer further confirmation for its reality.

6 The word order universals

It should now be clear why the empirical generalizations stated in section 1 are predicted to hold universally. Lack of inflectional morphology implies fixed order of direct nominal arguments (*modulo* Ā-movement of operators) because these are the only sources of morphosyntactic case, which is required in every language to license θ-role assignment. Therefore, a language that has no morphological case must make use of positional case to license arguments by (30).

The second generalization, that the order of licensing A-positions is the same in all languages, follows if we assume that both the assignment of abstract case by (25) and the assignment of positional case by (30) are universal.

The third generalization (due to Haider), is that the fixed word order of nonscrambling languages is the same as the contextually unmarked 'neutral' word order of scrambling languages. The formal account requires more apparatus than I have presented here, but the general idea should be transparent: even when positional case is recessive, so that scrambling is permitted, the thematic ordering is observed in the unmarked case, that is, whenever other factors (such as functional sentence perspective) do not override it.

An apparent problem for this claim is the existence of a class of verbs with reversible arguments in Icelandic. The key to the solution is Haider's observation that, in these very cases, there is also no single neutral or preferred order in German. Careful examination of the lexical semantics and argument structure of these verbs shows that the word order follows the general principles in these cases as well.

For most verbs with three arguments, we derive the correct basic constituent order in both languages. Privative verbs such as *deprive* are straightforward:

(39) a. Icelandic: *svipta* 'deprive', *ræna* 'rob' (NOM–ACC–DAT)
 b. German: *nehmen* 'take', *entziehen* 'withdraw', *abgewöhnen* 'wean someone from something', *verbieten* 'prohibit' (NOM–DAT–ACC), *entledigen* 'relieve (someone of something)' (NOM–ACC–GEN)

Their θ-structure is

(40) *deprive*: λzλyλx [x CAUSE [BECOME [y NOT HAVE z]]]

In Icelandic, the objects appear in the fixed order predicted by (40), (allowing for Heavy NP-Shift), and only the first object passivizes, regardless of case.

(41) a. Sjórinn svipti hana$_i$ manni sínum$_i$
 the-sea deprived her-ACC husband-DAT her(REFL)-DAT
 'The sea deprived her of her husband'
 b. *Sjórinn svipti manninum$_i$ gömlu konuna sína$_i$
 the-sea deprived the-man-DAT old-DAT the-wife-DAT his(REFL)-DAT
 'The sea deprived of the man his old wife'

In German, they are preferentially in that order, and only the accusative (direct) object passivizes. Both the similarities and the differences are as predicted.

(42) a. Sie verbietet ihrem Sohn das Rauchen
 she-NOM forbid-3SG her-DAT son-DAT the-ACC smoking-ACC
 'She forbade her son to smoke'
 b. Sie verbot das Rauchen ihrem Sohn

Verbs of direct causation also work as predicted:[23]

(43) a. Hávaðinn veldur verkamönnunum höfudverk
    the noise causes workers-DAT headache-ACC
    'The noise gives the workers a headache'
  b. *Hávadinn veldur höfudverk verkamönnunum
    'The noise gives the workers a headache'

A large class of verbs with a dative Recipient and an accusative Theme allow both orders as basic in both languages:

(44) a. Icelandic: *gefa* 'give', *vísa* 'show', *selja* 'sell'
  b. German: geben 'give', *zeigen* 'show', *verkaufen* 'sell', *empfehlen* 'recommend'

Neither (45a) nor (45b) seems to require any special discourse conditions:

(45) a. Ich gab das Geld meinem Bruder
  b. Ich gab meinem Bruder das Geld

In Icelandic, the corresponding verbs, also with a dative Recipient and an accusative Theme, allow both object orders freely (Zaenen, Maling & Thráinsson 1990:188):

(46) a. Eg gaf konungi ambáttina sína
    I-NOM gave king-DAT slave-ACC self's-ACC
    'I gave the king his maidservant'
  b. Eg gaf ambáttina konungi sínum
    I-NOM gave slave-the-ACC king-DAT self's-DAT
    'I gave the maidservant to her king'

In the passive, the difference is again that only the accusative passivizes in German, while either object passivizes in Icelandic, and it is in that case obligatorily in initial position:

(47) a. Das Geld wurde meinem Bruder gegeben
  b. Meinem Bruder wurde das Geld gegeben
(48) a. Honum voru oft gefnar baekur
    him-DAT were often given books-NOM
    'He was often given books'
  b. Bókin var gefin honum
    book-the-NOM was given him-DAT
    'The book was given him'

In certain 2-place predicates as well, dative and nominative are reversible in Icelandic, see (49), as noted by Smith (1992):

(49) a. Hefur honum nokkurn tíma staðið þetta til boða?
    has him-DAT any-ACC time-ACC stood this-NOM for offer
    'Has he ever had this on offer?'
  b. Hefur þetta nokkurn tíma staðið honum til boða?
    has this-NOM any-ACC time-ACC stood him-DAT for offer
    'Has this ever been on offer to him?'

Correspondingly, German has both orders without special emphasis or focussing:

(50) a. Hat das ihm zur Verfügung gestanden?
   has that him-DAT to disposal stood
   'Has that been at his disposal?'
   b. Hat ihm das zur Verfügung gestanden?
   has him-DAT that to disposal stood
   'Has he had that at his disposal?'

This dual character of *give*-type verbs can be traced to a semantic ambiguity between a *recipient-oriented* sense ($give_1$ 'X causes Y to get Z') and a *transfer sense* ($give_2$ 'X transfers Z from X to Y'):

(51) a. $give_1$ λxλyλz [x CAUSE [BECOME [y HAVE z]]]
   b. $give_2$ λxλyλz [x CAUSE [z GO [FROM x TO y]]]

The common meaning of (51a) and (51b) is that after the event (of giving, teaching, showing, etc.) there is a relation R(y,z) (of having, knowing, seeing, etc.) between Recipient and Theme. The additional meaning in (51b) is that prior to the event (at least) the corresponding relation R(x,z) holds between Agent (Causer) and Theme. Assuming as before that the θ-hierarchy is a projection of the depth of semantic embedding, we arrive at the desired two θ-structures and correlate them with the meaning difference in the right way. In English this difference is apparent in the semantic conditioning of the 'dative shift' alternation. As noted by Oehrle (1976), the *to*-dative version is only permitted in the transfer sense:

(52)
   a. Regular yoga exercises gave Bill { the ability to concentrate / powerful thighs / a heart attack }

   b. *Regular yoga exercises gave { the ability to concentrate / powerful thighs / a heart attack } to Bill

Similarly, $teach_1$, $show_1$, $offer_1$...imply simple causing to learn, see, have available ..., while $teach_2$, $show_2$, $offer_2$... imply that the thing taught, shown is previously known or seen by the Causer of the event (thus involving an abstract transfer of knowledge, vision or availability). Accordingly, (53b) is strange because the transfer meaning is inappropriate:

(53)
   a. The landslide { showed the people the need for a new party / offered the president an excuse to resign }

   b. ??The landslide { showed the need for a new party to the people / offered an excuse to resign to the president }

In the case of such verbs as *skila* 'return', the order is obligatorily Agent–Recipient–Theme:

(54) a. Ég skilaði   henni   peningunum
        I   returned her-DAT money-the-DAT
        'I returned the money to her'
     b. *Ég skiladi   peningunum   henni
        I   returned money-the-DAT her-DAT
        'I returned the money to her'

As predicted, only the thematically higher object, the Recipient, may passivize:

(55) a. Henni   var skilað   peningunum
        her-DAT was returned money-the-DAT
        'She was given back the money'
     b. *Peningunum   var skilað   henni
        money-the-DAT was returned her-DAT
        'The money was given back to her'

The transfer component of *skila* is motivated by its essentially locative character, revealed by the fact that *skila* — unlike *gefa*-type verbs — allows a prepositional phrase instead of the Dative:

(56) Ég skilaði   peningunum   til hennar
     I   returned money-the-DAT to her-GEN
     'I returned the money to her'

In discussion, H. Thráinsson raised the question why *gefa*, unlike *skila*, does not allow *til* in Icelandic. I assume that *til* is semantically incompatible with the particular kind of transfer denoted by *gefa*, presumably because it is generally restricted to transfer or extent in space or time, and hence (unlike English *to*) does not sit well with verbs denoting abstract transfer of possession. This would imply that (56) implies actual bringing, and (unlike its English translation) would not be used to refer, say, to signing a legal document. A corollary is that for any verb which has only the transfer meaning, the Theme (accusative) argument comes first in the basic order. This is the case for all change-of-place verbs, hence the position of Directional Locatives below Theme in the hierarchy. However, verbs of abstract transfer pattern exactly like change-of-place verbs:

(57) a. Icelandic: (all take PP complements)
     b. German: *aussetzen* 'set out, expose', *ausliefern* 'hand over, extradite', *unterwerfen* 'subject', *zuführen* 'bring to'

On the other hand, if the verb has no transfer component whatever, the basic order is fixed, with Theme in last place. This class includes all verbs where there is no transfer involved, notably verbs denoting intentional mental states:

(58) a. Icelandic: óska 'wish', lofa 'promise', spá 'predict'
b. German: wünschen 'wish', versprechen 'promise', zutrauen 'think someone capable of something', verübeln 'begrudge', gönnen 'not begrudge', verweigern 'deny'

Hence the predicted fixed order illustrated in Icelandic (59), and the passivization pattern in (60):

(59) a. þú   hefur   óskaþ   henni   þess
       you-NOM have-2SG wish-PP her-DAT this-GEN
       'You have wished her this'
   b. *þú   hefur   óskaþ   þess   henni
       you-NOM have-2SG wish-PP this-GEN her-DAT

(60) a. Ég   tel   þess   hafa   veriþ   óskaþ (*henni)
       I-NOM believe this-GEN have-INF wish-PP her-DAT
       'I believe this to have been wished her'
   b. Ég   tel   henni   hafa   veriþ   óskaþ þess
       I-NOM believe her-DAT have-INF wish-PP this-GEN
       'I believe her to have been wished this'

Correspondingly, since *to* denotes a transfer (change of possession or change of location), the same class of verbs in English only take double objects (in the relevant meaning).

7 From morphological to positional licensing

There is an obvious inherent asymmetry between position and morphology in that the property of linearity guarantees the availability of position as a potential licenser (whether recessive or dominant), whereas case and agreement may simply be lacking in the morphology. A language may lose its inflections but it cannot 'lose its word order' in the same sense: it must go on putting one word after another, even when it does not grammatically exploit or constrain word order. A corollary is that position is always ready to pick up the licensing function when morphology ceases to be able to handle it. Therefore, since θ-role assignment to arguments must be licensed by case features, loss of inflections automatically brings about a shift to positional licensing, with all the consequences that this entails.

With this in mind, let us return to the momentous syntactic events at the end of the ME period. These were of two kinds. On the one hand, at this point a number of syntactic innovations that had steadily gained ground through the ME period went to completion. A subject in Spec,IP position became obligatory in finite clauses, filled either by an argument or by an expletive pronoun. NP objects became fixed in post-verbal position, losing at once their ability to precede the verb within the VP and to scramble with each other after the V, as in the double object construction. In a concurrent development, inherent lexical ('quirky') case is gradually eliminated. On the other hand, several characteristic features of Modern English syntax show up for the first time in the historical record at this time: *do*-support, split infinitives, *pro*-infinitives, new modal auxiliaries, and the recipient passive. These convergent innovations can now be seen to have a common structural cause. They are consequences, some direct, others indirect, of a single grammatical change, itself ultimately a consequence of the erosion of case morphology in ME. This triggered the loss of inherent case, and caused NP arguments to become restricted to fixed licensing positions, entailing both the freezing of objects within the VP and the obligatoriness of the subject licensing position, Spec,IP, hence of the functional category I. The obligatoriness of I in turn caused *to* and the modals to become recategorized as I elements. In the course of the ME period, phonological and morphological changes resulted in the complete loss of case marking on nominal arguments. This dismantling of case inflection proceeded at its own rather leisurely pace. By 1200, nouns had ceased to be inflected for case, and dative case had merged with accusative case. After this time, NPs could still be marked for accusative case on the definite article (less often on the indefinite article) into the thirteenth century, in the conservative southern (Kentish) dialects through the fourteenth century (Allen 1995: ch. 5). The *OED*'s last examples of accusative inflection on NP arguments are:

(61) a. He ne may naȝt þolye þane guode smel ... ne more þanne
     he not may not tolerate the good smell no more than
     þe boterel þanne smel of þe vine   (Ayenbite 187, 1340)
     the toad the smell of the vine'
b. Ate laste þan gurdel he fond   (Sir Ferumb. 2419, c. 1380)
   at last the girdle he found
c. To Egremoure þon riche cite   (Sowdone of Babylone 108, c. 1400)
   to Egremoure the rich city

Chronologically, the impoverishment of morphological case marking on NPs goes hand in hand with the increasing fixation of word order. After the complete loss of noun and article inflection, the only remaining morphological case marking was on pronouns (where accusative had not been distinguished from dative since about 1200). Let us assume that if case never occurs on any lexical NP, then it cannot be assumed to be morphologically present on them either (as a zero morpheme or the like).[24] Agreement remained reasonably robust for some time, and could in principle have supplied the licensing nominative case features for subjects. For NP objects, however, no morphological licensing was available after articles ceased to be inflected. At this point, positional licensing had to become obligatory for them. A priori, it would have been possible that at this point a mixed licensing system could develop in which NP objects have to be positionally licensed, while subjects and pronominal objects continue to be morphologically licensed. The *Orrmulum* may give us a glimpse of just such a system (Allen 1995: 232-6). This text seems to treat nominal and pronominal experiencers differently; the former, already uninflected, are normally construed as nominative subjects, licensed positionally and/or by morphological agreement on the verb, the latter, retaining lexical case, behave as objects, and trigger no verb agreement.[25]

(62) a. ðat alle ... well georne birdenn clennsenn hemm
that all-NOM well truly behooved-PL cleanse them
b. & wel itt birrð uss trowwenn, ðatt ...
and well it behooves-SG us-ACC to believe that

As far as is known, the *Orrmulum*'s mixed licensing system does not occur elsewhere in ME.[26] Its marginal status is not surprising if we consider that mixed licensing systems are crosslinguistically quite rare (the Uniform Licensing tendency discussed at the end of section 5). All licensing morphology (case and agreement inflections) and all licensing positions are normally either dominant or not, across the board. The instability of systems like that of the *Orrmulum* thus lends additional support to the Uniform Licensing generalization. In general, then, when NPs become uninflected, and objects are assigned their licensing case features by position, the licensing of pronouns changes as well. The assignment of morphosyntactic case features to objects of whatever kind becomes uniformly based on position, and the residual case inflections of pronouns cease to have a morphosyntactic licensing function. This shift has a number of consequences. Pre-verbal NP objects disappear entirely (since their licensing positions are fixed). Simultaneously, in virtue of (30), the mutual order of objects in the double object construction becomes fixed in the same way as in Swedish, Dutch, or any other positional licensing language.

At the same time that these changes are completed in the second half of the fourteenth century, the new passive construction *John was given a book* enters the language (Allen 1992, 1995: 395). Three-place predicates begin to passivize the formerly dative (thematically higher) object, at first alongside the older passivization of the former accusative ('Theme') object. Allen's earliest example of this 'recipient passive' is from 1375.

This innovation can also be understood as a consequence of the loss of the licensing function of morphological case. In Germanic, the higher object of ditransitives was protected from passivization by its inherent morphosyntactic dative case (that is, by the feature complex [−HR, −LR]), see (33). This inherent morphosyntactic case was lexically assigned by a general rule to the middle θ-role of three-place predicates. While positionally licensed dative Experiencer subjects were introduced into OE, the first objects of ditransitives continued to resist passivization, at which point this class of arguments had to be marked as ineligible to become the subject in the passive. (Recall that passivization is demotion of the highest θ-role, upon which the subject role should fall on the next highest eligible θ-role.) After their morphosyntactic dative case ceased to be morphologically realized, its licensing function being taken over by position, they stood as simple unmotivated exceptions to the passive. This complication then began to be eliminated from the system.[27]

The single objects of verbs like *þancian* 'thank' had originally also failed to passivize in virtue of being inherently specified as dative in the lexicon, and turned into exceptions to passivization after dative subjects became possible. However, unlike the lexical case on the middle θ-role of ditransitives, which could be assigned by a general (albeit unmotivated) rule, the lexical case on the objects of these monotransitives was truly 'quirky' case: there is no way to predict the fact that *swican* 'betray' takes a dative object while *forsacan* 'forsake' takes an accusative object. After the morphological merger of dative and accusative case (which dates to around 1200), former single dative objects were in effect idiosyncratic exceptions to passivization, rather than systematic exceptions as the first objects of ditransitives were. These idiosyncratic exceptions were lost as soon as distinct dative case was lost, nearly two centuries before the systematic exceptions that the first objects of ditransitives constituted.

What these two classes of lexical case marking had in common is that the lexical case was assigned to an argument that would have received the same case by structural case assignment anyway (except precisely in the passive, as we have just seen). The lexical case marking was thus 'opaque' and had to be learned on the basis of the indirect evidence presented by the object's failure to passivize, presumably a point of difficulty for the learner. This is not the case for a third class of arguments with lexical case, the OE dative subjects of impersonal verbs such as *lician* 'like, please' and *þyncan* 'think' (see (34)). The lexical case there appears on the logical subject, where it blocks nominative morphology and subject–verb agreement. This class of lexical case marking is about as unpredictable as the previous class, but it differs in being straightforwardly accessible to the learner from the core data of active sentences (such as *me thinks..., the men thinks...*) and does not involve exceptionality with respect to passivization. Because of its relative transparency, it is eliminated rather more gradually than the other two classes of cases (Allen 1995: ch. 6), and indeed survives in fixed expressions such as *if you please* to this day.

Uniform Licensing manifests itself in still another way. When positional licensing is instituted for objects, it is at the same time extended to subjects as well. The unrestricted licensing position that confers nominative case is Spec,IP.[28] Thus subjects had to fill the Spec,IP position, and therefore to be non-empty. That is, impersonal constructions disappear (acquiring as subject either one of their formerly oblique arguments, or an expletive, as discussed above).

An immediate corollary of the obligatoriness of the Spec,IP position is that every finite clause has an I, to which the finite verb must move. This, together with the VO order required by positional licensing of objects, excludes three of the four OE phrase structures in (21). Only (21c), the modern phrase structure, satisfies both licensing constraints. Thus, the basic phrase structure of present-day English is the outcome of the fundamental shift to positional licensing in late ME.

The obligatoriness of the category I in finite clauses has more indirect consequences as well. It leads to the creation of a non-finite counterpart, by the recategorization of *to* as an I, as well as to the introduction (or expansion) of the category of modals.

As verb inflection recedes, the main verb begins to remain in VP and verb fronting is restricted to auxiliaries and modals. *Do*-support expands in lockstep with the loss of V-to-I until the change goes to completion in the eighteenth or early nineteenth century (Kroch 1989). This means that the rise of periphrastic *do* is not a result of the introduction of I but both are indirect results of the loss of inflectional morphology.

We have now traced the connections among the major syntactic innovations of the second half of the fourteenth century and shown how they follow from the loss of morphological licensing. There remains one syntactic change which has been connected to this complex, but which I suspect does not really belong there. This is the loss of V2 after fronted constituents other than those governed by an operator such as *wh*, *neg*, or *so*, a change which Hulk & van Kemenade connect to the rise of obligatory subjects.

For purposes of the discussion, I will assume the analysis of OE fronting processes in Kiparsky (1996) (section 3.3). According to this analysis, the specifier of CP is a Focus position, obligatorily followed by the finite verb in C. It hosts not only *wh*-phrases, *neg*-phrases and certain demonstratives, as in Modern English, but also other Focussed (contrastive or emphatic) elements. Topicalized constituents, on the other hand, are adjoined to the highest projection, where they can be followed by a focussed element in Spec,CP, or (if the highest projection is not CP) by the subject, preceding the finite verb.[29] As in Modern English, NPs regularly leave a resumptive pronoun in such cases, while adverbs and PPs do not (this being the only difference between 'Left Dislocation' and Topicalization proper).

What this means is that Topicalization is essentially the same process today as it was in OE. It is Focussing that has changed, by the imposition of a constraint requiring elements in Spec,CP to be licensed by an overt operator (*wh*, *neg*, *so*). Constituents not so licensed, such as ordinary PPs and NPs, are not eligible to move to the Focus position in Spec,CP, though they can be base-generated in the adjunction position (i.e. Topicalization and Left Dislocation, respectively). Since V2 is triggered by Focussing to Spec,CP but not by adjunction, the effect of this change is that V2 becomes restricted to overt operator contexts such as *wh*-questions.

In the theory proposed in the present chapter, this limitation of V2 to operator contexts cannot have a direct causal connection to the rise of obligatory subjects or to the loss of morphological case. The reason is that movement to Ā-positions, Spec,CP included, is not constrained by licensing requirements. It can take place as freely in languages with positional licensing as in languages with morphological licensing. The empirical point is clear from the continental Scandinavian languages, among others. They have lost both case and agreement, yet maintain fully general V2, with movement to Spec,CP of both Focussed and Topicalized constituents. How then could the loss of case and agreement have caused the radical curtailment of the same V2 system in English?

The chronology of the change points in the same direction. According to Allen (1995:417), preposing of dative (Recipient) objects becomes rare in the thirteenth century, and ceases entirely by the middle of the fourteenth century. On the other hand, preposing of accusative objects persists into the sixteenth century, too long after positional licensing becomes mandatory for a simple causal connection to be plausible.[30] Thus the curtailment of the V2 system may not really belong in the transitional period under discussion. For these reasons I will assume that it is a separate historical change.

8 Conclusion

A group of changes in English clause structure which occur together around 1375 are consequences of a single syntactic shift, by which structural position became the only bearer of licensing features. I analysed these changes in the framework of a theory of case and argument licensing which links the levels of morphology, syntactic structure and Semantic Form. This licensing theory allows us to go beyond the gross typological correlation between free word order and rich inflectional morphology, to the grammatical detail of their interaction. Synchronically, it provides a natural account of non-canonical alignments between case and grammatical function, such as 'quirky subjects' and nominative objects, including such previously unexplained phenomena as the fixed position of quirky subjects in otherwise freely scrambling languages, OE among them. Historically, we have seen that it succeeds in revealing the common theme behind the major syntactic processes that transformed ME into Modern English.

Notes

1. For example, *wh*-movement is of course allowed even in languages with rigid word order. Following Zwart (1993:246) and Neeleman (to appear) I also assume that so-called focus scrambling is a case of Ā-movement. VP-internal scrambling however is meant to be covered by the implicational universal stated in the text.
2. These data were kindly provided by Andreas Ludwig in consultation with other native speakers of Grisons; see also H. Smith (1992, 1993).
3. As far as I know, this generalization was first made explicit by Haider (1993), and it is implicit in a number of earlier works, such as Uszkoreit (1985) and Wechsler (1991).
4. Van Kemenade (1987) suggests that in another dialect, represented by Chaucer, pronouns instead adopted the nominal pattern, presumably through decliticization.
5. Cf. Modern English *I called up the man/*you*, and Shakespeare's *I know not the man/*thee* (vs *I know thee not*).
6. Here Platzack supposes that the reanalysis is mediated by the disappearance of object clitics, which makes subject clitics harder to interpret.
7. The classic reanalysis account of the syntactic change in verbs such as *like* (Jespersen 1927; Lightfoot 1979) actually makes the opposite assumption, that pronouns are not part of the triggering experience. According to this story (which is trenchantly criticized

by Allen 1986a), preposed indirect objects denoting Experiencers in hypothetical sentences like *þam cynge licodon peras* 'the king liked pears' were reanalysed as subjects when inflections were lost, a scenario which presupposes that learners ignored the evidence from pronouns.

8. *For-to* split infinitives are even earlier, but *for* and *to* are probably complementizers (van Gelderen 1993: ch. 4).

9. Van Kemenade (1993: 156) and Warner (1992, 1993) have suggested that *wile* 'will' and perhaps one or two other verbs, such as *sceal* 'shall' (van Kemenade) or *must* (Warner), might already be modals in OE, though both emphasize that the evidence is insufficient to exclude the alternative analysis as main verbs.

10. They surely are IPs in Modern English, but more evidence is needed before we can conclude that they are IPs when they come into the language in late ME. For example, they might start out as VPs, which is what Haider (1993) argues they are in German. Split infinitives in the accusative and infinitive construction would be good evidence of IP status.

11. Moreover, the putatively extraposed clauses might be expected to be islands. This however is a theory-internal argument and not necessarily compelling, as Zwart himself concedes.

12. This still leaves several descriptive options open. If the finite verb does not merge with I in the overt syntax, it must bear inflectional features in the lexicon; it might still move to I at LF. The issues here are complex and their very formulation is highly theory-dependent. For present purposes I will follow Reuland in assuming that V and I merge in the lexicon and constitute a complex category V/I in the overt syntax. Zwart instead posits a left-headed IP in Dutch (cf. Kayne 1994), with covert V-to-I movement at LF. Ackema, Neeleman & Weerman do away with I as a syntactic category altogether, and restrict each lexical category to a single functional projection in the syntax (see also Weerman 1989: 81).

13. As to how rich the overt morphology must be to license V-to-I movement, see Holmberg & Platzack (1988), Roberts (1993a), Falk (1993), Rohrbacher (1994a). According to Roberts, singular and plural must be overtly marked. According to Rohrbacher, all three persons must be overtly marked. Any of the proposed versions of the generalization would draw the distinction between German and Dutch in the way we intend here, so that, if there were an I in both these languages, we should expect the finite V to move to it in German, and not in Dutch.

14. When there is a preposed PP or locative adverbial, the expletive subject can be missing, under conditions which differ somewhat from language to language and even from one individual to another. See Falk (1993, especially chs. 4 and 9).

15. Although, as Allen is careful to point out, there is not enough data to establish this with full certainty.

16. For example, *Thou knowest yourself* or *You know thyself* were not used during the period when *Thou knowest thyself* competed with *You know yourself*.

17. Of course, empirical generalizations can be proposed within those theories, such as the connection of *pro*-drop or V-to-I movement to rich inflection, but these are not consequences of the theory, but extrinsic conditions added to it.

18. The Semantic Form of nouns and verbs includes in addition a referential argument, which is bound by a functional category (C, I in the case of verbs, D in the case of nouns). The referential argument of a verb, omitted from consideration here, is an event. CAUSE stands for a predicate which denotes, above and beyond simple causation, the direct and continuous participation of the Agent in the event in its scope.

19. Another corollary is that 'quirky case' is not a lexical association of abstract case, but of morphosyntactic case.

20. Here and in what follows I list the θ-roles with the highest role on the left, reversing the order of the λ-notation. This is easier to follow because it makes the θ-role schemata agree with the conventional enumeration as well as with the order of arguments in languages with positional licensing.

21. Such an account should generalize to other related phenomena, which form a family of restrictions on position and on morphological case involving properties such as animacy and humanness in addition to specificity. They are not restricted to subjects: Turkish has, in addition to its unrestricted accusative case, a (+SPECIFIC) accusative licensing position. On the semantics of specificity and on its role in Turkish object licensing, see Enč (1991).
22. For purposes of licensing, the accusative and infinitive and similar constructions will be treated as complex predicates, derived by combining the Semantic Form of the governing verb with the Semantic Form of the complement. Within this entire complex predicate, the accusative has the status of an object, and gets assigned (–HR). The accusative is, however, the subject of the contained complement, in virtue of being the highest θ-role in it which is licensed by structural case. The extent to which the Semantic Form of the embedded complement of a complex predicate is syntactically visible is subject to systematic variation within and across languages.
23. Thanks to Johanna Bárddal for these examples.
24. This is an empirical assumption with some support in morphological theory. Evidence for it can be found in the behaviour of case in languages where nouns and pronouns mark different case distinctions (for example, in ergative languages where nouns mark accusative and pronouns mark ergative case). See Kiparsky (to appear) for discussion.
25. Expressions like *methinks* could be seen as a residue of such a split system where pronouns preserved lexical case after nouns had lost it.
26. There do exist some other licensing asymmetries between pronouns and full NPs in late ME and early Modern English, which might be connected to the fact that only the former bear morphological case (see Allen 1995: 420, 426–30), who however offers a different account of these asymmetries).
27. Allen (1995: ch. 9) proposes the fixing of the order of objects as the cause of the new recipient passive. The present proposal connects these two changes in a slightly different way: both follow from the loss of morphosyntactic case, the first directly, the second as an indirect consequence.
28. In addition, Spec,VP is a restricted licensing position available only for (–SPECIFIC) subjects.
29. Thus OE is not a strict V2 language of the German type, in that not all its main clauses are CPs.
30. On theoretical grounds, there are unlikely to have been θ-role-specific preposing rules or conditions at work. The reason dative objects lose their preposability before accusative objects do is surely connected with the well-known object extraction asymmetries between Themes and Recipients (e.g. in *Which patient did the doctor show the nurse?* many speakers get only the reading where *Which patient* is the Theme, not where it is the Recipient). What seems to be going on is that Recipients under certain poorly understood conditions cannot be Focussed.

18 The chapters by Kiparsky, Roberts and Weerman: an epilogue

Höskuldur Thráinsson

1 Introduction

The chapters by Kiparsky, Roberts and Weerman share certain major goals and they are even concerned with the same or similar facts. At the same time, their approaches, their basic assumptions and even their interpretation of certain key facts are quite different. For this reason a comparison of these chapters sheds interesting light on the current situation in theoretical syntax in general and historical syntax in particular.

The purpose of this epilogue is to help the reader enjoy, evaluate and learn from the chapters discussed rather than, say, try to list some empirical problems that each chapter may have, or comment on all aspects of the analyses. I think it is more interesting to try to use these chapters to try to evaluate where we stand, in what respects we have made real progress in diachronic syntax by adopting methods and principles of modern theoretical syntax, and what we could concentrate on to make more progress. With this in mind, this epilogue is organized as follows: section 2 focusses on common properties of the chapters and tries to illustrate the similarities of their goals and how they differ from more traditional approaches to diachronic syntax; section 3 brings out some of the main differences in the approaches selected by the authors and the claims they make; section 4 contains some suggestions about the nature of the differences, suggests alternative accounts and points out a few remaining problems; section 5 is the conclusion.

2 Some common properties of the chapters

2.1 Taking overt morphology seriously

One quite obvious property that all the chapters under discussion have in common is that they want to take seriously the evidence offered by overt morphology and make the most of it. This is of course by no means a novel idea, since traditional studies in historical syntax pay close attention to morphological distinctions and their fate in the course of history. It seems also almost self-evident that this is what one must do when working on issues in the diachronic syntax of Germanic and Romance, which is what these authors concentrate on, since very obvious morphological changes have occurred in the history of these languages and they seem to coincide roughly with important syntactic changes. But while traditional approaches to syntax tended to read too much into overt morphological distinctions, assuming, for instance, that the overt case marking of arguments was the safest clue to their syntactic or grammatical role, some modern approaches to theoretical syntax have had relatively little to say about overt morphology and have concentrated on structural relations that are not always manifested overtly. Hence one could claim that it is not immediately obvious how to relate morphological and syntactic changes under such approaches. While that is undeniably true, it must also be kept in mind that it has never been obvious how to do this. Thus traditional approaches to diachronic syntax do not as a rule have very illuminating things to say about the relationship between morphological and syntactic change because their concept of syntactic structure is usually quite underdeveloped.

With this in mind, one could say that the authors of the chapters under discussion are trying to get the best of both worlds — the overt morphological world that traditional grammars have described, tabulated and classified, and the partially covert world of intricate syntactic relations that modern syntactic theory has discovered. Thus, the common positive aspects of these chapters can be summarized as follows: the authors are looking for generalizations and genuine explanations by trying to tie syntactic and morphological change together, explaining why certain changes take place at the same time. Kiparsky and Roberts, for instance, look for ways to account for the fact that changes in the VP seem to roughly cooccur with changes in the IP in the history of English. Similarly, Kiparsky, Roberts and Weerman all want to relate changes in overt case morphology to changes in the distribution of objects in the history of various Germanic languages. Common to all the chapters is that they try to explain syntactic changes by reference to concomitant morphological changes. At the same time, they recognize that overt morphology cannot tell the whole story and some of the observed developments can only be explained by reference to fairly abstract syntactic structures and general syntactic principles discovered by recent research in theoretical syntax. In this respect the chapters differ from traditional accounts of syntactic changes. But while this approach seems to be the right way to go, it becomes clear from reading these chapters that the road signs can be interpreted in different ways. The conclusion that somebody must be going the wrong way seems unavoidable. The following section illustrates this.

3 Some differences between the chapters

In this section I will first point out some areas where the chapters make theoretically incompatible assumptions which make it difficult to add up the results that the authors maintain they have obtained. Then I will focus on functional categories and show how different ideas about their nature lead to incompatible claims about the nature of some syntactic changes in the history of English.

3.1 Theoretical incompatibility of the analyses

First, note that the authors assume partially different frameworks. That does not necessarily mean that the theoretical assumptions they make will be incompatible. Kiparsky, for instance, assumes the framework he has been developing for some time, partially in cooperation with Manfred Bierwisch. While this framework assumes a close connection between syntactic argument structure and lexical semantics and proposes a separate level of Semantic Form (the level at which conceptual knowledge is expressed in linguistic terms) not assumed in, say, standard GB-type work (in the spirit of Chomsky 1981) or the Minimalist Programme (see, e.g., Chomsky 1993a), it is not entirely clear to what extent Kiparsky's approach would be incompatible with GB-type work or Minimalist work since very few GB and minimalist chapters are explicit about the role and nature of argument structure and the relationship between the conceptual system and syntax. Thus note that Chomsky (1993: 2) assumes, for instance, that LF provides 'instructions' for the conceptual–intentional system as to how to relate the relevant linguistic expression to 'the world' as it were, but admits that the 'status and character' of this interface level has been controversial. Thus it is unclear to what extent insights of work like Kiparsky's on the relationship between syntax and semantics (or for that matter work by Jackendoff 1983 and Bierwisch 1983, for instance, cited by Kiparsky) can be integrated into a Minimalist approach of the type assumed in Roberts' chapter.

Among clearer cases of incompatibility one could mention the fact that Weerman's account crucially relies on the GB notion of government, which has no formal status in a Minimalist Programme of the sort assumed by Roberts (see, e.g., Chomsky 1993a: 10). One could even go as far as claiming that the ever-multiplying definitions of government and its subvarieties in the GB literature were among the main reasons for the 'fresh start' that Chomsky wanted to make by getting rid of the increasingly heavy baggage of intricate machinery assumed in the GB literature and starting from scratch, as it were, with minimal assumptions in the Minimalist Programme. At the same time it is clear that government-based notions like the ECP have done a lot of useful work in GB type research so there must be something right about them. Hence one has to be careful not to throw the baby out with the bathwater here. But if the water is getting too dirty, it must be replaced.

Furthermore, it should be noted here that Kiparsky bases his account on the common assumption that headedness of lexical categories like VP can vary parametrically.[1] Thus he assumes that VP was right-headed in earlier stages of English. Roberts, on the other hand, is trying to account for syntactic changes in English by assuming uniformly left-headed projections, following the model suggested by Kayne (1994) where directionality plays no role in underlying structures. Hence there is a certain incompatibility between the models assumed by Kiparsky and Roberts. In addition, Weerman suggests that the ECP may be 'sensitive to direction'. While the syntactic status of such sensitivity to 'directionality' in that sense is unclear, he points out that it may indicate that the ECP has a 'PF character', referring to work by Aoun *et al.* (1987) in that connection without explaining this statement further. It is well known, of course, that phenomena having to do with word order frequently have phonological or phonetic properties. This is especially well known in the case of certain types of clitics, but it has also been suggested that the V2 phenomenon in Germanic is a phonological constraint (see most recently Chomsky 1995: 368). It should be noted, however, that one need not necessarily assume that when it is difficult to make sense of certain aspects of a particular syntactic account the reason is that there is a phonological aspect to it. That may very well be true, of course, but the other possibility is that there is something syntactically wrong with the syntactic account. In the case at hand, it remains to be seen how well this aspect of Weerman's analysis will age. We will return to some related questions in section 4 below.

3.2 Role and nature of functional categories

The most interesting case of incompatibility is to my mind the difference in treatment of functional categories by Kiparsky and Roberts. The reason this difference is of particular interest is that it illuminates a fundamental weakness in modern syntactic theory: hypotheses about functional categories are much too unconstrained. This can be seen very clearly when we consider the following difference between Kiparsky's and Roberts' approaches to the development of functional structure in the history of English.

According to Kiparsky, one of the most important syntactic changes in fourteenth-century English was 'the change to obligatory I'. He maintains that certain syntactic facts in Old English (OE) suggest that it did not have 'an obligatory Spec,IP position'. But when morphological case was lost, arguments could no longer be morphologically licensed. One of the consequences was that subjects had to be assigned a positional nominative and thus had to move to Spec,IP. This in turn meant that I (the head of IP) was 'obligatorily filled, with the consequence that verb-final clauses disappear'. Later, however, '[l]oss of the licensing function of inflection triggers the loss of the movement of finite verbs to I' with the well-kown consequence that in Modern English (ModE) 'verb fronting is restricted to auxiliaries and modals'.

Now it is clear that Kiparsky wants to capture the apparent relation between verb morphology and verb movement, just like Roberts. As the reader will recall, Roberts based his account on his principle (36a), repeated here as (1) for convenience:

(1) If a head H has the relevant L-morphology, then H has strong L-features.

Roberts intends this principle to relate rich agreement morphology on verbs and overt verb movement to I, which is something Kiparsky also wants to capture. But since OE obviously had rich verbal agreement, it is not clear how to reconcile this with Kiparsky's claim that OE did not have an obligatory I. This raises the more general question of the nature of functional projections and their relationship to morphology. We will return to that question in section 4 below. But note that in the strict lexicalist framework standardly assumed in Minimalist work, it is not clear what it means for a functional head to '[have] the relevant L-morphology'. If lexical elements emerge from the lexicon fully inflected, then it must be spelled out in some detail what it means for functional heads to 'have' the morphology.

Another interesting difference is the following: Roberts wants to relate overt movement of objects (scrambling or object shift) to rich case morphology. His principle in (1) is meant to relate movement for case checking (or assignment) purposes to rich case morphology. In his system, therefore, objects will move overtly for case checking if they have rich case morphology. In Kiparsky's system, on the other hand, arguments have to move to get 'positional case' if they do *not* have rich case morphology which can license them '*in situ*'. In this respect, Weerman's account is more like Kiparsky's in nature, although Weerman states that he wants to eliminate Case Theory.

Without going into further details, therefore, we can conclude that despite interesting similarities in spirit and goals, there are considerable and to some extent irreconcilable differences between the chapters. The following section of this epilogue is devoted to this state of affairs.

4 Suggestions, solutions and problems

4.1 A reason for the differences

I believe that the main reason for the differences between the chapters under discussion is that the theory on morphosyntax is underdeveloped. Morphosyntactic theory is too unconstrained, we do not really know how to begin to explain the relation and interaction between morphology and syntax. Hence we have a situation where one linguist can argue that the loss of case morphology will force arguments to move to a specifier position of a functional projection (Kiparsky on subjects) and another can argue that the loss of case morphology will stop arguments from moving to a specifier position of a functional projection (Roberts on objects).

4.2 A more restrictive theory of functional categories

The way morphosyntactic questions are framed in much of syntactic theory today, one can argue that the basic problem is a lack of a constrained theory about functional categories. We tend to propose new functional categories when we need additional positions in the syntax to account for word order facts. We give these functional categories names which suggest that they have something to do with morphology, such as Inflectional Phrase (IP) or Agreement Phrase (for subjects — Agr_SP) or Tense Phrase (TP) and so on. Thus a partial clause structure along the lines of (2) is frequently assumed in recent syntactic work, following initial suggestions by Pollock (1989), Chomsky (1991), Belletti (1990) and others. It is in fact similar to the structure assumed by Roberts in the chapter we have been discussing:

(2)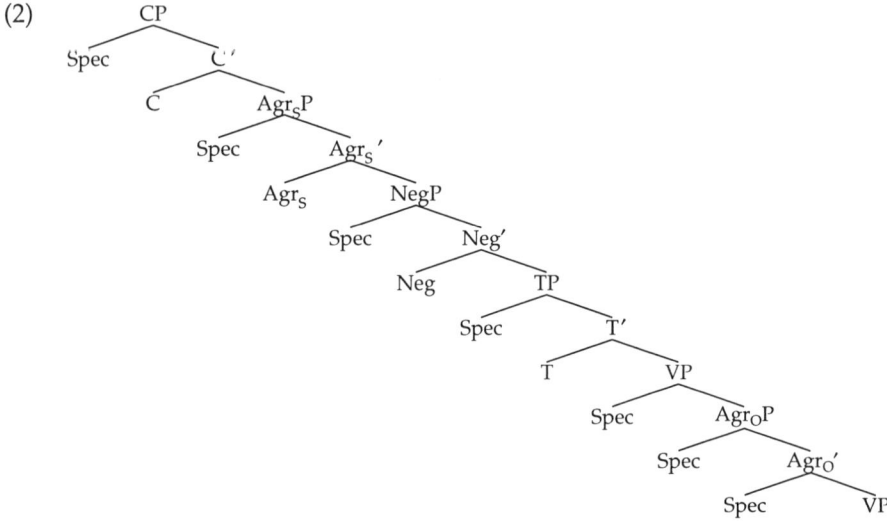

We claim further that arguments need to stand in a special relationship to some of these functional categories, if not overtly then at least covertly. When they do not, expletive elements can step in and fill their place, if not overtly then at least covertly. But the real danger is that without a restrictive theory about functional projections (and expletive elements) our claims will be vacuous and there will be nothing to stop us from making completely opposite claims on the basis of similar kinds of data (or even the same data). With this in mind, I would like to outline an account which is more restrictive than most theories of functional categories. It is also similar in spirit to the chapters under discussion, but at the same time it rules out some of the analyses suggested in these chapters. In addition, it suggests that it is possible to make some sense of the mysterious but elusive relationship between verbal inflection and verb movement.

Suppose we take seriously the suggestion that IP has something to do with verbal inflection. Then the question arises to what extent the structure of IP will reflect crosslinguistic differences in verbal inflection. One possibility that suggests itself is that Agr$_S$P and TP may be separate projections in some languages but not others since it is well known that only some languages have separate inflectional morphemes to indicate agreement and tense. Thus there are no verb forms in ModE, for instance, where an overt agreement marker exists in addition to a tense marker. Such a separation of agreement and tense markers is easily demonstrable for Modern Icelandic, on the other hand. This is illustrated in (3) (cf. Thráinsson 1996; Bobaljik 1995a, b; Bobaljik & Thráinsson, in prep., and references cited there):

(3)
	Icelandic		English	
	present	*past*	*present*	*past*
SG 1	reyk-i	reyk-t-i	smoke	smoke-d
SG 2	reyk-ir	reyk-t-ir	smoke	smoke-d
SG 3	reyk-ir	reyk-t-i	smoke-s	smoke-d
PL 1	reykj-um	reyk-t-um	smoke	smoke-d
PL 2	reyk-ið	reyk-t-uð	smoke	smoke-d
PL 3	reykj-a	reyk-t-u	smoke	smoke-d
	smoke-AGR	smoke-T-AGR	smoke-AGR	smoke-T

Obviously, OE was more like Modern Icelandic than ModE in this respect, but the ageement morphology changed during the Middle English (ME) period. This is illustrated in (4) (based on Quirk & Wrenn 1957: 43; Pyles & Algeo 1993: 160–1):

(4)
	Old English:		Middle English (Midland dialects):	
	present	*past*	*present*	*past*
SG 1	dēm-e	dēm-d-e	thank-e	thanke-d(-e)
SG 2	dēm-st	dēm-d-est	thanke-st	thanke-d-est
SG 3	dēm-ð	dēm-d-e	thank-e	thanke-d(-e)
PL 1,2,3	dēm-að	dēm-d-on	thanke(-n)(-s)	thanke-d(-en)
	'judge'		'thank'	

Now the question is why overt verbal morphology might be related to functional structure of sentences. One way of explaining that is to assume that Baker's Mirror Principle (1988: 13) is basically correct and that it can be translated into a lexicalist checking theory framework as follows (see Thráinsson, to appear; see also Chomsky 1993: 28): one could say that the morphological features that need to be checked are not associated with the inflected verb form as a whole but rather with the relevant overt inflectional morphemes, when such morphemes are available, namely with *-t-* and *-um* for Icelandic *reyk-t-um* 'smoked' (past, 1pl) and *-d-* and *-est-* for OE *dēm-d-est* 'judged' (past, 2sg), for instance. The morphological features associated with the inflectional morphemes are then checked off in a cyclic fashion, starting from the 'innermost' morpheme (the one closest to the verb stem, in these cases the tense morpheme), as the verb form is adjoined to the relevant functional head. Thus when the verb moves and adjoins to T in a split-IP structure the tense features associated with the tense morpheme are checked off, and when it adjoins to Agr_S the agreement features are checked.

The question is now whether this should be interpreted as a claim to the effect that a language cannot have a 'split IP' (i.e. a separate Agr_S-projection and a separate T-projection) unless it has separate agreement and tense morphemes. That does not seem to be a necessary conclusion. The weaker claim would be that *if* the language has separate agreement and tense morphemes *then* it must have a split IP. This amounts to saying that the child learning the language takes the overt morphological evidence as a clue to the functional syntactic structure (the functional architecture) of the language in question. One can also assume that there may be clear evidence for the 'fusion' of morphological categories in the inflectional morphology of a given language and in such cases the child will assume that the language in question does not have a 'split IP' but rather a fused IP. But in many cases the morphology will be ambiguous and then the child will have to rely on the syntax for clues. The basic idea would be, however, that the language acquirer does not assume separate functional categories unless there is positive evidence for them (morphological and/or syntactic) in the language in question. With respect to the morphological evidence, the possibilities can be summarized as in (5) (see Thráinsson, to appear):

(5)

Tense and agreement morphology	Fused IP	Split IP
fused morphology	necessary	impossible
split morphology	impossible	necessary
ambiguous morphology	possible	possible

The basic idea, then, is that some languages have a 'split IP' but others do not. One of the main syntactic consequences of having a split IP is that an 'extra subject position' is created (see, e.g., the discussion in Jonas & Bobaljik 1993; Jonas 1995; Thráinsson 1996, and references cited there). This extra subject position is argued to be Spec,TP and it is arguably occupied by the subject in transitive expletive constructions as those illustrated in (6):

(6) Það lásu margir málfræðingar aldrei þessa doktorsritgerð
there read many linguists never this doctoral dissertation
'Many linguists never read this doctoral dissertation'

As is well known, transitive expletive constructions are not acceptable in all Germanic languages. The claim is that they are only possible in languages with an extra subject position, namely a split IP.[2]

It is not immediately obvious, however, why having a split IP would correlate with (overt) verb movement out of the VP (to a functional head lower than C) and an unsplit IP would correlate with the lack of such movement. But as originally suggested by Bobaljik (1995b) and further discussed in Bobaljik & Thráinsson (in prep.), it can be argued that there is no motivation for verb movement out of the VP in an IP-VP language because there is arguably a feature-checking relationship between I which takes a VP as its complement and the V of that complement, even when this V is *in situ*. This is so because the features of V percolate up to the VP (maximal projections carry the features of their heads) and VP is the sister of I in such a structure. In a language with a split IP, on the other hand, there will be intervening projections between V in the VP and the heads of T and Agr (see the diagram in (2)). Hence the verb has to raise out of its VP to get into a checking relationship with the relevant functional heads (T and Agr_S) in such languages. Thus it follows that V-movement to an 'inflectional' head (i.e. a functional projection lower than CP) is forced in languages with split IP but unnecessary and hence disallowed for reasons of economy in languages with an unsplit IP.[3]

Now what does this mean in the context of the present chapters and in what sense is this more restrictive than the theories assumed there? If we look at Modern Germanic languages, for instance, there is a rather nice correlation between 'split morphology', evidence for an extra subject position and evidence for overt verb movement (see the discussion in Jonas 1995; Bobaljik 1995a, b; Thráinsson 1996; Bobaljik & Thráinsson, in prep.). With respect to diachronic syntax, then, we must assume that OE did not only have an 'obligatory IP' (contrary to what Kiparsky assumes in his chapter in this volume — and also contrary to van Gelderen 1993) but in fact a 'split IP', namely both an obligatory Agr_SP and an obligatory TP in finite clauses. Hence it is incumbent on me to at least make some suggestions as to where one might look for solutions to the problems which Kiparsky wants to explain by reference to an 'optional IP' in OE vs an 'obligatory IP' in ME (and later) — or explain how they could be interpreted in a different fashion. I will do so in the next subsection.

4.3 Some re-solved problems

First, it is useful to review what kinds of facts motivated Kiparsky's claim that OE only had an optional IP. The evidence includes 'verb-final main clauses, ... dative subjects, ... absence of an obligatory Definiteness Effect, and ... the absence of obligatory expletives'. For reasons of space I will only comment on the arguments that have to do with the definiteness effect and obligatory expletives as these issues form a natural class.

If we first consider the definiteness argument, it has frequently been observed that there is a definiteness restriction on expletive constructions in many (or most) languages: the associate of the expletive (the 'logical subject') cannot be a definite NP. Typical minimal pairs are given in (7):

(7) a. There is a man/*John outside
 b. Es ist ein Junge/*Jens draussen (German)
 c Það er strákur/*Jón úti (Icelandic)

While a number of theories have been put forth to explain this, one can distinguish two basic ways of looking at the problem. One is to argue that this phenomenon has to do with the position of the associate — it occurs in a position which is somehow reserved for indefinites. The other is to suggest that this is related to the role and nature of the expletive itself. More specifically, within a checking framework one could say that the expletive can serve to check certain features and this checking is only compatible with indefinite associates. I shall try to clarify this further.

It is well known that expletive elements do not seem to inflect for case and many of them do not seem to trigger agreement either. This is true of the English *there*, German *es* and Icelandic *það*, for instance. Therefore it seems natural to assume that such expletives neither check case nor agreement in Minimalist terms. But they must check something. One possibility is that they check a feature typically associated with DPs (or definite NPs) — we can call it a D-feature (or even definiteness feature for concreteness). If we assume that Spec,Agr$_S$P needs an element which can check this feature on the Agr$_S$ head, we can say that the insertion of an expletive in Spec,Agr$_S$P is a 'last resort' solution to have this feature checked. This is a solution that is available when the subject is indefinite, i.e. does not have a D-feature to check against the corresponding feature of the Agr$_S$-head. When it is definite, on the other hand, it presumably has the D-feature. Hence it will always be raised to Spec,Agr$_S$P to check its D-feature against the D-feature of the Agr$_S$ head. That rules out the insertion of an expletive in Spec,Agr$_S$P.[4]

Now Kiparsky is not assuming a checking framework but he has to make some assumptions about the role of the expletive. Note also that he is not assuming a split-IP analysis. As a result he has 'fewer subject positions' and cannot distinguish between the role of Spec,Agr$_S$P and Spec,TP with respect to the definiteness effect and the nature of expletive constructions. That may be relevant.

The first part of Kiparsky's argument involves a comparison of Swedish, Dutch, German and OE examples of the following sort:

(8) a. att det arbetar någon/en pojke/*Jan där (Swedish)
  that there works somebody/a boy/Jan there
 b. dat er iemand/een jongen/*Jan werkt (Dutch)
  that there somebody/a boy/Jan works
 c. daß da jemand/ein Junge/Jens arbeitet (German)
  that there somebody/a boy/Jens works
 d. Ond þa æfter þon þe ðær wæron ða halgan lofsangas (OE)
  and then after it that there were the holy praise-songs

Kiparsky's main point is that the definite subject *Jens* is apparently acceptable in the German example in (8c) whereas definite NPs like names are unacceptable in the Swedish and Dutch examples. Since the OE example contains a definite NP, Kiparsky argues that this indicates that OE lacked the definiteness effect and wants to relate this to the lack of (obligatory) IP. Note, however, that the German example does not involve the overt German expletive *es* 'there' at all (the 'there'-expletive does not occur in embedded clauses of this sort in German) but only a locative adverb. This contrasts with the Swedish example and possibly also with the Dutch example. Hence the examples are not entirely comparable if the definiteness effect has something to do with the inherent nature of the overt expletive, as suggested above. The OE example, on the other hand, appears to contain an overt *there*-expletive, although it is sometimes difficult to distinguish these from a locative 'there'. This is somewhat surprising, however, since it is usually assumed that OE did not have an expletive *there* at all (see, e.g., Breivik 1983). It would be interesting to look at more examples to check to what extent the definiteness effect is really absent in OE and to what extent that is related to the absence of an overt expletive.

Kiparsky further points out that OE impersonal passives 'hardly ever have *hit* [i.e. the *it*-expletive] if there is a preposed constituent'. He does not give any examples of such constructions with *hit* and without a preposed constituent, and based on expletive selection in other languages with something similar to the *there/it*-distinction, it is not clear that we would expect the *it*-expletive in those constructions anyway. And if there was no *there*-expletive in OE, it is not surprising that it does not show up when something is preposed. But the question remains, of course, why expletives develop and how that is related to changes in syntactic structure. The development seems to be parallel in many Germanic languages (see, e.g., Falk 1993 and references cited there). Note in particular that it is not directly related to loss of morphological case distinctions in all instances since Old Icelandic did not have overt expletives but Modern Icelandic does, despite the fact that the case system has not changed (see, e.g., Rögnvaldsson 1992, 1995). Kiparsky's account of morphological vs positional licensing does not rule out such a development but it calls for an explanation. Such a call takes us to the subsection listing a few remaining and intriguing problems.

4.4 Some remaining problems

This subsection mentions a couple of remaining problems as food for thought, in case the reader is beginning to feel that there is nothing left to do in diachronic syntax. These are not only problems that remain under the analyses suggested by Kiparsky, Roberts and Weerman but also under most other analyses, as far as I know.

First, given the apparent relationship between rich case morphology and scrambling, it is difficult to understand why Modern Icelandic does not allow scrambling to the extent Old Icelandic seems to have done, despite the fact that case morphology appears to be just as rich in Modern Icelandic as it was in Old Icelandic. Thus it seems to be the case that certain word orders are allowed in, say, German and Old Icelandic but not in Modern Icelandic. This is illustrated below.

First, consider the following examples from Modern German and Modern Icelandic:

(9) a. ... daß du ihr den Hut geben wirst (German)
 that you her(DAT) the hat(ACC) give will
 '... that you will give her the hat'
 b. *... að þú munt henni gefa hattinn (Icelandic)
 that you will her(DAT) give hat-the(ACC)
 c. ... daß er das Buch dem Kind gegeben hat (German)
 that he the book the child given has
 '... that he has given the book to the child'
 d. *... að hann hefur bókina gefið barninu (Icelandic)
 that he has book-the(ACC) given child-the(DAT)

If we abstract away from the position of the finite verb, the pairs (9a, b) and (9c,d) are very similar, but the German versions are good and the Icelandic ones bad. In addition, it can be shown that sentences corresponding to (9b, d) occur in Old Icelandic. Thus the examples in (10) are actually attested in the Icelandic sagas (cf. Rögnvaldsson 1992, 1995):

(10) a. ... og muntu henni gefa moturinn (*Laxdæla saga*, p. 1602)
 and will-you her(DAT) give cap-the(ACC)
 b. ... að hann hefir líf gefið barninu
 that he has life(ACC) given child-the(DAT)
 (*Harðar saga og Hólmverja*, p. 1259)

While it is not clear how Roberts or Weerman would even try to express this, Kiparsky can give an account by saying that although Modern Icelandic is a language with rich case morphology it has to rely on 'positional licensing' (at least to some extent) while Old Icelandic apparently did not. But why this change has taken place and what it is related to is not so clear.

The second problem I want to point out here is a related one. As the reader will recall, one of Weerman's main arguments is that 'case-marked DPs are to some extent syntactically comparable to PPs'. In German, for instance, case-marked DPs and PPs can scramble. Interestingly, however, there is a clear contrast between case-marked DP-arguments and PP-arguments in Icelandic. Assuming the 'expanded' or 'split IP' structure partially described above and in Roberts' chapter, this contrast can be expressed as in (11):

(11) PPs cannot occur in Spec,Agr$_O$P, case-marked DPs (objects) can, regardless of their morphological case.

Thus if we believe (following Holmberg 1986; vanden Wyngaerd 1989; Déprez 1989 and others) that an object preceding a negation or a sentential adverb has been shifted to Spec,Agr$_O$P, then the minimal pairs in (12)–(13) show this contrast:

(12) a. Ég snerti   ekki bókina
         I   touched not the book
     b. Ég snerti   bókina   ekki
         I   touched the book not
         'I did not touch the book'

(13) a. Ég kom ekki við   bókina
         I   came not with the book
         'I did not touch the book'
     b. *Ég kom við   bókina ekki
          I   came with the book not
     c. *Ég kom bókina   ekki við
          I   came the book not with

This indicates that Weerman may not be able to completely do away with case assignment or case checking, as the explanation that immediately suggests itself here is that this difference has something to do with case checking (or assignment). Note also that it does not matter which morphological case the object has. In the example in (12) we have an accusative object, but a dative, genitive or even nominative object would have worked just as well, as illustrated in (14)–(16):

(14) a. Ég stal   ekki bókinni
         I   stole not the book(DAT)
     b. Ég stal   bókinni ekki
         I   stole the book not
         'I did not steal the book'

(15) a. Ég sakna ekki þessarar stelpu
         I   miss not this   girl(GEN)
     b. Ég sakna þessarar stelpu ekki
         I   miss this   girl   not
         'I do not miss this girl'

(16) a. Mér líkar ekki þessi bíll
         me likes not this car(NOM)
     b. Mér líkar þessi bíll ekki
         me likes this car not
         'I do not like this car'

Thus even the lexically assigned (or irregular or quirky) cases do not prevent objects from shifting just as if they carried the more structurally determined(?) accusative.

5 Conclusion

The main purpose of this epilogue to the chapters by Kiparsky, Roberts and Weerman was to show the following.

(17) a. That the chapters share similar goals and the general approach is similar: use morphological evidence but also make use of intricate syntactic structures and principles.
   b. That the chapters differ in their assumptions and this sometimes leads to different interpretations of the same or similar facts.
   c. That we need a more restrictive syntactic theory, especially a more restrictive and explicit theory about the nature of functional categories and how they relate to morphology, and about the role of expletives.
   d. That various interesting and intriguing problems have been turned up by recent syntactic research, both synchronic and diachronic, and that includes problems raised in the present chapters.

All the chapters make interesting contributions to diachronic syntax and they all suggest further research to the reader, sometimes by being explicit and making testable predictions, sometimes by not being as explicit as one would like and thus challenging the reader to come up with a more explicit and more restrictive account. All of this, both the positive and negative results, will lead to more progress in the field of diachronic syntax. It has certainly become a really interesting field in its own right in the past decades, both as a field where linguists can make new empirical discoveries and as a field where they can continue to test their theoretical hypotheses. Such work must go hand in hand — and it does in the chapters under discussion.

Notes

1. He wants to maintain, however, that functional categories are always left-headed, thus limiting crosslinguistic variation, although some readers may wonder what to do with languages like Japanese or Turkish, for instance. But with the increase in literature trying to explain apparent right-headedness away, such readers will have enough reading material the next couple of years, even though some of it may also argue against the existence of right-headed VPs.
2. For a somewhat different account see Jonas (1995), who assumes that all Germanic langages have a split IP but Spec,TP is only available in those languages that have overt V-to-T movement. A different proposal is made in Chomsky (1995), who argues that the extra subject position is found in those languages which allow multiple specifiers of TP.
3. This is obviously a very schematic discussion of a complex issue. As the references indicate, the basic idea outlined here as to how to capture the relationship between a split IP and forced V-movement was originally proposed by Bobaljik (1995b) and it turned out to be very compatible to ideas presented in Thráinsson (to appear). Hence Bobaljik & Thráinsson (in prep).
4. See also Jonas (1995) for a similar line of argument.

Sources

Old Icelandic examples are taken from *Íslendinga sögur*, edited by Bragi Halldórsson, Jón Torfason, Sverrir Tómasson and Örnólfur Thorsson and published by Svart á hvítu, Reykjavík, 1985–1986. As the reader may have noted, they found their way into this epilogue via Eiríkur Rögnvaldsson's work.

References

Abeillé, A. & D. Godard. 1994a. 'The Complementation of Tense Auxiliaries in French.' *Proceedings of WCCFL* 13.
Abeillé, A. & D. Godard. 1994b. 'The Complementation of French Auxiliaries.' Ms., UFRL & CNRS, Université de Paris 7.
Abney, S. 1986. 'Functional Elements and Licensing.' Ms., MIT.
Abney, S. 1987. 'The English Noun Phrase in its Sentential Aspect.' Doctoral dissertation, MIT.
Abraham, W. 1988. 'Ergative Subjekte, die Partitivlösung und die DP/NP-Frage.' - *Groninger Arbeiten zur Germanistischen Linguistik* 29: 161–89.
Abraham, W. 1990. 'A Note on the Aspect–syntax Interface.' In J. Mascaró & M. Nespor eds., *Progress in Linguistics*, 1–12. Dordrecht.
Abraham, W. 1991a. 'Aktionsartsemantik und Auxiliarisierung im Deutschen.' In E. Feldbusch, R. Pogarell & C. Weiß eds., *Neue Fragen der Linguistik. Linguistische Arbeiten 270*, vol. 1: 125–33. Tübingen: Niemeyer.
Abraham, W. 1991b. 'Syntaktische und Semantische Korrelate von Modalverben.' In K. H. Klein, F. Pouradier Duteil & K. H. Wagner eds., *Betriebslinguistik und Linguistikbetrieb. Linguistische Arbeiten 261*, vol. 2: 1–13. Tübingen: Niemeyer.
Abraham, W. 1992a. 'The Emergence of the Periphrastic Passive in Gothic.' *Leuvense Bijdragen* 81: 1–3, 1–15.
Abraham, W. 1992b. 'Clausal Focus versus Discourse Rhema in German: a Programmatic View.' In D. Gilbers & S. Looyenga eds., *Language and Cognition. Yearbook University of Groningen 1992*, 1–18. Groningen.
Abraham, W. 1993a. 'The Focus Interface Hypothesis and the Historical Decay of the Verbal Genitive in German.' In A. de Boer *et al.* eds., *Language and Cognition III. Yearbook of the Research Group for Linguistic Theory and Knowledge Representation of the University of Groningen*, 1–10. Groningen.
Abraham, W. 1993b. 'Ergativa sind Terminativa.' *Groninger Arbeiten zur germanistischen Linguistik* 36: 103–23.
Abraham, W. 1993c. 'Null Subjects in the History of German: from IP to CP.' In A. van Kemenade & A. Hulk eds., *Null Subjects in Diachrony*. Special issue of *Lingua* 89: 2/3: 117–42.
Abraham, W. 1994. 'Ergativa sind Terminativa.' *Zeitschrift für Sprachwissenschaft* 12/2 (1993): 157–84.

Abraham, W. 1995a. *Deutsche Syntax im Sprachenvergleich. Grundlegung einer Typologischen Syntax des Deutschen*. Tübingen: Niemeyer. [Studien zur deutschen Grammatik 41].

Abraham, W. 1995b. 'Case Assignment without Functional Categories in Modern German.' In A. Wiegel *et al.* eds., *Yearbook Linguistics in Groningen 1995*. Groningen.

Ackema, P., A. Neeleman & F. Weerman 1993. 'Deriving Functional Projections.' *NELS* 23: vol. 1.

Adams, J. N. 1994a. 'Wackernagel's Law and the Position of Unstressed Pronouns in Classical Latin.' *Transactions of the Philological Society* 92: 103–78.

Adams, J. N. 1994b. *Wackernagel's Law and the Placement of the Copula* esse *in Classical Latin*. (Supplementary Vol. 18) The Cambridge Philological Society.

Adams, M. P. 1987. 'Old French, Null Subjects, and Verb Second Phenomena.' Doctoral dissertation, UCLA.

Adger, D. 1995a. 'Meaning, Movement and Economy.' *Proceedings of WCCFL 13*.

Adger, D. 1995b. 'Economy and Optionality: Interpretations of Subjects in Italian.' *York Papers in Linguistics* 17, 1–21.

Aebischer, P. 1948. 'Contribution à la proto-histoire des articles *ille* et *ipse* dans les langues romanes.' *Cultura Neolatina* 8: 181–203.

Allen, C. 1977. 'Topics in Diachronic Syntax.' Doctoral dissertation, University of Massachusetts, Amherst.

Allen, C. 1986a. 'Reconsidering the History of *like*.' *Journal of Linguistics* 22: 375–409.

Allen, C. 1986b. 'Dummy Subjects and the Verb-second "target" in Old English.' *English Studies* 67: 465–9.

Allen, C. 1992. 'Variation and Syntactic Change: the English "impersonal" Constructions.' Second Diachronic Generative Syntax Workshop, Preprints. Institute for Research in Cognitive Science, University of Pennsylvania.

Allen, C. 1995. *Case Marking and Reanalysis*. Oxford: Clarendon Press.

Alsina, A. 1993. 'A Theory of Complex Predicates: Evidence from Causatives in Bantu and Romance.' Forthcoming in A. Alsing, J. Bresnan & P. Sells eds., *Complex Predicates*. Stanford: CLSI.

Andersen, H. 1973. 'Abductive and Deductive Change.' *Language* 49(4): 765–93.

Anderson, J. 1988. 'The Type of Old English Impersonals.' In J. Anderson & N. Macleod eds., *Edinburgh Studies in the English Language*, vol. 1. Edinburgh: John Donald.

Anderson, S. R. 1988. 'Morphological Change.' In F. Newmeyer ed., *Linguistics: the Cambridge Survey*, 324–62. Cambridge University Press.

Anderson, S. R. 1992. *A-Morphous Morphology*. Cambridge University Press.

Anderson, S. R. 1993. 'Wackernagel's Revenge: Clitics, Morphology, and the Syntax of Second Position.' *Language* 69: 68–98.

Anderson, S. R. & E. Keenan 1985. 'Deixis.' In T. Shopen ed., *Language Typology and Syntactic Description*, 259–308. Cambridge University Press.

Andersson, A. B. & O. Dahl 1974. 'Against the Penthouse Principle.' *Linguistic Inquiry* 5: 451–4.

Andrieu, G., J. Piolle & M. Plouzeau 1974. *Le Roman de Tristan de Béroul. Concordancier Complet des Formes Graphiques Occurrentes*. Aix-en-Provence: Université de Provence.

Andrieu, G., J. Piolle & M. Plouzeau 1978. *Le Roman de la Rose ou de Guillaume de Dole de Jean Renart. Concordancier Complet des Formes Graphiques Occurrentes*. Aix-en-Provence: CREL-France CUERMA.

Aoun, J., N. Hornstein, D. Lightfoot & A. Weinberg 1987. 'Two Types of Locality.' *Linguistic Inquiry* 18: 537–77.

Appel, R., & P. Muysken. 1987. *Language Contact and Bilingualism*. London: Edward Arnold.

Baker, M.C. 1988. *Incorporation. A Theory of Grammatical Function Changing*. The University of Chicago Press.

Baker, M.C. 1991. 'On Some Subject/Object Non-asymmetries in Mohawk.' *Natural Language and Linguistic Theory* 9: 537–76.

Baker, M.C. 1992 'The Polysynthesis Parameter.' Ms., McGill University.

Baldes, H. 1882. *Der Genetiv bei Verbis im Althochdeutschen*. Straßburg.

Barwise, J. & R. Cooper 1981. 'Generalized Quantifiers and Natural Language.' *Linguistics and Philosophy* 4: 159–219.

Battaglia, Salvatore 1961. *Grande Dizionario della Lingua Italiana*. Turin: Unione Tipografico-Editrice Torinese.

Battye, A., & I. Roberts eds. 1995. *Clause Structure and Language Change*. Oxford University Press.

Bayer, J. 1983. 'COMP in Bavarian Syntax.' *The Linguistic Review* 3: 209–74.

Bean, M. 1983. *The Development of Word Order Patterns in Old English*. London: Croom Helm.

Behaghel, O. 1923. *Deutsche Syntax*. Heidelberg.

Behaghel, O. 1924. *Deutsche Syntax*. Heidelberg: Carl Winters Universitätsbuchhandlung.

Behaghel, O. 1932. *Deutsche Syntax. Eine geschichtliche Darstellung*, vol. 4. Heidelberg: Winter.

Belletti, A. 1988. 'The Case of Unaccusatives.' *Linguistic Inquiry* 19: 1–34.

Belletti, A. 1990. *Generalized Verb Movement: Aspects of Verb Syntax*. Turin: Rosenberg & Sellier.

Benincà, P. 1995. 'Complement Clitics in Medieval Romance: the Tobler–Mussafia Law.' In A. Battye & I. Roberts eds., *Clause Structure and Language Change*, 325–44. Oxford & New York: Oxford University Press.

Benincà, P., & G. Cinque 1993. 'Su alcune differenze fra enclisi e proclisi.' In *Omaggio a Gianfranco Folena*, 2313–36. Padua: Editoriale Programma.

Benincà, P., & C. Poletto. 1994. '*Bisogna* and its Companions: the Verbs of Necessity.' In G. Cinque et al. eds., *Paths towards Universal Grammar*, 35–58. Washington D.C: Georgetown University Press.

Bennett, J. A. W., & G. V. Smithers 1966. *Early Middle English Verse and Prose*. Oxford: Clarendon Press.

Bennis, H. 1987. *Gaps and Dummies*. Dordrecht: Foris.

Bennis, H., & T. Hoekstra 1986. 'Gaps and Parasitic Gaps.' *The Linguistic Review* 4: 29–87.

Benveniste, E. 1946. 'Structure des relations de personne dans le verbe.' In E. Benveniste ed., *Problèmes de linguistique générale I*, 225–36. Paris: Gallimard.

Berg, E. v.d. 1986. 'Sur les traces de l'objet au génitif: l'évolution de la construction impersonelle.' *Études Germaniques* 41: 403–17.

Béroul. *The Romance of Tristran*. A. Ewert ed., Vol. I. Oxford: Basil Blackwell, 1939.

Bertinetto, P. 1993. 'Il Verbo.' In L. Renzi & G. Salvi eds., *Grande grammatica di consultazione*. Vol II, 113–61. Bologna: Il Mulino.
Bertrand, R. 1984. *Guillaume de Lorris: le Roman de la Rose. Concordancier complet des formes graphiques occurrentes*. 2 volumes. Aix-en-Provence: Publications CUERMA.
Berwick, R. 1985. *The Acquisition of Syntactic Knowledge*. Cambridge, Mass.: MIT Press.
Besten, H. den 1983. 'On the Interaction of Root Transformations and Lexical Deletive Rules.' In W. Abraham ed., *On the Formal Syntax of the Westgermania*. Amsterdam: John Benjamins, 47–131.
Besten, H. den 1985. 'The Ergative Hypothesis and Free Word Order in Dutch.' Ms., University of Amsterdam.
Besten, H. den 1989. *Studies in West Germanic Syntax*. Amsterdam: Rodopi.
Besten, H. den, & J. Edmonson 1983. 'The Verbal Complex in Continental West Germanic.' In W. Abraham ed., *On the Formal Syntax of the Westgermania*. Amsterdam: John Benjamins.
Besten, H. den & G. Webelhuth 1990. 'Stranding.' In G. Grewendorf & W. Sternefeld eds., *Scrambling and Barriers*. Amsterdam: John Benjamins.
Beukema, F., & P. Coopmans 1989. 'A Government-Binding Perspective on the Imperative in English.' *Journal of Linguistics* 25: 417–36.
Bierwisch, M. 1983. 'Semantische und Konzeptuelle Repräsentation Lexikalischer Einheiten. In W. Motsch & R. Růzicka eds., *Untersuchungen zur Semantik*, 61–99. Berlin: Akademie-Verlag.
Bierwisch, M. 1986. 'On the Nature of Semantic Form in Natural Language.' In F. Klix & H. Hangendorf eds., *Human Memory and Cognitive Capabilities*, Part B: 765–783. Amsterdam: Elsevier (North-Holland).
Bierwisch, M., & R. Schreuder 1992. 'From Concepts to Lexical Items.' *Cognition* 42: 23–60.
Birkenmaier, W. 1977. 'Aspekt, Aktionsart und nominale Determination im Russischen.' *Zeitschrift für Slavische Philologie* 39: 398–417.
Birkenmaier, W. 1979. *Artikelfunktionen in einer Artikellosen Sprache. Studien zur Nominalen Determination im Russischen*. Munich. [*Forum Slavicum* 34].
Bittner, M. 1991. 'Case and Scope.' Ms., Rutgers University.
Bittner, M., & K. Hale 1993. 'Ergativity: towards a Theory of a Heterogeneous Class.' Ms., Rutgers University.
Bittner, M., & K. Hale 1996. 'The Structural Determination of Case and Agreement.' *Linguistic Inquiry* 27: 1–69.
Blake, B. 1994. *Case*. Cambridge University Press.
Blasco-Ferrer. E. 1984. *Storia linguistica della Sardegna*. Tübingen: Niemeyer.
Blumenthal, D. Dittmar no date. 'Johann Michael Moscherosch and his Use of Verbs with the Prefix.' Unpublished doctoral dissertation, University of Pennsylvania.
Bobaljik, J. 1995a. 'Morphosyntax: the Syntax of Verbal Inflection.' Doctoral dissertation, MIT.
Bobaljik, J. 1995b. 'Free Agr!' Paper presented at the 11th Comparative Germanic Syntax Workshop, Rutgers University, November 1995.
Bobaljik, J., & D. Jonas 1992. 'Subject Positions and the Role of TP.' Paper presented at the GLOW colloquium, Lund, Sweden.
Bobaljik, J., & D. Jonas 1993. 'Specs for Subjects: the Role of TP in Icelandic.' *MIT Working Papers in Linguistics* 59–98.

Bobaljik, J., & H. Thráinsson in preparation. 'Two Heads Aren't Always Better than One.' Ms., Harvard University, MIT and University of Iceland.
Boccaccio, G. 1370. *Decameron*. Turin: Einaudi.
Borer, H. 1984. *Parametric Syntax*. Dordrecht: Foris.
Bosque, I. 1987. 'Constricciones morfológicas sobre la coordinación.' *Lingüística Española Actual* 9: 83–100.
Bouchard, D. 1983. *On the Content of Empty Categories*. Dordrecht: Foris.
Bowers 1988. 'Extended X-Bar-Theory, the ECP, and the Left Branch Condition.' *Proceedings of the West Coast Conference on Formal Linguistics* 7: 47–62.
Brandi, L., & P. Cordin 1989. 'Two Italian Dialects and the Null Subject Parameter.' In O. Jaeggli & K. Safir eds., *The Null Subject Parameter*, 111–42. Dordrecht: Kluwer.
Braune, W., & W. Mitzka 1963. *Althochdeutsche Grammatik*. Tübingen. 11th edition.
Breivik, L. 1983. *Existential There. A Synchronic and Diachronic Study*. Studia Anglistica Norwegica 2. University of Bergen.
Bresnan, J. 1982. 'Control and Complementation.' *Linguistic Inquiry* 13: 343–434.
Bresnan, J., & J. Kanerva 1989. 'Locative Inversion in Chicheŵa: a Case Study of Factorization in Grammar.' *Linguistic Inquiry* 20(1): 1–50.
Bresnan, J., & L. Moshi 1990. 'Object Asymmetries in Comparative Bantu Syntax.' *Linguistic Inquiry* 21(2): 147–86.
Broekhuis, H. 1992. 'Chain-government.' HIL dissertation 2, Amsterdam. Distributed by Holland Academic Graphics, The Hague.
Browne, W. 1974. 'On the Problem of Enclitic Placement in Serbo-Croatian.' In R. D. Brecht & C. V. Chvany eds., *Slavic Transformational Syntax*, 36–52. Ann Arbor, Mich.: Slavic Publications.
Browne, W. 1975. 'Serbo-Croatian for English-speaking learners.' *Kontrastiva Analizaengleskog i Hrvatskog ili Srpskog Jezika*. Zagreb: Institut za lingvistiku Filosofskog fakulteta.
Bruin, C. de 1970. *Het Luikse Diatesseron*. Leiden: Brill.
Brunhuber, B. 1983. 'Aspekt und Determiniertheit im Russischen.' *Die slawischen Sprachen* 3: 5–13.
Brunner, K. 1938. *Abriß der Mittelenglischen Grammatik*. Halle/Saale: Max Niemeyer.
Brunner, K. 1965. *Altenglische Grammatik*. Tübingen: Max Niemeyer.
Brunot, F. 1924. *Histoire de la langue française des origines à 1900*. Paris: Armand Colin.
Burridge, K. 1993. *Syntactic Change in Germanic: Aspects of Language Change in Germanic; with Particular Reference to Middle Dutch*. Amsterdam: John Benjamins.
Burzio, L. 1986. *Italian Syntax: a Government-Binding Approach*. Dordrecht: Reidel.
Butler, M.Ch. 1980. *Grammatically Motivated Subjects in Early English*. Texas Linguistic Forum 16.
Bybee, J, P. Revere & B. Pagliuca 1994. *The Evolution of Grammar: Tense, Aspect and Modality in the Languages of the World*. The University of Chicago Press.
Canale, M. 1978. 'Word Order Change in Old English: Base Reanalysis in Generative Grammar.' Doctoral dissertation, McGill University.
Cardinaletti, A. 1992. 'On Cliticization in Germanic Languages.' *Rivista di Grammatica Generativa* 17.
Cardinaletti, A. to appear. 'On the Internal Structure of Pronominal DPs.' To appear in *The Linguistic Review*.
Cardinaletti, A., & I. Roberts 1991. 'Clause Structure and X-Second.' To appear in W. Chao & G. Horrocks eds., *Levels of Representation*. Mouton de Gruyter.

Cardinaletti, A., & M. Starke 1994. 'The Typology of Structural Deficiency: On the Three Grammatical Classes.' To appear in van Riemsdijk (forthcoming).
Cavar, D., & Ch. Wilder 1994. 'Long Head Movement? Verb Movement and Cliticization in Croatian.' *Lingua* 93: 1–58.
Changeux, J.-P. 1983. *L'Homme neuronal*. Fayard.
Chao, W. 1980. 'PRO-drop languages and non-obligatory control.' *University of Massachusetts Occasional Papers in Linguistics* 10.
Chatterjee, R. 1988. *Aspect and Meaning in Slavic and Indic*. [Current Issues in Linguistic Theory 51.] Amsterdam: John Benjamins.
Chenery, W. H. 1905. 'Object Pronouns in Dependent Clauses: a Study of Old Spanish Word Order.' *PMLA* 20: 1–151.
Chesterman, A. 1991. *On Definiteness. A Study with Special Reference to English and Finnish*. Cambridge University Press.
Chomsky, N. 1975. *The Logical Structure of Linguistic Theory*. New York: Plenum.
Chomsky, N. 1977. *Essays on Form and Interpretation*. Amsterdam: Elsevier (North Holland).
Chomsky, N. 1981. *Lectures on Government and Binding*. Dordrecht: Foris.
Chomsky, N. 1982. *Some Concepts and Consequences of the Theory of Government and Binding*. Cambridge, Mass.: MIT Press.
Chomsky, N. 1986a. *Barriers*. Cambridge, Mass.: MIT Press.
Chomsky, N. 1986b. *Knowledge of Language: its Nature, Origins and Use*. New York: Praeger.
Chomsky, N. 1988. 'Some Notes on Economy of Representation.' Unpublished ms., MIT.
Chomsky, N. 1991. 'Some Notes on Economy of Derivation and Representation.' In R. Freidin ed., *Principles and Parameters in Comparative Grammar*, 417–54. Cambridge, Mass.: MIT Press. [Originally published in *MITWPL* 10: 43–74. Cambridge. Mass.: MIT Press, 1989.].
Chomsky, N. 1993a. 'A Minimalist Program for Linguistic Theory.' In K. Hale & S. J. Keyser eds., *The View From Building 20*, 1–52. Cambridge, Mass.: MIT Press.
Chomsky, N. 1993b. *Language and Thought*. London: Moyer Bell, Wakefield.
Chomsky, N. 1994. 'Bare Phrase Structure.' In G. Webelhuth ed., *Government and Binding Theory and the Minimalist Program*, 383–440. Oxford: Blackwell.
Chomsky, N. 1995. *The Minimalist Program*. Cambridge, Mass.: MIT Press.
Chomsky, N., & H. Lasnik 1993. 'Principles and Parameters Theory.' In J. Jacobs, A. von Stechow, W. Sternefeld & T. Vennemann eds., *Syntax: an International Handbook of Contemporary Research*, 506–69. Berlin: Walter de Gruyter.
Chrétien de Troyes. *Le Conte du Graal (Perceval)*. F. Lecoy ed., vol. V of *Les Romans de Chrétien de Troyes*. Paris: Honoré Champion, 1972.
Chrétien de Troyes. *Erec et Enide*. M. Roques ed., vol. I of *Les Romans de Chrétien de Troyes*. Paris: Honoré Champion, 1981.
Chrétien de Troyes. *Le Chevalier au Lion (Yvain)*. M. Roques ed., vol. IV of *Les Romans de Chrétien de Troyes*. Paris: Honoré Champion, 1960.
Chrétien de Troyes. *Cligès*. A. Micha ed., vol. II of *Les Romans de Chrétien de Troyes*. Paris: Honoré Champion, 1982.
Chrétien de Troyes. *Le Chevalier de la Charrette*. M. Roques ed., vol. III of *Les Romans de Chrétien de Troyes*. Paris: Honoré Champion, 1958.
Chrétien de Troyes. *Le Roman de Perceval ou le Conte du Graal*. W. Roach ed., Geneva: Droz, 1959.

Chung, S. 1978. *Case Marking and Grammatical Relations in Polynesian*. University of Texas Press.
Cinque, G. 1990. *Types of A'-dependencies*. Cambridge, Mass.: MIT Press.
Cinque, G. 1993a. 'A Null Theory of Phrase and Compound Stress.' *Linguistic Inquiry* 24/2: 239–98.
Cinque, G. 1993b. 'On the Evidence for Partial N-movement in Romance NP.' Ms., University of Venice.
Cinque, G. 1995. 'Adverbs and the Universal Hierarchy of Functional Projections.' *Glow Newsletter* 14–15.
Clahsen, H., S. Eissenbeiss & A. Vainikka 1994. 'The Seeds of Structure.' In T. Hoekstra & B.D. Schwartz eds., *Language Acquisition Studies in Generative Grammar*, 85–118. Amsterdam: John Benjamins.
Clahsen, H., & P. Muysken 1986. 'The Availability of Universal Grammar to Adult & Child Learners — A Study of the Acquisition of German Word Order.' *Second Language Research* 2: 91–119.
Clahsen, H.-D., & K.-D. Smolka 1986. 'Psycholinguistic Evidence and the Description of V2 in German.' In Haider & Prinzhorn eds., *Verb Second Phenomena in Germanic Languages*. Dordrecht: Foris.
Clark, R. 1989. 'Causality and Parameter Setting.' *Behavioral and Brain Sciences* 12: 2.
Clark, R., & I. Roberts 1993. 'A Computational Approach to Language Learnability and Language Change.' *Linguistic Inquiry* 24: 299–345.
Clark, R., & I. Roberts in progress. 'Complexity and Language Change.' Ms., University of Pennsylvania/University of Wales.
Collins, C., & H. Thráinsson 1993. 'Double Object Constructions and the Theory of Case.' *MIT Working Papers in Linguistics* 19.
Collins, C., & H. Thráinsson, to appear. 'VP-Internal Structure and Object Shift in Icelandic.' To appear in *Linguistic Inquiry* 27: 3.
Collodi C. 1883. *Fiabe e Racconti. I Racconti delle Fate, le Avventure di Pinocchio, Storie Allegre*. Rome: Newton, 1992.
Comrie, B., & S. Thompson 1985. 'Lexical Nominalization.' In T. Shopen ed., *Language Typology and Syntactic Description*, Vol. III: 309–98. Cambridge University Press.
Corver, N., & H. van Riemsdijk eds. 1994. *Studies on Scrambling*. Berlin: Mouton de Gruyter.
Culicover, P.W. 1991. 'Topicalization, Inversion, and Complementizers in English.' In D. Delfitto, M. Everaert, A. Evers & F. Stuurman eds., *Going Romance and Beyond*. OTS Working Papers, University of Utrecht.
Czepluch, H. 1988. 'Kasusmorphologie und Kasusrelationen: Überlegungen zur Kasustheorie am Beispiel des Deutschen.' *Linguistische Berichte* 116: 275–310.
Dahlstedt, A. 1903. *The Word-Order of the Ancren Riwle*. Sundsvall: Sahlin.
Dalrymple, M., S. Shieber & F. Pereira 1991. 'Ellipsis and Higher-order Unification.' *Linguistics and Philosophy* 14(4): 399–452.
Damen, M. 1994. 'De Historische Ontwikkeling van Genitief Objecten.' MA thesis, Utrecht University.
Darby, H.C. 1936. 'The Economic Geography of England, AD 1000–1250.' In H.C. Darby ed., *An Historical Geography of England Before AD 1800*. Cambridge University Press.
Darwin, C. 1859. *On the Origin of Species*. London: John Murray.
De Dardel, R. 1993. 'Review of Harris & Vincent 1988.' *Vox Romanica*.

Dees, A. 1971. *Études sur l'évolution des démonstratifs en ancien et en moyen français.* Groningen: Wolters-Noordhoff.
Delbrück, B. 1904. *Synkretismus. Ein Beitrag zur Germanischen Kasuslehre.* Strasbourg: Karl Trübner Verlag.
Denison, D. 1990a. 'The Old English Impersonals revived.' In S. Adamson et al. eds., *Papers from the Fifth International Conference on English Historical Linguistics,* 111–41. Amsterdam: John Benjamins.
Denison, D. 1990b. 'Auxiliary + Impersonal in Old English.' In *Folia Linguistica Historica* 9.1: 139–66.
Denison, D. 1993. *English Historical Syntax.* London: Longmans.
Denison, N. 1957. *The Partitive in Finnish.* Helsinki. [*Actes Academiae Scientiarum Fennicae,* Ser. B 108].
Déprez, V. 1989. "On the Typology of Syntactic Projections and the Nature of Chains: Move α to the Specifier of Functional Projections." Doctoral dissertation, MIT.
Déprez, V. 1994. 'Parameters of Object Movement.' In N. Corver & H. van Riemsdijk eds., *Scrambling,* 101–52. Berlin: Mouton de Gruyter.
Diesing, M. 1990. 'Verb Movement and the Subject Position in Yiddish.' *Natural Language and Linguistic Theory* 8(1): 41–81.
Diesing, M. 1992. *Indefinites.* Cambridge, Mass.: MIT Press.
Dijk, K. van 1994a. 'The Origins of the IPP-effect in Dutch.' Ms., University of Amsterdam.
Dijk, K. van 1994b. 'The IPP-effect, Perfect Tense, and Applicative Constructions.' Ms., University of Amsterdam.
Dikken, M. den 1992. 'Empty Operator Movement in Dutch Imperatives.' Ms., University of Leiden.
Dimitrova-Vulchanova, M. 1993. 'Clitics in Slavic.' In L. Hellan ed., *Clitics in Germanic and Slavic,* 1–50. Eurotyp Working Papers. European Science Foundation, Strasbourg.
Donati, C., & A. Tomaselli. 1994. 'Language Types and Generative Grammar. A Review of some Consequences of the Universal VO Hypothesis.' Paper presented at the Tilburg Conference on Rightwards Movement (to be published in the Proceedings).
Donhauser, K. 1991. 'Moderne Kasuskonzeptionen und die Kasussetzung im Althochdeutschen.' In A. Betten ed., *Neuere Forschungen zur historischen Syntax des Deutschen,* 98–112. Tübingen: Max Niemeyer Verlag.
Donhauser, K. 1992. 'Das Genitivproblem in der Historischen Kasusforschung. Ein Beitrag zur Diachronie des deutschen Kasussytems.' Habilitation thesis, University of Passau.
Dowty, D. 1979. *Word Meaning and Montague Grammar. The Semantics of Verbs and Times in Generative Grammar and in Montague's PTQ.* Dordrecht: Reidel.
Drosdowski, G. et al. 1984. *Duden: Grammatik der deutschen Gegenwartsprache.* Mannheim: Dudenverlag.
Drubig, B. 1991. 'Zur Frage der Grammatischen Repräsentation Thetischer und Kategorischer Sätze.' In J. Jacobs ed., *Informationsstruktur und Grammatik* (Linguistische Berichte, Sonderheft 4), 142–96.
Duggan, J.J. 1969. *A Concordance of the Chanson de Roland.* Columbus: Ohio State University Press.

Dupuis, F. 1989. 'L'Expression du sujet dans les subordonnées en ancien français.' Doctoral dissertation, Université de Montréal.
Ebert, R. P. 1986. *Historische Syntax des Deutschen, II: 1300–1750*. Bern: Lang.
Ekwall, E. 1936. 'The Scandinavian Settlement.' In H. C. Darby ed., *An Historical Geography of England Before AD 1800*. Cambridge University Press.
Ellegård, A. 1953. *The Auxiliary 'Do': the Establishment and Regulation of its Use in English*. Stockholm: Almqvist & Wiksell.
Elmer, W. 1981. *Diachronic Grammar: the History of Old and Middle English Subjectless Constructions*. Tübingen: Niemeyer.
Elst, G. v. d. 1984. 'Zur Entwicklung des Deutschen Kasussystems.' *Zeitschrift für Germanistische Linguistik* 12: 275–312.
Emonds, J. 1976. *A Transformational Approach to English Syntax*. New York & London: Academic Press.
Enç, M. 1991. 'The Semantics of Specificity.' *Linguistic Inquiry* 22(1): 1–25.
Erdmann, O. 1973. *Untersuchungen über die Syntax der Sprache Otfrids*. Hildesheim: Georg Ohms Verlag.
Eriksson, O. 1985. *La suppléance verbale en français moderne*. Göteborg: Acta Universitatis Gothoburgensis.
Eroms, H.-W. 1992. 'Das Deutsche Passiv in Historischer Sicht.' In L. Hoffmann ed., *Deutsche Syntax. Ansichten und Aussichten* [Jahrbuch für deutsche Sprache 1991], 225–49. Berlin.
Es, G. van 1938. *De Attributieve Genitief in het Middelnederlandsch*. Assen: Van Gorcum.
Evers, A. 1975. 'The Transformational Cycle in Dutch and German.' Doctoral dissertation, University of Utrecht. Distributed by Indiana University Linguistics Club.
Evers, A. 1986. 'Long Rule Accessible Arguments in French and German.' In P. Coopmans et al. eds., *Formal Parameters of Generative Grammar*. Dordrecht: Foris.
Ewen, R. C. 1979. 'A Grammar of Bulgarian Clitics.' Doctoral dissertation, University of Washington, Seattle.
Faarlund, J.-T. 1990. *Syntactic Change. Toward a Theory of Historical Syntax*. Berlin: Mouton.
Falk, C. 1993. 'Non-Referential Subjects in the History of Swedish.' Doctoral dissertation, University of Lund.
Fanselow, G. 1987. *Konfigurationalität: Untersuchungen zur Universalgrammatik am Beispiel des Deutschen*. Tübingen: Gunter Narr.
Fanselow, G. 1990. 'Scrambling as NP-Movement.' In G. Grewendorf & W. Sternefeld eds., *Scrambling and Barriers*. Amsterdam: John Benjamins.
Fassi Fehri, A. 1993. *Issues in the Structure of Arabic Clauses and Words*. Dordrecht: Kluwer.
Firbas, J. 1992. *Functional Sentence Perspective*. Cambridge University Press.
Fischer, O. 1990. 'Syntactic Change and Causation: Developments in Infinitival Constructions in English.' Doctoral dissertation, University of Amsterdam.
Fischer, O. 1992. 'Syntax.' In N. Blake ed., *The Cambridge History of the English Language Vol 2: 1066–1476*, 207–409. Cambridge University Press.
Fodor, J. D., & I. A. Sag 1982. 'Referential and Quantificational Indefinites.' *Linguistics and Philosophy* 5: 355–98.
Foley, W., & R. Van Valin Jr. 1984. *Functional Syntax and Universal Grammar*. Cambridge University Press.

Fontana, J. M. 1993. 'Phrase Structure and the Syntax of Clitics in the History of Spanish.' Doctoral dissertation. University of Pennsylvania. IRCS Report No. 93-24.
Fontana, J. M. 1994. 'A Residual A-bar Position in Spanish.' In E. Duncan, D. Farkas & P. Spaelti eds., *Proceedings of WCCFL XII*.
Fontana, J. M. in press. 'Phonology and Syntax in the Interpretation of the Tobler–Mussafia Law.' To appear in A. Halpern and A. Zwicky eds., *Second Position Clitics and Related Phenomena*. Stanford: CSLI Press.
Foulet, L. 1961. *Petite syntaxe de l'ancien français*. Paris: Champion. 3rd edition.
Fourquet, J. 1938. *L'ordre des éléments de la phrase en germanique ancien*. Paris: Les Belles Lettres.
Fraenkel, E. 1932-3. *Kolon und Satz I, II*. Göttingen, Nachtrichten der Göttinger Gesellschaft der Wiss., Phil.-hist. Klasse.
Fraenkel, E. 1965. *Noch Einmal Kolon und Satz*. Munich, Bayerische Akademie der Wiss., Phil.-hist. Klasse, Sitzungsberichte.
Franks, S. 1981. 'Deep and Surface Case.' *Proceedings of NELS XI*. University of Massachusetts, Amherst.
Freidin, R. 1991. 'Introduction.' In R. Freidin ed., *Principles and Parameters in Comparative Grammar*, 1–6. Cambridge, Mass.: MIT Press.
Frisch, S. 1994. 'Reanalysis Precedes Syntactic Change: Evidence from Middle English.' Ms., Northwestern University. To appear in *Proceedings of FLSM 5*. Studies in the Linguistic Sciences 24.
Fukui, N. 1986. 'A Theory of Category Projection and its Application.' Doctoral dissertation. MIT.
Fukui, N., & M. Speas 1986. 'Specifiers and Projection.' *MIT Working Papers in Linguistics* 8: 128-72.
Galilei, G. 1970 (1632). *Dialogo intorno ai massimi sistemi*. Turin: Einaudi.
Geipel, J. 1971. *The Viking Legacy*. Newton Abbott, England: David & Charles.
Gelderen, E. van 1993. *The Rise of Functional Categories*. Amsterdam: John Benjamins.
Gerdts, D. 1993. 'Mapping Halkomelem Grammatical Relations.' *Linguistics* 31: 591-621.
Gessner, E. 1893. 'Das Spanische Personalpronomen.' *Zeitschrift für romanische Philologie* 17: 1-54.
Gestel, F. van, J. Nijen Twilhaar, T. Rinkel & F. Weerman 1992. *Oude Zinnen; Grammaticale Analyse van het Nederlands tussen 1200-1700*. Leiden: Martinus Nijhoff.
Gildersleeve, B. L., & G. Lodge 1895. *Latin Grammar*. London: Macmillan.
Giorgi, A., & F. Pianesi 1991. 'Towards a Syntax of Temporal Representation.' *Probus* 3: 1-27.
Giusti, G. 1993. 'A Unified Structural Representation of (Abstract) Case and Article. Evidences from Germanic.' Ms., University of Venice.
Givón, T. 1981. 'On the Development of the Numeral One as an Indefinite Marker.' *Folia Linguistica Historica* II: 35-53.
Givón, T. 1984. *Syntax: a Functional-Typological Introduction*, vol. 1. Amsterdam: John Benjamins.
Graffi, G. 1995. 'The Language of Logical Form.' Paper presented on the occasion of the International Conference 'Languages of Science', Bologna, October 1995.

Greenberg, J. 1963. 'Some Universals of Grammar with Particular Reference to the Order of Meaningful Elements.' In J. Greenberg ed., *Universals of Language*. Cambridge, Mass.: MIT Press.

Greenberg, J. 1991. 'The Last Stage of Grammatical Elements: Contractive and Expansive Desemanticization.' In E.C. Traugott & B. Heine eds., *Approaches to Grammaticalization* Vol I, 301–14. Amsterdam: John Benjamins.

Grewendorf, G. 1989. *Ergativity in German*. Dordrecht: Foris.

Grimm, J. 1837. *Deutsche Grammatik*, Bd. IV. Göttingen: Dieterich'sche Buchhandlung.

Grimshaw, J. 1990. *Argument Structure*. Cambridge, Mass.: MIT Press.

Grimshaw, J. 1991. 'Extended Projection.' Ms., Brandeis University.

Grimshaw, J. 1993. 'Minimal Projection, Heads, and Optimality.' Ms., Rutgers University.

Guillaume de Lorris. *Le Roman de la Rose*. F. Lecoy ed., Paris: Honoré Champion (CFMA), 1965. *La Mort le Roi Artu*. J. Frappier ed., Geneva: Droz, 1956. *Les Cent Nouvelles Nouvelles*. F. P. Sweetser ed., Geneva: Droz, 1966.

Haan, G. de & F. Weerman 1986. 'Finiteness and Verb Fronting in Frisian.' In H. Haider & M. Prinzhorn eds., *Verb Second Phenomena in Germanic Languages*, 77–110. Dordrecht: Foris.

Haase 1930 (1898). *Syntaxe française du XVIIe siècle. Nouvelle édition traduite et remaniée par M. Obert*. Paris: Delagrave.

Haeberli, E., & L. Haegeman 1995. 'Clause Structure in Old English: Evidence from Negative Concord.' *Journal of Linguistics* 31: 81–108.

Haegeman, L. 1992. *Generative Syntax: Theory and Description. A Case Study in West Flemish*. Cambridge University Press.

Haegeman, L. 1993. 'Object Clitics in West Flemish.' *Geneva Generative Papers* 2.

Haegeman, L. 1994a. 'Some Speculations on Argument Shift, Clitics and Crossing in West Flemish.' To appear in *Linguistische Berichte*.

Haegeman, L. 1994b. *Introduction to Government and Binding Theory*. Oxford: Blackwell.

Haegeman, L., & H. van Riemsdijk 1986. 'Verb Projection Raising, Scope and the Typology of Rules Affecting Verbs.' *Linguistic Inquiry* 17: 417–66.

Haegeman, L., & R. Zanuttini 1991. 'Negative Heads and the Neg Criterion.' *The Linguistic Review* 8: 233–51.

Haider, H. 1993. *Deutsche Syntax Generativ*. Tübingen: Narr.

Haider, H., & M. Prinzhorn 1986. *Verb Second Phenomena in Germanic*. Dordrecht: Foris.

Hale, K. 1982. 'Preliminary Remarks on Configurationality.' *NELS* 12: 86–96.

Hale, K. 1983. 'Warlpiri and the Grammar of Non-configurational Languages.' *NLLT* 1: 5–47.

Halle, M., & A. Marantz 1993. 'Distributed Morphology and the Pieces of Inflection.' In K. Hale & S. J. Keyser eds., *A View from Building 20*, 111–76. Cambridge, Mass.: MIT Press.

Halpern, A. L. 1992. 'Topics in the Placement and Morphology of Clitics.' Doctoral dissertation, Stanford University.

Halpern, A. L., & J. M. Fontana 1993. 'X^0 and X^{max} Clitics.' *Proceedings of WCCFL* 12: 251–66.

Hankamer, J. 1976. 'Multiple analyses.' In N. Li Charles ed., *Mechanisms of Syntactic Change*, 583–607. Austin: University of Texas Press.

Hankamer, J., & I. Sag 1976. 'Deep and Surface Anaphora.' *Linguistic Inquiry* 7: 391–426.
Hardt, D. 1993. 'Verb Phrase Ellipsis: Form, Meaning, Processing.' Unpublished doctoral dissertation, University of Pennsylvania, IRCS Report 93–23.
Harris, A., & L. Campbell 1995. *Historical Syntax in Cross-linguistic Perspective*. Cambridge University Press.
Harris, M. B. 1978a. *The Evolution of French Syntax: a Comparative Approach*. Harlow: Longman.
Harris, M. B. 1978b. 'The Interrelationship between Phonological and Grammatical Change.' In J. Fisiak ed., *Recent Developments in Historical Phonology*, 159–172. Berlin: Mouton de Gruyter.
Harris, M. B. 1980a. 'The Marking of Definiteness in Romance.' In J. Fisiak ed., *Historical Morphology*, 141–56. Berlin: Mouton de Gruyter.
Harris, M. B. 1980b. 'Noun Phrases and Verb Phrases in Romance.' *Transactions of the Philological Society* 1980: 62–80.
Hauge, K. R. 1976. *The Word Order of Predicate Clitics in Bulgarian*. Meddelelser 10. Slavic-Baltic Institute, University of Oslo.
Haverkort, M. 1994. 'Germanic Clitics and the Theory of Parameters.' To appear in K. Beals *et al.* eds., *Papers from CLS 30*.
Hawkins, J. 1983. *Explaining Language Universals*. London: Croom Helm.
Heidolph, K. E. *et al.* 1981. *Grundzüge einer Deutschen Grammatik*. Berlin. [Akademiegrammatik].
Heim, I. 1982. 'The Semantics of Definite and Indefinite NPs.' Doctoral dissertation, University of Massachussets, Amherst.
Heim, I. 1991. 'Artikel und Definitheit.' A. v. Stechow & D. Wunderlich eds., *Semantik/Semantics. An International Handbook*. Berlin: Mouton de Gruyter.
Heine, B. 1993. *Auxiliaries*. Oxford University Press.
Heine, B., U. Claudi, *et al.* 1991. *Grammaticalization: a Conceptual Framework*. The University of Chicago Press.
Heinrichs, H-M. 1954. *Studien zum Bestimmten Artikel in den Germanischen Sprachen*. Giessen: Wilhelm Schmitz Verlag.
Henry, A. 1995. *Belfast English and Standard English: Dialect Variation and Parameter Setting*. Oxford University Press.
Herman, J. 1963. *La Formation du système roman des conjonctions de subordination*. Berlin: Akademie Verlag.
Heycock, C. 1994. *Layers of Predication: the Non-Lexical Syntax of Clauses*. New York: Garland.
Heycock, C., & A. Kroch 1994. 'Verb Movement and Coordination in a Dynamic Theory of Licensing.' *The Linguistic Review* 11: 257–83.
Higginbotham, J. 1985. 'On Semantics.' *Linguistic Inquiry* 16(4): 547–93.
Higginbotham, J. 1987. 'Indefiniteness and Predication.' In E. Reuland & A. Ter Meulen eds., *The Representation of (In)definiteness*, 43–70. Cambridge, Mass.: MIT Press.
Higgins, F. R. 1988. 'Where the Old English sentence begins.' Ms., University of Massachussets, Amherst.
Higgins, F. R. 1992. 'SVO Order in Old English Subordinate Clauses.' Paper presented at Harvard University, 17 April, 1992.
Hirschbühler, P. 1989. Computerized Concordance of *Les cent nouvelles nouvelles* (based on the edition by Franklin P. Sweetser. Geneva: Droz, 1966).

Hirschbühler, P. 1990. 'La légitimation de la construction V1 à sujet nul dans la prose et le vers en ancien français.' *Revue québécoise de linguistique* 19: 32–55.
Hirschbühler, P., & M. O. Junker. 1988. Computerized Concordance of Philippe de Vigneulles, *Les Cent Nouvelles Nouvelles* (based on the edition by Charles H. Livingstone. Geneva: Droz, 1972).
Hoekstra, T. 1986. 'Passives and Participles.' In F. Beukema & A. Hulk eds., *Linguistics in the Netherlands 1986*, 95–104. Dordrecht: Foris.
Holmberg, A. 1985. 'Case and Word Order in Icelandic and Swedish.' Ms., Academy of Finland.
Holmberg, A. 1986. 'Word Order and Syntactic Features in the Scandinavian Languages and English.' Doctoral dissertation, University of Stockholm.
Holmberg, A. 1992. 'On the Representation of Case.' Paper presented at the GLOW colloquium, Lund, Sweden.
Holmberg, A. 1993. 'On the Representation of Case.' *GLOW-Newsletter* 30: 36–7.
Holmberg, A., & C. Platzack 1988. 'On the Role of Inflection in Scandinavian Syntax.' *Working Papers in Scandinavian Syntax* 50: 1–24.
Hoop, H. de 1992. 'Case Configuration and Noun Phrase Interpretation.' Doctoral dissertation, University of Groningen.
Hopper, P. 1991. 'On Some Principles of Grammaticization.' In E. Traugott & B. Heine ed., *Approaches to Grammaticalization*, 17–35. Amsterdam: John Benjamins.
Hopper, P. J., & E. C. Traugott 1993. *Grammaticalization*. Cambridge University Press.
Horst, J. van der 1981. *Kleine Middelnederlandse Syntaxis*. Amsterdam: Huis aan de drie grachten.
Hout, A. van, J. Randall & J. Weissenborn 1993. 'Acquiring the Unergative-unaccusative Distinction.' In M. Verrips & F. Wijnen eds., *The Acquisition of Dutch*. Universiteit van Amsterdam Instituut voor Algemene Taalwetenschap, Amsterdam Series in Child Language Development, Publication No. 60.
Huang, J. 1993. 'Reconstruction and the Structure of VP: Some Theoretical Consequences.' *Linguistic Inquiry* 24(1): 103–38.
Hudson, W. 1989. 'Functional Categories and the Saturation of Noun Phrases.' *Proceedings of NELS 19*. GLSA Amherst.
Huguet, E. 1925–73. *Dictionnaire de la langue française au 16e siècle*. Paris: Champion.
Hulk, A. 1993. 'Residual V2 and the Licensing of Functional Features.' *Probus* 5: 127–54.
Hulk, A., & A. van Kemenade 1988. 'Nominative Identification in Germanic and Romance languages.' In P. Coopmans & A. Hulk eds., *Linguistics in the Netherlands 1988*, 69–79. Dordrecht: Foris.
Hulk, A., & A. van Kemenade 1993a. 'Null Subjects in Diachrony.' Special issue of *Lingua* 89.2/3.
Hulk, A., & A. van Kemenade 1993b. 'Subjects, Nominative Case, Agreement, and Functional Heads.' *Lingua* 89: 181–215.
Hulk, A., & A. van Kemenade 1995. 'Verb-second, *Pro*-drop, Functional Projections, and Language Change.' In A. Battye & I. Roberts eds., *Clause Structure and Language Change*, 227–56. Oxford University Press.
Hummel, R. D. 1973. 'The Syntactical Distribution of MHG Preverbal in Selected Urkunden of the 13th century from Basel-Colmar-Freiburg'. Br. dissertation, University of Chicago.
Iatridou, S. 1990. 'About Agr(P).' *Linguistic Inquiry* 21: 551–77.

Iatridou, S., & A. Kroch 1992. 'The Licensing of CP-recursion and its Relevance to the Germanic Verb-second Phenomenon.' Ms., University of Pennsylvania.
Jackendoff, R. 1972. *Semantic Interpretation in Generative Grammar*. Cambridge, Mass.: MIT Press.
Jackendoff, R. 1983. *Semantics and Cognition*. Cambridge, Mass.: MIT Press.
Jackendoff, R. 1990. *Semantic Structures*. Cambridge, Mass.: MIT Press.
Jacobsson, B. 1951. *Inversion in English with Special Reference to the Early Modern English Period*. Uppsala: Almqvist and Wiksell.
Jaeggli, O. 1982. *Topics in Romance Syntax*. Dordrecht: Foris.
Jaeggli, O., & N. Hyams 1993. 'On the Independence and Interdependence of Syntactic and Morphological Properties: English Aspectual come and go.' *Natural Language and Linguistic Theory* 11: 313–46.
Jäger, P. 1917. *Der Gebrauch des bestimmten Artikels bei Isidor und Tatian vergleichend dargestellt*. Weida, Thüringen: Druck von Thomas & Hubert.
Jehan R. 1948. *Le Lai de l'Ombre*. J. Orr ed. Edinburgh University Press.
Jehan R. 1963. *Le Roman de la Rose ou de Guillaume de Dole*. F. Lecoy ed., Paris: Honoré Champion (CFMA).
Jespersen, O. 1938. *Growth and Structure of the English Language*. Garden City, N.Y.: Doubleday.
Johnson, K. 1991. 'Object Positions.' *Natural Language and Linguistic Theory* 9(4): 577–636.
Jonas, D. 1995. 'Clause Structure and Verb Syntax in Scandinavian and English.' Doctoral dissertation, Harvard University.
Jonas, D., & J. Bobaljik 1993. 'Specs for Subjects: the Role of TP in Icelandic.' *MIT Working Papers in Linguistics* 18: 59–98.
Jones, M. 1993. *Sardinian Syntax*. London: Routledge.
Kamp, H. 1981. 'A Theory of Truth and Semantic Representation.' In J. Groenendijk, T. Janssen & M. Stockhof eds., *Formal Methods in the Study of Language*, 227–30. Amsterdam: Mathematical Centre.
Karlsson, F. 1982. *Finnische Grammatik*. Hamburg.
Kayne, R. S. 1975. *French Syntax: the Transformational Cycle*. Cambridge, Mass.: MIT Press.
Kayne, R. S. 1989. 'Null Subjects and Clitic Climbing.' In O. Jaeggli & K. Safir eds., *The Null Subject Parameter*, 239–61. Dordrecht: Kluwer.
Kayne, R. S. 1991. 'Romance Clitics, Verb Movement and PRO.' *Linguistic Inquiry* 22: 647–86.
Kayne, R. S. 1993. 'Towards a Modular Theory of Auxiliary Selection.' *Studia Linguistica* 47: 3–31.
Kayne, R. S. 1994. *The Antisymmetry of Syntax*. Cambridge, Mass: MIT Press.
Keenan, E. 1987. 'A Semantic Definition of "Indefinite NP".' In E. Reuland & A. ter Meulen eds., *The Representation of (In)definiteness*, 286–317. Cambridge, Mass.: MIT Press.
Kemenade, A. van 1987. *Syntactic Case and Morphological Case in the History of English*. Dordrecht: Foris.
Kemenade, A. van 1992. 'V2, embedded topicalization, and the development of impersonals in Old and Middle English.' Second Diachronic Generative Syntax Workshop, Preprints. Institute for Research in Cognitive Science, University of Pennsylvania.

Kemenade, A. van 1993a. 'Syntactic Changes in late Middle English.' In H. Aertsen & R. Jeffers eds., *Historical Linguistics 1989*, 235–48. Amsterdam: John Benjamins.
Kemenade, A. van 1993a. 'The History of the English Modals: a Reanalysis.' *Folia Linguistica Historica* XIII/1–2: 143–66.
Kemenade, A. van 1993b. 'V2, Scrambling, and Cliticisation in Old and Middle English.' Paper given at the GLOW workshop on language change, Lund, April 1993.
Kemenade, A. van, forthcoming a. *Subject and Verb in the History of English*.
Kemenade, A. van, forthcoming b. 'Sentential Negation in Old and Middle English.'
Kemenade, A. van, & A. Hulk eds. 1993. *Null Subjects in Diachrony*. Special issue of *Lingua* 89.2/3.
Keyser, S. J., & W. O'Neil 1985. *Rule Generalization and Optionality in Language Change*. Dordrecht: Foris.
King, T. H. 1993. 'Licensing Left-Edge Focus in Russian.' Ms., Stanford University. Paper read at the LSA Annual Meeting.
Kiparsky, P. 1968. 'Phonological Change.' Unpublished doctoral dissertation, MIT.
Kiparsky, P. 1994. 'The Shift to Head-initial VP in Germanic.' Ms., Stanford.
Kiparsky, P. 1995. 'The Indo-European Origins of Germanic Syntax.' In A. Battye & I. Roberts eds., *Clause Structure and Language Change*, 140–70. Oxford University Press.
Kiparsky, P. 1996. 'The Shift to Head-initial VP in Germanic.' In H. Thrainsson and S. Epstein eds., *Proceedings of the Germanic Syntax Conference*.
Kiparsky, P. to appear. 'Structural Case.' Ms., Stanford University.
Klavans, J. L. 1982. *Some Problems in a Theory of Clitics*. Bloomington: Indiana University Linguistics Club.
Kock, E. A. 1902. *Three Middle-English Versions of the Rule of St. Benet*. Early English Text Society, Original Series 120. London: Kegan Paul.
Kohonen, V. 1978. *On the Development of English Word Order in Religious Prose around 1000 and 1200 AD: a Quantitive Study of Word Order in Context*. Åbo: Research Institute of the Åbo Akademi Foundation.
Kok, A. de 1985. *La place du pronom personnel régime conjoint en français*. Amsterdam: Rodopi.
Kolvenbach, M. 1973. 'Das Objekt im Deutschen. Seine Interrelationen zu Präpositionalphrasen und zum Akkusativ.' In *Festgabe für Paul Grebe zum 65. Geburtstag*, 123–34. Vol. 2. Mannheim [Sprache der Gegenwart 24].
Koopman, H. 1984. *The Syntax of Verbs*. Dordrecht: Foris.
Koopman, H. 1992. 'On the Absence of Case Chains in Bambara.' *NLLT* 10.4.
Koopman, W. 1990. 'Word Order in Old English.' Dissertation, University of Amsterdam.
Koopman, W. F. 1992. 'Old English Clitic Pronouns: some Remarks.' In F. Colman ed., *Evidence for Old English*, 44–87. Edinburgh: John Donald.
Koopman, W. 1993. 'The Order of Dative and Accusative Objects in Old English and Scrambling.' *Studia Anglica Posnaniensia* XXV-XXVII: 109–21.
Koopman, W. 1994. 'Adverbs: Clitics in Old English?' Ms.
Korchmáros, V. 1983. *Definiteness as Semantic Content and its Realisation in Grammatical Form*. Szeged. [*Studia Uralo-Altaica* 1983].
Koster, J. 1975. 'Dutch as an SOV Language.' *Linguistic Analysis*, 1.
Koster, J. 1993. 'Predicate Incorporation and the Word Order of Dutch.' Ms., University of Groningen.

Koziol, H. 1932. *Grundzüge der Syntax der Mittelenglischen Stabreimdichtungen.* Weiner Beiträge zur Englischen Philologie 58. Vienna: Braumüller.

Krause, M. 1987. *Sémantique et syntaxe des préverbes en goitique.* Thèse Paris-Sorbonne IV. Paris.

Kroch, A. 1989. 'The Loss of the Verb-Second Constraint in Middle English and Middle French.' Paper presented at the 9th Annual Meeting of the Association Québécoise de Linguistique, Montreal, Quebec.

Kroch, A. 1991. 'Reflexes of Grammar in Patterns of Language Change.' *Language Variation and Change* 1: 199–244.

Kroch, A. 1992. 'Syntactic change.' *Oxford International Encyclopedia of Linguistics.* Oxford & New York: Oxford University Press. Vol. 4: 111–14.

Kroch, A. 1994. 'Morphosyntactic Variation.' In K. Beals ed., *Proceedings of the Thirtieth Annual Meeting of the Chicago Linguistics Society*, vol. 2, 180–201. Chicago Linguistics Society.

Kroch, A., & A. Taylor 1993. 'The Syntax of Verb Movement in Middle English: Dialect Variation and Language Contact.' Ms., University of Pennsylvania.

Kroch, A., & A. Taylor 1994. 'Remarks on the XV/VX alternation in Middle English.' Paper given at the Third Diachronic Generative Syntax Conference, Amsterdam.

Kroch, A., & A. Taylor eds. 1994. *Penn-Helsinki Parsed Corpus of Middle English.* Philadelphia: University of Pennsylvania.

Kroch, A., A. Taylor & D. Ringe 1995. 'The Middle English Verb-Second Constraint: a Case Study in Language Contact and Language Change.' In S. Herring, P. van Reenen & L. Schoesler eds., *Textual Parameters.* Philadelphia: John Benjamins.

Kudra, D. 1993. 'Long Head Movement and Cliticization: Serbo-Croatian and Slovenian.' Ms., University of Ottawa.

Kuipers, A. H. 1967. *The Squamish Language.* The Hague: Mouton.

Kuno, S. 1981. 'Conditions for Verb Phrase Deletion.' *CLS* 17, 136–55.

Kunstmann, P., & M. Dubé. 1982. *Concordance analytique de la Mort le Roi Artu.* Ottawa: Editions de l'Université d'Ottawa.

Kural, M. 1994. 'Postverbal Constituents in Turkish.' Ms., UCLA.

Kytö, M. 1993. *Manual to the Diachronic Part of the Helsinki Corpus of English Texts: Coding Conventions and Lists of Source Texts.* Helsinki: Department of English, University of Helsinki. 2nd edition.

Laka, I. 1990. 'Negation in Syntax: on the Nature of Functional Categories and Projections.' Doctoral dissertation, MIT.

Lamontagne, G., & L. Travis 1987. 'The Syntax of Adjacency.' *Proceedings of the West Coast Conference on Formal Linguistics* 6: 173–86.

Langacker, R. 1977. 'Syntactic Reanalysis.' In C. Li ed. *Mechanisms of Syntactic Change*, 57–139. Austin: University of Texas Press.

Larsson, L.-G. 1983. *Studien zum Partitivgebrauch in den ostseefinnischen Sprachen.* Uppsala. [*Acta Universitatis Upsaliensis. Studia Uralica et Altaica Upsaliensia* 15.]

Lasnik, H. 1993. *Lectures on Minimalist Syntax.* University of Connecticut Working Papers in Linguistics. Occasional Papers. Issue 1.

Lasnik, H. 1994. 'Weakness and Greed: a Consideration of some Minimalist Concepts.' Paper presented at University of Maryland Minimalist Fest.

Lass, R. 1992. 'Phonology and Morphology.' In N. Blake ed., *The Cambridge History of the English Language, Vol 2: 1066–1476*, 23–155. Cambridge University Press.

Laughren, M. 1989. 'The Configurationality Parameter and Warlpiri.' In L. Marácz & P. Muysken eds., *Configurationality: the Typology of Asymmetries*, 319–53. Dordrecht: Foris.
Leake, R. E. 1981. *Concordance des Essais de Montaigne*. Genève: Droz.
Lee, Y.-S., & B. Santorini 1994. 'Towards Resolving Webelhuth's Paradox: Evidence from German and Korean.' In N. Corver & H. van Riemsdijk eds., *Scrambling*, 257–300. Berlin: Mouton de Gruyter.
Leiss, E. 1989. 'Grammatische Kategorien und Sprachlicher Wandel. Erklärung des Genitivschwunds im Deutschen.' In W. Bahrner, J. Schildt & D. Viehweger eds., *Proceedings of the 14th International Congress of Linguistics*. Part II, 1406–9. Berlin/DDR (August 1987).
Leiss, E. 1992. *Die Verbalkategorien des Deutschen*. [Studia Linguistica Germanica 31.] Berlin.
Leiss, E. 1994. 'Die Entstehung des Artikels im Deutschen.' *Sprachwissenschaft* 19: 307–19.
Lema, J., & M.-L. Rivero 1989. 'Long Head Movement: ECP vs. HMC.' In *Proceedings of NELS*, vol. 20, 333–47.
Lema, J., & M.-L. Rivero 1991. 'Types of Verbal Movement in Old Spanish: Modals, Futures, and Perfects.' *Probus* 3(3): 237–78.
Lenerz, J. 1977. *Zur Abfolge Nominaler Satzglieder im Deutschen*. Tübingen: G. Narr Verlag.
Lenerz, J. 1984. *Syntaktischer Wandel und Grammatiktheorie*. Tübingen: Niemeyer.
Lerch, E. 1925. *Historische Französische Syntax*, vol. 1. Leipzig: Reisland.
Levin, B. & M. Rappaport Hovav 1992. 'The Lexical Semantics of Verbs of Motion.' In I. Roca ed., *Thematic Structure: Its Role in Grammar*. Dordrecht: Foris.
Levin, B. & M. Rappaport Hovav 1995. *Unaccusativity*. Cambridge, Mass.: MIT Press.
Levin, N. S. 1986 (1979). *Main Verb Ellipsis in Spoken English*. New York: Garland (Published version of her 1979 Ohio State University Doctoral thesis).
Li, C., & S. Thompson 1976. 'Subject and Topic: a New Typology of Language. In C. Li ed., *Subject and Topic*, 457–90. New York: Academic Press.
Lightfoot, D. W. 1979. *Principles of Diachronic Syntax*. Cambridge University Press.
Lightfoot, D. W. 1987. Review of Keyser & O'Neil. *Language* 63(1): 151–4.
Lightfoot, D. W. 1988. 'Syntactic Change.' In F. Newmeyer ed., *Linguistics: the Cambridge Survey*. Vol I: *Linguistic Theory: Foundations*, 303–323. Cambridge University Press.
Lightfoot, D. W. 1991. *How to Set Parameters: Arguments from Language Change*. Cambridge, Mass.: MIT Press.
Lightfoot, D. W. 1993a. 'Why UG Needs a Learning Theory: Triggering Verb Movement.' In C. Jones ed., *Historical Linguistics: Problems and Perspectives*, 190–214. London: Longman.
Lightfoot, D. W. 1993b. 'Degree-0 Learnability.' *University of Maryland Working Papers in Linguistics*, vol. 1. To appear in B. Lust, G. Hermon & J. Kornfilt eds., *Syntactic Theory and First Language Acquisition: Crosslinguistic Perspectives*. Vol. 2 *Binding Dependency and Learnability*. Lawrence Erlbaum.
Lightfoot, D. W. 1995. 'Grammars for People.' *Journal of Linguistics* 31: 393–9.
Lightfoot, D. W., & N. Hornstein eds. 1994. *Verb movement*. Cambridge, Cambridge University Press.

Longobardi, G. 1991. 'Alcune riflessioni informali sulla posizione del verbo in gotico e le prospettive di una sintassi comparata dei complementatori generici.' Ms., University of Venice.
Longobardi, G. 1992. 'Proper Names and the Theory of N-Movement in Syntax and Logical Form.' Ms., University of Venice.
Longobardi, G. 1994. 'Reference and Proper Names: a Theory of N-movement in Syntax and Logical Form.' *Linguistic Inquiry* 25: 609–66.
Lyons, C. in prep. *Definiteness*. Cambridge, Cambridge University Press.
Machiavelli, N. 1796 (1513) *Il Principe* Turin: Unione Tipografico-Editrice Torinese.
MacLeish, A. 1969. *The Middle English Subject-Verb Cluster*. Janua Linguarum, Series Practica 26. The Hague: Mouton.
Magnússon, F. 1990. 'Kjarnafærsla og Það-innskot "Aukasetningum" Islensku.' Master's thesis, Málvísindastofnun Háskóla Islands.
Mahajan, A. 1990. 'The A/A' Distinction and Movement Theory.' Doctoral dissertation, MIT.
Maling, J. 1990. 'Inversion in embedded clauses in Modern Icelandic.' In J. Maling & A. Zaenen eds., *Modern Icelandic Syntax*, Syntax and Semantics 24, 71–95. San Diego: Academic Press.
Manzini, R. 1983. 'Restructuring and Reanalysis.' Doctoral dissertation, MIT.
Marantz, A. 1988. 'Clitics, Morphological Merger, and the Mapping to Phonological Structure.' In M. Hammond & M. Noonan eds., *Theoretical Morphology*, 253–70. New York: Academic Press.
Marantz, A. 1992. 'Case and Licensing.' *ESCOL '91*, 234–53. The Ohio State University.
Marchello-Nizia, C. 1979. *Histoire de la langue française aux XIVe et XVe siècles*. Paris: Bordas.
Marchello-Nizia, C. 1985. *Dire le vrai: l'adverbe 'si' en français médiéval*. Geneva: Droz.
Martin, R., & M. Wilmet 1980. *Manuel du français du moyen âge*. Volume 2: *Syntaxe du moyen français*. Bordeaux: SOBODI.
Mascaró, J., & M. Nespor eds. 1990. *Grammar in Progress: GLOW Essays for Henk van Riemsdijk*. Dordrecht: Foris.
Matthews, P. 1981. *Syntax*. Cambridge University Press.
McCawley, J. D. 1988. *The Syntactic Phenomena of English*. The University of Chicago Press.
McCloskey, J. 1992. 'Adjunction, Selection and Embedded Verb Second.' Ms., University of California at Santa Cruz.
McIntosh, A., M. L. Samuels & M. Benskin. 1986. *A Linguistic Atlas of Late Mediaeval English*. New York: Aberdeen University Press.
Meillet, A. 1912. 'L'évolution des formes grammaticales.' Repr. in A. Meillet 1958. *Linguistique Historique et Linguistique Générale*, 130–48. Paris: Champion.
Meinunger, A. 1993. 'Case Configuration and Referentiality.' In *Proceedings of ConSole II*. The Hague: Holland Academic Graphics.
Ménard, P. 1973. *Syntaxe de l'ancien français*. Bordeaux: SOBODI.
Meyer-Lübke, W. 1890–96. *Grammaire des langues romanes*. Paris: Welter.
Meyer-Lübke, W. 1897. 'Zur Stellung der Tonlosen Objektspronomina'. *Zeitschrift für romanische Philologie* 21: 313–34.
Miller, P. H. 1990. 'Pseudogapping and *do so* Substitution.' *Proceedings of CLS 26*, 293–305.

Miller, P. H. 1991. 'Clitics and Constituents in Phrase Structure Grammar.' Doctoral dissertation, Rijksuniversiteit Utrecht.
Miller, P. H. 1992. *Clitics and Constituents in Phrase Structure Grammar*. New York: Garland (Published version of 1991 doctoral dissertation, University of Utrecht).
Milroy, J. 1992. *Processes of Linguistic Change*. Oxford: Blackwell.
Milsark, G. 1977. 'Toward an Explanation of Certain Peculiarities of the Existential Construction in English.' *Linguistic Analysis* 3(1): 1–29.
Minkova, D., & R. Stockwell 1992. 'Poetic Influence on Prose Word Order in Old English.' In F. Colman ed., *Evidence for Old English*, 142–54. Edinburgh: John Donald.
Mitchell, B. 1964. 'Syntax and Word Order in the Peterborough Chronicle 1122–54.' *Neuphilologische Mitteilungen* 65: 113–44.
Mitchell, B. 1985. *Old English Syntax*, 2 vols. Oxford University Press.
Mitchell, B. 1989. *A Guide to Old English*. Oxford: Clarendon Press.
Moignet, G. 1973. *Grammaire de l'ancien français*. Paris: Klincksieck.
Moignet, G. 1974 (1960). 'La Suppléance du Verbe en Français.' In *Etudes de Psychosystématique Française*, 13–35. Paris: Klincksieck.
Moro, A. 1993. *I predicati nominali e la struttura della frase*. Unipress: Padua, in press; *The Raising of Predicates: Predicative NP and the Theory of Clause Structure*. Cambridge University Press.
Morpurgo D. A. 1996. *La linguistica dell'Ottocento*. Bologna: il Mulino.
Morse-Gagné, E. 1992. 'The Borrowing Hierarchy in the English Acquisition of Scandinavian Pronouns.' Ms., University of Pennsylvania.
Morse-Gagné, E. 1993. 'The Grammar of Viking Pronouns on Both Sides of the North Sea.' Ms., University of Pennsylvania.
Mossé, F. 1968. *Manual of Middle English*. Baltimore: Johns Hopkins Press.
Mussafia, A. 1886. 'Una particolarità sintattica della lingua italiana dei primi secoli.' *Miscellanea di Filologia e Linguistica in Memoria di N. Caix et U. A. Canello*, 255–61. Florence: Le Monnier.
Mussafia, A. 1888. 'Enclisi o proclisi del pronome personale atono quale oggetto.' *Romania* 27: 145–6.
Mustanoja, T. 1960. *A Middle English Syntax*. Mémoires de la Société Néophilologique de Helsinki xxiii. Helsinki: Société Néophilologique.
Neale, S. 1990. *Descriptions*. Cambridge, Mass.: MIT Press.
Neeleman, A. 1994. 'Complex predicates.' Utrecht: Onderzoeksinstituut voor Taal en Spraak.
Neeleman, A. to appear. 'Scrambling as a D-structure phenomenon.' In N. Corver & H. van Riemsdijk eds., *Scrambling*. Berlin: Mouton de Gruyter.
Neeleman, A., & F. Weerman 1993. 'Case Theory and the Diachrony of Complex Predicates in Dutch.' *Folia Linguistica Historica* 13: 189–217.
Newport, E. C., H. Gleitman & L. R. Gleitman 1977. 'Mother, I'd rather do It Myself: Some Effects and Non-effects of Maternal Speech Style.' In C. Snow & C. Ferguson eds., *Talking to Children: Language Input and Acquisition*. Cambridge University Press.
Nichols, J. 1986. 'Head-marking and Dependent Marking Grammar.' *Language* 62: 56–119.
Nichols, J. 1992. *Linguistic Diversity in Space and Time*. The University of Chicago Press.

Nocentini, A. 1990. 'L'uso dei dimostrativi nella *Peregrinatio Egeriae* e la genesi dell'Articolo Romanzo.' In *Atti del Convegno Internazionale sulla Peregrinatio Egeriae*, 137–58. Arezzo: Accademia Petrarca di Lettere Arti e Scienze.

Noonan, M. 1985. 'Complementation.' In T. Shopen ed., *Language Typology and Syntactic Description*, Vol. II: 42–140. Cambridge University Press.

Noreen, A. 1923. *Altisländische und Altnordische Grammatik*. Halle/Saale: Max Niemeyer.

Oehrle, R. 1976. 'The Grammatical Status of the English Dative Alternation.' Doctoral dissertation, MIT.

Ollier, M.-L. 1986. *Lexique et concordance de Chrétien de Troyes*. Montreal: Institut d'Etudes Médiévales, Université de Montréal.

Orr, J. 1962. *Old French and Modern English Idiom*. Oxford: Blackwell.

Oubuzar, E. 1974. 'Über die Ausbildung der Zusammengesetzten Verbformen im Deutschen Verbalsystem.' *Beiträge zur Geschichte der deutschen Sprache und Literatur* (Halle) 95: 5–96.

Paul, H. 1959. *Deutsche Grammatik*. Halle: Niemeyer.

Paul, H., P. Wiehl & S. Grosse 1989. *Mittelhochdeutsche Grammatik*. Tübingen. 23rd edition.

Pearce, E. 1990. *Parameters in Old French Syntax*. Dordrecht: Kluwer.

Pesetsky, D. 'Complementizer-Trace Phenomena and the Nominative Island Condition.' *The Linguistic Review* 1: 297–345.

Philippaki-Warburton, I., & B. Joseph 1987. *Modern Greek*. New York: Croom Helm.

Philippe de Vigneulles. *Les Cent Nouvelles Nouvelles*. C. H. Livingstone ed., Geneva: Droz, 1972.

Philippi, J. 1992. 'Die historische Entwicklung der DP.' MA Thesis, University of Hamburg.

Philippi, J. 1994. 'The Historical Rise of DP.' University of Stuttgart.

Philippi, J., & F. Weerman 1993. 'The Rise of DP.' Research project. University of Utrecht.

Pickering, M., & G. Barry 1991. 'Sentence Processing without Empty Categories.' *Language and Cognitive Processes* 6(3): 229–59.

Pintzuk, S. 1991. 'Phrase Structures in Competition: Variation and Change in Old English Word Order.' University of Pennsylvania doctoral dissertation.

Pintzuk, S. 1992. 'Phrase Structure Variation in Old English.' Second Diachronic Generative Syntax Workshop, Preprints. Institute for Research in Cognitive Science, University of Pennsylvania.

Pintzuk, S. 1993. 'Verb Seconding in Old English: Verb Movement to Infl.' *The Linguistic Review* 10: 5–35.

Pintzuk, S. 1994. 'Cliticization in Old English'. To appear in A. Halpern & A. Zwicky eds., *Second Position Clitics and Related Phenomena*. Stanford: CSLI.

Pintzuk, S., & A. Kroch 1985. 'Reconciling an Exceptional Feature of Old English Clause Structure.' In J.T. Faarlund ed., *Germanic Linguistics: Papers from a Symposium at the University of Chicago*. Indiana University Linguistics Club.

Pintzuk, S., & A. Kroch 1989. 'The Rightward Movement of Complements and Adjuncts in the Old English of *Beowulf*.' *Language Variation and Change* 1: 115–43.

Plank, F. 1984. 'The Modals Story Retold.' *Studies in Language* 8.3: 305–64.

Platzack, C. 1982. 'Transitive Adjectives in Swedish.' *The Linguistic Review* 2: 39–56.

Platzack, C. 1986. 'Comp, Infl, and Germanic Word Order.' In L. Hellan & K. Koch Christensen eds., *Topics in Scandinavian Syntax*. Dordrecht: Reidel.

Platzack, C. 1988. 'The Emergence of a Word Order Difference in Scandinavian Subordinate Clauses.' *McGill Working Papers in Linguistics*, Special Issue on Comparative Germanic Syntax. 215–38.

Platzack, C. 1995. 'The Loss of Verb Second in French and English.' In A. Battye & I. Roberts eds., *Clause Structure and Language Change*, 200–26. Oxford University Press.

Platzack, C., & A. Holmberg 1989. 'The Role of Agr and Finiteness in Germanic VO Languages.' *Working Papers in Scandinavian Syntax* 43: 51–76.

Poletto, C. 1993. *La sintassi del soggetto nei dialetti italiani settentrionali*. Padua: Unipress.

Pollard, C., & I.A. Sag 1987. *Information-Based Syntax and Semantics. Vol. 1, Fundamentals*. Stanford: CSLI Publications.

Pollard, C., & I.A. Sag 1994. *Head-Driven Phrase Structure Grammar*. Chicago: University of Chicago Press and CSLI Publications.

Pollock, J.-Y. 1989. 'Verb Movement, Universal Grammar, and the Structure of IP.' *Linguistic Inquiry* 20: 365–424.

Pollock, Jean-Yves 1993. 'Notes on Clause Structure.' Université of Amiens, Ms.

Postma, G.-J. 1995. 'Zero Semantics.' Leiden: HIL dissertation 13. Distributed by Holland Academic Graphics, The Hague.

Prinzhorn, M. 1990. 'Head Movement and Scrambling Domains.' In G. Grewendorf & W. Sternefeld eds., *Scrambling and Barriers*. Amsterdam: John Benjamins.

Progovac, L. in press. 'Clitics in Serbian/Croatian: Comp as the Second Position.' To appear in A. Halpern & A. Zwicky eds., *Second Position Clitics and Related Phenomena*. Stanford: CSLI Press.

Pyles, T., & J. Algeo 1993. *The Origins and Development of the English Language*. Fort Worth: Harcourt Brace Jovanovich. 4th edition.

Quirk, R., & C.L. Wrenn 1957. *An Old English Grammar*. London: Methuen. 2nd edition.

Radanovic-Kocic, Vesna 1988. 'The Grammar of Serbo-Croatian Clitics: a Synchronic and Diachronic Perspective.' Unpublished doctoral dissertation, University of Illinois, Urbana.

Ramsden, Herbert 1963. *Weak Pronoun Position in the Early Romance Languages*. Manchester University Press.

Rappaport Hovav, M., & B. Levin 1992. 'Classifying Single Argument Verbs' Ms., Bar Ilan University and Northwestern University, Evanston, Ill.

Renzi, L. 1976. 'Grammatica e storia dell'articolo italiano.' *Studi di Grammatica Italiana* 5: 5–42.

Renzi, L. 1983. 'Fiorentino e italiano: storia dei pronomi personali soggetto.' In F. Albano Leoni ed., *Italia Linguistica: Idee, Storia, Strutture*, 223–39. Bologna: Il Mulino.

Renzi, L. 1989. 'Two Types of Clitics in Natural Language.' *Rivista di Linguistica* 1: 355–72.

Renzi, L. 1992. 'Le développement de l'article en roman.' *Revue Roumaine de Linguistique* 37: 161–76.

Renzi, L. 1993. 'Vestiges de la flexion casuelle dans les langues romanes.' In *Actes du XXème Congrès Internationale de Linguistique et Philologie Romanes*, Vol. II, 672–77. Berne: Francke.

Reuland, E. 1990. 'Head movement and the Relation between Morphology and Syntax.' *Yearbook of Morphology* 3: 129–161.

Richards, B.J. 1990. *Language Development and Individual Differences: a Study of Auxiliary Verb Learning*. Cambridge University Press.

Riemsdijk, H. van 1978. *A Case Study in Syntactic Markedness: the Binding Nature of Prepositional Phrases*. Dordrecht: Foris.

Riemsdijk, H. van 1983. 'The Case of German Adjectives.' In F. Heny & T. Richards eds., *Auxiliaries and Related Puzzles*, 223–52. Dordrecht: Reidel.

Riemsdijk, H. van ed. forthcoming. *Clitics*. Berlin: Mouton de Gruyter.

Ritchie-Graeme, R.-L. 1907. *Recherche sur la syntaxe de la conjonction 'que' dans l'ancien français*. Paris: Champion.

Ritter, E., & S.T. Rosen 1994. 'Weak and Strong Predicates.' Paper LSA Boston. January 1994.

Rivero, M.-L. 1984. 'Diachronic Syntax and Learnability: Free Relatives in 13th Century Spanish.' *Journal of Linguistics* 20: 81–129.

Rivero, M.-L. 1986. 'Parameters in the Typology of Clitics in Romance and Old Spanish.' *Language* 62: 774–807.

Rivero, M.-L. 1991. 'Long Head Movement and Negation: Serbo-Croatian vs. Slovak and Czech.' *The Linguistic Review* 8: 319–51.

Rivero, M.-L. 1992. 'Clitic and NP Climbing in Old Spanish.' In H. Campos & F. Martínez-Gil eds., *Current Studies in Spanish Linguistics*. 241–82. Washington, D.C.: Georgetown University Press.

Rivero, M.-L. 1993a. 'Long Head Movement vs. V2, and Null Subjects in Old Romance.' *Lingua* 89: 113–41.

Rivero, M.-L. 1993b. 'Bulgarian and Serbo-Croatian Yes-No Questions. V^0-raising to -li vs. Li-Hopping.' *Linguistic Inquiry* 24: 567–75.

Rivero, M.-L. 1993c. 'Finiteness and Second Position in Long Head Movement Languages: Breton and Slavic.' Ms., University of Ottawa.

Rivero, M.-L. 1994a. [circulated in 1988]. 'The Structure of the Clause and V-movement in the Languages of the Balkans.' *Natural Language and Linguistic Theory* 12: 63–120.

Rivero, M.-L. 1994b. 'Negation, Imperatives, and Wackernagel effects.' *Rivista di Linguistica* 6(1): 91–118.

Rivero, M.-L., & A. Terzi 1994. 'Directionality Effects in the Syntax of Imperatives.' Paper presented at the GLOW Colloquium, Vienna.

Rivero, M.-L., & A. Terzi 1995. 'Imperatives, V-movement and Logical Mood.' *Journal of Linguistics* 31.2: 301–32.

Rizzi, L. 1982. *Issues in Italian Syntax*. Dordrecht: Foris.

Rizzi, L. 1986a. 'On the Status of Subject Clitics in Romance.' In O. Jaeggli & C. Silva-Corvalán eds., *Studies in Romance Linguistics*, 391–419. Dordrecht: Foris.

Rizzi, L. 1986b. 'Null Objects in Italian and the Theory of *pro*.' *Linguistic Inquiry* 17: 501–57.

Rizzi, L. 1990a. 'Some Speculations on Residual V2 Phenomena.' In J. Mascaró & M. Nespor eds.

Rizzi, L. 1990b. *Relativized Minimality*, Cambridge, Mass.: MIT Press.

Rizzi, L. 1991. 'Residual Verb Second and the *wh*-Criterion.' *University of Geneva Technical Reports in Formal and Computational Linguistics* 2.

Rizzi, L. 1993. Talk given at EUROTYP Clitics Workshop, University of Durham.

Rizzi, L., & I. Roberts 1989. 'Complex Inversion in French', *Probus* 1(1): 1–30.

Roberts, I. 1985a. 'The Representation of Implicit and Dethematized Subjects.' Dissertation, USC.

Roberts, I. 1985b. 'Agreement Parameters and the Development of English Modal Auxiliaries.' *Natural Language and Linguistic Theory* 3: 21–58.
Roberts, I. 1991. 'Excorporation and Minimality.' *Linguistic Inquiry* 22: 209–18.
Roberts, I. 1993a. *Verbs and Diachronic Syntax: a Comparative History of English and French*. Dordrecht: Kluwer.
Roberts, I. 1993b. 'A Formal Account of Grammaticalization in the History of Romance Futures.' *Folia Linguistica Historica* 13: 219–58.
Roberts, I. 1994a. 'Second Position Effects and Agreement in Comp.' Ms. University of Maryland.
Roberts, I. 1994b. 'Restructuring, Head Movement and Locality.' Ms. University of Wales, to appear in *Linguistic Inquiry*.
Roberts, I. 1995. 'Object Movement and Verb Movement in Early Modern English.' In H. Haider, S. Olsen & S. Vikner eds., *Studies in Comparative Germanic Syntax*, 269–84. Dordrecht: Kluwer.
Roberts, I. (forthcoming). 'Verb Movement and Markedness.' In M. deGraff & A. Pierce eds., *Language Acquisition, Language Change and Creolization*. Cambridge, Mass.: MIT Press.
Roeper, T., & J. Weissenborn 1990. 'How to make parameters work.' In L. Frazier & J. de Villiers eds., *Language processing and language acquisition*. Dordrecht: Kluwer.
Rögnvaldsson, E. 1992. 'Word Order Changes in the VP in Icelandic.' A paper given at the Second Diachronic Generative Syntax Conference, University of Pennsylvania, Philadelphia, November 1992.
Rögnvaldsson, E. 1995. 'Old Icelandic: a Non-Configurational Language?' *NOWELE* 26: 3–29.
Rögnvaldsson, E., & H. Thráinsson 1990. 'On Icelandic Word Order Once More'. In J. Maling & A. Zaenen eds., *Modern Icelandic Syntax*, Syntax and Semantics 24; San Diego: Academic Press, 3–41.
Rohlfs, G. 1966–8. *Grammatica storica dell'italiano e dei suoi dialetti*. Turin: Einaudi.
Rohrbacher, B. 1994a. 'The Germanic Languages and the Full Paradigm: a Theory of V to I Raising.' Doctoral dissertation, University of Massachusetts, Amherst.
Rohrbacher, B. 1994b. 'Notes on the Antisymmetry of Syntax.' Ms. University of Pennsylvania.
Rooryck, J. 1992. 'Romance Enclitic Ordering and Universal Grammar.' *The Linguistic Review* 9: 219–50.
Rosén, H. 1994. 'The Definite Article in the Making, Nominal Constituent Order, and Related Phenomena.' In J. Herman ed., *Linguistic studies on Latin*, 130–50. Amsterdam: John Benjamins.
Ross, J.R. 1967. 'Constraints on Variables in Syntax.' Doctoral dissertation, MIT.
Ross, J.R. 1973. 'The Penthouse Principle and the Order of Constituents.' In C. Corum, T.C. Smith-Stark & A. Weiser eds., *You take the high node and I'll take the low node*. Chicago Linguistic Society.
Rouquier, M. 1990. 'Le terme "ce que" régissant une complétive en ancien français.' *Revue Romane* 25: 47–72.
Rouveret, A. 1992. 'Clitic Placement, Focus and the Wackernagel Position in European Portuguese.' In L. Rizzi ed., *Clitics in Romance and Germanic*. 103–39. Eurotyp Working Papers. Strasbourg: European Science Foundation.
Rouveret, A., & J. Vergnaud 1980. 'Specifying Reference to the Subject.' *Linguistic Inquiry* 11: 417–67.

Rudin, C. 1986. *Aspects of Bulgarian syntax: Complementizers and wh-constructions.* Columbus: Slavica.
Rudin, C. 1988. 'On Multiple Questions and Multiple *wh*-fronting.' *Natural Language and Linguistic Theory* 6: 445–501.
Rudin, C. 1993. 'On Focus Position and Focus Marking in Bulgarian questions.' Ms., Wayne State College, Wayne, Nebr. Paper read at FLSM IV.
Runner, J. 1993. 'Quantificational Objects and AGR-O.' To appear in *Proceedings of the SCIL5.* MITWPL#20.
Rutten, J. 1991. *Infinitival Complements and Auxiliaries. Amsterdam Studies in Generative Grammar* 4.
Ruys, E. 1993. 'The Scope of Indefinites.' Doctoral dissertation, University of Utrecht.
Saez, L. A. 1991. 'The Structure of Comp in Slavic: Some Evidence from Slovak.' *International Journal of Basque Linguistics and Philology* XXV-2: 515–42.
Safir, K. 1987. 'What explains the Definiteness Effect?' In E. Reuland & A. ter Meulen eds., *The Representation of (In)definiteness*, 71–97. Cambridge Mass: MIT Press.
Sag, I. A. 1976. 'Deletion and Logical Form.' Doctoral dissertation, MIT. Published by IULC, 1977.
Saito, M. 1985. 'Some Asymmetries in Japanese and Their Theoretical Implications.' Doctoral dissertation, MIT.
Salmon, V. 1965. 'Sentence Structures in Colloquial Shakespearean English.' *Transactions of the Philological Society.* 105–40.
Salvi, G. 1988. 'La costruzione passiva.' In L. Renzi ed., *Grande grammatica Italiana di consultazione.* Bologna: Il Mulino.
Santorini, B. 1989. 'The Generalization of the Verb-Second Constraint in the History of Yiddish.' Doctoral dissertation, University of Pennsylvania.
Santorini, B. 1992. 'Variation and change in Yiddish subordinate clause word order.' *Natural Language and Linguistic Theory* 10: 595–640.
Scatton, E. 1984. *A Reference Grammar of Modern Bulgarian.* Columbus: Slavica.
Schachter, P. 1978. 'English Propredicates.' *Linguistic Analysis* 4(3): 187–224.
Schayik, D. van 1995. 'De Genitief in de 13e, 14e en 15e Eeuw.' MA Thesis, Utrecht University.
Schmidt, D. A. 1980. 'A History of Inversion in English.' Doctoral dissertation, Ohio State University.
Schrodt, R. 1992. 'Die Opposition von Objektsgenitiv und Objektsakkusativ in der Deutschen Sprachgeschichte: Syntax oder Semantik oder Beides?' *Beiträge zur Geschichte der Deutschen Sprache und Literatur* 114/3: 361–94.
Schrodt, R. 1994. 'Ist der Genitivverfall im Deutschen überhaupt erklärbar?' Paper University of Vienna, read in Stuttgart (Dec. 1994).
Schumacher, T. 1963. '*Uurdun sum Erkorene, sume sâr Verlorane.* Zum Ludwigslied, v. 11–18.' *Beiträge zur Geschichte der Deutschen Sprache und Literatur* 85: 57–64.
Schwegler, A. 1990. *Analyticity and Syntheticity. A Diachronic Perspective with Special Reference to Romance Languages.* Berlin: Mouton de Gruyter.
Selig, M. 1992. *Die Entwicklung der Nominaldeterminanten im Spätlatein.* Tübingen: Niemeyer.
Shibatani, M. 1990. *The Languages of Japan.* Cambridge University Press.
Shlonsky, Ur. 1994. 'Agreement in Comp.' *The Linguistic Review* 11: 351–76.

Sigurðsson, H. Á. 1986. 'Verb Post-Second in a V2 Language.' In Ö. Dahl & A. Holmberg eds., *Scandinavian Syntax*, 138–49. Institute of Linguistics, University of Stockholm.
Sigurðsson, H. Á. 1989. 'Verbal Syntax and Case in Icelandic.' Dissertation, University of Lund.
Sigurðsson, H. Á. 1990. 'V1 Declaratives and Verb Raising in Icelandic.' In J. Maling & A. Zaenen eds., *The Syntax of Modern Icelandic*, Syntax and Semantics 24. New York: Academic Press. 41–69.
Sigurðsson, H. Á. 1991. 'Icelandic Case-marked PRO and the Licensing of Lexical A-positions.' *Natural Language and Linguistic Theory* 9.2:327–65.
Sigurðsson, H. Á. 1992. 'Verbal Syntax and Case in Icelandic.' Unpublished doctoral dissertation, University of Lund.
Simpson, J. 1993. *Warlpiri Morpho-syntax*. Dordrecht: Kluwer.
Skeat, W. W. 1881–7. *The Holy Gospels in Anglo-Saxon, Northumbrian and Old Mercian Versions*. Cambridge University Press.
Smith, C. 1991. *The Parameter of Aspect*. Dordrecht: Kluwer.
Smith, H. 1992. 'Restrictiveness in Case Theory.' Ph.D. Diss., Stanford.
Smith, H. 1993. 'Dative Sickness in Germany.' *Natural Language and Linguistic Theory* 12.4:677–737.
Smyth, H. W. 1920. *A Greek Grammar*. N.Y.: American Book Co.
Sportiche, D. 1988. 'A Theory of Floating Quantifiers and its Corollaries for Constituent Structure.' *Linguistic Inquiry* 19: 425–51.
Sportiche, D. 1990. 'Movement, Case and Agreement.' Ms., UCLA.
Sportiche, D. 1995. 'Clitic Constructions.' In J. Rooryk & L. Zaring eds., *Phrase Structure and the Lexicon*, 213–76. Dordrecht: Kluwer.
Stasse, M. 1979. *Jehan Renart: Le Lai de l'Ombre. Concordances et Index*. Publications de l'Institut de Lexicologie Française de l'Université de Liège.
Steever, S. B. 1993. *Analysis to Synthesis: the Development of Complex Verb Morphology in the Dravidian Languages*. Oxford University Press.
Stengel, E. 1879. 'Die Ältesten Anleitungsschriften zur Erlernung der Französischen Sprache.' *Zeitschrift für Neufranzösische Sprache und Literatur* 1: 1–40.
Stenton, F. M. 1967. *Anglo-Saxon England*. Oxford: The Clarendon Press.
Stockwell, R. 1977. 'Motivations for exbraciation in Old English.' In C. Li ed., *Mechanisms of Syntactic Change*, University of Texas Press.
Stockwell, R. 1984. 'On the History of the Verb-second Rule in English.' In J. Fisiak ed., *Historical Syntax*. Berlin: Mouton de Gruyter.
Stowell, T. 1981. 'Origins of Phrase Structure.' Doctoral dissertation. Cambridge, Mass.: MIT Press.
Stowell, T. 1982. 'The Tense of Infinitives.' *Linguistic Inquiry* 13: 561–70.
Streitberg, W. 1891. 'Perfective und Imperfective Aktionsart im Germanischen.' *PBB* 15: 70–177.
Swan, T. 1994. 'Old English and Old Norse Initial Adverbials and Word Order.' In T. Swan, E. Morck & O. J. Westvik eds., *Language Change and Language Structure: Older Germanic Languages in Comparative Perspective*. Berlin: Mouton de Gruyter.
Swieczkowski, W. 1962. *Word Order Patterning in Middle English*. Janua Linguarum 19. The Hague: Mouton.
Tabor, W. 1994. 'Syntactic Innovation: a Connectionist Model.' Doctoral dissertation, Stanford University.

Taylor, A. 1990. 'Clitics and Configurationality in Ancient Greek.' Doctoral dissertation, University of Pennsylvania.
Taylor, A. 1994. 'The Change from SOV to SVO in Ancient Greek.' *Language Variation and Change* 6: 1–37.
Tekačić, P. 1980. *Grammatica storica dell'italiano*. Bologna: Il Mulino.
Tenny, C. 1989. 'The Aspectual Interface Hypothesis.' MIT Lexicon Project Working Papers 31.
Thomason, S. G., & T. Kaufman 1988. *Language Contact, Creolization and Genetic Linguistics*. Berkeley: University of California Press.
Thráinsson, H. 1986. 'V1, V2, V3 in Icelandic.' In H. Haider & M. Prinzhorn eds., *Verb-Second Phenomena in Germanic Languages*, 169–94. Dordrecht: Foris.
Thráinsson, H. 1994. 'Comments on the paper by Vikner.' In D. Lightfoot & N. Hornstein eds., *Verb Movement*, 149–62. Cambridge University Press.
Thráinsson, H. 1996. 'On the (Non-)Universality of Functional Categories.' In W. Abraham, S. D. Epstein, H. Thráinsson & Jan-Wouter Zwart eds., *Minimal Ideas: Syntactic Studies in the Minimalist Framework*, 253–81. Amsterdam: John Benjamins.
Tieken-Boon van Ostade, I. 1987. *The Auxiliary Do in Eighteenth-century English: a Sociohistorical-linguistic Approach*. Dordrecht: Foris.
Tobler, A. 1875 (=1912). 'Review of J. Le Coultre's *De l'ordre des mots dans Chrétien de Troyes*.' *Vermischte Beiträge zur französischen Grammatik*, 395–414. Hirzel, Leipzig.
Tobler, A. 1905. *Mélanges de grammaire française*. Paris.
Tobler, A., & E. Lommatzsch 1915–89. *Altfransözische Wörterbuch*. (= T&L).
Toman, J. 1986. 'Cliticization from NPs in Czech and Comparable Phenomena in French and Italian.' In H. Borer ed., *The Syntax of Pronominal Clitics*, 123–45. New York: Academic Press.
Toman, J. 1993. 'A Note on Clitics and Prosody.' In L. Hellan ed., *Clitics in Germanic and Slavic*, 113–18. Eurotyp Working Paper VIII.4. European Science Foundation, Strasbourg.
Tomaselli, A. 1989. 'La sintassi del verbo finito nelle lingue germaniche.' Doctoral dissertation. University of Pavia.
Tomaselli, A. 1990. *La sintassi del verbo finito nelle lingue germaniche*. Padua: Unipress.
Tomaselli, A. 1995. 'Cases of V3 in Old High German.' In A. Ballye & I. Roberts eds., *Clause Structure and Language Change*, 345–69. Oxford University Press.
Tommaseo, N., & B. Bellini 1929. *Dizionario della lingua italiana*. Turin: UTET.
Traugott, E. 1985. 'Conditional Markers.' In J. Haiman ed., *Iconicity in syntax*, 289–307. Amsterdam: John Benjamin.
Traugott, E. 1992. 'Syntax.' In R. Hogg ed., *The Cambridge History of the English Language, Volume I: The Origins to 1066*. Cambridge University Press.
Traugott, E., & B. Heine eds. 1991. *Approaches to Grammaticalization*. Amsterdam: Benjamins, 2 vols.
Traugott, E., & H. Smith 1993. 'Arguments from Language Change.' *Journal of Linguistics* 29: 431–47.
Travis, L. de Mena 1984. 'Parameters and Effects of Word Order Variation.' Doctoral dissertation, MIT.
Trudgill, P. 1994. *Dialects*. London: Routledge.
Uriagereka, J. 1988. 'On Government.' Ms., University of Connecticut.

Uriagereka, J. 1992a. 'Extraction Parameters: a Case Study of Underspecification.' Doctoral dissertation University of Connecticut.
Uriagereka, J. 1992b. 'A Focus Position in Western Romance.' Ms., University of Maryland. To appear in K. E. Kiss ed., *Discourse Configurational Languages*.
Uriagereka, J. 1995. 'Aspects of the Syntax of Clitic Placement in Western Romance.' *Linguistic Inquiry* 26: 79–123.
Uszkoreit, H. 1985. 'Constraints on order.' Stanford: SRI and CSLI 39.
Väänänen, V. 1987. *Le journal-épître d'Égérie (Itinerarium Egeriae). Étude linguistique*. Helsinki: Academia Scientiarum Fennica.
Vainikka, A. 1991. 'The Three Structural Cases in Finnish.' In A. Holmberg & U. Nikanne eds., *Case and other Topics in Finnish*. Berlin: Mouton de Gruyter.
Vallduví, E. forthcoming. 'On Rheme and Contrast.' In P. Culicover & L. McNally eds., *The Limits of Syntax*. New York: Academic Press.
Valois, D. 1991. *The Internal Syntax of DPs*. Unpublished doctoral dissertation, UCLA.
Van Valin, R. D., Jr. 1990. 'Semantic Parameters of Split Ergativity.' *Language* 66: 221–60.
Vance, B. 1989. 'Null Subjects and Syntactic Change in Medieval French.' Doctoral dissertation, Cornell University.
Vanden Wyngaerd, G. 1989. 'Object Shift as an A-Movement Rule.' *MIT Working Papers in Linguistics* 11: 256–71.
Vanelli, L. 1987. 'I pronomi soggetto nei dialetti italiani settentrionali dal medioevo e oggi.' *Medioevo Romanzo* 12: 173–211.
Vennemann, T. 1974. 'Topics, Subjects and Word Order: from SXV to SVX via TVX.' In J. Anderson & C. Jones eds., *Historical Linguistics. Vol. 1*, 339–76. Amsterdam: North Holland.
Verkuyl, H. 1988. 'Aspectual Asymmetry and Quantification.' In H. Vater & V. Ehrich eds., *Temporalsemantik. Beiträge zur Linguistik der Zeitreferenz*. Tübingen: Max Niemeyer Verlag.
Verkuyl, H. 1993. *A Theory of Aspectuality: the Interaction between Temporal and Atemporal Structure*. Cambridge University Press.
Vikner, S. 1990. 'Verb Movement and the Licensing of NP Positions in the Germanic Languages.' Doctoral dissertation, Université de Genève.
Vikner, S. 1994a. 'Finite Verb Movement in Scandinavian Embedded Clauses.' In Lightfoot & Hornstein, eds.
Vikner, S. 1994b. 'Scandinavian Object Shift and West Germanic Scrambling.' In N. Corver & H. van Riemsdijk eds., *Scrambling*, 487–517. Berlin: Mouton de Gruyter.
Vikner, S. 1995a. *Verb Movement and Expletive Subjects in the Germanic Languages*. Oxford University Press.
Vikner, S. 1995b. 'V^0-to-I^0 Movement and Inflection for Person in All Tenses.' *Working Papers in Scandinavian Syntax* 55: 1–27.
Vikner, S., & B. Schwartz to appear. 'The Verb Always leaves IP in V2 Clauses.' In A. Belletti & L. Rizzi eds., *Parameters and Functional Heads*. Oxford University Press.
Vincent, N. 1987. 'The Interaction of Periphrasis and Inflection: Some Romance Examples.' In M. Harris & P. Ramat eds., *Historical Development of Auxiliaries*, 237–56. Berlin: Mouton De Gruyter.
Vincent, N. 1988. 'Latin.' In M. Harris & N. Vincent ed., *The Romance Languages*, 26–78. London: Routledge.

Vincent, N. 1993. 'Head versus Dependent Marking: the Case of the Clause.' In G. Corbett et al. eds., *Heads in Grammatical Theory*, 140–63. Cambridge University Press.
Vincent, N. 1994. 'Syntactic Change.' In R. Asher ed., *Encyclopedia of Language and Linguistics*, 4391–6. Oxford: Pergamon Press.
Vincent, N. 1995. 'Exaptation and Grammaticalization.' In H. Andersen ed., *Historical Linguistics 1993*, 433–45. Amsterdam: John Benjamins.
Vincent, N. 1996. 'Synthetic and Analytic Structures.' In M. Maiden & M. Parry ed., *The Dialects of Italy*, London: Routledge.
Visser, F. T. 1963–73. *An Historical Syntax of the English Language. Part I, Syntactic Units with one Verb.* Leiden: Brill.
Vocabolario dell 'Accademia della Crusca. Florence: Tipografia Galileiana. 1863.
Wackernagel, J. 1892. 'Über ein Gesetz der Indogermanischen Wortstellung.' *Indogermanischen Forschungen* 1: 333–436.
Wanner, D. 1987. *The Development of Romance Clitic Pronouns: From Latin to Old Romance.* Berlin: Mouton de Gruyter.
Wanner, D. 1992a. 'The Tobler–Mussafia Law in Old Spanish.' In H. Campos & F. Martínez-Gil eds., *Current Studies in Spanish Linguistics*, 313–78. Washington, D.C: Georgetown University Press.
Wanner, D. 1992b. 'Subjects in Old Spanish: Conflicts between Typology, Syntax, and Dynamics.' In P. Hirschbühler & K. Koerner eds., *Romance Languages and Modern Linguistic Theory*, 339–72. Amsterdam: John Benjamins.
Warner, A. R. 1982. *Complementation in Middle English and the Methodology of Historical Syntax.* London: Croom Helm.
Warner, A. R. 1990. 'Reworking the History of the English Auxiliaries.' In Adamson, S., V. A. Law, N. Vincent & S. Wright eds., *Papers from the 5th International Conference on English Historical Linguistics*, 537–59. Amsterdam: John Benjamins.
Warner, A. R. 1992. 'Elliptical and Impersonal Constructions: Evidence for Auxiliaries in Old English?' In J. Anderson & N. Macleod eds., *Evidence for Old English*. Edinburgh Studies in the English Language, Vol. 2. Edinburgh: John Donald.
Warner, A. R. 1993. *English Auxiliaries: Structure and History.* Cambridge University Press.
Warner, A. R. 1995. 'Predicting the Progressive Passive: Parametric Change within a Lexicalist Framework.' *Language* 71: 533–57.
Webber, B. L. 1979. *A Formal Approach to Discourse Anaphora.* New York: Garland.
Webelhuth, G. 1991. *Syntactic Saturation Phenomena and the Modern Germanic Languages.* Oxford University Press.
Webelhuth, G. 1995. *Government and Binding Theory and the Minimalist Program.* Oxford: Blackwell.
Wechsler, S. 1990. 'Verb Second and Illocutionary Force in Swedish.' *Edinburgh Working Papers in Cognitive Science* 6: 229–34.
Wechsler, S. 1991. 'Argument Structure and Linking.' Doctoral dissertation, Stanford University.
Weerman, F. 1987. 'The Change from OV to VO as a Possible Change.' In F. Beukema & P. Coopmans eds., *Linguistics in the Netherlands 1987*, 223–32. Dordrecht: Foris.

Weerman, F. 1987. 'Modern Dutch could be Middle Dutcher than you think (and vice versa).' In W. Koopman, F. Van der Leek, O. Fischer & R. Eaton eds., *Explanation and Linguistic Change*. Amsterdam: John Benjamins.
Weerman, F. 1989. *The V2 Conspiracy*. Dordrecht: Foris.
Weerman, F. 1993. 'Reconsidering the Role of Parameters and "Peripheral" Rules.' In *Language Change*. Handbook for the 11th International Conference on Historical Linguistics, UCLA.
Weerman, F. 1995. 'Asymmetries between Nominative, Accusative and Inherent Case.' Ms., Utrecht University.
Wells, J. E. 1916. *A Manual of the Writings in Middle English 1050–1400*. New Haven: Yale University Press.
Wexler, P. 1976. 'On the Non-lexical Expression of Determinedness (with Special Reference to Russian and Finnish).' *Studia Linguistica* 30: 34–67.
Wexler, K. 1994. 'Optional Infinitives, Head Movement, and the Economy of Derivations.' In D. Lightfoot & N. Hornstein eds., *Verb Movement*, 305–50. Cambridge University Press.
Wexler, K., & R. M. Manzini 1987. 'Parameters, Binding Theory, and Learnability.' *Linguistic Inquiry* 18: 413–44.
Whitelock, D. 1967. *Sweet's Anglo-Saxon Reader*. Oxford University Press.
Wilder C., & D. Cavar 1994. 'Word Order Variation, Verb Movement, and Economy Principles.' *Studia Linguistica* 48: 46–86.
Williams, E. S. 1977. 'Discourse and Logical Form.' *Linguistic Inquiry* 8(1): 101–39.
Williams, E. S. 1981. 'Argument Structure and Morphology.' *The Linguistic Review* 1: 81–141.
Williams, E. S. 1987. 'Introduction.' In T. Roeper & E. Williams eds., *Parameter Setting*, vii–xix. Dordrecht: Reidel.
Wunderli, P. 1978. '"Ce Neutre" en moyen français: Étude de syntaxo-sémantique phrastique et transphrastique.' In M. Wilmet ed., *Sémantique lexicale et sémantique grammaticale en moyen français. Actes du Colloque organisé par le Centre d'Études Linguistiques et Littéraires de la Vrije Universiteit Brussel (28–29 Sept. 1978)*. Brussels: V.U.B. Centrum voor Taal-en Literatuurwetenschap.
Wurff, W. van der 1990, 'Diffusion and Reanalysis.' Doctoral dissertation, University of Amsterdam.
Wurff, W. van der 1993. 'Null Objects and Learnability: the Case of Latin.' Paper presented at ICHL 11, UCLA, August 1993.
Zaenen, A. 1993. 'Unaccusativity in Dutch: an Integrated Approach.' In J. Pustejovsky ed., *Semantics and the Lexicon*. Dordrecht: Kluwer.
Zaenen, A., J. Maling & H. Thráinsson 1985. 'Case and Grammatical Functions: the Icelandic Passive.' *Natural Language and Linguistic Theory* 3: 441–83. Reprinted in J. Maling & A. Zaenen eds., *Modern Icelandic Syntax*, Syntax and Semantics 24. New York: Academic Press. 95–137.
Zanuttini, R. 1994. 'Speculations on Negative Imperatives.' *Rivista di Linguistica* 6.1. Special issue on Negation edited by L. Haegeman.
Zaring, L. 1991. 'On Prepositions and Case-Marking in French.' *Canadian Journal of Linguistics* 36: 363–77.
Zaring, L. 1992. 'French *ce* as a Clausal Determiner.' *Probus* 4: 53–80.
Zaring, L. 1993. 'On a Type of Argument-Island in French.' *Natural Language and Linguistic Theory* 11(1): 121–74.

Zhang, S. 1991. 'Negation in Imperatives and Interrogatives: Arguments against Inversion.' Ms., University of Arizona.
Zwart, C. J.-W. 1991. 'Clitics in Dutch: Evidence for the Position of INFL.' Paper presented at the Giselle Conference, Girona.
Zwart, C. J.-W. 1993. 'Dutch Syntax: a Minimalist Approach.' Groningen: Groningen Dissertations in Linguistics, 40.
Zwarts, J. 1992. 'X'-Syntax-X'-Semantics. On the Interpretation of Functional and Lexical Heads.' Doctoral dissertation, Utrecht University.
Zwicky, A. 1977. *On Clitics*. Bloomington: IULC.
Zwicky, A. 1985. 'Heads.' *Journal of Linguistics* 21: 1–29.
Zwicky, A. 1994. 'Clitics.' In R. Asher ed., *Encyclopedia of Language and Linguistics*. Oxford: Pergamon Press.

Index

Languages

Arabic 62

Bantu 22
Basso Polesano 117
Bernese 215, 216, 235, 236
Bulgarian 42, 60, 170, 176, 182, 184, 202, 217, 218, 222, 232, 233, 243

Catalan 155, 177
Chinese 42, 64, 473
Czech 42, 44, 173, 175, 203, 205, 209

Danish 9, 278, 298, 299, 325, 328, 461
Dutch 3, 9, 15, 16, 18, 19, 32, 36, 41, 48, 64, 210, 214–216, 219, 235, 236, 248, 256, 263–265, 270, 288, 297, 300, 301, 309, 322–324, 328, 330–332, 334, 398, 400–403, 408, 409, 412–415, 417, 418, 419, 422, 425–428, 430, 431, 433–436, 438, 441, 443–445, 447–451, 453–455, 458, 459, 461, 462, 465, 467–469, 482, 489, 493, 504, 505
   Middle Dutch 18, 19, 41, 214–216, 235, 236, 417, 425–428, 432–438, 440, 441, 445

English 12, 19, 21, 36, 119, 120, 123, 125, 126, 130–132, 139, 179, 198, 199, 240, 329, 330, 426, 498, 501
   Belfast English 10, 273–284, 286, 287, 289, 290, 292–294, 384
   Early Modern English 63, 382, 399, 423, 426, 494

Hiberno-English 24, 273, 275
Middle English 2, 15, 60, 63, 65, 80, 82, 83, 86, 88–90, 99, 100, 106, 109, 113, 114, 120, 121, 123, 128, 129, 132, 133, 137, 143, 144, 146, 150, 151, 167, 169, 172, 177, 188–190, 194, 205, 223, 246, 248, 254, 256, 258, 262, 264–268, 269, 272, 275–278, 285, 292, 297, 298, 301, 305, 310–315, 317, 318, 319, 320, 322–326, 333, 335, 336, 339–341, 344–348, 352, 353, 356, 359, 360, 363–365, 367, 368, 369, 380, 382, 387–391, 393, 397–399, 419–423, 425, 429, 433, 445, 458–461, 463, 465, 469, 473, 479, 487–490, 492–494, 501, 503, 507
Northern English 299
Old English 2, 5, 15, 62, 63, 82, 85–89, 92, 166, 210, 212–214, 216, 221, 225, 227, 228, 229, 235–237, 239–241, 244–246, 248, 249, 264, 270, 271, 286, 298–306, 308–314, 316–324, 326, 332–334, 336, 338–340, 342, 346–348, 351, 352, 387, 388, 392, 397–426, 432–435, 437, 460–463, 465–467, 469–472, 478, 480, 489–494, 498, 499, 501, 503–505
Southern English 390

Finnish 34, 42, 44, 59–62, 65, 74, 75, 78, 79, 92, 454
Flemish 173, 174, 181, 182, 193, 194, 205, 215, 216, 271, 402, 409, 461
Florentine 114
French 7, 9, 11, 22–24, 117, 119, 120, 122, 124, 127, 129–131, 132, 134, 144, 145, 176, 191, 194, 212, 213, 223, 229, 150, 151, 159, 162, 164, 165, 167, 255, 261–263, 268, 272, 298, 328–330, 351, 353–356, 361, 371, 372, 373, 375–379, 386, 399, 411, 425, 437, 438
  Middle French 22, 119–122, 124, 125, 127, 131–134, 144, 145, 354, 355
  Old French 9, 22, 119–125, 127, 130–133, 159, 162, 176, 194, 212–214, 216, 218, 220, 222, 225, 228, 229, 235–245, 247, 248, 328, 353, 354, 375, 425
Frisian 9, 32, 328, 431, 461

German 3, 8, 9, 11, 20, 29, 30, 32–35, 42–45, 47–49, 51, 52, 54–56, 59–64, 68, 70, 71, 75, 81, 84, 87, 88, 89, 90, 92, 93, 134, 140, 153, 171, 181–183, 204, 210, 215, 216, 219–221, 235–238, 256, 263, 264, 265, 270, 271, 283, 297, 301, 304, 305, 308–310, 314, 322, 323, 327, 328, 330–332, 334, 400–403, 409, 415, 417–419, 425, 430, 431, 433, 435, 453–455, 459, 461–463, 465, 467–469, 471, 473, 478–480, 483–487, 493, 494, 504–506
  Middle High German 29, 30, 33, 35, 38, 39, 41, 45–48, 53–57, 59, 63, 65, 78, 82, 88–90, 136, 137, 425
  Old High German 30, 33–35, 37, 39–43, 45–50, 53–59, 61, 62–65, 75, 76, 79, 82, 85–89, 92, 134, 139, 140, 221, 407, 426, 435, 437, 453
  Swiss German 215, 402, 462
Germanic 11, 20–22, 62, 73, 92, 134, 136, 153, 164, 168, 205, 210, 214, 216–218, 222–224, 227, 228, 229, 234, 236–238, 243, 244, 247–249, 297, 299–306, 315, 321, 323, 324, 330, 338, 351, 397, 402–407, 411, 414, 416–418, 420, 422, 424–427, 429–431, 440, 452, 453, 457, 458, 461, 462, 467, 489, 496, 498, 502, 503, 505, 508
Gothic 11, 37, 42–44, 47, 50, 56, 61, 62, 74, 78, 85, 87–89, 92
Greek
  Ancient Greek 43, 60, 64, 84, 171, 181–183, 204
  Homeric Greek 208, 209, 216, 218, 222, 229, 230
  Modern Greek 29, 43, 60, 61, 64, 84, 170, 171, 181–183, 186–188, 194, 204, 208, 209, 216, 218, 222, 229, 230, 377
Grisons 462, 463, 480, 492

Hebrew 226

Icelandic 10, 15, 16, 43, 62, 210, 219, 227, 239, 245, 297, 300, 301, 307, 309, 322, 323, 328, 330, 339, 351, 393, 422, 425, 437, 440, 462, 463, 479, 480, 483, 484, 486, 487, 501, 504–506, 508
Irish, Old 43
Italian 94–99, 101, 102, 107–114, 116–118, 140, 143–145, 176, 194, 218, 239, 242, 151, 158–160, 162–165, 167, 280, 330, 332, 411
  Old Italian 95, 109–112, 114, 116, 118, 176, 218, 239, 242

Japanese 168, 268, 426, 442, 473, 508

Lakhota 377
Latin 11–13, 18, 20, 41, 60, 63, 117, 149–154, 158–161, 163–169, 245, 254, 298, 315, 316, 320–322, 324, 325, 370, 371, 373, 374, 400, 426
  Classical Latin 11, 117, 152, 159, 165, 370

Mohawk 15

Norwegian 84, 265, 298, 299, 313, 461

Polish 20, 34, 42, 44, 60, 232
Portuguese 11, 151, 186, 194–196, 205, 242, 280
Provençal 239

Romance 12, 18, 20–23, 43, 63, 64, 105, 149–154, 158–160, 162–169, 171, 176, 186, 187, 193, 194, 201, 203, 204, 208, 213, 217, 218, 220, 221, 223, 229, 231, 232, 234, 236–239, 242, 243, 249, 316, 338, 371, 374, 377, 407, 408, 411, 412, 416, 424, 426, 496
Rumanian 152, 232, 233, 426
Russian 20, 30, 34, 42–46, 53, 54, 58–62, 64, 74, 78, 92, 93, 134, 135, 202, 426, 437

Sanskrit 43
Saxon, Old 34, 37, 62
Scandinavian 8, 9, 24, 210, 264, 277–279, 297–300, 310, 311, 314, 315, 317, 319, 320, 322, 324, 325, 328, 348, 351, 424, 426, 465, 468, 469, 491
Continental Scandinavian, 9, 24, 328, 350, 491
Serbo-Croatian (SC) 44, 170–200, 202–206, 208, 209, 216–218, 222, 232, 234, 243, 249
Spanish 175, 176, 178, 188–190, 195, 206, 229, 249
Old Spanish 170–184, 187–193, 195–206, 213, 217, 218, 222, 223, 225–231, 233–249
Squamish 377
Swedish 5, 264

Turkish 75, 442, 494, 508

Warlpiri 15

Yiddish 10, 204, 210, 219, 227, 271, 297, 301, 307–309, 322, 323, 328, 397, 462, 465

Subjects

agreement morphology 331, 489
argument structure 14, 16, 17, 20, 23, 29, 134, 144, 473–477, 483, 497
articles 1, 7, 20–22, 24, 29, 30, 42, 43, 47, 39, 59–61, 62–65, 73, 82, 84, 86, 88, 90, 93, 210, 149, 150, 152–155, 158, 160, 163, 165, 166, 168, 169, 419, 425, 488
  definite vs indefinite 20–22, 29, 32, 35, 43, 45
aspect 14, 18, 20–23, 29, 30, 34, 40, 42–44, 47, 52–56, 59–61, 77–79, 88, 91, 92, 105, 134, 139, 168, 180, 181, 198, 224, 231, 232, 259, 260, 498
  perfective vs imperfective 35, 37, 38, 42, 105
auxiliaries vs main verbs 120, 121, 129–131

bridge verbs 9, 246, 298, 328, 333, 338, 342, 352

C-oriented 166, 169, 170–173, 175, 178–180, 182–184, 186, 188, 190, 199, 202–204, 222, 327, 329, 330, 332, 333, 341, 349–351, 407, 408, 426
Case
  abstract case 13, 15, 17, 19, 24, 75, 91, 427, 439, 473–479, 483, 493
  accusative vs genitive 29, 30, 32
  default case 36, 68, 71, 74, 77, 91, 92, 138
  morphological case 7, 12, 13, 18, 21, 22, 76, 91, 153, 160, 161, 163–165, 419–423, 425–443, 445, 446, 448, 450–458, 463, 473, 475, 479, 480, 482, 488, 489, 491, 494, 498, 511, 512, 513
  recessive case features 480
  syntactic case 13, 427–429
chain government 332, 338, 463
change in progress 24, 273, 274, 292, 296

clausal determiner 354, 371, 373–376
cliticization 212, 229, 230, 249, 271, 325, 334, 339, 348, 388, 405, 415, 419, 423, 426, 431
clitics 21–24, 95, 97, 98, 103, 104, 107, 108, 115, 116, 141, 147, 149–154, 158–161, 163–206, 207–220, 222–226, 228–239, 241, 242, 243, 247–249, 266, 278, 303, 304, 306, 313–315, 323, 333, 338, 351, 352, 368, 388, 393, 405–408, 411, 412, 418–420, 422, 423, 426, 463, 476, 492, 498
   2nd position 172, 179, 181, 182, 184, 188, 199, 202, 204, 205, 207–212, 216–218, 223, 225, 226, 229–237, 239, 241–244, 247, 248
   C-oriented vs I-oriented 166, 169, 170–173, 175, 178–180, 182–184, 190, 199, 202–204, 222, 327, 329, 330
   loss of clitics 380, 387, 388, 390, 392, 393, 420, 492
complementizer 9, 10, 66, 170, 172, 205, 208, 215, 221, 222, 229, 283, 298, 299, 308, 315–317, 327–329, 348, 350, 351, 353, 354, 370, 376, 405, 407, 435, 446, 468
CP-recursion 9, 172–175, 177, 180, 191, 298, 305–307, 309, 310, 316, 318, 323, 325, 328, 338, 342

definiteness 20, 23, 35, 37, 41, 43–45, 51, 53–60, 62, 63, 65, 72, 73, 77, 78, 80, 82, 89, 90, 139, 144, 155, 158, 161, 162, 165, 168, 169, 468, 471, 472, 477, 509–511
degree-0 learnability 4
diachronic reanalysis 267, 354
directionality parameter 14, 166, 397, 420
doubly filled Comp 175, 315
DP hypothesis 21, 66, 151

embedded topicalization 239, 326, 332, 338–342, 344, 347, 352
Empty Category Principle (ECP) 18, 19, 197, 257, 429, 442–446, 448, 451, 453, 455, 458, 497, 498

empty expletive 307, 308, 320, 323
extended projection 68, 353, 354, 372, 373, 375, 379, 386, 450, 456
Extended Projection Principle 386, 456
extraposition 300, 354, 358–371, 373, 374, 379, 400, 402, 403, 412, 416, 448, 453, 459, 467

focus 18, 24, 32, 149, 151, 157, 159, 162, 165, 166, 187, 199, 202, 205, 212, 231, 249, 261, 299, 353, 381, 384, 389, 403, 416, 431, 459, 462, 469, 491, 492, 497
functional categories 6, 7, 14, 20–22, 149, 197, 372, 373, 375, 378, 386, 387, 392, 426, 460, 466, 472, 497, 498, 500, 502, 514
functional heads 6, 7, 103–105, 178, 332, 372, 399, 412, 416, 499, 509

Gap Hypothesis 441, 443, 448, 451–453
grammatical relations 13, 16, 17, 299, 460, 473–476, 479
grammaticalization 1, 2, 4, 21–23, 94, 95, 158, 160–163, 166, 167

head movement 7, 8, 84, 88, 90, 177, 186, 191, 205, 211, 237, 411

I-oriented 169–173, 176, 178–180, 182, 184, 186, 188, 190, 199, 202–204, 222, 327, 329, 330, 349, 350, 351, 387, 392, 407
imperatives 10, 24, 206, 211, 214, 226, 233, 235, 272–296, 386, 392
interpolation 174, 189, 190, 192, 196, 199, 205, 229, 242

language acquisition 3–6, 253, 254, 268, 269, 273, 274, 293, 294, 318, 354, 372, 374, 377, 423, 454
language contact 297, 318, 348
Least Effort Strategy 268, 354, 374
licensing
   morphological licensing 15, 482, 488, 491
   positional licensing 460, 480, 482, 487–493, 511, 512

mapping hypothesis 70–74, 76, 91, 138
Mapping theories 13, 16, 17, 19, 25
marking
  argument marking 24, 27, 161, 163–165, 395
  head- vs dependent- 15, 16, 21, 161, 164
  modals 1, 2, 4, 99, 101–103, 105, 107, 116, 117, 145, 267, 336, 339, 352, 382–384, 392, 465, 466, 471, 472, 488, 491, 493, 498
  mood 2, 22, 23, 94, 105, 107, 282, 286, 373, 383, 384

nominative–dative inversion 331, 337

object shift 277–280, 319, 325, 422, 424, 425, 499
overt morphology 8, 11, 15, 18, 319, 473, 493, 495, 496

parameter setting 4, 259, 260, 262, 263, 268, 269, 376, 382, 385–387, 391, 464
parametric change 3–7, 24, 268, 380, 381, 383, 384, 392
pro
  pro-drop 32, 151, 246, 254, 280–282, 321, 330–332, 334, 336, 338, 346, 349, 350, 464, 465, 493
  expletive *pro*-drop 330, 332, 334, 338, 346, 349, 350, 464, 465
  pro-licensing 330
  referential *pro*-drop 330, 331, 336, 338, 350
pronouns
  demonstratives 62, 64, 82, 84, 86–88, 90, 153, 356, 374, 390, 469, 491
  weak 21, 150, 160, 165, 166, 168, 169, 278, 279, 281, 285, 406, 407, 411, 412, 426
  weak object pronouns 277–280, 285
pseudogapping 119, 120, 122, 123, 131, 144

reanalysis 2, 4, 131, 132, 160, 167, 259, 267, 301, 318, 319, 354, 371, 373, 374, 377, 390–392, 422, 461, 463, 464, 466, 492

recomplementation 246
referentiality 29, 34, 35, 40, 42–45, 48, 55, 57, 60, 65, 74, 92, 134, 136, 138, 144
Restricted Inversion dialect 274, 276, 285, 287–295, 384, 385, 392

scrambling 15, 18, 70, 71, 73, 76, 77, 203, 248, 303, 347, 400, 403–405, 410–412, 415, 417, 419, 420, 422–426, 430, 431, 433, 462, 473, 478, 480, 483, 492, 499, 511, 512
  loss of scrambling 419, 422–424, 426
second position 11, 166, 172, 181, 207–210, 212, 216–218, 226, 228, 229, 231, 238, 241, 248, 256, 257, 270, 302, 400
Semantic Form 473–476, 479, 492–494, 497
Spec–head agreement 16, 19, 66, 137, 198, 219, 220, 231, 307, 319, 331, 350, 378, 463
specificity 44, 426, 477, 494
subject–verb agreement 166, 263, 290, 307, 470, 490
subset principle 354, 375, 377, 383, 465
synchronic variation 5, 405

telicity 60, 61, 80, 81, 93, 139, 288
tense 3, 6–8, 22, 94, 96, 107, 117, 41, 45, 54, 59, 176, 197, 198, 204, 230, 243, 286, 287, 290–294, 317, 319, 320, 372, 383, 384, 500–502
θ-hierarchy 474, 485
Tobler–Mussafia law 176, 209, 222, 249
topic 10, 36, 104, 140, 155, 157–159, 162, 166, 188, 197, 199, 270, 302–309, 311, 313, 316, 318, 319, 320–323, 326, 329, 333, 338–348, 352, 380, 387, 415, 418
triggering experience 260–263, 464, 492

unaccusatives 92, 274, 276, 285, 288–290, 292, 296, 346
unification 93, 474, 475, 477, 480

544   *Index*

Unrestricted Inversion dialect 274–276, 280, 283–285, 288, 291–295, 385, 392

V-movement 8, 10, 11, 24, 205, 251, 338, 340, 380, 406, 411–414, 416, 424, 509, 514
  V-to-C movement 11, 310, 463, 466
  V-to-I movement 10, 24, 204, 228, 260–265, 271, 272, 318, 329, 339, 351, 352, 380–385, 390, 392, 399, 406, 421, 435, 466–469, 472, 491, 493
V-projection raising 270, 271, 409–412, 416, 417, 425
V-raising 187, 193, 196–198, 200–202, 205, 206, 261, 270, 408, 409, 412, 416, 418, 424, 425
V2 3, 4, 8–11, 24, 74, 171, 186, 189, 190, 193, 194, 204, 205, 207, 209–212, 214–217, 221, 223, 225, 226, 227, 228, 230, 231, 233–245, 247, 248, 257, 262, 264–267, 270–273, 289, 297–325, 326, 327, 328–330, 332, 333, 338, 340–342, 344–352, 356, 357, 367, 380, 384, 387, 388, 390, 392, 393, 399, 412, 413, 415, 418, 419, 424, 430, 434, 460, 463–466, 468–471, 491, 492, 494, 498
  asymmetric V2 9, 10, 347, 348
  CP-V2 10, 297, 298, 300, 301, 304–306, 312, 314, 316, 318, 320–325, 388, 390, 393
  IP-V2 271, 297, 298, 300–307, 309, 317, 318, 322, 323, 325, 388, 390, 393
  loss of V2 4, 11, 245, 247, 273, 310, 348–350, 352, 380, 387, 388, 390, 399, 419, 463, 491
  symmetric V2 10, 204
visibility 13, 25
VP-Ellipsis 119, 120, 122, 131, 144, 145

Wackernagel position 181, 182, 160, 407
weak/strong NP 35, 38, 53, 58, 66–70, 73–75, 77, 91, 137, 291
wh-criterion 306, 330
word order 3, 7, 8, 12, 14, 15, 163–166, 174, 177, 183, 189, 198, 203, 209–211, 217, 218, 219, 228, 235, 244, 245, 297, 298, 300–302, 304–306, 309, 310, 314, 318, 321–323, 325, 351, 397, 399, 400, 402–404, 418–420, 422, 423, 426, 429, 431, 432, 434, 439–441, 445, 451, 452, 454, 455, 459, 460, 462, 473, 479, 482–483, 487, 488, 492, 498, 500

X^{max} vs X^0 related categories 222, 224, 234, 243

OHIO UNIVERSITY LIBRARY

Please return this book as soon as you have finished with it. In order to avoid a fine it must be returned by the latest date stamped below. All books are subject to recall after two weeks or immediately if needed for reserve.

MAR 2 7 2000

MAR 1 4 2000

CF